Corruption: A Violation of Human Rights and a Crime Under International Law?

Martine Boersma

intersentia
Cambridge – Antwerp – Portland

Intersentia Ltd
Trinity House | Cambridge Business Park | Cowley Road
Cambridge | CB4 0WZ | United Kingdom
Tel.: +44 1223 393 753 | mail@intersentia.co.uk

Martine Boersma
Corruption: A Violation of Human Rights and a Crime Under International Law?

ISBN 978-1-78068-105-4
D/2012/7849/95
NUR 828

British Library Cataloguing in Publication Data. A catalogue record for this book is available from the British Library.

Dedicated to my parents,
Veur mien awwers,

Alexander Boersma &
Eleonora Boersma-Francot

Acknowledgements

The four-year period in which I had the privilege to work at the Law Faculty of Maastricht University and within the broader context of the Netherlands School of Human Rights Research has offered me a myriad of opportunities for professional and personal development. At the end of this journey, I should not forget to thank the persons whose support was invaluable.

First of all, I thank my supervisors Prof. Menno Kamminga and Prof. Hans Nelen for carefully reading and commenting upon the various drafts of the chapters of this dissertation. Our fruitful discussions, the combination of your respective areas of expertise, and especially your confidence in this endeavour were a great help. I also thank the members of the Assessment Committee, Prof. Fons Coomans, Prof. Cees Flinterman, Prof. John Hatchard, Prof. David Nelken, and Dr. Fabián Raimondo, for their willingness to read the manuscript and to provide comments.

I thank a number of persons who have helped me to improve my dissertation, amongst others my colleagues from the Maastricht Centre for Human Rights, by commenting on ideas and providing suggestions for improvement. Also a word of thanks for the co-organisers of the conference 'Corruption and Human Rights', which took place on October 22–23, 2009: Hans Nelen, Fons Coomans, Paul Frielink, Roland Moerland, and David Roef. All have contributed to making this event and the resulting publication in the Maastricht Series in Human Rights something to be proud of.

Furthermore, I owe a lot to Chantal Kuypers, administrator of the Maastricht Centre for Human Rights, for her help with organisational and practical aspects and for being the wonderful and friendly colleague that she is. I also acknowledge the support of Laura Visser, former student-assistant of the Centre, *inter alia* for some research assistance and for having to photocopy an awful lot of library books for me.

Moreover, the English language review of this dissertation was skilfully conducted by Carol Ní Ghiollarnáth, Ph.D. from Legal English Services, whose work I can warmly recommend – and not just because of her residence on the sunny island of Aruba.

A *very* special word of thanks to my former colleagues at the Faculty of Law, some of which deserve particular praise. Jennifer Sellin, we've experienced the entire Ph.D. phase together, literally from day one. Your friendship and support was indispensable, and having you as my paranymph means a lot to me. Marelle Attinger, my other paranymph, who would have guessed some ten years ago when volunteering at the Vrouwenrechtswinkel that we would become colleagues again when both pursuing a Ph.D? I greatly value your down-to-earth attitude and friendship. Jasper Krommendijk, you are by far the best possible person with whom to share an office. Our critical discussions on human rights and politics, as well as our laughs accompanied by *un pèlske in de kaffees vaan Mestreech* were always inspiring and encouraging.

Finally, I'd like to express my utmost gratitude to my parents Eleonora and Alexander, to whom this book is dedicated. *Vaanoet de grond vaan mien hart daank iech uuch veur alle steun, mèt zoe väöl dinger. Dit 'beukske' is veerdig, en iech hoop tot geer gruuts kint zien. Unne hiele groete merci!*

Maastricht, July 2012

Contents

Acknowledgements vii
List of Abbreviations xxi

General Introduction 1

1. A Day in the Life of John and Jane Doe 1
2. Overview of Contemporary Research 2
   2.1. Corruption as a Violation of Human Rights? 2
   2.2. Corruption as a Crime under International Law? 7
3. Main Research Questions 9
4. Structure 9
   4.1. Part A: The Phenomenon of Corruption: An Introductory Analysis 9
   4.2. Part B: Responsibility of States: Corruption as a Violation of Human Rights? 10
   4.3. Part C: Individual Responsibility: Corruption as a Crime under International Law? 11
   4.4. Part D: Summary, Reflections and Recommendations 12
5. Methodology 12
   5.1. Part A: The Phenomenon of Corruption: An Introductory Analysis 12
   5.2. Part B: Responsibility of States: Corruption as a Violation of Human Rights? 13
      5.2.1. Data Collection and Organisation 13
      5.2.2. Interpretation of Results 19
   5.3. Part C: Individual Responsibility: Corruption as a Crime under International Law? 20
      5.3.1. Data Collection and Organisation 20
      5.3.2. Interpretation of Results 21

Part A
The Phenomenon of Corruption: An Introductory Analysis

Chapter I
Basic Issues 25

1. Introduction 25
2. Defining 'Corruption' 27
   2.1. Public and Private Sector Corruption 27
   2.2. Grand and Petty Corruption 29

2.3. Corruption *vis-à-vis* Other Concepts . . . 30
2.4. Cultural Connotations . . . 32
3. Typology of Corruption . . . 33
3.1. Introductory Remarks . . . 33
3.2. Bribery . . . 33
3.3. Embezzlement . . . 35
3.4. Trading in Influence . . . 35
3.5. Abuse of Functions . . . 36
3.5.1. Patronage . . . 36
3.5.2. Nepotism . . . 37
3.6. Illicit Enrichment . . . 38
4. Measuring Corruption . . . 38
5. The Harmfulness of Corruption . . . 40
5.1. Introductory Remarks . . . 40
5.2. Political Consequences . . . 41
5.2.1. Erosion of Democracy and Legitimacy . . . 41
5.2.2. Armed Conflict . . . 41
5.3. Economic Consequences . . . 45
5.4. Social Consequences . . . 48
5.5. Environmental Consequences . . . 49
6. Concluding Remarks . . . 51

Chapter II
Global and Regional Legal Framework Against Corruption . . . 53

1. Introduction . . . 53
2. International Regulation of Corruption . . . 54
2.1. The Precursory Role of the US Foreign Corrupt Practices Act . . . 54
2.1.1. Content . . . 54
2.1.2. Underlying Motives for Adoption . . . 55
2.1.3. Criticisms and Resulting Amendments . . . 56
2.1.4. Enforcement and Effectiveness . . . 58
2.2. Rationales for International Legislative Efforts . . . 61
2.2.1. US Lobbying Efforts . . . 61
2.2.2. Societal Developments . . . 62
3. Legal Instruments on the Global and Regional Plane . . . 64
3.1. Inter-American Convention Against Corruption (1996) . . . 64
3.1.1. Content . . . 64
3.1.2. Follow-up Mechanism (MESICIC) . . . 67
3.2. European Union . . . 70
3.2.1. PFI Convention (1995), First Protocol (1996) and Second Protocol (1997) . . . 70

3.2.2. Convention on the Fight Against Corruption Involving Officials of the European Communities or Officials of EU Member States (1997) 71
3.2.3. Other Developments 72
3.3. OECD Convention on Combating Bribery of Foreign Public Officials in International Business Transactions (1997) 73
3.3.1. Content 73
3.3.2. Monitoring Mechanism 77
3.4. Council of Europe 81
3.4.1. Criminal Law Convention on Corruption (1999) and Additional Protocol (2003) 81
3.4.2. Civil Law Convention on Corruption (1999) 82
3.4.3. Recommendation on Codes of Conduct for Public Officials (2000) 83
3.4.4. Recommendation on Common Rules against Corruption in the Funding of Political Parties and Electoral Campaigns (2003) 83
3.4.5. GRECO: the COE's Monitoring Mechanism 84
3.5. African Instruments 85
3.5.1. SADC Protocol Against Corruption (2001) 85
3.5.2. ECOWAS Protocol on the Fight Against Corruption (2001) 88
3.5.3. African Union Convention on Preventing and Combating Corruption (2003) 88
3.6. United Nations 92
3.6.1. United Nations Convention Against Transnational Organized Crime (2000) 92
3.6.2. United Nations Convention Against Corruption (2003) 93
4. Comparative Analysis 97

PART B
RESPONSIBILITY OF STATES: CORRUPTION AS A VIOLATION OF HUMAN RIGHTS?

Chapter III
Treaty-Based System: Corruption as a Topic in the Work of the UN Human Rights Treaty Bodies 103

1. Introduction 103
2. State Reporting Procedure 104
2.1. Overview 104
2.2. Language Employed in the Treaty Bodies' Concluding Observations . . 105
3. Individual Complaints Procedure 108
4. Human Rights Committee (HRC) 109
4.1. Concluding Observations 109

4.1.1. The Right to Equality Before Courts and Tribunals and to a Fair Trial 109
4.1.2. The Prohibition of Human Trafficking 112
4.1.3. The Right to Freedom of Movement 112
4.1.4. Miscellaneous Observations 113
4.2. Views on Individual Complaints 114
5. Committee on Economic, Social and Cultural Rights (CESCR) 116
6. Committee on the Rights of the Child (CRC) 120
7. Committee on the Elimination of All Forms of Discrimination Against Women (CEDAW) 125
8. Committee on the Elimination of Racial Discrimination (CERD) 126
9. Committee Against Torture (CAT) 128
10. Concluding Remarks 130

Chapter IV
Charter-Based System: Corruption as a Topic in the UPR and the Special Procedures of the UN Human Rights Council 135

1. Introduction 135
2. Universal Periodic Review 135
2.1. Background 135
2.2. Discussion of Corruption During the UPR Dialogue 136
2.2.1. Statements by States under Review 137
2.2.2. Comments and Questions by Reviewing States 139
2.2.3. Recommendations Made to States under Review 141
2.2.4. Countries in Respect of Which Corruption is Discussed 142
2.2.5. Countries Commenting, Asking, Recommending about Corruption 143
2.2.6. The Relationship Between Corruption and Human Rights Violations 144
2.3. Concluding Remarks 145
3. Special Procedures of the UN Human Rights Council 145
3.1. Background 145
3.2. The Former Special Rapporteur on Corruption and Its Impact on the Full Enjoyment of Human Rights, in Particular Economic, Social and Cultural Rights 147
3.2.1. Introduction 147
3.2.2. Outcomes 148
3.2.3. Assessment 150
3.3. Other Selected Thematic Mandates 150
3.3.1. Introduction 150
3.3.2. Outcomes 151
3.3.3. Assessment 164

3.4. Country Mandates 165
3.4.1. Introduction 165
3.4.2. Outcomes 166
3.4.3. Assessment 174
3.5. Concluding Remarks 174

Chapter V
Regional Human Rights Practice on the Topic of Corruption 177

1. Introduction 177
2. Europe 177
2.1. Background 177
2.2. Practice of the European Court of Human Rights 178
2.2.1. Whistleblowers' Right to Freedom of Expression (Article 10 ECHR) 178
2.2.2. Rights of Persons Accused of Corruption 181
3. The Americas 185
3.1. Background 185
3.2. Practice of the Inter-American Commission on Human Rights 186
3.2.1. Corruption in the Judiciary 186
3.2.2. Rights of Whistleblowers 188
3.2.3. Economic, Social and Cultural Rights 188
3.2.4. Other Issues 189
3.3. Practice of the Inter-American Court of Human Rights 190
4. Africa 192
4.1. Background 192
4.2. Practice of the African Commission on Human and Peoples' Rights 192
5. Concluding Remarks 193

Chapter VI
Taking It Further: Corruption as a Human Rights Violation 195

1. Introduction 195
2. Clarifying the Corruption and Human Rights Connection 195
2.1. Introduction 195
2.2. ICHRP's Approach: Various Types of 'Violations' 196
2.3. Alternative Approach: 'Dimensions' of the Corruption and Human Rights Connection 197
2.4. Opposition to the Corruption and Human Rights Connection 200
3. Corruption as a Violation of Civil and Political Rights 202
3.1. The Right to Equality and Non-Discrimination 202
3.1.1. Introduction 202
3.1.2. The Right to Equality Before the Law 204

3.1.3. The Right to Equal Protection of the Law 204
3.1.4. The Prohibition of Discrimination 204
3.2. The Right to Equality Before Courts and Tribunals and the Right to a Fair Trial 205
3.2.1. Introduction. 205
3.2.2. The Right to Equality Before Courts and Tribunals. 207
3.2.3. The Right to a Fair Trial 209
3.2.4. The Presumption of Innocence. 211
3.2.5. Rights of Persons Charged with a Criminal Offense 211
3.2.6. The Right to a Remedy. 212
3.3. Rights of Political Participation. 212
3.3.1. Introduction. 212
3.3.2. The Right to Take Part in the Conduct of Public Affairs 214
3.3.3. The Right to Vote 214
3.3.4. The Right to be Elected. 215
3.3.5. The Right of Equal Access to Public Service. 216
3.4. The Prohibition of Human Trafficking 216
3.4.1. Introduction. 216
3.4.2. State Obligations under the Trafficking Protocol 218
3.4.3. Article 8 ICCPR 218
3.5. The Rights of Detainees to be Treated with Humanity and Dignity. . . . 222
3.5.1. Introduction. 222
3.5.2. Article 10 ICCPR 222
3.6. The Right to Freedom of Movement 224
3.6.1. Introduction. 224
3.6.2. The Right to Liberty of Movement and Freedom to Choose Residence 225
3.6.3. The Freedom to Leave a Country and Liberty of Emigration . . . 226
3.6.4. The Right to Enter One's Own Country. 228
4. Corruption as a Violation of Economic, Social and Cultural Rights 228
4.1. State Party Obligations under Article 2(1) ICESCR 228
4.1.1. Introduction. 228
4.1.2. 'Undertakes To Take Steps' 229
4.1.3. 'Individually and Through International Assistance and Co-operation, Especially Economic and Technical'. 230
4.1.4. 'To the Maximum of Its Available Resources' 231
4.1.5. 'With a View to Achieving Progressively the Full Realisation of the Rights Recognised in the Covenant' 232
4.1.6. 'By all Appropriate Means, Including Particularly the Adoption of Legislative Measures'. 233
4.2. The Right to Food 234
4.2.1. Introduction. 234
4.2.2. Content 235

4.2.3. State Obligations and Violations. 236
4.2. The Right to Adequate Housing 239
4.3.1. Introduction. 239
4.3.2. Content 240
4.3.3. State Obligations and Violations. 242
4.4. The Right to Education 244
4.4.1. Introduction. 244
4.4.2. Content 246
4.4.3. State Obligations and Violations. 250
4.5. The Right to Health 252
4.5.1. Introduction. 252
4.5.2. Content 254
4.5.3. State Obligations and Violations. 258
5. Towards a New Human Right to a Corruption-Free Society? 264
6. Concluding Remarks: The Merits and Limits of the Human Rights Approach to Corruption 267
6.1. General Conclusions 267
6.2. Employing the UN Treaty Bodies 268
6.3. The Role of the Human Rights Council: UPR and Special Procedures . 269
6.4. Bringing Corruption Before Regional Human Rights Instances 270
6.5. Domestic Human Rights Litigation. 271
6.6. National Human Rights Institutions (NHRIs). 272
6.7. Cooperation between Human Rights Actors and Anti-Corruption Organisations. 274

Part C
Individual Responsibility: Corruption as a Crime under International Law?

Chapter VII
Situating Corruption Within International Criminal Law 277

1. Introduction. 277
2. Key Concepts 278
2.1. ICL *largo sensu:* ICL *stricto sensu* and Transnational Criminal Law . . 278
2.2. International Crimes: Crimes under International Law and Transnational Crimes. 279
3. Corruption in International Criminal Law from a Historical Perspective . . . 283
3.1. Developments until World War I 283
3.2. Post-World War I 284
3.3. Post-World War II 285
3.4. The International Criminal Court 287
3.4.1. Developments Leading to the ICC's Establishment 287

3.4.2. *Travaux Préparatoires* of the Rome Statute 291
3.5. Findings 294
4. Rationales for the International Criminalisation of Corruption 295
4.1. Introduction: Developing a Model for International Criminalisation . . . 295
4.2. Feasibility and Motivation of Harm 296
4.2.1. Content 296
4.2.2. Defining 'Harm' at the International Level: Bassiouni's Criteria for International Criminalisation 296
4.2.3. Application 299
4.3. Tolerance 301
4.3.1. Content 301
4.3.2. Application 302
4.4. Subsidiarity 302
4.4.1. Content 302
4.4.2. Application 302
4.5. Proportionality 304
4.5.1. Content 304
4.5.2. Application 305
4.6. Legality 305
4.6.1. Content 305
4.6.2. Application 305
4.7. Practical Applicability and Effectivity 306
4.7.1. Content 306
4.7.2. Application 306
4.8. Findings 308
5. Objectives of Punishment in International Criminal Law 308
5.1. Introduction 308
5.2. Retributivism 309
5.3. Consequentialism 310
5.3.1. Deterrence 310
5.3.2. Incapacitation 311
5.3.3. Rehabilitation 311
5.4. Expressivism 311
5.5. Other Goals 313
5.6. Findings 313
6. Types of Corruption Eligible for International Criminalisation *de lege ferenda* 314
6.1. Demand-side Corruption: Tackling the Public Sector 314
6.2. Focus on Grand Corruption 314
6.3. Types of Corruption – UNCAC 316
7. Concluding Remarks 317

Chapter VIII
Corruption as a Crime Against Humanity under International Law *de lege lata*? . . . 319

1. Introduction . . . 319
2. Elements of Crimes Against Humanity: General Framework . . . 320
   2.1. Article 7 Rome Statute . . . 320
   2.2. *Actus Reus* . . . 322
   2.3. *Mens Rea* . . . 322
      2.3.1. 'Intent' . . . 323
      2.3.2. 'Knowledge' . . . 325
   2.4. Contextual Element: 'Widespread or Systematic Attack Directed Against Any Civilian Population' . . . 326
      2.4.1. 'Widespread' . . . 326
      2.4.2. 'Systematic' . . . 326
      2.4.3. 'Attack' . . . 327
      2.4.4. 'Directed Against Any Civilian Population' . . . 328
   2.5. Individual Criminal Responsibility . . . 328
3. Corruption as 'Extermination'? . . . 329
   3.1. Introduction . . . 329
   3.2. Elements of Extermination . . . 330
   3.3. Application . . . 331
4. Corruption as 'an Other Inhumane Act'? . . . 333
   4.1. Introduction . . . 333
   4.2. Elements of an Other Inhumane Act . . . 334
   4.3. Application . . . 336
5. Concluding Remarks . . . 338

Chapter IX
Possibilities of Combating Corruption under International Criminal Law *de lege ferenda*? . . . 339

1. Introduction . . . 339
2. Possible Content of an Anti-Corruption Provision in the Rome Statute . . . 340
   2.1. Inclusion of a Separate Anti-Corruption Provision? . . . 340
      2.1.1. Introduction . . . 340
      2.1.2. Passive Bribery . . . 341
      2.1.3. Embezzlement . . . 344
   2.2. Inclusion of New Crimes Against Humanity? . . . 344
3. Practical Challenges of International Prosecution Before the ICC . . . 345
4. Feasibility of Including an Anti-Corruption Provision into the Rome Statute . . . 346
5. Addressing Grand Corruption in Present Cases before the ICC . . . 347

6. Establishing an Anti-Corruption Tribunal: A Possible Alternative? 348
6.1. A Permanent Anti-Corruption Court? 348
6.2. An Ad Hoc Anti-Corruption Tribunal? 348
7. Concluding Remarks 349

PART D
SUMMARY, REFLECTIONS AND RECOMMENDATIONS

Chapter X
Summary 353

1. Introduction 353
2. Part A: The Phenomenon of Corruption: An Introductory Analysis 353
2.1. Defining and Measuring Corruption 353
2.2. Harmful Consequences of Corruption 354
2.3. Global and Regional Legal Framework 355
3. Part B: Responsibility of States: Corruption as a Violation of Human Rights? 356
3.1. Human Rights Practice 356
3.1.1. UN Human Rights Treaty Bodies 357
3.1.2. Universal Periodic Review 359
3.1.3. Special Procedures of the Human Rights Council 360
3.1.4. Regional Human Rights Mechanisms 363
3.2. Further Links 365
3.2.1. General Conclusions 365
3.2.2. Merits and Limits of the Human Rights Approach to Corruption 366
4. Part C: Individual Responsibility: Corruption as a Crime under International Law? 367
4.1. Theoretical Considerations 368
4.2. *De lege lata* Perspective 370
4.2.1. Introductory Remarks 370
4.2.2. Corruption as Extermination (Article 7(1)(b) Rome Statute)? ... 371
4.2.3. Corruption as an Other Inhumane Act (Article 7(1)(k) Rome Statute)? 372
4.3. *De Lege Ferenda* Perspective 373

Chapter XI
Reflections and Recommendations 375

1. Introduction 375
2. Corruption and International Human Rights Law 375
2.1. Paradigm Shift: Corruption as a Violation of Human Rights 375

2.2. Human Rights Treaty Bodies of the United Nations 376
2.3. Universal Periodic Review of the Human Rights Council 378
2.4. Special Procedures of the Human Rights Council 378
2.5. Regional Human Rights Mechanisms 379
3. Corruption and International Criminal Law 380
4. Final Remarks 381

Samenvatting 383
Annex 1. Overview of Concluding Observations on Corruption 407
Annex 2. General Comment on Corruption and Human Rights: A Draft Proposal 411
Bibliography 437
United Nations Documents 469
Table of Cases 481
Index 485
Curriculum Vitae 489

List of Abbreviations

ACHR	American Convention on Human Rights
AfChHPR	African Charter on Human and Peoples'Rights
AfCionHPR	African Commission on Human and Peoples'Rights
AI	Amnesty International
AU	African Union
BPI	Bribe Payers Index
CAT	Committee Against Torture
CCL 10	Allied Control Council Law No. 10
CERD	Committee on the Elimination of Racial Discrimination
CESCR	Committee on Economic, Social and Cultural Rights
CEDAW	Committee on the Elimination of All Forms of Discrimination Against Women
CITES	Convention on International Trade in Endangered Species
CO	Concluding Observations
COE	Council of Europe
CPI	Corruption Perceptions Index
CRC	Committee on the Rights of the Child
DCC	Dutch Criminal Code
DGD	Day of General Discussion
DOJ	US Department of Justice
ECHR	European Convention on Human Rights
ECtHR	European Court of Human Rights
ECOWAS	Economic Community of West African States
ECOWAS CCJ	ECOWAS Community Court of Justice
EU	European Union
FAO	Food and Agriculture Organisation
FATF	Financial Action Task Force
FCPA	Foreign Corrupt Practices Act
FDI	Foreign Direct Investment
FEC	Far Eastern Commission
GA	General Assembly of the United Nations
GC	General Comment
GCB	Global Corruption Barometer
GCR	Global Corruption Report
GRECO	Group of States Against Corruption (COE)
HRC	UN Human Rights Committee
HRCion	Human Rights Commission
HRCouncil	Human Rights Council
HRW	Human Rights Watch

IACAC	Inter-American Convention Against Corruption
IACionHR	Inter-American Commission on Human Rights
IACtHR	Inter-American Court of Human Rights
ICC	International Criminal Court
ICCPR	International Covenant on Civil and Political Rights
ICESCR	International Covenant on Economic, Social and Cultural Rights
ICHRP	International Council on Human Rights Policy
ICJ	International Court of Justice
ICL	International Criminal Law
ICPRMW	International Convention on the Protection of Rights of Migrant Workers
ICTR	International Criminal Tribunal for Rwanda
ICTY	International Criminal Tribunal for the Former Yugoslavia
ICVS	International Crime Victims Survey
ILC	International Law Commission
IMF	International Monetary Fund
KNCHR	Kenya National Commission on Human Rights
MESICIC	Follow-up Mechanism to the Inter-American Convention Against Corruption
MGs	Maastricht Guidelines on Violations of Economic, Social and Cultural Rights
MNC	Multinational Corporation
NGO	Non-governmental organisation
NHRI	National human rights institution
OAS	Organization of American States
OECD	Organisation for Economic Co-operation and Development
OHCHR	Office of the High Commissioner for Human Rights
PCIJ	Permanent Court of International Justice
PFI Convention	Convention on the Protection of the European Communities' Financial Interests
PIL	Public Interest Litigation
SADC	Southern African Development Community
SC	Security Council of the United Nations
SEC	Securities and Exchange Commission
SERAP	Social Economic Rights and Accountability Project
SR	Special Rapporteur
TI	Transparency International
UDHR	Universal Declaration of Human Rights
UN	United Nations
UNCAC	United Nations Convention Against Corruption
UNCRC	United Nations Convention on the Rights of the Child
UNCh	Charter of the United Nations

UNCTOC	United Nations Convention Against Transnational Organized Crime
UN.GIFT	United Nations Global Initiative to Fight Human Trafficking
UNODC	United Nations Office on Drugs and Crime
UNWCC	United Nations War Crimes Commission
UPR	Universal Periodic Review
VCLT	Vienna Convention on the Law of Treaties
WB	World Bank
WGB	Working Group on Bribery (OECD)
WGC	working Group on Communications
WGS	Working Group on Situations
WTO	World Trade Organization
WW I	First World War
WW II	Second World War
WWF	World Wide Fund

General Introduction

'Earth provides enough to satisfy every man's need, but not every man's greed.'

~ Mahatma Gandhi ~

1. A Day in the Life of John and Jane Doe

Societal problems, including corruption, are often examined by researchers and policymakers at the abstract macro-level. Yet, it is sometimes more appropriate to step out of the bubble of statistics, tables and graphs, by considering corruption's actual impact on human dignity at the micro-level. This section therefore takes the reader on a journey to a developing country, be it in Africa, Latin America or Asia, offering insights into the life of an average working class family that can barely make ends meet.[1]

Out of a meager salary, John Doe, the male head of the family, supports himself, his wife Jane, their three children and a number of elderly relatives living with them. On an ordinary weekday, John takes the bus from his house in a rural village to his poorly paid job in the city. On the way to the city, the bus driver is stopped by a police officer, who apparently identified a traffic violation. For the bus to continue the journey, the driver has to pay 'a little something extra' to the policeman. During his workday at the factory, producing goods for a multinational footwear manufacturer, John is exposed to toxic substances, while appropriate protective clothing is absent. Although labour inspectors did visit the factory recently, it is believed that they did not report violations of health and safety regulations to their superiors.

Meanwhile, Jane walks two of her children to the village school. Today, she also wishes to register her youngest son there, so that he can also attend school next month. While primary education in the country is supposed to be free, Jane has to pay a sum of money to the school's headmaster. Otherwise, enrolment at school will not be possible. Jane is also worried about her daughter's complaints about the lack of school books and pencils, and about the school building, which is in a state of

1 Inspired by the short story about a day in the life of Juma Ali, as described by Laurence Cockroft, 'Corruption and Human Rights: A Crucial Link', *Working Paper* (Berlin: Transparency International, 19 October 1998) and by the fictional case study of 'Painland' in Brigit Toebes, 'Health Sector Corruption and Human Rights: A Case Study', in Martine Boersma and Hans Nelen (eds.), *Corruption and Human Rights: Interdisciplinary Perspectives* (Maastricht Series in Human Rights; Antwerp: Intersentia, 2010, p. 91–123.

near collapse. Rumour has it that officials from the provincial authorities made educational funds somehow 'disappear.'

After bringing the children to school, Jane takes her 75-year-old mother-in-law to the local hospital, since she is suffering from an unknown illness. However, upon arrival at the poorly equipped public clinic, the nurses pay no attention to the women, and they have to wait for hours and hours. At the same time, Jane observes that some persons arriving much later do receive proper medical care, and realises that those people get privileged treatment because they can afford to bribe the nurses, whose salaries were not paid in the last few months. When finally a doctor comes to see the old lady, he cannot help her because the medication is allegedly no longer available. He does offer to provide treatment at a private health clinic, run by himself.

At the end of the afternoon, Jane has to attend a court case about a dispute with the landlord. However, since the latter can afford to bribe the judge, the Doe family loses the case. Before evening falls, John and Jane head for the ballot box to vote in the country's elections. The couple hopes that the opposition party will be able to deliver its promises to combat the looting of the country's natural resource wealth by the current Government. Jane read in the newspaper that many government officials inhabit palatial mansions, and that their wives engage in shopping sprees in European capitals. She was sad to find out that the journalist responsible for this information was recently arrested. While standing in line near the election office, John and Jane are approached by 'supporters' of the current President, offering them money to vote for the ruling party, which they decline. Later, the couple finds out that this party wins the elections with a massive 80 per cent of the votes, and they tell each other that voting in the next round of elections will not be of use anyway. Another day has ended for the Doe family.

2. Overview of Contemporary Research

2.1. Corruption as a Violation of Human Rights?

As illustrated by the short fictional case study above, corruption in the public sector can have a severe negative impact upon human dignity. However, the idea that this practice may be a violation of human rights is relatively new. No global or regional human rights instrument contains specific reference to corruption, and anti-corruption treaties only rarely refer to human rights.[2] Nevertheless, in recent times

2 Also pointed out by Daniel Kaufmann, 'Human Rights and Governance: The Empirical Challenge', in Philip Alston and Mary Robinson (eds.), *Human Rights and Development: Towards Mutual Reinforcement* (Oxford: Oxford University Press, 2005), p. 352–402 at p. 370–371. An exception is the African Union Convention on Preventing and Combating Corruption, stating in its Preamble that the AU's Member States are 'aware of the need to respect human dignity and to foster the promotion of economic, social, and political rights in conformity with the provisions of the African Charter on Human and People's Rights and other relevant human

a number of scholars have started the discussion on linking corruption to the human rights field. The present section gives a (mainly chronological) overview of key literature on the topic.

One of the first scholars to take up the relationship between corruption and human rights was Kofele-Kale. This author placed corruption within the discourse of human rights and international criminal law.[3] *Inter alia*, Kofele-Kale argued for the establishment of an independent human right to a corruption-free society, flowing from the right to permanent sovereignty over natural resources as enshrined in common Article 1 ICCPR and ICESCR, as well as from the right to development.[4] Since it can be seriously doubted whether the proposal of new or 'emerging' human rights actually leads to improved human rights protection,[5] this is not the approach adopted in the present work. Nevertheless, proposals to formulate a new anti-corruption human right are examined in more detail in a later chapter.[6]

Two short Transparency International working papers released in 1998 take the approach of focusing on existing human rights. Cockroft described the links between anti-corruption campaigns and actions to advance human rights.[7] Jayawickrama went more into detail. He found that corruption can constitute a violation of existing human rights because (i) it perpetuates discrimination; (ii) it prevents the full realization of economic, social and cultural rights; and (iii) it leads to the infringement of several civil and political rights.[8] This view was embraced in

---

rights instruments.' Furthermore, the Preamble of the Council of Europe's Criminal Law Convention on Corruption provides that the Member States emphasise that 'corruption threatens the rule of law, democracy and human rights, undermines good governance, fairness and social justice, distorts competition, hinders economic development and endangers the stability of democratic institutions and the moral foundations of society.' A similar reference to human rights can be found in the Preamble of the Council of Europe's Civil Law Convention on Corruption. For an analysis of the existing anti-corruption treaties, the reader is referred to chapter II.

3 Ndiva Kofele-Kale, 'Patrimonicide: The International Economic Crime of Indigenous Spoliation', *Vanderbilt Journal of Transnational Law*, 28 (1995), p. 45–118; Ndiva Kofele-Kale, 'The Right to a Corruption-Free Society as an Individual and Collective Human Right: Elevating Official Corruption to a Crime under International Law', *The International Lawyer*, 34 (2000), p. 149–178; Ndiva Kofele-Kale, *The International Law of Responsibility for Economic Crimes: Holding State Officials Individually Liable for Acts of Fraudulent Enrichment* (2 edn.; Aldershot: Ashgate, 2006); Ndiva Kofele-Kale, 'Change or the Illusion of Change: The War against Official Corruption in Africa', *George Washington International Law Review*, 38/4 (2006), p. 697–747.

4 See *inter alia* Kofele-Kale, 'The Right to a Corruption-Free Society as an Individual and Collective Human Right: Elevating Official Corruption to a Crime under International Law', at p. 163 *et seq.*

5 For example, the 'emerging human right' to tobacco control, as proposed by Carolyn Dresler and Stephen P. Marks, 'The Emerging Human Right to Tobacco Control' *Human Rights Quarterly*, 28 (2006), p. 599–651.

6 See chapter VI, §5.

7 Cockroft, 'Corruption and Human Rights: A Crucial Link.'

8 Nihal Jayawickrama, 'Corruption – a Violation of Human Rights?' (Sofia, 1–2 June 1998).

2002 by Peter Eigen, founder and then Chairman of Transparency International.[9] In 2008, Transparency International released a new brief working paper on human rights and corruption.[10]

Another author who further developed an actual international human rights approach to corruption is Pearson. She noted that 'moving from an economic and political perspective on corruption to a human rights approach involves shifting from viewing corruption as a misappropriation of wealth and distortion of expenditure [...], to viewing corruption and the tolerance of corruption by States as also being a breach of fundamental human rights.'[11] Pearson listed a number of human rights, and explained how these might be violated by corruption. In this respect, she distinguished between the following groups of rights: (i) rights to affiliation; (ii) rights to life, bodily health and integrity; (iii) rights to political participation; (iv) rights to non-discrimination and the rule of law; and (v) rights to social and economic development.[12] Interestingly, Pearson cited a number of concluding observations of the human rights treaty bodies to support her argument.

Dowell-Jones also took the practice of the human rights treaty bodies into account. In a broader study of the practice of the Committee on Economic, Social and Cultural Rights when dealing with economic matters, she reviewed the Committee's summary records between 1996 and 2000, and concluded *inter alia* that the Committee experiences considerable difficulties in addressing the topic of corruption.[13]

In 2002, a piece by Buckley shed light on the relationship between corruption and human rights. She set out what anti-corruption and human rights have in common and where the two do not intersect, discussed how corruption impacts human rights, explored the aims of the anti-corruption movement, and examined dilemmas of radicalism and pragmatism in anti-corruption work. Finally, she considered the potentials of a coalition between the anti-corruption movement and human rights work.[14]

Furthermore, in the work of Raj Kumar, the central idea is that corruption can be framed as a violation of human rights.[15] Following the arguments of Kofele-

---

9 Peter Eigen, 'Corruption in a Globalized World', *SAIS Review*, 22 (2002), p. 45–59 at p. 48–50.

10 Transparency International, 'Human Rights and Corruption', *Working Paper* (2008).

11 Zoe Pearson, 'An International Human Rights Approach to Corruption', in Peter Larmour & Nick Wolanin (ed.), *Corruption and Anti-Corruption* (Canberra: Asia Pacific Press, 2001), p. 30–61 at p. 46.

12 *Ibid.* at p. 45–46.

13 Mary Dowell-Jones, *Contextualising the International Covenant on Economic, Social and Cultural Rights: Assessing the Economic Deficit* (International Studies in Human Rights, 80; Leiden Martinus Nijhoff Publishers, 2004) at p. 81–96.

14 Marella Buckley, 'Anti-Corruption Initiatives and Human Rights: The Potentials', in Hans-Otto Sano and Gudmundur Alfredsson (eds.), *Human Rights and Good Governance. Building Bridges* (The Raoul Wallenberg Institute Human Rights Library, 9; The Hague: Kluwer Law International, 2002), p. 173–201.

15 C Raj Kumar, 'Corruption and Human Rights: Promoting Transparency in Governance and the Fundamental Right to Corruption-Free Service in India', *Columbia Journal of Asian Law*, 17

Kale, Raj Kumar argued in favour of a separate fundamental human right to a corruption-free society.[16] Moreover, Raj Kumar linked corruption to violations of the principle of non-discrimination (Article 26 ICCPR and Article 2(2) ICESCR).[17] In addition, he found that Article 2(1) ICESCR obliges States to take efforts against corruption, and that the rights laid down in Article 25 ICCPR are impinged by electoral corruption.[18] Finally, he discussed the relevance of Article 19 ICCPR on the freedom of information, in respect of fighting corruption.[19]

During the 12th International Anti-Corruption Conference (the world's main gathering on anti-corruption) in 2006, Morten Kjaerum (then member of the Committee on the Elimination of Racial Discrimination) argued that in the human rights world, too little attention has been paid to the effects of corruption on human rights. He held that the UN Committees do address corruption, but not to the extent the issue deserves, and that the development of strategies by human rights institutions and NGOs at the national level was at the early stages. He then went on to note the added value of involving human rights in combating corruption.[20] Kjaerum's claim about the lack of attention paid to corruption by the treaty bodies is an interesting one, and will be verified in a later chapter of the present thesis.[21]

Within the UN context, attention for corruption and human rights is also emerging. In 2007, a study was conducted for the United Nations Development Program by Sunga and Bottigliero, linking anti-corruption and human rights. Amongst other things, it examined how corruption can threaten human rights; how weak human rights promotion and protection can create conditions increasing corruption; and considered how human rights based approaches in anti-corruption strategies can strengthen democracy and the rule of law and promote the enjoyment of human rights. Recommendations were formulated, directed to the work of the UNDP.[22] In addition, in a 2007 report, the Office of the High Commissioner for

---

(2003), p. 31–72 at p. 35. Similar arguments are made in C Raj Kumar, 'Corruption and Human Rights – II', *Frontline,* 19/20 (12–25 October 2002); C Raj Kumar, 'Corruption and Human Rights – I', *Frontline,* 19/19 (14–27 September 2002). C Raj Kumar, 'Corruption as a Human Rights Issue in South Asia: Law, Development and Governance', *Human Rights 2006: the Year in Review* (Castan Centre for Human Rights Law, Monash University, Melbourne, 1 December 2006).

16 See Raj Kumar, 'Corruption and Human Rights: Promoting Transparency in Governance and the Fundamental Right to Corruption-Free Service in India', at p. 35 *et seq.*

17 *Ibid.* at p. 58 *et seq.*

18 *Ibid.* at p. 59.

19 *Ibid.* at p. 59–60.

20 Morten Kjaerum, 'Breaking the Vicious Cycle: Corruption and Poverty; Obstacles to Social and Economic Rights. A Human Rights Based Bottom-up Approach.' *12th International Anti-Corruption Conference* (Guatemala City and Antigua, Guatemala, 2006), to be consulted at <www.12iacc.org/archivos/KJAERUM.pdf>, accessed 8 August 2011.

21 See chapter III.

22 Lyal S. Sunga and Ilaria Bottigliero, 'In-Depth Study on the Linkages between Anti-Corruption and Human Rights for the United Nations Development Program', (Raoul Wallenberg Institute, 15 January 2007).

Human Rights linked corruption to human rights and offered case studies in which anti-corruption efforts relied on human rights and good governance principles, including accountability, transparency and inclusion, and which have had a positive impact on human rights protection.[23]

The recent project by the International Council on Human Rights Policy (hereafter: ICHRP), a Swiss NGO, is thus by far the most elaborate one on the topic of corruption and human rights. Two reports and a number of working papers were published.[24] One of the key working papers was written by Bacio Terracino.[25] Unlike the position taken by Kofele-Kale and Raj Kumar, the ICHRP's work did not argue as such for the recognition of a separate right to a corruption-free society. Rather it focused, like Jayawickrama and Pearson, upon the human rights contained in the existing international human rights treaties, and examined how various forms of corruption may violate these rights.[26] This is the approach also adopted in the present work.[27]

Other authors who have examined the matter of corruption and human rights in one way or another are Kaufmann,[28] Gathii,[29] Chun,[30] and Mendes.[31] Furthermore,

---

23 Office of the United Nations High Commissioner for Human Rights, 'Good Governance Practices for the Protection of Human Rights', (Geneva, 2007) at p. 59–79, to be consulted through <www.ohchr.org/Documents/Publications/GoodGovernance.pdf>, accessed 8 August 2011.

24 Reports: International Council on Human Rights Policy, *Corruption and Human Rights: Making the Connection* (Versoix, Switzerland, 2009); International Council on Human Rights Policy, *Integrating Human Rights in the Anti-Corruption Agenda: Challenges, Possibilities and Opportunities* (Geneva, Switzerland, 2010). The main findings of the ICHRP can also be found in Magdalena Sepúlveda Carmona and Julio Bacio Terracino, 'Corruption and Human Rights: Making the Connection', in Martine Boersma and Hans Nelen (eds.), *Corruption & Human Rights: Interdisciplinary Perspectives* (Antwerp: Intersentia, 2010), p. 25–49. The 2009 report and accompanying working papers can be consulted through <www.ichrp.org/en/projects/131>. The 2010 report can be consulted through <www.ichrp.org/en/projects/1312>, accessed 3 September 2010.

25 Julio Bacio Terracino, 'Hard Law Connections between Corruption and Human Rights', *Working Paper* (Geneva: International Council on Human Rights Policy, 2007), to be consulted through <www.ichrp.org/files/papers/130/131_-_Julio_Bacio_Terracino_-_2007.pdf>, accessed 3 September 2010.

26 International Council on Human Rights Policy, *Corruption and Human Rights: Making the Connection* at p. 3.

27 See in particular chapter VI.

28 Kaufmann, 'Human Rights and Governance: The Empirical Challenge.'

29 James Thuo Gathii, 'Defining the Relationship between Human Rights and Corruption', *University of Pennsylvania Journal of International Law*, 31 (2009), p. 125–202.

30 Liu Chun, 'The Control of Corruption and Protection of Human Rights', in Errol P. Mendes and Anik Lalonde-Roussy (eds.), *Bridging the Global Divide on Human Rights: A Canada-China Dialogue* (Aldershot: Ashgate, 2003), p. 305–327, offering insights into the Chinese context.

31 Errol P. Mendes, 'Corruption: The Cancer of the International Bill of Rights – Democracy and Freedom of Expression, the Main Treatments?' in Errol P. Mendes and Anik Lalonde-Roussy (eds.), *Bridging the Global Divide on Human Rights: A Canada-China Dialogue* (Aldershot: Ashgate, 2003), p. 287–302, linking corruption and human rights to democracy and to the freedom of expression.

in 2009 the Council of Europe Commissioner for Human Rights, Thomas Hammarberg, firmly stated that 'corruption is a major human rights problem.'[32] Moreover, recent research on corruption and human rights can be found in a conference volume by the Maastricht Centre for Human Rights, encompassing contributions from various disciplines.[33] While the majority of contributing authors is in favour of using human rights to fight corruption, some contributors firmly oppose this approach.[34] Their arguments will be considered below.[35]

The present work aims to elaborate further on existing research, by taking individual human rights as a starting point and by closely examining how corruption can violate these rights. What is largely absent in the research described above, is a thorough analysis of the ways in which corruption is being dealt with in the human rights supervisory mechanisms at the global and regional level. Although Pearson and Dowell-Jones did touch upon the concluding observations and summary records of the treaty bodies, a comprehensive study of human rights practice in relation to corruption was not yet conducted. Hence, the current dissertation departs from human rights practice rather than from theory, by examining case law, treaty body practice, and other output of human rights supervisory bodies, thus providing an inclusive analysis of corruption and human rights *de lege lata.* After this analysis, the remaining links are further elaborated upon, and recommendations are provided.

2.2. Corruption as a Crime under International Law?

In the field of international criminal law, little scholarly attention has been paid thus far to corruption. Kofele-Kale argued that the breach of the independent right to a corruption-free society should be treated as a crime under international law.[36] He even went as far as claiming that 'one can safely conclude that an emerging customary law norm that treats corruption as a crime under international law draws strong support [...].'[37]

32 Thomas Hammarberg, 'Corruption Is a Major Human Rights Problem', *CommDH/Speech (2009)9* (Strassbourg, 5 October 2009).

33 Martine Boersma and Hans Nelen (eds.), *Corruption & Human Rights: Interdisciplinary Perspectives* (Maastricht Series in Human Rights Antwerp: Intersentia, 2010).

34 Morag Goodwin and Kate Rose-Sender, 'Linking Corruption and Human Rights: An Unwelcome Addition to the Development Discourse', in Martine Boersma and Hans Nelen (eds.), *Corruption & Human Rights: Interdisciplinary Perspectives* (Maastricht Series in Human Rights Antwerp: Intersentia, 2010), p. 221–240.

35 See chapter VI, §2.4.

36 See for example Kofele-Kale, 'The Right to a Corruption-Free Society as an Individual and Collective Human Right: Elevating Official Corruption to a Crime under International Law', at p. 152.

37 *Ibid.* at p. 172–173.

Other authors suggesting that corruption deserves to be a crime under international law, or even that it already has acquired that status, are Acheampong,[38] Ocheje,[39] Acquaah-Gaisie,[40] Eboe-Osuji,[41] Davidsson,[42] Bantekas,[43] Starr,[44] and Evans Webster.[45] For instance, Bantekas suggested that corruption might fulfil the requirements of the crime of extermination (Article 7(2)(b) of the Rome Statute),[46] while Starr and Acquaah-Gaisie argued that the requirements of an 'other inhumane act' (Article 7(2)(k) of the Rome Statute) can be met by grand corruption.[47]

While the scholars in question have certainly contributed to placing corruption within the debate on international criminalisation, their analysis is far from exhaustive. They have not examined in a comprehensive manner whether certain forms of corruption can be qualified as crimes under international law as it currently stands, taking relevant theory and practice into account. Nor have they explored the possible content of a future provision on corruption, to be inserted into the Rome Statute, or other ways in which international criminal law may be used to fight corruption. These matters are addressed in this dissertation, where necessary elaborating upon previous research.

---

38 Kenneth Asamoa Acheampong, 'Combating Grand Corruption: The Potential Impact of a United Nations Convention on the Prevention and Punishment of the Crime of Economic Genocide', *Revue Africaine des Droits de l'Homme*, 7 (1998), p. 38–55.

39 Paul D. Ocheje, 'Refocusing International Law on the Quest for Accountability in Africa: The Case against The "Other" Impunity', *Leiden Journal of International Law*, 15 (2002), p. 749–779.

40 Gerald Acquaah-Gaisie, 'Grand Corruption – a Crime against Humanity'. *The Global Business and Technology Association International Conference* (Lisbon, 2005); Gerald Acquaah-Gaisie, 'Curbing Financial Crime among Third World Elites', *Journal of Money Laundering Control*, 8 (2005), p. 371–381.

41 Chile Eboe-Osuji, 'Kleptocracy: A Desired Subject of International Criminal Law That Is in Dire Need of Prosecution by Universal Jurisdiction', in Evelyn A. Ankumah and Edward K. Kwakwa (eds.), *African Perspectives on International Criminal Justice* (Special Series, 3; Accra-Maastricht-Pretoria: Africa Legal Aid, 2005), p. 121–132.

42 Elias Davidsson, 'Economic Oppression as an International Wrong or as a Crime against Humanity', *Netherlands Quarterly of Human Rights*, 23 (2005), p. 173–212.

43 Ilias Bantekas, 'Corruption as an International Crime and a Crime against Humanity: An Outline of Supplementary Criminal Justice Policies', *Journal of International Criminal Justice*, 4 (2006), p. 466–484.

44 Sonja Starr, 'Extraordinary Crimes at Ordinary Times: International Justice Beyond Crisis Situations', *Northwestern University Law Review*, 101 (2007), p. 1257–1314.

45 Mary Evans Webster, 'Fifteen Minutes of Shame: The Growing Notoriety of Grand Corruption', *Hastings International and Comparative Law Review*, 31 (2008), p. 807–826.

46 Bantekas, 'Corruption as an International Crime and a Crime against Humanity: An Outline of Supplementary Criminal Justice Policies', at p. 474 *et seq.*

47 Starr, 'Extraordinary Crimes at Ordinary Times: International Justice Beyond Crisis Situations', at p. 1297. Acquaah-Gaisie, 'Grand Corruption – a Crime against Humanity' at p. 1, 5–6; Acquaah-Gaisie, 'Curbing Financial Crime among Third World Elites', at p. 379. Effeh also touched upon Article 7(2)(k), see Ubong E. Effeh, 'Sub-Saharan Africa: A Case Study on How Not to Realize Economic, Social and Cultural Rights, and a Proposal for Change', *Northwestern Journal of International Human Rights*, 3 (2005).

3. Main Research Questions

Having taken stock of scholarly work done so far on the linkages between corruption on the one hand and human rights law and international criminal law on the other, the present work seeks to answer the following questions:

(1) What global and regional legal framework currently exists to curb corruption, and how does it function?

(2) Is it possible to conceptualise (certain forms of) public sector corruption as a violation of human rights?
  a) What does the practice of global and regional human rights supervisory mechanisms reveal about the links between corruption and human rights violations?
  b) What further links can be established between corruption and human rights violations, and what are the merits and limits of such an approach?

(3) Is it possible to conceptualise (certain forms of) public sector corruption as a crime under international law?
  a) Should the system of international criminal law be used to fight corruption, and if so, which forms of corruption would qualify for this approach?
  b) Can certain forms of corruption be conceptualised under the Rome Statute as a crime against humanity *de lege lata*?
  c) What possibilities does international criminal law *de lege ferenda* offer to combat corruption at the international level?

4. Structure

4.1. Part A: The Phenomenon of Corruption: An Introductory Analysis

Part A analyses the problem of corruption with the purpose of providing a general framework as a basis for the entire study. To begin with, chapter I (*Basic Issues*) formulates a working definition of corruption, and contains an inventory of the various types of corrupt practices. Moreover, attention is paid to the ways in which corruption can possibly be measured, and to the harmful consequences of corruption.

Subsequently, chapter II (*Global and Regional Legal Framework Against Corruption*) concerns the content and functioning of the global and regional anti-corruption treaties which are in force at this very moment. Otherwise, it would not be possible to give a sound opinion on the potential existence of an accountability gap which these instruments might leave. Hence, this second chapter aims to answer research question (1).

4.2. Part B: Responsibility of States: Corruption as a Violation of Human Rights?

Part B concerns the obligations on the part of the State: human rights obligations in international law. It determines whether it is possible to conceptualise (certain forms of) public sector corruption as a violation of human rights. Hence, this part answers overall research question (2).

Sub-question 2(a), asking how corruption is dealt with in global and regional human rights practice, is answered in chapters III, IV and V. The essence of these chapters lies in discussing the practice of the human rights supervisory organs in order to determine what attention they have devoted to corruption in relation to human rights (*de lege lata*). Do they find that forms of corruption are in themselves a violation of a certain right? What are the differences between the various supervisory organs in dealing with corruption? Therefore, chapter III (*Treaty-Based System*) discusses how the UN human rights treaty bodies, supervising State compliance with the international human rights treaties, have dealt with corruption so far. Chapter IV (*Charter-Based System*) examines the outcome of the Universal Periodic Review of the UN Human Rights Council, and a number of the Council's Special Procedures. Chapter V considers the practice of the regional mechanisms for human rights protection in Europe, the Americas and Africa.

Sub-question 2(b) is dealt with in chapter VI (*Taking it Further*), which elaborates on the findings of the preceding chapters. As pointed out by Pearson, 'an examination of corruption in terms of the effects that it has on human rights involves highlighting specific rights and how they may be violated.'[48] Whenever there appears to be a gap in the reasoning of the human rights supervisory bodies, the further links between corruption and violations of the right concerned are developed. The chapter links actual or hypothetical cases of corruption to the precise obligations of States under the provisions of human rights treaties, and tries to demonstrate that corrupt practices can indeed violate these rights. The examples mentioned do not intend to provide an exhaustive overview of all possible forms of corruption in a certain area impacting upon human rights. Rather, they offer illustrations of potential violations that can serve as an inspiration to scholars, civil society organisations and governmental organisations. Moreover, this chapter discusses the added value, as well as the limits, of using human rights law in the fight against corruption.

---

48 Pearson, 'An International Human Rights Approach to Corruption', at p. 50.

4.3. Part C: Individual Responsibility: Corruption as a Crime under International Law?

Part C analyses whether it is possible to conceptualise (certain forms of) public sector corruption as a crime under international law, and thus aims to provide a satisfactory answer to research question (3).

Chapter VII (*Situating Corruption within International Criminal Law*) aims to determine whether international criminal law is an appropriate system to combat corruption, i.e. sub-question 3(a). First, the notions 'international criminal law' (*largo sensu* and *stricto sensu*) and 'transnational criminal law' are clarified, as well as the concepts 'international crimes', 'crimes under international law', and 'transnational crimes'. Second, a brief study of the historical roots of international criminal law is conducted, in order to find out what attention has been paid to corruption in recent history. Third, the underlying rationales of international criminalisation are examined, so as to determine whether it would make proper sense to criminalise corrupt offences at the international plane, even if this might not be self-evident from the historical analysis. Attention is paid to the criteria of harm, tolerance, subsidiarity, proportionality, legality, and practical applicability and effectiveness. Fourth, the objectives of punishment in international law are considered, to establish whether these can be met by criminalising corruption internationally. These objectives are retributivism, consequentialism, expressivism, and a number of other goals of punishment at the international level. Finally, whenever one concludes that anti-corruption would fit within the area of international criminal law, it has to be ascertained which forms of corruption qualify for international criminalisation. This is done by taking the provisions of the United Nations Convention Against Corruption as a starting point.

After having situated corruption within the system of international criminal law, chapter VIII (*Corruption as a Crime Against Humanity under International Law* de lege lata) addresses question 3(b), and considers whether corruption can constitute a crime against humanity under Article 7 of the Rome Statute. To this end, the general concept of crimes against humanity is examined, by studying its components: (i) *actus reus*; (ii) *mens rea*; and (iii) the contextual element. Subsequently, a number of crimes against humanity that are currently criminalised in the Rome Statute are considered, in order to determine whether these offences can possibly cover corrupt practices. Scholarly claims arguing that corruption can be seen as either extermination (Article 7(1)(b)), or as another inhumane act (Article 7 (1)(k)), are carefully scrutinised.

Chapter IX (*Possibilities of Combating Corruption under International Criminal Law* de lege ferenda?) explores the possible content of a new anti-corruption provision in the Rome Statute, as well as the practical and political feasibility of such a provision. Moreover, it examines whether corruption can be dealt with in current cases before the ICC, and/or whether the establishment of a separate anti-corruption tribunal is an option (sub-question 3(c)).

4.4. Part D: Summary, Reflections and Recommendations

Chapter X (*Summary*) summarises the findings of the entire study and draws conclusions from Parts A, B and C. The final chapter XI (*Reflections and Recommendations*) provides some further reflections on the topic and issues recommendations on how to cope with corruption in the future in the context of international human rights law and international criminal law. In this regard, a draft proposal for a joint General Comment on Corruption and Human Rights is included, which can be of use to the Human Rights Committee and the Committee on Economic, Social and Cultural Rights, but which may also be valuable to the other treaty bodies and to non-governmental organisations, scholars and practitioners working in the field of human rights.

5. Methodology

Given the significance of methodology in legal research in general,[49] and in human rights research in particular, the current section discusses for the three parts of the present study (i) how relevant information has been collected; (ii) how this information has been organised; and (iii) how the results are interpreted.[50] At the outset it can be noted that the thesis, consisting of desktop research, attempts to draw general conclusions by means of inductive reasoning, moving from specific observations to broader generalisations and theories (bottom-up approach).[51]

5.1. Part A: The Phenomenon of Corruption: An Introductory Analysis

The research method adopted in chapter I is the study of a wide range of secondary literature. Since corruption is a complex societal phenomenon, one cannot confine him- or herself to an examination of legal writings only. Therefore, sources in other disciplines such as economics, political science, anthropology and criminology were also taken into account. Chapter I thus aims to provide an interdisciplinary view of the topic, with the limitation that the author remains a lawyer by training. Literature used in chapter I was primarily selected from the Dutch library database

---

49 A particularly refreshing and revealing work in this respect is Hervé Tijssen, *De Juridische Dissertatie Onder de Loep. De Verantwoording van Methodologische Keuzes in Juridische Dissertaties* (Den Haag: Boom Juridische Uitgevers, 2009).

50 This trichotomy was noted by Fons Coomans, Fred Grünfeld, and Menno T. Kamminga, 'A Primer', in Fons Coomans, Fred Grünfeld, and Menno Kamminga (eds.), *Methods of Human Rights Research* (Maastricht Series in Human Rights; Antwerp: Intersentia, 2009), p. 11–17 at p. 14.

51 Observations => Patterns => Tentative hypothesis => Theory. See William M.K. Trochim (Cornell University), 'Research Methods Knowledge Base', <www.socialresearchmethods.net/kb/dedind.php>, accessed 26 May 2009.

Picarta,[52] and from the international legal journal databases Hein Online[53] and Westlaw.[54] Whenever reference is made in chapter I, or in other chapters of the dissertation, to research done by actors such as the World Bank and Transparency International, this does not necessarily entail that the author endorses the broader policies and views of these organisations.

The method employed in chapter II is an analysis of the texts of all anti-corruption treaties at the global and regional plane. Use was also made of explanatory documents, including those published by the international or regional organisations in which context the treaties came into being. These documents can be found on the websites of the organisations concerned, such as the UN, the Council of Europe, the European Union, the OECD, the African Union and the Organization of American States. In addition, scholarly commentaries on the legal instruments were taken into account, which can be found by searching through Picarta, Hein Online and Westlaw, as well as by exploring the Internet. Finally, NGO documents – many by anti-corruption NGO Transparency International – were consulted.

5.2. Part B: Responsibility of States: Corruption as a Violation of Human Rights?

5.2.1. Data Collection and Organisation

- UN Treaty Bodies: Concluding Observations

The UN human rights treaty bodies are quasi-judicial organs which can be considered the highest authorities in the field of human rights at the universal level. Chapter III discusses the practice on corruption of the Human Rights Committee; the Committee on Economic, Social and Cultural Rights; the Committee on the Rights of the Child; the Committee on the Elimination of All Forms of Discrimination Against Women; the Committee on the Elimination of Racial Discrimination; and the Committee Against Torture. Important output of these bodies are the concluding observations, adopted by the committees as a result of the

---

52 Picarta, <www.picarta.nl> provides access to the library collections (books, journal articles, and electronic resources in all disciplines) of all Dutch universities, public libraries, many ministries and a large number of specialised libraries.

53 Hein Online, <www.heinonline.org> is a database containing articles from legal journals.

54 Westlaw, <www.westlaw.com> is a database containing case law, US State and federal statutes, administrative codes, newspaper and magazine articles, public records, law journals, law reviews, treatises, legal forms and other information resources.

examination of State reports in the State reporting procedure.[55] These observations are not binding: they are recommendations to the State in question.[56]

The concluding observations about corruption were collected as follows. In order to search through the observations by keyword, the Universal Human Rights Index of the United Nations may be used.[57] However, this database does not contain the concluding observations before the year 2000. Moreover, the treaty body document search on the website of the Office of the UN High Commissioner for Human Rights does not facilitate browsing by keyword.[58] Given these shortcomings of the two UN databases, the online database of the Netherlands Institute of Human Rights (SIM) of the Utrecht School of Law was consulted.[59] This database contains all concluding observations of the HRC, CESCR, CERD, CAT, CEDAW and the CRC. The search terms that were used were the following: corrupt*, brib*, misappropriat* and embezzle*. The wildcards (*) serve to include derivatives of a certain term, for example 'bribes' as well as 'bribery'.[60] The keyword corrupt* generated the majority of results.

As examples, a number of concluding observations are quoted in full, also to grasp the wording that is used by the treaty bodies to condemn corruption. The other observations are referred to in footnotes, and an overview can be found at the end of the present work in Annex 1. All observations issued until 15 June 2011 were taken into account.

- UN Treaty Bodies: Views on Individual Complaints

Chapter III on treaty body practice also discusses the views that were adopted in individual complaints procedures by the Human Rights Committee, the Committee Against Torture, the Committee on the Elimination of Racial Discrimination, and the Committee on the Elimination of Discrimination Against Women. These views carry great moral authority, but they are not binding under international law.[61] The views were collected by making use of SIM's database, using the four keywords listed above. All views adopted until 15 June 2011 were taken into account.

---

55 For more on the concluding observations of the Human Rights Committee, see Manfred Nowak, *UN Covenant on Civil and Political Rights: CCPR Commentary* (2 edn.; Kehl: Engel, 2005) at p. 739–746, §48–60.

56 Michael O'Flaherty, 'The Concluding Observations of the United Nations Human Rights Treaty Bodies', *Human Rights Law Review*, 6 (2006), p. 27–52 at p. 33.

57 United Nations, Universal Human Rights Index, <www.universalhumanrightsindex.org >.

58 Office of the United Nations High Commissioner for Human Rights, Treaty Body Document Search, <http://tb.ohchr.org/default.aspx>.

59 Netherlands Institute of Human Rights (SIM), Documentation Site <http://sim.law.uu.nl/sim/Dochome.nsf>.

60 See chapter I, section 3 for a discussion of the various forms of corruption, which gave rise to the selection of these keywords.

61 Nowak, *UN Covenant on Civil and Political Rights: CCPR Commentary* at p. XXII, §6 and p. 894–897, §39–44.

- UN Human Rights Council: Universal Periodic Review

Chapter IV pays attention to the way in which corruption is discussed by States during the Universal Periodic Review, a peer review mechanism under the UN Human Rights Council, established in 2006. The added value of a study into this system lies *inter alia* in the fact that the human rights record of all 192 UN Member States is reviewed every four years, regardless of whether they are Parties to a particular human rights treaty or not. When conducting a study into the UPR, the website of UPR Info, a Geneva-based NGO is a useful tool. UPR Info developed a database containing all UPR recommendations made in the first seven UPR sessions, categorised by topic. Interestingly, the issue of corruption is among the standard classification keywords, and therefore all recommendations about corruption to States under review can be easily accessed.[62] Nevertheless, not only the ultimate recommendations are relevant. Also remarks of the State under review, and comments not being recommendations should be taken into account. Therefore, the present study was based on the Working Group's outcome reports of the first eight UPR sessions. All 128 outcome reports were obtained from the database on the website of the Office of the UN High Commissioner for Human Rights.[63] Use was made of the keyword 'corrupt', also generating results for derivations. This search generated most instances in which corruption is discussed in the outcome reports.

- UN Human Rights Council: Special Procedures

A wide variety of Special Procedures exists under the Human Rights Council, both thematic mandates and country mandates.[64] There are currently thirty-three thematic mandates. Since it is not feasible to examine all of them, a selection was made of ten relevant thematic Procedures for the purpose of the present study: (i) the former Special Rapporteur on corruption and its impact on the full enjoyment of human rights, in particular economic, social and cultural rights; (ii) the Independent Expert on the question of human rights and extreme poverty; (iii) the Special Rapporteur on the right to adequate housing; (iv) the Special Rapporteur on the right to education; (v) the Special Rapporteur on the right to food; (vi) the Special Rapporteur on the right to health; (vii) the Special Representative of the S-G on human rights and transnational corporations and other business enterprises; (viii) the Special Rapporteur on the independence of judges and lawyers; (ix) the Special Rapporteur on trafficking in persons, especially in women and children; and (x) the Special Rapporteur on the sale of children, child prostitution and child

---

62 UPR Info, Database of UPR Recommendations, <www.upr-info.org/database/>, accessed 21 June 2011.

63 <www.ohchr.org/EN/HRBodies/UPR/Pages/Documentation.aspx>.

64 For more on the Special Procedures, see Ingrid Nifosi, *The UN Special Procedures in the Field of Human Rights* (Antwerp: Intersentia, 2005).

pornography. The leading criterion in the selection is the topic of the mandate. Some procedures are at first sight more relevant in the context of corruption compared to other mandates. For instance, the mandate of the Special Rapporteur on the independence of judges and lawyers seems more related to corruption than the mandate on contemporary forms of racism, although links can nevertheless exist. The Special Procedures which are not dealt with here can be considered material for further research on the topic.

As regards the country mandates, there are at present eight country-specific Procedures: Independent Experts for Burundi, Haïti, Somalia, and the Sudan, a Special Representative for Cambodia, and Special Rapporteurs for the Democratic People's Republic of Korea, Myanmar, and the Occupied Palestinian Territories. All these mandates were considered.

The reports that are examined in this study are the annual reports of the selected thematic mandates and the country mandates to the Human Rights Council, the former Human Rights Commission and the General Assembly, as well as the reports resulting from country visits. Moreover, the subsequent resolutions of the Human Rights Council and the former Commission on Human Rights were studied. The basis of the study is the list of thematic and country mandates available on the website of the Office of the UN High Commissioner for Human Rights, using the same search terms as indicated above.[65] It must be noted that the findings of the persons fulfilling the mandates do not have the same status as the treaty bodies' General Comments, concluding observations and views. Although the findings of the Special Procedures are not binding, they can have political and moral implications.[66] Furthermore, the resolutions adopted by the Council and the Commission as a result of findings of a Special Rapporteur carry more weight than the reports of the Special Rapporteur him- or herself. All documents released until 1 January 2011 were taken into account.

- European Court of Human Rights

European human rights practice was consulted by making use of the HUDOC database, searching through all the judgments of the European Court of Human Rights in English, by using the terms corrupt*.[67] This generated over 100 results, of

---

65 The list of thematic mandates is available at: Office of the United Nations High Commissioner for Human Rights, Special Procedures Assumed by the Human Rights Council – Thematic Mandates, <www2.ohchr.org/english/bodies/chr/special/themes.htm>, accessed 2 December 2010. The list of country mandates is available at: Office of the United Nations High Commissioner for Human Rights, 'Special Procedures Assumed by the Human Rights Council – Country Mandates', <www2.ohchr.org/english/bodies/chr/special/countries.htm>, accessed 10 February 2011.

66 Ingrid Westendorp, *Women and Housing: Gender Makes a Difference* (School of Human Rights Research Series, 23; Antwerp: Intersentia, 2007, at p. 308.

67 European Court of Human Rights, HUDOC Database <www.echr.coe.int/ECHR/EN/Header/Case-Law/Hudoc/Hudoc+database/>.

which the first 100 (in descending relevance) are considered. Moreover, the SIM database, containing the summaries of all cases of the ECtHR (including those in French) from 1960 to January 2011, was consulted next to HUDOC, also by using the keyword corrupt* and bribe*.[68]

- Inter-American Commission on Human Rights

Concerning the Inter-American Commission on Human Rights, a proper database containing all cases before the Inter-American Commission on Human Rights is not available. While the Cion's annual reports (from 1970 to 2009) describe the activities of the Commission, contain the petitions and cases before the Commission and before the Court, deal with human rights developments in the region, and discuss follow-up reports, the website of the Commission does not facilitate a proper search function through these annual reports.[69] The Cion's website only has a general search function, giving an unusable and polluted list of results.[70] Hence, in order to obtain an impression about cases on corruption before the Cion, the search function of the Human Rights Library of the University of Minnesota was used.[71] This tool provides an overview of the Commission's annual reports (from 1991 to 2009)[72] which is accompanied by a search function for the individual cases.[73] Therefore, this was used to search the individual cases, by keywords corrupt,* bribe,* embezzle*, and misappropriat*.

Other official publications of the Commission are the country reports, thematic reports and other publications, and resolutions, all of which are accessible online.[74] These documents were all scrutinised individually by making use of the keywords corrupt*, bribe*, embezzle* and misappropriat*.[75]

---

68 <http://sim.law.uu.nl/SIM/CaseLaw/hof.nsf/(Date)?OpenView>.

69 Inter-American Commission on Human Rights, Annual Reports <www.cidh.oas.org/annual.eng.htm>, accessed 12 January 2011. Wilson points out that there might be a number of reasons for the difficulties in accessing the decisions of the Commission: (i) relative newness; (ii) lack of internal resources at the Cion for dissemination; (iii) different perceptions of the value of legal precedent in the civil law systems of Central and South America; (iv) lack of rigour or substance in the decisions; (v) the possibility of intentionally political motives to hide the decisions from public view; and (vi) the general obscurity of international case law decisions in the US 'mainstream' legal research databases due to lack of commercial interest. See Richard J. Wilson, 'Researching the Jurisprudence of the Inter-American Commission on Human Rights: A Litigator's Perspective.'

70 Inter-American Commission on Human Rights, <www.cidh.org/search/advcidh.asp>.

71 University of Minnesota Human Rights Library, <www1.umn.edu/humanrts/google/localsearch.html> containing the annual reports from 1991–2009.

72 University of Minnesota Human Rights Library, <www1.umn.edu/humanrts/cases/commissn.htm>.

73 <www1.umn.edu/humanrts/google/localsearch.html>.

74 Inter-American Commission on Human Rights, Official Publications, < www.cidh.oas.org/publi.eng.htm>.

75 Documents released up to 15 August 2010 are taken into account in the present study.

- Inter-American Court of Human Rights

For the examination of the case law of the Inter-American Court of Human Rights, the database on its website was used.[76] Keywords: corrupt*, bribe*, embezzle* and misappropriat*.

- African Commission on Human and Peoples' Rights

The website of the Commission is not a particularly useful tool. As regards the decisions of the Commission on individual communications, all decisions are listed on its website.[77] In order to search through these decisions, the Human Rights Library of the University of Minnesota was used[78]: keywords corrupt, corruption, bribe, bribery.

- Information on the Content of Human Rights Treaty Provisions

Chapter VI examines the content of a number of rights, and analyses how these may be violated by corruption. The obvious starting point for this exercise is the text of the provisions of the ICCPR and the ICESCR. The primary sources for clarifying these provisions are the General Comments/General Recommendations drafted by the treaty bodies.[79] These can be found on the website of the Office of the UN High Commissioner for Human Rights.[80] Nowak has observed that the Human Rights Committee's General Comments 'are considered to be the most authoritative interpretation of the Covenant's provisions'.[81] The same is true for the General Comments/General Recommendations of the other treaty bodies. Even though these documents are not binding, Tomuschat opined that they 'have become a treasury of rules and principles which should guide every enlightened State Party to the relevant human rights instruments in discharging its obligations.'[82] In addition to the General Comments/General Recommendations, relevant writings of legal scholars, as found in the literature databases mentioned earlier, were taken into consideration as a complementary source of information.

---

76 Inter-American Court of Human Rights, <www.corteidh.or.cr/buscadores.cfm>.

77 African Commission on Human and Peoples' Rights, Decisions on Individual Communications, <www.achpr.org/english/_info/List_Decision_Communications.html>.

78 University of Minnesota Human Rights Library, <www1.umn.edu/humanrts/google/localsearch.html>.

79 The General Comments of CERD and CEDAW are named General Recommendations.

80 Office of the United Nations High Commissioner for Human Rights, Human Rights Bodies – General Comments, <www2.ohchr.org/english/bodies/treaty/comments.htm>.

81 Nowak, *UN Covenant on Civil and Political Rights: CCPR Commentary*, at p. XXII, §6.

82 Christian Tomuschat, *Human Rights: Between Idealism and Realism* (2 edn., The Collected Courses of the Academy of European Law, XIII/1; Oxford: Oxford University Press, 2008) at p. 191.

5.2.2. Interpretation of Results

The methodology used in Part B is in conformity with the rules of treaty interpretation as enshrined in the Vienna Convention on the Law of Treaties (hereafter: VCLT). Article 31(1) VCLT contains the general rules of treaty interpretation. Treaties have to be interpreted in good faith, by analysing the ordinary meaning of the terms of the treaty in their context and in the light of the instrument's object and purpose. Moreover, Article 31(3)(b) stipulates that, together with the context, 'any subsequent practice in the application of the treaty which establishes the agreement of the Parties regarding its implementation' shall be taken into account. What can be seen as 'any subsequent practice' in respect of human rights treaties? According to Scheinin,

> 'on the basis of the preparatory works, it appears clear that this clause does not merely refer to explicit acceptance by all State Parties to a multilateral treaty, but covers also the tacit approval of a practice engaging only some of the Parties. Hence, it would be legitimate to treat to the outcomes of the human rights treaty monitoring procedures, such as final views on individual complaints, concluding observations on State Party reports, and general comments as codifications of earlier practice, as various forms of 'subsequent practice' in the meaning of VCLT Article 31(3)(b) – at least in the vast majority of instances where no formal objection is made by State Parties'.[83]

Mechlem also held that the treaty bodies and States Parties to human rights treaties jointly generate 'subsequent practice'.[84] Since the treaty bodies are human rights treaties' main interpreters, they are also the principal generators of subsequent practice. The committees have a special role as compared with other multilateral treaties, and therefore it would be inappropriate to confine 'practice' to State practice.[85] Thus, the present work discusses the practice of the treaty bodies as being 'subsequent practice' that must be taken into account together with the context. Additionally, the practice of the Special Rapporteurs is also considered, although it should be stressed that the value of these reports in legal terms is considerably less than the practice of the treaty bodies.

In addition to the general rules of interpretation of Article 31, Article 32 VCLT contains the supplementary means of treaty interpretation. The treaty's *travaux préparatoires* and circumstances of conclusion can be consulted: (i) in order to confirm the meaning resulting from the application of Article 31; or (ii) to determine the meaning whenever interpretation according to Article 31: (a) leaves the meaning

---

83 Martin Scheinin, 'Impact on the Law of Treaties', in Menno T. Kamminga and Martin Scheinin (eds.), *The Impact of Human Rights Law on General International Law* (Oxford: Oxford University Press, 2009), p. 23–36 at p. 33.

84 Kerstin Mechlem, 'Treaty Bodies and the Interpretation of Human Rights', *Vanderbilt Journal of Transnational Law*, 42 (2009), p. 905–947 at p. 912.

85 *Ibid.* at p. 920.

ambiguous or obscure; or (b) leads to a result which is manifestly absurd or unreasonable. As the text of Article 32 already indicates, the *travaux préparatoires* and the circumstances of treaty conclusion only come into play whenever the general rules of interpretation have proven to be insufficient. Some argue that even if the results of the general rules are sufficient, the *travaux préparatoires* can still be used, not just to confirm the result, but also to replace the result of the general rules of interpretation (the so-called 'pro-preparatory-work position'). However, Linderfalk convincingly argued that arguments used to break the hierarchy of Articles 31 and 32 are not valid.[86] For this reason, the present work only considers the human rights treaties' preparatory works whenever the methods laid down in Article 31 are inadequate – which is rarely the case in the present dissertation.

5.3. Part C: Individual Responsibility: Corruption as a Crime under International Law?

5.3.1. Data Collection and Organisation

Research conducted into international criminal law is largely based on writings of scholars. In order to gather this information, the library and journal databases mentioned earlier were consulted. Also, the case law of the ICTY, the ICTR and the ICC was used, accessible online.[87] The study into the historical roots of international criminal law considers *inter alia* whether offences of an economic nature, including corruption, were at any point taken into consideration during the Rome Conference of 1998. To this end, the *travaux préparatoires* of the Conference, i.e. the official records of the negotiations on the Rome Statute were searched. The core of the *travaux*, compiled in three volumes, were made available on the Internet by the UN.[88] In order to obtain the desired information, these volumes were

---

86 Ulf Linderfalk, 'Is the Hierarchical Structure of Articles 31 and 32 of the Vienna Convention on the Law of Treaties Real or Not? Interpreting the Rules of Interpretation', *Netherlands International Law Review*, 54 (2007), p. 133–154. For an elaborate discussion of the VCLT, the reader is referred to Ulf Linderfalk, *On the Interpretation of Treaties: The Modern International Law as Expressed in the 1969 Vienna Convention on the Law of Treaties* (Dordrecht: Springer, 2007).

87 International Criminal Tribunal for the Former Yugoslavia: <www.icty.org/action/cases/4> International Criminal Tribunal for Rwanda: <www.ictrcaselaw.org> International Criminal Court: <www.icc-cpi.int/Menus/ICC/Situations+and+Cases/Cases>.

88 Travaux Préparatoires <http://untreaty.un.org/cod/icc/rome/proceedings/contents.htm>. Volume I contains the Final Documents (i.e. the Rome Statute and Final Act of the Conference); Volume II contains the relevant General Assembly resolutions, the agenda, the Rules of Procedure, the lists of delegations, Officers of the Conference and its Committees and the secretariat of the Conference, as well as the summary records of the plenary meetings of the Conference and of the meetings of the Committee of the Whole. Volume III contains the Reports of the Credentials Committee, the PrepCom, the Committee of the Whole, and the Drafting Committee; as well as the documents of the plenary and the documents of the Committee of the Whole. UN Doc. A/CONF/183/13.

examined by making use of the keywords: 'economic', 'corrupt', 'bribe', 'launder'; and 'financial'.[89] In addition to the *travaux* compiled by the UN, the ICC Legal Tools project of the ICC Office of the Prosecutor, an electronic library on international criminal law, includes a database of the ICC preparatory works.[90] This database contains over 16,000 documents related to the negotiation and drafting of the ICC Statute, the Rules of Procedure and Evidence, and the Elements of Crimes document. These documents were produced by States, NGOs, academic institutions, the UN, and other international organisations between December 1989 and September 2002.[91] As pointed out by Schabas, many of the individual documents are not strictly speaking official, and therefore there is some doubt as to whether these documents can be labelled as *travaux stricto sensu*.[92] Nonetheless, these documents might reveal certain discussions or NGO suggestions. The following search terms were used: 'corrupt', 'corruption', 'bribe', 'bribery', 'laundering', 'economic crime', and 'financial crime'.

5.3.2. Interpretation of Results

Concerning the interpretation of the provisions in the Rome Statute, Articles 31 and 32 of the Vienna Convention on the Law of Treaties apply, see section 5.2.2 *supra*.

---

89 These terms also cover extended versions of the words used, e.g. 'corruption' instead of 'corrupt.'

90 The ICC Legal Tools can be consulted through <www.legal-tools.org/en/go-to-database/ltfolder/0_3960/#results>, accessed 11 January 2010.

91 For information on the content of the ICC Legal Tools, see <www.legal-tools.org/en/overview-of-the-tools/>, accessed 11 January 2010.

92 William A. Schabas, 'Travaux Préparatoires of the Rome Statute' (9 April 2008), <http://humanrightsdoctorate.blogspot.com/2008/04/travaux-prparatoires-of-rome-statute.html>, accessed 11 January 2010.

Part A

The Phenomenon of Corruption: An Introductory Analysis

Chapter I
Basic Issues

1. Introduction

Most people will 'know corruption when they see it'.[1] Yet, regardless of how easy it may be to label certain conduct in a specific case as 'corrupt', the notion of 'corruption' is generally surrounded by a great deal of confusion. Many definitions have been formulated over the years, none of them being fully satisfactory for everyone.[2]

Why is 'corruption' so difficult to define? First of all, the problem is very complex. As elaborated upon in section 3, corruption is a broad concept consisting of different practices, which vary in nature.[3] Also, what is seen as corruption may to a certain extent depend on the cultural context.[4] What is regarded in some societies as being unacceptable may be a rather common practice in others.[5] Moreover, the topic of corruption is studied by various disciplines.[6] Law, economics, political science, criminology, anthropology and other disciplines each have their own approach, and also within one discipline numerous definitions have

---

1 Phrase used by US Supreme Court Justice Potter Stewart in his concurring opinion in *Jacobellis v. Ohio* (1964), describing the threshold test for pornography. See Paul Gewirtz, 'On "I Know It When I See It"', *Yale Law Journal,* 105 (1996), p. 1023–1047.

2 For a useful overview of theories defining corruption, particularly from a political science perspective, see A.J. Brown, 'What Are We Trying to Measure? Reviewing the Basics of Corruption Definition', in Charles Sampford et al. (eds.), *Measuring Corruption* (Aldershot: Ashgate, 2006), p. 57–79.

3 Angela Gorta, 'Research. A Tool for Building Corruption Resistance', in Peter Larmour and Nick Wolanin (eds.), *Corruption and Anti-Corruption* (Canberra: Asia Pacific Press, 2001), p. 11–29 at p. 14; Zoe Pearson, 'An International Human Rights Approach to Corruption', in Peter Larmour & Nick Wolanin (ed.), *Corruption and Anti-Corruption* (Canberra: Asia Pacific Press, 2001), p. 30–61 at p. 32; World Bank, 'Helping Countries Combat Corruption. The Role of the World Bank', p. 8, <www1.worldbank.org/publicsector/anticorrupt/corruptn/corrptn.pdf>, accessed 12 April 2010.

4 Kenneth Asamoa Acheampong, 'Combating Grand Corruption: The Potential Impact of a United Nations Convention on the Prevention and Punishment of the Crime of Economic Genocide', *Revue Africaine des Droits de l'Homme*, 7 (1998), p. 38–55 at p. 39–40; David H. Bayley, 'The Effects of Corruption in a Developing Nation', in Arnold J. Heidenheimer, Michael Johnston, and Victor T. Levine (eds.), *Political Corruption: A Handbook* (New Brunswick: Transaction, 1989), p. 935–952 at p. 937–939; Peter Csonka, 'Corruption: The Council of Europe's Approach', in Barry Rider (ed.), *Corruption: The Enemy Within* (The Hague – London – Boston: Kluwer Law International, 1997), p. 343–353 at p. 346; John Gardiner, 'Defining Corruption', in Arnold J. Heidenheimer and Michael Johnston (eds.), *Political Corruption: Concepts and Contexts.* (New Brunswick: Transaction, 2002), p. 25–40 at p. 36–38; Pearson, 'An International Human Rights Approach to Corruption', at p. 33–34.

5 See §2.4 hereafter for a discussion of these cultural aspects.

6 Pearson, 'An International Human Rights Approach to Corruption' at p. 32.

been formulated. Yet, it has been noted that the respective definitions also show a great deal of overlap.[7]

Like any other thorough study of the phenomenon of corruption, the present work is in need of a useful working definition. Even though endless debating about definitional issues does not contribute to the solution of the problem, over-simplification of this highly complex topic should also be avoided. Where does one start the search for a definition of corruption? Since this is first and foremost a legal dissertation, it would make proper sense to start with an examination of legal sources. However, most national laws do not define the notion, and the same is true for most global and regional treaties concluded in the recent past.[8] Not even the leading international treaty, the United Nations Convention Against Corruption (hereafter: UNCAC) indicates how corruption should be defined.[9] Therefore, the present work departs from the definitions employed by key players in the field of anti-corruption, such as Transparency International and the World Bank. This however does not imply that the present work supports the policies of these organisations, or the views they may have on (anti-) corruption. Furthermore, conclusions are drawn from research done by scholars in various disciplines, particularly political science. This is discussed in section 2.

However, for the purpose of (international) law, a single overall definition does not suffice to cover the 'multi-headed monster' of corruption. For that reason, section 3 presents a further classification of its various forms. The distinctions made in the global and regional anti-corruption treaties, most notably the UNCAC, are taken as a starting point.

After the matter of defining corruption, the relevance of measuring it comes into play. Since corruption is by its nature a secretive practice, it is difficult to estimate how much corruption takes place in a certain country or continent. Nonetheless, several tools were developed to determine corruption levels. These are discussed in section 4.

In order to understand the destructiveness of corruption in its entirety, it is important to take note of its consequences. Section 5 concisely sets out the harm that corruption causes. Conclusions are drawn from research done in various disciplines and from information made available by civil society organisations. One must keep in mind that the consequences listed in the classification are closely intertwined. Political, economic, social, and environmental factors are interrelated and can rarely be fully separated. Furthermore, the overview does not strive for full exhaustiveness. Whenever appropriate, references are provided to further reading on the matter. Finally, section 6 provides a number of concluding remarks.

---

7 Arnold J. Heidenheimer and Michael Johnston (eds.), *Political Corruption: Concepts and Contexts* (3rd edn., New Brunswick: Transaction, 2002) at p. 13.

8 Only the SADC Protocol Against Corruption defines 'corruption' as such. See *infra* chapter II, §3.5.1.

9 The content of the United Nations Convention Against Corruption is discussed in chapter II, §3.6.2.

2. Defining 'Corruption'

2.1. Public and Private Sector Corruption

A useful starting point in the quest for an appropriate definition is Transparency International (hereafter: TI), the main NGO working in the field of anti-corruption.[10] TI characterises corruption as 'the abuse of *entrusted* power for private gain' [emphasis added, MB].[11] This definition contains three elements: i) an abuse of power; ii) a power that is entrusted; and iii) a private benefit. Regarding the second element, TI does not distinguish between power that is entrusted in the public sector or in the private sector. In respect of the third element, the benefit does not necessarily have to accrue to the person in power; it is also possible that his or her immediate family or friends benefit.[12]

Another organisation concerned with anti-corruption is the World Bank.[13] Since the late 1990s, the Bank is very active in this area,[14] but previously the 'c-word' was a taboo subject considered to be too politically sensitive.[15] Currently, the Bank provides that corruption is 'the abuse of *public* office for private gain' [emphasis added, MB].[16] This definition contains the same three elements as TI's definition, with one major difference: the World Bank's definition only covers corruption in the public sector, not corruption in the private sector.

The difference in the definitions employed by the two organisations reveals the main forms of corruption: public sector corruption and private sector corruption. Public sector corruption takes place within the public domain, involving State actors. However, non-State actors are often involved, for example when a corporation bribes a public official. Private sector corruption occurs within and between non-State actors, such as corporations, non-governmental organisations and other private institutions.[17]

---

10 Transparency International, founded in 1993, is a prominent anti-corruption NGO with a Berlin-based Secretariat and many National Chapters worldwide. Its mission is 'to create change towards a world free of corruption'. See TI's website <www.transparency.org>.

11 Definition can be found on <www.transparency.org/about_us>, accessed 17 May 2011.

12 Jeremy Pope, *TI Source Book 2000. Confronting Corruption: The Elements of a National Integrity System* (Berlin: Transparency International, 2000) at p. 1 footnote 2.

13 Although the World Bank has become a major player in the field of anti-corruption, it has not been able to ban the problem in its own organisation. This was painfully demonstrated in September 2007 by the resignation of president Paul Wolfowitz, who abused his powerful position to increase the salary of a friend. Also corruption within projects funded by the Bank has been reported. For more on this topic, see Steve Berkman, *The World Bank and the Gods of Lending* (Sterling, VA: Kumarian Press, 2008).

14 For a comprehensive study of the World Bank's anti-corruption work, see Heather Marquette, *Corruption, Politics and Development: The Role of the World Bank* (Hampshire: Palgrave Macmillan, 2003).

15 World Bank (ed.), *Voice for the World's Poor: Selected Speeches and Writings of World Bank President James D. Wolfensohn, 1995–2005* (Washington, DC, 2005) at p. 177.

16 World Bank, 'Helping Countries Combat Corruption. The Role of the World Bank', p. 8.

17 Pearson, 'An International Human Rights Approach to Corruption', at p. 32–33.

Given the wide range of TI's activities, it is understandable that this NGO aims to cover a broad spectrum of both public and private conduct. In the past however, TI did employ a definition of corruption which was limited to the public sector only. Now, its working sphere is broadened by including private sector corruption as well.[18] Nevertheless, a majority of scholars in the field of law,[19] political science[20] and economics[21] define corruption in a way similar to the World Bank's definition by focusing upon public sector corruption. This approach dates back to 1931[22] and, since then, corruption is most frequently defined in terms of conduct in the public sector. When looking at the various global and regional anti-corruption treaties, we also find that these are primarily aimed at addressing public sector corruption, although provisions on private sector corruption may also be included.[23]

The present thesis focuses upon public sector corruption, since, in the field of human rights, the State is still the main actor.[24] Thus, where the term 'corruption' is used, this refers to acts or omissions in which State actors are involved. The current work employs the definition *'the abuse of public office for private or political gain'*. As TI pointed out, corruption does not necessarily have to benefit the person engaging in it. Family and friends can also be beneficiaries, for instance when a luxury car is given to the spouse of a judge, in order to influence the judge's decision in a certain case. Moreover, corruption may not only benefit the officeholder (or his/her family and friends) in the private sphere, but also or exclusively in his/her professional capacity. *Inter alia*, this occurs when the gains of corruption accrue to the official's political party.[25] It is therefore appropriate to extend the phrase 'for private gain' to 'for private or political gain'.

---

18 Michel van Hulten, 'Hier Geen Corruptie? Dat Lijkt Maar Zo.' *NRC Handelsblad*, 26 September 2007.

19 For example, Jayawickrama, 'Corruption – a Violation of Human Rights?' *Working Paper* (Berlin: Transparency International, 1998); Pearson, 'An International Human Rights Approach to Corruption.'

20 For example, Bayley, 'The Effects of Corruption in a Developing Nation', at p. 936–937; Gunnar Myrdal, 'Corruption: Its Causes and Effects', in Arnold J. Heidenheimer, Michael Johnston, and Victor T. Levine (eds.), *Political Corruption: A Handbook* (New Brunswick Transaction, 1989), 953–62; Joseph S. Nye, 'Corruption and Political Development: A Cost-Benefit Analysis', in Arnold J. Heidenheimer and Michael Johnston (eds.), *Political Corruption: Concepts and Contexts* (New Brunswick: Transaction, 2002), p. 281–300.

21 See Jens Chr. Andvig et al., 'Corruption: A Review of Contemporary Research', *CMI Report, R 2001:7* (Bergen: Chr. Michelsen Institute 2001).

22 It was defined by J.J Senturia, 'Corruption, Political', in E.R.A. Seligman (ed.), *Encyclopaedia of the Social Sciences* (New York: Macmillan, 1931), p. 448–452.

23 See chapter II for a comprehensive overview of the current treaty regime governing corruption.

24 Human rights responsibilities may also rest upon private actors, including multinational corporations. Nonetheless, their conduct largely falls outside of the scope of the present work.

25 Gardiner, 'Defining Corruption' at p. 26.

2.2. Grand and Petty Corruption

Apart from the public-private sector divide, it follows from scholarly literature that it is possible to distinguish between grand and petty corruption.[26] These terms do not refer to the scale of the corruption or to the size of the resources involved, but to the level of authority where corruption takes place.[27]

Grand corruption occurs at the policy formulation end of politics, and involves public officials operating at the highest levels of the State. It is sometimes referred to as *political corruption*.[28] Quite recently, other concepts were invented to refer to high-level corruption, such as patrimonicide and indigenous spoliation. *Patrimonicide* is a combination of 'patrimonium', which is the estate or property belonging by ancient right to an institution, corporation or class, and 'cide', meaning killing.[29] *Indigenous spoliation* is defined as 'an illegal act of depredation committed for private ends by constitutionally responsible rulers, public officials, or private individuals'.[30] However, the use of these two notions is not widespread and the meaning of the words may not be immediately clear to everyone. Moreover, adding more terminology to the already complicated discourse about corruption does not serve any purpose. Therefore, this thesis prefers the notion of grand corruption, also since most established languages contain terms resembling 'corruption' because they were taken over from Latin.[31]

Two concepts closely related to grand corruption are kleptocracy and State capture. *Kleptocracy* is composed of '*klepto*', i.e. to steal, and '*kratos*', i.e. rule. Hence, the term means 'rule by looters'. It stands for 'a political system dominated by those who steal from State coffers and practice extortion as their *modus*

---

26 The term 'grand corruption' seems to originate from the work of George Moody-Stuart, see *inter alia* George Moody-Stuart, *Grand Corruption in Third World Development* (Oxford: WorldView Publishing, 1997).

27 Inge Amundsen, 'Political Corruption: An Introduction to the Issues', *Working Paper, 1999:7* (Bergen: Chr. Michelsen Institute, 1999) at p. 3–4; Inge Amundsen, 'Political Corruption', *U4 Issue, 6:2006* (Bergen: Chr. Michelsen Institute, 2006) at p. 3, 8; Andvig et al., 'Corruption: A Review of Contemporary Research', at p. 10–12; Jens Chr. Andvig et al., 'Research on Corruption. A Policy Oriented Survey', (Bergen/Oslo: Chr. Michelsen Institute (CMI) & Norwegian Institute of International Affairs (NUPI), 2000) at p. 18–20.

28 Amundsen, 'Political Corruption: An Introduction to the Issues', at p. 3–4; Amundsen, 'Political Corruption', at p. 3, 5, 8–9; Andvig et al., 'Corruption: A Review of Contemporary Research', at p. 10–12; Andvig et al., 'Research on Corruption. A Policy Oriented Survey', at p. 18–20.

29 Ndiva Kofele-Kale, 'Patrimonicide: The International Economic Crime of Indigenous Spoliation', *Vanderbilt Journal of Transnational Law,* 28 (1995), p. 45–118 at p. 58; Ndiva Kofele-Kale, *The International Law of Responsibility for Economic Crimes: Holding State Officials Individually Liable for Acts of Fraudulent Enrichment* (2nd edn.; Aldershot: Ashgate, 2006) at p. 13.

30 Kofele-Kale, 'Patrimonicide: The International Economic Crime of Indigenous Spoliation', at p. 56; Kofele-Kale, *The International Law of Responsibility for Economic Crimes: Holding State Officials Individually Liable for Acts of Fraudulent Enrichment* at p. 9.

31 A.J. Heidenheimer, M. Johnston, and V. Le Vine (eds.), *Political Corruption: A Handbook* (New Brunswick: Transaction, 1989) at p. 12.

operandi.' Examples are 'Papa Doc' Duvalier (Haiti), Mobutu Sese Seko (Zaïre), Bokassa (Central African Republic), and Suharto (Indonesia).[32] While not every instance of grand corruption necessarily means that the particular State is a kleptocracy, whenever grand corruption is systemic, this will often be the case. *State capture* is defined as 'the undue and illicit influence of the elite in shaping the laws, policies and regulations of the State. In essence, this form of capture is a manifestation of 'grand' corruption.'[33]

Petty corruption is also named bureaucratic corruption, administrative corruption, survival corruption, street-level or low corruption. It is committed at the implementation end of politics, where citizens meet public officials. Examples are junior customs officials, low-ranking policemen, or teachers at public schools demanding bribes.[34] Unlike grand corruption, petty corruption may be committed by low level officials in order to supplement wages that are below subsistence level.

Both grand and petty corruption can occur within the private and the public sector. In the private sector, petty corruption is committed by a low-ranking employee, while grand corruption is committed by a CEO for instance. Yet, as indicated above, this thesis only concerns public sector corruption. The terms 'grand' and 'petty' will therefore refer to State action or inaction, although private actors may certainly be involved.

In part B of the present study, concerning the links between corruption and human rights violations, both grand and petty corruption are relevant. In part C, which deals with corruption from an international criminal law perspective, the emphasis is on grand corruption.[35]

2.3. Corruption *vis-à-vis* Other Concepts

Corruption, as a term, may easily be confused with a number of related or (partly) overlapping concepts, such as economic crime, white collar crime, fraud, and collusion. For the purpose of clarity, these concepts will be briefly defined here. *Economic crime* is a term lacking a universally accepted definition. We may consider it to be an umbrella concept, covering a wide range of offences in the private and the public sector which possess a financial component, and which also includes certain forms of corruption. Nevertheless, not all economic crime is corruption, and not all corrupt acts are necessarily economic per se, since the gain

32 U4 Anti-Corruption Resource Centre, 'Corruption Glossary', <www.u4.no/document/glossary.cfm>, accessed 18 May 2011.

33 Daniel Kaufmann, 'Human Rights and Governance: The Empirical Challenge', in Philip Alston and Mary Robinson (eds.), *Human Rights and Development: Towards Mutual Reinforcement* (Oxford: Oxford University Press, 2005), p. 352–402 at p. 373.

34 Amundsen, 'Political Corruption: An Introduction to the Issues', at p. 3–4; Amundsen, 'Political Corruption', at p. 3, 5, 8–9; Andvig et al., 'Corruption: A Review of Contemporary Research', at p. 10–12; Andvig et al., 'Research on Corruption. A Policy Oriented Survey', at p. 18–20.

35 The focus on grand corruption for the purpose of part C is explained in chapter VII, §6.

obtained by corruption does not have to be economic in itself; also political advantages are covered.

White collar crime is a notion first defined by Sutherland in the 1940s, although debate continues on the precise delimitations of the concept.[36] A commonly used definition is that white collar crime is:

> ... a heterogeneous group of offences committed by people of relatively high status or enjoying relatively high levels of trust, and made possible by their legitimate employment. Such crimes typically include fraud, embezzlement, tax violations and other accounting offences, and various forms of workplace theft and fiddling in which the organization, its customers or other organizations are victims.[37]

Hence, the notions of corruption and white collar crime may overlap, but this is not always the case. Not all forms of corruption are white collar crime (think of bribes demanded by a nurse at a public hospital, who does not enjoy high status), and not all white collar crime is corruption (e.g. since white collar crime also covers offences in the private sector only).

Fraud is another broad concept with varying definitions, depending on context and discipline. In the literature about corruption, we find that fraud is defined as 'economic crime involving deceit, trickery or false pretences, by which someone gains unlawfully.'[38] While it is argued by some that fraud is a form of corruption,[39] the present work does not support that view. Rather, fraud is a way of committing certain corrupt acts. For example, embezzlement (i.e. theft of State funds by a public official) can be committed by means of fraud. At the same time, one may also argue that corruption is a specific type of fraud.

Finally, *collusion* is described by Van den Heuvel as a 'secret agreement for a fraudulent or deceitful purpose, especially to defeat the course of law.' Collusion can be seen as a cause, condition or explanation of corruption.[40] Collusion may ultimately lead to corruption.

---

36 See *inter alia* David Nelken, 'White-Collar and Corporate Crime', in Mike Maguire, Rod Morgan, and Robert Reiner (eds.), *The Oxford Handbook of Criminology* (4th edn.; Oxford: Oxford University Press 2007), p. 733–770.

37 Steve Tombs and Dave Whyte, 'White Collar Crime', in Eugene Mclaughlin and John Muncie (eds.), *The Sage Dictionary of Criminology* (2nd edn.; London: SAGE Publications, 2005), p. 462–464 at p. 462.

38 U4 Anti-Corruption Resource Centre, 'Corruption Glossary.'

39 Argued by Andvig et al., 'Corruption: A Review of Contemporary Research', at p. 9.

40 Grat van den Heuvel, 'The Parliamentary Enquiry on Fraud in the Dutch Construction Industry: Collusion as Concept between Corruption and State-Corporate Crime', *Crime, Law & Social Change*, 44 (2005), p. 133–151 at p. 133.

2.4. Cultural Connotations

Corruption is a notion with a strong cultural connotation. Occasionally, corruption may be justified by using the argument 'that this is the way we do things over here, it is a cultural thing.' Also, it is sometimes argued that some peoples, regions, or countries are 'by nature' more corrupt than others because of their 'culture'. Both positions ought to be dismissed as inaccurate. Yet, at the same time, cultural or contextual factors cannot be completely disregarded in the corruption discourse. Recently, we see a growing anthropological interest in corruption, which we should welcome.[41]

One of the key issues in the discussion on corruption and culture is the fact that the commonly used definition of corruption being 'the abuse of public office for private gain' implies a clear demarcation between the public and the private sphere. However, it is argued that the line between what is public and what is private cannot be drawn sharply in all countries.[42]

Another aspect that should be taken into account is the legacy of colonialism. The new rulers, after decolonisation, inherited a corrupt political and legal system.[43] This explains, at least in part, the worryingly high levels of perceived corruption in many developing countries, including in the African continent.

In sum, the study of corruption should be conducted in a particular cultural context. When looking at the causes and consequences of corruption, and when designing and implementing anti-corruption policies, the particular societal aspects have to be taken into account, to avoid a one-size-fits-all solution that may not work. Nevertheless, certain universal standards, such as enshrined in the United Nations Convention Against Corruption, should be upheld globally. Also, the standards laid down in the Universal Declaration of Human Rights, and the two subsequent Covenants should guide all nations.

---

41 A number of key anthropological works on corruption are Georgio Blundo and J.P. Olivier de Sardan (eds.), *Everyday Corruption and the State. Citizens and Public Officials in Africa* (Cape Town: David Philip, 2006); Dieter Haller and Cris Shore (eds.), *Corruption: Anthropological Perspectives*, eds. Thomas Hylland Eriksen and Jon P. Mitchell (Anthropology, Culture and Society, London, Ann Arbor, MI: Pluto Press, 2005); Tone Kristin Sissener, 'Anthropological Perspectives on Corruption', *Working Paper, 2001:5* (Bergen: Chr. Michelsen Institute, 2001); Daniel Jordan Smith, *A Culture of Corruption. Everyday Deception and Popular Discontent in Nigeria* (Princeton: Princeton University Press, 2007).

42 Argument made by Akhil Gupta, 'Blurred Boundaries: The Discourse of Corruption, the Culture of Politics, and the Imagined State', *American Ethnologist*, 22/2 (1995), p. 375–402 and elaborated upon by Cris Shore and Dieter Haller, 'Introduction – Sharp Practice: Anthropology and the Study of Corruption', in Dieter Haller and Cris Shore (eds.), *Corruption: Anthropological Perspectives* (London: Pluto Press, 2005), p. 1–26 at p. 5 *et seq* as well as by Sissener, 'Anthropological Perspectives on Corruption', at p. 7 *et seq*.

43 Brought forward by Sissener, 'Anthropological Perspectives on Corruption' and by economists Luis Angeles and Kyriakos C. Neanidis, 'Colonialism, Elite Formation and Corruption', *Discussion paper series no. 144* (Centre for Growth & Business Cycle – University of Manchester, June 2010).

3. Typology of Corruption

3.1. Introductory Remarks

Corruption comes in many disguises. From a legal perspective, it makes proper sense not only to define corruption in a broad manner, but to distinguish between separate offences, each falling under the larger umbrella of corruption. If corruption is perceived as one problem, it is too large and too vague to combat it properly.[44] In order to categorise the main types of corruption, the UNCAC is a good point of departure. This treaty is the only truly global anti-corruption instrument, drafted quite recently in 2003. The definitions it provides are supported by a great number of countries: 154 States are Party to the Convention.[45] The UNCAC, which does not distinguish between grand and petty corruption, classifies five types of corruption: bribery, embezzlement, trading in influence, abuse of functions and illicit enrichment.[46] In practice, however, it might not be easy to separate these various types. Yet, a general framework is needed in order to get a grip on the topic. The classification below therefore functions as the basis for parts B and C of the present study.

3.2. Bribery

In popular expression, a number of scholarly works and in some international and regional legal instruments,[47] corruption and bribery are used as synonyms. This can be explained by the fact that the offence of bribery forms the 'hard core' of corruption. Nonetheless, corruption covers a much wider range of conduct. This is also reflected in the key anti-corruption treaties, such as the UNCAC, the Inter-American Convention Against Corruption and the African Union Convention on Preventing and Combating Corruption.

Bribery is a form of corruption which necessarily involves two parties, and therefore two forms of bribery can be distinguished. *Active bribery* is committed by the bribe-payer, the supply side. In cases of grand corruption, multinational corporations frequently fulfil this role. By transferring a significant sum of money to the bank account of a high-level official, a corporation has a competitive advantage in, for example, the award of the concession of oil exploitation over corporations who do not bribe. *Passive bribery* on the other hand is committed by the bribe-taker. This demand side is played with vigour by some high-level

---

44 Gorta, 'Research. A Tool for Building Corruption Resistance', at p. 14.

45 United Nations Treaty Collection, <http://treaties.un.org>, accessed 19 November 2011.

46 See chapter III, §3.6.2 for an overview of the content of UNCAC.

47 Some anti-corruption treaties only cover bribery: the EU Protocols to the PFI Convention, the Convention on the Fight Against Corruption Involving Officials of the European Communities or Officials of EU Member States and the COE's Civil Law Convention on Corruption. See chapter II.

government officials, often eager for additional sources of income to facilitate their lifestyle.

One must keep in mind that bribes can be offered voluntarily by the supply side. This is so-called *transactive corruption*, in which there is an agreement between the bribe-payer and the bribe-taker, which benefits both. However, corporations more and more contend that the bribes they are paying are extorted by powerful, greedy public officials. They argue that they are confronted with the choice of either bribing or waiting for a competitor to bribe and thus losing the business deal. This is known as *extortive corruption*, which leaves no other possibility for the bribing party. The public official thus commits passive bribery in a legal sense, but in reality s/he was the most active party.[48] It should nonetheless be kept in mind that instances of extortive petty bribery may not be the result of greed on the part of the public official, but rather of bare necessity: in many developing countries, public officials, such as school teachers, nurses or policemen, are underpaid. This often leaves them no other choice than collecting additional sources of income from bribes in order to provide a livelihood for their own families.[49]

The counter-obligation which the bribe-taking public official has to fulfil can be either *according to the law* or *against the law*. The former happens, for example, if, after the payment of bribes, a contract is awarded to a corporation which was legally entitled to this. By contrast, the latter happens if by the law, the contract should have been granted to another corporation. Yet, it must be recognised that such decision making leaves a lot of room for discretion, and determining which corporation should have been granted the contract is often difficult.

Informal synonyms for bribery are speed money, grease payments,[50] kickbacks, baksheesh, sweeteners and pay-offs.[51] These terms conceal the seriousness of the offence and intend to indicate that bribes are sometimes a necessary evil to 'speed things up' or 'grease the palms' of a public official. Currently, all global and regional anti-corruption treaties oblige State Parties to criminalise (certain types of) bribery at the national level.

A useful legal definition of bribery is provided by the UNCAC in Article 15. Active bribery (the supply-side) is defined as 'the promise, offering or giving, to a public official, directly or indirectly, of an undue advantage, for the official himself

---

48 Syed Hussein Alatas, *Corruption: Its Nature, Causes and Functions* (Aldershot; Brookfield, Vt., USA: Avebury, 1990) at p. 3.

49 Yet, we should be careful in stating that higher wages in the public sector equal less corruption. Other factors must also be taken into account. See William D. Savedoff, 'Pay for Honesty? Lessons on Wages and Corruption from Public Hospitals', in Taryn Vian, William D. Savedoff, and Harald Mathisen (eds.), *Anticorruption in the Health Sector: Strategies for Transparency and Accountability* (Sterling, VA: Kumarian Press, 2010), p. 69–76. Also relevant is Susan Rose-Ackerman, *Corruption and Government: Causes, Consequences and Reform* (Cambridge: Cambridge University Press, 1999) at p. 71–75.

50 Jayawickrama, 'Corruption – a Violation of Human Rights?' at p. 658.

51 Amundsen, 'Political Corruption: An Introduction to the Issues', at p. 11.

or herself or another person or entity in order that the official act or refrain from acting in the exercise of his or her official duties'. Passive bribery (the demand side) is defined as 'the solicitation or acceptance by a public official, directly or indirectly, of an undue advantage, for the official himself or herself or another person or entity, in order that the official act or refrain from acting in the exercise of his or her official duties'. The definitions in the other instruments are very much similar to the definitions in the UNCAC.

3.3. Embezzlement

A second form of corruption is embezzlement. Frequently used synonyms are misappropriation, pillaging of State assets, diversion of property and simply theft.[52] Unlikely bribery, embezzlement does not necessarily include two parties; it is a form of 'autocorruption'.[53] Embezzlement can take many forms. The World Bank lists as examples: spontaneous privatisation of State assets, theft of financial resources of the government, theft of cash from treasuries, extended advances to public officials which were never paid back and payments for fictitious ghost workers.[54]

The UNCAC provides a definition of embezzlement in Article 16: 'the embezzlement, misappropriation or other diversion by a public official for his or her benefit or the benefit of another person of entity, of any property, public or private funds or securities or any other thing of value entrusted to the public official by virtue of his or her position'. Embezzlement is also qualified as an act of corruption in the Inter-American Convention Against Corruption (Article XI(1)(d)) and is included in the SADC Protocol (Article 3(1)(d)) and in the African Union Convention on Preventing and Combating Corruption (Article 4(1)(d)).

3.4. Trading in Influence

Like bribery, trading in influence has an active and a passive side. Article 18(a) UNCAC defines active trading in influence as: '... the promise, offering or giving to a public official or any other person directly or indirectly, of an undue advantage in order that the public official or the person abuse his real or supposed influence with a view to obtaining from an administration or public authority an undue advantage for the original instigator of the act or for any other person.'

---

52 *Ibid.* at p. 11–12; Amanda L. Morgan, 'Corruption: Causes, Consequences and Policy Implications. A Literature Review', *Working Paper nr. 9* (Asia Foundation, October 1998) at p. 29–30.

53 Alatas, *Corruption: Its Nature, Causes and Functions*, at p. 2.

54 World Bank, 'Helping Countries Combat Corruption. The Role of the World Bank', p. 10.

The other side of the coin, passive trading in influence, is described in Article 18(b) UNCAC as: '... the solicitation or acceptance by a public official or any other person, directly or indirectly, of an undue advantage for himself or herself or for another person in order that the public official or the person abuse his or her real or supposed influence with a view to obtaining from an administration or public authority an undue advantage.'

The Criminal Law Convention on Corruption of the Council of Europe also includes reference to trading in influence (Article 12), as well as the African Union Convention (Article 4(1)(f)) and the SADC Protocol (Article 3(1)(f)).

3.5. Abuse of Functions

Abuse of functions is defined in Article 19 UNCAC as 'the performance of or failure to perform an act, in violation of laws, by a public official in the discharge of his or her functions, for the purpose of obtaining an undue advantage for himself or herself or for another person or entity'. Hence, abuse of functions appears to be some sort of remaining category, in order to capture conduct that cannot be qualified as either bribery, embezzlement or trading in influence. From a practical perspective, this is to be welcomed, yet it should be noted that this offence is made dependent upon the State's domestic legislation, since the act needs to be 'in violation of laws'. In the author's view, it is very well possible to classify two types of behaviour as an 'abuse of functions': patronage and nepotism. These practices are not included in an anti-corruption treaty as such, but they are generally regarded as types of corruption.

3.5.1. Patronage

According to the Oxford English Dictionary, one of the main definitions of patronage is 'the power or right to control appointments to public office or the right to privileges. In modern use often with the connotation of the abuse of this power by the appointing to office of political allies.'[55] Scholars in various disciplines as well as the World Bank and other organisations perceive of patronage (also named clientelism) as a specific type of corruption.[56] The description of patronage also perfectly fits the definition of corruption: the officeholder abuses his or her public function in order to advance (a person belonging to) a particular group, in order to

---

55 Oxford English Dictionary <www.oed.com>.

56 Amundsen, 'Political Corruption'; Kenneth M. Gibbons, 'Variations in Attitudes Towards Corruption in Canada', in Arnold J. Heidenheimer, Michael Johnston, and Victor T. Levine (eds.), *Political Corruption: A Handbook* (New Brunswick: Transaction, 1989), 763–80 at p. 763; Morgan, 'Corruption: Causes, Consequences and Policy Implications. A Literature Review', at p. 32–34; World Bank, 'Helping Countries Combat Corruption. The Role of the World Bank', p. 8.

obtain political support. The advantage can consist of employment in bureaucracies, access to public goods and services, property rights or the right to participate in the market system.[57]

Patronage can be very harmful. If political supporters are awarded public offices, the requirements of fulfilling such a function are often disregarded. Thus, the newly appointed civil servant frequently lacks the necessary knowledge, which can harm public interest. Moreover, it is likely that he or she will use the function as his or her own private business by engaging in corruption.

Patronage is a form of corruption which public officials usually engage in because of political gain, instead of private benefit.[58] This illustrates the necessity of broadening the definition of public sector corruption as noted in section 2.1 above.

3.5.2. Nepotism

Like patronage, the global and regional legal instruments do not make specific reference to nepotism (also known as cryonism). The dictionary definition of this concept is 'the showing of special favour or unfair preference to a relative in conferring a position, job, privilege, etc'.[59] This already indicates that nepotism is a form of favouritism which is more personalised and specific than patronage.[60] Nepotism refers to the beneficial treatment of close family, while patronage covers a larger group, such as political supporters or a particular ethnic group.

Nepotism is generally considered to be a form of corruption,[61] which is correct since it falls within the notion of corruption as indicated *supra*. A notorious example of nepotism took place within the family of the late Suharto. The former ruler of Indonesia distributed wealth to his wife, six children, half-brother and grandsons in the form of licenses and monopolies. His wife held a State monopoly on the import and milling of wheat, a son controlled the clove trade, a daughter controlled the toll-roads and another son held the license for mobile phones.[62] It is clear that this kind of privatisation, in which State property is treated as if it were the family business, is absolutely unacceptable.

---

57 Morgan, 'Corruption: Causes, Consequences and Policy Implications. A Literature Review', at p. 32.

58 *Ibid.* at p. 32–34.

59 Oxford English Dictionary <www.oed.com>.

60 Amundsen, 'Political Corruption: An Introduction to the Issues', at p. 14–15; Morgan, 'Corruption: Causes, Consequences and Policy Implications. A Literature Review', at p. 34.

61 Gibbons, 'Variations in Attitudes Towards Corruption in Canada', at p. 764; Nye, 'Corruption and Political Development: A Cost-Benefit Analysis', at p. 284.

62 The Economist, 2 February 2008, p. 85.

3.6. Illicit Enrichment

Illicit enrichment, according to Article 20 UNCAC, is 'a significant increase in the assets of a public official that he or she cannot reasonably explain in relation to his or her lawful income'. It is also codified in the African Union Convention (Article 4 (1) (g)) and in the Inter-American Convention Against Corruption (Article IX). Illicit enrichment is a somewhat problematic concept. To begin with, one could reasonably argue that an unexplainable increase in income does not constitute corruption *in itself*. The money could also come from other illegal sources. Furthermore, even if we assume that the increase consists of means collected through acts of corruption, then 'illicit enrichment' is more likely to refer to the *result* of corruption, rather than to a specific type of corruption. Moreover, the concept can be problematic as far as the burden of proof is concerned. The alleged corrupt public official has to demonstrate that the increase in income is caused by legal means, which can cause problems of incompatibility with national legislation. Moreover, the presumption of innocence might be at stake.[63] Despite these difficulties, the concept of illicit enrichment is included in the UNCAC.[64]

4. Measuring Corruption

The key characteristic of corruption is secrecy. Measuring how much corruption occurs is therefore a daunting task. Over the years, researchers have developed a number of tools to get an idea of the amount of corruption, in order to compare countries and to detect trends over time. Generally, there are three approaches in measuring corruption: (i) gathering the views of relevant stakeholders (i.e. surveys of firms, public officials, NGOs, donors, etc.); (ii) tracking the institutional features of countries (e.g. procurement practices and budget transparency); (iii) auditing of specific projects.[65] Since a comprehensive analysis of all instruments for measuring corruption falls outside of the scope of the present section, the following discussion focuses upon the most prominent ways of measurement, all of which are stakeholder surveys as indicated above under (i).[66]

The tool that generates most publicity worldwide is Transparency International's annual *Corruption Perceptions Index* (hereafter: CPI), which was first launched in

63 Peter W. Schroth, 'The African Union Convention on Preventing and Combating Corruption', *Journal of African Law*, 49 (2005), p. 24–38 at p. 27–30.

64 See chapter VI, §2.3 for more on this topic.

65 Daniel Kaufmann, Aart Kraay, and Massimo Mastruzzi, 'Measuring Corruption: Myths and Realities', in Transparency International (ed.), *Global Corruption Report 2007: Corruption in Judicial Systems* (Cambridge: Cambridge University Press, 2007), p. 318–323, at p. 318–319.

66 For on overview of many corruption-related indicators, see Maks Kobonbaev and Sharon Eicher, 'Quantifying the Immeasurable', in Sharon Eicher (ed.), *Corruption in International Business: The Challenge of Cultural and Legal Diversity* (Corporate Social Responsibility Series: Gower, 2009), p. 61–79.

1995. The founding father of this instrument is Lambsdorff. As the name indicates, the CPI measures people's *perceptions* of public sector corruption (rather than its occurrence).[67] The Index contains the large majority of the world's countries, and on the basis of expert assessments and opinion surveys among business people, these countries are ranked from 1 to 183. At the top of the list, we find the countries with the lowest levels of perceived corruption, while at the bottom of the list, we find the countries that are perceived to be most corrupt. In 2011, New Zealand was perceived to be the cleanest country, holding the no. 1 position, while Somalia was perceived to be most tainted by corruption at no. 182.[68] While the CPI is by far the index most referred to, there are also strong criticisms on its methodology.[69] *Inter alia,* it is stated that across countries and years, there are significant differences in the sources used. Also, the perceptions of business leaders and experts may influence each other, which may lead to distorted outcomes. In addition, it is questionable whether the CPI, which intends to measure a wide range of corrupt practices, can actually reflect improvements in the actual extent of particular types of corruption. Hence, successes in certain areas (e.g. customs or traffic police) may not be reflected in the index.[70]

The CPI is complemented by the *Bribe Payers Index* (hereafter: BPI), also developed by TI. The BPI focuses on the supply-side of corruption, i.e. the likelihood of corporations from industrialised countries to bribe officials abroad. The last BPI was published in 2008, ranking 22 countries. The number one position is the country whose firms are least likely to bribe (Belgium and Canada), while the final position is occupied by the State whose firms are most likely to bribe (Russia).[71] Furthermore, another instrument that aims to obtain insights into the supply side is the *European Fraud Survey* by Ernst & Young.[72] The 2011 edition is based on interviews with 2,365 employees of large corporations in 25 European

---

67 For an explanation of the methodology behind the CPI, see Johann Graf Lambsdorff, 'Measuring Corruption – the Validity and Precision of Subjective Indicators (CPI)', in Charles Sampford et al. (eds.), *Measuring Corruption* (Aldershot: Ashgate, 2006), p. 81–99.

68 For more on the CPI 2011, see <http://cpi.transparency.org/cpi2011/result> accessed 10 December 2011.

69 For an extensive analysis, see Fredrik Galtung, 'Measuring the Immeasurable: Boundaries and Functions of (Macro) Corruption Indices', in Charles Sampford et al. (eds.), *Measuring Corruption* (Aldershot: Ashgate, 2006), p. 102–130. Mark Philp, 'Corruption Definition and Measurement', in Charles Sampford et al. (eds.), *Measuring Corruption* (Aldershot: Ashgate, 2006), p. 45–56 at p. 49 *et seq.* A general critique of corruption indicators can be found in Maks Kobonbaev, Donald Jacobsen, and Sharon Eicher, 'Critiquing the Indicators of Corruption and Government', in Sharon Eicher (ed.), *Corruption in International Business: The Challenge of Cultural and Legal Diversity* (Corporate Social Responsibility Series: Gower, 2009), p. 81–89.

70 As summarised by Jan van Dijk, *The World of Crime. Breaking the Silence on Problems of Security, Justice and Development across the World* (Thousand Oaks, CA: Sage, 2008), at p. 182.

71 For more on the BPI 2008 and its methodology, see <www.transparency.org/policy_research/surveys_indices/bpi/bpi_2008>, accessed 18 May 2011.

72 Ernst & Young, *European Fraud Survey 2011: Recovery, Regulation and Integrity* (2011).

countries. The survey includes questions on employee perception of fraud, bribery and corruption, company responses to the challenges posed by fraud risks, and the response of regulators and law enforcement.[73]

TI releases the *Global Corruption Barometer* (hereafter: GCB), a survey assessing the general attitudes of the public towards corruption, as well as the public's experience of corruption. The GCB of 2010 captures the views of over 91,500 people in 86 countries. It shows that six out of ten people around the world find that corruption has increased over the past three years. Moreover, one out of four people reported that in the past year, they have paid bribes.[74]

Furthermore, the *International Crime Victims Survey* (hereafter: ICVS) includes a question about the respondent's experiences with street-level corruption in the past year. It is held that this is 'arguably the most reliable source of truly comparative information on corruption prevalence.'[75] We must bear in mind that this tool is limited to measuring petty corruption.

While all methods of measuring corruption undoubtedly have their flaws, the need remains to measure corruption levels in order to keep track of progress made by States. Yet, not all progress may be shown by the mentioned surveys.

5. The Harmfulness of Corruption

5.1. Introductory Remarks

Whereas the previous sections explored definitions of corruption, discussed its various forms and touched upon the instruments by which it can possibly be measured, it is now time to assess the various ways in which corruption is harmful. Following Transparency International's classification, the current section explores a number of consequences of corruption (i) politically; (ii) economically; (iii) socially; and (iv) environmentally.[76] Yet, while the following overview touches upon a number of important aspects, it does not claim to be exhaustive. Also, care should be taken to avoid generalisations. Corruption is highly contextualised, and both its causes and consequences will vary depending on the type of corruption (grand or petty, bribery or other forms), its nature (endemic or sporadic), as well as on the particular country situation. One must also bear in mind that the four sets of consequences are undoubtedly interrelated.

---

73 See <www.ey.com/GL/en/Services/Assurance/Fraud-Investigation---Dispute-Services/European-fraud-survey–2011--recovery--regulation-and-integrity>, accessed 18 May 2011.

74 For more on the GCB 2010, see <www.transparency.org/policy_research/surveys_indices/gcb/2010>, accessed 18 May 2011.

75 Van Dijk, *The World of Crime. Breaking the Silence on Problems of Security, Justice and Development across the World* at p. 182.

76 Transparency International, 'Frequently Asked Questions About Corruption', <www.transparency.org/news_room/faq/corruption_faq>, accessed 20 May 2011.

5.2. Political Consequences

5.2.1. Erosion of Democracy and Legitimacy

As argued by Johnston, 'the question of the political implications of corruption has no single answer'.[77] What seems to be clear, however, is that it is generally believed that 'the effect of corruption on politics is that corruption renders the State incapacitated and impotent.'[78] One of the dangers of corruption is that it threatens democratic governance. In case of rigged elections, for example, those who obtain power are not accountable to the public, and will not care so much about the actual needs of the population.[79] When there is widespread corruption, citizens lose their trust in the political system, which will be perceived as illegitimate. As a result, citizens will turn their back on the system.[80] Another aspect concerns tax collection. The State's capacity to extract taxes may be affected when the public becomes aware of the embezzlement of taxes by public officials. The willingness of the public to pay taxes decreases, tax revenues decline, and less money is available for public services.[81] Furthermore, in a corrupt political system, decision-making is distorted since priority will be given to projects that offer opportunities for self-enrichment, but which do not meet the actual needs of citizens.[82]

5.2.2. Armed Conflict

Under certain circumstances, corruption may be related to armed conflict. Particularly the presence of natural resources can play a prominent role. The relationship between corruption, a country's natural resource wealth, and armed conflict, as captured in figure 1 below, is multi-faceted. Although the outbreak of armed conflict is often a complex, multi-causal process that cannot be easily simplified, the present section aims to identify a number of important connections, without claiming to be fully exhaustive.

---

77 Michael Johnston, 'Public Officials, Private Interests, and Sustainable Democracy: When Politics and Corruption Meet', in Kimberley Ann Elliott (ed.), *Corruption and the Global Economy* (Washington, D.C.: Institute for International Economics, 1997), p. 61–82 at p. 62.

78 Andvig et al., 'Corruption: A Review of Contemporary Research', at p. 43–44.

79 Ebenezer Durojaye, 'Corruption as a Threat to Human Security in Africa', in Ademola Abass (ed.), *Protecting Human Security in Africa* (Oxford: Oxford University Press, 2010), p. 217–243 at p. 224.

80 Transparency International, 'Frequently Asked Questions About Corruption'; Andvig et al., 'Corruption: A Review of Contemporary Research'. Susan Rose-Ackerman, 'The Political Economy of Corruption', in Kimberley Ann Elliott (ed.), *Corruption and the Global Economy* (Washington, D.C.: Institute for International Economics, 1997), p. 31–60 at p. 45.

81 Andvig et al., 'Corruption: A Review of Contemporary Research', at p. 44.

82 *Ibid.*

(i) Corruption → Armed Conflict, and Armed Conflict → Corruption

Corruption can bring about armed conflict, and hence may contribute to the commission of crimes under international law, since these crimes are often perpetrated during such conflicts. Le Billon suggested that under certain conditions, corruption can lead to violent conflict, particularly when there are changes in the system of corruption.[83] He found that corruption can fuel war due to three interrelated processes.

Corruption can increase grievances and conflicting demands for political change. The negative economic consequences of corruption (see *infra*), and the fact that corrupt practices can deepen inequalities, can lead to discontent.[84] The same holds true for the political consequences of corruption.[85] This dissatisfaction created by corruption feeds political instability, because people will support movements advocating political change. Le Billon suggested that most leaders of (violent) coups declare that they will tackle the corrupt practices of the previous government, in order to obtain popular support.[86]

Furthermore, those groups or individuals who manage to capture the State through armed conflict, and become its future leaders, will be awarded with the availability of rents. Hence, the opportunity to engage in corrupt practices (e.g. through the exploitation of natural resources) may be a driving force behind conflict. The rents that become available to the new leaders can be used for themselves (i.e. greed-driven), and/or to reward a group of supporters.[87]

Moreover, political corruption undermines institutionalised public affairs, including processes of political change and conflict resolution mechanisms. Whenever corruption denies people e.g. fair elections, or a fair trial, this can lead to violence because (i) the ruling group may use force to stay in power; and (ii) people may turn to radical movements to claim their rights.[88]

In sum, Le Billon pointed out that 'whether motivated by greed or grievances, conflict often has much to do with corruption',[89] but he also noted that the character of corruption in a given situation should be taken into account. It is important to determine whether forms of corruption are considered to be legitimate or illegitimate within a certain political context.[90] Hence, he concluded by stating that 'corruption is not in itself a sufficient or even necessary factor in the outbreak of armed conflict. Different types of corruption have different relations with conflict,

---

83 Philippe Le Billon, 'Buying Peace or Fuelling War: The Role of Corruption in Armed Conflicts', *Journal of International Development,* 15 (2003), p. 413–426.

84 *Ibid.* at p. 417.

85 *Ibid.* at p. 418.

86 *Ibid.*

87 *Ibid.* at p. 418–419.

88 *Ibid.* at p. 419.

89 *Ibid.*

90 *Ibid.* at p. 420.

thus requiring a differentiation of the types of corruption and an examination of the factors affecting their legitimacy and functions.'[91]

Furthermore, it must be noted that corruption can also influence the duration of armed conflict: (i) it is a breeding ground for corruption; and (ii) it undermines the efficiency and morale of the armed forces, particularly on the side of the government.[92]

While corruption can lead to armed conflict, the reverse is also true: conflict can cause corruption. War situations offer an abundance of opportunities for participants to engage in corrupt practices, e.g. through defence contracts and wages of ghost soldiers.[93]

(ii) Natural Resource Wealth → Armed Conflict

Natural resource wealth and armed conflict are closely linked. In this respect, the term 'conflict resources' is often used. Global Witness defined these as 'natural resources whose systematic exploitation and trade in a context of conflict contribute to, benefit from or result in the commission of serious violations of human rights, violations of international humanitarian law or violations amounting to crimes under international law.'[94]

First of all, natural resource wealth can be used to fund ongoing conflict. Also, natural resource wealth can constitute the reason why armed conflict takes place. This is the so-called 'greed theory', as identified by Collier and others, which sets out that armed conflict is initiated to gain control over valuable resources.[95] This view is mitigated by Ballentine, who pointed out that:

> ... very few contemporary conflicts can be adequately captured as pure instances of 'resource wars' or conflicts caused by 'loot-seeking', on the part of either insurgents or State actors. Economic incentives and opportunities have not been the only or even the primary cause of these armed conflicts; rather, to varying degrees, they interacted with socioeconomic and political grievances, interethnic disputes, and security dilemmas in triggering the outbreak of warfare. However, these studies also suggest that, in certain circumstances, combatant access to economic resources has been a salient factor shaping a permissive opportunity for sustaining hostilities and has had important effects on the duration, intensity, and character of conflict.[96]

---

91 *Ibid.* at p. 424.

92 *Ibid.* at p. 422–423.

93 *Ibid.* at p. 422.

94 Global Witness, 'The Sinews of War – Eliminating the Trade in Conflict Resources', (Washington DC, November 2006) at p. 1.

95 Karen Ballentine and Jake Sherman, 'Introduction', in Karen Ballentine and Jake Sherman (eds.), *The Political Economy of Armed Conflict: Beyond Greed and Grievance* (A Project of the International Peace Academy; Boulder: Lynne Rienner Publishers, 2003), p. 1–15.

96 Karen Ballentine, 'Beyond Greed and Grievance: Reconsidering the Economic Dynamics of Armed Conflict', *Ibid.* p. 259–283 at p. 259–260.

Further research done by Humpreys identified five ways in which natural resource wealth is linked with conflict: (i) rent seeking (resource curse); (ii) grievances: an uneven distribution of resource wealth and the socio-economic impact of extractive industries lead to discontent; (iii) economic instability; (iv) financing of conflict; and (v) peace spoiling.[97]

Another important factor is whether the resources are lootable (e.g. diamonds, timber) or unlootable (e.g. oil and gas). Lootable resources tend to lead to non-separatist insurgencies, while unlootable resources are more likely to play a role in separatist conflicts.[98]

(iii) Natural Resource Wealth → Corruption

The presence of an abundance of natural resources can result in corruption. Since it is generally the State which ultimately holds control over natural resources, there are opportunities for those working in the public sector to obtain private benefits (rent-seeking) through corruption.

These are important observations, revealing that there can be various causal relationships between corruption, armed conflict and natural resource wealth. This concise analysis, however, does not intend to simplify other complex factors that should also be taken into account.

Figure 1. Triangle of Corruption – Armed Conflict – Natural Resource Wealth

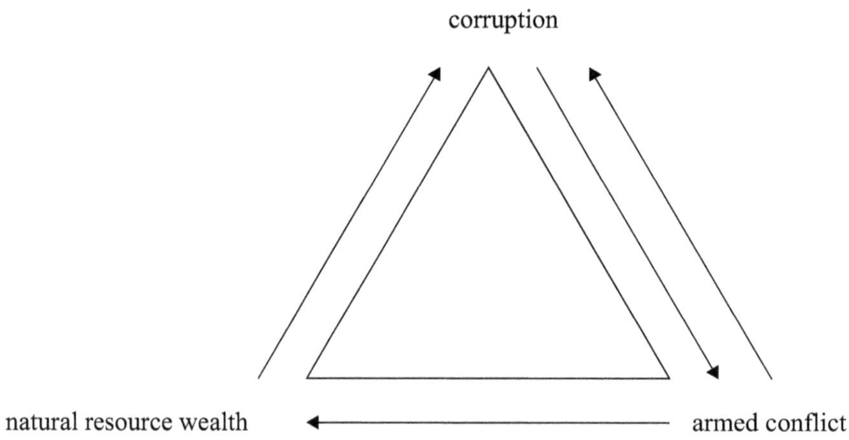

97 Macartan Humphreys, 'Natural Resources and Armed Conflicts: Issues and Options', in Karen Ballentine and Heiko Nitzschke (eds.), *Profiting from Peace: Managing the Resource Dimension of Civil War* (Boulder: Lynne Rienner Publishers 2005), p. 25–44. The five points mentioned are summed up by Karen Ballentine and Heiko Nitzschke, 'Introduction', in Karen Ballentine and Heiko Nitzschke (eds.), *Profiting from Peace: Managing the Resource Dimension of Civil War* (Boulder: Lynne Rienner Publishers 2005), p. 1–24 at p. 5–6.

98 Ballentine and Nitzschke, 'Introduction', at p. 3.

5.3. Economic Consequences

What influence does corruption have upon a country's economy? In an article that first appeared in 1964, Leff focused upon the benefits of bureaucratic corruption for the economic development of underdeveloped countries. In his view, bureaucratic corruption is the bribing of bureaucrats who are responsible for the formulation and administration of governmental economic policies.[99] According to Leff, this practice has several positive effects. It can serve to trigger the attention of a government that is indifferent or hostile to economic activities and it can make economic activities a priority for governments and activate bureaucracy. Furthermore, bureaucratic corruption reduces uncertainty and increases investment, it can lead to innovation, it increases competition and efficiency and it serves as a protection against bad economic policies.[100] In the same line of reasoning, Huntington noted that a certain amount of corruption can function as a welcome lubricant in a traditional, relatively uncorrupt society where traditional norms prevail. In this way, corruption was considered to be a tool to achieve modernisation.[101]

However, in this day and age, the view of corruption as beneficial to an economic system is abandoned by the large majority of economists. The World Bank noted that studies that aim to demonstrate that corruption can have positive economic effects are only concerned with static short term effects. Over longer periods of time, corruption will be harmful.[102] Moreover, Rose-Ackerman pointed out that the argument of corruption as a tool to increase efficiency by speeding up bureaucrats will work in the opposite direction: public officials may introduce even more unnecessary regulations and delays, in order for them to demand or to be offered bribes.[103]

A large number of work is currently available on the various economic consequences of corruption.[104] The work of Mauro is cited frequently. Drawing from his own work and research done by others, he listed several ways in which

---

99 Nathaniel H. Leff, 'Economic Development through Bureaucratic Corruption', in Arnold J. Heidenheimer and Michael Johnston (eds.), *Political Corruption: Concepts and Contexts* (3rd edn.; New Brunswick: Transaction, 2002), p. 307–320 at p. 307–308.

100 *Ibid.* at p. 311–315.

101 Samuel P. Huntington, 'Modernization and Corruption', in Arnold J. Heidenheimer and Michael Johnston (eds.), *Political Corruption: Concepts and Contexts* (3rd edn.; New Brunswick: Transaction, 2002), p. 253–263 at p. 261. This article was first published in 1968.

102 World Bank, 'Helping Countries Combat Corruption. The Role of the World Bank', p. 15.

103 Rose-Ackerman, 'The Political Economy of Corruption', at p. 43; Rose-Ackerman, *Corruption and Government: Causes, Consequences and Reform* at p. 15–17.

104 A useful overview is provided by Andvig et al., 'Corruption: A Review of Contemporary Research', at chapter 7 and by Kimberley Ann Elliott, 'Corruption as an International Policy Problem: Overview and Recommendations', in Kimberley Ann Elliott (ed.), *Corruption and the Global Economy* (Washington, D.C.: Institute for International Economics, 1997), p. 175–233 at p. 186–196.

corruption may lower economic growth.[105] Mauro's classification is taken as a starting point, and supplemented with data from other scholars.

First, entrepreneurs will perceive the paying of bribes as a kind of tax, which has a negative impact upon private investment, lowering economic growth.[106] Several other studies support Mauro's conclusions on the influence of corruption on investment.[107] In addition, it was pointed out by the World Bank and Campos *et al.* that not only the level of corruption (i.e. the size of corruption) impacts investments, but also its nature. In this respect, it is the predictability of corruption that matters. For example, is it foreseeable how much bribes have to be paid and will the desired benefit be ultimately obtained by the bribe-payer? Studies show that countries with more predictable corruption have higher investment rates than countries with more unpredictable corruption. However, countries remain better off without any corruption.[108] Furthermore, Wei found that corruption also lowers foreign direct investment.[109]

Also, according to Murphy *et al.*, in situations where rent seeking is more profitable than entrepreneurship, it is likely that talented and well-educated people will choose rent seeking rather than productive job opportunities. This misallocation of talent has a negative influence on growth.[110]

In addition, corruption might reduce the effectiveness of aid flows, where funds are embezzled.[111] Cremer found that corruption in development projects is a serious problem. His study reveals *inter alia* corruption in a World Bank project in Indonesia, and misappropriation by development NGOs.[112]

Furthermore, in cases where corruption results in tax evasion or the improper use of discretionary tax exemptions (e.g. awarded to a corporation which has bribed a public official), there is a loss of tax revenue.[113] This lowers the government's

---

105 Paolo Mauro, 'The Effects of Corruption on Growth and Public Expenditure', in Arnold J. Heidenheimer and Michael Johnston (eds.), *Political Corruption: Concepts and Contexts* (3rd edn.; New Brunswick: Transaction, 2002), p. 339–352 at p. 342–344.

106 *Ibid.* at p. 342; Paolo Mauro, 'Corruption and Growth', *The Quarterly Journal of Economics,* 110 (1995), p. 681–712.

107 Andvig et al., 'Corruption: A Review of Contemporary Research', at p. 72–73.

108 World Bank, *World Development Report 1997: The State in a Changing World* (New York: Oxford University Press, 1997) at p. 103; J. Edgardo Campos, Donald Lien, and Sanjay Pradhan, 'The Impact of Corruption on Investment: Predictability Matters', *World Development,* 27 (1999), p. 1059–1067 at p. 1065.

109 Shang-Jin Wei, 'How Taxing Is Corruption on International Investors?' *NBER Working Papers, number 6030* (Cambridge, Massachusetts: National Bureau of Economic Research, February 1997).

110 Mauro, 'The Effects of Corruption on Growth and Public Expenditure', at p. 343; Kevin M. Murphy, Andrei Shleifer, and Robert W. Vishny, 'The Allocation of Talent: Implications for Growth', *The Quarterly Journal of Economics,* 106 (1991), p. 503–530.

111 Mauro, 'The Effects of Corruption on Growth and Public Expenditure', at p. 343.

112 Georg Cremer, *Corruption and Development Aid: Confronting the Challenges* (Freiburg: Lambertus Verlag, 2008).

113 Mauro, 'The Effects of Corruption on Growth and Public Expenditure', at p. 343.

ability to provide essential goods and services and will worsen the problem of low wages in the public sector, thus breeding even more corruption.[114]

As touched upon earlier, there are negative budgetary consequences when tax collection is reduced or the level of public expenditure is raised.[115]

Moreover, corruption in public procurement can lead to an inferior quality of public infrastructure and service. For example, when bribes are paid to a public official in order to obtain the contract, this official might allow the use of cheaper, substandard materials in the construction of a bridge or school building.[116]

Finally, corruption influences the composition of government expenditure. For example, officials are more likely to spend the governmental budget on large projects (such as the purchase of military aircraft) than on small projects (such as providing school books), because larger, more complex projects offer more opportunities to obtain personal gain through bribes.[117] Research provides suggestive evidence that corruption is negatively associated with government expenditure on education and possibly on health.[118] A report from Human Rights Watch demonstrates that large-scale corruption within the local governments of the Niger Delta's River State has led to very poor basic health care and primary education.[119] In this context, the term 'white elephant project' deserves to be mentioned.[120] A white elephant project is a project which generates money for public officials and suppliers, while its public purpose is limited or non-existent.[121]

On a final note, some actual figures may be appropriate. It was mentioned that according to estimates of the African Union and the African Development Bank, corruption costs African economies more than US$148 billion dollars every year,

---

114 Elliott, 'Corruption as an International Policy Problem: Overview and Recommendations', at p. 191.

115 Mauro, 'The Effects of Corruption on Growth and Public Expenditure', at p. 343.

116 *Ibid.* at p. 343. For more on corruption in procurement, see Tina Søreide, 'Corruption in Public Procurement. Causes, Consequences and Cures', *CMI Report, R 2002:1* (Bergen, Chr. Michelsen Institute, 2002).

117 Mauro, 'The Effects of Corruption on Growth and Public Expenditure', at p. 343–344; Elliott, 'Corruption as an International Policy Problem: Overview and Recommendations', at p. 192.

118 Mauro, 'The Effects of Corruption on Growth and Public Expenditure', at p. 343–344, 347–349.

119 Human Rights Watch, 'Chop Fine. The Human Rights Impact of Local Government Corruption and Mismanagement in Rivers State, Nigeria.' *Report, Volume 19, No. 2(A)* (New York, January 2007).

120 Named after Mark Twain's short story 'The Stolen White Elephant' (1882), which describes the theft of a white elephant, a gift from the King of Siam to the Queen of England, during transport from India to Britain. Even though the animal is very large, the police department searching for him is unable to find the elephant.

121 Elliott, 'Corruption as an International Policy Problem: Overview and Recommendations'; Augustine Ruzindana, 'The Importance of Leadership in Fighting Corruption in Uganda', in Kimberley Ann Elliott (ed.), *Corruption and the Global Economy* (Washington, D.C.: Institute for International Economics, 1997), p. 133–145 at p. 137.

leading to a loss of 50 per cent in tax revenue, increasing the costs of African goods by 20 per cent and eating away 25 per cent of Africa's GDP.[122]

5.4. Social Consequences

While the previous sub-section already demonstrated that corruption may hamper economic growth, it also increases inequalities in how wealth is distributed.[123] Economists found that 'the impact of corruption upon income inequality and poverty is considerable.'[124] Hence, the social consequences of corruption may be adequately captured by the phrase that the practice benefits the 'haves' over the 'have-nots'.[125] The poor are disproportionately affected, since those who can afford to pay bribes can obtain an advantage over those who cannot afford to do so. Public funds embezzled by officials for their private ends can no longer be used for the realisation of social goals such as health care, housing, and education. This is of course closely intertwined with the political and economic consequences as discussed *supra*. Lower economic growth is generally linked to poverty, and with poverty come poor living conditions, low life-expectancy, high infant-mortality and a high illiteracy rate.[126] Rather than affecting merely the current generation, corruption infects future generations for decades to come.

Corruption does not always divide the rich from the poor in an arbitrary way. Divisions can also run along ethnic lines.[127] In certain States, corrupt rulers will favour their own ethnic group, and reward their 'own people' with certain benefits (e.g. social services, water supply, or financial resources) which are not provided to other groups. As suggested by Githongo, 'in ethnically heterogeneous African States with a tradition of political patronage, economic inequality is manifested

122 William De Maria, 'Cross Cultural Trespass: Assessing African Anti-Corruption Capacity', *International Journal of Cross Cultural Management,* 8/3 (2008), p. 317–341 at p. 317. These figures are also mentioned by Transparency International, see Transparency International, 'Frequently Asked Questions on Corruption and Africa', <www.transparency.org/news_room/in_focus/2005/g8_summit/faq>, accessed 23 May 2011.

123 Rose-Ackerman, 'The Political Economy of Corruption', at p. 44.

124 Sanjeev Gupta, Hamid R. Davoodi, and Rosa Alonso-Terme, 'Does Corruption Affect Income Inequality and Poverty?' in George T. Abed and Sanjeev Gupta (eds.), *Governance, Corruption & Economic Performance* (Washington, DC: International Monetary Fund, 2002), p. 458–486 at p. 478.

125 Johnston noted that 'Most corruption will tend to benefit the haves at the political, as well as material, expense of the have-nots.' Johnston, 'Public Officials, Private Interests, and Sustainable Democracy: When Politics and Corruption Meet', at p. 63.

126 For more on poverty and corruption, see Transparency International, 'Poverty and Corruption', *Working Paper 02/2008* (2008) and Eric Chetwynd, Frances Chetwynd, and Bertram Spector, 'Corruption and Poverty: A Review of Recent Literature', (Washington, DC: Management Systems International, January 2003).

127 U4 Anti-Corruption Resource Centre, 'FAQs: Causes and Consequences of Corruption', <www.u4.no/helpdesk/faq/faqs1.cfm>, accessed 20 May 2011.

along ethnic and regional lines.'[128] Interestingly, he also pointed out that 'ironically, it's not the corruption in itself that people object to but the fact that it is perpetrated predominantly by an elite from one ethnic group to the exclusion of others, *especially theirs*' [original emphasis].[129] Such ethnic tensions can clearly fuel violent conflict (see *supra* at 5.3).

5.5. Environmental Consequences

In examining corruption's effects, it is important to adopt a holistic approach towards the issue and to pay due respect not just to the human factor, but also to the wider environment and non-human animals. Corruption has a severe negative impact upon the natural environment in various ways.[130]

As elaborated upon earlier, the presence of natural resources may prompt corrupt practices. The resulting exploitation of those resources is not likely to be sustainable. An obvious example is illegal logging as a result of, or part of, corrupt practices, having a severe negative impact upon the conservation of nature. Corruption exacerbates illegal logging by allowing it to take place, and by not enforcing regulations and not punishing perpetrators. Those officials who benefit from illegal logging will also oppose to anti-corruption measures.[131] Research shows that corruption may be a key factor in the loss of tropical forests because of unsustainable or illegal logging. This also impacts upon the various mammals inhabiting those areas.[132] TRAFFIC[133] reports that corruption is a major cause of deforestation in Tanzania.[134]

As regards the exploitation of natural resources, particularly in the extractive industries, pollution frequently occurs. In a globalised economic order, most

---

128 John Githongo, 'Inequality, Ethnicity and the Fight against Corruption in Africa: A Kenyan Perspective', *Economic Affairs*, 26/4 (2006), p. 19–23 at p. 19.

129 *Ibid.* at p. 21.

130 A group of graduate students of Columbia University conducted research on this matter: Environmental Science and Policy Workshop, 'Corruption & the Environment. A Project for Transparency International' (Columbia University, School of International and Public Affairs, April 2006).

131 Joyotee Smith et al., 'Illegal Logging, Collusive Corruption and Fragmented Governments in Kalimantan, Indonesia', in Luca Tacconi (ed.), *Illegal Logging: Law Enforcement, Livelihoods and the Timber Trade* (London: Earthscan, 2007), p. 91–109 at p. 91.

132 R.J. Smith and M.J. Walpole, 'Should Conservationists Pay More Attention to Corruption?' *Oryx*, 39 (2005), p. 251–256 at p. 252.

133 TRAFFIC is the wildlife trade monitoring network. It is governed by the TRAFFIC Committee, which consists of members of TRAFFIC's partner organisations: the World Wildlife Fund (WWF) and the International Union for Conservation of Nature (IUCN). See <www.traffic.org>.

134 Simon A.H. Milledge, Ised K Gelvas, and Antje Ahrends, 'Forestry, Governance and National Development: Lessons Learned from a Logging Boom in Southern Tanzania', (Dar es Salaam: TRAFFIC East/Southern Africa / Tanzania Development Partners Group / Ministry of Natural Resources and Tourism, 2007).

multinational corporations aim to do business in countries with low taxes, cheap labour and lax environmental regulations. In striving for profit-maximization, businesses and individuals may bribe public officials in order to circumvent environmental regulations. Resulting pollution does not only affect the natural environment, it will also affect the standard of living of the persons living in a certain area. Especially the living circumstances of indigenous peoples may be at stake. Their rights to health, food, housing etcetera are often dependent on the natural environment. Meanwhile, the multi-billion dollar profits resulting from corporate activity will often not benefit the local population. Also, outside the context of natural resource exploitation, corruption can have negative environmental consequences. This was recently demonstrated when Monsanto, a US agrochemical corporation, admitted that it had bribed a high level official at the Indonesian ministry of environment, so that the ministry would not assess the environmental impact of Monsanto's genetically modified cotton.[135]

Corruption is also detrimental to wildlife conservation. One can think of various forms of corruption in this respect. Public officials responsible for conservation of wildlife can be bribed to turn a blind eye to poaching. Corruption can also occur at various places in the supply chain of the (il)legal trade in animals or animal 'products'. Moreover, money intended for anti-poaching and conservation efforts is frequently embezzled by public officials.[136] It has been noted that this is a larger problem than bribery of wildlife officials.[137] Research shows that corruption is more damaging to wildlife than other factors such as the level of poverty or the growth of the human population. High corruption rates in Africa correspond with the decrease in the number of elephants and black rhinoceros.[138] In respect of endangered species, some argue that trade bans might not be effective since they only lead to the enrichment of corrupt officials if the demand for the animal or 'product' is high.[139] Examples of corruption in the trade in endangered species are the elephant and ivory trade in Myanmar and neighbouring countries. For instance, Myanmar allows the legal sale of ivory tusks and tusk tips from elephants that have died a natural death, if these elephants were owned by the government or private citizens. This creates opportunities for corruption. In 2006, some 9,000 ivory items, such as chopsticks, and 16 whole tusks (together originating from 116 bulls) were

---

135 BBC News Online, 'Monsanto Fined $1.5m for Bribery', <http://news.bbc.co.uk/2/hi/business/4153635.stm>, accessed 8 January 2009; Greenpeace, 'Monsanto Pays Up', <www.greenpeace.org/international/news/monsanto-pays-fine-for-bribery>, accessed 12 January 2009. As a consequence, Monsanto had to pay a fine of $1.5 million, because bribery by US individuals and corporations is criminalised by the US Foreign Corrupt Practices Act, as discussed in chapter II, §2.1 hereafter.

136 Smith and Walpole, 'Should Conservationists Pay More Attention to Corruption?', at p. 252.

137 Stefan Lovgren, 'Corruption Top Threat to African Animals, Study Says', (National Geographic News, 5 November 2003).

138 R.J. Smith et al., 'Governance and the Loss of Biodiversity', *Nature*, 426 (6 November 2003), p. 67–70.

139 *Ibid.*

offered for sale at markets in Myanmar and border markets in Thailand and China. Furthermore, live elephants are smuggled out of Myanmar for abuse in Thailand's tourist industry.[140] These facts and figures show that corruption is not only a human rights topic, but also an issue that can no longer be ignored within the debate on animal welfare and animal rights.[141]

6. Concluding Remarks

Although corruption is hard to define, all work on the topic is in need of a useful working definition. The present chapter made clear that the thesis focuses on corruption in the public sector, defined as *'the abuse of public office for private or political gain'*. This is a slightly adapted version of the definition employed by the World Bank, in order to include political gain as well. Corruption can take place at the policy formulation end of politics, committed by high-level officials. This is known as grand corruption. On the other hand, petty corruption entails corrupt practices committed by lower-level officials at the policy implementation end of politics. Furthermore, while corruption may be closely related to concepts such as economic crime, white-collar crime, fraud, and collusion, these should not be used as synonyms.

The umbrella term 'corruption' does not suffice for a legal study of the matter. For this reason, the terminology of the United Nations Convention Against Corruption is used as a framework for distinguishing between the various faces of corruption. The treaty sets out five main types of corruption, i.e. (i) bribery; (ii) embezzlement, (iii) trading in influence; (iv) abuse of functions and (v) illicit enrichment.

While defining corruption is difficult enough, measuring it may be an even more challenging task. Nonetheless, a number of instruments were developed to estimate how much corruption is taking place in a given country. These are the Corruption Perceptions Index, the Bribe Payers Index, the Global Corruption Barometer, and the International Crime Victims Survey. While none of these is flawless, they offer valuable insights into corruption research.

From the study of the consequences of corruption that aimed to provide a short overview of key issues in current research, it follows that political, economic, social and environmental factors are intertwined. In all of these areas, it is beyond doubt that corruption is a serious evil. From a political perspective, corruption erodes democracy and legitimacy, and may be related to the occurrence and duration of armed conflict, particularly in countries with natural resource wealth. Economically, corruption may lower economic growth in various ways, and leads to larger income

140 Chris R. Shepherd and Vincent Nijman, 'Elephant and Ivory Trade in Myanmar', (Petaling Jaya, Selangor, Malaysia: TRAFFIC Southeast Asia, 2008).

141 For an excellent basic introduction into animal rights theory, see Peter Singer, *Animal Liberation* (New York: Harper Collins, 1975).

inequality and poverty. Environmentally, corruption is detrimental to the natural environment in cases of unsustainable exploitation of natural resources, and severely affects wildlife conservation. How corruption impacts upon human rights is specifically dealt with in part B.

Having set out the basic issues in the discussion about corruption, the following chapter II is dedicated to the content and functioning of the various global and regional legal instruments which aim to prevent and combat corrupt practices.

Chapter II
Global and Regional Legal Framework Against Corruption

1. Introduction

As the problem of corruption was defined and explained more precisely in the previous chapter, it is relevant to elaborate upon the legal instruments that were adopted over the years in order to prevent and combat the issue. Starting in the mid–1990s, a true proliferation of anti-corruption instruments can be witnessed. A precursory role was played even earlier by the US in the form of the Foreign Corrupt Practices Act (hereafter: FCPA).

Section 2 elaborates upon the content of the FCPA, the motives for its adoption, the criticisms it has received and the amendments resulting therefrom, as well as the enforcement and effectiveness of this novel piece of legislation. This section also discusses the underlying reasons for the global explosion of anti-corruption efforts that followed the FCPA.

Subsequently, the global and regional legal instruments which have recently come into being are discussed in section 3. This part concisely discusses the content of each instrument and contains a critical analysis of the positive and negative aspects of the anti-corruption instruments and, whenever established, the accompanying monitoring mechanisms. It must be noted that effectiveness of legislation can be difficult to measure, particularly where it concerns anti-corruption provisions. It is an inherent feature of corruption that it occurs in secret, and therefore it is hard to determine whether the level of corruption has actually diminished as a result of legal instruments. It goes far beyond the scope of the current thesis to conduct empirical research in order to determine how effective each and every instrument and the monitoring thereof actually is. Therefore, this chapter draws its main conclusions from information provided by the organisations which have developed the instruments, from NGO reports (particularly Transparency International) and from scholarly research. The instruments are (mostly) discussed in chronological order of adoption, elucidating how the legal framework has developed over the years.

Finally, a comparative analysis follows in section 4, discussing the main similarities and differences between the instruments and the shortcomings of the present regime. Moreover, the concluding section argues that the current legal framework at the global and regional level leaves an accountability gap, which calls for additional approaches to the problem of corruption. These approaches, in the field of human rights law and international criminal law, are the topic of Parts B and C of the current work.

2. International Regulation of Corruption

2.1. The Precursory Role of the US Foreign Corrupt Practices Act

2.1.1. Content

Prior to the mid–1990s, no global or regional instruments existed on the topic of corruption. Corruption was primarily seen as an issue of domestic rather than international concern. Therefore, most countries did have national legislation prohibiting certain corrupt acts within their territories, particularly the bribery of *domestic* public officials.[1] Legislation prohibiting the active bribery of *foreign* public officials was lacking. The only exception to the rule was the United States Foreign Corrupt Practices Act which came into being as early as 1977.[2] This piece of legislation aims to prevent active bribery of foreign public officials by US corporations and citizens. To this end, the FCPA contains both anti-bribery provisions and accounting and recordkeeping provisions. The anti-bribery provisions criminalise active bribery of a foreign public official (regardless of rank), a foreign political party or party official or any candidate for a political office by issuers, domestic concerns and persons other than issuers and domestic concerns.[3] The accounting and recordkeeping provisions impose accounting and recordkeeping standards upon issuers.[4]

Violators of FCPA provisions face criminal and civil penalties. For each violation of the anti-bribery provisions, corporations and other business entities risk criminal fines up to US$2 million, as well as a civil penalty up to $10,000. Individuals are subject to criminal fines up to US$100,000 and/or a prison sentence with a maximum of 5 years. They are also subject to a civil penalty up to US$10,000. Fines imposed upon individuals may not be paid, directly or indirectly,

---

1 E.C. Lashbrooke, 'The Foreign Corrupt Practices Act of 1977: A Unilateral Solution to an International Problem', *Cornell International Law Journal,* 12 (1979), p. 227–243 at p. 228.

2 15 U.S.C. §§78m, 78dd–1, 78dd–2, 78dd–3 and 78ff.

3 15 U.S.C. §78dd–1 (a), §78dd–2 (a), §78dd–3 (a). 'Issuers' are entities that have registered securities in accordance with the Securities and Exchange Act. Stuart H. Deming, *The Foreign Corrupt Practices Act and the New International Norms* (International Practitioner's Deskbook Series; Chicago: Section of International Law and Practice, American Bar Association, 2005) at p. 8. A 'domestic concern' means 'any individual who is a citizen, national, or resident of the United States; and any corporation, partnership, association, joint-stock company, business trust, unincorporated organization, or sole proprietorship which has its principal place of business in the US, or which is organized under the laws of a State of the US or a territory, possession, or commonwealth of the US'; 15 U.S.C §78dd–2 (h) (1). 'Persons other than issuers and domestic concerns' means nearly everyone in the US engaging in international trade by any means of doing business. Thomas R. Snider and Won Kidane, 'Combating Corruption through International Law in Africa: A Comparative Analysis', *Cornell International Law Journal*, 40 (2007), p. 691–748 at p. 701.

4 15 U.S.C. §78m; Deming, *The Foreign Corrupt Practices Act and the New International Norms*, at p. 21–27.

by the person's employer.[5] For the violation of the accounting and recordkeeping provisions, corporations and other business entities can be imposed fines up to US$25 million, while individuals risk fines up to US$5 million and/or imprisonment for a duration of a maximum of 20 years.[6] Moreover, the actual fines may be much higher under the Alternative Fines Act: they can amount to twice the benefit that the defendant intended to gain from paying the bribe.[7]

2.1.2. Underlying Motives for Adoption

The FCPA was a novel piece of legislation, causing quite some controversy. What were the motives of the US to unilaterally adopt legislation limiting corporate conduct abroad? When answering this question, one must bear in mind that the FCPA has its origins in the Watergate scandal in the early nineteen-seventies. It was revealed that several corporations kept secret funds that were not only used to make illegal contributions to the Republican election campaign, but also to pay substantial amounts in bribes to foreign public officials. Subsequently, the US Securities and Exchange Commission (hereafter: SEC)[8] started investigations as well as a voluntary disclosure programme. This demonstrated the massive scale of the bribery. Reportedly over 400 US corporations (including 117 of the Fortune 500 corporations) admitted that they had made questionable or illegal payments to foreign government officials, politicians and political parties in excess of US$300 million. Subsequently, US Congress took up the issue by establishing hearings, and following those events, it decided to adopt legislation to address the problem: the FCPA was born.[9] Several reasons, which are in fact closely related, were underlying this decision.

First of all, bribery was seen as unethical conduct, contrary to US values. Thus, the FCPA was partly based on moral grounds. This idea also fitted the policy of the

---

5 15 U.S.C. §78dd–2 (g); 78-dd–3(e); 78ff(c).

6 15 U.S.C. §78ff (a).

7 Deming, *The Foreign Corrupt Practices Act and the New International Norms*, at p. 41–45; United States Department of Justice, 'Lay-Person's Guide to FCPA', (Washington United States Department of Justice) at p. 6.

8 The SEC is an agency of the US government aiming 'to protect investors, maintain fair, orderly, and efficient markets, and facilitate capital formation.' Securities and Exchange Commission Website, <www.sec.gov>, accessed 7 October 2008.

9 Laura E. Longobardi, 'Reviewing the Situation: What Is to Be Done with the Foreign Corrupt Practices Act?' *Vanderbilt Journal of Transnational Law*, 20 (1987), p. 431–494 at p. 433–435; Marvin G. Pickholz, 'The United States Foreign Corrupt Practices Act as a Civil Remedy', in Barry Rider (ed.), *Corruption: The Enemy Within* (The Hague/London/Boston: Kluwer Law International 1997), p. 231–252 at p. 231–233; Stanley Sporkin, 'The Worldwide Banning of Schmiergeld: A Look at the Foreign Corrupt Practices Act on Its Twentieth Birthday', *Northwestern Journal of International Law & Business*, 18 (1998), p. 269–281 at p. 271–277.

Carter Administration, which in general stressed the importance of morality and human rights.[10]

Reputational concerns also played a part in the adoption of the FCPA. The misconduct of well-known corporations such as Lockheed, Exxon, Gulf Oil and Mobil Oil received large media coverage and led to public outcry. The FCPA aimed to restore the confidence of both the American public and foreign relations in US businesses. Moreover, scandals of US corporations involved in the bribery of officials in foreign States could endanger the relations with these States.[11]

Finally, apart from moral and reputational reasons, US trade interests were important in the creation of the new Act on foreign bribery. Bribery was seen as a non-tariff barrier to trade, distorting competition by favouring the corporation willing to provide the largest bribe.[12]

2.1.3. Criticisms and Resulting Amendments

The FCPA has received several criticisms, particularly from the business side. To begin with, it was frequently contended that the FCPA has led to a competitive disadvantage for US corporations, since they were not allowed to pay bribes abroad, while non-US companies were not hindered to do so by any law. In many countries bribes were even tax-deductible.[13] In practice, it is of course quite difficult to

---

10 Wesley Cragg and William Woof, 'The US Foreign Corrupt Practices Act: A Study of Its Effectiveness', *Business and Society Review,* 107 (2002), p. 98–144 at p. 109 and 117–118; Beverly Earle, 'The United States' Foreign Corrupt Practices Act and the OECD Anti-Bribery Recommendation: When Moral Suasion Won't Work, Try the Money Argument', *Dickinson Journal of International Law,* 14 (1996), p. 207–242 at p. 208 and 224; Lashbrooke, 'The Foreign Corrupt Practices Act of 1977: A Unilateral Solution to an International Problem', at p. 231–232; Agnieszka Klich, 'Bribery in Economies in Transition: The Foreign Corrupt Practices Act', *Stanford Journal of International Law,* 32 (1996), p. 121–147 at p. 123–124; Pickholz, 'The United States Foreign Corrupt Practices Act as a Civil Remedy', at p. 233; Henry H. Rossbacher and Tracy W. Young, 'The Foreign Corrupt Practices Act: An American Response to Corruption', in Barry Rider (ed.), *Corruption: The Enemy Within* (The Hague/London/Boston: Kluwer Law International, 1997), p. 209–230 at p. 217–218.

11 Cragg and Woof, 'The US Foreign Corrupt Practices Act: A Study of Its Effectiveness', at p. 108; Lashbrooke, 'The Foreign Corrupt Practices Act of 1977: A Unilateral Solution to an International Problem', at p. 231–232; Pickholz, 'The United States Foreign Corrupt Practices Act as a Civil Remedy', at p. 233; Rossbacher and Young, 'The Foreign Corrupt Practices Act: An American Response to Corruption', at p. 217.

12 Earle, 'The United States' Foreign Corrupt Practices Act and the OECD Anti-Bribery Recommendation: When Moral Suasion Won't Work, Try the Money Argument', at p. 224; Lashbrooke, 'The Foreign Corrupt Practices Act of 1977: A Unilateral Solution to an International Problem', at p. 231; Pickholz, 'The United States Foreign Corrupt Practices Act as a Civil Remedy', at p. 233.

13 Christopher F. Corr and Judd Lawler, 'Damned If You Do, Damned If You Don't? The OECD Convention and the Globalization of Anti-Bribery Measures.' *Vanderbilt Journal of Transnational Law,* 32 (1999), p. 1249–1344 at p. 1253.

determine whether and, if so, how much US corporations have actually lost due to the US prohibition on foreign bribery. Opinions seem to differ on this matter.[14]

A second critique concerns the wording of the Act. It has been noted that this is too vague. Several important notions are not defined, which might have possibly led corporations to be too cautious in conducting business abroad because of uncertainty about the applicability of the FCPA on their conduct.[15]

Furthermore, it has been argued by a limited number of scholars that laws such as the FCPA prohibiting bribery of public officials outside the territory of the US constitute an undesired imposition of Western values upon other countries.[16] However, others have contended that bribery is universally shameful, in all cultures.[17]

In order to address some of these criticisms, mainly the concern about the alleged decrease in competitiveness of US firms, the FCPA was amended in 1988. The most important changes are as follows. First, certain small bribes, so-called 'facilitating payments for routine governmental actions' or 'grease payments' no

---

14 David Chaikin, 'Extraterritoriality and the Criminalization of Foreign Bribes', in Barry Rider (ed.), *Corruption: The Enemy Within* (The Hague/London/Boston: Kluwer Law International 1997), p. 285–301 at p. 289; Corr and Lawler, 'Damned If You Do, Damned If You Don't? The OECD Convention and the Globalization of Anti-Bribery Measures.' at p. 1253–1254; Christopher L. Hall, 'The Foreign Corrupt Practices Act: A Competitive Disadvantage, but for How Long?' *Tulane Journal of International and Comparative Law,* 2 (1994), p. 289–316 at p. 302–309; Klich, 'Bribery in Economies in Transition: The Foreign Corrupt Practices Act', at p. 141–142; Tor Krever, 'Curbing Corruption? The Efficacy of the Foreign Corrupt Practices Act', *North Carolina Journal of International Law & Commercial Regulation,* 33 (2007), p. 83–102 at p. 89–92; Rossbacher and Young, 'The Foreign Corrupt Practices Act: An American Response to Corruption', at p. 227; Duane Windsor and Kathleen A. Getz, 'Multilateral Cooperation to Combat Corruption: Normative Regimes Despite Mixed Motives and Diverse Values', *Cornell International Law Journal,* 33 (2000), p. 731–772 at p. 760–762.

15 Barbara Crutchfield George, Kathleen A. Lacey, and Jutta Birmele, 'On the Treshold of the Adoption of Global Antibribery Legislation: A Critical Analysis of Current Domestic and International Efforts toward the Reduction of Business Corruption', *Vanderbilt Journal of Transnational Law,* 32 (1999), p. 1–48 at p. 20–21; Hall, 'The Foreign Corrupt Practices Act: A Competitive Disadvantage, but for How Long?' at p. 304; Philip M. Nichols, 'Regulating Transnational Bribery in Times of Globalization and Fragmentation', *Yale Journal of International Law,* 24 (1999), p. 257–303 at p. 287–288; Rossbacher and Young, 'The Foreign Corrupt Practices Act: An American Response to Corruption', at p. 223.

16 Steven R. Salbu, 'Bribery in the Global Market: A Critical Analysis of the Foreign Corrupt Practices Act', *Washington and Lee Law Review,* 54 (1997), p. 229–287; Steven R. Salbu, 'The Foreign Corrupt Practices Act as a Threat to Global Harmony', *Michigan Journal of International Law,* 20 (1999), p. 419–449; Steven R. Salbu, 'Extraterritorial Restriction of Bribery: A Premature Evocation of the Normative Global Village', *Yale Journal of International Law,* 24 (1999), p. 223–255; Kenneth U. Surjadinata, 'Revisiting Corrupt Practices from a Market Perspective', *Emory International Law Review,* 12 (1998), p. 1021–1090.

17 John T. Noonan Jr., *Bribes* (New York: Macmillan Publishing Company, 1984) at p. 702–703. This author noted that 'Significantly, it is often the Westerner with ethnocentric prejudice who supposes that a modern Asian or African society does not regard the act of bribery as shameful in the way Westerners regard it.'

longer fall under the scope of the FCPA.[18] Examples of such routine governmental action are obtaining permits or licenses, processing governmental papers such as visas, providing police protection etcetera.[19] Any decision by a foreign public official to award new businesses or to continue business with a certain party is not a routine governmental action.[20] It has been noted that the exemption for grease payments is undesirable given the harmfulness of low level corruption and that the FCPA should therefore be amended once again to include small facilitating payments.[21]

In addition, a number of affirmative defenses were included in the FCPA. If the payment of bribes (other than facilitating payments) is lawful under the written laws of the foreign country, or if the payment was a bona fide business expenditure (e.g. payment of travel and lodging) or if the money was spent as part of demonstrating a product or performing a contractual obligation, this can be asserted by those charged with a violation of the anti-bribery provisions.[22]

Lastly, the 1977 FCPA determined that intent was established if the defendant 'knew or had reason to know' that bribes had been paid. Given the uncertainty about the actual content of the 'reason to know' standard, this phrase was eliminated.[23]

2.1.4. Enforcement and Effectiveness

Enforcement of the FCPA is in the hands of the US Department of Justice (hereafter: DOJ) and the SEC. The DOJ takes care of all criminal enforcement, while civil enforcement is functionally divided between the DOJ and the SEC. The SEC has civil enforcement authority over issuers, their officers, directors, employees, agents

---

18 15 U.S.C. §78dd–1(b); §78dd–2(b); §78dd–3(b) See: Barbara Crutchfield George and Kathleen A. Lacey, 'A Coalition of Industrialized Nations, Developing Nations, Multilateral Development Banks, and Non-Governmental Organizations: A Pivotal Complement to Current Anti-Corruption Initiatives', *Cornell International Law Journal,* 33 (2000), p. 547–592 at p. 560–562; Deming, *The Foreign Corrupt Practices Act and the New International Norms*, at p. 15–16; United States Department of Justice, 'Lay-Person's Guide to FCPA', at p. 5.

19 15 U.S.C. §78dd–1(f) (3) (A); §78dd–2(h) (4) (A); §78dd–3(f) (4) (A).

20 15 U.S.C. §78dd–1(f) (3) (B); §78dd–2(h) (4) (B); §78dd–3(f) (4) (B).

21 Alexandros Zervos, 'Amending the Foreign Corrupt Practices Act: Repealing the Exemption For "Routine Government Action" Payments', *Penn State International Law Review,* 25 (2006–2007), p. 251–294.

22 15 U.S.C. §78dd–1(c); §78dd–2(c); §78dd–3(c). See Crutchfield George and Lacey, 'A Coalition of Industrialized Nations, Developing Nations, Multilateral Development Banks, and Non-Governmental Organizations: A Pivotal Complement to Current Anti-Corruption Initiatives', at p. 562; Deming, *The Foreign Corrupt Practices Act and the New International Norms* at p. 16–18; United States Department of Justice, 'Lay-Person's Guide to FCPA', at p. 5.

23 Crutchfield George and Lacey, 'A Coalition of Industrialized Nations, Developing Nations, Multilateral Development Banks, and Non-Governmental Organizations: A Pivotal Complement to Current Anti-Corruption Initiatives', at p. 561.

and stockholders acting on their behalf. The DOJ has competence over all other civil enforcement.[24]

In order to avoid violation of the anti-bribery provisions of the FCPA and possible resulting penalties, US corporations and nationals can request an opinion from the Attorney General under the Opinion Procedure.[25] This procedure, which has not been widely used by companies,[26] makes it possible to ask whether or not certain specified future conduct is in conformity with the enforcement policy of the Department of Justice regarding the anti-bribery provisions.[27]

The question now arises whether or not the DOJ and the SEC have actively enforced the FCPA during its thirty years of existence and whether the law is truly effective in its goal of substantially reducing the amount of bribes paid by US corporations to foreign public officials.

On the issue of enforcement, there appear to be several trends in the entire period 1977–2008. In the initial stage, immediately after adoption of the FCPA, enforcement appeared to be relatively active. However, when the Reagan administration came into power, enforcement activity decreased. Only a few authorisations for prosecutions under the FCPA were given and funding for the DOJ and the SEC decreased.[28] In the period 1977–1995, only 16 separate criminal prosecutions were brought for violation of the anti-bribery provisions.[29] There are also indications that during the Administrations of Reagan and Bush Sr., foreign policy considerations (such as the Cold War) were underlying decisions to prosecute or not.[30] A new development towards more aggressive enforcement is visible since the mid–1990s when the Clinton Administration came into power.[31] This trend continued in an even stronger form between 2003–2007. In that period, there is a reported growth in the frequency as well as the severity of enforcement. There is a

---

24 Deming, *The Foreign Corrupt Practices Act and the New International Norms*, at p. 41.

25 Opinion Procedure Regulations 28 C.F.R. §§80.1-.16.

26 Rossbacher and Young, 'The Foreign Corrupt Practices Act: An American Response to Corruption', at p. 222. For an overview of the Opinion Procedure Releases from 1993 onwards, see <www.usdoj.gov/criminal/fraud/fcpa/opinion>.

27 For more information about this procedure, see: Longobardi, 'Reviewing the Situation: What Is to Be Done with the Foreign Corrupt Practices Act?' at p. 461–476; United States Department of Justice, 'Lay-Person's Guide to FCPA', at p. 7.

28 Cragg and Woof, 'The US Foreign Corrupt Practices Act: A Study of Its Effectiveness', at p. 116.

29 William F. Pendergast, 'Foreign Corrupt Practices Act: An Overview of Almost Twenty Years of Foreign Bribery Prosecution', *International Quarterly*, 7 (1995), p. 187. as cited in Rossbacher and Young, 'The Foreign Corrupt Practices Act: An American Response to Corruption', at p. 222.

30 Cragg and Woof, 'The US Foreign Corrupt Practices Act: A Study of Its Effectiveness', at p. 119–129; Krever, 'Curbing Corruption? The Efficacy of the Foreign Corrupt Practices Act', at p. 93.

31 Cragg and Woof, 'The US Foreign Corrupt Practices Act: A Study of Its Effectiveness', at p. 130; Crutchfield George, Lacey, and Birmele, 'On the Threshold of the Adoption of Global Antibribery Legislation: A Critical Analysis of Current Domestic and International Efforts toward the Reduction of Business Corruption', at p. 4, 12–17.

trend towards more aggressive investigations and enforcement proceedings by the DOJ and the SEC. The number of proceedings targeting individuals has also risen.[32] Moreover, punishment has become more severe. For example, in April 2007, the oilfield services company Baker Hughes agreed to pay US$44 million, the largest FCPA fine ever.[33] On a comparative note: the annual operating profit of this corporation is approximately US$2,000 million.[34]

Notwithstanding these recent trends, for the entire existence of the FCPA, the overall picture of enforcement of the anti-bribery provisions is not very positive: between 1977 and 2006, there were a total of 63 successful FCPA prosecutions or decrees (so this is both criminal and civil) for violation of the anti-bribery provisions.[35] Moreover, it has been argued that of these 63 cases, no less than 36 incidents may be characterised as 'easy' cases for the authorities to handle. In those instances, bribery was discovered because it had not been properly disguised by companies or individuals.[36]

What reasons might account for the apparently low rate of FCPA enforcement? To begin with, investigations that require financial detection are very expensive.[37] Also, the transnational character of FCPA investigations might hinder enforcement, since witnesses and evidence may be present on foreign territory.[38] What may also have impeded enforcement of the FCPA is the alleged competitive disadvantage felt by US businesses, which lowered the motivation of the US to enforce the Act in an active manner.[39]

When considering the effectiveness of anti-corruption legislation, including the FCPA, one must bear in mind that this is difficult, if not impossible, to measure. Corruption occurs secretively, and 'hard' evidence of foreign bribery – or the lack

---

32 Danforth Newcomb and Philip Urofsky, 'FCPA Digest of Cases and Review Releases Relating to Bribes to Foreign Officials under the Foreign Corrupt Practices Act of 1977', (New York: Shearman & Sterling LLP, 2008) at p. 2–10; Mike Koehler, 'Compliance Lessons from an Active Year in FCPA Enforcement', *White Collar Crime Report,* 3 (15 February 2008) at p. 1; Priya Cherian Huskins, 'FCPA Prosecutions: Liability Trend to Watch', *Stanford Law Review,* 60 (2008), p. 1447–1457 at p. 1449–1450.

33 Newcomb and Urofsky, 'FCPA Digest of Cases and Review Releases Relating to Bribes to Foreign Officials under the Foreign Corrupt Practices Act of 1977', at p. 5.

34 See <www.aboutus.org/BakerHughes.com>, accessed 24 May 2011.

35 Philip Segal, 'Coming Clean on Dirty Dealing: Time for a Fact-Based Evaluation of the Foreign Corrupt Practices Act', *Florida Journal of International Law,* 18 (2006), p. 169–210 at p. 186–187.

36 *Ibid.* at p. 186–195.

37 Rossbacher and Young, 'The Foreign Corrupt Practices Act: An American Response to Corruption', at p. 223; Segal, 'Coming Clean on Dirty Dealing: Time for a Fact-Based Evaluation of the Foreign Corrupt Practices Act', at p. 187–188.

38 Klich, 'Bribery in Economies in Transition: The Foreign Corrupt Practices Act', at p. 122; Rossbacher and Young, 'The Foreign Corrupt Practices Act: An American Response to Corruption', at p. 223; Segal, 'Coming Clean on Dirty Dealing: Time for a Fact-Based Evaluation of the Foreign Corrupt Practices Act', at p. 188.

39 Segal, 'Coming Clean on Dirty Dealing: Time for a Fact-Based Evaluation of the Foreign Corrupt Practices Act', at p. 186.

thereof – is often unavailable. However, most research seems to indicate that, thus far, the FCPA did not have a significant impact upon the incidence of foreign bribery by US corporations and individuals.[40] In order to support this conclusion, reference is frequently made, amongst others, to the Bribe Payers Index (hereafter: BPI).[41] This survey lists 22 leading export countries as to the amount of bribes their companies are perceived to pay abroad. In the BPI 2008, the US is listed and ranked at the 9th place.[42] Finally, what may also account for the FCPA's limited effectiveness is its limited enforcement, as discussed above.[43] At the same time, the value of legislation such as the FCPA lies not solely in its retributivist or deterrent function. Rather, the existence of an Act which prohibits foreign bribery also has a value expressive function: it communicates to businesses and to society at large that foreign bribery is (morally) unacceptable and worthy of punishment.[44]

2.2. Rationales for International Legislative Efforts

2.2.1. US Lobbying Efforts

For many years, the US was the only country prohibiting the bribery of public officials abroad. Given the idea that this isolated position harmed US corporations, the 1988 amendments to the FCPA (as discussed *supra* also called upon the US President to lobby for the internationalisation of the FCPA within the context of the OECD.[45] These efforts remained fruitless for quite some time. Corruption was not considered to be a topic worthy of international regulation.[46] But eventually,

40 Cragg and Woof, 'The US Foreign Corrupt Practices Act: A Study of Its Effectiveness', at p. 129–131; David A. Gantz, 'Globalizing Sanctions against Foreign Bribery: The Emergence of a New International Legal Consensus', *Northwestern Journal of International Law & Business,* 18 (1998), p. 457–497 at p. 462–465; Krever, 'Curbing Corruption? The Efficacy of the Foreign Corrupt Practices Act', at p. 92–93; Rossbacher and Young, 'The Foreign Corrupt Practices Act: An American Response to Corruption', at p. 227–229.

41 Cragg and Woof, 'The US Foreign Corrupt Practices Act: A Study of Its Effectiveness', at p. 98, 114; Krever, 'Curbing Corruption? The Efficacy of the Foreign Corrupt Practices Act', at p. 93; Segal, 'Coming Clean on Dirty Dealing: Time for a Fact-Based Evaluation of the Foreign Corrupt Practices Act', at p. 177–178.

42 See <www.transparency.org/policy_research/surveys_indices/bpi/bpi_2008>, accessed 24 May 2011.

43 Krever, 'Curbing Corruption? The Efficacy of the Foreign Corrupt Practices Act', at p. 93.

44 For more on the functions of punishment in criminal law, see chapter VII, §5, in particular §5.4 on the theory of expressivism.

45 Crutchfield George and Lacey, 'A Coalition of Industrialized Nations, Developing Nations, Multilateral Development Banks, and Non-Governmental Organizations: A Pivotal Complement to Current Anti-Corruption Initiatives', at p. 562–563.

46 Lucinda A. Low, 'The United Nations Convention against Corruption: The Globalization of Anticorruption Standards', *Conference of the International Bar Association, International Chamber of Commerce & Organization for Economic Cooperation and Development: The Awakening Giant of Anticorruption Enforcement* (London, England, 4–5 May 2006) at p. 1.

pressure by the Clinton Administration resulted in the adoption of the OECD Convention on Combating Bribery of Foreign Public Officials in International Business Transactions in 1997 – twenty years after the coming into being of the FCPA. This instrument (discussed *infra* in §3.3) largely resembles the FCPA. Moreover, from the mid–1990s a wider range of global and regional anti-corruption instruments was drafted and adopted and the majority of those instruments contain provisions on the criminalisation of active foreign bribery.[47] This means that many countries that are Party to anti-corruption treaties are now also under the obligation to criminalise active foreign bribery by their MNCs and citizens. A prominent example of domestic legislation is the recent UK Bribery Act, which entered into force on 1 July 2011. At the same time, it is by no means certain that the legal provisions on bribery are actively enforced. A recent report noted that enforcement activities by the DOJ and the SEC are much more aggressive and extraterritorial than efforts in other countries.[48]

The FCPA functioned as a model for legislation, particularly because it showed that it was possible to tackle the supply side of bribery instead of the demand side.[49] But lobbying by the US was not the only reason for the emergence of an international anti-corruption regime. Rather it was set in motion by a wider range of interrelated societal changes and developments and by the self-interest of States.

2.2.2. Societal Developments

The main development characterising the period from the 1990s onwards is economic globalisation. Countries have become more and more interdependent and one global market has emerged. This process, in part facilitated by technological developments,[50] led to an increasing power of multinational corporations (hereafter: MNCs), actors able to thrive in a world with fading borders. It was noted that globalisation led to a larger amount of corruption, since competition for profitable contracts had increased.[51] This is particularly true in the context of Central and Eastern Europe after the end of the Cold War. With the fall of the Berlin Wall and the collapse of the Soviet Union, democracy spread and societies became more open. Capitalism was embraced as the one remaining ideology and Western

---

47 Treaties criminalising the active bribery of foreign public officials (although this might be subject to safeguard clauses): the Inter-American Convention Against Corruption (Article VIII), the Council of Europe's Criminal Law Convention on Corruption, the SADC Protocol Against Corruption (Article 6), the UN Convention Against Corruption (Article 16 (1)).

48 Ernst & Young, 'Corruption or Compliance – Weighing the Costs: 10th Global Fraud Survey', (2008) at p. 1.

49 Crutchfield George, Lacey, and Birmele, 'On the Threshold of the Adoption of Global Antibribery Legislation: A Critical Analysis of Current Domestic and International Efforts toward the Reduction of Business Corruption', at p. 18–22.

50 *Ibid.* at p. 26.

51 Crutchfield George and Lacey, 'A Coalition of Industrialized Nations, Developing Nations, Multilateral Development Banks, and Non-Governmental Organizations: A Pivotal Complement to Current Anti-Corruption Initiatives', at p. 553.

companies took advantage of the new investment opportunities in Central and Eastern Europe. But in this region, corruption also spread during this period. Corporations hence encountered widespread corruption and both companies and governments became aware of its costs and distortive effects.[52] Also related to the end of the Cold War is the diminished incentive for governments to sponsor corrupt dictators in developing countries, such as on the African continent.[53] Another factor contributing to the rise of an anti-corruption regime were the sentiments of the general public due to a number of corruption scandals which took place in several Western European countries.[54] Furthermore, it was noted that the character of the present anti-corruption regime is more normative (based upon harmonised behaviour) than moral (based upon intrinsic commitment to shared values). Self-interest of States was an important rationale for taking measures to combat corruption, since the practice was seen as 'the ultimate non-tariff barrier to trade'.[55] What also deserves to be mentioned is the growing international attention for organised crime and the combating thereof as of the mid–1990s. Anti-corruption neatly fitted that trend.

Another push towards the establishment of various anti-corruption instruments and programmes came from the international financial institutions. Especially the World Bank is a prominent player in the field of anti-corruption since the late 1990s. Before then, the subject was considered to fall outside of its mandate, since it was found that its Articles of Agreement did not allow work on 'political issues' such as corruption ('the c-word') or human rights.[56] But partly due to the societal developments described above, the Bank came to acknowledge that, in the words of key figure Wolfensohn, 'corruption was not just political, but the single most significant factor in bringing about development, equity and social justice.'[57] In the same period, NGOs also started to work on anti-corruption. Most prominently, Transparency International was founded in 1993 by Peter Eigen, former regional director for the World Bank.[58]

52 Crutchfield George, Lacey, and Birmele, 'On the Treshold of the Adoption of Global Antibribery Legislation: A Critical Analysis of Current Domestic and International Efforts toward the Reduction of Business Corruption', at p. 22–23; Low, 'The United Nations Convention against Corruption: The Globalization of Anticorruption Standards', at p. 2; Klich, 'Bribery in Economies in Transition: The Foreign Corrupt Practices Act', at p. 131–133.

53 Patrick Glynn, Stephen J. Kobrin, and Moisés Naím, 'The Globalization of Corruption', in Kimberley Ann Elliott (ed.), *Corruption and the Global Economy* (Washington, D.C.: Institute for International Economics, 1997), p. 7–27 at p. 10–11.

54 Windsor and Getz, 'Multilateral Cooperation to Combat Corruption: Normative Regimes Despite Mixed Motives and Diverse Values', at p. 768.

55 Pickholz, 'The United States Foreign Corrupt Practices Act as a Civil Remedy.'

56 Heather Marquette, *Corruption, Politics and Development: The Role of the World Bank* (Hampshire: Palgrave Macmillan, 2003) at p. 1, for an analysis of the changes in the position of the Bank on corruption.

57 World Bank (ed.), *Voice for the World's Poor: Selected Speeches and Writings of World Bank President James D. Wolfensohn, 1995–2005* (Washington, DC, 2005) at p. 177–178.

58 See <www.transparency.org/about_us/organisation/adv_council>, accessed 25 May 2011.

3. Legal Instruments on the Global and Regional Plane

3.1. Inter-American Convention Against Corruption (1996)

3.1.1. Content

The first regional legal instrument designed to address corruption is the Inter-American Convention Against Corruption (hereafter: IACAC), which was adopted on 29 March 1996 and entered into force on 6 March 1997. It came into being within the context of the Organization of American States (hereafter: OAS) and it currently has thirty-three State Parties.[59]

The instrument does not provide for a definition of 'corruption'. Rather it refers to certain 'acts of corruption' in the public sector to which the Convention applies. No distinction is made between grand and petty corruption: the instrument refers to public officials at any level of the State's hierarchy.[60] State obligations under the IACAC can be grouped into three categories: prevention, criminalisation and cooperation and post-corruption measures.

The Convention contains a wide list of *preventive measures*: adoption of codes of conduct for public officials and enforcement mechanisms,[61] instructions to government personnel,[62] registration and disclosure of the income of public officials,[63] open, equitable and efficient hiring and procurement systems,[64] revenue collection and control systems that deter corruption,[65] abolishment of favourable tax treatment of corruption,[66] whistleblower protection,[67] establishment of anti-corruption bodies,[68] book- and recordkeeping requirements,[69] civil society and NGO participation[70] and the study of further preventive measures.[71] Although this is an extensive list, adoption of one or more preventive measures is optional for State Parties, since they merely have to 'consider' their applicability.[72]

---

59 Organisation of American States, 'Signatures and Ratifications of the Inter-American Convention against Corruption', <www.oas.org/juridico/english/Sigs/b–58.html>, accessed 24 May 2011.
60 Article I IACAC.
61 Article III(1) and (2) IACAC.
62 Article III(3) IACAC.
63 Article III(4) IACAC.
64 Article III(5) IACAC.
65 Article III(6) IACAC.
66 Article III(7) IACAC.
67 Article III(8) IACAC.
68 Article III(9) IACAC.
69 Article III(10) IACAC.
70 Article III(11) IACAC.
71 Article III(12) IACAC.
72 Article III IACAC; Giorleny D. Altamirano, 'The Impact of the Inter-American Convention against Corruption', *The University of Miami Inter-American Law Review,* 38 (2007), 487–547 at p. 503; Conference, 'The Experts Roundtable: A Hemispheric Approach to Combating

Also, the IACAC obliges States to *criminalise* certain 'acts of corruption'. What is relevant, however, is that the instrument separates three groups of offences, to which different levels of obligations apply. In the first place, the Convention is applicable to the following 'acts of corruption' in the public sector: (i) passive bribery at the national level;[73] (ii) active bribery[74] at the national level; (iii) any act or omission in the discharge of duties by a government official or a person performing public functions in order to illicitly obtain benefit;[75] (iv) the fraudulent use or concealment of property derived from corrupt acts[76] and (v) several modes of participation in corrupt offences.[77] State Parties are obliged to criminalise these acts in their national legislation, which can be derived from the wording 'shall adopt', which makes this a mandatory provision.[78] The Convention recognises that the list of 'acts of corruption' as described above is not exhaustive. The IACAC also applies by mutual agreement between or among States with respect to other acts of corruption.[79] In the second place, the IACAC describes the offences of transnational (active) bribery[80] and illicit enrichment.[81] These offences also have to be criminalised by State Parties ('shall adopt'), but this is subject to a safeguard clause which notes that criminalisation must be in conformity with the Constitution and the fundamental legal principles of the national legal systems. States can thus escape criminalisation of both offences without making reservations to the IACAC, which limits the effectiveness of the Convention.[82] Among States which have indeed criminalised transnational bribery and illicit enrichment, these offences shall also be considered an 'act of corruption'.[83] Thus, these provisions are, although mandatory, less strongly worded than the first set of corrupt acts.[84] In the third place, the IACAC contains a set of corrupt practices which State Parties

Corruption', *American University International Law Review,* 15 (2000), p. 768–780 at p. 774–775; Gillian Dell, 'Anti-Corruption Conventions in the Americas. What Civil Society Can Do to Make Them Work', (Berlin: Transparency International 2006) at p. 13, 16. For an analysis of Article III, see Carlos A. Manfroni, updated by Richard S. Werksman, *The Inter-American Convention against Corruption,* trans. Michael Ford (Lanham: Lexington Books, 2003) at p. 18–32.

73 Article VI(1)(a) IACAC.

74 Article VI(1)(b) IACAC.

75 Article VI(1)(c) IACAC.

76 Article VI(1)(d) IACAC.

77 Article VI(1)(e) IACAC.

78 Article VII IACAC; Altamirano, 'The Impact of the Inter-American Convention against Corruption', at p. 501; Dell, 'Anti-Corruption Conventions in the Americas. What Civil Society Can Do to Make Them Work', at p. 13.

79 Article VI(2) IACAC.

80 Article VIII IACAC.

81 Article IX IACAC.

82 Conference, 'The Experts Roundtable: A Hemispheric Approach to Combating Corruption', at p. 772–773.

83 Articles VIII and IX IACAC.

84 Dell, 'Anti-Corruption Conventions in the Americas. What Civil Society Can Do to Make Them Work', at p. 13.

'undertake to consider' to criminalise in their national laws. These are (i) the improper use of classified information;[85] (ii) the improper use of State property;[86] (iii) the seeking of illicit benefit by a private individual,[87] and (iv) the diversion of property (embezzlement or misappropriation).[88] Given the soft wording of the Article containing these offences, State Parties do not have a strict legal obligation to criminalise these acts, the Article is merely aspirational.[89] If States have criminalised the offences, they are qualified as 'acts of corruption'.[90]

Furthermore, the instrument contains provisions in respect of *cooperation and post-corruption measures.* The Convention contains a provision on extradition.[91] Also, States have to afford one another the widest measure of mutual assistance in the investigation and prosecution of acts of corruption as well as mutual technical cooperation in the prevention, detection, investigation and punishment of acts of corruption.[92] The Convention also obliges cooperation in the field of asset recovery.[93] Furthermore, States cannot invoke bank secrecy as an excuse for refusing cooperation with other States.[94] All these provisions are mandatory. Finally, the IACAC notes that for the purposes of the mentioned Articles:

> … the fact that the property obtained or derived from an act of corruption was intended for political purposes, or that it is alleged that an act of corruption was committed for political motives or purposes, shall not suffice in and of itself to qualify the act as a political offense or as a common offense related to a political offense.[95]

Having seen the basic content of the Convention, how should we now assess it? It was noted that the IACAC, being the first regional instrument, has contributed to raising awareness of the problem of corruption and that it offers good opportunities to combat it.[96] The instrument's broad approach recognises the diversity of the problem, since it covers a wide range of corrupt offences, not merely bribery.

---

85 Article XI(1)(a) IACAC.

86 Article XI(1)(b) IACAC.

87 Article XI(1)(c) IACAC.

88 Article XI(1)(d) IACAC.

89 Altamirano, 'The Impact of the Inter-American Convention against Corruption', at p. 504; Conference, 'The Experts Roundtable: A Hemispheric Approach to Combating Corruption', at p. 774; Manfroni, *The Inter-American Convention against Corruption*, at p. 75.

90 Article XI(2) IACAC.

91 Article XIII IACAC.

92 Article XIV IACAC.

93 Article XV IACAC.

94 Article XVI IACAC.

95 Article XVII IACAC.

96 Altamirano, 'The Impact of the Inter-American Convention against Corruption', at p. 539–540; Norma Parker *et al.*, 'Corruption in Latin America: A Desk Assessment', *Americas' Accountability Anti-Corruption Project* (Alexandria, Virginia: Casals & Associates, 2004) at p. 19, 39.

Furthermore, the provisions on cooperation and post-corruption measures are mandatory. Particularly positive is the above-mentioned article on bank secrecy.[97]

But several flaws can also be identified. The adoption of preventive measures is merely optional and there are three different levels of obligations in respect of criminalisation. Thus, not all 'acts of corruption' are treated the same. This is particularly problematic in respect of embezzlement, which is not obligatory to criminalise. Furthermore, the safeguard clauses concerning transnational active bribery and illicit enrichment can hinder criminalisation. It was pointed out that the Convention lacks provisions on the sanctions which States have to impose in case of a violation of national anti-corruption legislation.[98] No reference is made either to political party financing.[99] Undoubtedly these flaws are the result of unavoidable political compromises, made in the process of drafting.

3.1.2. Follow-up Mechanism (MESICIC)

Although the IACAC itself does not provide for a monitoring procedure, a Follow-up Mechanism (MESICIC is the acronym of its Spanish name)[100] was established in 2001. It was therefore possible for the drafters to take the experiences of other, previously established, anti-corruption mechanisms into account elsewhere.[101]

The Follow-up Mechanism consists of a process of peer review, the main structure of which is contained in the Report of Buenos Aires.[102] The purposes of the Follow-up Mechanism are (a) the promotion of the implementation of the IACAC, (b) the follow-up of commitments of the State Parties and the study of their implementation and (c) the facilitation of technical cooperation activities, the exchange of information and the harmonization of States Parties' legislation.[103] The Follow-Up Mechanism is composed of two bodies: the Conference of States Parties and the Committee of Experts.[104] The Conference of States Parties is the principal organ consisting of the Parties to the IACAC which are members of the

---

97 Article XVI(1) IACAC; Manfroni, *The Inter-American Convention against Corruption* at p. 93.

98 Altamirano, 'The Impact of the Inter-American Convention against Corruption', at p. 500–501.

99 *Ibid.* p. 487–547 at p. 500; Parker *et al.*, 'Corruption in Latin America: A Desk Assessment', at p. 41.

100 MESICIC: Mecanismo de Seguimiento de la Implementación de la Convención Interamericana contra la Corrupción.

101 The monitoring mechanisms of the OECD and the COE – discussed *infra* in §3.3 and 3.4 – were established prior to MESICIC. Roberto de Michele, 'The Follow-up Mechanism of the Inter-American Convention against Corruption: A Preliminary Assessment: Is the Glass Half Empty?' *Southwestern Journal of Law and Trade in the Americas,* 10 (2004), p. 295–318 at p. 300.

102 Organisation of American States, 'Report of Buenos Aires on the Mechanism for Follow-up on the Implementation of the Inter-American Convention against Corruption', (4 May 2001).

103 Report of Buenos Aires, §1.

104 Report of Buenos Aires, §5.

Mechanism.[105] The Committee of Experts consists of experts who are appointed by the States Parties to the Mechanism[106] and is responsible for the technical analysis of the implementation of the IACAC by States in different 'rounds'.[107]

Each review round consists of three phases.[108] In the first phase, the Committee makes a selection of the provisions of the Convention which will be analysed in that particular round and adopts a review methodology.[109] Furthermore, the order in which the countries will be reviewed is determined[110] and the Committee divides itself into subgroups of two experts.[111] During the second phase, States Parties have to submit the answers to the questionnaire which has been prepared by the Committee.[112] It is also possible for civil society organisations to respond, and the experts can seek information from these organisations on their own initiative.[113] The subgroups will then review the State information and will draft a preliminary report, upon which the State Party concerned can comment. This leads to a revised version of the report, which is presented in a plenary meeting of the Committee.[114] In the third phase the Committee issues the final report on each State Party, including recommendations, which is published subsequently.[115]

It has been noted that this Follow-up Mechanism suffers from several weaknesses, one of which is the duration of the review mechanism. The respective rounds are very time-consuming.[116]

The functioning of the Committee of Experts is often criticised. Since each State Party appoints its own experts, they are selected on the basis of political loyalty, while they frequently lack the necessary expertise. The Rules of Procedure of the Committee of Experts do not contain any requirements which the appointees have to fulfil. This lack of expertise is likely to impact upon the quality of the review and can partly explain the lengthy procedures. Furthermore, the duration of

---

105 Organisation of American States, 'Rules of Procedure of the Conference of States Parties to the Mechanism for Follow-up on Implementation of the Inter-American Convention against Corruption', (2 April 2004) at Article 3.

106 Organisation of American States, 'Rules of Procedure of the Committee of Experts and Other Provisions', (29 June 2007) at Article 2.

107 Report of Buenos Aires, §5 and 7.

108 Dell, 'Anti-Corruption Conventions in the Americas. What Civil Society Can Do to Make Them Work', at p. 100–101.

109 Report of Buenos Aires, §7 (b)(i).

110 Report of Buenos Aires, §7 (b)(ii).

111 Report of Buenos Aires, §7 (b)(iii).

112 Report of Buenos Aires, §7 (b)(i).

113 Report of Buenos Aires, §8.

114 Report of Buenos Aires, §7 (b)(iii).

115 Report of Buenos Aires, §7 (b)(iv).

116 Altamirano, 'The Impact of the Inter-American Convention against Corruption', at p. 541; Dell, 'Anti-Corruption Conventions in the Americas. What Civil Society Can Do to Make Them Work', at p. 101; Michele, 'The Follow-up Mechanism of the Inter-American Convention against Corruption: A Preliminary Assessment: Is the Glass Half Empty?' at p. 313.

the mandate of the experts is not fixed, which makes the experts vulnerable to replacement at the discretion of the State Party.[117]

Furthermore, the Secretariat of the OAS, which serves as the headquarter for the Follow-up Mechanism[118] also fulfils other tasks and is therefore not solely dedicated to the Mechanism. It suffers from a lack of financial resources and personnel, which might also account for the time-consuming review process.[119]

There are also some difficulties regarding the input of civil society organisations in the review mechanism. The experts are able to receive or ask for additional information from NGOs, which supplements the answers to the questionnaire given by the State Party. However, there are also State Parties that do not have such NGOs which can provide information. In such a case, the experts can only rely on the governmental information.[120] Furthermore, the quality of the NGO reports which have been produced to this date varies.[121] Moreover, it also appeared that there are no financial means for the translation of civil society reports into the various languages of the OAS.[122]

Fifth, the implementation of the recommendations of the Committee of Experts which are given in the final report is not monitored. If the State concerned does not take action, the consequences remain political.[123] The Mechanism does not entail the adoption of sanctions either,[124] which is understandable given the intergovernmental nature of the procedure,[125] but it results in a peer review procedure that lacks sharp teeth.

Nevertheless, a promising development is the introduction of country visits as part of the evaluation process, as agreed upon during the Third Meeting of the Conference of States Parties. These visits will be commenced during the Fourth Round of MESICIC, starting in 2011.[126]

---

117 Altamirano, 'The Impact of the Inter-American Convention against Corruption', at p. 506, 541–542; Dell, 'Anti-Corruption Conventions in the Americas. What Civil Society Can Do to Make Them Work', at p. 101; Michele, 'The Follow-up Mechanism of the Inter-American Convention against Corruption: A Preliminary Assessment: Is the Glass Half Empty?' at p. 314.

118 Report of Buenos Aires, §6.

119 Altamirano, 'The Impact of the Inter-American Convention against Corruption', at p. 541, 543; Dell, 'Anti-Corruption Conventions in the Americas. What Civil Society Can Do to Make Them Work', at p. 101; Michele, 'The Follow-up Mechanism of the Inter-American Convention against Corruption: A Preliminary Assessment: Is the Glass Half Empty?' at p. 313, 317.

120 Michele, 'The Follow-up Mechanism of the Inter-American Convention against Corruption: A Preliminary Assessment: Is the Glass Half Empty?' at p. 314–316.

121 *Ibid.* at p. 315.

122 *Ibid.* at p. 316 footnote 378.

123 *Ibid.* at p. 315–316; Parker *et al.*, 'Corruption in Latin America: A Desk Assessment', at p. 40.

124 Report of Buenos Aires, §3 (c).

125 Report of Buenos Aires, §3.

126 Transparency International, 'Inter-American Anti-Corruption Convention Strengthened by Member States', <www.transparency.org/news_room/latest_news/press_releases/2010/2010_12_15_cosp_third_meeting_en>, accessed 25 May 2011.

It is difficult to determine precisely how effective the IACAC has been so far in lowering corruption in the States that are Party to the instrument. However, a recently conducted study of Guatemala, Honduras, Jamaica and Trinidad and Tobago seems to indicate that although the Convention has led to the adoption of new anti-corruption legislation in these countries, this has neither led to an improvement in corruption perception (as measured by the CPI), nor to a lower level of corruption risks.[127]

In sum, the IACAC is a comprehensive instrument that paved the way for the adoption of instruments within international organisations in other parts of the world. At the same time, one must take note of the shortcomings of the Convention itself, as well as the Follow-up Mechanism. If the IACAC is to produce a significant decline in corruption in the American continent, a stronger method of enforcement, coupled with political will, is absolutely crucial.

3.2. European Union

3.2.1. PFI Convention (1995), First Protocol (1996) and Second Protocol (1997)

The Treaty of the European Union refers to the prevention and combating of corruption in Article 29, which forms part of the EU's third pillar.[128] In 1995, use was made of this provision by adopting the Convention on the Protection of the European Communities' Financial Interests (hereafter: the PFI Convention).[129] It entered into force on 17 October 2002. The PFI Convention does not deal with corruption as such, but concerns fraud affecting the European Communities' financial interests. The instrument distinguishes expenditure fraud and revenue fraud. Expenditure fraud is defined as:

> ... any intentional act or omission relating to the use or presentation of false, incorrect or incomplete statements or documents, which has as its effect the misappropriation or wrongful retention of funds from the general budget of the European Communities or budgets managed by, or on behalf of, the European Communities; the non-disclosure of information in violation of a specific obligation, with the same effect; or the misapplication of such funds for purposes other than those for which they were originally granted.[130]

Revenue fraud consists of:

> ... any intentional act or omission relating to the use or presentation of false, incorrect or incomplete statements or documents, which has as its effect the illegal

---

127 Altamirano, 'The Impact of the Inter-American Convention against Corruption.'

128 Mireille Delmas-Marty, 'The European Union and Penal Law', *European Law Journal* 4(1998), 87–115 at p. 108.

129 OJ C 316, 27/11/1995, p. 49–57.

130 Article 1(1)(a) PFI Convention.

diminution of the resources of the general budget of the European Communities or budgets managed by, or behalf of, the European Communities; the non-disclosure of information in violation of a specific obligation, with the same effect or the misapplication of a legally obtained benefit, with the same effect.[131]

The main obligation under the PFI Convention is the criminalisation by State Parties in their national legislation of the above-mentioned offences,[132] as well as of the intentional preparation or supply of false, incorrect or incomplete statements or documents having a fraudulent effect.[133] States must also provide for criminal sanctions for violators.[134]

The First Protocol to the PFI Convention, which was adopted in 1996 and entered into force on 17 October 2002, introduces the term 'corruption'.[135] A distinction is made between active corruption[136] and passive corruption[137], but these concepts merely encompass active and passive bribery involving Community or Member State officials. The Parties to the Protocol are under the obligation to criminalise both offences if the financial interests of the European Communities are at stake.

In 1997, the Second Protocol to the PFI Convention was adopted,[138] entering into force on 17 October 2002. This instrument, *inter alia,* obliges State Parties to establish money laundering as a criminal offence[139] and to take measures which ensure that legal persons can be held liable and can be punished for fraud, active corruption (= bribery) and money laundering.[140]

No monitoring mechanism exists in respect of the PFI Convention and its two Protocols, meaning that the prosecution of officials is left to the Member States. Nonetheless, the European Court of Justice has the competence to interpret the instruments and to judge the disputes.[141]

3.2.2. Convention on the Fight Against Corruption Involving Officials of the European Communities or Officials of EU Member States (1997)

In 1997, the Convention on the Fight Against Corruption Involving Officials of the European Communities or Officials of Member States of the European Union came

---

131 Article 1(1)(b) PFI Convention.
132 Article 1(2) PFI Convention.
133 Article 1(3) PFI Convention.
134 Article 2 PFI Convention.
135 OJ C 313, 23/10/1996, p. 2–10.
136 Article 3 First Protocol to the PFI Convention.
137 Article 2 First Protocol to the PFI Convention.
138 OJ C 221, 19/07/1997, p. 12–22.
139 Article 2 Second Protocol to the PFI Convention.
140 Article 3 and 4 Second Protocol to the PFI Convention.
141 Article 8 PFI Convention; Article 8 First Protocol to the PFI Convention; Article 13 Second Protocol to the PFI Convention.

into being and entered into force on 28 September 2005.[142] As in the Protocols to the PFI Convention, corruption is only defined in terms of active and passive bribery, which is a rather limited approach.[143] However, the limitation included in the previous three instruments that the EC's financial interests have to be at stake has been removed. Member States have to ensure that in their national criminal legislation, active and passive bribery committed by or against its Government Ministers, Members of Parliament, members of the highest courts in the exercise of their functions, is equally criminalised as the same offences committed by members of the European Commission, the European Parliament, the Court of Justice and the Court of Auditors.[144] Furthermore, judicial cooperation is an important element of the Convention. If officials are involved in active or passive corruption which concerns at least two Member States, those States have to cooperate in an effective manner in the investigation, prosecution and enforcement of the penalties.[145] There is no specific monitoring mechanism attached to the Convention, but again, the European Court of Justice has the competence to interpret the Convention and the rule in disputes which may arise.[146]

3.2.3. Other Developments

After the adoption of the three legal instruments described above, several anti-corruption initiatives were taken within the EU. A main overview can be found in the European Commission's Communication 'On a Comprehensive EU Policy Against Corruption', released in 2003.[147] Noteworthy is the establishment in 1999 of OLAF, the European Anti-Fraud Office, which combats fraud and other illegal activities which are harmful to the Community's interests.[148]

The 2003 Communication also makes clear that the Commission employs a broad definition of 'corruption', as used by the UN Global Programme against Corruption: 'the abuse of power for private benefit'. It aims to focus on both public and private sector corruption. Nevertheless, the Commission also acknowledged that the definition of corruption included in the EU's legal instruments remains limited to bribery. According to the Commission, this narrow definition is

---

142 OJ C 195, 25/06/1997, p. 2–11.

143 COM (2003) 317 final, p. 6.

144 Article 4(1) Convention on the Fight Against Corruption Involving Officials of the EC's or of EU MS.

145 Article 9(1) Convention on the Fight Against Corruption Involving Officials of the EC's or of EU MS; Laura Ferola, 'Anti-Bribery Measures in the European Union: A Comparison with the Italian Legal Order', *International Journal of Legal Info,* 28 (2000), 512–557 at p. 525–526.

146 Article 12 Convention on the Fight Against Corruption Involving Officials of the EC's or of EU MS.

147 Communication from the Commission to the Council, the European Parliament and the European Economic and Social Committee – On a comprehensive EU policy against corruption [COM (2003) 317 final – Not published in the Official Journal].

148 OLAF website, <http://ec.europa.eu/anti_fraud/index_en.html>, accessed 8 August 2011.

necessary in criminal law, while the broader notion of corruption can be used in the context of prevention.[149]

As elaborated upon previously, the two Conventions and Protocols are not subject to a specific review mechanism. According to the Commission, duplication of efforts has to be avoided. Therefore, the Commission aims for the European Community to become a Member of GRECO, the anti-corruption monitoring mechanism of the Council of Europe (see *infra* §3.4).[150] The Commission is currently negotiating with GRECO about overcoming legal obstacles to its accession.[151] If GRECO membership is not possible, the Commission would consider setting up a separate EU mutual evaluation and monitoring mechanism.[152]

The EU's activities in the field of anti-corruption are of course to be welcomed. Although the scope of the current instruments is relatively narrow, this might be understandable given the fact that other organisations within Europe such as the Council of Europe are already dealing with the issue and that many EU Member States are Party to other anti-corruption treaties. In the author's view it is nonetheless relevant to bear in mind that the EU institutions themselves do not have a spotless record on corruption. The revelations from 1998 onwards of Dutch whistleblower Paul van Buitenen, former European civil servant and then member of the European Parliament, proved the existence of corrupt practices within the EU and eventually led to the collapse of the European Commission.[153]

3.3. OECD Convention on Combating Bribery of Foreign Public Officials in International Business Transactions (1997)

3.3.1. Content

On 21 November 1997 the Organisation for Economic Co-operation and Development (hereafter: OECD) adopted the Convention on Combating Bribery of Foreign Public Officials in International Business Transactions (hereafter: the Anti-Bribery Convention), which entered into force on 15 February 1999. Thus far 40 countries are Party to the Convention, 6 of which are not Members of the OECD.[154]

149 COM (2003) 317 final, p. 6.

150 COM (2003) 317 final, p. 9.

151 Open Society Institute's EU Monitoring and Advocacy Program (EUMAP), 'Corruption and Anti-Corruption Policy', <www.eumap.org/topics/corruption>, accessed 6 March 2008.

152 COM (2003) 317 final, p. 9.

153 Paul van Buitenen, *Strijd Voor Europa* (Baarn: Ten Have, 1999).

154 OECD, List of Ratifying Countries (OECD Member Countries), <www.oecd.org/infobycountry/0,3380,en_2649_34859_1_1_1_2_37447,00.html>, accessed 24 May 2011; OECD, List of Ratifying Countries (Non-Member Countries), <www.oecd.org/infobycountry/0,3380,en_2649_34859_1_1_1_3_37447,00.html>, accessed 24 May 2011. The non-OECD members that have ratified the Anti-Bribery Convention are Argentina, Brazil, Bulgaria, Indonesia, Russia, and South-Africa.

The Convention should be viewed in conjunction with the Revised Recommendation of the Council of the OECD on Combating Bribery in International Business Transactions. The original Recommendation originates from 1994 while the revised version was adopted on 23 May 1997, prior to the establishment of the Convention. It contains provisions on the criminalisation of active bribery of foreign public officials,[155] the removal of tax deductibility of bribes,[156] accounting and audit requirements,[157] public procurement,[158] and international cooperation.[159] The Recommendation is subject to the same monitoring mechanism as the Anti-Bribery Convention, as discussed below.[160]

The Anti-Bribery Convention focuses on a single issue of the Recommendation: the criminalisation and punishment by State Parties of active bribery of foreign public officials in international business transactions. Those who intentionally offer, promise or give bribes to public officials abroad (also in non-OECD countries) must be held criminally liable by their home countries.[161] State Parties must also ensure that legal persons can be held liable for such conduct.[162] In addition, States must provide for an effective, proportionate and dissuasive sanctions regime, also for legal persons.[163] Furthermore, the Convention includes *inter alia* provisions on money laundering,[164] accounting standards[165] and international cooperation.[166]

Hence, by focusing on the supply side of foreign bribery, the OECD Anti-Bribery Convention can be regarded content-wise as an internationalised version of the American FCPA. For interpretation of the Convention, one can turn to the Commentaries adopted by the State Parties, which can be regarded as authoritative although they are not binding.[167] From the Commentaries it can be learned that

---

155 Recommendation No. III.

156 Recommendation No. IV; Regarding tax deductibility, the 1996 Recommendation of the Council on the Tax Deductability of Bribes to Foreign Public Officials is also relevant.

157 Recommendation No. V.

158 Recommendation No. VI.

159 Recommendation No. VII.

160 Recommendation No. VIII – X.

161 Article 1 OECD Anti-Bribery Convention.

162 Article 2 OECD Anti-Bribery Convention; see: Mark Pieth, 'Article 2. The Responsibility of Legal Persons', in Mark Pieth, Lucinda A. Low, and Peter J. Cullen (eds.), *The OECD Convention on Bribery: A Commentary* (Cambridge: Cambridge University Press, 2007), p. 173–206.

163 Article 3 OECD Anti-Bribery Convention; see: Peter J. Cullen, 'Article 3. Sanctions', *Ibid.*, 207–266.

164 Article 7 OECD Anti-Bribery Convention; see: Mark Pieth, 'Article 7. Money Laundering', *Ibid.*, 355–376.

165 Article 8 OECD Anti-Bribery Convention; see: Gregory S. Bruch and Akita N. Adkins, 'Article 8. Accounting', *Ibid.*, 377–405.

166 Articles 9, 10, 11 OECD Anti-Bribery Convention, see: Maurice Harari and Anne Valérie Julen Berthod, 'Articles 9, 10 and 11. International Co-Operation', *Ibid.*, 406–444.

167 Commentaries on the Convention on Combating Bribery of Foreign Public Officials in International Business Transactions, Adopted by the Negotiating Conference on 21 November 1997.

what matters in the fulfillment of State obligations is functional equivalence: not the exact wording of the national criminal law provisions is relevant, but the actual effects of a country's legal system.[168] In 2009, the OECD issued its 2009 Recommendation of the Council for Further Combating Bribery of Foreign Public Officials in International Business Transactions.[169]

A major strength of the Anti-Bribery Convention is that its State Parties are the home States of most MNCs, accounting for an approximate 70 per cent of all exports and 90 per cent of Foreign Direct Investment (hereafter: FDI).[170] The instrument thus offers the opportunity to tackle the supply side of bribery. The limited scope of the Convention enables States to focus on adequately tackling one problem. It is also understandable that the OECD does not have the competence to deal with the internal affairs of non-Member States by covering bribe-taking by foreign officials.

Nevertheless, home-State criminalisation of active bribery by corporations is only one part of the solution. Mark Pieth, chairperson of the OECD Working Group on Bribery (hereafter: WGB) noted quite optimistically that 'the recipient of bribes will be taken to court by the "victim state"'.[171] Yet it is by no means certain that this will actually happen. The State of the bribe-taker may not have adopted adequate anti-bribery legislation or may lack the political will to address the issue. It is particularly possible for high-level officials to avoid prosecution. In addition, where bribes are extorted from corporations by the bribe-taker, complying with the demands of this public official might be very hard to resist for corporate actors, particularly if large business interests are at stake. If corporation X is not willing to bribe, corporation Y with less scruples might be eager to take its place. As a result, the latter will obtain, for instance, a concession to drill for oil. Thus, being overly reliant on well-behaving corporations is not wise. Instruments such as the Anti-Bribery Convention should be supplemented with adequate legislation in the host States and political will on the part of foreign public officials. But of course, this is not a task which the OECD has to fulfil.

Another troublesome aspect of the Convention is that MNCs can use their corporate veil to circumvent the prohibition on bribery. Foreign subsidiaries of MNCs are not covered by the Convention, and therefore they can be used to

---

168 Commentaries, 'General' paragraph 2.

169 26 November 2009.

170 Mark Pieth, 'Introduction', in Mark Pieth, Lucinda A. Low, and Peter J. Cullen (eds.), *The OECD Convention on Bribery. A Commentary* (Cambridge: Cambridge University Press 2007), 3–41 at p. 21.

171 Mark Pieth, 'Taking Stock: Making the OECD Initiative against Corruption Work', <www.oas.org/juridico/english/pieth2000.htm>, accessed 6 March 2008.

pay the bribes.[172] This gap could be closed by obliging parent companies to ensure that effective anti-bribery policies are put in place by their subsidiaries.[173]

Furthermore, it is problematic that the Anti-Bribery Convention, unlike the FCPA, does not cover the bribery of political parties and of members of a political party who are not (yet) public officials. Therefore it is still possible to bribe future office-holders[174] or those powerful people who are surrounding public officials. As noted earlier, the FCPA is stricter on this issue. It is also not clear whether the Anti-Bribery Convention prohibits bribery of family members of foreign public officials.[175]

Furthermore, it is relevant to note that small 'facilitation payments' (i.e. petty bribes) are excluded from the scope of the Convention: only grand or at least straightforward bribery by corporations is covered.[176] The same is true for the amended FCPA. In practice it can be difficult for corporations to determine where 'facilitation payments' end and substantial bribery begins. It has been argued that the exemption of petty bribes should be abandoned, also because this type of bribery is organised top-down and very harmful.[177] On moral grounds this is a valid argument. However, it is not likely that State Parties to the Convention will

---

172 Laurence Cockroft, 'Implementation of the OECD Convention: The Conditions for Success', *Seminar Corruption and Bribery in Foreign Business Transactions: New Global and Canadian Standards* (Vancouver, Canada 4–5 February 1999) at p. 3–4; Zoe Gounari, 'The OECD Convention on Combating Bribery of Foreign Public Officials in International Business Transactions: Theory and Practice', at p. 10–11; Fritz Heimann, 'Will the OECD Convention Stop Foreign Bribery?' in Transparency International (ed.), *Global Corruption Report 2004. Political Corruption* (2004) at p. 131–132; Fritz Heimann and Gillian Dell, 'Progress Report 2007. Enforcement of the OECD Convention on Combating Bribery of Foreign Public Officials', (Berlin: Transparency International 2007) at p. 38; International Monetary Fund (IMF), 'OECD Convention on Combating Bribery of Foreign Public Officials in International Business Transactions', (2001) at §32–33.

173 Heimann, 'Will the OECD Convention Stop Foreign Bribery?' at p. 132.

174 Cockroft, 'Implementation of the OECD Convention: The Conditions for Success', at p. 3–4; Gounari, 'The OECD Convention on Combating Bribery of Foreign Public Officials in International Business Transactions: Theory and Practice', at p. 11; Heimann, 'Will the OECD Convention Stop Foreign Bribery?' at p. 132; Heimann and Dell, 'Progress Report 2007. Enforcement of the OECD Convention on Combating Bribery of Foreign Public Officials', at p. 38; International Monetary Fund (IMF), 'OECD Convention on Combating Bribery of Foreign Public Officials in International Business Transactions', at p. 32–33; O. Thomas Johnson and Donald J. Ridings, 'The OECD Convention and the Emergence of an International Anti-Bribery Regime', in Carol J. Holgren and Anita M. Stover (eds.), *Private Investors Abroad: Problems and Solutions in International Business in 1998* (New York: Matthew Bender, 1998), 6.1–6.21 at 6.03[03]; OECD, 'Fighting Bribery and Corruption: Frequently Asked Questions', (2007).

175 Alejandro Posadas, 'Combating Corruption under International Law', *Duke Journal of Comparative & International Law,* 10 (2000), p. 345–414 at p. 381.

176 Commentaries paragraph 9.

177 Heimann and Dell, 'Progress Report 2007. Enforcement of the OECD Convention on Combating Bribery of Foreign Public Officials', at p. 38.

actually prosecute corporations for having paid relatively small amounts of money to public officials abroad. Moreover, it will be nearly impossible to detect that small bribes were paid. Thus, including small facilitation payments will be of symbolical value only, with little practical effect.

As a final remark on the actual content of the Anti-Bribery Convention, it is relevant to take note of the suggestion that the Convention could be strengthened by including provisions which provide for a statute of limitations with a minimum of five years and provisions which call for more severe sanctions for both natural and legal persons.[178] Regarding the call for higher penalties, one must not lose sight of the fact that the severity of sanctions imposed on bribe-paying corporations has to be more or less in conformity with the average level of sanctions in a State Party to the Anti-Bribery Convention. Inclusion of sanction standards in the Convention text might therefore be unwise, given differences across State Parties.

3.3.2. Monitoring Mechanism

The OECD Working Group on Bribery (hereafter: WGB) consists of government experts of all State Parties and monitors implementation of and compliance with the Convention and the 1997 Revised Recommendation. To this end, a monitoring mechanism has been set up, which consists of two consecutive phases.

In the first phase (which took place between 1999 to 2001) it was examined whether State Parties have adequately *implemented* the Convention in their national legislation. First, the Parties had to submit their replies to a questionnaire. Then, experts of two State Parties (lead examiners) examined these replies in the provisional review, upon which the country concerned could comment. Subsequently, two rounds of consultation took place within the WGB, which ended with the adoption of an evaluation report. Finally, the WGB adopted a final report on each State Party by means of a written procedure. These reports were then reported to the OECD's Ministerial Conferences and published on the OECD's website. The implementation of the actions recommended by the WGB is monitored and periodical Phase 1 "bis" reviews have taken place.[179] Overall, this first phase

---

178 Christopher K. Carlberg, 'A Truly Level Playing Field for International Business: Improving the OECD Convention on Combating Bribery Using Clear Standards', *Boston College International and Comparative Law Review,* 26 (2003), p. 95–112.

179 Nicola Bonucci, 'Article 12. Monitoring and Follow-Up', in Mark Pieth, Lucinda A. Low, and Peter J. Cullen (eds.), *The OECD Convention on Bribery: A Commentary* (Cambridge: Cambridge University Press, 2007), 445–475.
OECD, 'OECD Anti-Bribery Convention: Procedure of Self- and Mutual Evaluation – Phase 1', <www.oecd.org/document/21/0,3343,en_2649_37447_2022613_1_1_1_37447,00.html>, accessed 15 October 2008.

has been quite successful. A large majority of the State Parties has ensured that its national laws are in conformity with the requirements of the Convention.[180]

The second phase (from 2001 to 2007) aimed to assess whether States have also *applied* the legislation in an effective manner.[181] The procedure of the second phase resembles the first phase, with the major difference being that, in Phase 2, on-site country visits have taken place. Furthermore, the scope of the second Phase was broader and the depth was greater. There is also a Follow-up procedure to the second Phase.[182] At this moment, it is being debated within the OECD whether a possible third phase of monitoring should be established, but nothing has been decided yet.[183]

As the current monitoring mechanism has been functioning for quite some years, what can be said about the actual application and enforcement of the legislation implemented by State Parties? In this respect, it is useful to make use of information from various sources: the view of the WGB itself, the studies conducted by Transparency International, the opinions of the representatives of the business side, i.e. the International Chamber of Commerce, and research done by scholars on the effectiveness of the Convention.

The chairperson of the WGB, Mark Pieth, noted that a lot of progress has been made. The Convention has been able to convince countries to criminalise active bribery of public officials abroad and approximately 150 investigations are or have been conducted. But Pieth also acknowledged that few investigations have led to actual convictions, since investigations are time-consuming. Pieth also stressed that we must not focus too much on the criminal side, since the actual goal of the Convention is to motivate companies to set up preventive measures, particularly compliance mechanisms. For businesses, this is the biggest challenge. Regarding law enforcement, it is relevant that mutual legal assistance networks will be established. Finally, Pieth noted that the new emerging economies (China, Russia, India, South-Africa and Israel) also have to get on board.[184]

It is also noteworthy that in the beginning of 2008, the WGB started a review of the OECD's anti-bribery instruments. To this end, the WGB released a consultation paper[185] upon which various organisations and legal experts could

---

180 Gounari, 'The OECD Convention on Combating Bribery of Foreign Public Officials in International Business Transactions: Theory and Practice', at 8.

181 Pieth, 'Taking Stock: Making the OECD Initiative against Corruption Work',.

182 Bonucci, 'Article 12. Monitoring and Follow-Up'.; OECD, 'OECD Anti-Bribery Convention: Procedure of Self- and Mutual Evaluation – Phase 2', <www.oecd.org/document/27/0,3343,en_2649_37447_2022939_1_1_1_37447,00.html>, accessed 15 October 2008.

183 Bonucci, 'Article 12. Monitoring and Follow-Up', at p. 473–474; Pieth, 'Introduction', at p. 36.

184 Interview with Mark Pieth, can be consulted at the OECD website <www.oecd.org>.

185 OECD Working Group on Bribery in International Business Transactions, 'Consultation Paper. Review of the OECD Instruments on Combating Bribery of Foreign Public Officials in International Business Transactions Ten Years after Adoption', <www.oecd.org/dataoecd/18/25/39882963.pdf>, accessed 15 October 2008.

comment.[186] Amongst others, TI noted that the consultation paper 'presents a disturbing picture of inadequate enforcement and considerable deficiencies in how governments have implemented or interpreted the Convention'. TI was less positive about the actual outcomes of the Convention than Pieth and pointed out that in 2007, there was significant enforcement of the Convention in 14 countries, but there has been little or no enforcement in half of the Parties, including 3 of the largest exporters.[187]

The International Chamber of Commerce was also quite critical. It held that:

> ... all the expectations raised by the OECD instruments have not been fulfilled, and that business leaders are often left with the impression that what is not allowed in one place, is condoned in another. The level playing field which has been promised so many times, has not or only partly become a reality. This is a source of frustration for business, as the lack of common rules directly affects free and fair competition between market players.[188]

The Chamber pointed to, amongst other things, the differences in enforcement between Member States and the wide variety in the number investigations and prosecutions. Furthermore, the Chamber stressed that the demand side of bribery should also be addressed.[189] Several researchers hold the opinion that, thus far, the Anti-Bribery Convention has not been very effective.[190]

In sum, it is reasonable to draw the conclusion from these sources that, although progress has been made, the actual enforcement of the anti-bribery provisions by State Parties to the OECD Convention is not yet at the desired level. There are several possible explanations for the difficulties in enforcement.

First, preparation of foreign bribery cases is troublesome for national prosecutors, given the secretive nature of bribery and the fact that investigations also have to be conducted abroad, in the country of the bribe-taker and possibly in the country where the bribes have been deposited. Thus, prosecutors have to rely heavily upon the cooperation they receive from the States of the bribe-takers, who

---

186 For an overview of all responses, see: OECD, 'Review of the OECD Anti-Bribery Instruments. Compilation of Responses to Consultation Paper', (OECD, 2008).

187 Fritz Heimann and Christiaan Poortman, 'TI Comments on OECD Consultation Paper', (Berlin: Transparency International, 5 March 2008) at p. 1. See also: Heimann and Dell, 'Progress Report 2007. Enforcement of the OECD Convention on Combating Bribery of Foreign Public Officials', at p. 6.

188 International Chamber of Commerce, 'ICC Note On "The Most Important Obstacle to the Effective Enforcement of the OECD Anti-Bribery Convention"', (11 June 2007). See also: ICC Commission on Anti-Corruption, 'Responses to the Consultation Paper on the Review of the OECD Anti-Bribery Instruments', (International Chamber of Commerce, 2008).

189 *Ibid.*

190 Kathleen A. Getz, 'The Effectiveness of Global Prohibition Regimes: Corruption and the Antibribery Convention', *Business & Society,* 45 (2006), 254–281; Daniel K. Tarullo, 'The Limits of Institutional Design: Implementing the OECD Anti-Bribery Convention', *Virginia Journal of International Law,* 44 (2004), p. 665–710.

are not under an obligation to provide assistance and who might even object to investigations.[191]

Second, the offices of the prosecution lack professional resources. It is necessary to set up centralised offices to prosecute foreign bribery cases, equipped with specialised staff and resources.[192]

Third, in certain State Parties to the Anti-Bribery Convention (e.g. Germany and Canada), criminal prosecution is a decentralised task at the state or provincial level, not at the national level. Some have argued that for local prosecutors, investigating and prosecuting foreign bribery might not be a priority.[193] However, it has not been demonstrated that countries with a centralised system are more active in bringing cases than countries with a decentralised system of prosecution.

Fourth, the lack of political willingness of States to prosecute bribing corporations might pose a threat to enforcement of the Convention's rules. The prosecution of corporations which generate employment can be politically sensitive.[194]

Fifth, there is a lack of complaints about bribery of foreign public officials. This can be explained by a wide variety of reasons. Public awareness about the prohibition of foreign bribery is said to be insufficient; there is often no accessible complaint procedure or adequate whistleblower protection. Furthermore, corporations who are aware of competitors engaged in bribery of foreign public officials will probably be reluctant to file a complaint since hard evidence might be difficult to acquire and possible defamation suits might be brought against them.[195]

All in all, the OECD Anti-Bribery Convention is a necessary instrument, since corporations do play a large role in the occurrence of bribery. The Convention is an acknowledgement of the fact that both developing and developed countries are equally responsible for bribery in business transactions. It is therefore of pivotal importance that, after the second phase of monitoring, the WGB continues to ensure that the legislative measures adopted by State Parties are actively enforced. Moreover, the efforts of the home-States of multinational corporations should be complemented with measures taken in their host-States. Again, political will to address corruption is crucial in this respect.

---

191 Gounari, 'The OECD Convention on Combating Bribery of Foreign Public Officials in International Business Transactions: Theory and Practice', at p. 9–10; Heimann, 'Will the OECD Convention Stop Foreign Bribery?' at p. 129.

192 Heimann, 'Will the OECD Convention Stop Foreign Bribery?' at p. 129; Heimann and Dell, 'Progress Report 2007. Enforcement of the OECD Convention on Combating Bribery of Foreign Public Officials', at p. 36.

193 Heimann, 'Will the OECD Convention Stop Foreign Bribery?' at p. 129.

194 *Ibid.*

195 Gounari, 'The OECD Convention on Combating Bribery of Foreign Public Officials in International Business Transactions: Theory and Practice', at p. 9–10; Heimann, 'Will the OECD Convention Stop Foreign Bribery?' at p. 129; Heimann and Dell, 'Progress Report 2007. Enforcement of the OECD Convention on Combating Bribery of Foreign Public Officials', at p. 36.

3.4. Council of Europe

3.4.1. Criminal Law Convention on Corruption (1999) and Additional Protocol (2003)

The Council of Europe's efforts to address corruption became institutionalised in 1995 with the establishment of the Multidisciplinary Group on Corruption (hereafter: GMC after its French acronym '*Groupe Multidisciplinaire sur la Corruption*'), which adopted a Programme of Action against Corruption in 1996. Subsequently, in 1997 the Twenty Guiding Principles against Corruption came into being.[196] These principles are of political importance but they are not legally binding.[197] Actual binding standard-setting commenced in 1999 when the Criminal Law Convention on Corruption was adopted.[198] This instrument, which entered into force in July 2002, has 41 State Parties.[199] Non-COE Members also can – and indeed have – become Party to the Convention. What is interesting is that the preamble of the Convention specifically notes that 'corruption threatens [...] human rights'.

The Criminal Law Convention contains obligations concerning criminalisation and international cooperation. Regarding *criminalisation*, the Convention obliges State Parties to criminalise several forms of corruption in their domestic legislation. These are (i) active and passive bribery of domestic and foreign public officials;[200] (ii) active and passive bribery of members of domestic, foreign and international public assemblies;[201] (iii) active and passive bribery of officials of international organisations;[202] (iv) active and passive bribery of judges and officials of international courts[203] and (v) active and passive bribery in the private sector.[204] Furthermore, State Parties have to criminalise trading in influence,[205] money

---

196 Resolution (97) 24 on the twenty guiding principles for the fight against corruption, adopted by the Committtee of Ministers on 6 November 1997 at the 101st Session of the Committee of Ministers.

197 Guy de Vel and Peter Csonka, 'The Council of Europe Activities against Corruption', in Cyrille Fijnaut and Leo Huberts (eds.), *Corruption, Integrity and Law Enforcement* (The Hague: Kluwer Law International, 2002), p. 361–380 at p. 363.

198 Criminal Law Convention on Corruption, adopted on 27 January 1999.

199 Council of Europe, 'Criminal Law Convention on Corruption – Signatures and Ratifications', <http://conventions.coe.int/Treaty/Commun/ChercheSig.asp?NT=173&CM=7&DF=10/7/2008&CL=ENG>, accessed 24 May 2011.

200 Article 2, 3 and 5 Criminal Law Convention on Corruption.

201 Article 4, 6 and 10 Criminal Law Convention on Corruption.

202 Article 9 Criminal Law Convention on Corruption.

203 Article 11 Criminal Law Convention on Corruption.

204 Article 7 and 8 Criminal Law Convention on Corruption.

205 Article 12 Criminal Law Convention on Corruption.

laundering,[206] account offences[207] and aiding and abetting.[208] The Convention also requires that State Parties establish corporate liability for active bribery, trading in influence and money laundering.[209] The Convention contains provisions on sanctions and measures to be imposed.[210]

On the topic of *international cooperation*, the Convention provides that Parties have to cooperate to the widest extent possible in respect of investigations and proceedings concerning the criminal offences that are dealt with by the Convention.[211] Furthermore, the Convention contains provisions on mutual assistance,[212] extradition,[213] the provision of spontaneous information,[214] the designation of a central authority,[215] direct communication between central authorities[216] and the sharing of information between Parties.[217]

In 2003, the Additional Protocol to the Criminal Law Convention on Corruption was adopted, entering into force on 1 March 2005.[218] State Parties to this instrument are under the obligation to criminalise active and passive bribery of both domestic and foreign arbitrators and jurors in their national laws.[219] The Protocol has been ratified by 23 States.[220]

Regarding the scope of the Convention and its Protocol, it is clear that these are mainly aimed at tackling bribery and trading in influence. Other forms of corruption, such as embezzlement, have not been taken into account. On the other hand, the instrument takes a comprehensive approach to both active and passive bribery, by including various forms as noted above. This is a necessary first step in combating corruption as a whole.

3.4.2. Civil Law Convention on Corruption (1999)

The year 1999 also saw the adoption of a second Convention on the topic, the Civil Law Convention on Corruption,[221] which entered into force on 1 November 2003.

---

206 Article 13 Criminal Law Convention on Corruption.
207 Article 14 Criminal Law Convention on Corruption.
208 Article 15 Criminal Law Convention on Corruption.
209 Article 18 Criminal Law Convention on Corruption.
210 Article 19 Criminal Law Convention on Corruption.
211 Article 25 Criminal Law Convention on Corruption.
212 Article 26 Criminal Law Convention on Corruption.
213 Article 27 Criminal Law Convention on Corruption.
214 Article 28 Criminal Law Convention on Corruption.
215 Article 29 Criminal Law Convention on Corruption.
216 Article 30 Criminal Law Convention on Corruption.
217 Article 31 Criminal Law Convention on Corruption.
218 Additional Protocol to the Criminal Law Convention on Corruption, adopted on 15 April 2003.
219 Articles 2 – 6 Additional Protocol.
220 Council of Europe, 'Additional Protocol to the Criminal Law Convention on Corruption – Signatures and Ratifications', <http://conventions.coe.int/Treaty/Commun/ChercheSig.asp?NT=191&CM=1&DF=6/4/2008&CL=ENG>, accessed 7 October 2008.
221 Civil Law Convention on Corruption, adopted on 9 September 1999.

Currently, 33 States are Party to the Civil Law Convention.[222] This treaty notes that, for the purpose of the Convention, corruption is equated with bribery.[223] The Convention obliges State Parties to provide for effective remedies for persons who have suffered damage due to acts of corruption, including the possibility to obtain compensation for damage, in their domestic legislation.[224] This compensation may cover material damage, loss of profits and non-pecuniary loss.[225] State Parties must also provide for procedures for victims of public sector corruption.[226] This is a very important provision. Furthermore, States must provide that any contract or clause thereof which provides for corruption is null and void in their national laws.[227] Finally, States have to put in place appropriate legal whistleblower protection for employees.[228]

In essence, the content of this Convention is promising. When properly implemented, its provisions give victims of bribery practical possibilities to obtain compensation for harm they have suffered. Unfortunately, it is not entirely clear to what extent the Parties to the Convention have put such legislation in place and how it functions in practice. Hopefully, attention for the Civil Law Convention will increase in the near future.

3.4.3. Recommendation on Codes of Conduct for Public Officials (2000)

In 2000, the Recommendation on Codes of Conduct for Public Officials was adopted.[229] This instrument recommends that the governments of COE Member States promote the adoption of national codes of conduct for public officials, based on a model code of conduct annexed to the Recommendation. However, it is unclear how many countries have adopted an enforceable code of conduct.

3.4.4. Recommendation on Common Rules against Corruption in the Funding of Political Parties and Electoral Campaigns (2003)

The Recommendation on Common Rules against Corruption in the Funding of Political Parties and Electoral Campaigns came into being in 2003.[230] This non-

222 Council of Europe, 'Civil Law Convention on Corruption – Signatures and Ratifications', <http://conventions.coe.int/Treaty/Commun/ChercheSig.asp?NT=174&CM=7&DF=10/7/2008&CL=ENG>, accessed 24 May 2011.

223 Article 2 Civil Law Convention on Corruption.

224 Article 1 Civil Law Convention on Corruption.

225 Article 3 Civil Law Convention on Corruption.

226 Article 5 Civil Law Convention on Corruption.

227 Article 8 Civil Law Convention on Corruption.

228 Article 9 Civil Law Convention on Corruption.

229 Recommendation No. R(2000)10 of the Committee of Ministers to member states on codes of conduct for public officials, adopted on 11 May 2000.

230 Recommendation Rec(2003)4 of the Committee of Ministers to member states on common rules against corruption in the funding of political parties and electoral campaigns, adopted on 8 April 2003.

binding instrument recommends that governments of Member States of the COE adopt rules against corruption in the funding of political parties and electoral campaigns in their national legislation. The appendix to the Recommendation provides for a set of common rules which States can use.

3.4.5. GRECO: the COE's Monitoring Mechanism

Compliance with the Twenty Guiding Principles, the two Conventions, the Additional Protocol and the two Recommendations is monitored by the Group of States against Corruption (*Group d'États Contre la Corruption*, GRECO). GRECO was established in 1999 and is comprised of the States Parties to the Criminal and Civil Law Conventions and other States.[231] Currently, GRECO has 46 Member States while each State appoints two delegates.[232] The essence of its monitoring process lies in mutual evaluation and peer pressure.[233]

The evaluation procedure takes place in consecutive rounds and each round is dedicated to a particular theme. Evaluations are carried out by evaluation teams, composed of experts previously delivered by Members.[234] The countries under evaluation have to submit written replies to GRECO questionnaires.[235] Furthermore, during country visits, information is gathered from public officials and civil society representatives.[236] Subsequently, the evaluation team will draft a first version of the evaluation report, upon which the country concerned can comment.[237] Then, GRECO will examine and discuss the report, and eventually, it will be adopted.[238] The evaluation report concludes on whether the country's legislation and practice is in conformity with its obligations and can contain observations, which are not subject to any follow-up procedure, and/or recommendations. Recommendations require Members to take measures within the next 18 months.[239] A special compliance procedure will then monitor the implementation of these recommendations.[240] The decision whether or not the country has actually implemented the recommendations is based on written situation reports submitted by the country.[241] If it appears that the country is not in compliance with certain recommendations, GRECO will monitor this during a new 18 month period.[242] The compliance reports which GRECO adopts contain an

---

231 GRECO Statute Article 4.

232 GRECO Statute Article 6 (1).

233 GRECO Statute Article 1; GRECO Rules of Procedure, Rule 22 (2).

234 GRECO Statute Article 10 and 12; GRECO Rules of Procedure, Rule 25 (1) and 26.

235 GRECO Statute Article 11; GRECO Rules of Procedure, Rule 24.

236 GRECO Statute Article 13; GRECO Rules of Procedure, Rule 27.

237 GRECO Statute Article 14; GRECO Rules of Procedure, Rule 28.

238 GRECO Statute Article 15; GRECO Rules of Procedure, Rule 29.

239 GRECO Statute Article 15 (6) and GRECO Rules of Procedure, Rule 30 (1).

240 GRECO Rules of Procedure, Rule 31.

241 GRECO Statute Article 15 (6) and GRECO Rules of Procedure, Rule 30 (2).

242 GRECO Rules of Procedure, Rule 31.

overall conclusion on the implementation of all recommendations, in order to decide whether the compliance procedure can be terminated. Members who have responded to GRECO's recommendations in a globally unsatisfactory manner are subject to a special, third, procedure.[243]

The approach of GRECO is a 'soft' one. This can be a seen as a strength, since countries are able to discuss freely about the issue. Reports are freely accessible on the Internet, meaning that countries' compliance with the COE's instruments can be discussed in public. However, among the general public, GRECO might not be very well known. Like other peer review mechanisms, the overall effectiveness of GRECO proceedings will depend upon the political willingness of the participating countries. The compliance procedure does not contain any forceful measures which can be imposed on States that do not implement the evaluation report's recommendations. The consequences of non-compliance thus remain political.

3.5. African Instruments

3.5.1. SADC Protocol Against Corruption (2001)

The Southern African Development Community (hereafter: SADC) was established in 1992, as the successor to the Southern African Development Coordination Conference (SADCC) originating from 1980. The SADC is an intergovernmental organisation consisting of 15 States[244] which has as its overall objective 'to build a Region in which there will be a high degree of harmonisation and rationalisation to enable the pooling of resources to achieve collective self-reliance in order to improve the living standards of the people of the region.'[245]

In 2001, the SADC Protocol against Corruption was adopted. It entered into force on 6 July 2005. Currently, 14 States have signed the instrument, while 9 States are Party.[246] Unlike most other anti-corruption instruments, the SADC Protocol provides a definition of corruption:

> ... any act referred to in Article 3 and includes bribery or any other behaviour in relation to persons entrusted with responsibilities in the public and private sectors which violates their duties as public officials, private employees, independent agents

---

243 GRECO Website, 'How Does GRECO Work?' <www.coe.int/t/dg1/greco/general/4.%20 How%20does%20GRECO%20work_en.asp>, accessed 7 October 2008.

244 SADC Member States: Angola, Botswana, Lesotho, Malawi, Mozambique, Swaziland, Tanzania, Zambia, Zimbabwe, Namibia, South Africa, Mauritius, Democratic Republic of the Congo, Madagascar and Seychelles.

245 Southern African Development Community Website, <www.sadc.int>, accessed 7 October 2008. For the full list of objectives see Article 5 (1) Treaty of the Southern African Development Community.

246 The ratifying countries are: Botswana, Lesotho, Malawi, Mauritius, Namibia, South Africa, Tanzania, Zambia and Zimbabwe.

or other relationships of that kind and aimed at obtaining undue advantage of any kind for themselves or others.[247]

The mentioned provision determines that the Protocol applies to the following acts of corruption: (i) passive bribery in the public sector;[248] (ii) active bribery in the public sector;[249] (iii) an act or omission by a public official in order to illicitly obtain benefits;[250] (iv) diversion of property in the public sector;[251] (v) active and passive bribery in the private sector;[252] (vi) active and passive trading in influence in the public and private sector;[253] (vii) the fraudulent use or concealment of property derived from other corrupt acts[254] and (viii) several modes of participation in acts of corruption.[255] This list is not exhaustive, since the Protocol also applies by mutual agreement between or among States with respect to acts of corruption that are not covered by the instrument.[256] Also, the Protocol contains an FCPA-like reference to active bribery of foreign public officials.[257]

The obligations of States with regard to the above-mentioned acts of corruption fall into three main groups: prevention, criminalisation and cooperation and post-corruption measures. First, concerning *prevention*, States are obliged to adopt measures which create, maintain and strengthen: codes of conduct for public officials as well as mechanisms to enforce them,[258] transparent, equitable and efficient government hiring and procurement systems,[259] revenue collection and control systems that deter corruption and deny the tax-deductibility of bribes,[260] mechanisms to promote access to information,[261] whistleblower protection and protection against false claims,[262] anti-corruption institutions,[263] deterrents to bribery such as bookkeeping and accounting requirements,[264] media, civil society and NGO participation[265] and measures in the field of public education and

247 Article 1 SADC Protocol Against Corruption.
248 Article 3 (1) (a) SADC Protocol Against Corruption.
249 Article 3 (1) (b) SADC Protocol Against Corruption.
250 Article 3 (1) (c) SADC Protocol Against Corruption.
251 Article 3 (1) (d) SADC Protocol Against Corruption.
252 Article 3 (1) (e) SADC Protocol Against Corruption.
253 Article 3 (1) (f) SADC Protocol Against Corruption.
254 Article 3 (1) (g) SADC Protocol Against Corruption.
255 Article 3 (1) (h) SADC Protocol Against Corruption.
256 Article 3 (2) SADC Protocol Against Corruption.
257 Article 6 SADC Protocol Against Corruption.
258 Article 4 (1) (a) SADC Protocol Against Corruption.
259 Article 4 (1) (b) SADC Protocol Against Corruption.
260 Article 4 (1) (c) SADC Protocol Against Corruption.
261 Article 4 (1) (d) SADC Protocol Against Corruption.
262 Article 4 (1) (e) and (f) SADC Protocol Against Corruption.
263 Article 4 (1) (g) SADC Protocol Against Corruption.
264 Article 4 (1) (h) SADC Protocol Against Corruption.
265 Article 4 (1) (i) SADC Protocol Against Corruption.

awareness raising.[266] Finally, Parties have to take measures to prevent private sector corruption.[267]

States also have the obligation *to criminalise* the acts of corruption listed in Article 3, as described above, in their national legislation.[268] States are also obliged, 'to the extent possible' to develop and harmonise their policies and national legislation.[269] Furthermore, bribery of foreign public officials also has to be criminalised, although such criminalisation is subject to the domestic legislation of State Parties.[270]

In addition, the Protocol contains provisions on *judicial cooperation and mutual legal assistance* between States,[271] confiscation and seizure of proceeds of corruption offences[272] and extradition.[273] In sum, the Protocol adopts a comprehensive approach by covering a wide range of offenses in both the public and the private sector.

As a means of overseeing the implementation of the Protocol, the instrument establishes a Committee of State Parties.[274] States have to report to this Committee within one year after becoming a Party, and subsequently every two years.[275] The Committee has the task to gather and disseminate information amongst Parties, to organise training programmes, to evaluate the programmes to be put in place and a programme of cooperation for the implementation of the Protocol, to provide any other related assistance to Parties as and when appropriate and to regularly report to the SADC's Council of Ministers about the compliance of Parties to the Protocol.[276] Unfortunately, very little information is available on the functioning of the Committee and on the implementation of State obligations under the Protocol. The SADC's website does not provide clarifications on this topic. This is a pity, since the instrument itself is promising. Unfortunately, it can be severely doubted whether a State Party such as Zimbabwe has actively worked to live up to the standards of the Protocol.[277]

---

266 Article 4 (1) (j) SADC Protocol Against Corruption.

267 Article 4 (2) SADC Protocol Against Corruption.

268 Article 7 (2) SADC Protocol Against Corruption.

269 Article 7 (1) SADC Protocol Against Corruption.

270 Article 6 (1) SADC Protocol Against Corruption.

271 Article 10 SADC Protocol Against Corruption.

272 Article 8 SADC Protocol Against Corruption.

273 Article 9 SADC Protocol Against Corruption.

274 Article 11 (1) SADC Protocol Against Corruption.

275 Article 11 (2) SADC Protocol Against Corruption.

276 Article 11 (3) SADC Protocol Against Corruption.

277 For a 2002 overview of trends in corruption, a review of existing legislation and an analysis of anti-corruption practices in the SADC Member States, see United Nations Office on Drugs and Crime (Regional Office for Southern Africa). Edited by Ugljesa Zvekic, 'Corruption & Anti-Corruption in Southern Africa. Analysis Based on the Results of the Regional Seminar on Anti-Corruption Investigating Strategies with Particular Regard to Drug Control for the SADC Member States. <www.unodc.org/pdf/southafrica/southafrica_corruption.pdf>, accessed 21 October 2008.

3.5.2. *ECOWAS Protocol on the Fight Against Corruption (2001)*

The Economic Community of West African States (hereafter: ECOWAS), founded in 1975, is a group of 15 West African countries[278] aiming:

> ... to promote co-operation and integration, leading to the establishment of an economic union in West Africa in order to raise the living standards of its peoples, and to maintain and enhance economic stability, foster relations among Member States and contribute to the progress and development of the African Continent.[279]

On 21 December 2001, the Protocol on the Fight against Corruption was adopted, covering prevention, criminalisation and international cooperation in the field of corruption and calling for the establishment of a Technical Commission to monitor the implementation of the instrument. To date, only one State has ratified the instrument, and therefore the Protocol has not yet entered into force.[280]

3.5.3. *African Union Convention on Preventing and Combating Corruption (2003)*

(i) Content

The African Union Convention on Preventing and Combating Corruption was adopted on 11 July 2003 and entered into force on 5 August 2006. It was signed by 45 out of 53 African Union Member States, of which 31 have ratified it.[281] The AU Convention, which strongly resembles the IACAC,[282] concerns both private and public sector corruption[283] and does not distinguish between grand and petty corruption.[284] The instrument rests upon three pillars: prevention, criminalisation and cooperation.

Prevention of corruption is a central element. The Convention aims to achieve this goal, amongst others, by obliging State Parties to set up national anti-corruption

---

278 ECOWAS Member States: Benin, Burkina Faso, Cabo Verde, Côte d'Ivoire, Gambia, Ghana, Guinee, Guinee Bissau, Liberia, Mali, Niger, Nigeria, Senegal, Sierra Leone and Togo.

279 Article 3 (1) Treaty of ECOWAS.

280 See <www.transparency.org/global_priorities/international_conventions/conventions_instruments/ecowas_protocol>, accessed 24 May 2011.

281 The ratifying countries are: Algeria, Benin, Burkina Faso, Burundi, Comoros, Congo, Ethiopia, Gabon, Gambia, Ghana, Kenya, Libya, Lesotho, Liberia, Madagascar, Malawi, Mali, Mozambique, Namibia, Nigeria, Niger, Rwanda, Seychelles, Sierra Leone, South Africa, Senegal, Tanzania, Togo, Uganda, Zambia, and. Zimbabwe.

282 Kolawole Olaniyan, 'The African Union Convention on Preventing and Combating Corruption: A Critical Appraisal', *African Human Rights Law Journal,* 4 (2004), 74–92 at 78.

283 Akere Muna, 'The African Union Convention against Corruption', in Transparency International (ed.), *Global Corruption Report 2004. Political Corruption* (2004), 116–121 at 118.

284 See Article 1 which refers to public officials at any level of the State hierarchy.

bodies[285] and accounting and auditing systems,[286] by making declarations of assets by public officials mandatory[287] and by requiring States to adopt and monitor codes of conduct.[288] The Convention also stresses the importance of raising public awareness about corruption and emphasises the role of the media and civil society in that process.[289] States are obliged to ensure the right of access to information, required to fight corruption.[290]

The Convention also aims at a harmonised *criminalisation* of acts of corruption and related offences at the national level.[291] Like most other instruments, the Convention does not define 'corruption' itself. Rather it refers to a number of 'acts and practices including related offences' which constitute corruption within the meaning of the instrument.[292] These are (i) passive and active bribery in the public sector;[293] (ii) illicitly obtaining benefits;[294] (iii) embezzlement;[295] (iv) active and passive bribery in the private sector;[296] (v) trading in influence;[297] (vi) illicit enrichment;[298] (vii) the use or concealment of proceeds of corrupt acts;[299] (viii) and participation in corrupt offences.[300] All these acts of corruption are under the same regime of obligatory criminalisation by State Parties.[301] In addition, the Convention leaves room for 'other acts of practices of corruption' which are not listed in the Convention.[302] Money laundering also has to be made an offence.[303] This wide approach, which clearly also sees embezzlement and trading in influence as forms of corruption, is to be welcomed.

Cooperation among State Parties is a third important element: the Convention contains provisions on jurisdiction,[304] extradition,[305] confiscation and seizure of

---

285 Article 5 (3) AU Convention.
286 Article 5 (4) AU Convention.
287 Article 7 (1) AU Convention.
288 Article 7 (2) AU Convention.
289 Article 5 (8) and Article 12 AU Convention.
290 Article 9 AU Convention.
291 Article 2 (3) AU Convention.
292 Article 1 AU Convention.
293 Article 4 (1) (a) and (b) AU Convention.
294 Article 4 (1) (c) AU Convention.
295 Article 4 (1) (d) AU Convention.
296 Article 4 (1) (e) AU Convention.
297 Article 4 (1) (f) AU Convention.
298 Article 4 (1) (g) AU Convention.
299 Article 4 (1) (h) AU Convention.
300 Article 4 (1) (i) AU Convention.
301 Article 5 (1) AU Convention.
302 Article 4 (2) AU Convention.
303 Article 6 AU Convention.
304 Article 13 AU Convention.
305 Article 15 AU Convention.

assets,[306] the lifting of bank secrecy,[307] mutual legal assistance[308] and international cooperation.[309]

It is very positive that such a wide-ranging anti-corruption instrument as the African Convention has been adopted in Africa, a continent plagued by corruption. Particularly promising and innovative is the provision obliging public officials to declare their assets at the beginning and the end of public office. Nonetheless, one must also recognise the deficiencies from which the AU Convention suffers.

The first one is technical remark, relating to the actual text of the Convention. Reportedly, the four language versions of the Convention (i.e. English, French, Portuguese and Arabic) are not 'equally authentic' as claimed in Article 28. The texts state different things and, in the English version, words are missing. The origin of these inconsistencies can be found in the drafting process, in which amendments were made to draft versions of the Convention.[310]

Second, the Convention makes use of safeguard clauses, making certain provisions dependent upon national laws.[311] This is particularly problematic in respect of the provision on immunity, stating that 'any immunity granted to public officials shall not be an obstacle to the investigation of allegations against and the prosecution of such officials'. Yet, this is made 'subject to the provisions of domestic legislation'.[312] Thus, in practice, national laws can (and usually do) give public officials immunity for deeds done while in office.[313]

Third, the provisions on whistleblower protection might cause problems. State Parties are obliged to take measures to protect informants and witnesses in corruption and related offences and States have to protect their identities.[314] Also, they must make sure that citizens report corruption without having to fear punishment for doing so.[315] However, the effectiveness of these provisions can be strongly undermined by the subsequent provision which obliges States to 'adopt national legislative measures in order to punish those who make false and malicious reports against innocent persons in corruption and related offences'.[316] It is not unlikely that such a threat of being punished will keep honest people from reporting

306 Article 16 AU Convention.

307 Article 17 AU Convention.

308 Article 18 AU Convention.

309 Article 19 AU Convention.

310 Peter W. Schroth, 'The African Union Convention on Preventing and Combating Corruption', *Journal of African Law,* 49 (2005), p. 24–38 at p. 25–27.

311 Olaniyan, 'The African Union Convention on Preventing and Combating Corruption: A Critical Appraisal', at p. 85–86.

312 Article 7 (5) AU Convention.

313 Olaniyan, 'The African Union Convention on Preventing and Combating Corruption: A Critical Appraisal', at p. 85–86; Nsongurua J. Udombana, 'Fighting Corruption Seriously? Africa's Anti-Corruption Convention', *Singapore Journal of International and Comparative Law,* 7 (2003), p. 447–488 at p. 469.

314 Article 5 (5) AU Convention.

315 Article 5 (6) AU Convention.

316 Article 5 (7) AU Convention.

corruption, since allegations of corruption are usually difficult to prove and the opposing party accused of corruption might be very powerful.[317]

Fourth, although the involvement of civil society organisations is very important in preventing and combating corruption, it can pose problems of representation and legitimacy. It is of prime importance that truly independent, African NGOs are involved, which are supported by the people, instead of Westerns organisations without grassroots support.[318] In addition, political oppression of societal groups might not be uncommon in undemocratic regimes.[319]

Fifth, as is the case with most instruments discussed in the present chapter, the AU Convention relies heavily upon the national laws and legal systems of State Parties. National anti-corruption agencies are awarded an important role. It is therefore crucial that these institutions are themselves independent and free from corruption. Unfortunately, this is currently not the case in many African countries.[320]

(ii) Monitoring Mechanism

Monitoring of State Parties' obligations under the Convention takes place by means of the Advisory Board on Corruption within the African Union, comprised of 11 experts and which reports to the AU's Executive Council on the compliance by each State Party with the Convention.[321] Unfortunately, this system does not consist of actual mutual evaluation or enforcement.[322] The Board reports to the AU's Executive Council on the basis of reports submitted by national anti-corruption agencies, but if these do not report, no sanctions can be put in place.[323] The Board does not possess investigative powers and does not have the mandate to denounce acts of corruption.[324] Furthermore, the independence of the Board's members is uncertain, since they are proposed by the States themselves.[325] The members do not have to fulfil any educational requirements.[326] Given this lack of enforcement possibilities, it has been suggested that the Convention should become a Protocol to the African Convention on Human and Peoples' Rights, so that the anti-corruption

317 Muna, 'The African Union Convention against Corruption', at p. 120; Schroth, 'The African Union Convention on Preventing and Combating Corruption', at p. 33–34.

318 Indira Carr, 'Corruption in Africa: Is the African Union Convention on Combating Corruption the Answer?' *Journal of Business Law,* March (2007), p. 111–136 at p. 126–127.

319 Muna, 'The African Union Convention against Corruption', at p. 120.

320 Udombana, 'Fighting Corruption Seriously? Africa's Anti-Corruption Convention', at p. 479–481.

321 Article 22 AU Convention.

322 Udombana, 'Fighting Corruption Seriously? Africa's Anti-Corruption Convention', at p. 475.

323 Muna, 'The African Union Convention against Corruption', at p. 119.

324 *Ibid.*

325 *Ibid.*

326 Udombana, 'Fighting Corruption Seriously? Africa's Anti-Corruption Convention', at p. 474.

provisions would be brought under the competence of the African Commission and the African Court of Human and Peoples' Rights.[327]

In sum, the AU Convention on Preventing and Combating Corruption is a relatively new instrument, which should be welcomed despite its obvious shortcomings. It is likely that some more time is needed in order to decide upon its functioning in the long term. In a continent tainted by corruption, one cannot expect instant miracles from a legal instrument. But what is already certain is that – like all anti-corruption initiatives – the AU Convention needs to be backed by a strong political will in order to achieve true progress. At this moment it seems unlikely that corrupt public officials will limit their own actions by actually putting into place and enforcing adequate anti-corruption legislation.[328]

3.6. United Nations

3.6.1. United Nations Convention Against Transnational Organized Crime (2000)

United Nations' efforts to address corruption commenced in 1996, when the General Assembly adopted two Resolutions on the topic: the International Code of Conduct for Public Officials[329] and the UN Declaration against Corruption and Bribery in International Commercial Transactions.[330] Subsequently, 1997 saw the birth of the GA Resolution International Cooperation Against Corruption and Bribery in International Commercial Transactions,[331] which was taken further in 1998 with the Action Against Corruption and Bribery in International Commercial Transaction Resolution.[332] In 1999, another GA Resolution was adopted,[333] while in 2000 the first Convention in the field came into being: the UN Convention Against Transnational Organized Crime (hereafter: UNCTOC).[334] This instrument entered into force on 29 September 2003 and currently has 147 State Parties.[335]

---

327 Olaniyan, 'The African Union Convention on Preventing and Combating Corruption: A Critical Appraisal', at p. 86–89.

328 Jennifer L. Akre, 'Overcoming Chad's Oil Curse: The African Union Convention on Preventing and Combating Corruption as a Framework for Securing Foreign Investments', <http://works.bepress.com/cgi/viewcontent.cgi?article=1000&context=jennifer_akre>, accessed 10 November 2008; Carr, 'Corruption in Africa: Is the African Union Convention on Combating Corruption the Answer?' at p. 135; Muna, 'The African Union Convention against Corruption', at p. 120; Udombana, 'Fighting Corruption Seriously? Africa's Anti-Corruption Convention', at p. 488.

329 UN Doc. A/RES/51/59 (12/12/1996).

330 UN Doc. A/RES/51/191 (16/12/1996).

331 UN Doc. A/RES/52/87 (12/12/1997).

332 UN Doc. A/RES/53/176 (15/12/1998).

333 UN Doc. A/RES/54/128 (17/12/1999).

334 UN Doc. A/RES/55/25 (15/12/2000).

335 United Nations Office on Drugs and Crime, 'Signatories to the United Nations Convention against Transnational Organized Crime', <www.unodc.org/unodc/en/treaties/CTOC/countrylist.html>, accessed 26 May 2011.

The UNCTOC does not define corruption itself, but it distinguishes between active and passive bribery of national public officials[336] and active and passive bribery of foreign public officials or international civil servants.[337] It is recognised that there are also other forms of corruption.[338]

State obligations under the Convention are threefold: prevention,[339] criminalisation and international cooperation. Regarding the second element, State Parties are obliged to criminalise active and passive domestic bribery,[340] while they merely have to consider criminalisation of active and passive bribery of foreign public officials and other forms of corruption.[341] In addition, money laundering has to be criminalised. The Conference of Parties is responsible for periodically reviewing the implementation of the Convention.[342]

3.6.2. United Nations Convention Against Corruption (2003)

(i) Content

The first global legal instrument against corruption, the UN Convention Against Corruption, was adopted in 2003 and entered into force on 14 December 2005. Currently, there are 154 State Parties to the Convention.[343] The UNCAC is an extensive instrument, consisting of 71 articles. The obligations of States fall into four groups, i.e. prevention, criminalisation, international cooperation and asset recovery.

Regarding the *prevention* of corruption, the UNCAC contains a wide range of measures in the public as well as the private sector.[344] The effectiveness of several provisions might be undermined by their wording: frequently, the non-mandatory language 'States shall endeavour to' and 'States shall consider to' is used instead of the much stronger 'States shall'. This makes numerous preventive provisions optional.[345]

---

336 Article 8(1) UNCTOC.
337 Article 8(2) UNCTOC.
338 Article 8(2) UNCTOC.
339 Articles 9 and 31 UNCTOC.
340 Article 8(1) UNCTOC.
341 Article 8(2) UNCTOC.
342 Article 32 UNCTOC.
343 United Nations Office on Drugs and Crime, 'Signatories to the United Nations Convention against Corruption', <www.unodc.org/unodc/en/treaties/CAC/signatories.html>, accessed 18 November 2011.
344 UNCAC Chapter II 'Preventive measures.'
345 Philippa Webb, 'The United Nations Convention against Corruption: Global Achievement or Missed Opportunity?' *Journal of International Economic Law*, 8 (2005), p. 191–229 at p. 205–206.

The UNCAC also contains obligations *to criminalise* certain corrupt practices and related offences in both the public and private sphere.[346] Again, what is actually understood by 'corruption' is not defined; instead a number of offences are listed. Unlike for example the IACAC, the UNCAC does not clearly indicate what conduct can be seen as an 'act of corruption'. What must be noted is that States do not have the same obligations with respect to all offences. A distinction is made between offences that are mandatory to criminalise, and offences that are only optional to criminalise.[347] The first group consists of (i) active and passive bribery of national public officials;[348] (ii) active bribery of foreign public officials and officials of public international organisations;[349] (iii) embezzlement;[350] (iv) laundering of the proceeds of corruption;[351] (v) obstruction of justice[352] and (vi) participation.[353] The second group is comprised of (i) passive bribery of foreign public officials and officials of public international organisations;[354] (ii) trading in influence;[355] (iii) abuse of functions;[356] (iv) illicit enrichment;[357] (v) private sector bribery;[358] (vi) private sector embezzlement;[359] (vii) concealment;[360] and (viii) attempt and preparation.[361] It is very positive that the Convention adopts a comprehensive approach towards corruption by including numerous forms of corruption, going beyond the traditional anti-bribery provisions.[362] Yet, the distinction between separate levels of obligations – a result of political compromise – is a weak point of the Convention.

International cooperation is a third main element of the Convention which, *inter alia*, consists of provisions on mutual legal assistance and extradition.[363] Unlike the

---

346 UNCAC Chapter III 'Criminalization and law enforcement.'

347 Indira Carr, 'The United Nations Convention on Corruption: Making a Real Difference to the Quality of Life of Millions?' *Manchester Journal of International Economic Law,* 3 (2006), p. 3–44 at p. 19–25; Low, 'The United Nations Convention against Corruption: The Globalization of Anticorruption Standards', at p. 7–12.

348 Article 15 UNCAC.

349 Article 16 (1) UNCAC.

350 Article 17 UNCAC.

351 Article 23 UNCAC.

352 Article 25 UNCAC.

353 Article 27 (1) UNCAC.

354 Article 16 (2) UNCAC.

355 Article 18 UNCAC.

356 Article 19 UNCAC.

357 Article 20 UNCAC.

358 Article 21 UNCAC.

359 Article 22 UNCAC.

360 Article 24 UNCAC.

361 Article 27 (2) and (3) UNCAC.

362 Low, 'The United Nations Convention against Corruption: The Globalization of Anticorruption Standards', at p. 13; R Rajesh Babu, 'The United Nations Convention against Corruption: A Critical Overview', *Social Science Research Network,* (1 March 2006) at p. 9.

363 UNCAC Chapter IV 'International cooperation.'

provisions that require criminalisation at the national level, most of the provisions regarding international cooperation are self-executing.[364]

Finally, the UNCAC contains a wide range of measures on asset recovery, which are more far-reaching than other existing international legal obligations. The provisions include not only seizure and freezing but also repatriation of assets to home States.[365] This is definitely a strong point of the Convention, which also generated a large amount of political will among the negotiating Parties.[366]

Another positive aspect is the provision under which States have to take measures to address the consequences of corruption, such as through the annulment or rescission of contracts, the withdrawal of concessions or by taking remedial action.[367] Moreover, States are obliged to ensure that the persons or entities who have suffered damage due to corruption have the right to ask for compensation in legal proceedings.[368] This provision resembles the COE's Civil Law Convention on Corruption.[369]

The UNCAC is the most detailed and far-reaching international instrument against corruption to date.[370] It must also be recognised that the Convention suffers from a number of deficits. Apart from the many optional provisions which the UNCAC contains, the use of numerous safeguard clauses can harm the effectiveness of the instrument. Several provisions are made subject to principles of domestic law, national constitutions etcetera.[371] Furthermore, the provision on immunity[372] is problematic since it provides States with several possibilities to grant immunity to corrupt (former) officials.[373]

---

364 Low, 'The United Nations Convention against Corruption: The Globalization of Anticorruption Standards', at p. 4, 18–19.

365 UNCAC Chapter V 'Asset recovery'. For more information on the topic of repatriation, see: Linda M. Samuel, 'Repatriation Obligations under the United Nations Convention against Corruption', *Resource Material Series,* 65 (2005), p. 58–64.

366 Webb, 'The United Nations Convention against Corruption: Global Achievement or Missed Opportunity?' at p. 206–212.

367 Article 34 UN Convention against Corruption; Low, 'The United Nations Convention against Corruption: The Globalization of Anticorruption Standards', at p. 15–16.

368 Article 35 UNCAC; *Ibid.* at p. 16–17.

369 *Ibid.* at p. 17.

370 *Ibid.* at p. 3.

371 *Ibid.* at p. 4; Webb, 'The United Nations Convention against Corruption: Global Achievement or Missed Opportunity?' at p. 206.

372 Article 30 (2) UN Convention Against Corruption.

373 Carr, 'The United Nations Convention on Corruption: Making a Real Difference to the Quality of Life of Millions?' at p. 36; Commonwealth Secretariat & Chatham House, 'Anti-Corruption Conference: The UN Convention against Corruption. Implementation and Enforcement: Meeting the Challenges', (Chatham House, London, 24–25 April 2006) at p. 33; Low, 'The United Nations Convention against Corruption: The Globalization of Anticorruption Standards', at p. 13.

As a final note it is remarkable and worrisome that three G20-countries have not ratified the UNCAC: Germany, Japan and Saudi-Arabia.[374] In Europe, the non-State Parties, except Germany, are Ireland and the Czech Republic. Another country that is not a Party is New Zealand, which is peculiar given its excellent CPI score.[375] Other non-ratifying States include Sudan, Chad, Guinea, Ivory Coast, Equatorial Guinea, Eritrea, Somalia, Swaziland, Oman, Syria, Myanmar, North Korea, Belize and Suriname.

(ii) Monitoring and Enforcement

As regards the monitoring and enforcement of State obligations under the UNCAC, the Convention itself stipulates that the Conference of States Parties has the task to improve the capacity of and cooperation between State Parties to achieve the Convention's objectives and to promote and review its implementation.[376] The Article concerned lists a number of activities which the Conference should fulfil. Amongst others, the Conference shall establish 'if it deems necessary, any appropriate mechanism or body to assist in the effective implementation of the Convention'.[377]

During the first Conference of States Parties in 2006, the importance of a review mechanism was acknowledged. A self-assessment checklist was developed and 16 countries took part in a voluntary pilot programme. Subsequently, a Working Group on the Review of Implementation was formed.[378] A good opportunity to adopt a concrete monitoring mechanism was missed during the second Conference of States Parties in the end of January 2008. State Parties could not agree about the form of a possible monitoring mechanism, about the transparency of the process and the participation of civil society. However, it was decided that the self-assessment programme, as well as the pilot programme, would be expanded. The next possibility for the establishment of a monitoring mechanism arose in late 2009 during the third Conference of States Parties in Doha.[379] During this event, States finally agreed upon the establishment of a Review Mechanism.[380]

---

374 Christian Humborg, 'In the Fight Against Corruption, Germany Falls Behind', http://blog.transparency.org/2011/05/16/in-the-fight-against-corruption-germany-falls-behind/> accessed 26 May 2011.

375 In 2010, New Zealand shared the no.1 position on the CPI with Denmark and Singapore.

376 Article 63 (1) UNCAC.

377 Article 63 (7) UNCAC.

378 Transparency International, 'Effectively Monitoring the United Nations Convention against Corruption', *Policy Position Paper 1* (2008) at p. 3.

379 Transparency International, 'UN Corruption Conference: Failure to Act on Critical Issue a 'Major Setback' for the Fight against Corruption', *Press Release* (1 February 2008).

380 Conference of State Parties to the UNCAC, Resolution 3/1.

The UNCAC review process consists of a review of every State Party by two other State Parties, or to be more precise, their governmental experts.[381] One of these two reviewing States shall be from the same geographical region as the State under review.[382] The review results in a country review report, which includes successes, good practices, challenges and observations for the implementation of UNCAC.[383] These reports will remain confidential,[384] but may be published by the State under review,[385] and States shall, upon request, endeavour to make the review report accessible to other States.[386] Oversight of the UNCAC review process is in the hands of the Implementation Review Group (hereafter: IRG), consisting of State Party representatives.[387] The IRG meets at least once a year in Vienna[388] and reports to the Conference.[389] Currently, there are 26 first year country reviews under way, a number of which include country visits.[390]

4. Comparative Analysis

The previous section 3 demonstrated that a wide range of legal anti-corruption instruments is available in the global and regional sphere. What are the main similarities, differences, and shortcomings?

Regarding the content of the instruments, the following can be said. None of the instruments provides a clear, exhaustive definition of corruption and its various forms. As elaborated upon in chapter I, this is indeed a difficult task. The instruments therefore resort to an enumeration of various possible forms of corruption. Acts such as money laundering (which can be seen as a result, rather than type of corruption) are sometimes also labelled as 'acts of corruption'. Some instruments are much more narrow in scope than others. For example, the EU Convention remains limited to tackling bribery involving officials of the European Communities or officials of EU Member States. The OECD Convention only tackles the supply side of transnational bribery. The IACAC, the SADC and ECOWAS Protocols, the AU Convention and the UNCAC are much more comprehensive. Particularly relevant is the fact that all instruments mainly oblige State Parties to tackle corruption at the national level. Although most treaties call

---

381 Terms of reference for the Mechanism for the Review of Implementation of the United Nations Convention against Corruption, §18.

382 *Ibid.* §19.

383 *Ibid.* §33.

384 *Ibid.* §37.

385 *Ibid.* §38.

386 *Ibid.* §39.

387 *Ibid.* §42.

388 *Ibid.* §43.

389 *Ibid.* §42.

390 Gillian Dell, 'Update on the UNCAC Review Process', <www.uncaccoalition.org/en/home/166-update-on-the-uncac-review-process-government-self-assessments-online-and-irg-meeting.html>, accessed 26 May 2011.

for international cooperation, the criminalisation of corrupt offences thus remains a matter of national concern.

Obviously, the geographical scope of the instruments differs. The IACAC, the EU Conventions, the COE Conventions, the SADC and ECOWAS Protocols and the AU Convention are regional instruments, while ratification of the OECD Convention and the UNCAC is open to countries around the world.

Concerning monitoring and enforcement, there are some differences. The IACAC, the OECD Convention, COE Conventions, the SADC Protocol, the AU Convention and the UNCAC do have a follow-up mechanism, while the EU Conventions do not. The quality of the monitoring also differs: the mechanisms of the OECD and the COE seem to be the most developed. However, none of the mechanisms truly has teeth. It is especially a pity that the newly established UNCAC peer review mechanism results in confidential reports, and that the first round of assessments will take no less than 15 years to complete.[391]

It must be noted that the attention for corruption since the 1990s is a positive development. But unfortunately, the recently developed instruments share a number of weaknesses. First, the wording of several provisions is too soft. This is particularly true in respect of the UNCAC and the IACAC. For example, the criminalisation of embezzlement under the IACAC is only optional, as well as the adoption of preventive measures. In respect of the UNCAC, we find that a number of corrupt acts are optional, instead of mandatory for States to criminalise. The same holds true for the adoption of preventive measures.

The use of safeguard clauses also limits the effectiveness of legal instruments. Mainly the IACAC and the AU Convention suffer from this defect. Such clauses make certain provisions of the treaty dependent upon national legislation.

Furthermore, the existence of numerous instruments might be an issue of concern, since there is possible overlap and duplication of efforts regarding reporting procedures. States may be reluctant to look into each and every treaty provision in a meticulous way. Poor State Parties may also lack the staff, resources and expertise to implement the provisions of the anti-corruption treaties. In this respect, capacity-building is required to turn anti-corruption treaties into a success.

Moreover, as noted above, the main pillars of all treaties are prevention, criminalisation and enforcement at the national level. Although this is undoubtedly necessary, it is left to the discretion of State Parties whether they will adequately combat corruption. Moreover, given the lack of *binding* review mechanisms and the lack of enforcement possibilities if States do not comply, it depends upon national political will whether corruption is sufficiently addressed or not. Particularly in countries with rampant corruption at the top-level, the current instruments do not suffice. It is unlikely that heads of States and upper-level government officials involved in corruption themselves will adopt and enforce effective anti-corruption policies. If these actors will target the issue, their efforts will probably remain

[391] Stuart Levey, 'Fighting Corruption after the Arab Spring', *Foreign Affairs,* (16 June 2011).

limited to addressing the 'small fish', i.e. petty corruption, in order to divert attention from their own practices, or they will address alleged corruption by political opponents. As noted by Mbaku:

> ... throughout many African countries, anti-corruption programs initiated and implemented by the government are often administered selectively and capriciously and aimed primarily at the opponents of the incumbent government. In many instances, these programs are not designed to affect high-ranking government officials (including especially members of the ruling party), even if there is overwhelming evidence supporting the complicity of these individuals in venality. In fact, many African countries, such individuals are called 'untouchables'.[392]

More specifically within the Nigerian context, it was pointed out that there is a lack of political will to combat corruption, as well as a great deal of selectiveness as to who is prosecuted and who is not.[393] In addition, Hatchard pointed to the relatively few reported convictions for corruption worldwide, and called into question the use of criminal law as a main pillar for the fight against corruption.[394] Moreover, cases of grand corruption often possess a transnational element, which makes domestic prosecution difficult.[395] These matters certainly merit an analysis of anti-corruption strategies at the international level.

Thus, there are no clear assurances that the present instruments are able to effectively tackle corruption, particularly by those at the top-level of the State. Although the relevance of having anti-corruption treaties should not be downplayed, it is appropriate to examine whether additional approaches towards fighting corruption can be detected in the field of human rights and international criminal law. In these areas of law, it might be possible to tackle corruption at the international plane, which could facilitate the accountability of high-level officials.

---

392 John Mukum Mbaku, *Corruption in Africa: Causes, Consequences and Cleanups* (Plymouth: Lexington Books, 2007) at p. 145.

393 Ebenezer Durojaye, 'Corruption as a Threat to Human Security in Africa', in Ademola Abass (ed.), *Protecting Human Security in Africa* (Oxford: Oxford University Press, 2010), p. 217–243 at p. 236 *et seq.*

394 John Hatchard, 'Adopting a Human Rights Approach Towards Combating Corruption', in Martine Boersma and Hans Nelen (eds.), *Corruption & Human Rights: Interdisciplinary Perspectives* (Maastricht Series in Human Rights; Antwerp: Intersentia, 2010), p. 7–23 at p. 14.

395 *Ibid.* at p. 15.

Part B

Responsibility of States: Corruption as a Violation of Human Rights?

Chapter III
Treaty-Based System: Corruption as a Topic in the Work of the UN Human Rights Treaty Bodies

1. Introduction

The treaty-based system of international human rights protection consists of nine core human rights treaties.[1] Supervision of State Parties' compliance with the obligations laid down in these instruments is a task of the UN human rights treaty bodies. Each treaty establishes its own treaty body,[2] i.e. a Committee consisting of independent and impartial experts. The present chapter examines the output of two procedures of these treaty bodies: the State reporting procedure and the individual complaints procedure, the content of which is briefly described in sections 2 and 3 hereafter.[3] In order to discover what attention is being paid by the HRC, CESCR, CRC, CEDAW, CERD and CAT, in the two procedures, to the relationship between corruption and human rights, sections 4 to 9 consider, *inter alia*, the following questions. Which countries are scrutinised for corruption? In the context of which human rights is corruption discussed? What wording do the Committees adopt to condemn corrupt practices? Are there perhaps differences between the treaty bodies? Is it possible to detect any trends over time? At the outset it must be noted that up to 15 June 2011, the six treaty bodies have produced a total of 131 concluding observations in which corruption is discussed.[4] A table containing the full list of

---

1 In chronological order: the International Convention on the Elimination of All Forms of Racial Discrimination (ICERD, 1965); the International Covenant on Civil and Political Rights (ICCPR, 1966); the International Covenant on Economic, Social and Cultural Rights (ICESCR, 1966); the Covenant on the Elimination of All Forms of Discrimination Against Women (CEDAW, 1979); the Convention against Torture and Other Cruel, Inhuman or Degrading Treatment or Punishment (CAT, 1984); the United Nations Convention on the Rights of the Child (UNCRC, 1989); the International Convention on the Protection of the Rights of All Migrant Workers and Their Families (ICRMW, 1990); the International Convention for the Protection of All Persons from Enforced Disappearance (CPPED, 2006); and the Convention on the Rights of Persons with Disabilities (CRPD, 2006).

2 Note that the Committee on Economic, Social and Cultural Rights was not established by the Covenant itself, but by ECOSOC Resolution 1985/17 of 28 May 1985. The Members of the Committee were elected in May 1986, and the Committee's first session was held in March 1987. See Christian Tomuschat, *Human Rights: Between Idealism and Realism* 2 edn., The Collected Courses of the Academy of European Law, XIII/1; Oxford: Oxford University Press, 2008) at p. 172.

3 Other procedures of the UN treaty bodies are the inter-State complaints procedure and the inquiry procedure, which fall outside of the scope of the present work.

4 While there are nine core human rights treaties, only six treaty bodies are examined since, at the time of writing, (i) the Committee on Enforced Disappearances (CED) did not yet function; (ii) the Committee on Migrant Workers (CMW) started functioning only very recently; and (iii) the Committee on the Rights of Persons with Disabilities (CRPD) had not yet adopted any concluding observations.

observations, organised alphabetically per country and including the scores on the 2011 Corruption Perceptions Index, can be found in Annex 1. After discussing treaty body practice, conclusions are drawn in section 10.

2. State Reporting Procedure

2.1. Overview

The main method of monitoring compliance with human rights treaty obligations is the process of State reporting, which is contained in all core human rights treaties at the international level. Under this procedure, each State Party must submit a periodic report (every two to five years, depending on the treaty), on the implementation of its obligations under each treaty to which it is a Party.[5] When writing the report, States ought to follow the reporting guidelines of the treaty bodies. In 2008, a set of harmonised guidelines on reporting under the international human rights treaties was adopted, in order to simplify the reporting procedures of the various treaty bodies.[6] Under the new procedure, State Parties have to submit reports that consist of (i) a common core document; and (ii) treaty-specific documents. In Appendix 3 to the new harmonised guidelines, we can find a list of indicators for assessing the implementation of human rights, on which States have to report. These are demographic indicators; social, economic and cultural indicators; indicators on the political system; and indicators on crime and the administration of justice. None of these lists of indicators includes reference to the level of corruption in a country.

After the State has submitted its documents, the treaty body presents the State with a list of issues and questions based on concerns raised by the State report.[7] The State may write a reply to the list of issues and questions. Hereafter, a so-called

---

5 Office of the United Nations High Commissioner for Human Rights, The United Nations Human Rights Treaty System: An Introduction to the Core Human Rights Treaties and the Treaty Bodies, *Fact sheet No. 30* <www2.ohchr.org/english/bodies/docs/OHCHR-FactSheet30.pdf>, accessed 20 June 2011, at p. 29–33. and Office of the United Nations High Commissioner for Human Rights, The Reporting Cycle under the Human Rights Treaties, <www2.ohchr.org/english/bodies/docs/ReportingCycle.gif>. For an extensive analysis of the functioning of the treaty bodies and the State reporting procedures, see Philip Alston and James Crawford (eds.), *The Future of UN Human Rights Treaty Monitoring* (Cambridge: Cambridge University Press, 2000); Anne F. Bayefsky (ed.), *The UN Human Rights Treaty System in the 21st Century* (The Hague: Kluwer Law International, 2000); Michael O'Flaherty, *Human Rights and the UN: Practice before the Treaty Bodies* (2 edn., Nijhoff Law Specials, 54; The Hague: Kluwer Law International, 2002).

6 Compilation of guidelines on the form and content of reports to be submitted by States parties to the international human rights treaties, 3 June 2009, UN Doc. HRI/GEN/2/Rev.6.

7 CAT and CERD do not adopt lists of issues, and CEDAW does not adopt lists of issues for initial reports. Anne F. Bayefsky, *The UN Human Rights Treaty System: Universality at the Crossroads* (Ardsley, NY: Transnational Publishers, 2001) at p. 35.

constructive dialogue takes place between the Committee and the delegates of the State Party. This oral dialogue results in the adoption of concluding observations by the treaty body, which are non-binding yet authoritative recommendations addressed to the State concerned.[8] In respect of follow-up procedures to the concluding observations, the practice varies among treaty bodies.[9]

2.2. Language Employed in the Treaty Bodies' Concluding Observations

Before considering the various concluding observations of the treaty bodies on the specific matter of corruption, some remarks must be made about the way in which the observations of the Committees are formulated. Various authors have commented upon the language used by the treaty bodies in their concluding observations. Particularly the observations of the CESCR have received a great deal of attention from scholars.

In 1993, Coomans elaborated upon the phraseology of the CESCR. He noted that the observations in which the CESCR expresses its '(serious) concern' deal with grave situations where the CESCR has in fact concluded that a State does not comply with its treaty obligations. In some cases, the CESCR found that a violation of one or more treaty provisions has taken place. Coomans noted the reluctance of the CESCR to qualify a certain situation as a violation of the Covenant or to label a State as a violator. The CESCR has done so primarily with regard to the right to housing. The CESCR seems to reserve the qualification 'violation' for serious matters where a State Party has unequivocally disrespected the provisions of the Covenant, for example in cases of the large-scale forced evictions in the Dominican Republic and Panama. This stance is affirmed in the CESCR's General Comment No. 4. Coomans observed that the reluctant attitude of the CESCR is probably due to the difficulties it has in qualifying what amounts to a violation. Furthermore, it might not be clear what the content of a treaty norm is and what State obligations it entails.[10] More generally, in international fora it is not quickly concluded that a

8 Office of the United Nations High Commissioner for Human Rights, 'The United Nations Human Rights Treaty System: An Introduction to the Core Human Rights Treaties and the Treaty Bodies', at p. 29–33. On the legal status of concluding observations, see Michael O'Flaherty, 'The Concluding Observations of the United Nations Human Rights Treaty Bodies', Human Rights Law Review, 6 (2006), p. 27–52 at p. 32–37.

9 For more on the follow-up to concluding observations, see O'Flaherty, 'The Concluding Observations of the United Nations Human Rights Treaty Bodies', at p. 47–51, as well as Bert G. Ramcharan, 'Follow-up of the Treaty Body Conclusions by the Treaty Mechanisms and the UN Mechanisms Beyond', in: Anne F. Bayefsky (ed.), *The UN Human Rights Treaty System in the 21st Century* (The Hague: Kluwer Law International, 2000), p. 277–283; Markus G. Schmidt, 'Follow-up Mechanisms before UN Human Rights Treaty Bodies and the UN Mechanisms Beyond', in: Anne F. Bayefsky (ed.), *The UN Human Rights Treaty System in the 21st Century* (The Hague: Kluwer Law International, 2000), p. 233–249.

10 Fons Coomans, 'Schendingen Van Economische, Sociale En Culturele Rechten', in: Fons Coomans, A.W. Heringa, and Ingrid Westendorp (eds.), *De Toenemende Betekenis Van*

violation of an economic, social or cultural right has taken place. Usually it is determined that a State Party does not (entirely) comply with the norm, or that practice is not (entirely) in conformity with the norm. Often these expressions conceal the fact that a supervisory body has not been able to univocally assess whether a State Party acts in conformity with the international norm.[11]

Similarly, Chapman noted in 1996 the reluctance of the CESCR 'to use explicit violations terminology, preferring to express its 'principal subjects of concern', and to make 'suggestions and recommendations'.[12] In her view, 'like many other actors within the UN system, the Committee is inclined to diplomatic formulations and disinclined to label inadequacies and problems as violations.'[13] Moreover, 'while the Committee comes close to using the language of violations, it is reluctant to use it explicitly.' In her work on the violations approach, Chapman noted that she has translated 'concerns' and 'recommendations' into violations.[14] In a piece from 2007, Chapman noted that 'when reviewing the performance of specific States parties, the Committee still prefers the language of 'concerns' to 'violations', but it has been willing to label serious problems as violations.'[15]

Leckie pointed out in 1998 that:

> ... even the Committee on Economic, Social and Cultural Rights, with its incomparable overall record regarding its supervisory functions in raising the stature of the ICESCR, has only infrequently, and then often softly, declared violators of the ICESCR as violators. Moreover, numerous factors may further limit the future use of violations terminology: ongoing tension between the Committee's desire for constructive dialogue (the role of 'honest broker' or inquisitor) and the designation of violations (the role of adjudicator, adversary, or truth seeker); re-election fears of particular members; discomfort about alienating States parties (often at the expense of victims of abuse); and frequent expression of questionable ideological points of view fundamentally at odds with the object and purpose of the ICESCR itself by several current Committee members.[16]

Sepúlveda noted in 2003 that the wording used by the CESCR in its concluding observations is 'rather diplomatic and soft.' However, she observed that:

Economische, Sociale En Culturele Mensenrechten (Leiden: Stichting NJCM-Boekerij, 1994), p. 59–73 at p. 65.

11 *Ibid.* at p. 66.

12 Audrey R. Chapman, 'A "Violations Approach" For Monitoring the International Covenant on Economic, Social and Cultural Rights', *Human Rights Quarterly*, 18 (1996), p. 23–66 at p. 41.

13 *Ibid.* at p. 48.

14 *Ibid.* at p. 49.

15 Audrey R. Chapman, 'The Status of Efforts to Monitor Economic, Social and Cultural Rights', in: Shareen Hertel and Lanse Minkler (eds.), *Economic Rights: Conceptual, Measurement and Policy Issues* (Cambridge University Press, 2007), p. 143–164 at p. 156.

16 Scott Leckie, 'Another Step Towards Indivisibility: Identifying the Key Features of Violations of Economic, Social and Cultural Rights', *Human Rights Quarterly*, 20 (1998), p. 81–124 at p. 122.

> ... over the years the Committee has gradually begun to take a more adversarial position. Nowadays, it is not rare for the Committee to explicitly state that there has been a 'violation' or a 'breach' of the Covenant or that a given action or omission is 'incompatible' with the Covenant. More frequently, the Committee comes close to stating that a violation has occurred by using the terms 'urge', 'calls upon States', to do or not to do something, or expresses 'concern' or 'grave concern' with respect to specific State actions or omissions. When we consider that the concluding observations generally adopt cautions, diplomatic wording and that the Committee usually only 'recommends' that State parties should adopt or abstain from a given course of action, these expressions indeed constitute 'imperative language'. As they emanate from an authoritative body, they allow us to identify the obligations of the Covenant without great speculation.[17]

In sum, there is a slight shift in the terminology used by the CESCR in its concluding observations. The use of 'violations language' is less uncommon nowadays than it used to be in the mid-1990s. When the treaty bodies are 'deeply/seriously/gravely concerned' about a certain practice, and '(strongly) urge' or 'call upon' the State Party to take action, this is an indication that a State does not comply with its obligations under the particular treaty. Nevertheless, also the more soft and diplomatic statements made by the treaty bodies must be taken into account. Given the fact that corruption is a topic with a high degree of political sensitivity, one would indeed expect the use of diplomatic terms.

There is also criticism on the differentiation in formulation by the treaty bodies. O'Flaherty found that:

> ... this form of prioritisation carries with it a particular danger of arbitrary or capricious application, not least given the perils of attempting to hierarchically rank the sentiments lying behind specific verbs, adverbs and adjectives. [...] If it is to be applied at all, it would seem to be important that attempts be made to do so within the confines of a strictly defined lexicography which ensures consistent application.[18]

It was then noted that the CAT only uses the terms 'expresses concern' and 'recommends'. CERD, CESCR and the HRC employ 'concerned', 'notes with 'regret/concern', 'recommends', 'invites', 'should', 'urges', etc., while words such as 'very' and 'strongly' are occasionally added.[19] O'Flaherty pointed out that:

> ... it is not clear though why some matters merit terms such as 'very concerned' and 'strongly recommended', while others do not. The matter is all the more unclear where a treaty body is 'deeply concerned' but then no more than 'recommends' a

---

17 Magdalena Sepúlveda, *The Nature of the Obligations under the International Covenant on Economic, Social and Cultural Rights* (School of Human Rights Research, 18; Antwerpen: Intersentia, 2003) at p. 211.

18 O'Flaherty, 'The Concluding Observations of the United Nations Human Rights Treaty Bodies', at p. 45–46.

19 *Ibid.* at p. 46.

> remedial action. Practice in CRC and CEDAW is somewhat more uneven, with a higher proportion of concerns which are 'deeply' held and actions which are 'urged' rather than 'recommended'. Also it is not uncommon for something to arouse 'deep concern for CRC but only result in a 'recommendation', and so forth. The typically lengthy and complex recommendations of CEDAW often simultaneously contain multiple verbs, such as 'urges'/'recommends', 'calls upon'/'invites' and 'requests'/'encourages'.[20]

Hence, the way in which concluding observations, including those on corruption, are formulated by the various treaty bodies should be taken with a considerable pinch of salt.

3. Individual Complaints Procedure

A number of treaty bodies are competent to consider complaints from individuals about alleged violations of their rights under the treaty concerned: the Human Rights Committee (under the First Optional Protocol to the ICCPR);[21] the Committee on Economic, Social and Cultural Rights (under the Optional Protocol to the ICESCR);[22] the Committee on the Elimination of Discrimination Against Women (under the Optional Protocol to the Women's Convention); the Committee Against Torture (under Article 22 CAT); the Committee on the Elimination of Racial Discrimination (under Article 14 CERD); the Committee on Migrant Workers (under Article 77 CMW); and the Committee on the Rights of Persons with Disabilities (under the Optional Protocol to the CRPD).[23]

Before it is possible for an individual to submit a complaint to one of the Committees, it is necessary that the State concerned has recognised the competence of the treaty body to consider complaints. This can be done by becoming a Party to

20 *Ibid.*

21 See Henry J. Steiner, 'Individual Claims in a World of Massive Violations: What Role for the Human Rights Committee?' in: Philip Alston and James Crawford (eds.), *The Future of UN Human Rights Treaty Monitoring* (Cambridge: Cambridge University Press, 2000), p. 15–53.

22 The Optional Protocol to the ICESCR is not yet in force. It will enter into force as soon as ten States have ratified/acceded. Currently, only five States are Party to the OP: Ecuador, Mongolia, Spain, Argentina and El Salvador, while it was signed by 39 States. See the database of the UN Treaty Collection at <http://treaties.un.org/Home.aspx?lang=en>, accessed 7 January 2012.

23 See Office of the United Nations High Commissioner for Human Rights, 'The United Nations Human Rights Treaty System: An Introduction to the Core Human Rights Treaties and the Treaty Bodies', at p. 33–34 and <www2.ohchr.org/english/bodies/complaints.htm>, accessed 20 June 2011. For more on the individual complaints procedures, see Andrew Byrnes, 'An Effective Complaints Procedure in the Context of International Human Rights Law', in: Anne F. Bayefsky (ed.), *The UN Human Rights Treaty System in the 21st Century* (The Hague: Kluwer Law International, 2000), p. 139–162. and David Kretzmer and Peter Burns, 'Commentary on Complaint Processes by Human Rights Committee and Torture Committee Members', in: Anne F. Bayefsky (ed.), *The UN Human Rights Treaty System in the 21st Century* (The Hague: Kluwer Law International, 2000), p. 163–167.

the mentioned Optional Protocols, or by making a declaration as required by the relevant provisions in CAT, CERD, and CMW.[24] Furthermore, it is required that individuals have exhausted domestic remedies, and it is not allowed for the issue at hand to be investigated under another international procedure.[25] The individual complaints procedure results in the adoption of so-called 'views' by the relevant Committee. These views are not binding, but are nevertheless regarded as highly authoritative.

4. Human Rights Committee (HRC)

4.1. Concluding Observations

The Human Rights Committee, supervising State compliance with the International Covenant on Civil and Political Rights, is composed of eighteen experts[26] and first met in 1977.[27] As of 1992, the HRC issues collective concluding observations, while previously, only a compilation of concluding observations of individual Committee members were issued.[28] In the Human Rights Committee's concluding observations,[29] the topic of corruption featured in 28 observations.[30] These can be classified into a number of thematic categories.

4.1.1. The Right to Equality Before Courts and Tribunals and to a Fair Trial

The large majority of the Human Rights Committee's observations about corruption are concerned with corruption in the judiciary, which is related to Article 14 of the

24 Office of the United Nations High Commissioner for Human Rights, 'The United Nations Human Rights Treaty System: An Introduction to the Core Human Rights Treaties and the Treaty Bodies', at p. 34.

25 See *inter alia* the First Optional Protocol to the ICCPR.

26 For more on the work of the HRC, see <www2.ohchr.org/english/bodies/hrc/index.htm>, accessed 15 June 2011.

27 Manfred Nowak, *UN Covenant on Civil and Political Rights: CCPR Commentary* (second edn.; Kehl: Engel, 2005) at p. XXIV, §12.

28 O'Flaherty, 'The Concluding Observations of the United Nations Human Rights Treaty Bodies', at p. 29–30.

29 For an extensive analysis of the reporting procedure under the ICCPR, see Ineke Boerefijn, The Reporting Procedure under the Covenant on Civil and Political Rights: Practice and Procedure of the Human Rights Committee (School of Human Rights Research Series, 2; Antwerp: Intersentia, 1999), as well as Yogesh Tyagi, *The UN Human Rights Committee: Practice and Procedure* (Cambridge: Cambridge University Press, 2011) at chapter 3.

30 In chronological order: Italy (1994); Macau (1997); Georgia (1997); Algeria (1998); Cambodia (1999); Macau (1999); Kyrgyz Republic (2000); Trinidad and Tobago (2000); Argentina (2000); Georgia (2002); Benin (2004); Albania (2004); Kenya (2005); Brazil (2005); Congo (2006); Central African Republic (2006); Kosovo (2006); Bosnia and Herzegovina (2006); Ukraine (2006); Georgia (2007); Macedonia (2008); Rwanda (2009); Chad (2009); Azerbaijan (2009), Moldova (2009); Russia (2009); Uzbekistan (2010); and Mongolia (2011).

ICCPR: the right to equality before courts and tribunals and the right to a fair trial. In the first observation on the matter, issued in 1999, the HRC stated, *inter alia*, that it 'is *concerned* that the justice system remains weak due to [...] [judges'] susceptibility to bribery and political pressure'. For this reason, the Committee found that Cambodia '*should take urgent measures* to strengthen the judiciary and to guarantee its independence, and to ensure that all allegations of corruption or undue pressure on the judiciary are dealt with promptly' [emphasis added, MB].[31]

Observations of a similar character were made in respect of Kyrgyzstan (2000),[32] Georgia (2002 and 2007),[33] Benin (2004),[34] Albania (2004),[35] Kenya (2005),[36] Brazil (2005),[37] Congo (2006),[38] the Central African Republic (2006),[39] Kosovo (2006),[40] Ukraine (2006)[41] Rwanda (2009),[42] Chad (2009),[43] Azerbaijan (2009),[44] Moldova (2009),[45] Russia (2009),[46] and Mongolia (2011).[47] In these observations, the Committee expressed its 'concern' about judicial corruption, and found that the particular State 'should' take necessary measures to combat the practice, to investigate complaints about the matter, and to punish perpetrators. On a few occasions, a brief mention was made of possible causes of corruption, such as low salaries and delays in the payment thereof, and the lack of security of tenure.[48]

The topic of judicial corruption is clearly placed by the Committee in the context of the obligations of Article 14 of the ICCPR: judicial independence, judicial impartiality and access to courts. For example, according to the observations on Kenya (2005), 'the Committee *notes with concern* that because of, *inter alia*, widespread corruption, the access of citizens to domestic courts and to judicial remedies is limited in practice.'[49] Consequently, according to the HRC, 'the State Party *should ensure* that all individuals subject to its jurisdiction have equal access

31 HRC CO Cambodia 27 July 1999, UN Doc. CCPR/C/79/Add.108, §. 8 and 10.
32 HRC CO Kyrgyzstan 24 July 2000, UN Doc. CCPR/CO/69/KGZ, §. 15.
33 HRC CO Georgia 19 April 2002, UN Doc. CCPR/CO/74/GEO, §12 and HRC CO Georgia 15 November 2007, UN Doc. CCPR/C/GEO/CO/3, §13.
34 HRC CO Benin 1 December 2004, UN Doc. CCPR/CO/82/BEN, §18.
35 HRC CO Albania 2 December 2004, UN Doc. CCPR/CO/82/ALB, §18.
36 HRC CO Kenya 29 April 2005, UN Doc. CCPR/CO/83/KEN, §9 and 20.
37 HRC CO Brazil 1 December 2005, UN Doc. CCPR/C/BRA/CO/2, §17.
38 HRC CO Congo 26 April 2006, UN Doc. CCPR/C/COD/CO/3, §21.
39 HRC CO Central African Republic 27 July 2006, UN Doc. CCPR/C/CAF/CO/2, §16.
40 HRC CO Kosovo 14 August 2006, UN Doc. CCPR/C/UNK/CO/1, §20.
41 HRC CO Ukraine 28 November 2006, UN Doc. CCPR/C/UKR/CO/6, §17.
42 HRC CO Rwanda 31 March 2009, UN Doc. CCPR/C/RWA/CO/3, §17.
43 HRC CO Chad 11 August 2009, UN Doc. CCPR/C/TCD/CO/1, §26.
44 HRC CO Azerbaijan 13 August 2009, UN Doc. CCPR/C/AZE/CO/3, §12.
45 HRC CO Moldova 4 November 2009, UN Doc. CCPR/C/MDA/CO/2, §23.
46 HRC CO Russia 24 November 2009, UN Doc. CCPR/C/RUS/CO/6, §21.
47 HRC CO Mongolia 2 May 2011, UN Doc. CCPR/C/MNG/CO/5, §17.
48 HRC CO Kyrgyzstan 24 July 2000, §15; HRC CO Georgia 19 April 2002, §12; HRC CO Congo 26 April 2006, §21; HRC CO Ukraine 28 November 2006, §17.
49 HRC CO Kenya 29 April 2005, UN Doc. CCPR/CO/83/KEN, §9.

to judicial and other remedies' [emphasis added, MB].[50] Later on in the same observations, the Committee stated that:

> ... it *remains concerned* about reports of serious dysfunctions in the administration of justice, owing primarily to the lack of human and material resources as well as the slow pace of proceedings. While the Committee *appreciates* recent Government measures such as the adoption of the Anti-Corruption and Economic Crimes Commission, which led to the resignation or suspension of many High Court and Court of Appeal judges, it *notes* that allegations of judicial corruption persist, a situation that *seriously undermines* the independence and impartiality of the judiciary (Article 2 and 14 of the Covenant).[51]

As a result, 'the State Party *should give priority* to its efforts to combat corruption in the judiciary and to address the need to provide increased resources to the administration of justice' [emphasis added, MB].[52] Although the Committee does not state *expressis verbis* that forms of judicial corruption constitute a 'violation' of component parts of Article 14, this is the closest the Human Rights Committee comes.

The Committee seems to take an increasing interest in judicial corruption, since the largest part of the observations is from a rather recent date. Furthermore, the countries that are being criticised for judicial corruption are located in many of the world's continents. However, since judicial corruption is rampant in many more countries than the 17 States listed, it remains unclear why the Committtee decided to issue observations in respect of these States, while not addressing the problem in countries with similar levels of judicial corruption. Perhaps the information provided by third parties (particularly NGOs), or the lack thereof, plays a role in this respect. At the moment, the matter appears to be addressed in a rather random fashion. Moreover, given the fact that the Human Rights Committee holds three sessions each year, and scrutinises multiple States during each of these sessions, the total number of concluding observations on judicial corruption is surprisingly low, particularly given the widespread nature of judicial corruption throughout the world.[53]

Nowhere does the Human Rights Committee specify what definition of corruption it employs. In its observations on Kyrgyzstan (2000), the Committee seems to distinguish between corruption and bribery,[54] although it is likely that not too much value should be attached to the single use of this phrase.

---

50 HRC CO Kenya 29 April 2005, UN Doc. CCPR/CO/83/KEN, §9.

51 HRC CO Kenya 29 April 2005, UN Doc. CCPR/CO/83/KEN, §20.

52 HRC CO Kenya 29 April 2005, UN Doc. CCPR/CO/83/KEN, §20.

53 As evidenced in Transparency International, Global Corruption Report 2007: Corruption in Judicial Systems (Cambridge: Cambridge University Press, 2007).

54 HRC CO Kyrgyzstan 24 July 2000, §15, stating 'The Committee notes that the applicable attestation procedure for judges, the requirement of re-evaluation every seven years, the low level of salaries and the uncertain tenure of judges may encourage corruption and bribery.'

4.1.2. The Prohibition of Human Trafficking

The relationship between the conduct of corrupt public officials and the occurrence of human trafficking is a topic that was discussed by the Human Rights Committee on four occasions: in respect of Cambodia (1999),[55] Albania (2004),[56] Brazil (2005),[57] and Bosnia and Herzegovina (2006).[58] The observations demonstrate that the Committee is 'concerned' about the role of (police or government) officials in human trafficking, and that States 'should' combat trafficking-related corruption. In respect of Bosnia and Herzegovina, the Committee found that judges, prosecutors and law enforcement officers should receive intensified training on the application of anti-trafficking and anti-corruption standards.[59]

In the concluding observations on the role of corruption in human trafficking, the HRC referred to Article 8 of the ICCPR, since it is generally understood that the prohibition of human trafficking falls under the scope of this provision, which lays down the prohibition of slavery and slave-trade, servitude, and forced or compulsory labour.[60]

4.1.3. The Right to Freedom of Movement

In three of its observations, the Committee briefly addressed the links between corruption and the right to freedom of movement as enshrined in Article 12 ICCPR: in respect of Georgia (1997),[61] Azerbaijan (2009),[62] and Uzbekistan (2010).[63] In the observations on Georgia, 'the Committee *regrets* that, despite the elimination of the *propiska* [i.e. the internal passport], there remain obstacles to freedom of movement within the country. It *notes with concern* that there continues to be a great deal of corruption in this area' [emphasis added, MB].[64] In its observations on Azerbaijan:

> … the Committee *remains concerned* that, in spite of the achievements by the State Party's authorities in addressing the problems of the large number of internally displaced persons following the 1991–94 conflict with Armenia, in particular in Nagorny Karabakh, such people continue to face problems in obtaining address registration (*propiska*), which may expose them to corrupt practices, depriving them of a large number of social entitlements and allowances and of the enjoyment of a

55 HRC CO Cambodia 27 July 1999, UN Doc. CCPR/C/79/Add.108, §16.
56 HRC CO Albania 2 December 2004, UN Doc. CCPR/CO/82.ALB, §15.
57 HRC CO Brazil 1 December 2005, UN Doc. CCPR/C/BRA/CO/2, §15.
58 HRC CO Bosnia and Herzegovina 22 November 2006, UN Doc. CCPR/C/BIH/CO/1, §16.
59 HRC CO Bosnia and Herzegovina 22 November 2006, UN Doc. CCPR/C/BIH/CO/1, §16.
60 Nowak, *UN Covenant on Civil and Political Rights: CCPR Commentary* at p. 200 at §213.
61 HRC CO Georgia 5 May 1997, UN Doc. CCPR/C/79/Add.75, §6.
62 HRC CO Azerbaijan 13 August 2009, UN Doc. CCPR/C/AZE/CO/3, §18.
63 HRC CO Uzbekistan 7 April 2010 CCPR/C/UZB/CO/3, §18.
64 HRC CO Georgia 5 May 1997, UN Doc. CCPR/C/79/Add.75,§6 and 19.

> number of rights, including in the areas of employment and health. In general, the Committee *reiterates its concern* that the existence of the address registration (*propiska*) system violates the right to freedom of movement and choice of residence under article 12 of the Covenant (Articles 2, 12 and 26) [emphasis added, MB].[65]

Therefore, 'the State Party *should* simplify its address registration procedure, so as to enable all individuals who reside legally in Azerbaijan, including internally displaced persons, to fully exercise their rights and freedoms under the Covenant' [emphasis added].[66] Furthermore, in respect of Uzbekistan:

> … the Committee remains concerned about the need for individuals to receive an exit visa in order to be able to travel abroad. It is also *concerned* that the State Party maintains the compulsory address registration of individuals (*propiska*), which may interfere with the enjoyment of a number of other rights under the Covenant, and may result in abuses and permit corruption (Article 12) [emphasis added].[67]

Hence, 'the State Party *should* abolish the exit visa system, and also ensure that its address registration system (*propiska*) is in compliance with the provisions of article 12 of the Covenant' [emphasis added, MB].[68] This observation reveals that the requirement of address registration (*propiska*) can enable corruption.

4.1.4. Miscellaneous Observations

A number of the Human Rights Committee's observations on corruption are not related to a specific civil or political human right. For example, the observations made in respect of Macedonia (2008) stated that:

> … the Committee, while commending the numerous efforts taken by the State party to combat corruption, be it high-level or small scale, with a view to achieving the 'zero tolerance' goal for corruption in the State party, *remains concerned* about the persistence of corruption and its negative impact on the full enjoyment of the rights guaranteed by the Covenant (Article 2). The State Party *should* continue its efforts to combat corruption so that attitudes in society change and corruption is not perceived as unavoidable [emphasis added, MB].[69]

Furthermore, the earliest observation on corruption, made in 1994 in respect of Italy, stated that the Committee '*notes* that there are difficulties in implementing the necessary struggle against organised crime and corruption, especially in the highest spheres of power, in a manner that is compatible with the provisions of the

---

65 HRC CO Azerbaijan 13 August 2009, UN Doc. CCPR/C/AZE/CO/3, §18.

66 *Ibid.* §18.

67 HRC CO Uzbekistan 7 April 2010, UN Doc. CCPR/C/UZB/CO/3, §18.

68 *Ibid.* §18.

69 HRC CO Macedonia 17 April 2008, UN Doc. CCPR/C/MKD/CO/2, §8.

Covenant' [emphasis added, MB].[70] This observation reveals the tension that may exist between combating corruption and respecting human rights while doing so.

The observations on Macau (1997) indicated that the Human Rights Committee sees an anti-corruption body as an institution to protect human rights, since it noted that it 'welcomes the setting up of new institutions and offices to protect human rights, such as the Public Information and Assistance Centre and the High Commission against Corruption and Administrative Illegality.'[71] In respect of Russia (2009), the Committee noted as positive aspects the 2008 adoption of the National Plan on Countering Corruption and the enactment of the Federal Law on Counteraction of Corruption.[72]

Moreover, the Committee once referred to the existence of corruption in prisons in Argentina (2000)[73] and to police corruption in Trinidad and Tobago (2000).[74] In the observations on Algeria (1998), the Committee found that in this country, freedom of expression is restricted where it concerns coverage of allegations and discussion of corruption and criticism of government officials.[75]

4.2. Views on Individual Complaints

When examining the Human Rights Committee's views on individual complaints, we find that only a small number of complaints are related to corruption.[76]

First of all, there are a few complaints about the maltreatment of persons who expose corrupt practices (whistleblowers). An example is *Philip Afuson Njaru v. Cameroon.*[77] Afuson Njaru is a Cameroon journalist and human rights advocate, who wrote articles in which he criticised police corruption and violence of the security forces. In response to this criticism, he was harassed, severely beaten, threatened and arrested by police officials on various occasions. Judicial authorities have not initiated investigations after Afuson Njaru filed complaints against his treatment. The Human Rights Committee found violations of several rights, including Article 19, i.e. the freedom of expression. It was stated that:

> ... in the circumstances of the author's case, the Committee concludes that the author has demonstrated the relationship between the treatment against him and his

---

70 HRC CO Italy 3 August 1994, UN Doc. CCPR/C/79/Add.37, §2.

71 HRC CO Portugal (Macau) 5 May 1997, UN Doc. CCPR/C/79/Add.77, §10. The HRC refers again to the Anti-Corruption Commission in the concluding observations of 4 November 1999, UN Doc. CCPR/C/79/Add.115, §8.

72 HRC CO Russia 24 November 2009, UN Doc. CCPR/C/RUS/CO/6.

73 HRC CO Argentina 15 November 2000, UN Doc. CCPR/CO/70/ARG, §11.

74 HRC CO Trinidad and Tobago 10 November 2000, UN Doc. CCPR/CO/70/TTO, §14.

75 HRC CO Algeria 18 August 1998, UN Doc. CCPR/C/79/Add.95, §16.

76 For more on the individual communication procedure of the HRC, see Tyagi, *The UN Human Rights Committee: Practice and Procedure*, at chapter 5.

77 Communication no. 1353/2005, *Philip Afuson Njaru v. Cameroon*, views of 19 March 2007, UN Doc. CCPR/C/89/D/1353/2005.

activities as journalist and therefore that there has been a violation of article 19, paragraph 2, in conjunction with article 2, paragraph 3 of the Covenant.[78]

Another case where a journalist was arrested for having criticised corruption is *Rafael Marques de Morais v. Angola.*[79]

Furthermore, there are a small number of cases in which the applicant claims that due to judicial corruption, he did not receive a fair trial in the State Party concerned. An example is *Munguwambuto Kabwe Peter Mwamba v. Zambia,*[80] where the author of the complaint (a high ranking police officer convicted of murder and sentenced to death by the High Court) argued, *inter alia,* that he did not receive a fair trial because the judge and the State prosecutor were bribed. Moreover, the Inspector of Police allegedly orchestrated the author's conviction, because the author had previously tried to remove this Inspector for corruption. The applicant suggested that police officers had been bribed to produce false evidence and testimonies, and that the judges were influenced by police statements in the media during the investigation phase.[81] Furthermore, the wife of the author was informed by public officials that upon appeal, the death sentence would be confirmed by the Supreme Court, because the author had lodged a number of complaints, including complaints of corruption on the part of the judge and the police.[82] While the Committee found violations of Articles 6(1); 10(1); 14(2); 14(3)(c); 14(5); 6; and 7 for a number of reasons, it did not address the matter of judicial corruption in its views. In particular, it is peculiar that the Committee does not discuss the requirement of judicial impartiality of Article 14(1) in the context of the factual situation as described by the complainant. Another case in which the applicant argued that he did not receive a fair trial due to corruption is *Zdzislaw Bator v. Poland.* This case was found inadmissible because domestic remedies in respect of the claim of judicial corruption were not exhausted.[83]

Moreover, there is one substantial reference to prison corruption, in *Michael and Brian Hill v. Spain* (1997).[84] The case concerned two British brothers who were arrested in Spain, on suspicion of having firebombed a bar. Amongst other things, they complain that, during their police custody, they did not receive any food or drink for five days and very little during the remaining period of five days, because

---

78 *Philip Afuson Njaru v. Cameroon*, §6.4.

79 Communication no. 1128/2002, *Rafael Marques de Morais v. Angola*, views of 29 March 2005, UN Doc. CCPR/C/83/D/1128/2002.

80 Communication no. 1520/2006, *Munguwambuto Kabwe Peter Mwamba v. Zambia,* views of 10 March 2010, UN Doc. CCPR/C/98/D/1520/2006.

81 *Munguwambuto Kabwe Peter Mwamba v. Zambia,* §2.4.

82 *Munguwambuto Kabwe Peter Mwamba v. Zambia,* §2.6.

83 Communication no. 1037/2001, *Zdzislaw Bator v. Poland,* inadmissibility decision of 22 July 2005, UN Doc. CCPR/C/84/D/1037/2001.

84 Communication no. 526/1993, *Michael and Brian Hill v. Spain*, views of 22 June 1997, UN Doc. CCPR/C/59/D/526/1993.

the allocation of funds specifically for this purpose were misappropriated.[85] The HRC found that such treatment of detainees amounts to a violation of Article 10 of the ICCPR. This case demonstrates that corrupt acts, such as misappropriation of funds intended for food, can lead to a violation of Article 10.

5. Committee on Economic, Social and Cultural Rights (CESCR)

Unlike the other treaty bodies, the Committee on Economic, Social and Cultural Rights (hereafter: CESCR) was not established by the human rights treaty itself. Rather, supervision of the International Covenant on Economic, Social and Cultural Rights (hereafter: ICESCR) was left to ECOSOC. In its turn, ECOSOC created two successive Working Groups which had the task of monitoring State compliance with the Covenant. Because of discontent with the work of these Working Groups, the Committee on Economic, Social and Cultural Rights was established by ECOSOC in 1985. The first session of the CESCR took place in 1987,[86] and the Committee started to adopt country-specific observations in 1990.[87] The CESCR consists of eighteen experts.[88]

In 31 of the Committee's observations, the topic of corruption was addressed. A number of observations show that, in the view of the Committee, corruption has a negative impact upon the (equal) enjoyment, implementation, realisation, or (full) exercise of economic, social and cultural rights. These are the observations on Nigeria (1998),[89] Mexico (1999),[90] Guatemala (2003),[91] Moldova (2003),[92] Tajikistan (2006),[93] Latvia (2008),[94] Kenya (2008),[95] Madagascar (2009),[96] Sri Lanka (2010),[97] and Russia (2011).[98] In other observations, the committee expresses in general its '(deep) concern' about corrupt practices, and 'recommends' or '(strongly) urges' States to address the problem. Such observations were made in

85 §2.7 and 10.4.

86 Sepúlveda, *The Nature of the Obligations under the International Covenant on Economic, Social and Cultural Rights,* at p. 29–31.

87 O'Flaherty, 'The Concluding Observations of the United Nations Human Rights Treaty Bodies', at p. 30.

88 For more on the work of CESCR, see <www2.ohchr.org/english/bodies/cescr/index.htm>, accessed 20 June 2011.

89 CESCR CO Nigeria 13 May 1998, UN Doc. E/C.12/1/Add.23, §3 and 25.

90 CESCR CO Mexico 8 December 1999, UN Doc. E/C.12/1/Add.41, §19 and 32.

91 CESCR CO Guatemala 12 December 2003, UN Doc. E/C.12/1/Add.93, §10.

92 CESCR CO Moldova 12 December 2003, UN Doc. E/C.12/1/Add.91, §12.

93 CESCR CO Tajikistan 24 November 2006, UN Doc. E/C.12/TJK/CO/1, §13.

94 CESCR CO Latvia 7 January 2008, UN Doc. E/C.12/LVA/CO/1, §9.

95 CESCR CO Kenya 1 December 2008, UN Doc. E/C.12/KEN/CO/1, §10.

96 CESCR CO Madagascar 16 December 2009, UN Doc. E/C.12/MDG/CO/2, §11.

97 CESCR CO Sri Lanka 9 December 2010, UN Doc. E/C.12/LKA/CO/2–4, §12.

98 CESCR CO Russia 1 June 2011, UN Doc. E/C.12/RUS/CO/5, §6.

respect of Russia (1997),[99] Albania (2006),[100] Philippines (2008),[101] Chad (2009),[102] and Algeria (2009).[103]

A small number of observations specifically mention the issue of the availability of resources for social programmes: the observations on Azerbaijan (2007)[104] and Georgia (2002).[105] The observations on Yemen (2011) stated that the impact of serious resource constraints of the State Party was aggravated by widespread corruption. The Committee therefore drew attention to General Comment No. 3, and to the obligation contained therein to ensure the satisfaction of, at the very least, minimum essential levels of each of the rights.[106]

Among all of the Committee's observations about corruption, the topic of judicial corruption featured prominently. The observations reveal that the Committee is '(deeply) concerned' about judicial corruption, and therefore it 'recommends' or '(strongly) urges' States to combat the practice. Amongst others, the Committee frequently called for an increase in the salary of judges. The CESCR discussed judicial corruption in respect of eleven countries, and most of the observations are very recent. This is interesting, given the mandate of the Committee which focuses upon economic, social and cultural rights. Nevertheless, the Committee found that judicial corruption also impacts upon the enjoyment of economic, social and cultural rights. The earliest observation on the topic was issued in 1996, on the Dominican Republic.[107] In 1997, the topic was addressed again in respect of this State.[108] Dowell-Jones conducted a study into the Summary Records of the CESCR of Sessions 14 to 22 (1996–2000),[109] which revealed that during the constructive dialogue between Committee members and the delegation of the Dominican Republic, the country 'did receive a detailed analysis of the preponderance of corruption under various articles of the Covenant.'[110] This is clearly reflected in the Committee's observations. Dowell-Jones suggested that:

> … the Committee's analysis of the second periodic report of the Dominican Republic is a valuable example of how the Committee could proceed in integrating a comprehensive scrutiny of issues of corruption into its review of State Party reports

---

99 CESCR CO Russia 20 May 1997, UN Doc. E/C.12/1/Add.13, §13.

100 CESCR CO Albania 21 November 2006, UN Doc. E/C.12/ALB/CO/1, §17.

101 CESCR CO Philippines 1 December 2008, UN Doc. E/C.12/PHL/CO/4, §14.

102 CESCR CO Chad 16 December 2009, UN Doc. E/C.12/TCD/CO/3, §11.

103 CESCR CO Algeria 7 June 2010, UN Doc. E/C.12/DZA/CO/4, §7.

104 CESCR CO Azerbaijan 22 December 1997, UN Doc. E/C.12/1/Add.20, §10.

105 CESCR CO Georgia 19 December 2002, UN Doc. E/C.12/1/Add.83, §11.

106 CESCR CO Yemen 1 June 2011, UN Doc. E/C.12/YEM/CO/2, §4.

107 CESCR CO Dominican Republic 3 December 1996, UN Doc. E/C.12/1/Add.6, §16.

108 CESCR CO Dominican Republic 12 December 1997, UN Doc. E/C.12/1/Add.16, §4 and 29.

109 Mary Dowell-Jones, Contextualising the International Covenant on Economic, Social and Cultural Rights: Assessing the Economic Deficit (International Studies in Human Rights, 80; Leiden Martinus Nijhoff Publishers, 2004), at p. 59.

110 *Ibid.* at p. 93–95.

as it details corruption's broad effects as well as analysing some of the particular effects under individual articles of the Covenant.[111]

Other observations on judicial corruption were made by the CESCR in respect of Bolivia (2001),[112] Moldova (2003),[113] Azerbaijan (2004),[114] Latvia (2008),[115] Angola (2008),[116] Cambodia (2009),[117] Congo (2009),[118] Kazakhstan (2010),[119] and Afghanistan (2010).[120] It is remains unclear why the judicial corruption in these countries is discussed, but not in others. Furthermore, it is difficult to determine why the Human Rights Committee (partly) scrutinises other countries than the CESCR for corruption. Furthermore, another related concern of the CESCR, made in respect of Sri Lanka (2011), is that the country's President appoints the chairpersons and members of the Commission to Investigate Allegations of Bribery or Corruption.[121]

It is also noteworthy that only rarely does the Committee link corruption to a specific right as enshrined in the ICESCR. An exception are the observations on India (2008), which expressed the 'concern' of the Committee 'about reports of corruption, inefficiency and discrimination that hamper access to food, particularly by the disadvantaged and marginalised groups of society who have been excluded from the benefits of the State Party's economic growth.'[122] Another example can be found in the observations on Yemen (2011), in which the CESCR is concerned about the reported misappropriation of social insurance benefits by State officials or tribal leaders. In this regard, Article 9 is mentioned, i.e. the right to social security. The Committee '*recommends* that the State Party step up its efforts to combat corruption and misappropriation of State funds in the area of social security, including social insurance benefits, and prosecute those responsible' [emphasis added, MB].[123] The issue of corruption in social security systems was also dealt with in the observations on Sri Lanka (2010).[124]

Other issues dealt with by the Committee were the involvement of corrupt officials in human trafficking in Serbia and Montenegro (2005),[125] corruption

---

111 *Ibid.* at p. 95.
112 CESCR CO Bolivia 21 May 2001, UN Doc. E/C.12/1/Add.60, §12.
113 CESCR CO Moldova 12 December 2003, UN Doc. E/C.12/1/Add.91, §12 and 33.
114 CESCR CO Azerbaijan 14 December 2004, UN Doc. E/C.12/1/Add.104, §6, 13 and 38.
115 CESCR CO Latvia 7 January 2008, UN Doc. E/C.12/LVA/CO/1, §9 and 35.
116 CESCR CO Angola 1 December 2008, UN Doc. E/C.12/AGO/CO/3, §10 and 12.
117 CESCR CO Cambodia 22 May 2009, UN Doc. E/C.12/KHM/CO/1, §14.
118 CESCR CO Congo 20 November 2009, UN Doc. E/C.12/COD/CO/4, §10–11.
119 CESCR CO Kazakhstan 7 June 2010, UN Doc. E/C.12/KAZ/CO/1, §11.
120 CESCR CO Afghanistan 7 June 2010, UN Doc. E/C.12/AFG/CO/2–4, §15.
121 CESCR CO Sri Lanka 9 December 2010, UN Doc. E/C.12/LKA/CO/2–4, §9.
122 CESCR CO India May 2008, UN Doc. E/C.12/IND/CO/5, §25.
123 CESCR CO Yemen 1 June 2011, UN Doc. E/C.12/YEM/CO/2, §16.
124 CESCR CO Sri Lanka 9 December 2010, UN Doc. E/C.12/LKA/CO/2–4, §23.
125 CESCR CO Serbia and Montenegro 23 June 2005, UN Doc. E/C.12/1/Add.108, §52.

connected to drug trafficking in Colombia and Mauritius (both in 2010),[126] corruption relating to housing loans in Kazahkstan (2010),[127] and corruption in land allocation schemes in Afghanistan (2010).[128]

In its observations, the CESCR welcomed specific anti-corruption efforts, such as accession to anti-corruption treaties, the adoption of domestic anti-corruption legislation and the establishment of anti-corruption institutions. Examples are the observations on Azerbaijan (2004)[129] and Tajikistan (2006).[130]

It is particularly interesting to note that the CESCR's observations about corruption (especially judicial corruption) seem to become more and more elaborate, since the Committee is increasingly outspoken about the anti-corruption measures that should be taken by State Parties. Moreover, the Committee requested the States to report in their next periodic report about progress and difficulties in the fight against corruption.

An example of such a more sophisticated observation is the one directed to Congo (2009), where 'the Committee *expresses deep concern* at the state of the justice system characterized by a severe shortage of judges, lack of adequate resources, political and military interference and high levels of corruption [...]'. Hence:

> ... the Committee *urges* the State Party to strengthen its efforts to build an independent, efficient, adequately resourced and accountable justice system. The Committee *calls upon* the State Party to exercise greater political will in fighting impunity by allocating the necessary resources for a prompt and full implementation of the recently adopted Plan of Action for Justice Reform and for the well functioning of the High Judicial Council. The State Party should also urgently create a school for magistrates and promulgate a code of conduct for magistrates. The Committee further *calls upon* the State Party to respect fully the authority of the High Judicial Council regarding the nomination and dismissal of magistrates.[131]

Moreover:

> ... the Committee *notes with concern* that corruption remains endemic in the State Party, and that the only State institution in charge of combating corruption, the Professional Ethic Code Observatory (*Observatoire du code de l'Ethique Professionelle*) lacks resources, independence and credibility. The Committee also *regrets* that the tripartite agreement signed in February 2008 with South Africa and UNODC to fight corruption has not yet been implemented.

---

126 CESCR Colombia 21 May 2010, UN Doc. E/C.12/COL/CO/5, §28; CESCR CO Mauritius 8 June 2010, UN Doc. E/C.12/MUS/CO/4, §8.

127 CESCR CO Kazakhstan 7 June 2010, UN Doc. E/C.12/KAZ/CO/1, §30.

128 CESCR CO Afghanistan 7 June 2010, UN Doc. E/C.12/AFG/CO/2–4, §36.

129 CESCR CO Azerbaijan 14 December 2004, UN Doc. E/C.12/1/Add.104, §6.

130 CESCR CO Tajikistan 24 November 2006, UN Doc. E/C.12/TJK/CO/1, §6.

131 CESCR CO Congo 20 November 2009, UN Doc. E/C.12/COD/CO/4, §10.

For this reason:

> … the Committee *urges* the State Party to adopt strong, efficient and time-framed measures to promote good governance and combat corruption. In this respect, the Committee *urges* the State Party to:
> (a) Recognize the urgency of eradicating corruption within all government agencies, including police forces at national, provincial and locals levels;
> (b) Raise awareness of politicians, law makers, national and local civil servants and law enforcement officers on the negative impact of corruption;
> (c) Train judges, prosecutors, the police and other law enforcement officers on the strict application of anti-corruption laws;
> (d) Review its sentencing policy for corruption-related offences;
> (e) Ensure that civil servants and military personnel do not resort to extortion from civilians by taking the necessary measures to this end, including payment of adequate salaries;
> (f) Ensure the transparency of the conduct of public authorities, in law and in practice;
> (g) Implement the tripartite agreement signed with South Africa and UNODC; and
> (h) Provide in its next periodic report detailed information about anti-corruption initiatives, progress made, and obstacles encountered, in combating corruption. [emphasis added, MB][132]

It is certainly recommended that the CESCR continues to take such a clear stance against corruption, by specifying the concrete actions that have to be taken by State Parties to combat corruption.

6. Committee on the Rights of the Child (CRC)

The Committee on the Rights of the Child (hereafter: CRC), composed of eighteen experts,[133] started its work in 1993, and adopted concluding observations from then on.[134] It is interesting to observe that out of the 131 concluding observations issued by the six treaty bodies, 50 emanate from the Committee on the Rights of the Child (hereafter: CRC).[135] This means that in terms of quantity, this Committee issued

---

132 CESCR CO Congo 20 November 2009, UN Doc. E/C.12/COD/CO/4, §11.

133 For more on the work of CRC, see <www2.ohchr.org/english/bodies/crc/index.htm>, accessed 15 June 2011.

134 O'Flaherty, 'The Concluding Observations of the United Nations Human Rights Treaty Bodies', at p. 30.

135 For more on the State reporting procedure of the Committee on the Rights of the Child, see Judith Karp, 'Reporting and the Committee on the Rights of the Child', in: Anne F. Bayefsky (ed.), *The UN Human Rights Treaty System in the 21st Century* (The Hague: Kluwer Law International, 2000), p. 35–44. and Gerison Lansdown, 'The Reporting Process under the Convention on the Rights of the Child', in: Philip Alston and James Crawford (eds.), *The Future of UN Human Rights Treaty Monitoring* (Cambridge: Cambridge University Press, 2000), p. 113–128.

more observations on corruption than any of the other treaty bodies. The question arises in which context corruption is being discussed by the CRC, and how the relatively large attention paid by the Committee to the topic can possibly be explained.

With regard to a number of States, the Committee made more general remarks about the fight against corruption. In respect of Thailand (1998), the first observation on corruption was made, which noted the establishment of the Corrupt Practices Commission, but in which the Committee found that the need to strengthen law enforcement and combat corrupt practices in all areas covered by the Convention was still of 'particular concern' to the Committee, and therefore was 'recommended' that Thailand takes all appropriate measures, including training, to strengthen law enforcement and prevent corrupt practices.[136] Furthermore, the observations on Ukraine (2011) stated that the CRC was 'seriously concerned at the high level of corruption in the State Party',[137] and that it 'urged' the country to adopt the law on principles of prevention and combating corruption without delay.[138] Moreover, the observations on Sierra Leone (2010) under the Optional Protocol to the Convention recommended that the country addressed in its national action plan, the constraints to implementing the OP, including corruption and the perpetuation of harmful practices which render children vulnerable to violations of their rights under the OP.[139] Also, the observations on Afghanistan (2011) stated that the CRC was concerned about the low implementation of legislation in the field of rights of the child, due to, *inter alia*, widespread corruption.[140]

In its observations on Tajikistan (2000), the CRC found that the country had to face a number of problems, including corruption, which had an especially severe impact on children belonging to the most vulnerable segments of society.[141] Similar comments were made in the observations on Kenya (2001),[142] Georgia (2002),[143] Malawi (2002),[144] Zambia (2003),[145] Kyrgyzstan (2004),[146] Moldova (2009),[147] and Tajikistan (2010).[148] Furthermore, in the observations on Cameroon (2001), the CRC '*recommends* that the State Party continue efforts to develop good governance strategy and to combat corruption, especially in the social sector' [emphasis added,

136 CRC CO Thailand 26 October 1998, UN Doc. CRC/C/15/Add.97, §10.
137 CRC CO Ukraine 21 April 2011, UN Doc. CRC/C/UKR/CO/3–4, §64.
138 CRC CO Ukraine 21 April 2011, UN Doc. CRC/C/UKR/CO/3–4, §65.
139 CRC CO Sierra Leone, 14 October 2010, UN Doc. CRC/C/OPSC/SLE/CO/1, §13.
140 CRC CO Afghanistan 8 April 2011, UN Doc. CRC/C/AFG/CO/1, §7.
141 CRC CO Tajikistan 23 October 2000, UN Doc. CRC/C/15/Add.136, §5.
142 CRC CO Kenya 7 November 2001, UN Doc. CRC/C/15/Add.160, §9.
143 CRC CO Georgia 27 October 2003, UN Doc. CRC/C/15/Add.222, §54.
144 CRC CO Malawi 2 April 2002, UN Doc. CRC/C/15/Add.174, §5.
145 CRC CO Zambia 2 July 2003, UN Doc. CRC/C/15/Add.206, §4.
146 CRC CO Kyrgyzstan 3 November 2004, UN Doc. CRC/C/15/Add.244, §6.
147 CRC CO Moldova 30 January 2009, UN Doc. CRC/C/MDA/CO/3, §6.
148 CRC CO Tajikistan 5 February 2010, UN Doc. CRC/C/TJK/CO/2, §5.

MB].[149] Almost identical recommendations were made in respect of Gabon (2002),[150] and Mongolia (2005).[151]

By far the most prominent issue in the CRC's concluding observations on corruption is that of the allocation by States of resources for the realisation of children's rights. Pursuant to Article 4 of the Convention on the Rights of the Child (a provision resembling Article 2(1) ICESCR):

> States Parties shall undertake all appropriate legislative, administrative, and other measures for the implementation of the rights recognized in the present Convention. With regard to economic, social and cultural rights, States Parties shall undertake such measures *to the maximum extent of their available resources* and, where needed, within the framework of international co-operation [emphasis added, MB].

In 29 of its concluding observations, the CRC discussed corruption in the context of a State's maximum available resources: Georgia (2000),[152] Malawi (2002),[153] Zambia (2003),[154] Georgia (2003),[155] Sao Tome and Principe (2004),[156] Angola (2004,)[157] Liberia (2004),[158]Albania (2005),[159] Togo (2005),[160] Nigeria (2005),[161] Russia (2005),[162] Uzbekistan (2006),[163] Benin (2006),[164] Congo (2006),[165] Sierra Leone (2008),[166] Bulgaria (2008),[167] Bangladesh (2009),[168] Niger (2009),[169] Romania (2009),[170] Philippines (2009),[171] Mozambique (2009),[172] Burkina Faso

149 CRC CO Cameroon 6 November 2001, UN Doc. CRC/C/15/Add.164, §14(b).
150 CRC CO Gabon 3 April 2002, UN Doc. CRC/C/15/Add.171, §11(b).
151 CRC CO Mongolia 21 September 2005, UN Doc. CRC/C/15/Add.264, §14.
152 CRC CO Georgia 28 June 2000, UN Doc. CRC/C/15/Add.124, §18–19.
153 CRC CO Malawi 2 April 2002, UN Doc. CRC/C/15/Add.174, §5, 14–15.
154 CRC CO Zambia 2 July 2003, UN Doc. CRC/C/15/Add.206, §4, 15–16.
155 CRC CO Georgia 27 October 2003, UN Doc. CRC/C/15/Add.222, §13–14, 54.
156 CRC CO Sao Tome and Principe 1 July 2004, UN Doc. CRC/C/15/Add.235, §15.
157 CRC CO Angola 3 November 2004, UN Doc. CRC/C/15/Add.246, §14.
158 CRC CO Liberia 4 June 2004, UN Doc. CRC/C/15/Add.236, §14.
159 CRC CO Albania 31 March 2005, UN Doc. CRC/C/15/Add.249, §15–16.
160 CRC CO Togo 31 March 2005, UN Doc. CRC/C/15/Add.255, §17.
161 CRC CO Nigeria 13 April 2005, UN Doc. CRC/C/15/Add.257, §21–22.
162 CRC CO Russia 23 November 2005, UN Doc. CRC/C/RUS/CO/3, §19–20.
163 CRC CO Uzbekistan 2 June 2006, UN Doc. CRC/C/UZB/CO/2, §52–53(c).
164 CRC CO Benin 20 October 2006, UN Doc. CRC/C/BEN/CO/2, §17–18.
165 CRC CO Congo 20 October 2006, UN Doc. CRC/C/COG/CO/1, §14–15.
166 CRC CO Sierra Leone 20 June 2008, UN Doc. CRC/C/SLE/CO/2, §18.
167 CRC CO Bulgaria 23 June 2008, UN Doc. CRC/C/BGR/CO/2, §16–17.
168 CRC CO Bangladesh 12 June 2009, UN Doc. CRC/C/BGD/CO/4, §22–23.
169 CRC CO Niger 12 June 2009, UN Doc. CRC/C/NER/CO/2, §17–18(f).
170 CRC CO Romania 12 June 2009, UN Doc. CRC/C/ROM/CO/4, §15–16.
171 CRC CO Philippines 22 October 2009, UN Doc. CRC/C/PHL/CO/3–4, §19–20(d).
172 CRC CO Mozambique 4 November 2009, UN Doc. CRC/C/MOZ/CO/2, §17–18(f).

(2010),[173] Mongolia (2010),[174] Cameroon (2010),[175] Tajikistan (2010),[176] El Salvador (2010),[177] Nigeria (2010)[178] Sri Lanka (2010),[179] and Afghanistan (2011).[180] In these observations, the Committee expressed its '(serious) concern' about corruption, and 'recommends' or 'urges' that States take action to prevent and eradicate corruption, amongst others by implementing legislation, by undertaking investigations, by ratifying the UN Convention Against Corruption, and by prosecuting the persons responsible. The CRC made clear that corruption impacts negatively upon the resources of the State Party to realise children's rights, for example in the areas of education or health. The observations imply that due to corruption, the State Party does not meet its obligations under Article 4 to devote the maximum available resources.

The impact of corruption upon children's health was discussed by the Committee in its observations on Pakistan (2003), which stated that the CRC is 'extremely concerned' about the very poor health situation of children and the unavailability of children's health care services. As a particular matter of concern, the CRC listed, *inter alia*, the poor provision of health care, especially in rural areas, which is in part due to corruption within the framework of projects supported by international organisations.[181] Moreover, in its observations on Kenya (2007), the CRC '*recommends* that the State Party step-up anti-corruption measures relating to the management of funds for the health sector' [emphasis added, MB].[182] The observations on Benin (2006) also mentioned the impact of corruption on the resources available for children's health,[183] as well as the observations on Congo (2006),[184] Bulgaria (2008),[185] Philippines (2009),[186] and Afghanistan (2011).[187]

Children's right to education was addressed by the Committee in its observations on Mozambique (2002), expressing the concern of the CRC that 'there is alleged corruption and sexual abuse and economic exploitation of pupils by professionals, including teachers, in the school system', and the CRC 'recommends' that Mozambique ends these practices.[188] In the observations on Benin (2006),[189] the

173 CRC CO Burkina Faso 9 February 2010, UN Doc. CRC/C/BFA/CO/3–4, §16–17(e).
174 CRC CO Mongolia 29 January 2010, UN Doc. CRC/C/MNG/CO/3–4, §17–18(e).
175 CRC CO Cameroon 18 February 2010, UN Doc. CRC/C/CMR/CO/2, §17–18(f).
176 CRC CO Tajikistan 5 February 2010, UN Doc. CRC/C/CMR/CO/2, §17(e).
177 CRC CO El Salvador 17 February 2010, UN Doc. CRC/C/SLV/CO/3–4, §18(f).
178 CRC CO Nigeria 11 June 2010, UN Doc. CRC/C/NGA/CO3–4, §16–17(a).
179 CRC CO Sri Lanka 19 October 2010, UN Doc. CRC/C/LKA/CO/3–4, §16(c) and 17(f).
180 CRC CO Afghanistan 8 April 2011, UN Doc. CRC/C/AFG/CO/1, §17–18.
181 CRC CO Pakistan 27 October 2003, UN Doc. CRC/C/15/Add.217, §52.
182 CRC CO Kenya 19 June 2007, UN Doc. CRC/C/KEN/CO/2, §48 (g).
183 CRC CO Benin 20 October 2006, UN Doc. CRC/C/BEN/CO/2, §17.
184 CRC CO Congo 20 October 2006, UN Doc. CRC/C/COG/CO/1, §14.
185 CRC CO Bulgaria 23 June 2008, UN Doc. CRC/C/BGR/CO/2, §16–17.
186 CRC CO Philippines 22 October 2009, UN Doc. CRC/C/PHL/CO/3–4, §19.
187 CRC CO Afghanistan 8 April 2011, UN Doc. CRC/C/AFG/CO/1, §17.
188 CRC CO Mozambique 3 April 2002, UN Doc. CRC/C/15/Add.172, §56 and 57.
189 CRC CO Benin 20 October 2006, UN Doc. CRC/C/BEN/CO/2, §17.

impact of corruption upon the resources available for education is briefly mentioned, as well as in the observations on Congo (2006),[190] Bulgaria (2008),[191] Philippines (2009),[192] Sri Lanka (2010)[193] and Afghanistan (2011).[194] The observations on Sri Lanka also expressed the concern of the Committee that 'school fees continue to be charged despite the constitutional guarantee of free education, introducing discrimination against children from poor families and facilitating corruption in school admissions.'[195] In addition, the observations on Afghanistan recommended that the State 'strengthen efforts to stop all forms of corruption in the educational system.'[196]

In its observations on Cambodia (2000), the Committee expressed its concern about corruption in the country's adoption procedures.[197] Likewise, the observations on Ukraine (2007) stated that the CRC '*regrets* that there are still numerous corruption-related obstacles to a transparent procedure for legal adoptions' and '*recommends* the State Party to continue and enforce its anti-corruption measures in order to combat the sale of children for adoption [...]' [emphasis added, MB].[198] Similar observations were made in respect of Bulgaria (2008).[199] Furthermore, in the observations on Russia (2005), the CRC stated that it is '*seriously concerned* that widespread corruption, *inter alia* in the health and education sectors as well as in adoption procedures, is affecting children in the full enjoyment of their rights' [emphasis added].[200] Finally, the observations on Guatemala (2011)[201] also addressed corruption in relation to adoption.

The role of corruption in trafficking in children was addressed in a small number of observations. In its observations under the Optional Protocol to the Convention on the Rights of the Child, the CRC observed in respect of Kazakhstan (2006) that it '*remains concerned* about allegations of complicity by State officials in trafficking and that corruption impedes the effectiveness of prevention measures' [emphasis added, MB].[202] The same observations were made in respect of Kyrgyzstan (2007).[203] Furthermore, the Committee 'recommends' that Mozambique (2009) prosecute and punish corrupt officials involved in the sale, trafficking and abduction of children.[204] Finally, the concluding observations on Mexico (2011)

---

190 CRC CO Congo 20 October 2006, UN Doc. CRC/C/COG/CO/1, §14.
191 CRC CO Bulgaria 23 June 2008, UN Doc. CRC/C/BGR/CO/2, §16–17.
192 CRC CO Philippines 22 October 2009, UN Doc. CRC/C/COG/CO/1, §19.
193 CRC CO Sri Lanka 19 October 2010, UN Doc. CRC/C/LKA/CO/3–4, §16(c).
194 CRC CO Afghanistan 8 April 2011, UN Doc. CRC/C/AFG/CO/1, §17.
195 CRC CO Sri Lanka 19 October 2010, UN Doc. CRC/C/LKA/CO/3–4, §62(c).
196 CRC CO Afghanistan 8 April 2011, UN Doc. CRC/C/AFG/CO/1, §61(b).
197 CRC CO Cambodia 28 June 2000, UN Doc. CRC/C/15/Add.128, §40.
198 CRC CO Ukraine 28 June 2007, UN Doc. CRC/C/OPSC/UKR/CO/1, §29–30.
199 CRC CO Bulgaria 21 January 2008, UN Doc. CRC/C/OPSC/UKR/CO/1, §26.
200 CRC CO Russia 23 November 2005, UN Doc. CRC/C/RUS/CO/3, §19.
201 CRC CO Guatemala 1 October 2010, UN Doc. CRC/C/GTM/CO/3–4, §61.
202 CRC CO Kazakhstan 17 March 2006, UN Doc. CRC/C/OPSC/KAZ/CO/1, §23–24.
203 CRC CO Kyrgyzstan 4 May 2007, UN Doc. CRC/C/OPSC/KGZ/CO/1, §25.
204 CRC CO Mozambique 4 November 2009, UN Doc. CRC/C/MOZ/CO/2, §87(b).

under the Optional Protocol on the sale of children, child prostitution and child pornography expressed the concern of the CRC about 'reports of corruption and impunity relating to the offences under the Optional Protocol.'[205]

Finally, the observations on Burundi (2010) mentioned serious problems of corruption within the criminal juvenile justice system.[206]

The fact that the Committee on the Rights of the Child has produced more concluding observations on corruption than any of the other treaty bodies, might be related to Bayefsky's finding that the CRC's observations are generally more than twice the length of the observations of the other treaty bodies. In her opinion, this is a direct reflection of the input of UNICEF and the NGO-CRC Group, and the staffing resources of the CRC.[207] Furthermore, O'Flaherty also commented upon the length of the CRC's observations. He pointed out that Members of the CRC deem the length necessary because of the wide range of issues addressed by the Convention on the Rights of the Child.[208]

7. Committee on the Elimination of All Forms of Discrimination Against Women (CEDAW)

The Committee on the Elimination of all Forms of Discrimination Against Women, consisting of twenty-three experts,[209] was established in 1982.[210] Concluding observations are being issued since 1994.[211] It appears that corruption was mentioned by this treaty body in only 3 concluding observations. Moreover, no individual complaints to the Committee were concerned with corruption.

In the observations on China (1999), the Committee expressed its 'concern' about corrupt public officials who were reportedly involved or colluding in the trafficking of women, including through payments from prostitutes.[212] Furthermore, in the observations on Thailand (2006), 'the Committee *urges* the State Party to

---

205 CRC CO Mexico 7 April 2011, UN Doc. CRC/C/OPSC/MEX/CO/1, §29(e).

206 CRC CO Burundi 1 October 2010, UN Doc. CRC/C/BDI/CO/2, §76.

207 Bayefsky, *The UN Human Rights Treaty System: Universality at the Crossroads*, at p. 62.

208 O'Flaherty, 'The Concluding Observations of the United Nations Human Rights Treaty Bodies', at p. 31.

209 For more on the work of CEDAW, see <www2.ohchr.org/english/bodies/cedaw/index.htm>, accessed 20 June 2011.

210 For more on the State Reporting Procedure of CEDAW, see Carmel Shalev, 'State Reporting and the Convention on the Elimination of All Forms of Discrimination against Women', in: Anne F. Bayefsky (ed.), *The UN Human Rights Treaty System in the 21st Century* (The Hague: Kluwer Law International, 2000), p. 23–34. See also Mara R. Bustelo, 'The Committee on the Elimination of Discrimination against Women at the Crossroads', in: Philip Alston and James Crawford (eds.), *The Future of UN Human Rights Treaty Monitoring* (Cambridge: Cambridge University Press, 2000), p. 79–111.

211 O'Flaherty, 'The Concluding Observations of the United Nations Human Rights Treaty Bodies', at p. 30.

212 CEDAW CO China 5 February 1999, UN Doc. CEDAW/C/1999/I/L.1/Add.7, §40.

adopt measures that will facilitate and accelerate the process for obtaining citizenship by hill tribe women, including by addressing any corrupt practices by public officials responsible for determining the citizenship of applicants' [emphasis added, MB][213] Finally, in its observations on Uganda (2010), the Committee discussed violence against women. In that context, corruption in police stations was mentioned. Allegedly, some police officers illegally charge fees for free services.[214]

CEDAW's lack of attention is noteworthy given the suggestions in recent literature that corruption has a disproportionate impact upon women as compared to men, especially in three areas: the political dimension, the law enforcement dimension, and the socio-economic dimension. One of the overall causes of the fact that corruption is particularly harmful to women, is the given fact that women generally have less financial resources than men. Hence, they cannot afford to pay bribes to obtain certain public goods or services.[215]

8. Committee on the Elimination of Racial Discrimination (CERD)

The Committee on the Elimination of Racial Discrimination (hereafter: CERD), comprised of eighteen experts,[216] operates as of 1969 and issues collective concluding observations since 1993.[217] The topic of corruption features in seven of the Committee's concluding observations, all of which were released between 2003 and 2010. The Committee discussed corruption in relation to a number of topics.

In a few observations, the Committee made general remarks about States' progress in the fight against corruption. In 2003, CERD *commends* Albania for taking action against organized crime and corruption, which are said to be particularly harmful to the most vulnerable social groups.[218] In its observations on Bulgaria (2009), the Committee 'is aware of the efforts the State Party must make in particular to strengthen the independence of the judiciary and to eliminate

213 CEDAW CO Thailand 3 February 2006, UN Doc. CEDAW/C/THA/CO/5, §38.

214 CEDAW CO Uganda 5 November 2010, UN Doc. CEDAW/C/UGA/CO/7, §23.

215 For more on this topic, and a review of existing literature, see Martine Boersma, 'The Impact of Corruption Upon Women's Rights: A Neglected Area?' in: Ingrid Westendorp (ed.), *The Women's Convention Turned 30: Achievements, Setbacks and Prospects* (Antwerp: Intersentia, 2010).

216 For more on the work of CERD, see <www2.ohchr.org/english/bodies/cerd/index.htm>, accessed 15 June 2011, and Michael Banton, 'Decision-Taking in the Committee on the Elimination of Racial Discrimination', in: Philip Alston and James Crawford (eds.), *The Future of UN Human Rights Treaty Monitoring* (Cambridge: Cambridge University Press, 2000), p. 55–78.

217 O'Flaherty, 'The Concluding Observations of the United Nations Human Rights Treaty Bodies', at p. 30.

218 CERD CO Albania 10 December 2003, UN Doc. CERD/C/63/CO/1, §6.

corruption and organized crime in the country.'[219] Furthermore, in its observations on Azerbaijan:

> ... the Committee, while recognising the adoption of a wide range of anti-discrimination policies by the State Party, is *concerned* that a certain number of those policies and projects, such as the National Strategy on the increase of transparency and the fight against corruption [...] have yet to be implemented or evaluated (Article 2).

The Committee then '*urges* the State Party to fully implement all anti-discrimination policies that have been adopted, to closely monitor and evaluate progress in implementation of the Convention at national and local levels and to make an assessment of the impact of the measures already implemented in its next periodic report.'[220] [emphasis added, MB.]

In respect of Madagascar (2004), the Committee '*notes with interest* the establishment of such national human rights machinery as the Office of the Ombudsman, the National Human Rights Commission and the High Council to Combat Corruption.'[221] [emphasis added, MB.] This reveals that CERD sees an anti-corruption body as part of the human rights framework.

The observation on Uzbekistan (2006) addressed the relationship between corruption and the right to freedom of movement as laid down in Article 5 (d) (i) and (ii) of the ICERD: the Committee is:

> ... *concerned* about the continuing existence of a compulsory residence registration system (*propiska*) in the State Party. While acknowledging that it is maintained for purposes of address registration, retention of this system may affect *de facto* the enjoyment of a number of rights and freedoms. Allegations of corruption in this regard *are also of concern* (article 5, paragraph d (i) and (ii).[222] [emphasis added, MB.]

Two observations were concerned with corruption in the judiciary, i.e. those on Chad (2009)[223] and Cambodia (2010).[224] In these observations, CERD also 'recommends' that the States concerned take measures to address corruption in the justice system.

There are no views of CERD on individual complaints relating to corruption.

---

219 CERD CO Bulgaria 23 March 2009, UN Doc. CERD/C/BGR/CO/19, §3.
220 CERD CO Azerbaijan 26 August 2009, UN Doc. CERD/C/AZE/CO/6, §8.
221 CERD CO Madagascar 10 December 2004, UN Doc. CERD/C/65/CO/4, §7.
222 CERD CO Uzbekistan 4 April 2006, UN Doc. CERD/C/UZB/CO/5, §16.
223 CERD CO Chad 21 September 2009, UN Doc. CERD/C/TCD/15, §11.
224 CERD CO Cambodia 16 March 2010, UN Doc. CERD/C/KHM/CO/8–13.

9. Committee Against Torture (CAT)

The Committee Against Torture, composed of ten experts,[225] was established in 1987 and commenced issuing concluding observations in 1993.[226] In 12 of its observations, CAT addressed the topic of corruption. The first observations date back to 1995, where the Committee stated in respect of Italy that 'the existence of a large number of public officials involved in acts of corruption is not a positive contribution.'[227]

In the observations on Tajikistan (2006), the Committee noted as a positive measure that the country ratified important instruments that contribute to human rights protection, including the UN Convention Against Corruption.[228] In respect of Indonesia (2008), CAT welcomed the establishment of a number of anti-corruption institutions, as to safeguard human rights protection.[229] CAT's observations on Cambodia (2011) welcomed the country's ratification or accession to the UNCAC, as well as the adoption of an anti-corruption law.[230] Hence, it can be detected that in the view of CAT, anti-corruption legislation and institutions fall within the framework of human rights protection.

The majority of CAT's observations are concerned with corruption in the criminal justice system (the police and judicial sector), i.e. those on Cambodia (2003),[231] Nepal (2007),[232] Benin (2008),[233] Indonesia (2008),[234] Kenya (2009),[235] Chad (2009)[236] and Cambodia (2011).[237] These observations show that the Committee is '(deeply) concerned' about corruption in the criminal justice system, and it 'recommends' or 'urges' the particular States to take the necessary measures, including the adoption of legislation and preventive measures. In respect of Benin it was also noted that the State's next periodic report should contain statistics on corruption among law enforcement officials and penalties imposed.[238]

The observations on Ecuador (2006) related to the rights of detainees under the Convention Against Torture. Here we find that the Committee is rather specific, by stating that it:

---

225 For more on the work of CAT, see <www2.ohchr.org/english/bodies/cat/index.htm>, accessed 15 June 2011.

226 O'Flaherty, 'The Concluding Observations of the United Nations Human Rights Treaty Bodies', at p. 30.

227 CAT CO Italy 26 July 1995, UN Doc. A/50/44, §146–158 at §153.

228 CAT CO Tajikistan 7 December 2006, UN Doc. CAT/C/TJK/CO/1, §4(b).

229 CAT CO Indonesia 2 July 2008, UN Doc. CAT/C/IDN/CO/2, §4.

230 CAT CO Cambodia 20 January 2011, UN Doc. CAT/C/KHM/CO/2, §6(c) and 7(a).

231 CAT CO Cambodia 5 February 2004, UN Doc. CAT/C/CR/31/7, §6(e).

232 CAT CO Nepal 13 April 2007, UN Doc. CAT/C/NPL/CO/2, §16.

233 CAT CO Benin 19 February 2008, UN Doc. CAT/C/BEN/CO/2, §13, 29.

234 CAT CO Indonesia 2 July 2008, UN Doc. CAT/C/IDN/CO/2, §22.

235 CAT CO Kenya 19 January 2009, UN Doc. CAT/C/KEN/CO/1, §12.

236 CAT CO Chad 19 May 2009, UN Doc. CAT/C/TCD/CO/1, §24.

237 CAT CO Cambodia 20 January 2011, UN Doc. CAT/C/KHM/CO/2, §13.

238 CAT CO Benin 19 February 2009, UN Doc. CAT/C/BEN/CO/2, §29(d).

> ... *deeply deplores* the situation in detention centres, and especially in social rehabilitation centres where prisoners' human rights are constantly violated. The overcrowding, *corruption* and poor physical conditions prevailing in prisons, and especially the lack of hygiene, proper food and appropriate medical care, *constitute violations of rights* which are protected under the Convention (article 11) [emphasis added, MB].

Subsequently, the Committee finds that Ecuador 'should' adopt effective measures to remedy this situation.[239] Furthermore, the observations on Benin also addressed the problem of corruption in prisons, stating that the State 'should' take measures to end it.[240] Moreover, the observations on Chad also mentioned prison corruption and the Committee found that Chad 'should take urgent measures' to stop this practice.[241] Like Benin, Chad has to supply the Committee with statistics on corruption among law enforcement officials and penalties imposed.[242] The observations on Cameroon (2010) stated that CAT has received reports about corruption, such as the renting of prison cells and sale of medical equipment, and finds that Cameroon should take 'urgent steps' to put an end to these practices.[243]

The observations on Austria (2010) concerned the newly established Federal Bureau of Anti-Corruption. The Committee found that the State Party should provide further information on the mandate of this institution, which is an independent body outside of the traditional Austrian law enforcement structures, and which conducts independent investigations in cooperation with the public prosecutors.[244]

It is noteworthy that the Committee's most recent observations on corruption, i.e. those on Cambodia (2011), contain the most elaborate discussion of the topic thus far. Among the Committee's 'principal subjects of concern and recommendations', an entire section is devoted to corruption, in which the Committee provides detailed instructions to the State:

> The Committee is *deeply concerned* at reports of widespread and systemic corruption throughout the country. The Committee considers that the rule of law is the cornerstone for the protection of the rights set forth in the Convention and, while *welcoming* the new Anti-Corruption Law and other measures taken by the State Party, it *notes with concern* reports of political interference and corruption affecting the judicial bodies and the functioning of some public services, including the police and other law enforcement services. In this respect, the Committee *expresses its concern* at reports that police officers are promoted for convictions and that police stations are given special incentives for convictions, amounting to a rewards system,

239 CAT CO Ecuador 8 February 2006, UN Doc. CAT/C/ECU/CO/3, §24.
240 CAT CO Benin 19 February 2008, UN Doc. CAT/C/BEN/CO/2, §18.
241 CAT CO Chad 19 May 2009, UN Doc. CAT/C/TCD/CO/1, §25.
242 CAT CO Chad 19 May 2009, UN Doc. CAT/C/TCD/CO/1, §40.
243 CAT CO Cameroon 19 May 2010, UN Doc. CAT/C/CMR/CO/4, §15.
244 CAT CO Austria 20 May 2010, UN Doc. CAT/C/AUT/CO/2–5, §19.

> as well as reports of police officers benefitting financially from informal arrangements or extrajudicial settlements. The Committee is also *concerned* that the Anti-Corruption Unit established under the new Anti-Corruption Law has not yet taken any steps against alleged perpetrators of corruption and is not yet fully operational. (arts. 2, 10 and 12) The State Party *should* take immediate and urgent measures to eradicate corruption throughout the country which is one of the most serious impediments to the rule of law and the implementation of the Convention. Such measures should include effective implementation of the anti-corruption legislation and the expeditious operationalization of the Anti-Corruption Unit, which should consist of independent members. The State Party *should* also increase its capacity to investigate and prosecute cases of corruption. The State Party *should* establish a programme of witness and whistle-blower protection to assist in ensuring confidentiality and to protect those who lodge allegations of corruption, and ensure that sufficient funding be allocated for its effective functioning. Furthermore, the State Party *should* undertake training and capacity-building programmes for the police and other law enforcement officers, prosecutors and judges, on the strict application of anti-corruption legislation as well as on relevant professional codes of ethics, and adopt effective mechanisms to ensure transparency in the conduct of public officials, in law and in practice. The Committee *requests* the State Party to report back on progress achieved, and the difficulties encountered, in combating corruption. The Committee also *requests* the State Party to provide information on the number of officials, including senior officials that have been prosecuted and punished on account of corruption charges. [emphasis added, MB.][245]

It is certainly recommended that the Committee continues to scrutinise corruption insuch a manner.

Finally, when examining CAT's decisions on individual complaints, we find a number of cases which showed that persons exposing corruption face torture or inhumane treatment, as a result, decide to request asylum abroad. An example of such a factual situation is *M.M.K. v. Sweden*.[246] There are no decisions in which CAT discusses corruption itself.

10. Concluding Remarks

Having analysed all 131 concluding observations of the treaty bodies discussing corruption, and a small set of views on individual complaints, it is possible to draw a number of conclusions. As an interpretative tool, a table can be found in Annex 1, containing the full list of observations, organised alphabetically by country. Also added to the table is the country's score on the Corruption Perceptions Index 2011

245 CAT CO Cambodia 20 January 2011, UN Doc. CAT/C/KHM/CO/2, §12.

246 Communication no. 221/2002, *M.M.K. v. Sweden*, decision of 15 May 2005, UN Doc. CAT/C/34/D/221/2002.

of Transparency International, ranking 183 countries. A high score signifies a high level of perceived corruption.[247]

As shown in figure 2 below, there is *a noticeable imbalance* with regard to the attention paid to corruption by the six treaty bodies. While the lower level of attention to corruption by CERD can possibly be explained by the subject-matter of their work (i.e. racial discrimination, which might have less to do with corruption), the lack of attention paid to corruption by CEDAW is striking and appears difficult to justify given the disproportionate impact which corruption has on women.

Figure 2. Treaty body attention for corruption

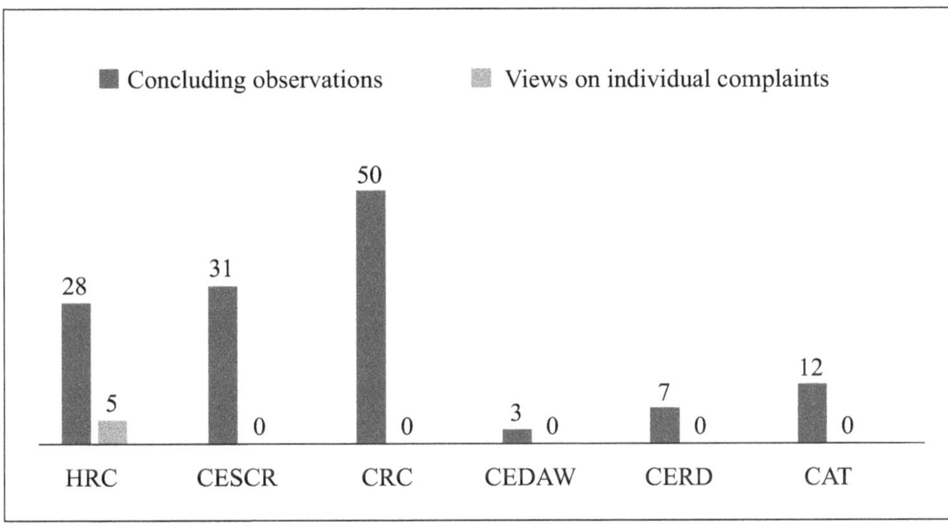

In respect of *the countries that were scrutinised by the Committees*, we find that observations were made in respect of 67 States. Many of these are developing countries. Figure 3 below shows a geographical overview of the observations, demonstrating that most observations were made on Sub-Saharan Africa. When considering the CPI score of the scrutinised countries, we find that the large majority of countries are located at the lower level of the index, because of the high level of perceived corruption. Hence, it seems that the practice of the human rights treaty bodies does reflect real perceptions about corruption. Nevertheless, the CPI ranks many more States with high-levels of corruption, which are not scrutinised by the Committees. It is possible that this absence can be partly explained by the problem of late or non-submission of State reports, and the fact that some countries might not be Parties to all six human rights treaties.

247 For more on the measurement of corruption, including the CPI, see chapter I.

Figure 3. Geographical overview of concluding observations

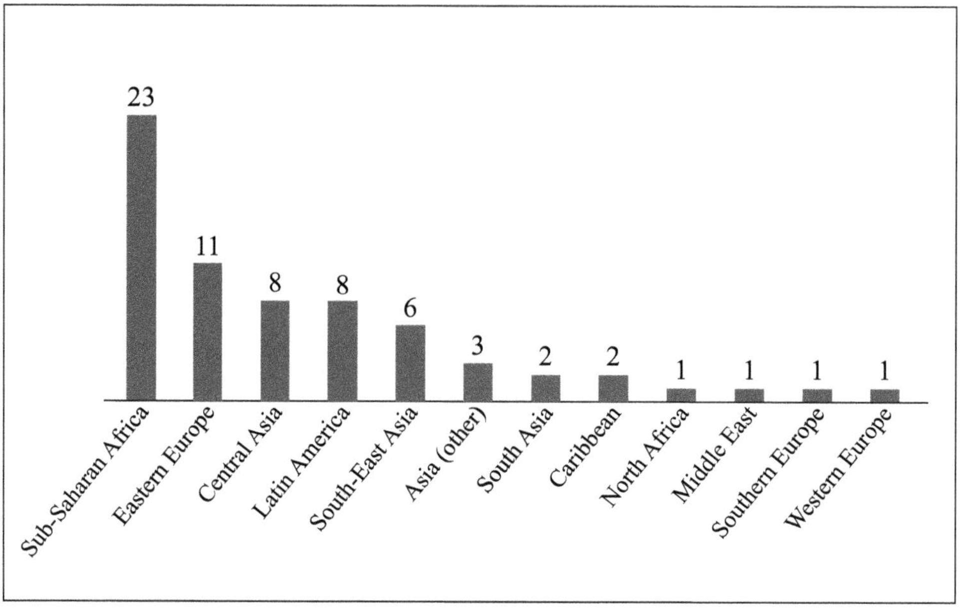

As to *the human rights in relation to which corruption is discussed*, the following deserves to be mentioned. Corruption in the judiciary, which impacts on the right to equality before courts and tribunals and to a fair trial, is by far the most prominent topic in the work of the HRC. Also the CESCR and CAT pay attention to this matter. Other civil and political rights in relation to which corruption is discussed by the HRC, CERD, and CAT are the prohibition of human trafficking, the right to freedom of movement, and the rights of detainees. Remarkably absent in the concluding observations of the Human Rights Committee are statements on the impact of corruption on political rights (Article 25 ICCPR), an important topic in relation to irregularities during elections.

In respect of economic, social and cultural rights, it can be concluded that the CESCR does not often link corruption to the obligations of States under a *particular* right under the ICESCR. This was only done in respect of the right to food, and the right to social security. Also, while the Committee makes clear that corruption has a negative impact upon the equal enjoyment/implementation/realisation/exercise of economic social and cultural rights, and that corruption affects a State's resources available for social programmes, this issue could be developed much further, by examining the specific obligations under Article 2(1). The CRC does pay quite some attention to the impact of corruption on the maximum available resources. This Committee also refers on a number of occasions to the rights to health and education. Other issues discussed by the CRC are the role of corruption in adoption procedures and in trafficking in children.

When we consider the *language* used by the Committees to condemn corruption, we can observe that this does not significantly differ from the language used to discuss other human rights problems. Bayefsky already pointed out that 'concluding observations are often extremely general. [...] Too often they identify areas of concern without specifying specific laws or practices, or connecting those concerns to specific recommendations.'[248] Although none of the observations specifically state that a certain corrupt practice 'violates' a human right, there are clear indications that this is actually the case. The best example is the observation of the Human Rights Committee in respect of Kenya (2005), stating that allegations of judicial corruption 'seriously undermine' the independence and impartiality of the judiciary', which are components of the right to a fair trial. Also, the fact that for example the CESCR 'urges' Congo (2009) to take a clear set of anti-corruption measures,[249] might show that in such a case, the State Party does not meet its obligations under the ICESCR, although it does remain unclear what provision of the treaty is at stake here. It is certainly to be desired that the Committees link corrupt practice to clear obligations under the treaties.

It is clear that most observations on corruption, particularly the more elaborate ones, are *from a rather recent date.* There is thus a trend towards greater scrutiny of corruption by the treaty bodies. As discussed in chapter II *supra* attention for corruption emerged in the second half of the 1990s, and increased in the beginning of the 2000s. Hence, the increase in global attention for corruption in this period is reflected as well in the practice of the treaty bodies.

It needs to be kept in mind that the treaty bodies need to maintain the cooperation of States in the reporting procedure. Discussing politically sensitive issues such as corruption within the State apparatus can thus be a difficult task.[250] Yet, we see that the Committees no longer shy away from doing so.

Concerning the views on individual complaints, we found very few complaints where corruption played a substantial role. The Human Rights Committee dealt with a number of complaints concerning maltreatment of persons exposing corrupt practices (whistleblowers), most notably *Philip Afuson Njaru v. Cameroon*.[251] Other complaints concerned allegations that the applicant did not receive a fair trial due to judicial corruption. Furthermore, it flows from the HRC's views in *Michael and Brian Hill v. Spain* that misappropriation of funds for food or drinks for prisoners can lead to a violation of Article 10 ICCPR, containing detainees' rights.[252] Furthermore, a small number of complaints brought before the Committee Against

---

248 Bayefsky, The UN Human Rights Treaty System: Universality at the Crossroads, at p. 62.

249 CESCR CO Congo 20 November 2009, UN Doc. E/C.12/COD/CO/4, §11.

250 In respect of the CESCR, this was noted by Dowell-Jones, *Contextualising the International Covenant on Economic, Social and Cultural Rights: Assessing the Economic Deficit* at p. 83.

251 Communication no. 1353/2005, *Philip Afuson Njaru v. Cameroon*, views of 19 March 2007, UN Doc. CCPR/C/89/D/1353/2005.

252 Communication no. 526/1993, *Michael and Brian Hill v. Spain*, views of 22 June 1997, UN Doc. CCPR/C/59/D/526/1993.

Torture showed that persons exposing corruption may face torture or inhumane treatment and therefore request asylum abroad. Finally, neither CERD nor CEDAW issued any relevant views on corruption.

CHAPTER IV
CHARTER-BASED SYSTEM: CORRUPTION AS A TOPIC IN THE UPR AND THE SPECIAL PROCEDURES OF THE UN HUMAN RIGHTS COUNCIL

1. INTRODUCTION

While the previous chapter discussed the treaty-based monitoring mechanisms, the current chapter considers the Charter-based method of human rights supervision, i.e. the system based on the UN Charter, in particular Article 55. The key organ in this respect is the UN Human Rights Council (hereafter: the Council). The Council, composed of 47 UN Members, was established by the General Assembly in 2006 and replaces the former UN Human Rights Commission.[1] Mechanisms of the Council are the Universal Periodic Review (hereafter: UPR), as well as various Special Procedures: Special Rapporteurs, Working Groups, Independent Experts and Special Representatives. Sections 2 and 3 hereafter (i) concisely describe the functioning of the mechanisms mentioned; (ii) discuss how corruption is dealt with in these processes; and (iii) draw conclusions.

2. UNIVERSAL PERIODIC REVIEW

2.1. Background

The UPR is a procedure of the UN Human Rights Council, established in 2006 by the General Assembly.[2] Under the UPR, the human rights situation of all 192 UN Member States is periodically reviewed in cycles of four years. The first session of the first cycle started in 2008, and from then on, three sessions take place every year. In each session, 16 States are reviewed, meaning 48 States each year.[3]

Given the fact that the UPR is an inter-State mechanism, the essence of the system is that States report about their human rights situation to other States, which have the opportunity to ask questions and make comments and recommendations to the State under review. The reviews are conducted by the UPR Working Group, composed of the 47 members of the Council, but other UN Member States can also participate in the dialogue. The review of each State is assisted by so-called 'troikas': groups of three States serving as rapporteurs.[4]

---

1 The Human Rights Council was established on 15 March 2006 by General Assembly Resolution 60/251, UN Doc. A/RES/60/251.

2 Info about the UPR can be found on <www.ohchr.org/EN/HRBodies/UPR/Pages/UPRMain.aspx>, accessed 21 June 2011. The UPR was established together with the Council on 15 March 2006 by General Assembly Resolution 60/251, UN Doc. A/RES/60/251.

3 All UPR sessions: <www.ohchr.org/EN/HRBodies/UPR/Pages/UPRSessions.aspx>, accessed 21 June 2011.

4 Basic facts about the UPR: <www.ohchr.org/EN/HRBodies/UPR/Pages/BasicFacts.aspx>, accessed 21 June 2011.

The review commences with the submission by the State under review of a State report. Also, the Office of the High Commissioner for Human Rights (hereafter: OHCHR) submits a compilation of UN information, drawn *inter alia* from the Special Procedures of the Council and the work of the UN treaty bodies. There is also room for NGOs to submit information, which results in the so-called summary of stakeholders' information. The State report is discussed in Geneva during a three-hour oral dialogue with other UN Member States. Before this dialogue, States are able to submit advance questions to the State under review, but during the oral discussion, other topics can also be brought up. Ultimately, the dialogue results in an outcome report prepared by the troika. This report summarises the dialogue, including the questions asked, the replies of the State concerned, and the comments and recommendations.[5]

The human rights obligations assessed during the UPR are those contained in: (i) the UN Charter; (ii) the UDHR; (iii) human rights treaties to which the State is a Party; (iv) voluntary pledges and commitments, such as national human rights policies and programmes; and (v) international humanitarian law. One must recognise that the UPR process is a politicised mechanism. The Members of the Human Rights Council are State representatives, unlike the members of the treaty bodies, who are independent experts. As a result, State comments during the UPR dialogue may be coloured by political motives.

2.2. Discussion of Corruption During the UPR Dialogue

When examining the outcome reports of the first eight UPR sessions, during which a total of 128 UN Member States were reviewed, we find that corruption is a topic frequently discussed in the dialogue with the State under review: discussions on corruption are present in the outcome reports of 77 countries.[6] Understandably, the

5 *Ibid.* See also Human Rights Council document 8/PRST/1, titled Modalities and practices for the universal periodic review process.

6 Own search through all outcome reports of the first eight UPR sessions, keyword 'corrupt'. It is possible that the keyword 'corrupt' might not have captured all instances in which corruption is discussed in more disguised terms. Nevertheless, the author believes that the search covers the large majority of the discussions on corruption, also when compared to the list of recommendations on corruption during the first seven UPR sessions, as compiled by UPR Info, and accessible on <www.upr-info.org/database>, accessed 18 November 2010. The 76 States concerned are: Afghanistan, Albania, Angola, Azerbaijan, Bahrein, Bangladesh, Barbados, Belarus, Belize, Benin, Bhutan, Bolivia, Bosnia and Herzegovina, Botswana, Brazil, Brunei, Burkina Faso, Burundi, Cambodia, Cameroon, Cape Verde, Chad, Comoros, Congo, Côte d'Ivoire, Czech Republic, Democratic Republic of Congo, Dominica, Dominican Republic, Ecuador, Egypt, El Salvador, Equatorial Guinea, Eritrea, Finland, Gambia, Germany, Ghana, Grenada, Guatemala, Guinea-Bissau, India, Iraq, Kazakhstan, Kenya, Korea, Kyrgyzstan, Lesotho, Macedonia, Madagascar, Malaysia, Mali, Mauritius, Mexico, Montenegro, Morocco, Nicaragua, Nigeria, Norway, Peru, Poland, Qatar, Romania, Russia, Saudi Arabia, Serbia, South Africa, Tonga, Turkey, Turkmenistan, Tuvalu, Ukraine, Uruguay, Vanuatu, Vietnam, Yemen, and Zambia.

depth of the discussion varies among countries, for example depending on the extent of the problem of corruption in the State concerned. The main findings which can be drawn from the outcome reports are discussed hereafter.[7]

2.2.1. Statements by States under Review

It appears that States report to the Council about problems they experience with corruption in their territory, and about the actions they have taken or will take to address this. The outcome reports then reveal that questions were asked by reviewing States, which were answered by the State under review. Ultimately, the discussion can result in recommendations.

For example, Albania stated that:

> ... corruption, as a typical phenomenon in all post-communist societies, has also affected the country for years. The Albanian Government is convinced that corruption can be successfully combated only through vigorous legal and organizational measures designed to disrupt its sources, which in their essence affect human rights. The preparation of a clear strategy on combating corruption has already yielded fruit. Specialized anticorruption structures are attached to the Prime Minister's Office, the Ministry of the Interior, the Ministry of Finance and others. As to the field of education, the Government has taken concrete measures for the eradication of corruption and has endorsed the legislation for the organization of exams at universities.[8]

This was followed by remarks and questions from Belgium[9] and Russia,[10] a reply from Albania,[11] comments and questions by Italy,[12] again a reply from the Albanian government on the action taken against corruption,[13] remarks and questions by Korea,[14] Slovenia,[15] Greece,[16] the United Kingdom[17] and

---

7 The reader may contact the author to obtain a copy of the full overview, containing all comments, questions and responses, and recommendations on corruption, organised alphabetically per country. This overview also includes countries' CPI score, as well as the character of the comments and questions (e.g. whether they are positive remarks about progress made in the fight against corruption, critical calls for actions, or requests for information).

8 UN HRC, UPR Working Group outcome report Albania, 6th session (2009), UN Doc. A/HRC/13/6, §6. See also the National Report submitted by Albania, UN Doc. A/HRC/WG.6/6/ALB/1, in particular §108–114.

9 *Ibid.* §9.

10 *Ibid.* §16.

11 *Ibid.* §20.

12 *Ibid.* §26.

13 *Ibid.* §47.

14 *Ibid.* §52.

15 *Ibid.* §53.

16 *Ibid.* §54.

17 *Ibid.* §55.

Kyrgyzstan.[18] The discussion ended with recommendations made by Belgium,[19] Slovenia,[20] and the United Kingdom.[21]

When examining the statements made by States under review, it is possible to identify which actions they are currently taking to address corruption. First, a number of States reported on the fact that they have become, or will become, a Party to anti-corruption treaties, particularly the United Nations Convention Against Corruption. *Inter alia*, this is the case with Afghanistan,[22] Madagascar,[23] Serbia,[24] and Turkey. The latter stated that 'Turkey is a State Party to the anti-corruption conventions of the United Nations, the Council of Europe and OECD, and actively participates in GRECO of the Council of Europe.'[25] Furthermore, it is interesting that anti-corruption instruments were mentioned together with 'classic' human rights treaties. For instance, Vanuatu held that:

> … it is not in a position to ratify the International Covenant on Economic, Social and Cultural Rights due to the high threshold of its obligations and the financial constraints, but it is in the preliminary stage of ratification of the Convention Against Torture and Other Cruel, Inhuman or Degrading Treatment or Punishment and the United Nations Convention Against Corruption. Draft policy papers for the ratification of the two Conventions will soon be submitted to the Council of Ministers for endorsement.[26]

States frequently referred to the adoption or amendment of domestic anti-corruption legislation, for example Burundi,[27] Cambodia,[28] Grenada,[29] and Macedonia.[30] Also, on many occasions countries reported on the establishment of domestic anti-

18 *Ibid.* §59.
19 *Ibid.* §67 ad 27.
20 *Ibid.* §67 ad 28.
21 *Ibid.* §69 ad 12.
22 UN HRC, UPR Working Group outcome report Afghanistan, 5th session (2009), UN Doc. A/HRC/12/9, §88.
23 UN HRC, UPR Working Group outcome report Madagascar, 7th session (2010), UN Doc. A/HRC/14/13, §11.
24 UN HRC, UPR Working Group outcome report Serbia, 3rd session (2008), UN Doc. A/HRC/10/78, §8.
25 UN HRC, UPR Working Group outcome report Turkey, 8th session (2010), UN Doc. A/HRC/15/13, §15.
26 UN HRC, UPR Working Group outcome report Vanuatu, 5th session (2009), UN Doc. A/HRC/12/14, §19.
27 UN HRC, UPR Working Group outcome report Burundi, 3rd session (2008), UN Doc. A/HRC/10/71, §77.
28 UN HRC, UPR Working Group outcome report Cambodia, 6th session (2009), UN Doc. A/HRC/13/4, §18.
29 UN HRC, UPR Working Group outcome report Grenada, 8th session (2010), UN Doc. A/HRC/15/12, §19.
30 UN HRC, UPR Working Group outcome report Macedonia, 5th session (2009), UN Doc. A/HRC/12/15, §44.

corruption bodies, such as Guatemala,[31] Kenya,[32] Korea,[33] Malaysia,[34] Romania,[35] and Tonga.[36] A small number of countries, including Cambodia[37] and Serbia[38] referred to disciplinary actions or the prosecution of corrupt officials. Finally, other actions are taken against corruption, such as education campaigns (as mentioned by Cambodia).[39]

Occasional reference was made to the Corruption Perception Index. For example, Macedonia pointed out that its score on this index has improved from 106 to 74 in two years time.[40] Such statements show that States may value their position in the CPI. Also noteworthy are the ambitious pledges about corruption made by some States: Benin pointed out that 'according to the latest analysis, corruption is still not fully eradicated in Benin, but measures are being taken to reach level of zero corruption between now and 2015.'[41] This is a remarkable statement given the country's CPI ranking of 100, listing Benin as a country with a high level of perceived corruption.

2.2.2. Comments and Questions by Reviewing States

The outcome reports show that many comments were made by reviewing States about corruption in the State under review, and questions were asked. On many occasions, States praised the State under review for taking anti-corruption measures, such as the ratification of anti-corruption treaties including UNCAC and the Inter-American Convention Against Corruption. States were also commended for having established domestic anti-corruption bodies, and for having adopted or

---

31 UN HRC, UPR Working Group outcome report Guatemala, 2nd session (2008), UN Doc. A/HRC/8/38, §18.
32 UN HRC, UPR Working Group outcome report Kenya, 8th session (2010), UN Doc. A/HRC/15/8, §10.
33 UN HRC, UPR Working Group outcome report Korea, 2nd session (2008), UN Doc. A/HRC/8/40, §5.
34 UN HRC, UPR Working Group outcome report Malaysia, 4th session (2009), UN Doc. A/HRC/11/30, §17.
35 UN HRC, UPR Working Group outcome report Romania, 2nd session (2008), UN Doc. A/HRC/8/49, §34.
36 UN HRC, UPR Working Group outcome report Tonga, 2nd session (2008), UN Doc. A/HRC/8/48, §34.
37 UN HRC, UPR Working Group outcome report Cambodia, 6th session (2009), UN Doc. A/HRC/13/4, §18.
38 UN HRC, UPR Working Group outcome report Serbia, 3rd session (2008), UN Doc. A/HRC/10/78, §8.
39 UN HRC, UPR Working Group outcome report Cambodia, 6th session (2009), UN Doc. A/HRC/13/4, §18.
40 UN HRC, UPR Working Group outcome report Macedonia, 5th session (2009), UN Doc. A/HRC/12/15, §44.
41 UN HRC, UPR Working Group outcome report Benin, 2nd session (2008), UN Doc. A/HRC/8/39, §54.

amended anti-corruption legislation. An example of such a remark is the comment of the Netherlands in the review of Belize, where the Netherlands 'referred to the actions taken with regard to good governance mentioned in the national report, such as the new Prevention of Corruption Act, and the fact that Belize is party to the Inter-American Convention Against Corruption [...].'[42] Another example is the comment by Syria in the review of Zambia, stating that Syria 'welcomed the Government's efforts [...] to combat hunger, poverty and corruption. It noted that Zambia was among the foremost African States and 30th in the world in the fight against corruption, according to a report of Transparency International in 2004.'[43]

Yet, States were also critical about corruption in the State under review, and did not seem to hesitate whenever corruption posed serious problems. Regarding the topics which were discussed in relation to corruption, the following deserves to be mentioned. First, we find that corruption in the judiciary is a prominent issue, *inter alia*, in the reviews of Cambodia,[44] Czech Republic,[45] Ghana,[46] Macedonia,[47] Mali,[48] and Peru.[49] Also corruption in the police and the military was discussed, amongst others during the review of Chad,[50] El Salvador,[51] and Montenegro.[52] Furthermore, a recurring issue was the vulnerable position of persons exposing corrupt practices, in particular journalists, who often face harassment when they blow the whistle. Criticisms on such treatment can be found

---

42 UN HRC, UPR Working Group outcome report Belize, 5th session (2009), UN Doc. A/HRC/12/4, §35.

43 UN HRC, UPR Working Group outcome report Zambia, 2nd session (2008), UN Doc. A/HRC/8/43, §42.

44 UN HRC, UPR Working Group outcome report Cambodia, 6th session (2009, UN Doc. A/HRC/13/4, §29 (Belgium); 44 (Netherlands), 66 (USA); 67 (New Zealand); 70 (Slovakia); 82 ad 40 (recommendations); 82 ad 41 (recommendation Norway); 82 ad 42 (recommendation Israel); 82 ad 45 (recommendation Belgium).

45 UN HRC, UPR Working Group outcome report Czech Republic, 1st session (2008), UN Doc. A/HRC/8/33, §43.

46 UN HRC, UPR Working Group outcome report Ghana, 1st session (2008), UN Doc. A/HRC/8/36, §15 (Czech Republic); 67 (reply Ghana); 68 ad 4 (recommendation Czech Republic).

47 UN HRC, UPR Working Group outcome report Macedonia, 5th session (2009), UN Doc. A/HRC/12/15, §55 (Greece).

48 UN HRC, UPR Working Group outcome report Mali, 2nd session (2008), UN Doc. A/HRC/8/50, §27 (Canada); 30 (reply Mali); 36 ad 20 (recommendation Canada).

49 UN HRC, UPR Working Group outcome report Peru, 2nd session (2008), UN Doc A/HRC/8/37, §23 (Germany); 52 ad 11 (recommendation Germany).

50 UN HRC, UPR Working Group outcome report Chad, 5th session (2009), UN Doc. A/HRC/12/5, §66 (South Africa).

51 UN HRC, UPR Working Group outcome report El Salvador, 7th session (2010), UN Doc. A/HRC/14/5, §11 (recommendation Italy); 43 (recommendation Canada).

52 UN HRC, UPR Working Group outcome report Montenegro, 3rd session (2008), UN Doc. A/HRC/10/74, §51 (Slovakia).

in the reviews of Bosnia and Herzegovina,[53] Brazil,[54] Montenegro,[55] Peru,[56] Serbia,[57] and Vietnam.[58] Another topic is the role of public officials in human trafficking, as discussed *inter alia* in the review of Uruguay.[59]

2.2.3. Recommendations Made to States under Review

Not only did the outcome reports reveal comments and questions about corruption, but on many occasions the dialogue with the State under review resulted in recommendations on anti-corruption, specified in bold in the final sections of the outcome report under the header 'conclusions and recommendations'. While corruption was discussed in 77 outcome reports, 44 of these reports include one or more recommendations on the topic. A total of 80 recommendations were made. When considering that during the first seven sessions, a total of 10,262 recommendations were made, this seems little, but one must bear in mind that a wide variety of human rights topics are on the agenda during the UPR.[60]

Often, the recommendations on corruption were quite general. For example, in respect of Kyrgyzstan, Tajikistan and Afghanistan recommended that the country 'adopt a zero-tolerance policy towards corruption', while Jordan recommended that Kyrgyzstan 'fight corruption at all levels' and Singapore recommended that the State 'seize this opportunity to create a corruption-free environment.'[61] It was noted by UPR Info, an NGO monitoring the UPR process, that recommendations made by States during the UPR frequently tend to be general, so this is not merely a characteristic of recommendations on the topic of corruption.[62]

Nevertheless, there were also several recommendations on corruption which were more specified. It was frequently recommended that States should ratify anti-corruption treaties, including the UNCAC. *Inter alia*, this was recommended to the

---

53 UN HRC, UPR Working Group outcome report Bosnia and Herzegovina, 7th session (2010), UN Doc. A/HRC/14/16, §47 (Netherlands).

54 UN HRC, UPR Working Group outcome report Brazil, 1st session (2008), UN Doc. A/HRC/8/27, §39 (Norway).

55 UN HRC, UPR Working Group outcome report Montenegro, 3rd session (2008), UN Doc. A/HRC/10/74, §37 (Canada).

56 UN HRC, UPR Working Group outcome report Peru, 2nd session (2008), UN Doc. A/HRC/8/37, §41 (USA).

57 UN HRC, UPR Working Group outcome report Serbia, 3rd session (2008), UN Doc. A/HRC/10/78, §47 (Czech Republic).

58 UN HRC, UPR Working Group outcome report Vietnam, 5th session (2009), UN Doc. A/HRC/12/11, §35 (Canada); 61 (Switzerland); 99 ad 101 (recommendation Canada).

59 UN HRC, UPR Working Group outcome report Uruguay, 5th session (2009), UN Doc. A/HRC/12/12, §63 (USA).

60 UPR Info, 'Analytical Assessment of the Universal Periodic Review', (Geneva, 2010) at p. 9.

61 UN HRC, UPR Working Group outcome report Kyrgyzstan, 8th session (2010), UN Doc. A/HRC/15/2, §76 ad 27, 76 ad 28, and 76 ad 29, 76 ad 32.

62 UPR Info, 'Analytical Assessment of the Universal Periodic Review', at p. 9.

Dominican Republic by Algeria,[63] and to Equitorial Guinea by Australia.[64] It is interesting that in such recommendations, the recommending State sometimes mentions anti-corruption treaties side by side with traditional human rights treaties. For instance, the Netherlands recommended that Vanuatu ratifies the International Covenant on Economic, Social and Cultural Rights and the United Nations Convention Against Corruption.[65] Furthermore, it was mentioned multiple times that the State under review should adopt domestic anti-corruption legislation, and set up anti-corruption bodies, for example as recommended by multiple States to Cambodia.[66] In addition, there were other more specific recommendations. For example, Norway recommended Angola 'to consider partnership in the Extractive Industries Transparency Initiative, as a measure against corruption and a means towards poverty reduction.'[67] Furthermore, the USA recommended Vanuatu to 'allocate more funding to the Ombudsman to allow for more aggressive prosecution of corruption cases.'[68] Moreover, Canada recommended Vietnam to 'adopt a whistleblower law so that those who identify corruption are protected from prosecution or harassment.'[69] These specific recommendations are the most useful, since they give particular guidance to the State under review.

2.2.4. Countries in Respect of Which Corruption is Discussed

It is interesting to examine in respect of which countries corruption was discussed during the UPR. In this regard, it must be kept in mind that not all UN Member States were reviewed yet, since at the day of writing, sessions 9 to 11 were still to come. From the first eight sessions we can however conclude that the large majority of countries in respect of which corruption was discussed, are developing countries with high levels of perceived corruption according to the CPI, such as Afghanistan and Cambodia. Also countries ranking in the middle of the CPI are scrutinised. Fewer remarks were made about corruption, for example, in Western Europe.

Nevertheless, a small number of comments were made in respect of States which are not generally known for their pervasive corruption. In respect of Germany (with

---

63 UN HRC, UPR Working Group outcome report Dominican Republic, 6th session (2010), UN Doc. A/HRC/13/3, §12.

64 UN HRC, UPR Working Group outcome report Equatorial Guinea, 6th session (2010), UN Doc. A/HRC/13/16, §5.

65 UN HRC, UPR Working Group outcome report Vanuatu, 5th session (2009), UN Doc. A/HRC/12/14, §31 and 56 ad 4.

66 UN HRC, UPR Working Group outcome report Cambodia, 6th session (2009), UN Doc. A/HRC/13/4, §82 ad 35 *et seq.*

67 UN HRC, UPR Working Group outcome report Angola, 7th session (2010), UN Doc. A/HRC/14/11, §126.

68 UN HRC, UPR Working Group outcome report Vanuatu, 5th session (2009), UN Doc. A/HRC/12/14, §56 ad 17.

69 UN HRC, UPR Working Group outcome report Vietnam, 5th session (2009), UN Doc. A/HRC/12/11, §65 and 99 ad 101.

a CPI 2011 ranking of 14), Russia 'noted that Germany is not completely free from corruption. It recommended that Germany make additional efforts to combat corruption and to examine the possibility of ratifying the United Nations Convention Against Corruption.'[70] This comment and recommendation shows the usefulness of the UPR in assessing the human rights situation, including the status of corruption, in *all* countries, including Western nations. The fact that Germany is not (yet) a party to the UNCAC is certainly something that deserves to be noted, especially if the country criticises developing countries for corruption problems. As noted by Human Rights Watch, 'through the UPR, the Human Rights Council has examined country situations that are rarely spotlighted in international forums, and has shed light on human rights concerns in States with generally strong human rights performance where such issues would otherwise have been overlooked.'[71]

Another remarkable recommendation was made to Norway by Kyrgyzstan, stating that Norway should 'continue efforts to counter corruption and particularly look into the opportunity to adopt legislation in line with the United Nations Convention Against Corruption'.[72]

2.2.5. Countries Commenting, Asking, Recommending about Corruption

It is relevant to consider which countries are most critical about corrupt practices in other States. According to the broader analysis of the first seven UPR sessions conducted by NGO Info, it is generally true that the most active regional group at the review session is the regional group to which the State under review belongs.[73] On a few occasions, this pattern can also be detected in the comments and recommendations on corruption. For example, Tajikistan and Afghanistan made recommendations to nearby Kyrgyzstan.[74] But it is also clear that the discussions on corruption go far beyond regional boundaries. A variety of both developed and developing countries made comments, asked questions, and formulated recommendations about corruption. It is also noticeable that a number of developed States are rather active in this respect, in particular Canada and the USA. On the other hand, African States do not take on the role of criticising countries for corruption very often.

---

70 UN HRC, UPR Working Group outcome report Germany, 4th session (2009), UN Doc. A/HRC/11/15, §25 and 81 ad 26.

71 Human Rights Watch, 'Curing the Selectivity Syndrome: The 2011 Review of the Human Rights Council', (New York, June 2010) at p. 12. also quoted by UPR Info, 'Analytical Assessment of the Universal Periodic Review', at p. 10.

72 UN HRC, UPR Working Group outcome report Norway, 6th session (2009), UN Doc. A/HRC/13/5, §37.

73 UPR Info, 'Analytical Assessment of the Universal Periodic Review', at p. 8.

74 UN HRC, UPR Working Group outcome report Kyrgyzstan, 8th session (2010), UN Doc. A/HRC/15/2, §76 ad 27 and 76 ad 28.

2.2.6. The Relationship Between Corruption and Human Rights Violations

For the purposes of the present study, it is important to determine what was stated during the UPR sessions about the relationship between corruption and human rights. Do countries perceive corruption as a human rights violation in itself, or as a part of broader circumstances affecting human rights? A number of State remarks shed light on this matter. The Netherlands asked Guatemala about 'corruption as a source of human rights abuses.'[75] In the review of Guinea-Bissau, Indonesia pointed out that 'poverty, a lack of modern infrastructure and funding, a low literacy rate and rampant corruption were all obstacles to the effective promotion and protection of human rights and to development in the country.'[76] Furthermore, Mexico stated that its own national report is 'based on the premise that corruption, public insecurity and impunity are a threat to human rights.'[77] In the same review, Cuba noted that 'corruption and violence are among the largest obstacles to the full enjoyment of human rights.'[78] Moreover, Israel found that in Nicaragua, 'human rights violations remained prevalent, including [...] widespread corruption.'[79] Poland, during its own review, found that 'corruption is a serious obstacle to ensuring an environment conducive to the full enjoyment of human rights.'[80] In the recommendations on Vietnam, Iran argued that 'corruption negatively affects the enjoyment of the human rights of everyone'.[81] Canada recommended that Yemen 'implement strict judicial measures on corruption and bribery, which continue to have devastating effects on socio-economic rights.'[82] Finally, South Africa referred in Zambia's review 'to corruption and its negative impact on the enjoyment of economic, social and cultural rights.'[83]

These phrases point to the fact that corruption is clearly considered to be a human rights issue. However, the States concerned remained vague about the precise linkages between corruption and human rights violations. A clear

75 UN HRC, Working Group outcome report Guatemala, 2nd session (2008), UN Doc. A/HRC/8/38, §44.

76 UN HRC, UPR Working Group outcome report Guinea-Bissau, 8th session (2010), UN Doc. A/HRC/15/10, §25.

77 UN HRC, UPR Working Group outcome report Mexico, 4th session (2009), UN Doc. A/HRC/11/27, §12.

78 *Ibid.* §30.

79 UN HRC, UPR Working Group outcome report Nicaragua, 7th session (2010), UN Doc. A/HRC/14/3, §70.

80 UN HRC, UPR Working Group outcome report Poland, 1st session (2008), UN Doc. A/HRC/8/30, §52.

81 UN HRC, UPR Working Group outcome report Vietnam 5th session (2009), UN Doc. A/HRC/12/11, §99 ad 36.

82 UN HRC, UPR Working Group outcome report Yemen, 5th session (2009), UN Doc. A/HRC/12/13, §91 ad 71.

83 UN HRC, UPR Working Group outcome report Zambia, 2nd session (2008), UN Doc. A/HRC/8/43, §52.

recognition of the idea that corruption can in itself constitute a violation of human rights is absent, except perhaps in the remark by Israel.

2.3. Concluding Remarks

From the discussion above, it can be concluded that during the first 8 UPR sessions, a number of States under review reported about corruption on their own initiative in their national reports. States also discussed the anti-corruption activities they are undertaking, including the ratification of anti-corruption treaties, the adoption of national anti-corruption legislation, the establishment of domestic anti-corruption bodies, and disciplinary action/prosecution of officials. These are also issues on which the reviewing States commented, asked questions, and formulated recommendations. Topics discussed were, *inter alia*, corruption in the judiciary, and the vulnerable position of whistleblowers such as journalists.

From the statements made by the States under review, the questions asked by reviewing States, and the comments and recommendations made, it becomes unequivocally clear that corruption is often mentioned side by side with the 'traditional', 'classic' human rights topics such as the prohibition of torture, child labour and the abolition of the death penalty. Hence, one of the main conclusions of the present research is that, in the view of States, corruption clearly is a human rights issue, and the UPR is an appropriate forum to address it. Arguments stating that corruption should be kept out of the human rights discourse cannot be considered valid in the light of this recent State practice.[84] States did not seem reluctant to discuss corruption, albeit in abstract terms, and with little reference to cases of grand corruption. Nevertheless, there is no clear evidence that, although corruption is a human rights topic, States find that corruption is in itself a violation of certain human rights. There is still a need for further elaboration of the theory in this respect. This matter is addressed in a later chapter.[85]

3. Special Procedures of the UN Human Rights Council

3.1. Background

Under the Human Rights Council, a wide variety of Special Procedures exists. These procedures are either carried out by one person (Special Rapporteur, Special Representative of the Secretary-General, or Independent Expert), or by a group of

84 As argued by Morag Goodwin and Kate Rose-Sender, 'Linking Corruption and Human Rights: An Unwelcome Addition to the Development Discourse', in Martine Boersma and Hans Nelen (eds.), *Corruption & Human Rights: Interdisciplinary Perspectives* (Maastricht Series in Human Rights Antwerp: Intersentia, 2010), p. 221–240.

85 See chapter VI *infra*.

five (Working Group).[86] The differences in titles do not reflect major differences in responsibilities or working methods.[87] All mandate-holders are independent and impartial experts.[88] The Special Procedures address human rights issues on a certain topic (thematic mandates), or the human rights situation in a certain country (country mandates).[89] Since the Special Procedures are based on the UN Charter, they can cover all UN Member States, regardless of whether these States have ratified international human rights treaties or not. This is an important advantage compared to the work of the treaty bodies.[90]

The Special Procedures have the following tasks: (i) analysing the thematic issue or country situation, which includes country visits; (ii) advising on the measures which ought to be taken by governments and other actors; (iii) alerting UN organs and agencies (particularly the Human Rights Council), and the international community to the need to address specific situations and issues; the Special Procedures have an early warning role, and they can encourage preventive measures; (iv) advocating on behalf of victims of human rights violations, by requesting urgent action by States, and by calling upon governments to respond to specific allegations of human rights violations and provide redress (urgent appeals[91] and letters of allegation[92]); (v) activating and mobilising international and national communities and the Human Rights Council to address specific human rights issues and encouraging cooperation among governments, civil society and intergovernmental organisations; (vi) following up to recommendations.[93] Hence, the activities of the Special Procedures are of a much more practical nature than the procedures of the treaty bodies. The output of the Special Procedures is not binding but can nevertheless carry political and moral value.[94]

The present section 3 analyses what the practice of the Special Procedures reveals about the links between corruption and human rights violations. The related resolutions of the former Human Rights Commission, the current Human Rights Council, and the General Assembly are also taken into account. A selected number

---

86 Introduction to the Special Procedures of the Human Rights Council: <www2.ohchr.org/english/bodies/chr/special/index.htm>, accessed 25 June 2011.

87 Office of the United Nations High Commissioner for Human Rights, 'Manual of the United Nations Human Rights Special Procedures', (August 2008) at p. 6, footnote 5.

88 *Ibid.* at p. 7, §11.

89 Website OHCHR: <www2.ohchr.org/english/bodies/chr/special/index.htm>, accessed 25 June 2011.

90 Miko Lempinen, *Challenges Facing the System of Special Procedures of the United Nations Commission on Human Rights* (Turku/Abo: Institute for Human Rights, Abo Akademi University, 2001) at p. 1 and 34 *et seq.*

91 For more on urgent appeals, see Office of the United Nations High Commissioner for Human Rights, 'Manual of the United Nations Human Rights Special Procedures', at p. 14, §43–45.

92 For more on letters of allegation, see *Ibid.* at p. 15, §46–48.

93 *Ibid.* at p. 5, §5.

94 Ingrid Westendorp, *Women and Housing: Gender Makes a Difference* (School of Human Rights Research Series, 23; Antwerp: Intersentia, 2007) at p. 308.

of relevant thematic procedures are discussed first, followed by an analysis of the output of all current country mandates.

3.2. The Former Special Rapporteur on Corruption and Its Impact on the Full Enjoyment of Human Rights, in Particular Economic, Social and Cultural Rights

3.2.1. Introduction

The key mandate to consider is that of the former Special Rapporteur on corruption and its impact on the full enjoyment of human rights, in particular economic, social and cultural rights. Ms. Christy Mbonu (Nigerian) was appointed in 2003 by the former Sub-Commission on the Promotion and Protection of Human Rights,[95] after she had submitted a working paper to the Sub-Commission.[96] Because Mbonu was appointed by the Sub-Commission, her mandate was of a lower formal status within the UN than the mandates under the Commission itself (now: Council). Yet, the fact that a Special Procedure was dedicated to corruption constitutes a clear acknowledgement that corruption undoubtedly is a human rights issue. During the short period of her mandate, which ended in 2006 when the Sub-Commission was replaced by the Advisory Committee,[97] the Special Rapporteur delivered a preliminary report,[98] a progress report[99] and a final report.[100] The present section considers the findings of Mbonu as regards the specific links between corruption and human rights violations.

---

95 Sub-Commission on the Promotion and Protection of Human Rights, Resolution 2003/2, UN Doc. E/CN.4/Sub.2/RES/2003/2, which was endorsed by the Commission on Human Rights in its Decision 2004/106.

96 Working paper submitted by Ms. Christy Mbonu in accordance with Sub-Commission decision 2002/106, 14 May 2003, UN Doc. E/CN.4/Sub.2/2003/18.

97 As indicated on the website of the Office of the High Commissioner for Human Rights: <www2.ohchr.org/english/issues/development/governance/formerSR.htm>, accessed 25 June 2011. The Advisory Committee of the Human Rights Council is the new think-thank of the Human Rights Council, comprised of eighteen experts. See <www2.ohchr.org/english/bodies/hrcouncil/advisorycommittee.htm>, accessed 25 June 2011.

98 Preliminary report of the Special Rapporteur on corruption and its impact on the full enjoyment of human rights, in particular economic, social and cultural rights, Sub-Cion 56th session, 7 July 2004, UN Doc. E/CN.4/Sub.2/2004/23.

99 Progress report submitted by the Special Rapporteur on corruption and its impact on the full enjoyment of human rights, in particular economic, social and cultural rights, Sub-Cion 57th session, 22 June 2005, UN Doc. E/CN.4/Sub.2/2005/18.

100 Final report of the Special Rapporteur on corruption and its impact on the full enjoyment of human rights, in particular economic, social and cultural rights, Sub-Cion 58th session, 8 August 2006, UN Doc. A/HRC/Sub.1/58/CRP.10.

3.2.2. Outcomes

The mandate of the Special Rapporteur offered in itself an excellent opportunity within the UN system to examine closely whether, and, if so, how corruption violates human rights, and to raise awareness about this topic. Unfortunately, the study carried out by Mbonu remained rather descriptive and revealed little about the human rights dimension of corruption.

In her short initial working paper, Mbonu avoided defining 'corruption',[101] although she did set out the various forms of corruption in a non-exhaustive list. The distinctions she made were however rather peculiar.[102] She also pointed to a number of causes of corruption,[103] discussed its victims,[104] and paid attention to several actions taken against corruption (including treaties) at the national, regional and international level.[105] Finally, she suggested a number of remedies against corruption, none of which were specifically related to human rights.[106] As regards the links between corruption and human rights violations, she merely noted that 'the enjoyment of all regimes of rights, be they economic, social and cultural or civil and political, is seriously undermined by the phenomenon of corruption.'[107] It was also stressed that 'the negative impact of corruption on the enjoyment of all rights is therefore all-encompassing and should be dealt with in a holistic manner.'[108]

Mbonu's preliminary report discussed manifestations of corruption,[109] identified its victims,[110] and elaborated upon corruption's socio-economic, civil-political, and private sector consequences.[111] With regard to the civil and political consequences, mention was made of the rights of political participation (Article 21(1) UDHR and Article 25 ICCPR), and Mbonu linked the right to equality and non-discrimination (Article 26 ICCPR) to judicial corruption.[112] However, the piece clearly lacks a thorough legal analysis. Furthermore, the report discussed anti-corruption initiatives.[113] In her conclusions, Mbonu stated 'Suffice it to say that corruption,

---

101 Working paper, §3. She noted that 'It is perhaps not necessary here to waste time on the definition of corruption [...]'. This is a pity, since a Special Rapporteur on corruption should demarcate his/her main topic of concern.

102 She listed: (a) looted funds and wealth kept secretly abroad; (b) misappropriation of public funds; (c) money-laundering; (d) gratification; (e) abuse of office. Working paper, §11.

103 Working paper, §12.

104 Working paper, §13–14.

105 Working paper, §15–20.

106 Working paper, §21–22. Listed are (a) political leadership and political will; (b) anti-corruption legislation; (c) law enforcement and the judiciary; (d) provision of jobs, good pay and poverty eradication; (e) tougher sanctions; (f) role of civil society, the media, and the public; (g) moral regeneration.

107 Working paper §3. This is reiterated in the preliminary report, §7 and 40.

108 Working paper §13.

109 Preliminary report, §7–16.

110 *Ibid.* §17–21.

111 *Ibid.* §22–39.

112 *Ibid.* §30.

113 *Ibid.* §40–56.

whether systemic, endemic or petty, violates citizens' enjoyment of all the rights contained in all the international instruments.'[114] This is quite a bold claim, not supported by proper argumentation in the report itself. Subsequently, the Special Rapporteur formulated recommendations, but these were rather general anti-corruption suggestions, not paying attention to human rights-related remedies. The end of the report did call for 'periodic high-level meetings' in association with agencies such as the IMF, the World Bank, the ILO and the WHO, corporate representatives and the UN Office in Vienna. In the opinion of Mbonu, 'the focus of the meeting would be on the human rights dimension of corruption.'[115]

Likewise, the progress report offers few new insights. It was discussed how corruption erodes democratic institutional structures: the judiciary, law enforcement agencies, and political parties.[116] With regard to judicial corruption, mention was made of the right to a fair trial, and the right to equality before the law and non-discrimination.[117] In the discussion of political party corruption, rights to political participation were quoted.[118] The Special Rapporteur found that 'various manifestations of corruption in the political parties exist in many countries that invariably violate the rights of citizens. A fundamental right is violated if, due to poverty, vote buying by political parties denies the electorate from voting for the best candidates.'[119] Subsequently, the issue of corruption in procurement was dealt with,[120] as well as capital flight through corruption.[121] In respect of corruption in procurement, Mbonu held that this is an obstacle to the realisation of economic, social and cultural rights.[122] The remainder of the report dealt with partnerships in the fight against corruption.[123] Like the majority of the report, its conclusions and recommendations were not human rights-related.

The Special Rapporteur's final report shows that Mbonu had prepared a questionnaire on the fight against corruption, to be filled in by Member States and anti-corruption NGOs. It remains unknown what happened to this initiative after Mbonu's mandate ended.

As regards the core of the mandate, i.e. establishing links between corruption and violations of especially economic, social and cultural rights, the results of the Special Rapporteur are disappointing. Mbonu did stress that diversions of public funds by corrupt officials 'lead to the denial of rights, in particular economic, social

114 *Ibid.* §57.
115 *Ibid.* §60.
116 Progress report, §12–31.
117 *Ibid.* §13–14.
118 *Ibid.* §21.
119 *Ibid.* §24.
120 *Ibid.* §32–37.
121 *Ibid.* §38–40.
122 *Ibid.* §35, stating that 'Experts have identified procurement as one of the areas most prone to corruption and constituting a huge obstacle to States in meeting their obligation to gradually provide those rights adjudged to be "positive rights" to their citizens.' See also §63.
123 *Ibid.* §41–58.

and cultural rights.'[124] She argued that the diverted resources could no longer be used for education, housing and health care, and held that 'those deprived of these rights as enshrined in the International Bill of Human Rights can best be described as victims of corruption.'[125] Second, the Special Rapporteur seemed to acknowledge that corruption does not only lead to diversion of resources, but that it also impacts upon the way in which the remaining resources are spent. Resources are allocated inefficiently, the costs of investment are raised, and the quality of public sector projects and services is decreased.[126] These observations may very well be correct, but one would rightfully expect a more in-depth analysis from a Special Rapporteur.

In the resulting resolutions of the Sub-Commission, it was stated, *inter alia*, that the Sub-Commission is 'deeply concerned that the enjoyment of human rights, be they economic, social and cultural or civil and political, is seriously undermined by the phenomenon of corruption.' Recommendations to States to combat corruption did not elaborate any further on the links with human rights.[127]

3.2.3. Assessment

While the mandate of the Special Rapporteur had great potential for developing the topic of corruption and human rights, the few reports that were published are disappointing. Rather than focusing on corruption's links to human rights violations, the reports dealt with general aspects of corruption, adding little to existing literature. Moreover, the analysis by Mbonu remained rather superficial and was conducted in a haphazard fashion. For instance, Mbonu did not refer to the various State obligations under Article 2(1) of the ICESCR (e.g. the obligation to devote 'maximum available resources'), which would have been enabled stronger legal claims.[128] Now that the mandate was discontinued altogether, the opportunity was lost to advance the topic in this Special Procedure.

3.3. Other Selected Thematic Mandates

3.3.1. Introduction

At the time of writing, 33 thematic mandates exist.[129] Since an in-depth discussion of all these mandates in the present work is not feasible, a selection of ten relevant

124 Working paper §5.

125 *Ibid.* §13.

126 Working paper §5–6.

127 Sub-Commission on Human Rights Resolution, 5 August 2005, UN Doc. E/CN.4/Sub.2/2005/L.24/Rev.1.

128 See chapter VI hereafter for an analysis of State obligations under Article 2(1) of the ICESCR in relation to corruption.

129 Thematic mandates of the Human Rights Council: <www2.ohchr.org/english/bodies/chr/special/themes.htm>, accessed 25 June 2011.

Special Procedures was made for the purpose of this study. The leading criterion is the topic of the mandate. Some procedures are at first sight more relevant in the context of corruption compared to others. For example, the mandate on the independence of judges and lawyers seems more related to corruption than the mandate on contemporary forms of racism, although links can nevertheless exist.

Based on these limiting considerations, all output of the following Special Procedures is examined: (i) the former Special Rapporteur on corruption and its impact on the full enjoyment of human rights, in particular economic, social and cultural rights (as discussed *supra*; (ii) the Special Rapporteur on the independence of judges and lawyers; (iii) the Special Rapporteur on trafficking in persons, especially in women and children; (iv) the Special Rapporteur on the sale of children, child prostitution and child pornography; (v) the Special Rapporteur on the right to adequate housing; (vi) the Special Rapporteur on the right to education; (vii) the Special Rapporteur on the right to food; (viii) the Special Rapporteur on the right to health; (ix) the Independent Expert on the question of human rights and extreme poverty; and (x) the Special Representative of the S-G on human rights and transnational corporations and other business enterprises. The extent to which corruption was discussed by these mandates varies. The main findings are elaborated upon below.

3.3.2. Outcomes

(i) Special Rapporteur on the Independence of Judges and Lawyers

The Special Rapporteur on the independence of judges and lawyers[130] paid substantial attention to corruption, which can also be inferred from the Rapporteur's list of focus issues, which includes 'judicial corruption'.[131] Most of the Special Rapporteur's annual reports addressed corruption,[132] and so did a number of the country reports.[133] Amongst other things, the Special Rapporteur discussed why

---

130 The Special Rapporteur on the independence of judges and lawyers was appointed by Commission on Human Rights Resolution 1994/41. The mandate was extended in 2008 by Human Rights Council Resolution 8/6. The mandate is currently held by Ms. Gabriela Knaul. Previous mandate-holders were Mr. Leandro Despouy (August 2003 – July 2009), and Mr. Param Cumaraswamy (1994 – July 2003).

131 Issues in focus of the Special Rapporteur on the independence of judges and lawyers: <www2.ohchr.org/english/issues/judiciary/issues.htm>, accessed 27 June 2011. Office of the United Nations High Commissioner for Human Rights, Special Rapporteur on the Independence of Judges and Lawyers – Issues in Focus, <www2.ohchr.org/english/issues/judiciary/issues.htm>, accessed 15 September 2010.

132 Annual reports of the Special Rapporteur on the independence of judges and lawyers: <www2.ohchr.org/english/issues/judiciary/annual.htm>, accessed 27 June 2011.

133 Country reports of the Special Rapporteur on the independence of judges and lawyers: <www2.ohchr.org/english/issues/judiciary/visits.htm>, accessed 27 June 2011. Particularly the reports on Mexico, Indonesia, Kazakhstan, Tajikistan and Kyrgyzstan discuss corruption problems in the country concerned.

judicial corruption is harmful,[134] and addressed some of its causes.[135] On the specific links between corruption and human rights, a recent report held that:

> ... corruption is one of the most serious obstacles to the promotion and protection of human rights. Therefore, judges and lawyers should receive continued training on good governance, particularly in combating corruption in the public and private sectors, including in the judiciary. Corruption has a detrimental impact on human rights, the rule of law and democracy. Corruption makes national institutions weak and public trust in them is eroded. Corruption can be political, economic or corporate, but, in all its forms, it undermines democratic values and institutions and the enjoyment of human rights. Judicial integrity is a key element of impartial justice. Judges, prosecutors and lawyers should be trained in the need to combat corruption and in the international norms and declarations. In this aspect, particular attention should be given to the Bangalore Principles on Judicial Conduct. [emphasis added, MB.][136]

Another recent report noted that:

> ... judicial corruption has been identified as a factor contributing to impunity. Combating corruption is often complex as often there is no prima facie evidence of its existence and it may permeate all institutions in the criminal justice system. Corruption in one part of the judicial system may undermine efforts of the whole system to combat impunity; hence it is important that it be addressed holistically. To counter judicial corruption, concrete measures will have to be adopted, such as the disclosure of personal assets by judicial officials and other persons with significant responsibility in the criminal justice system; control mechanisms at the institutional level to ensure the transparency of operations; the establishment of internal oversight bodies and confidential complaint mechanisms; and the regular and systematic publication of activity reports. Additionally, efforts should be made to improve the salaries of judges, magistrates and judicial staff to reduce susceptibility to corruption.[137]

Sections such as these are useful because they provide more concrete guidance as to what actions ought to be taken by States.

---

134 Report of the SR on the independence of judges and lawyers, CHR 60th session, 31 December 2003, UN Doc. E/CN.4/2004/60, §39–40.

135 Report of the SR on the independence of judges and lawyers, CHR 60th session, 31 December 2003, UN Doc. E/CN.4/2004/60, §32; Report of the SR on the independence of judges and lawyers, GA 63rd session, 12 August 2008, UN Doc. A/63/271, §46; Report of the SR on the independence of judges and lawyers, HRC 11th session, 24 March 2009, UN Doc. A/HRC/11/41, §75; Report of the SR on the independence of judges and lawyers, HRC 4th session, 18 January 2007, UN Doc. A/HRC/4/25, §19.

136 Report of the SR on the independence of judges and lawyers, HRC 14th session, 25 March 2010, UN Doc. A/HRC/14/26, §73–74.

137 Report of the SR on the independence of judges and lawyers, GA 65th session, 10 August 2010, UN Doc. A/65/274, §44–45.

Moreover, it follows from the reports that the Special Rapporteur linked the World Bank with Transparency International, the Judicial Group on Strengthening Judicial Integrity, and other anti-corruption organisations.[138] Such a practical collaboration and exchange of ideas is highly desirable and should be continued. Finally, several communications and allegations sent to governments, as well as urgent appeals, dealt with corruption. These mainly concerned the punishment by States of persons who blow the whistle about judicial corruption,[139] or threats to persons who investigate corruption.[140]

(ii) Special Rapporteurs on Trafficking in Persons, and on the Sale of Children, Child Prostitution and Child Pornography

Since the mandate of the Special Rapporteur on trafficking in persons, especially in women and children, and the mandate of the Special Rapporteur on the sale of children, child prostitution and child pornography are related, as far as the subject-matter is concerned, these two procedures are considered together.

The Special Rapporteur on trafficking in persons, especially in women and children[141] has thus far paid surprisingly little explicit attention in the annual reports to the central role of corruption in human trafficking.[142] In 2009 the Rapporteur identified corruption as one of the root causes of trafficking, and found that it was insufficiently tackled.[143] One would certainly expect a thorough analysis of the topic given such a statement. In the country reports, the Rapporteur

---

138 Report of the SR on the independence of judges and lawyers, CHR 54th session, 12 February 1998, UN Doc. E/CN.4/1998/39, §21; Report of the SR on the independence of judges and lawyers, CHR 56th session, 21 February 2000, UN Doc. E/CN.4/2000/61, §26(d) and 29–30; Report of the SR on the independence of judges and lawyers, CHR 57th session, 1 February 2001, UN Doc. E/CN.4/2001/65, §28–29; Report of the SR on the independence of judges and lawyers, CHR 58th session, 11 February 2002, UN Doc. E/CN.4/2002/72, §25; Report of the SR on the independence of judges and lawyers, CHR 60th session, 31 December 2003, UN Doc. E/CN.4/2004/60, §68.

139 See e.g. Report of the SR on the independence of judges and lawyers, CHR 56th session, 21 February 2000, UN Doc. E/CN.4/2000/61, §187–188; Report of the SR on the independence of judges and lawyers, CHR 57th session, 1 February 2001, UN Doc. E/CN.4/2001/65, §132–133; Report of the SR on the independence of judges and lawyers, Addendum: Communications to and from governments, HRC 14th session, 18 June 2010, UN Doc. A/HRC/14/26/Add.1, §106, 118.

140 Report of the SR on the independence of judges and lawyers, CHR 59th session, 25 February 2003, UN Doc. E/CN.4/2003/65/Add.1, §65 and 67, and 251–253.

141 The SR on trafficking in persons, especially in women and children, was appointed by Commission on Human Rights Resolution 2004/110. The mandate was extended in 2008 by Human Rights Council Resolution 8/12. The mandate is currently held by Ms. Joy Ngozi Ezeilo. Previous mandate-holder was Ms. Sigma Huda (2004–2008).

142 Annual reports of the SR on trafficking in persons: <www2.ohchr.org/english/issues/trafficking/annual.htm>, accessed 27 June 2011.

143 Report of the SR on trafficking in persons, especially women and children, HRC 10th session, 20 February 2009, UN Doc. A/HRC/10/16, section Conclusions and Recommendations.

paid attention to corruption in respect of Bosnia and Herzegovina,[144] discussing, *inter alia*, the involvement of corrupt police officers in human trafficking, and measures were recommended to address this.[145] Brief reference was also made to corruption in the country report on Japan.[146] Regarding communications to and from governments,[147] the Rapporteur noted that a number of communications address factors causing or exacerbating human trafficking, such as corruption,[148] for example the communications sent to Congo[149] and India,[150] and the allegation letter to Myanmar.[151] As an aside, it is interesting to note that the first mandate-holder, Ms. Sigma Huda, was sentenced herself by a Bangladeshi court to three years of imprisonment for complicity in bribery, committed by her husband (a former government minister and barrister).[152]

The Special Rapporteur on the sale of children, child prostitution and child pornography[153] discussed corruption in a large number of annual reports.[154] It was repeatedly stressed that corrupt officials, be it police officers, politicians, judges, village headmen, border officials, immigration officials, or public inspectors, play an important part in facilitating the sale of children for prostitution or adoption. Amongst others, they can be involved in the recruitment of children, their transportation and the supply of the necessary documents. Hence, the Rapporteur called upon the States concerned to improve the quality of law

---

144 Country reports of the SR on trafficking in persons: <www2.ohchr.org/english/issues/trafficking/visits.htm>, accessed 27 June 2011.

145 Report of the SR on trafficking in persons, especially women and children, Mission to Bosnia and Herzegovina, CHR 62nd session, 30 November 2005, UN Doc. E/CN.4/2006/62/Add.2, §19, 28, 55, 82.

146 Report of the SR on trafficking in persons, especially women and children, Mission to Japan, HRC 14th session, 12 May 2010, UN Doc. A/HRC/14/32/Add.4, §24.

147 Communications of the SR on trafficking in persons: <www2.ohchr.org/english/issues/trafficking/communications.htm >, accessed 27 June 2011.

148 Report of the SR on trafficking in persons, especially women and children, Summary of cases transmitted to Governments and replies received, CHR 62nd session, 27 March 2006, UN Doc. E/CN.4/2006/62/Add.1, §5; Report of the SR on trafficking in persons, especially women and children, Summary of cases transmitted to Governments and replies received, HRC 4th session, 30 May 2007, UN Doc. A/HRC/4/23/Add.1, §6.

149 Report of the SR on trafficking in persons, especially women and children, Summary of cases transmitted to Governments and replies received, CHR 62nd session, 27 March 2006, UN Doc. E/CN.4/2006/62/Add.1, §32.

150 *Ibid.* §51.

151 *Ibid.* §92, 94 and 98.

152 *The Daily Star*, 28 August 2007, 'Huda gets 7 years, Sigma 3 yrs for graft.' <www.thedailystar.net/story.php?nid=1694>, accessed 27 June 2011.

153 The SR on the sale of children, child prostitution and child pornography was appointed by Commission on Human Rights Resolution 1990/68. The mandate was extended in 2008 by Human Rights Council Resolution 7/13. The mandate is currently held by Ms. Najat M'jid Maalla. Previously, the mandate was held by Mr. Vitit Muntarbhorn (1991–1994), Ms. Ofelia Calcetas-Santos (1994–2001) and Mr. Juan Miguel Petit (2001–2008).

154 Annual reports of the SR on the sale of children, child prostitution and child pornography: <www2.ohchr.org/english/issues/children/rapporteur/annual.htm>, accessed 27 June 2011.

enforcement by ensuring that officials receive adequate remuneration and training, and that they will be punished if they are complicit in trafficking. Powerful information campaigns may also be a tool to fight corruption. Furthermore, corrupt practices were addressed in communications, allegation letters and urgent appeals to governments.[155] Most of the Rapporteur's country reports also discussed corrupt practices in the country under scrutiny.[156] Comments were made in respect of Nepal,[157] Mexico,[158] Kenya,[159] Guatemala,[160] Belgium,[161] Russia,[162] Morocco,[163] South Africa,[164] Brazil,[165] Paraguay,[166] Romania,[167] Albania,[168] and Ukraine,[169] condemning the involvement of corrupt officials in the exploitation of children, and calling upon States to take measures.

---

155 Report of the SR on the sale of children, child prostitution and child pornography, CHR 62nd session, 27 March 2006, UN Doc. E/CN.4/2006/67/Add.1, §55–59; Report of the SR on the sale of children, child prostitution and child pornography, CHR 62nd session, 27 March 2006, UN Doc. E/CN.4/2006/67/Add.1, §88–90, 100.

156 Country reports of the SR on the sale of children, child prostitution and child pornography: <www2.ohchr.org/english/issues/children/rapporteur/visits.htm>, accessed 27 June 2011.

157 Report of the SR on the sale of children, child prostitution and child pornography, Mission to Nepal, CHR 50th session, 20 January 1994, UN Doc. E/CN.4/1994/84/Add.1, §24(f) and 60(2).

158 Report of the SR on the sale of children, child prostitution and child pornography, on the mission to Mexico, CHR 54th session, 23 February 1998, UN Doc. E/CN.4/1998/101/Add.2, §113; and Report of the SR on the sale of children, child prostitution and child pornography, on the mission to Mexico, HRC 7th session, 28 January 2008, UN Doc. A/HRC/7/8/Add.2, §9, 40, 46, 76, 77, 79.

159 Report of the SR on the sale of children, child prostitution and child pornography, on the mission to Kenya, 28 January 1998, UN Doc. E/CN.4/1998/101/Add.1, §36.

160 Report of the SR on the sale of children, child prostitution and child pornography, Mission to Guatemala, CHR 56th session, 27 January 2000, UN Doc. E/CN.4/2000/73/Add.2, §105.

161 Report of the SR on the sale of children, child prostitution and child pornography, Mission to Belgium, CHR 56th session, 22 December 1999, UN Doc. E/CN.4/2000/73/Add.1, §11.

162 Report of the SR on the sale of children, child prostitution and child pornography, Mission to Russia, CHR 57th session, 6 February 2001, UN Doc. E/CN.4/2001/78/Add.2, §6.

163 Report of the SR on the sale of children, child prostitution and child pornography, Mission to Morocco, CHR 57th session, 7 November 2000, UN Doc. E/CN.4/2001/78/Add.1, §67–68.

164 Report of the SR on the sale of children, child prostitution and child pornography, Mission to South Africa, CHR 59th session, 9 January 2003, UN Doc. E/CN.4/2003/79/Add.1, §29(b).

165 Report of the SR on the sale of children, child prostitution and child pornography, Mission to Brazil, CHR 60th session, 3 February 2004, UN Doc. E/CN.4/2004/9/Add.2, §58.

166 Report of the SR on the sale of children, child prostitution and child pornography, Mission to Paraguay, CHR 61st session, 9 December 2004, UN Doc. E/CN.4/2005/78/Add.1, §63, 66, 109 and 119.

167 Report of the SR on the sale of children, child prostitution and child pornography, Mission to Romania, CHR 61st session, 26 January 2005, UN Doc. E/CN.4/2005/78/Add.2, §21, 43, 61–62, 104, 112.

168 Report of the SR on the sale of children, child prostitution and child pornography, Mission to Albania, CHR 62nd session, 27 March 2006, UN Doc. E/CN.4/2006/67/Add.2, §6, 47, 61, 62, 87, 129.

169 Report of the SR on the sale of children, child prostitution and child pornography, Mission to Ukraine, HRC 4th session, 27 January 2007, UN Doc. A/HRC/4/Add.2, §62, 63, 64, 70, 76(d), 78, 79.

(iii) Economic, Social and Cultural Rights: Special Rapporteurs on the Rights to Housing, Education, Food, and Health

In order to examine how corruption may violate economic, social and cultural rights, the mandates of the four Special Rapporteurs on the rights to housing, education, food, and health are discussed jointly.

The Special Rapporteur on the right to adequate housing as a component of the right to an adequate standard of living, and on the right to non-discrimination in this context,[170] made a few brief remarks about corruption in the annual reports.[171] These remarks concerned corruption in relation to the privatisation of water services,[172] corruption in the distribution of aid, compensation and reconstruction work in case of natural disasters and humanitarian emergencies.[173] Furthermore, the Rapporteur held that he may have faced non-responsiveness by States 'because the violations of the right to adequate housing touch upon issues such as the pre-eminence given to land and housing as speculative capital, corruption, real-estate mobbing, land grabbing and illegal activities undertaken by land cartels and mafia. These issues negatively impact the efforts of individuals, civil society, and sometimes States themselves to implement the right to adequate housing.[174]

In addition, the country reports of the mandate reveal some discussions about corruption.[175] For example, the report on Afghanistan showed that in order to achieve the right to adequate housing, combating corruption (especially in the judicial system) was deemed necessary.[176] Another example is the report on Spain, discussing corruption in the reclassification of land.[177]

---

170 The SR on the right to adequate housing was appointed by Commission on Human Rights Resolution 2000/9. The mandate was extended in 2007 by Human Rights Council Resolution 15/8. The mandate is currently held by Ms. Raquel Rolnik. The previous mandate-holder was Mr. Miloon Kothari (2000–2008).

171 Annual reports of the SR on the right to adequate housing: <www2.ohchr.org/english/issues/housing/annual.htm>, accessed 27 June 2011.

172 Report of the SR on the right to adequate housing, CHR 58th Session, 1 March 2002, UN Doc. E/CN.4/2002/59, §62.

173 Report of the SR on the right to adequate housing, CHR 62nd Session, 14 March 2006, UN Doc. E/CN.4/2006/41, §29. Reiterated in Report of the SR on the right to adequate housing, HRC 7th Session, 13 February 2008, UN Doc. A/HRC/7/16, §81; and report of the SR on the right to adequate housing, GA 63rd Session, 13 August 2008, UN Doc. A/63/275, §28.

174 Report of the SR on the right to adequate housing, HRC 7th Session, 13 February 2008, UN Doc. A/HRC/7/16, §. 62.

175 Country reports of the SR on the right to housing: <www2.ohchr.org/english/issues/housing/visits.htm>, accessed 27 June 2011.

176 Report of the SR on the right to adequate housing, Mission to Afghanistan, CHR 60th session, 4 March 2004, UN Doc. E/CN.4/2004/48/Add.2, §17, 34, 97(j).

177 Report of the SR on the right to adequate housing, Mission to Spain, HRC 7th session, 7 February 2008, UN Doc. A/HRC/7/16/Add.2, §45–49, 94.

The Special Rapporteur on the right to education[178] hardly paid any attention to corruption in the annual reports.[179] Mention was made of letters sent to the Turkish government, asking for clarification of the case of the collapse of a school building that was not properly built, allegedly because of corruption. This resulted in the death of 84 children.[180] The country reports offer more insights into the topic.[181] Amongst other things, the reports on Uganda, Turkey, Indonesia and China discuss the impact of corruption upon the budgetary allocations for education. Due to corrupt practices, less money is available for education.[182]

The Special Rapporteur on the right to food[183] paid attention to corruption in the annual reports.[184] The first annual report to the Commission set out the main content of the right to food. In his discussion of the tripartite typology (to respect, to protect, to fulfil), the Rapporteur opined that *the obligation to protect* imposes a number of duties on the State, such as the duty to combat corruption.[185] Such a specific connection of corruption to a particular human rights obligation is generally very rare in Special Rapporteurs' reports. Moreover, the Rapporteur identified seven major problem areas which directly affect the realisation of the right to food. One of these areas is corruption.[186] The Rapporteur noted, *inter alia*, that the Rome Declaration of the 1996 World Food Summit expressly mentioned that corruption is one of the causes of food insecurity. The Rapporteur explained that corruption can take many forms and that it occurs in both the North and the South, but that the social consequences of corruption, particularly those affecting food security, are

---

178 The SR on the right to education was appointed by Commission on Human Rights Resolution 1998/33. The mandate was extended in 2008 by Human Rights Council Resolution 8/4. The mandate is currently held by Mr. Kishore Singh. Previous mandate-holders are Mr. Vernor Muñoz Villalobos (2004–2010) and Katarina Tomasevski (1998–2004).

179 Annual reports of the SR on the right to education: <www2.ohchr.org/english/issues/education/rapporteur/annual.htm>, accessed 27 June 2011.

180 Report of the SR on the right to education, CHR 60th Session, 15 January 2004, UN Doc. E/CN.4/2004/45, §51.

181 Country reports of the SR on the right to education: <www2. ohchr.org/english/issues/education/rapporteur/visits.htm>, accessed 27 June 2011.

182 Report of the SR on the right to education, Mission to Uganda, CHR 56th session, 9 August 1999, UN Doc. E/CN.4/2000/6/Add.1, §48; Report of the SR on the right to education, Mission to Turkey, CHR 58th session, 27 March 2002, UN Doc. E/CN.4/2002/60/Add.2, §9, 30, 31, 32; Report of the SR on the right to education, Mission to Indonesia, CHR 59th session, 4 November 2002, UN Doc. E/CN.4/2003/9/Add.1, §9, 47, 50, 63; Report of the SR on the right to education, Mission to China, CHR 60th session, 21 November 2003, UN Doc. E/CN.4/2004/45/Add.1, §15, 18, 32.

183 The SR on the right to food was appointed by Commission on Human Rights Resolution 2000/10. The mandate was extended in 2010 by Human Rights Council Resolution 13/4. The mandate is currently held by Mr. Olivier de Schutter. Previous mandate-holder was Mr. Jean Ziegler (2001–2008).

184 Annual reports of the SR on the right to food: <www2.ohchr.org/english/issues/food/annual.htm>, accessed 27 June 2011.

185 Report of the SR on the right to food, CHR 57th session, 7 February 2001, UN Doc. E/CN.4/2001/53, §28.

186 *Ibid.* §69(e).

the most serious in poor countries. A particular example of corruption in the context of World Bank aid to Chad was mentioned, and it was also stated that the Rapporteur would closely follow the efforts of the Bank, other intergovernmental organisations and NGOs such as TI to achieve transparency and to combat corruption.[187] Later annual reports mentioned corruption every now and then. *Inter alia,* the Rapporteur viewed corruption of the government as a key obstacle to the right to food, since it diverts essential resources away from social spending.[188]

The country reports elaborated upon corruption on various occasions.[189] The report on Niger made clear that misappropriation of food stocks for a certain social programme can constitute a violation of the right to food, for which judicial remedies ought to be available.[190] In addition, the report on Bangladesh included a specific case of a violation of the right to food, concerning the procurement by the government of a large amount of wheat from local farmers, for the purpose of creating emergency grain stocks. However, it emerged that no wheat was produced in Bangladesh at that time. Instead, the funds were largely misappropriated (apparently with involvement of senior government officials) and low-cost, poultry feed was imported from India and disguised as wheat from Bangladesh. Since the poultry feed was unsuitable for human consumption, distribution of the substance caused major health problems to the Bangladeshi people. The Rapporteur noted that these instances constituted violations of the obligation to respect the right to food. In addition, no legal action was taken and no action was taken against senior government officials, although some officials were removed from office. The Rapporteur therefore concluded that impunity from the law for corrupt practices continues.[191] The report observed that poor governance and mismanagement are obstacles to the realisation of the right to food. It was widely alleged that corruption is widespread in some institutions and authorities. The report referred to corruption in important procurement projects, leakages in funds and food aid for the poor and the control of access to resources by powerful criminal groups, often connected to the government structure.[192] Thus, it was recommended that 'remedies for violations of the right to food and water must be available through the courts in order to reduce impunity for these violations. This should include judicial action, or other forms of accountability, in cases of misappropriation of food stocks, or mismanagement in procurement methods. [...]. The proposed Anti-Corruption Commission should also be established to improve transparency and accountability,

---

187 *Ibid.* §75.

188 Report of the SR on the right to food, CHR 59th session, 10 January 2003, UN Doc. E/CN.4/2003/54, §27.

189 Country reports of the SR on the right to food: <www2.ohchr.org/english/issues/food/visits.htm>, accessed 27 June 2011.

190 Report of the SR on the right to food, Mission to Niger, CHR 58th session, 23 January 2002, UN Doc. E/CN.4/2002/58/Add.1, §52, 68(b).

191 Report of the SR on the right to food, Mission to Bangladesh, CHR 60th session, 29 October 2003, UN Doc. E/CN.4/2004/10/Add.1, §43.

192 *Ibid.* §49.

particularly in food distribution and procurement.'[193] Also, the study on India reported about various instances of corruption in relation to food, and recommended that this should be challenged, and the persons responsible must be held accountable.[194] Finally, some communications to governments were concerned with corruption in relation to food.[195]

The Special Rapporteur on the right of everyone to the enjoyment of the highest attainable standard of physical and mental health[196] regularly discussed corruption in relation to health in his annual reports, giving useful insights.[197] The first annual report to the Commission noted the problem of corruption in the provision of health services. The Rapporteur found that corruption disadvantages the poor and *corrodes the right to health*, for example when poor people are asked to pay for medication that ought to be free of charge. Hence, the Rappporteur held that 'corruption is an issue of both the right to health and poverty'.[198]

Furthermore, the report on the health-related Millennium Development Goals discussed the use of indicators and benchmarks as tools for monitoring the progressive realisation of the right to health in relation to child survival. It was noted that 'a failure to reach the benchmark does not necessarily mean that the State is in breach of its international right to health obligations. The State might have fallen short of the benchmark for reasons beyond its control. However, if the monitoring and accountability mechanism reveals that the 70 per cent benchmark was not reached because of – for example – corruption in the health sector, then it will probably follow that the State has failed to comply with its international right to health obligations.'[199]

Another report discussing the human right to medicines, and the responsibilities of States in this respect, noted that States have a legal obligation to ensure a reliable, efficient and transparent system for the supply of quality affordable medicines. This supply system must avoid corruption.[200] The report later discussed that in some

---

193 *Ibid.* §54(g).

194 Report of the SR on the right to food, Mission to India, CHR 62nd session, 20 March 2006, UN Doc. E/CN.4/2006/44/Add.2, §32–34, 48(i).

195 Report of the SR on the right to food, HRC 7th session, 29 February 2008, UN Doc. A/HRC/7/5/Add.1, §63, 67.

196 The SR on the right to health was appointed by Commission on Human Rights Resolution 2002/31. The mandate was extended in 2007 by Human Rights Council Resolution 15/22. The mandate is currently held by Mr. Anand Grover. Previously, the mandate was held by Mr. Paul Hunt (2002-July 2008).

197 Annual reports of the SR on the right to health: <www2.ohchr.org/english/issues/health/right/annual.htm>, accessed 27 June 2011.

198 Report of the SR on the right to health, CHR 59th session, 13 February 2003, UN Doc. E/CN.4/2003/58, §98.

199 Report of the SR on the right to health, GA 59th session, 8 October 2004, UN Doc. A/59/422, §77. The statement is repeated in the Report of the SR on the right to health, CHR 62nd Session, 3 March 2006, UN Doc. E/CN.4/2006/48, §44.

200 Report of the SR on the right to health, GA 61st session, 13 September 2006, UN Doc. A/61/338, §68.

medicine supply systems, there is endemic corruption; for example, products are diverted, unofficial 'fees' are required for customs clearance, and counterfeit medicines are permitted to circulate. Hence, corruption can be deadly. The Rapporteur cited the head of Nigeria's Food and Drug Authority, who stated that 'Drug counterfeiting, facilitated by corruption, kills en masse and anybody can be a victim'.[201] In the view of the Rapporteur, corruption in the health sector disproportionately affects the poor, since they are less able to afford the bribes required for free services, or to pay for private health care if corruption has depleted public services.[202] The Rapporteur went on the note that the right to health includes participation, access to information, transparency, monitoring and accountability, each of which helps to establish an environment in which corruption cannot survive. It was stated that 'a right-to-health policy is also an anti-corruption policy.' Therefore the application of the right to health can help to reduce corruption in health systems, and particularly in medicine supply systems.[203] The importance of access to health information was underscored in another report, and it was stated that health information enables individuals and communities to expose corruption.[204]

Moreover, a report on the responsibilities of pharmaceutical companies contained an annex with the Human Rights Guidelines for Pharmaceutical Companies in Relation to Access to Medicines. Guidelines 15 and 16 are concerned with corruption: '15. A company should publicly adopt effective anti-corruption policies and measures, and comply with relevant national law implementing the United Nations Convention Against Corruption. 16. In collaboration with States, the company should take all reasonable measures to address counterfeiting.' The Commentary to the Guidelines noted, *inter alia*, that 'corruption is a major obstacle to the enjoyment of the right to the highest attainable standard of health, including access to medicines.'[205]

Several country reports[206] discussed the problem of corruption in relation to health, i.e. the reports on Mozambique,[207] Peru,[208] Romania,[209] Uganda,[210] and

---

201 *Ibid.* §78.

202 *Ibid.* §79.

203 *Ibid.* §80.

204 Report of the SR on the right to health, HRC 7th session, 31 January 2008, UN Doc. A/HRC/7/11, §40.

205 Report of the SR on the right to health, GA 63rd session, 11 August 2008, UN Doc. A/63/263.

206 Country reports SR on the right to health: <www2.ohchr.org/english/issues/health/right/visits.htm>, accessed 27 June 2011.

207 Report of the SR on the right to health, Mission to Mozambique, CHR 61st session, 4 January 2005, UN Doc. E/CN.4/2005/51/Add.2, §41, 45–52, 59, 68–70, 88.

208 Report of the SR on the right to health, Mission to Peru, CHR 61st session, 4 February 2005, UN Doc. E/CN.4/2005/51/Add.3, §22.

209 Report of the SR on the right to health, Mission to Romania, CHR 61st session, 21 February 2005, UN Doc. E/CN.4/2005/51/Add.4, §22, 33–37.

210 Report of the SR on the right to health, Mission to Uganda, CHR 62nd session, 19 January 2006, UN Doc. E/CN.4/2006/48/Add.2, §21, 44.

India.[211] Several interesting observations were made about the relation of corruption to specific aspects of the right to health. First of all, in Mozambique, access to health care is hindered by corruption in the health sector.[212] The economic accessibility of the right to health is hindered by the illicit charging of user fees.[213] Whenever resources for health care are diverted, or bribery defines priorities, this is a severe constraint to the enjoyment of the right to health.[214] The report on India also discussed access. It was stated that:

> ... access has several dimensions, including financial access or affordability. There is only space to mention briefly one aspect of financial access in the present context. In some health facilities, there is a widespread practice of staff asking for money for services (e.g. transport, medicines and tests) that the Government has mandated are free. "Informal fees" undermine the JSY scheme and sometimes compel women and their families to take out loans at high interest rates. These corrupt practices disproportionately affect those living in poverty and are a barrier to equitable access. In relation to each health facility, the Special Rapporteur strongly recommends the strengthening of transparency, as well as community and patient participation in monitoring and accountability.[215]

Also, in his report on Mozambique, the Rapporteur noted that:

> in line with the obligation of the Government, including its civil servants, to respect the right to health, and the obligation of the Government to protect the right to health from interference by third parties, the Special Rapporteur urges it to take all appropriate action to combat corruption in the health sector. He recommends that the Ministry of Health integrate the right to health – including the features of transparency and accountability – into all its policies and programmes, and publicly renews its commitment to remove all corruption from the health sector.[216]

Accordingly, it appears that in the view of the Special Rapporteur, the obligations to respect and to protect the right to health include the obligation to combat health sector corruption.

Furthermore, in his report on Romania, corruption was discussed as being a serious financing issue,[217] and it was stated that corruption affects the right to health in various ways. The Rapporteur found that corruption is an obstacle to the realization of the right to health (of the poor), and is inconsistent with the principles

---

211 Report of the SR on the right to health, Mission to India, HRC 14th session, 15 April 2010, UN Doc. A/HRC/14/20/Add.2, §52.

212 Mission to Mozambique, §41.

213 *Ibid.* §45–52.

214 *Ibid.* §69.

215 Report of the SR on the right to health, Mission to India, HRC 14th session, 15 April 2010, UN Doc. A/HRC/14/20/Add.2, §52.

216 Mission to Mozambique, §70.

217 Mission to Romania, §33.

of non-discrimination and equality.[218] The report then went on to note some important measures taken by the Romanian government to combat corruption,[219] and subsequently, the Special Rapporteur urged the Government to take anti-corruption action the health sector, and formulated a specific set of measures.[220] In sum, the way in which the Special Rapporteur on the right to health has addressed corruption is a good example of how the Special Procedures can be used to put corruption on the human rights agenda and to press for change with the Government concerned.

(iv) Miscellaneous Mandates

A good recent example of how corruption can be addressed by the Special Procedures can be found in the 2010 country report on the mission to Zambia of *the Independent Expert on the question of human rights and extreme poverty.*[221] While earlier annual reports made clear how corruption and extreme poverty are linked,[222] the country report on Zambia revealed discussions on governmental attempts to tackle high-level corruption,[223] as well as the existing political obstacles to progress in the fight against corruption.[224] The Expert also gave detailed recommendations on anti-corruption actions that should be taken: the Government must (i) ensure full investigation of corruption cases, as well as accountability for those responsible; (ii) increase its support to the anti-corruption mechanisms by ensuring their total independence; (iii) strengthen the Anti-Corruption Commission by amending its statute so that it will report to the Parliament; (iv) adopt legal instruments protecting whistleblowers; (v) adopt an asset declaration act for authorities; (vi) take measures to ensure the harmonisation of existing anti-corruption legal instruments with the

---

218 *Ibid.* §34.

219 *Ibid.* §35.

220 *Ibid.* §36.

221 The Independent Expert was appointed by Commission on Human Rights Resolution 1998/25. The mandate was extended in 2008 by Human Rights Council Resolution 8/11. The mandate is currently held by Ms. Magdalena Sepúlveda Carmona, who also prepared two reports on corruption and human rights in the capacity of research director at the International Council for Human Rights Policy. Previous mandate-holders are Mr. Arjun Sengupta (August 2004-August 2008) and Ms. A.M. Lizin (April 1998-July 2004).

222 Annual reports of the SR on human rights and extreme poverty: <www.ohchr.org/EN/Issues/Poverty/Pages/AnnualReports.aspx>, accessed 27 June 2011. Country reports: <www.ohchr.org/EN/Issues/Poverty/Pages/CountryVisits.aspx>, accessed 27 June 2011. For discussions on how corruption and extreme poverty are linked, see Report of the Independent Expert on the question of human rights and extreme poverty, CHR 55th session, 29 January 1999, UN Doc. E/CN.4/1999/48, §145; Report of the IE on the question of human rights and extreme poverty, CHR 56th session, 25 February 2000, UN Doc. E/CN.4/2000/52, §92 and Report of the IE on the question of human rights and extreme poverty, GA 63rd session, 13 August 2008, UN Doc. A/63/274, §24.

223 Report of the IE on the question of human rights and extreme poverty, HRC 14th session, 11 May 2010, UN Doc. A/HRC/14/31/Add.1, §92–93.

224 *Ibid.* §94–96.

recently adopted National Anti-Corruption Policy; (vi) ensure freedom of expression, personal security of anti-corruption advocates and a free and independent media, in order to maintain an enabling environment for civil society involved in anti-corruption efforts.[225] Such a detailed recommendation offers clear guidance to the State concerned as to what actions ought to be taken, and can serve as a fine example for other Special Procedures.

The Special Representative of the S-G on the issue of human rights and transnational corporations and other business enterprises, John Ruggie, addressed corruption in his reports.[226] He held that 'bribery and corruption are often considered part of the human rights agenda since they are such significant impediments to the realization of rights, and many companies have adopted anti-bribery policies'.[227] Ruggie also pointed to the involvement of the extractive industries in corrupt practices,[228] and held that the endemic corruption in these industries and the misallocation of public revenues undermine the rule of law, impede the pursuit of social objectives and contribute to conflict that foster human rights abuse. In this context, the Extractive Industries Transparency Initiative (EITI) was mentioned,[229] as well as the Global Compact, which also contains an anti-corruption principle.[230] In addition, it was noted that human rights abuses involving corporations mainly take place in countries with high levels of perceived corruption.[231] Moreover, in a study into the scope and patterns of alleged human rights violations related to companies, corruption allegations were also recorded, including those in the labour context.[232] It is certainly justified that the mandate of the Special Representative deals with corruption, given the important role of corporations in corrupt conduct. However, his analysis on the links between corrupt corporate conduct and human rights violations remained rather limited and superficial.

---

225 *Ibid.* §112.

226 The Special Representative was appointed in 2005 by Commission on Human Rights Resolution 2005/69, and the mandate was extended in 2008 by Human Rights Council Resolution 8/7. Reports of the Special Representative: <www.ohchr.org/EN/Issues/TransnationalCorporations/Pages/Reports.aspx>, accessed 27 June 2011. OHCHR, Special Representative of the S-G on the Issue of Human Rights and Transnational Corporations and Other Business Enterprises – Reports, <www.ohchr.org/EN/Issues/TransnationalCorporations/Pages/Reports.aspx>, accessed 5 January 2011.

227 Report of the Special Representative of the S-G on the issue of human rights and transnational corporations and other business enterprises, HRC 4th session, 8 February 2007, UN Doc. A/HRC/4/35/Add.4, §96–99.

228 Interim report of the SR of the S-G on the issue of human rights and transnational corporations and other business enterprises, CHR 62nd session, 22 February 2006, UN Doc. E/CN.4/2006/97, §25.

229 *Ibid.* §45.

230 *Ibid.* §40.

231 *Ibid.* §27.

232 Report of the Special Representative of the S-G on the issue of human rights and transnational corporations and other business enterprises, HRC 8th session, 23 May 2008, UN Doc. A/HRC/8/5/Add.2, §14, 16, 20, 28, 54, 84, 86.

3.3.3. Assessment

Having analysed the reports of ten thematic procedures, it can be concluded that the extent to which corruption is dealt with in these procedures varies greatly. In the field of civil and political rights, the mandate of the Special Rapporteur on the independence of judges and lawyers paid prominent attention to corruption. Unfortunately, no links were established between corrupt practices within the judiciary and specific State obligations under Article 14 ICCPR. This is an exercise that ought to be conducted in future reports of this mandate. What is laudable is the cooperation of this Special Rapporteur with anti-corruption organisations, and the fact that a recent report formulated specific actions that ought to be taken by States. The Special Rapporteur on trafficking in persons did not address corruption in a way that is merited given the role that corruption plays in the perpetration of trafficking. At the same time, corruption is a recurrent topic in the work of a related procedure, i.e. the mandate of the Special Rapporteur on the sale of children, child prostitution and child pornography. Especially in these areas, corruption can be very well addressed during country visits, a practice that should certainly continue.

In the field of economic, social, and cultural rights, the Rapporteurs on the rights to housing and education paid too little attention to corruption. While they do seem to be aware of the problem, a proper analysis is lacking. In contrast, the Rapporteur on the right to food made clear how corruption can violate aspects of the right to food. Interestingly, Mr. Ziegler found that the obligation to protect the right to food imposes the duty upon States to combat corruption. Moreover, the Rapporteur on the right to health is to date the best example of how corruption should be taken into account by Special Procedures in the field of economic, social and cultural rights. He also seemed to hold the opinion that the obligation to combat corruption is part of the obligation to respect and to protect the right to health. Also, the economic accessibility of the right to health is hindered by corruption.

The mandate of the Independent Expert on human rights and extreme poverty, as fulfilled by Ms. Sepúlveda, is a proper example of how specific recommendations on corruption can be formulated by a Special Procedure. The mandate of Prof. Ruggie, Special-Representative of the S-G on business and human rights, also discussed corruption, but an in-depth study was lacking. This is a pity given the crucial role of transnational corporations in the occurrence of corrupt practices.

We may conclude that while some Procedures are more active in discussing and denouncing corruption within their mandates, in general most Procedures remain rather general and vague on the links between corruption and violations of specific human rights.

When considering the resolutions of the Human Rights Council, the former Commission and the General Assembly on the topics of the ten mandates considered, the outcomes are somewhat disappointing. With respect to the mandates of the Special Rapporteur on the independence of judges and lawyers, none of the resolutions adopted specifically mentioned judicial corruption, although the importance of judicial independence and impartiality is stressed.[233] In the resolutions regarding the mandate of the Special Rapporteur on the sale of children, child prostitution and child pornography, no reference was made to corrupt practices, disregarding the extensive attention paid to corruption by this Special Rapporteur.[234] Likewise, corruption was not mentioned in resolutions on the right to housing,[235] education,[236] food,[237] or health.[238] Nevertheless, in the resolutions adopted on human rights and extreme poverty,[239] reference to corruption was made by the Commission, which recalled in two subsequent resolutions:

> … that, as stated in the Plan of Implementation on Sustainable Development, held in Johannesburg, South Africa, in September 2002, good governance within each country and at the international level is essential for sustainable development; and that at the domestic level […] anti-corruption measures […] are the basis for sustainable development.'[240]

The fact that the problems discussed by the Special Procedures do not return in the resolutions of the Council/Commission is not limited to corruption. It is a general matter of concern that the resolutions of the Council/Commission do not properly reflect the issues discussed in the reports of the Special Procedures.

3.4. Country Mandates

3.4.1. Introduction

Currently, there are eight country mandates: Independent Experts on Burundi, Haiti, Somalia, and the Sudan, Special Rapporteurs on the Democratic People's Republic of Korea, Myanmar, and the Occupied Palestinian Territories, and a

---

233 Resolutions: <http://ap.ohchr.org/documents/dpage_e.aspx?m=87>, accessed 27 June 2011.

234 Resolutions: <http://www2.ohchr.org/english/issues/children/rapporteur/standards.htm>, accessed 27 June 2011.

235 Resolutions: <www.ohchr.org/EN/Issues/Housing/Pages/OverviewMandate.aspx>, accessed 27 June 2011.

236 Resolutions: <www2.ohchr.org/english/issues/education/rapporteur/overview.htm>, accessed 27 June 2011. However, the Commission did urge all States 'to enhance the status, morale and professionalism of teachers.' Reference to the morale and professionalism of teachers implies that they should abstain from demanding bribes or any other favour in exchange for educational services.

237 Resolutions: <http://www2.ohchr.org/english/issues/food/overview.htm>, accessed 27 June 2011.

238 Resolutions: <http://www2.ohchr.org/english/issues/health/right/overview.htm>, accessed 27 June 2011.

239 Resolutions: <www.ohchr.org/EN/Issues/Poverty/Pages/Resolutions.aspx>, accessed 27 June 2011.

240 Commission on Human Rights Resolution 2004/23 §2(b) and Resolution 2005/16, §2(b).

Special Representative of the Secretary-General on Cambodia.[241] The countries under scrutiny have very high levels of perceived corruption according to the Corruption Perceptions Index of 2011: Haïti ranks 175, Cambodia 164, Burundi 172, Sudan 177, Myanmar 180, while Somalia and North Korea are perceived to be the world's most corrupt countries, both ranking 182.[242] CPI data for the Occupied Palestinian Territories are not available. On the basis of the CPI scores of the five countries, one would therefore expect a great deal of attention for corruption in the reports of the Special Procedures. Nevertheless, this does not hold true for all country mandates.

3.4.2. Outcomes

The mandates on Burundi, Haïti and Cambodia are proper examples of how corruption can be addressed by the Special Procedures. Although these mandates do not specifically discuss how corrupt practices violate human rights, the reports do show that the mandate-holders are in the position to address corruption in the country concerned, to formulate recommendations, and to monitor the situation over a longer period of time.

The Independent Expert, and previously the Special Rapporteur, on the situation of human rights in *Burundi*[243] discussed corruption in quite a number of reports. Especially judicial corruption is an important topic,[244] as well as specific measures taken to address corruption.[245] In 2001 the Rapporteur stated that corruption is one

241 Country mandates of the Human Rights Council: <www2.ohchr.org/english/bodies/chr/special/countries.htm>, accessed 10 February 2010. Discontinued country mandates are not taken into account in the current chapter.

242 This does not come as a surprise since Somalia is a so-called 'failed State.'

243 The mandate was established in 2004 by Commission on Human Rights Resolution 2004/82, and was extended in 2008 by Human Rights Council Resolution 9/19. The mandate is currently held by Mr. Fatsah Ouguergouz. The Independent Expert on Burundi is the successor of the Special Rapporteur on Burundi. The reports of the former Special Rapporteur are also taken into account in the present discussion.

244 Comments about judicial corruption can be found in: Interim report of the SR on the situation of human rights in Burundi, GA 55th session, 7 September 2000, UN Doc. A/55/358, §75; Report of the SR on the situation of human rights in Burundi, CHR 57th session, 19 March 2001, UN Doc. E/CN.4/2001/44, §135; Interim report of the SR on the situation of human rights in Burundi, GA 56th session, 17 October 2001, UN Doc. A/56/479, §119; Interim report of the IE on the situation of human rights in Burundi, GA 61st session, 19 September 2006, UN Doc. A/61/360, §22; Interim report of the IE on the situation of human rights in Burundi, HRC 4th session, 26 February 2007, UN Doc. A/HRC/4/5, §39; Report of the IE on the situation of human rights in Burundi, GA 8 August 2007, 62nd session, UN Doc. A/62/213, §41; Report of the IE on the situation of human rights in Burundi, HRC 9th session, 15 August 2008, UN Doc. A/HRC/9/14, §72.

245 Report of the SR on the human rights situation in Burundi, CHR 57th session, 19 March 2001, UN Doc. E/CN.4/2001/44, §41; Interim report of the IE on the situation of human rights in Burundi, GA 61st session, 19 September 2006, UN Doc. A/61/360, §21.

of Burundi's major problems, which often goes unpunished.[246] Moreover, the Independent Expert spoke out against grand corruption, by stating in 2007 that:

> ... concerns were raised again regarding a general trend towards corruption and embezzlement, with scandals sometimes implicating high-ranking officials within the Government and the ruling party. Frequent strikes and the growing discontent of civil servants were often motivated by widespread poverty. While the Government should be commended for setting up an anti-corruption court, more action needs to be undertaken in order to demonstrate political will to fight corruption.[247]

Such statements show that the Special Procedures can be used to address high-level corruption as well.

In the work of the Independent Expert on the situation of human rights in *Haïti*, corruption is also a prominent topic.[248] The problem was briefly noted for the first time as early as 1995 and 1996,[249] and a 1997 report dedicated a particular sub-section to the matter.[250] More recent reports also deal with corruption in a rather extensive fashion, with particular attention for police corruption and corruption in the judicial system. Recommendations were also addressed to the Haitian government. The Expert clearly condemned the widespread nature of corruption in the country, and provided guidance on the actions that should be taken. For example, the report to the Human Rights Council in May 2010 stated, *inter alia*, that:

> ... during his various visits in 2008 and 2009, the Independent Expert gathered a considerable amount of evidence that corruption, one of the scourges of Haitian society, continued unabated at all levels, even though the fight against corruption figured in the action plans of the Ministry of Justice and of the forces of law and order. The succession of speeches delivered by President Préval since 2007 seemed to have given a clear and reaffirmed signal of the political will to make the fight

---

246 Report of the SR on the situation of human rights in Burundi, CHR 57th session, 19 March 2001, UN Doc. E/CN.4/2001/44, §41.

247 Report of the IE on the situation of human rights in Burundi, GA 62nd session, 8 August 2007, UN Doc. A/62/213, §49. Similar concerns about high-level corruption were also expressed in: Interim report of the Independent Expert on the situation of human rights in Burundi, HRC 4th session, 26 February 2007, UN Doc. A/HRC/4/5, §70.

248 The mandate of the Independent Expert on the situation of human rights in Haïti was established in 1995 by Commission on Human Rights Resolution 1995/70, and was extended in 2009 by Human Rights Council Resolution PRST/9/1. The mandate is currently held by Michel Forst. Prior to 1995, there was a SR on Haiti. All documents related to the mandate of the Independent Expert and the former SR, including HRC, CHR and GA resolutions: can be found through <http://ap.ohchr.org/documents/dpage_e.aspx?m=47>.

249 Report of the IE on the situation of human rights in Haïti, GA 50th session, 1 November 1995, UN Doc. A/50/714, §34; Report of the IE on the situation of human rights in Haïti, CHR 52nd session, 24 January 1996, UN Doc. E/CN.4/1996/94, §38 and 73.

250 Report of the IE on the situation of human rights in Haïti, CHR 53rd session, 7 February 1997, UN Doc. E/CN.4/1997/89, §33, 34, 50, 70–76, 85.

> against corruption a strategic aim (albeit one whose attainment seemed to be taking a long time).[251]

It was also stated that 'with the massive influx of humanitarian aid and reconstruction funds it is important to show that the aim of combating corruption remains a central focus of the Government.'[252] Hence, the Expert recommended that 'a) measures should be introduced for waging an effective campaign against corruption and thus demonstrating that combating corruption is a becoming a major focus of the Government; and b) particular attention should be paid in the fight against corruption to the management of humanitarian aid funds.'[253]

The Special Representative of the Secretary-General on the situation of human rights in *Cambodia* also paid a great deal of attention to corruption.[254] The topic is discussed in the majority of reports. In the view of the Representative, corruption is one of the four fundamental evils which affect Cambodian society and hamper the enjoyment of human rights by all the peoples in the country.[255] The Representative thoroughly discussed corruption and its causes, condemned it, and addressed recommendations to the Government to change the situation. It also follows from the reports that during his country visits, the Special Representative was able to discuss matters on the ground, which is a clear advantage of this method of human rights monitoring. A topic featuring prominently in the reports is corruption in the judicial branch,[256] and the role of the very low salaries paid to judges and court personnel.[257] Interestingly, the Rapporteur did not shy away from mentioning

---

251 Report of the IE on the situation of human rights in Haïti, HRC 14th session, 3 May 2010, UN Doc. A/HRC/14/44, §78.

252 *Ibid.* §79.

253 *Ibid.* §103.

254 The mandate was established in 1993 by Commission on Human Rights Resolution 1993/6, and was extended in 2009 by Human Rights Council Resolution 12/25. The mandate is currently held by Mr. Suraya Prasad Subedi. All documents related to the mandate, including the resolutions of the HRC, the former CHR and the GA: <http://ap.ohchr.org/documents/dpage_e.aspx?m=107>. For more on this mandate, see Surya P. Subedi, 'The UN Human Rights Mandate in Cambodia: The Challenge of a Country in Transition and the Experience of the SR for the Country', *The International Journal of Human Rights,* 15/2 (2011), p. 249–264.

255 Report of the Special Representative of the S-G on Cambodia, CHR 57th session, 24 January 2001, UN Doc. E/CN.4/2001/103, §22. This was reiterated in Report of the Special Representative of the S-G on Cambodia, CHR 61st session 20 December 2004, UN Doc. E/CN.4/2005/116, §76. The other evils identified by the Speical Representative are poverty, violence and lawlessness.

256 A lengthy discussion can be found *inter alia* in the Report of the Special Representative of the S-G on Cambodia, CHR 61st session, 20 December 2004, UN Doc.E/CN.4/2005/116, §21, 24, 28, 31, 32, 61/68, 76/77, and recommendations are formulated at §102–103.

257 This was discussed in many reports, *inter alia*, the Report of the Special Representative of the S-G on Cambodia, CHR 50th session, 21 February 1994, UN Doc. E/CN.4/1994/73/Add.1, §27; Report of the Special Representative of the S-G on Cambodia, CHR 52nd session, 26 February 1996, UN Doc. E/CN.4/1996/93, §35(a); Report of the Special Representative of the S-G on Cambodia, CHR 54th session, 20 February 1998, UN Doc. E/CN.4/1998/95, §81.

specific cases of judicial corruption. *Inter alia*, he discussed the trial and sentencing of a nephew of Cambodia's Prime Minister, who was accused of voluntary manslaughter but managed to escape punishment.[258] Furthermore, other topics discussed were prison corruption,[259] the role of corrupt public officials in human trafficking,[260] corruption in child adoption procedures,[261] corruption in education,[262] corruption in relation to land ownership and concessions,[263] corruption in the logging industry,[264] police corruption,[265] and corruption in the military.[266] This overview shows that the Representative's concerns about corruption are not limited to one aspect of Cambodian society. In addition, the Representative noted positive action taken by the Cambodian Government, but also frequently formulated anti-corruption recommendations, i*nter alia*, to investigate and prosecute cases of corruption, and to collect data to monitor progress.[267] It was also recommended on several occasions that the persons working in the judicial branch should receive appropriate remuneration and training.[268] Clear emphasis is placed on the adoption of domestic anti-corruption legislation,[269] and on the ratification of the UNCAC.[270] Finally, the reports of the UN Secretary-General also

---

258 Report of the Special Representative of the S-G on Cambodia, CHR 61st session, 20 December 2004, UN Doc.E/CN.4/2005/116, §24.

259 Report of the Special Representative of the S-G on Cambodia, CHR 57th session, 24 January 2001, UN Doc. E/CN.4/2001/103, §48; Report of the Special Representative of the S-G on Cambodia, GA 56th session 26 July 2001, UN Doc. A/56/209, §55, 60 and 92.

260 Report of the Special Representative of the S-G on Cambodia, CHR 54th session, 20 February 1998, UN Doc. E/CN.4/1998/95, §131; Report of the Special Representative of the S-G on Cambodia, CHR 59th session, 18 December 2002, UN Doc. E/CN.4/2003/114, §63; Report of the Special Representative of the S-G on Cambodia, GA 56th session, 26 July 2001, UN Doc. A/56/209, §72 and 97.

261 Report of the Special Representative of the S-G on Cambodia, CHR 60th session, 19 December 2003, UN Doc. E/CN.4/105, §25 and 64.

262 Report of the Special Representative of the S-G on Cambodia, GA 49th session, 3 November 1994, UN Doc. A/49/635, §50, 62; Report of the Special Representative of the S-G on Cambodia, GA 53rd session, 17 October 1997, UN Doc. A/52/489, §14, 128.

263 Report of the Special Representative of the S-G on Cambodia, CHR 55th session, 26 February 1999, UN Doc. E/CN.4/1999/101, §141; Report of the Special Representative of the S-G on Cambodia, CHR 60th session 19 December 2003, UN Doc. E/CN.4/105, §46.

264 Report of the Special Representative of the S-G on Cambodia, GA 56th session, 26 July 2001, UN Doc. A/56/209, §36 and 84.

265 Report of the Special Representative of the S-G on Cambodia, CHR 55th session, 26 February 1999, UN Doc. E/CN.4/1999/101, §54.

266 Recommendations of the Special Representative of the S-G on Cambodia, GA 49th session, 3 November 1994, UN Doc. A/49/635, §23.

267 Report of the Special Representative of the S-G on Cambodia, CHR 61st session, 20 December 2004, UN Doc. E/CN.4/2005/116, §102.

268 Report of the Special Representative of the S-G on Cambodia, CHR 57th session, 24 January 2001, UN Doc. E/CN.4/2001/103, §97.

269 Report of the Special Representative of the S-G on Cambodia, CHR 61st session, 20 December 2004, UN Doc.E/CN.4/2005/116, §64 and 104.

270 Report of the Special Representative of the S-G on Cambodia, CHR 60th session, 19 December 2003, UN Doc. E/CN.4/2004/105, §59; Report of the Special Representative of the SG on

addressed corruption, mostly by referring to the findings of the Rapporteur. For example, it was stated that 'the Special Representative paid particular attention to the problems of impunity and corruption, which impact negatively on the realization of a range of human rights and distort the allocation of economic resources further exacerbating existing inequalities.'[271] The Office of the High Commissioner in Cambodia is also actively involved in anti-corruption activities.[272]

Contrary to the three mandates discussed above, the five other country mandates hardly pay proper attention to corruption. The Independent Expert on the situation of human rights in *Somalia* discussed corruption only sporadically.[273] Some attention was paid to judicial corruption,[274] and the Expert met with the head of an international NGO consortium, with whom he discussed a number of 'key human rights issues', including corruption.[275] The Expert also pointed to the loss of foreign aid due to corruption,[276] and stated that the Government should dismiss corrupt officials.[277] While these comments reveal that corruption is a problem in Somalia, they do not show the pervasiveness of the phenomenon, nor its specific effects on the human rights situation in the country.

The same holds true for the Independent Expert on the situation of human rights in *Sudan*.[278] Some attention was paid to the diversion of food away from

Cambodia, HRC 4th session, 30 January 2007, UN Doc. A/HRC/4/36, §108.

271 Report of the Secretary-General, CHR 23 December 2004, UN Doc. E/CN.4/2005/111, §9.

272 *Ibid.*

273 The mandate was established in 1993 by Commission on Human Rights resolution 1993/86, and extended in 2009 by Human Rights Council Resolution 12/26. The mandate is currently held by Mr. Shamsul Bari. All documents related to the mandate of the Independent Expert (including resolutions of the HRC, the CHR and the GA): <http://ap.ohchr.org/documents/dpage_e.aspx?m=48>.

274 Report of the IE on the situation of human rights in Somalia, CHR 54th session, 16 January 1998, UN Doc. E/CN.4/1998/96, §47 and 76; Report of the IE on the situation of human rights in Somalia, CHR 56th session, 26 January 2000, UN Doc. E/CN.4/2000/110, §91; Report of the IE on the situation of human rights in Somalia, CHR 58th session, 14 January 2002, UN Doc. E/CN.4/2002/119, §97; Report of the IE on the Situation of Human Rights in Somalia, CHR 59th session, 31 December 2003, UN Doc. E/CN.4/2003/115, §31.

275 Report of the IE on the situation of human rights in Somalia, CHR 59th session, 31 December 2003, UN Doc. E/CN.4/2003/115, §89.

276 Report of the IE on the situation of human rights in Somalia, CHR 55th session, 18 February 1999, UN Doc. E/CN.4/1999/103, §12.

277 Report of the IE on the situation of human rights in Somalia, HRC 12th session, 17 September 2009, UN Doc. A/HRC/12/49, §86 (see also §76); and Report of the IE on the situation of human rights in Somalia, HRC 13th session, 22 March 2010, UN Doc. A/HRC/13/65, §92.

278 The Independent Expert is the successor of the SR on the situation of human rights in Sudan. The Expert's mandate was established in 2009 by Human Rights Council Resolution 11/10, and extended by Human Rights Council Decision 14/117. The mandate is currently held by Mr. Mohamed Chande Othman. All documents related to the mandate, including the resolutions of the HRC, the former CHR and the GA: <http://ap.ohchr.org/documents/dpage_e.aspx?m=95&m=172>.

recipients,[279] and to the adoption of a bill in Southern Sudan for the establishment of an anti-corruption commission.[280] Moreover, it was concluded that:

> ... the advancement of economic, social and cultural rights is going at an extremely slow pace. Widespread poverty, corruption, lack of transparency and marginalization continue to be sources of political unrest and dissatisfaction throughout the country. The situation is seriously inhibiting the delivery of basic social services, such as health care, education and water supply, especially in Southern Sudan.[281]

Likewise, the Special Rapporteur on the situation of human rights in *the Democratic People's Republic of Korea* hardly paid any attention to corruption,[282] although it was mentioned that citizens may escape the severe Governmental sanctions by bribing officials.[283] Furthermore, it was briefly discussed whether or not foreign food aid was diverted for other uses.[284] Given the particularly closed and oppressive nature of the North-Korean dictatorship of Kim Jong-Il, it does not come as a surprise that discussions about corruption are not present in the reports, even more so because NGOs are non-existent in the country.

Also in the work of the Special Rapporteur on the situation of human rights in *Myanmar* corruption is not a key issue.[285] The Rapporteur summed up to which human rights and humanitarian treaties Myanmar is a Party, and the UNCAC is included in this list.[286] Apparently, an anti-corruption treaty is also considered to

---

279 Commission on Human Rights, 55th session, 17 May 1999, UN Doc. E/CN.4/1999/38/Add.1, §55. See also Report by the SR on the Situation of Human Rights in the Sudan, GA 54th session, 14 October 1999, UN Doc. A/54/467, §56; CHR 56th session, 19 April 2000, UN Doc. E/CN.4/2000/36, §23.

280 Report of the SR on the situation of human rights in the Sudan, GA 62nd session, 24 September 2007, UN Doc. A/62/354, §60.

281 *Ibid.* at §86.

282 The mandate was established in 2004 by Commission on Human Rights Resolution 2004/13, and was extended in 2010 by Human Rights Council Resolution 13/14. The mandate is currently held by Mr. Marzuki Darusman. All documents related to the mandate, including the resolutions of the HRC, the former CHR and the GA: http://ap.ohchr.org/documents/dpage_e.aspx?c=50&su=59>.

283 Report of the SR on the situation of human rights in the DPR of Korea, HRC 10th session, 24 February 2009, UN Doc. A/HRC/10/18, §30 and Report of the SR on the situation of human rights in the DPR of Korea, HRC 13th session, 17 February 2010, UN Doc. A/HRC/13/47, §35–36.

284 Report of the SR on the situation of human rights in the DPR of Korea, GA 60th session, 29 August 2005, UN Doc. A/60/306, §13.

285 The mandate was established in 1992 by Commission on Human Rights Resolution 1992/58 and was extended in 2010 by Human Rights Council Resolution 13/25. The mandate is currently held by Mr. Tomás Ojea Quintana. All documents related to the mandate, including the resolutions of the HRC, the former CHR and the GA: <http://ap.ohchr.org/documents/dpage_e.aspx?m=89>.

286 Report of the SR on the situation of human rights in Myanmar, GA 61st session, 21 September 2006, UN Doc. A/61/369; Report of the SR on the situation of human rights in Myanmar, HRC 4th session, 12 February 2007, UN Doc. A/HRC/4/14, §75; Report of the SR on the situation of human rights in Myanmar, GA 62nd session, 13 August 2007, UN Doc. A/62/223; Report of the

be a human rights treaty. On a number of occasions, prison corruption was briefly mentioned,[287] and in the context of the right to education, it was also mentioned that bribes had to be paid to school authorities.[288] Furthermore, the Rapporteur noted that 'a once stable economy has been damaged through decades of misguided economic policies, rampant corruption, cronyism, and disproportionate spending on the military.'[289] He also found that 'corruption, which is on the rise, is a serious problem particularly as law enforcement and the administration of justice are casualties of military rule'.[290] Moreover, it was recommended that 'many mutually reinforcing reforms could be considered simultaneously in order to promote political reform, including [...] anti-corruption measures [...].'[291] Such a recommendation is unfortunately too vague to serve as an actual stimulus for change. Finally, the Special Rapporteur on the situation of human rights in *the Occupied Palestinian Territories* did not pay any attention to corruption.[292]

Not only the reports of the country mandates are important, the question also arises whether the concerns of the Special Procedures are ultimately translated into the resulting resolutions of the Human Rights Council, the former Commission, and the General Assembly. Overall, relatively few references to corruption can be found in the resolutions of these organs. No statements were made in the resolutions on *Burundi*.[293] As regards the mandate on *Haïti*, the President of the Human Rights Council stated in 2007 that the Council noted with satisfaction steps taken against corruption.[294] This statement seems to be at odds with the findings of the Independent

SR on the situation of human rights in Myanmar, HRC 6th session, 7 December 2007, UN Doc. A/HRC/6/14.

287 Report of the SR on the situation of human rights in Myanmar, CHR 52nd session, 2 May 1996, UN Doc. E/CN.4/1996/95, §111; Report of the SR on the situation of human rights in Myanmar, CHR 53rd session, 6 February 1997, UN Doc. E/CN.4/1997/64, §25; Report of the SR on the situation of human rights in Myanmar, CHR 55th session, 22 January 1999, UN Doc. E/CN.4/1999/35, §23; Report of the SR on the situation of human rights in Myanmar, CHR 58th session, 10 January 2002, UN Doc. E/CN.4/2002/45, §60; Report of the SR on the situation of human rights in Myanmar, CHR 60th session, 5 January 2004, UN Doc. E/CN.4/2004/33, §42.

288 Interim report of the SR on the situation of human rights in Myanmar, GA 55th session, 22 August 2000, UN Doc. A/HRC/55/359, §36.

289 Report of the SR on the situation of human rights in Myanmar, HRC 6th session, 7 December 2007, UN Doc. A/HRC/6/14, §14.

290 Report of the SR on the situation of human rights in Myanmar, CHR 55th session, 22 January 1999, UN Doc. E/CN.4/1999/35, §78.

291 Report of the SR on the situation of human rights in Myanmar, CHR 61st session, 2 December 2004, UN Doc. E/CN.4/2005/36, §62.

292 The mandate was established in 1993 by Commission on Human Rights Resolution 1993/2. The mandate is currently held by Mr. Richard Falk. All documents related to the mandate, including the resolutions of the HRC, the former CHR and the GA, can be found through <http://ap.ohchr.org/documents/dpage_e.aspx?m=91>.

293 Commission on Human Rights Resolutions: <http://ap.ohchr.org/documents/sdpage_e.aspx?b=1&c=30&t=11> accessed 2 December 2010. Human Rights Council and General Assembly Resolutions: <http://ap.ohchr.org/documents/sdpage_e.aspx?b=3&c=30&t=11> accessed 2 December 2010.

294 President's Statement, HRC 6th session, 28 September 2007, UN Doc. A/HRC/PRST/6/1, §5.

Expert on Haïti, who noted in 2009 that 'successive speeches by President Préval since 2007 appear to have sent out a clear and renewed signal of the political commitment to making to fight against corruption a strategic objective but implementation seems to be slow.'[295] Furthermore, with respect to *Sudan*, a few resolutions of the Commission and the General Assembly 'urge all parties to the continuing conflict in the Sudan, in particular the Sudan People's Liberation Army, not to divert relief supplies, including food, from their civilian recipients.'[296] Moreover, a Human Rights Council report of 2007 contained recommendations formulated by the Group of Experts on Darfur to the Sudanese government. The Government 'indicated that it was under an obligation to review the foreign funding of NGOs to ensure that all finances were disclosed publicly in line with international anti-money laundering and anti-corruption convention obligations.'[297] Moreover, in respect of *Cambodia,* the Commission stated in 2001 and 2003 that it:

> ... notes with concern the continued problems related to the rule of law and the functioning of the judiciary, *inter alia*, through corruption, including interference by the executive with the independence of the judiciary, welcomes the Government's continued commitment to reform the judiciary, commends its current efforts to prepare the laws and codes that are essential components of the basic legal framework, and urges the Government to continue to take the necessary measures to promote the independence and impartiality of the Supreme Council of the Magistracy and the judicial system as a whole.[298]

In October 2010, the Council stated that it 'welcomes the efforts made by the Government of Cambodia in combating corruption, including the adoption of the penal code and the anti-corruption law as well as the appointment of members of the National Council for Anti-Corruption', but also 'expresses its concern about some areas of human rights practices in Cambodia, and urges the Government of Cambodia to continue its efforts to combat corruption, including by the

---

295 Report of the IE on the situation of human rights in Haïti, HRC 11th session, 26 March 2009, UN Doc. A/HRC/11/5, §26.

296 Commission on Human Rights Resolution 1999/15, 23 April 1999, UN Doc. E/CN.4/RES/1999/15. Similar formulations were repeated in later resolutions: Commission on Human Rights Resolution 2000/27, 18 April 2000, UN Doc. E/CN.4/RES/2000/27; General Assembly Resolution 55/116, 12 March 2001, UN Doc. A/RES/55/116; Commission on Human Rights Resolution 2001/18, 20 April 2001, UN Doc. E/CN.4/RES/2001/18; GA Resolution 56/175, 28 February 2002, UN Doc. A/RES/56/175; Commission on Human Rights Resolution 2002/16, 19 April 2002, UN Doc. E/CN.4/RES/2002/16.

297 Final report on the situation of human rights in Darfur prepared by the group of experts mandated by the HRC in its resolution 4/8, HRC 62nd session, 24 September 2007, UN Doc. A/HRC/6/19, p. 84, recommendation 2.2.3.

298 Commission on Human Rights Resolution 2001/82, 25 April 2001, UN Doc. E/CN.4/RES/2001/82, §6; Commission on Human Rights Resolution 2003/79, 25 April 2003, UN Doc. E/CN.4/RES/2003/79, §5.

implementation of an anti-corruption law.'[299] Also the Resolutions of the General Assembly mentioned corruption. In 1998 the GA stated that it:

> ... notes with serious concern the comments of the Special Representative concerning corrupt practices within the judicial system and in the prison administration, and strongly urges the Government of Cambodia to address the problem of corrupt practices and to increase its efforts to create a functioning and impartial system of justice, including convening the Supreme Council of Magistracy, to institute a system to guarantee the essential sustenance of prisoners and to continue its efforts to improve the physical environment of prisons.[300]

Similar wordings were used in a 2002 resolution.[301]

3.4.3. Assessment

It can be concluded that there are considerable differences as to the depth with which corruption is discussed by the mandate-holders of the country procedures. The reports of only three out of eight mandates reveal that corruption is seriously considered. Differences cannot be explained by varying levels of corruption, since most countries under scrutiny suffer from high levels of perceived corruption according to the CPI.

The mandates on Burundi, Haïti, and especially the mandate on Cambodia address corruption in the State concerned, while the Procedures on Somalia, Sudan, North-Korea, Myanmar and the Occupied Palestinian territories paid too little or no attention to the matter. While none of the reports made clear how corruption can violate human rights, it is beyond doubt that corruption is considered to be a legitimate human rights concern. From the mandates that do address corruption more extensively, we can learn that especially judicial corruption is a key area of concern. From the mandate on Burundi and Cambodia it becomes clear that the Special Procedures can also be used to initiate discussions on grand corruption.

3.5. Concluding Remarks

From the examination of the outcomes of the selected Special Procedures, it emerged that corruption is a serious human rights concern. As regards the key thematic mandate, i.e. that of the former Special Rapporteur on corruption and its impact on the full enjoyment of human rights, the potential of this procedure was

---

299 Human Rights Council Resolution 15/20, 8 October 2010, UN Doc. A/HRC/RES/15/20, §4(f) and 5(c).

300 General Assembly Resolution 52/135, 27 February 1998, UN Doc. A/RES/52/135, §8.

301 General Assembly Resolution 56/169, 28 February 2002, 56th session, UN Doc. A/RES/56/169, §1.

certainly not realised, *inter alia*, because the quality of the few reports leaves a lot to be desired.

As regards the nine other thematic mandates that were examined, we can conclude that corruption is on the agenda of the mandate-holders. Nevertheless, there are significant differences as to how thoroughly the matter is discussed. To a certain extent, these differences might be related to the varying quality of some mandate-holders as compared to others.[302] The Rapporteur on the independence of judges and lawyers and the Rapporteur on the right to health are good examples of how the Special Procedures can be used to address corruption. Yet, a thorough legal analysis of how corruption violates specific aspects of particular human rights is more the exception than the rule. Perhaps this can also not be expected from the mandate-holders, who tend to deal with problems in a practical rather than a legalistic fashion.

Concerning the country mandates, we found that only three mandates (i.e. those on Burundi, Haiti and Cambodia) are good examples of how these procedures can be used to scrutinise corruption.

Thus far, in respect of the thematic procedures, corruption rarely returned in the resolutions of the Human Rights Council and the General Assembly.[303] Only on a few occasions did this happen in respect of the country mandates. Yet, this problem is not limited to discussions of corruption. It was pointed out that generally, the reports by the Special Procedures may not influence the resolutions of the former Commission on Human Rights. This has to do with the fact that the Commission (now: Council) is a political body, while the Special Rapporteurs are independent experts.[304]

Meanwhile, we must acknowledge certain weaknesses of the system of Special Procedures in general. These weaknesses undoubtedly affect the quality of reports, including the ways in which certain topics, such as corruption, are dealt with. Among the difficulties that can be identified are (i) the selection process of mandate-holders, which is in need of objective criteria;[305] (ii) the lack of financial

---

302 Lyal S. Sunga, 'The Special Procedures of the UN Commission on Human Rights: Should They Be Scrapped?', in Gudmundur Alfredsson et al (eds.), *International Human Rights Monitoring Mechanisms. Essays in Honour of Jakob Th. Möller* (The Raoul Wallenberg Institute Human Rights Library, 7; The Hague: Kluwer Law International 2001), p. 233–277, stating at p. 267 that 'it is also indisputable that some special rapporteurs bring a much higher level of expertise and exercise their functions much more diligently than others.

303 On the importance of resolutions of the Human Rights Council (in respect of the right to food), see Sally-Ann Way, 'The Role of the UN Human Rights Bodies in Promoting and Protecting the Right to Food', in Wende Barth Eide and Uwe Kracht (eds.), *Food and Human Rights in Development, Volume I* (Antwerp: Intersentia, 2005), p. 205–228 at p. 210.

304 Lempinen, *Challenges Facing the System of Special Procedures of the United Nations Commission on Human Rights* at p. 105 *et seq.*

305 Surya P. Subedi *et al.*, 'The Role of the Special Rapporteurs of the United Nations Human Rights Councol in the Development and Promotion of International Human Rights Norms', *The International Journal of Human Rights*, 15/2 (2011), p. 155–161 at p. 159.

and staff support by the Office of the High Commissioner for Human Rights;[306] (iii) the restriction on the maximum length of reports;[307] (iv) the refusal of governments concerned to cooperate with the Special Procedures;[308] and (v) the lack of a proper follow-up mechanism.[309]

Despite these issues, the value of the Special Procedures of the UN Human Rights Council in the fight against corruption lies in the advantage that the Special Procedures can examine the situation from a practical perspective, with (possible) access on the ground, and for a longer period of time. This is certainly a benefit when compared with the work of the treaty bodies who are bound by the human rights treaty concerned, and cannot undertake country visits during the State reporting procedure. Speaking from his own experience, Pinheiro stated that:

> ... the work of special rapporteurs remains a powerful tool for the powerless. Reports ask member states for clarifications about allegations, request responses to specific problems, expose perpetrators, develop analyses, and propose recommendations. They may not produce immediate changes, but they do contribute to the struggle for human rights; they increase transparency and accountability. This is not a minor accomplishment. And the victims appreciate the effort.[310]

It is precisely in the light of these goals that discussions of corruption by the Special Procedures are useful. The cross-fertilization of the Special Procedures with other relevant anti-corruption actors is certainly desirable. This was particularly visible in the work of the SR on the independence of judges and lawyers, who collaborated with a number of organisations.

---

306 Lempinen, *Challenges Facing the System of Special Procedures of the United Nations Commission on Human Rights* at p. 165–176. Joanne Naples-Mitchell, 'Perspectives of UN Special Rapporteurs on Their Role: Inherent Tensions and Unique Contributions to Human Rights', *The International Journal of Human Rights*, 15/2 (2011), p. 232–248 at p. 244, stating that 'the most urgently needed reforms in the rapporteur scheme, then, are not structural but budgetary. There should be a significant increase in the UN human rights budget so that OHCHR can provide each mandate-holder with four to five assistants.'

307 Lempinen, *Challenges Facing the System of Special Procedures of the United Nations Commission on Human Rights* at p. 163–165.

308 *Ibid.* at p. 1, stating that 'the most common challenge facing the special procedures is perhaps the refusal by a government to cooperate with a special rapporteur.'

309 Paulo Sérgio Pinheiro, 'Being a Special Rapporteur: A Delicate Balancing Act', *The International Journal of Human Rights*, 15/2 (2011), p. 162–171 at p. 169, concluding that 'the major problem is not just in the recommendations, but in the inexistence of any follow-up by the CHR and now by the HRC or the OHCHR, that just recently begun to consolidate the roster of recommendations, thanks to the exercise of the Universal Periodic Review.' See also Jeroen Gutter, 'Special Procedures and the Human Rights Council: Achievements and Challenges Ahead', *Human Rights Law Review*, 7 (2007), p. 93–107 at p. 105.

310 Paulo Sérgio Pinheiro, 'Musings of a UN Special Rapporteur on Human Rights', *Global Governance*, 9 (2003), p. 7–13.

Chapter V
Regional Human Rights Practice on the Topic of Corruption

1. Introduction

Whereas the preceding chapters III and IV examined the topic of corruption within the system of human rights protection at the global plane, the present chapter contains an analysis of the way in which corruption is dealt with by human rights monitoring mechanisms at the regional level: in Europe (section 2), the Americas (section 3), and Africa (section 4). An analysis of the situation in Asia is lacking since a similar regional system of human rights protection in that continent does not exist. After a brief discussion of the working of the systems, it is considered how corruption is discussed by the (semi)judicial monitoring bodies. What links do they find between corruption and human rights violations? The final section 5 draws conclusions. For an overview of the research methodology, the reader is referred to the General Introduction. At this point it deserves to be mentioned that the following sections cover a wide scope of available case law. Moreover, the results are placed in their context.

2. Europe

2.1. Background

The European Convention on Human Rights of 1950 (hereafter: ECHR, or the Convention) and its Protocols are the foundation of the system of human rights protection in Europe, complemented by the European Social Charter and other conventions within the context of the Council of Europe. Emphasis of the Convention is on civil and political rights. Currently, there are 47 State Parties, and supervision is in the hands of the European Court of Human Rights (hereafter: ECtHR). Individuals can directly lodge an application with the Court in Strasbourg.[1]

An examination of the Court's case law revealed (i) cases about whistleblowers' right to freedom of expression (Article 10 ECHR), especially with regard to civil servants and journalists; and (ii) cases about the rights of persons accused of corruption, including the rights enshrined in Articles 5, 6 and 8 ECHR. Cases in which the applicant held that his or her rights were violated by corrupt practices were not found.

1 For more on the ECHR, see David John Harris, Michael O'Boyle, and Colin Warbrick, *Law of the European Convention on Human Rights* (2nd edn.; Oxford: Oxford University Press, 2009).

2.2. Practice of the European Court of Human Rights

2.2.1. Whistleblowers' Right to Freedom of Expression (Article 10 ECHR)

A number of the Court's corruption-related cases are concerned with the right to freedom of expression, enshrined in Article 10 ECHR, of persons denouncing corruption. These are interesting cases on the topic of whistleblowers. Combating corruption requires the protection of their human rights. As argued by the International Council on Human Rights Policy, corruption is an indirect cause of human rights violations when authorities try to silence whistleblowers from exercising, for example, their right to freedom of expression. Corruption is then a necessary condition for the human rights violation to occur.[2] The ECtHR case law distinguishes between, on the one hand, civil servants who blow the whistle, and, on the other hand, journalists who expose corruption.

(i) Civil Servants

Regarding civil servants, an important case is *Guja v. Moldova* (2008),[3] brought by an applicant who served as Head of the Press Department of the Prosecutor General's Office in Moldova. Guja leaked documents to a newspaper, which showed that a high-ranking politician interfered with an ongoing corruption investigation. After the publication of newspaper articles on the matter, Guja was dismissed. He complained before the Court that this constituted a violation of Article 10, in particular the right to impart information. The Court had to determine whether the interference (i.e. the dismissal) was 'necessary in a democratic society', as required by Article 10(2).

The Court noted that, so far, it had not dealt with cases in which a civil servant publicly disclosed internal information.[4] The Court held that:

> ... a civil servant, in the course of his work, may become aware of in-house information, including secret information, whose divulgation or publication corresponds to a strong public interest. The Court thus considers that the signalling by a civil servant or an employee in the public sector of illegal conduct or wrongdoing in the workplace should, in certain circumstances, enjoy protection. This may be called for where the employee or civil servant concerned is the only person, or part of a small category of persons, aware of what is happening at work and is thus best placed to act in the public interest by alerting the employer or the public at large.[5]

---

2 International Council on Human Rights Policy, *Corruption and Human Rights: Making the Connection* (Versoix, Switzerland, 2009) at p. 27–28. For more on this topic, see p. 63–68 of the Council's report.

3 ECtHR Grand Chamber Judgment *Guja v. Moldova*, 12 February 2008, Application no. 14277/04.

4 *Ibid.* §72.

5 *Ibid.* §72.

The Court then formulated a number of criteria to determine whether the restrictions on whistleblowers (e.g. the dismissal of Guja) are 'necessary in a democratic society'. First, the whistleblower has to use alternative channels to address the matter, particularly one's superior or another competent body. Use of the media should be a last resort.[6] Second, the public interest in the disclosed information is important.[7] Third, the authenticity of the disclosed information is significant.[8] Fourth, the Court must weigh the damage suffered by the public authority because of the disclosure, and determine whether the damage outweighs the public interest.[9] Fifth, the motive of the reporting individual is of importance. Does the person act out of personal grievance or the expectation of personal gain, or out of public interest considerations? The individual must act in good faith, in the belief that the information was true, that the disclosure was in the public interest, and that no other more discreet means were available.[10] Sixth, the penalty imposed on the individual and its consequences must be taken into account.[11] By setting these criteria, the Grand Chamber of the Court offered a framework to use Article 10 for the protection of whistleblowers. In the present case, the Court found that Guja's dismissal was not necessary in a democratic society, and concluded that Article 10 was violated. *Inter alia*, it was stated that 'open discussion of topics of public concern is essential to democracy and regard must be had to the great importance of not discouraging members of the public from voicing their opinions on such matters.'[12]

As a final note, it is interesting to observe that in the section on relevant non-Convention materials, the Court quotes provisions on whistleblower protection contained in anti-corruption treaties: (i) Article 33 UNCAC (to which Moldova was not a Party);[13] (ii) parts of the Preamble and Article 22 of the Council of Europe's Criminal Law Convention on Corruption (to which Moldova is a Party) and the Explanatory Report;[14] (iii) parts of the Preamble and Article 9 of the Council of Europe's Civil Law Convention (to which Moldova is a Party), and the Explanatory Report;[15] and (iv) Article 11 and 12(5) and (6) of the Recommendation on Codes of Conduct for Public Officials adopted by the Council of Europe's Committee of Ministers.[16]

---

6 *Ibid.* §73.
7 *Ibid.* §74.
8 *Ibid.* §75.
9 *Ibid.* §76.
10 *Ibid.* §77.
11 *Ibid.* §78.
12 *Ibid.* §91.
13 *Ibid.* §44.
14 *Ibid.* §45.
15 *Ibid.* §46.
16 *Ibid.* §47.

Another interesting case is *Kudeshkina v. Russia* (2009), which concerned Russian judge Kudeshkina.[17] She was dismissed because she had made statements in the media criticising higher judicial officials, arguing that pressure was put on her in connection with a criminal case against a police investigator. The Court found a violation of Article 10, and stated that Kudeshkina had raised a very important matter of public interest, which had to be open to free debate in democratic society.[18] Even if Kudeshkina had allowed herself a certain degree of exaggeration and generalisation, the ECtHR found her statement to be a fair comment on a matter of great public importance.[19] Her dismissal was capable of having a 'chilling effect' on judges wishing to participate in the public debate on the effectiveness of judicial institutions. Hence, this penalty was found to be disproportionately severe.[20]

(ii) Journalists

A larger body of case law concerns journalists or newspaper editors, who published accusations of corruption, for example, in newspapers, and against whom legal proceedings (for defamation, slander, or insult) were started as a result. Relevant cases are, in reversed chronological order: *Fedchenko v. Russia* (2010);[21] *Mahmudov and Agazade v. Azerbaijan* (2008);[22] *Barb v. Romania* (2008);[23] *Alithia Publishing Company Ltd & Constantinides v. Cyprus* (2008);[24] *Timpul Info-Magazine and Anghel v. Moldova* (2007);[25] *Dyuldin and Kislov v. Russia* (2007);[26] *Diena and Ozolins v. Latvia* (2007);[27] *Gorelishvili v. Georgia* (2007);[28] *Stângu and Scutelnicu*

---

17 ECtHR, Judgment *Kudeshkina v. Russia*, 26 February 2009, Application no. 29492/05.

18 *Ibid.* §94.

19 *Ibid.* §95.

20 *Ibid.* §100.

21 ECtHR, Judgment *Fedchenko v. Russia* (no. 2), 11 February 2010, Application no. 48195/06. Violation of Article 10.

22 ECtHR, Judgment *Mahmudov and Agazade v. Azerbaijan*, 18 December 2008, Application no. 35877/04. Violation of Article 10.

23 ECtHR, Judgment *Barb v. Romania*, 7 October 2008, Application no. 5945/03. Violation of Article 10.

24 ECtHR, Judgment *Alithia Publishing Company Ltd & Constantinides v. Cyprus*, 22 May 2008, Application no. 17550/03. No violation of Article 10 (§71 stated 'As the applicants acted in flagrant disregard of the duties of responsible journalism and has thus undermined the Convention rights of others, the interference with the existence of their right to freedom of expression was justified.').

25 ECtHR, Judgment *Timpul Info-Magazin and Anghel v. Moldova*, 27 November 2007, Application no. 42864/05. Violation of Article 10.

26 ECtHR, Judgment *Dyuldin and Kislov v. Russia*, 31 July 2007, Application no. 25968/02. Violation of Article 10.

27 ECtHR, Judgment *Diena and Ozolins v. Latvia*, 12 July 2007, Application no. 16657/03. Violation of Article 10.

28 ECtHR, Judgment *Gorelishvili v. Georgia*, 5 June 2007, Application no. 12979/04. Violation of Article 10.

v. Romania (2006);[29] *Cumpana and Mazare v. Romania* (2004);[30] *Sabou and Pîrcalab v. Romania* (2004);[31] and *Thoma v. Luxemburg* (2001).[32] In most of these cases, the Court found that the State's interference with the right to freedom of expression of the journalists concerned was not justified, and concluded that Article 10 was violated.

In order to understand the reasoning of the Court, one of the above-mentioned cases is discussed by means of illustration. In *Cumpana and Mazare v. Romania* (2004), the applicants were journalists who wrote a newspaper article containing allegations of corruption by a politician and a judge, which was accompanied by a cartoon. The publication led to the criminal conviction of the journalists for insult and defamation. Before the ECtHR they complained that their right to freedom of expression was violated. The Grand Chamber of the Court examined whether the interference with Article 10 was 'necessary in a democratic society'. To this end, the conviction of the journalists first had to meet a 'pressing social need'.[33] In this respect, the vital role of 'public watchdog' performed by the press was stressed by the Court.[34] Second, the sanction imposed needed to be proportional.[35] In the present case, the Court found that the conviction did meet a pressing social need,[36] but the imposition of a prison sentence, as well as the disqualification of the journalists from exercising civil rights, and the prohibition of working as a journalist for one year, were found disproportional.[37] Hence, Article 10 was violated.

2.2.2. Rights of Persons Accused of Corruption

Another set of cases of the ECtHR sheds light on the human rights concerns that may arise in the fight against corruption. They show that anti-corruption efforts on the part of governments must meet the requirements of the Convention, including Articles 6, 5, and 8. While corruption may violate human rights, anti-corruption measures can also violate recognised human rights. Hence, there can be tensions between anti-corruption and human rights practice.[38] The following cases are

---

29 ECtHR, Judgment *Stângu and Scutelnicu v. Romania*, 31 January 2006, Application no. 53899/00. No violation of Article 10.

30 ECtHR Grand Chamber Judgment *Cumpana and Mazare v. Romania*, 17 December 2004, Application no. 33348/96.

31 ECtHR Judgment *Sabou and Pîrcaleb v. Romania*, 28 September 2004, Application no. 46572/99. Violation of Article 10.

32 ECtHR Judgment *Thoma v. Luxembourg,* 29 June 2001, Application no. 38432/97.

33 *Cumpana and Mazare v. Romania*, §88.

34 *Ibid.* §93.

35 *Ibid.* §90.

36 *Ibid.* §110.

37 *Ibid.* §116–119.

38 International Council on Human Rights Policy, *Integrating Human Rights in the Anti-Corruption Agenda: Challenges, Possibilities and Opportunities* (Geneva, Switzerland, 2010) at p. 63–69.

illustrative of the various human rights matters that can come into play when combating corruption.

(i) *Ramanauskas v. Lithuania* (2008): Article 6 ECHR

Ramanauskas v. Lithuania (2008) concerns Article 6, on the right to a fair trial of a person accused of corruption.[39] Applicant Ramanauskas was a prosecutor, who had been asked, through acquaintance VS, by individual AZ to secure the acquittal of a third person, and he was offered a bribe of $3,000 to do so. Initially the applicant had refused this offer, but later agreed after repeated offers. AZ turned out to be an officer of a special anti-corruption police unit of the Ministry of Interior. However, the authorities were not yet informed of the action at the time. Later the applicant was convicted, and he complained that he was incited to commit a criminal offense, and that the conviction for bribery was unfair. He also held that the principle of equality of arms and the rights of the defence under Article 6 were violated because neither the courts nor the parties had the opportunity to examine VS.

In the discussion of the case, the Court acknowledged that:

> ... corruption – including in the judicial sphere – has become a major problem in many countries, as is attested by the Council of Europe's Criminal Law Convention on the subject. This instrument authorises the use of special investigative techniques, such as undercover agents, that may be necessary for gathering evidence in this area, provided that the rights and undertakings deriving from international multilateral conventions concerning "special matters", for example human rights, are not affected. That being so, the use of special investigative methods – in particular, undercover techniques – cannot in itself infringe the right to a fair trial. However, on account of the risk of police incitement entailed by such techniques, their use must be kept within clear limits.[40]

The Court held in the present case that Article 6(1) was violated, since the actions of VS and AZ amounted to incitement, and that there was no indication that the offence of bribery would have been committed without their intervention.[41] An important factor was the *ex post facto* legitimisation by the authorities of the initial conduct of AZ. Other cases on incitement to bribery are *Ünel v. Turkey* (2008)[42] and *Milinienè v. Lithuania* (2008).[43]

---

39 ECtHR Judgment *Ramanauskas v. Lithuania*, 5 February 2008, Application no. 74420/01.

40 *Ibid.* §50–51. In the overview of relevant international law, the Court discussed Article 23 of the Council of Europe's Criminal Law Convention on Corruption, dealing with evidence gathering and special investigative techniques.

41 *Ibid.* §73–74.

42 ECtHR Judgment *Ünel v. Turkey*, 27 May 2008, Application no. 35686/02.

43 ECtHR Judgment *Milinienè v. Lithuania*, 24 June 2008, Application no. 74335/01.

(ii) *Craxi v. Italy* (2003): Article 8 ECHR

Craxi v. Italy (2003)[44] concerned the Italian 'clean hands' (*mani pulite*) campaign against corruption. As part of this campaign, Craxi (former Italian Prime Minister, and former general secretary of the Italian Socialist Party) was prosecuted in Italy for corruption, dishonest receipt of money by a public officer, concealment of dishonest gain, and offences against the legislation on the financing of political parties. In 1994, Craxi was sentenced to prison in absentia since he resided in Tunesia. The public prosecutor obtained an order so that Craxi's telephone calls between Italy and Tunisia could be intercepted, which was done by the Italian police in 1995. At a hearing in September 1995, the prosecutor asked the Court for the telephone transcripts to be admitted as evidence in the case against Craxi and for the transcripts to be deposited in the court registry. Subsequently, a number of extracts were read out in Court by the Prosecution and the content of certain telephone conversations and the names of the persons involved were published in the press. The local Court decided not to use the information in the conversations. In 1996, Craxi was sentenced to a prison sentence of 8 years and three months, and a fine of 150 million lire. In appeal, the sentence was reduced to four years and six months. Before the Court, applicant Craxi complained that the release into the public domain of the intercepted phone calls of a private nature constituted a breach of, *inter alia*, Article 8, i.e. the right to respect for private life. In particular, Craxi complained about the decision of the Prosecutor to deposit the transcripts with the registry of the Italian Court.

The ECtHR argued that there was indeed an interference with the rights laid down in Article 8. Some of the conversations published in the Italian press were strictly private, and had little or no connection with the criminal charges against Craxi.[45] Publication of these conversations by the press did not correspond to a pressing social need, and, as a result, the interference with Article 8 was not 'necessary in a democratic society'.[46] The question was whether this interference could be imputed to the Italian State.[47] Since the conversations of a private nature were not all read out in the Italian Court, the ECtHR found that the journalists had obtained their information from consulting the Court's registry.[48] However, this registry is only accessible to the Parties in a given case, so the journalists must have had access because of a malfunction of the registry or because one of the parties or their lawyers have given them information.[49] The Court then noted that there may be positive obligations for States to ensure the right to private life. In the present case, Italian authorities failed in their obligation to provide safe custody of the

44 ECtHR Judgment *Craxi v. Italy* (No. 2), 17 July 2003, Application no. 25337/94.
45 *Ibid.* §66.
46 *Ibid.* §67.
47 *Ibid.* §68.
48 *Ibid.* §69.
49 *Ibid.* §71–72.

transcripts of the telephone calls. The Court also found that Italy should have conducted an inquiry to find out how the journalists had obtained access to the documents.[50] As a result, the Court held that there was a violation of Article 8.[51]

As regards the reading out of the telephone calls by the Prosecutor at a Court hearing, the ECtHR found that the statutory procedures had not been followed, and, as a result, Craxi was deprived of a substantial procedural safeguard. The Court found that the interference with Article 8 was not 'in accordance with the law', and hence found a violation of Article 8.[52]

(iii) *Lietzow v. Germany* (2001): Article 5 ECHR

Lietzow v. Germany (2001) is another case about the rights of allegedly corrupt persons.[53] The applicant in this case, director of the Sewage Disposal Department, had regularly accepted payments from an engineering company's owner and his deputy. These payments, increased by at least 100 per cent, were then included in bills for public construction works financed by the Department. Lietzow also received a jacuzzi. There was an agreement between Lietzow and the engineering company that Lietzow would ensure that contracts were regularly awarded to the company. Because of the alleged risk of collusion, Lietzow was arrested. He argued that he was given little details about his case, and therefore he complained to the Court that his defence council did not obtain access to his criminal files, violating Article 5(4).[54] According to the prosecutor, this access was denied in the interest of ongoing investigations on economic crime, including corruption, involving a large number of public officials and employees. The Court found a violation of Article 5(4), arguing that it:

> ... acknowledges the need for criminal investigations to be conducted efficiently, which may imply that part of the information collected during them is to be kept secret in order to prevent suspects from tampering with evidence and undermining the course of justice. However, this legitimate goal cannot be pursued at the expense of substantial restrictions on the rights of the defence. Therefore, information which is essential for the assessment of the lawfulness of a person's detention should be made available in an appropriate manner to the suspect's lawyer.[55]

---

50 *Ibid.* §75.
51 *Ibid.* §76.
52 *Ibid.* §81–83.
53 ECtHR Judgment *Lietzow v. Germany*, 13 February 2001, Application no. 24479/94.
54 Article 5(4) of the ECHR states: 'Everyone who is deprived of his liberty by arrest and detention shall be entitled to take proceedings by which the lawfulness of his detention shall be decided speedily by a court and his release ordered if the detention is not lawful.'
55 *Lietzow v. Germany*, §47.

3. The Americas

3.1. Background

Under the auspices of the Organization of American States (hereafter: OAS), a number of regional human rights instruments came into being, most importantly the American Convention on the Protection of Human Rights of 1969 (hereafter: ACHR) and the Protocol of San Salvador of 1988. While the ACHR mainly focuses upon civil and political rights,[56] the Protocol is concerned with economic, social and cultural rights.[57] Out of the 35 Member States of OAS, there are currently 24 State Parties to the ACHR,[58] and 15 State Parties to the Protocol of San Salvador.[59] Monitoring of the Convention and the Protocol is carried out by the Inter-American Commission on Human Rights (hereafter: IACionHR) located in Washington, and the Inter-American Court of Human Rights (hereafter: IACtHR) in San José, Costa Rica.[60]

The Inter-American Commission on Human Rights (i) deals with petitions from individuals about alleged human rights violations (Articles 44–51 ACHR); (ii) observes the general human rights situation in State Parties and publishes country-specific reports; (iii) conducts country visits, usually resulting in a country report; (iv) stimulates public consciousness on human rights, and carries out thematic studies; (v) organises conferences, seminars and meetings with, *inter alia*, governmental representatives, academic institutions and NGOs to disseminate information and increase knowledge about the Inter-American human rights system; (vi) can recommend OAS Member States to adopt measures contributing to human rights protection; (vii) can request States to adopt precautionary measures to avoid serious and irreparable harm in urgent cases, and can request the Court to order provisional measures in urgent cases; (viii) submits cases to the Court and appears before the Court in the litigation of cases; (ix) can request advisory opinions from the Court about the interpretation of the ACHR.[61]

---

56 Article 26 ACHR is concerned with economic, social and cultural rights.

57 Other regional human rights instruments in the Americas are, *inter alia*, the Inter-American Convention to Prevent and Punish Torture, the Protocol to the ACHR to Abolish the Death Penalty, the Inter-American Convention on the Prevention, Punishment and Eradication of Violence Against Women, the Inter-American Convention on Forced Disappearance of Persons and the Inter-American Convention on the Elimination of all Forms of Discrimination Against Persons with Disabilities.

58 Ratification Status of the ACHR, <www.cidh.oas.org/Basicos/English/Basic4.Amer.Conv.Ratif.htm>, accessed 29 June 2011.

59 Ratification Status of the Protocol of San Salvador, <www.cidh.oas.org/Basicos/English/Basic6.Prot.Sn%20Salv%20Ratif.htm>, accessed 29 June 2011.

60 For more on the Inter-American Court of Human Rights, see Jo M. Pasqualucci, *The Practice and Procedure of the Inter-American Court of Human Rights* (Cambridge: Cambridge University Press 2003).

61 Background to the Inter-American Commission on Human Rights, <www.cidh.oas.org/what.htm>, accessed 29 June 2011.

As stated, individuals can file complaints with the Commission.[62] If the case is admissible, and a violation is found, the Commission addresses recommendations to the State concerned. If the State does not comply, the Commission can refer the case to the Court.[63] The same is true if the Commission finds that the case is of particular importance or legal interest. States can also bring cases,[64] while individuals do not have direct access to the Court. Furthermore, for the Court to have jurisdiction, it is required that the State concerned is a party to the ACHR and that it has recognised the jurisdiction of the Court.[65]

3.2. Practice of the Inter-American Commission on Human Rights

The Commission publishes various documents: (i) annual reports (containing case law); (ii) country reports;[66] (iii) thematic reports and other documents; and (iv) resolutions. The value of these documents in legal terms varies.

At the outset the following must be noted. First, only a small number of petitions before the Commission address corruption. Second, as regards the country reports, the Cion released 58 reports since 1962, many of which discuss corruption. One can detect a steady increase in attention for corruption in recent years, as of the mid–1990s. Third, the Cion's thematic reports and other publications have, up to now, dealt with corruption on a number of occasions.[67] Fourth, out of the eleven resolutions of the Commission, only two addressed corruption.[68] The following sections contain a thematic overview of the Commission's main concerns about corruption, as found in the sources mentioned above.

3.2.1. Corruption in the Judiciary

A small number of petitions before the Commission were brought by individuals who complain that their right to a fair trial was violated by judicial corruption. Because domestic remedies were not exhausted, the Commission declared these cases inadmissible.[69] Nevertheless, other cases reveal that the Commission does

---

62 Article 44 ACHR.

63 Article 61 ACHR.

64 Article 61 ACHR.

65 Article 62 ACHR.

66 On country reports, see Cecilia Medina, 'The Role of Country Reports in the Inter-American System of Human Rights', in David J. Harris and Stephen Livingstone (eds.), *The Inter-American System of Human Rights* (Oxford: Clarendon Press, 1998), p. 115–132.

67 Thematic reports and other publications of the Inter-American Commission on Human Rights, <www.cidh.oas.org/pais.eng.htm>, accessed 12 January 2011.

68 Resolutions of the Inter-American Commission on Human Rights, <www.cidh.org/publi.eng.htm>, accessed 12 January 2011.

69 Inter-American Commission on Human Rights, *Oscar Vila-Masot v. Venezuela*, case 11.216, report no. 87/98; *Gustavo Gomez Lopez v. Venezuela*, case 11.703, report no. 82/98.

consider itself competent to decide on matters concerning judicial corruption. It stated that it:

> ... has full authority to adjudicate irregularities of domestic judicial proceedings which result in manifest violations of due process or of any of the rights protected by the Convention. For example, if [the petitioner] presented information establishing that the trial was not impartial because the judges were corrupt, or were biased for racial, religious, or political reasons against him, the Commission would be competent to examine the case under Articles 8, 21 and 25 of the Convention.[70]

In many of the Commission's country reports, judicial corruption was also a matter of concern.[71] While discussions were mostly factual, the IACionHR made an interesting observation in its report on Paraguay (2001), stating that:

> Another point where corruption and human rights concerns come together, also in the context of impunity, is that the corruption of the judge in a particular trial undermines his or her independence when deciding the case, and may consequently constitute a violation by the State of the rights and guarantees enshrined in the American Convention, among them the guarantee that all persons will be judged by an independent and impartial judge, enshrined in Article 8(1) of the American Convention.'[72]

This makes unequivocally clear that according to the Commission, corruption may constitute a violation of human rights. Furthermore, we find that the Commission's thematic report on citizen security and human rights of 2009 stated, *inter alia*, that citizen security requires the elimination of corruption or impunity.[73] In its recommendations, the Commission noted that:

> A citizen security policy must be implemented in such a way that the right to due process and the right to judicial protection are observed. Member States must be especially mindful of their obligations to: [...] implement the mechanisms necessary to prevent, investigate and punish any form of corruption that prevents the system of administration of justice from functioning correctly.[74]

---

70 Inter-American Commission on Human Rights, *Santiago Marzioni v. Argentina*, case 11.673, report no. 39/96, §61 and 62. This was also stated in *Juan Milla Bermúdez v. Honduras*, case 11.206, report no. 46/96, §45.

71 See for example IACionHR, *Haïti: Failed Justice or the Rule of Law? Challenges Ahead for Haïti and the International Community*, 26 October 2005, OEA/Ser/L/V/II.123, Doc. 6 rev 1, §159–160.

72 IACionHR, Third report on the situation of human rights in Paraguay, 9 March 2001, OEA/Ser.L/V/II.110, chapter II, §47.

73 IACionHR, Report on Citizen Security and Human Rights, 31 December 2009, OEA/Ser.L/V/II, Doc. 57, §2. See also §33, 91, 99, 167, and 173.

74 *Ibid.* §232 B ad. 16.

Thus, in the view of the Commission, anti-corruption obligations are part of the right to due process and to judicial protection, as laid down in the ACHR.

3.2.2. Rights of Whistleblowers

A few individual cases brought before the Commission concerned the (lack of) protection of whistleblowers. One complaint concerned a Mexican journalist who denounced corruption, and was later assassinated. The Commission found that Mexico did not properly investigate the matter. As a result, violations of the rights to freedom of expression, fair trial, and judicial protection were found.[75] Furthermore, it appeared from the country reports that in many countries whistleblowers, especially journalists, face serious risks of prosecution or harassment when they expose corruption. *Inter alia*, this was made clear in the report on Peru (2000).[76]

3.2.3. Economic, Social and Cultural Rights

The country report on Paraguay (2001), already noted above, is one of the country reports dealing most elaborately with corruption.[77] According to the Cion, 'the phenomenon of corruption has to do not only with the legitimacy of public institutions, society, the integral development of peoples, and all other more general aspects mentioned *supra* but also has a specific impact on the effective enjoyment of human rights in society in general.'[78] Moreover, it is clear that the Commission drew inspiration from a working paper by Jayawickrama.[79] The Cion followed the reason of Jayawickrama by discussing, *inter alia*, that corruption has a major impact in the area of economic, social and cultural rights, since it is one of the factors that can stand in the way of the adoption by the State of 'the necessary measures ... to the extent allowed by their available resources, ... for the purpose of achieving progressively ... the full observance of' these rights (Article 1 of the Protocol of San Salvador).[80] The Cion then went on to discuss the relationship between corruption and the prohibition of discrimination of Article 1(1) of the

---

75 Inter-American Commission on Human Rights, *Victor Manuel Oropeza v. Mexico*, case 11.740, report no. 130/99, §57. Another case about critical journalists is *Horacio Verbitsky et al. v. Argentia*, case 12.128, report no. 3/04.

76 IACionHR, Second report on the situation of human rights in Peru, 2 June 2000, OEA/Ser.L/V/II.106, Doc. 59 rev., chapter V, §48, 67, 69, 88, 106.

77 IACionHR, Third report on the situation of human rights in Paraguay, 9 March 2001, OEA/Ser.L/V/II.110, chapter II, §section G (§41–56).

78 *Ibid.* §45.

79 Nihal Jayawickrama, 'Corruption – a Violation of Human Rights?' *Working Paper* (Sofia: Transparency International, 1–2 June 1998). The content of this working paper is discussed in the General Introduction of the present work.

80 IACionHR, Third report on the situation of human rights in Paraguay, 9 March 2001, OEA/Ser.L/V/II.110, chapter II, §48.

ACHR,[81] and the right to freedom of expression and political rights.[82] Subsequently, the Commission discussed the anti-corruption actions taken by Paraguay.[83]

Also worth mentioning are the Commission's Guidelines for the preparation of progress indicators in the area of economic, social and cultural rights (2008).[84] These guidelines deal with several kinds of indicators that can be used to monitor the progressive realisation of economic, social and cultural rights. A difference is made between structural indicators, process indicators and outcome indicators.[85] In the field of equality and non-discrimination, a structural indicator is the ratification by the State of the Inter-American Convention Against Corruption.[86] Furthermore, other structural indicators are (i) the existence of a specific anti-corruption monitoring agency, its responsibilities, jurisdiction and budget; (ii) the powers of such an agency to receive, process, resolve and/or refer complaints; and (iii) the existence of measures and actions in social policies to eradicate patronage.[87] A process indicator is the number of complaints received and resolved concerning corruption connected with access to social programmes and plans.[88] These indicators show that corruption cannot be disregarded in the discussion on the progressive realisation of economic, social and cultural rights.

3.2.4. Other Issues

Other corruption-related issues discussed in the country reports of the Commission were police corruption, for example as mentioned in the report on Mexico (1998),[89] and corruption in prisons, such as discussed in the report on Guatemala (2001).[90] Also, the Commission pointed out that the fight against corruption can also be used

---

81 *Ibid.* §50 and 51.

82 *Ibid.* §52.

83 *Ibid.* §53–56.

84 IACionHR, Guidelines for Preparation of Progress Indicators in the Area of Economic, Social and Cultural Rights, 19 July 2008, OEA/Ser.L/V/II.132, Doc. 14.

85 *Structural indicators* seek to determine what measures the State would be able to adopt to implement the rights in the Protocol of San Salvador. They collect information to evaluate how the State's institutional apparatus and legal system are organised to perform the obligations under the Protocol. *Ibid.* §30. *Process indicators* measure the quality and extent of State efforts to implement rights by measuring the scope, coverage, and content of strategies, plans, programs, or policies, or other specific activities and interventions designed to accomplish the goals necessary for the realisation of a given right. *Ibid.* §31. *Outcome indicators* measure the actual impact of government strategies, programs and interventions. *Ibid.* §32.

86 *Ibid.* table at p. 22.

87 *Ibid.* table at p. 23.

88 *Ibid.* table at p. 24.

89 IACionHR, Report on the situation of human rights in Mexico, 24 September 1998, OEA/Ser.L/V/II.100, Doc. 7 rev. 1, chapter V, §388 *et seq.*

90 IACionHR, Fifth report on the situation of human rights in Guatemala, 6 April 2001, OEA/Ser.L/V/II.111, Doc. 21 rev., chapter VIII, §17, 21, 22.

as a tool against political opponents; such was the case in Venezuela (2009), in respect of Manuel Rosales, opponent of Hugo Chavez in the elections of 2006.[91]

As regards prison corruption, we find that the Commission's Resolution 1/08 enunciates principles and best practices on the protection of persons deprived of liberty in the Americas. Principle XXIII, paragraph 1 lists preventive measures to combat violence and emergency situations, stating that:

> ... in accordance with international human rights law, appropriate and effective measures shall be adopted to prevent violence amongst persons deprived of liberty, or between persons deprived of liberty and the personnel. In order to achieve that, the following measures shall be taken, amongst others: [...] g) Prevent and combat all types of abuse of authority and corruption; and h) eradicate impunity by investigating and punishing all acts of violence and corruption in accordance with the law.[92]

3.3. Practice of the Inter-American Court of Human Rights

In a small number of cases of the Inter-American Court of Human Rights, corruption was an important issue. *Acevedo-Jaramillo et al. v. Peru* (2006) concerned the dismissal of workers, by the municipality, who wanted their jobs back, as well as payment of their salaries. This was already ordered by local courts, but Peru refused to comply with these domestic judgments.[93] Peru held before the IACtHR that non-compliance was justified because of widespread corrupt practices, in this case between the trade union, the national intelligence service and the judiciary. It was argued that the domestic judgments, which Peru did not comply with, were of an illegal nature. Evidence was submitted to the IACtHR to prove such corruption. The IACtHR did not accept Peru's argument, and found that the State violated Article 25(1) and 25(2)(c) of the ACHR, i.e. the right to judicial protection.

The case *Ivcher Bronstein v. Peru* (2001) concerned Bronstein, who was a majority shareholder, director and president of a television channel. He was deprived of his nationality title (which he had obtained through naturalization), allegedly so as to remove him from the editorial board of the channel, and to restrict his freedom of expression. The underlying reason was that the channel denounced grave violations of human rights and acts of corruption by State actors. The IACtHR ruled that various rights were violated, including the right to freedom of

---

91 IACionHR, Democracy and Human Rights in Venezuela, 30 December 2009, OEA/Ser.L/V/II. Doc 54, §102–103.

92 IACionHR, Resolution 1/08, Principles and Best Practices on the Protection of Persons Deprived of Liberty in the Americas. The other instance is Resolution 1/03 on trial for international crimes, mentioning the Inter-American Convention Against Corruption.

93 Inter-American Court of Human Rights, *Acevedo-Jaramillo et al. v. Peru*, Judgment of 7 February 2006.

expression under Article 13(1) and 13(3) of the ACHR.[94] This case shows the importance of the exercise of this right by the media in exposing corruption. Whistleblowers can invoke the right before domestic courts and human rights bodies.

Another case in which the right to freedom of expression was a central topic is *Ricardo Canese v. Paraguay* (2004). The case concerned former Paraguayan presidential candidate Ricardo Canese, who was convicted for slander and defamation because he was critical about Juan Carlos Wasmosy, who also ran for office. According to Canese, Wasmosy had ties to former dictator Stroessner and was involved in corrupt acts in the construction partnership CONEMPA, which was awarded a contract to build the Itaipú hydroelectric power plant, a joint project of Paraguay and Brazil. The case before the IACtHR concerned, *inter alia*, the question of whether Paraguay violated Canese's right to freedom of expression by convicting him. In the proceedings before the Court, the Commission held that 'freedom of expression is one of the most effective ways of denouncing corruption. Moreover, the rule should be that alleged acts of corruption are publicized.'[95] The Court found that:

> … there is no doubt that the statements made by Mr. Canese with regard to CONEMPA concern matters of public interest, because, when he made them, this company was involved in the construction of the said hydroelectric power plant. According to the body of evidence in the instant case […] the National Congress itself, through its Bicameral Unlawful Acts Investigation Committee, was investigating corruption at Itaipú, involving Juan Carlos Wasmosy and the said company.[96]

Hence, the Court found that Paraguay had violated, *inter alia*, Canese's the right to freedom of thought and expression as enshrined in Article 13 of the ACHR.

Apitz Barbera et al. v. Venezuela (2008) concerned a number of judges who were removed from office, allegedly because a recent ruling was politically sensitive/unfavourable. The judges were portrayed in the media by President Chavez as being corrupt. The IACtHR found a violation of Article 8(1), i.e. the right to a fair trial, and of Article 25(1), i.e. the right to judicial protection, and ruled that the judges had to receive compensation and had to be reinstated. This case shows that accusations of corruption can be used by those in power to silence (political) opponents.[97]

---

94 Inter-American Court of Human Rights, *Ivcher Bronstein v. Peru*, Judgment of 6 February 2001.

95 Inter-American Court of Human Rights, *Ricardo Canese v. Paraguay*, Judgment of 31 August 2004, §72d.

96 *Ibid.* §92.

97 Inter-American Court of Human Rights, *Apitz Barbera et al. v. Venezuela*, Judgment of 5 August 2008.

4. Africa

4.1. Background

The African Charter on Human and People's Rights (hereafter: AfCHPR, or the Banjul Charter) was adopted in 1981 by the Assembly of Heads of State and Government of the Organization of African Unity (OAU, replaced in 2002 by the African Union), and entered into force in 1986. The Charter has 53 State Parties.[98] Supervision of State obligations is in the hands of the African Commission on Human and Peoples' Rights (hereafter: African Commission), which was established in 1987, and began functioning in 1989. Its decisions became public as of 1994.[99] The Commission (i) considers complaints from individuals;[100] (ii) can consider inter-State complaints;[101] (iii) conducts on-site missions;[102] (iv) examines State reports;[103] and (v) has a number of Special Mechanisms, including Special Rapporteurs.[104] There is also an African Court on Human and Peoples' Rights, established in 2004, but this institution has not yet heard a case.[105]

4.2. Practice of the African Commission on Human and Peoples' Rights

Given the pervasiveness of corruption throughout Africa,[106] it is relevant to examine whether and, if so, how the African Commission has dealt with this subject in its decisions on individual complaints. An analysis of the few decisions in which corruption was mentioned reveals that the Commission has hardly done any work in this area. A rare example is *Ilesanmi v. Nigeria.*[107] In this case, complainant Ilesanmi was a consultant who had exposed widespread smuggling of various goods, in which public officials were allegedly involved. Ilesanmi claimed, *inter alia*, that the smugglers were also responsible for a number of assassinations. Moreover, he held that, as a result of his exposure of smuggling, his pregnant wife was murdered, and that he himself was abducted, imprisoned and poisoned. He

---

98 African Union, Ratification Status of the African Charter on Human and Peoples' Rights, <www.achpr.org/english/ratifications/ratification_african%20charter.pdf>.

99 Frans Viljoen, *International Human Rights Law in Africa* (Oxford: Oxford University Press, 2007) at p. 169.

100 *Ibid.* at p. 319–361.

101 *Ibid.* at p. 361–362.

102 *Ibid.* at p. 362–367.

103 *Ibid.* at p. 369–392.

104 *Ibid.* at p. 392–401.

105 For an extensive analysis of the African Court on Human and Peoples' Rights, see *Ibid.* at p. 418–475. See also George Mukundi Wachira, 'African Court on Human and Peoples' Rights: Ten Years on and Still No Justice', (Minority Rights Group International 2008).

106 See Viljoen, *International Human Rights Law in Africa*, at p. 292–295.

107 African Commission on Human and Peoples' Rights, *Ilesanmi v. Nigeria*, Communication 268/2003.

argued that Nigeria violated various rights under the Charter. The Commission declared the communication inadmissible due to non-exhaustion of local remedies. Moreover, the Commission found the complaint insulting to Nigeria, since Ilesanmi accused public officials, including (then) President Obasanjo, of corruption: 'the African Commission finds that the language used in the communication as intended to bring the institution of the president into ridicule and disrepute and thus insulting.'[108] This concerns the admissibility requirement contained in the African Charter that communications must not be written in disparaging or insulting language directed against the State concerned or its institutions.[109] The African Charter is the only human rights treaty containing such a requirement, which may constitute a barrier to submitting individual complaints about corruption. Accusations about corrupt conduct may often imply 'insults' to the State. Hopefully, the Commission will apply the requirement in a lenient way in the future.

5. Concluding Remarks

From the examination of regional human rights practice, a number of conclusions can be drawn. Since the study of African case law generated few relevant cases, the following will focus upon the European and Inter-American systems.

To begin with, corruption may constitute an indirect violation of the right to freedom of expression of whistleblowers. Those individuals who face dismissal or prosecution in their country for denouncing corruption can turn to the European Court of Human Rights so as to invoke their right to freedom of expression under Article 10 of the Convention. Likewise, complaints can be brought before the Inter-American Commission on Human Rights, and ultimately the Inter-American Court may rule on the matter.

Furthermore, European practice showed that anti-corruption measures can violate the rights of persons accused of corruption. Care must be taken to respect these rights, *inter alia*, those enshrined in Articles 5, 6 and 8 of the ECHR. The same considerations will undoubtedly also apply to the American context.

Moreover, the practice of the Inter-American Commission demonstrated that corruption in the judiciary may directly violate the right to a fair trial. Nevertheless, one would have perhaps expected a greater deal of complaints about corruption, including in the judiciary, both in Europe and the Americas. One would expect cases brought to the ECtHR and the IACionHR by individuals who claim that they are victims of corruption. An example would be an individual who did not receive a fair trial because the judge received bribes, which is a practice violating Article 6 of the European Convention, and Article 8 of the American Convention. However, within the European context, such cases were not found, and there were only a few relevant cases of the Inter-American Commission. This absence of cases may mean

---

108 *Ibid.* §40.

109 Article 56(3) ACHPR. See Viljoen, *International Human Rights Law in Africa* at p. 334–335.

that corruption in the judicial systems of Europe and the Americas is not so much of a problem, or that domestic systems are capable of dealing with the matter in a proper way. The first part of this hypothesis is unlikely, since perceived levels of judicial corruption in Latin America are reportedly high,[110] and many countries in Eastern and Southern Europe are also suffering from corruption problems. The second part of this hypothesis can only be examined by further research, falling outside of the scope of the present work. A second possible explanation for the lack of cases on judicial corruption may be that corrupt practices are well-concealed and that the affected individual has too little evidence to submit a case to the European Court or the Inter-American Commission. This is a more plausible explanation since corruption is secretive by its very nature. Finally, there might be various other reasons why cases do not reach Strasbourg or Washington. In any event, if such cases were brought before the ECtHR or the IACionHR, this would offer the opportunity to examine corruption in the light of the requirements posed by Article 6 of the European Convention and Article 8 of the American Convention.

110 Transparency International, *Global Corruption Report 2007: Corruption in Judicial Systems* (Cambridge: Cambridge University Press, 2007) at p. 12. For more on judicial corruption in Latin America, see Linn Hammergren, 'Fighting Judicial Corruption: A Comparative Perspective from Latin America', in Transparency International (ed.), *Global Corruption Report 2007: Corruption in Judicial Systems* (Cambridge: Cambridge University Press, 2007), p. 138–146.

Chapter VI
Taking It Further: Corruption as a Human Rights Violation

1. Introduction

In chapters III, IV and V, attention was paid to the ways in which corruption is dealt with in the global systems of human rights monitoring (both treaty-based and Charter-based), as well as in the regional mechanisms for the protection of human rights (in Europe, the Americas, and Africa). An overview of current human rights practice was provided, from which it appeared that corruption is indeed on the agenda of many monitoring bodies. Yet, a clear legal argumentation as to how corruption may exactly violate human rights is largely lacking in human rights practice, and the discussions on this matter leave a lot to be desired. Therefore, the present chapter takes as a starting point the rights that were discussed in the context of corruption by the various monitoring mechanisms, but which were not yet elaborated upon to the fullest extent. Before doing so, it is necessary to devote some preliminary considerations to the various ways in which corruption and human rights may be connected, and to the opposition that exists against making such a connection. These matters are addressed in section 2. Section 3 considers how corruption may violate a number of civil and political rights, as enshrined in the ICCPR. Section 4 is devoted to various economic, social and cultural rights, laid down in the ICESCR.[1] Section 5 examines whether or not there is any need for a new human right to a corruption-free society *de lege ferenda*. Finally, the chapter provides conclusions in section 6, which also includes an assessment of both the merits and limits of the human rights approach to corruption.

2. Clarifying the Corruption and Human Rights Connection

2.1. Introduction

From the analysis of human rights practice in previous chapters, it follows that corruption and human rights are intertwined in various ways. Not every corrupt act constitutes a human rights violation; rather the links may be of a different nature. In the discussion as to whether corruption may constitute a violation of human rights, the issue of causality is crucial. Does the corrupt act itself violate the right concerned, or are there other circumstances involved? At the outset of the present chapter it is imperative to examine the various 'dimensions' of the corruption and

---

1 This approach further develops the one adopted in International Council on Human Rights Policy, *Corruption and Human Rights: Making the Connection*, (Versoix, Switzerland, 2009).

human rights connection. The following sections of the chapter will then focus on one of these dimensions, as explained hereafter.

2.2. ICHRP's Approach: Various Types of 'Violations'

The question regarding the required causal link between a corrupt act and a human rights violation was addressed by the ICHRP in one of its reports. The NGO acknowledged that 'because all forms of corrupt practice may in the long run have an impact on human rights, it cannot be concluded mechanically that a given act of corruption violates a human right.'[2] Therefore, the ICHRP provided a framework distinguishing between (i) direct violations; (ii) indirect violations; and (iii) remote violations.

A *direct violation* occurs (a) when a corrupt act is deliberately used as a means to violate a right (for example, a judge who is bribed is no longer independent/ impartial, violating the right to a fair trial); (b) when the standard of due diligence is not met: if the violation is foreseeable, the official needs to exercise reasonable diligence to prevent the act; and (c) when a State acts or fails to act in a way that prevents individuals from having access to the right.[3]

An *indirect violation* occurs when corruption is an essential factor which contributes to a chain of events eventually leading to a violation. Corruption is thus a necessary condition for the violation, without which the violation would not have taken place. An example is the dumping of toxic waste, which took place because a public official was bribed. Without the bribe, the rights to health or life would not have been violated. Furthermore, it is argued that there is also an indirect violation when authorities violate the rights of persons who blow the whistle about corruption.[4]

A *remote violation* takes place when many other factors contribute to the human rights violation, for instance when electoral corruption leads to societal protests which are then violently repressed by the State.[5]

Although the ICHRP framework offers useful insights into the matter of causality, one can detect a number of flaws in the reasoning above. For instance, it was argued that there is an *indirect* violation of the right to health when bribery of a public official leads to the dumping of toxic waste in a residential area. Yet, under the right to health there is a State obligation 'to protect' individuals against infringements by third parties. Hence, by allowing the waste to be dumped, the State breaches its obligation to protect, which constitutes a *direct* violation of the right to health under Article 12 ICESCR.[6]

2 *Ibid.* at p. 24.
3 *Ibid.* at p. 27.
4 *Ibid.* at p. 27–28.
5 *Ibid.* at p. 28.
6 For a further analysis of the various State obligations under the right to health and their relation to corruption, see section 4.5 hereafter.

Moreover, the terminology of 'direct', 'indirect' and 'remote' violations leads to conceptual confusion and uncertainty in legal terms. Speaking of 'indirect' or 'remote' violations may not be useful. Hence, instead of applying the ICHRP framework, the author proposes to speak of various 'dimensions' of the corruption and human rights connection, which do show some overlap with the ICHRP categorisation, but which do not speak of various 'types' of violations. A right has either been violated, or not.

2.3. Alternative Approach: 'Dimensions' of the Corruption and Human Rights Connection

An inclusive 'corruption and human rights approach' should pay due regard to the following five dimensions.

(i) Shared Environment of Corruption and Human Rights Violations
The first dimension is the broadest one. Corruption and human rights violations thrive in the same environment, if a number of conditions are present or absent. This entails that corruption and human rights violations are both appearances of behaviour which lacks integrity.[7] A State with a highly corrupt leadership is less likely to respect human rights altogether, and a State with a poor human rights record is rarely 'clean'. This correlation can also be detected in the Corruption Perceptions Index, which reveals that human rights-respecting democracies are generally less corrupt than authoritarian States.[8] Moreover, a study demonstrated that more corrupt countries have worse records at protecting human rights, even after controlling for a number of other explanatory variables.[9] It was argued that while human rights violations can take place for various reasons, corruption should be seen as prior to human rights abuse since it undermines accountability and oversight mechanisms.[10]

(ii) Human Rights Necessary to Fight Corruption
The human rights of persons revealing corruption or protesting against it may be violated by State actors.[11] This aspect can be found in the case law of the European

---

7 Emile Kolthoff, *Integriteit, Mensenrechten en de Veiligheidsmythe* (Den Haag: Boom Juridische Uitgevers 2010) at p. 32.

8 For the results of the 2011 CPI, see <httphttp://cpi.transparency.org/cpi2011/>, accessed 7 January 2011.

9 Todd Landman and C.J.W. Schudel, 'Corruption and Human Rights: Empirical Relationships and Policy Advice', *Working Paper International Council on Human Rights Policy* (Geneva, 2007).

10 *Ibid.* at p. 5, §10.

11 For more on the protection of the rights of persons investigating corruption, see International Council on Human Rights Policy, *Corruption and Human Rights: Making the Connection*, at p. 63–68.

Court of Human Rights. The ECtHR elaborated upon the right to freedom of expression of whistleblowers, *inter alia*, in *Guja v. Moldova* (on civil servants)[12] and in *Cumpana and Mazare v. Romania* (on journalists).[13] The Inter-American Commission on Human Rights also paid attention to (violations of) whistleblowers' rights, as well as the Inter-American Court of Human Rights.[14] Furthermore, during the UPR, some comments were made about whistleblower protection.[15] Indeed, it is important to keep in mind that human rights are essential tools in the fight against corruption. Without the right to freedom of expression (including the right to seek, receive and impart information), the right of assembly, and the right to freedom of association, preventing, exposing and fighting corruption will be particularly difficult. It is often the case that corrupt regimes violate these rights, for reasons of power preservation.[16]

(iii) Human Rights of Persons Accused of Corruption

On the other hand, the human rights of persons accused of corruption may be violated by anti-corruption measures.[17] As pointed out by the ICHRP, three aspects deserve particular consideration. Firstly, the offence of illicit enrichment, as laid down in Article 20 UNCAC,[18] may pose problems with regard to the presumption of innocence, the burden of proof, and the guarantee against self-incrimination.[19] Secondly, special investigative techniques may violate the right to privacy, the right to a fair trial, and the prohibition of arbitrary arrest.[20] The right to a fair trial of a person accused of corruption was at stake before the ECtHR in *Ramanauskas v. Lithuania*,[21] while the right to respect for private life was an important issue in

---

12 ECtHR Grand Chamber Judgment *Guja v. Moldova*, 12 February 2008, Application no. 14277/04.

13 ECtHR Grand Chamber Judgment *Cumpana and Mazare v. Romania*, 17 December 2004, Application no. 33348/96.

14 The Inter-American Commission: see chapter V, §3.2.2; the Inter-American Court: see chapter V, §3.3.

15 See for example the recommendation from Canada to Vietnam to adopt a whistleblower law: UN HRC, UPR Working Group outcome report Vietnam, 5th session (2009), UN Doc. A/HRC/12/11, §65 and 99 ad 101.

16 See, *inter alia*, Marella Buckley, 'Anti-Corruption Initiatives and Human Rights: The Potentials', in Hans-Otto Sano and Gudmundur Alfredsson (eds.), *Human Rights and Good Governance. Building Bridges* (The Raoul Wallenberg Institute Human Rights Library, 9; The Hague: Kluwer Law International, 2002), p. 173–201 at p. 188–90.

17 A relevant report is Noel Kututwa, 'How to Combat Corruption While Respecting Human Rights', *Working Paper International Council on Human Rights Policy* (2007). See also Buckley, 'Anti-Corruption Initiatives and Human Rights: The Potentials', at p. 178.

18 Article 20 UNCAC defines illicit enrichment as 'a significant increase in the assets of a public official that he or she cannot reasonably explain in relation to his or her lawful income.'

19 International Council on Human Rights Policy, *Integrating Human Rights in the Anti-Corruption Agenda: Challenges, Possibilities and Opportunities* (Geneva, Switzerland, 2010) at p. 65–66.

20 *Ibid.* at p. 67–68.

21 ECtHR Judgment *Ramanauskas v. Lithuania*, 5 February 2008, Application no. 74420/01.

Craxi v. Italy.[22] Third, asset recovery processes may violate the right to property and the presumption of innocence.[23] From this dimension we can learn that a balance needs to be struck between, on the one hand, combating corruption as effectively as possible, and, on the other hand, guaranteeing the fundamental rights of the accused.

According to Gathii, drawing examples from the Kenyan context, corrupt high-level government officials use human rights claims to circumvent and avoid punishment and accountability. He concluded that:

> ... while it is often assumed that respect for human rights can help in combating corruption, it is also true that those who stand to lose most from the exposure of corruption are also more likely to seek to defend and vindicate their rights in the judiciary. Thus, human rights play a paradoxical role in relation to the fight against corruption – they help to expose corruption but also give those charged with corruption offenses opportunities to defend their due process rights in the criminal justice system.[24]

(iv) Anti-Corruption Reforms Negatively Impacting upon the Human Rights of Vulnerable Groups

Initiatives in the field of judicial reform and anti-corruption may run counter to the human rights of citizens, especially of poor, marginalised and disadvantaged groups in African States. This rarely explored dimension was elaborated upon by Gathii. He pointed out that (i) in reforms made in the judicial system, priority is often given to measures which accommodate the rights of investors, while the poor do not benefit from changes; and (ii) anti-corruption reforms privilege investors rather than vulnerable groups, since petty corruption (particularly affecting the poor) is rarely addressed.[25] This dimension makes clear that domestic anti-corruption measures should not merely focus upon grand corruption, but also pay attention to the rights of poor persons, whose everyday lives are affected by petty corruption.

(v) Corruption as a Violation of Human Rights

The final dimension entails that corrupt acts in themselves may constitute violations of human rights. It is precisely this topic to which most of the present chapter is devoted. Sections 3 and 4 provide insights into how corrupt acts can run counter to a State's international obligations in the field of human rights, by making use of the provisions of the ICCPR and the ICESCR.

---

22 ECtHR Judgment *Craxi v. Italy* (No. 2), 17 July 2003, Application no. 25337/94.

23 International Council on Human Rights Policy, *Integrating Human Rights in the Anti-Corruption Agenda: Challenges, Possibilities and Opportunities*, at p. 68.

24 James Thuo Gathii, 'Defining the Relationship between Human Rights and Corruption', *University of Pennsylvania Journal of International Law*, 31 (2009), p. 125–202 at p. 166.

25 *Ibid.* at p. 180–197.

2.4. Opposition to the Corruption and Human Rights Connection

While there is a great deal of support in literature for the approach of connecting corruption to human rights, there is also fierce criticism directed towards (i) anti-corruption efforts in general; and (ii) making the connection between corruption and human rights. To begin with, David Kennedy, while not being in favour of corruption, opposed the international campaign against corruption, and labelled his own position as 'anti-anti-corruption'.[26] Kennedy questioned whether one should have an anti-corruption campaign at all.[27] His main argument is that anti-corruption is an ideological tool, part of a neo-colonialist agenda.[28] He also held that 'corruption' cannot be properly defined, and that it is not necessarily bad for development.[29] These arguments obscure the fact that although some conduct may fall into a grey area, there is in fact a commonly used definition of corruption which suits many; and that there is a large body of evidence that corruption indeed has negative effects on development.[30] Moreover, the argument that anti-corruptionism is a neo-colonial project as such, should be firmly rejected. Kennedy's position ignores the strong calls from within developing countries to fight corruption. For instance, during the recent uprisings in the Middle-East (the 'Arab Spring'), heavy criticisms against corrupt leadership were, and are still being, voiced.[31]

Sharing Kennedy's concerns, Goodwin and Rose-Sender opposed the connection between corruption and human rights, stating that it is an unwelcome addition to the development discourse. First of all, they argued against anti-corruptionism in development policies. In their view, anti-corruptionism is not neutral, but rather a tool of neo-liberal policy of institutions such as the World Bank, focusing on the free market and using the law to limit the role of the State.[32] This reasoning follows the one by Kennedy. Indeed, as demonstrated in chapter I of the present work, it is true that anti-corruptionism has its roots, *inter alia*, in the work of the World Bank. Yet, that does not necessarily mean that all anti-corruption

---

26 David Kennedy, 'The International Anti-Corruption Campaign', *Connecticut Journal of International Law*, 14 (1999), p. 455–465 at p. 456.

27 *Ibid.* at p. 457, stating that 'there is a real question whether one should or should not have an anti-corruption campaign which is different from the question whether a campaign against corruption could have procedural or definitional excesses.'

28 *Ibid.* at p. 459–460, noting that 'my own instinct is that the anti-corruption campaign is vastly more significant as an ideological tool than as a policy to reduce departures from the rule of law or advance development' and that 'the campaign seems part of a broader ideological project of neo-colonialism.'

29 *Ibid.* at p. 460–462 on the definitional issue and p. 62–64 on the consequential issue.

30 See, *inter alia*, Toke S. Aidt, 'Corruption, Institutions and Economic Development', *Oxford Review of Economic Policy*, 25 (2009), p. 271–291.

31 Stuart Levey, 'Fighting Corruption after the Arab Spring', *Foreign Affairs,* (16 June 2011).

32 Morag Goodwin and Kate Rose-Sender, 'Linking Corruption and Human Rights: An Unwelcome Addition to the Development Discourse', in Martine Boersma and Hans Nelen (eds.), *Corruption & Human Rights: Interdisciplinary Perspectives* (Maastricht Series in Human Rights Antwerp: Intersentia, 2010), p. 221–240 at p. 223–227.

efforts are therefore suspect or neo-liberal. As it was eloquently formulated by Nelken, 'we should not take it for granted that anti-corruption or human rights proposals can only reinforce an approach to economic development that seeks to extend the sway of the free market.'[33] I do agree with Goodwin and Rose-Sender that one should be careful to point to corruption as being the reason why countries are still trapped in poverty, since there are much more factors that ought to be taken into account.[34] Furthermore, Goodwin and Rose-Sender are right when they point to the responsibility of Western governments and institutions for corrupt practices, for example during the Cold War, and for maintaining unfair global trade systems at the expense of developing countries.[35] Yet, I do not share their opinion that 'this predominating focus on developing government failures in the face of our own complicity in them has of course an undeniable smack of cultural imperialism to it.'[36] As noted earlier, there is a lot of genuine concern about corruption among citizens of developing countries, without this being imposed by the West. Moreover, human rights organisations in the developing world also make use of the language and tools of 'neo-colonial institutions': for instance, the Kenya National Commission on Human Rights, which issued reports about corruption and its connection to human rights, adopts the World Bank definition of corruption, considering it to be the most comprehensive.[37] In this light, the assumption that anti-corruptionism is an imperialist tool imposed on developing countries becomes untenable.

Second, Goodwin and Rose-Sender argued that the integration of corruption into human rights is part of a wider trend to integrate topics of international concern into the human rights discourse, and they are highly critical about this.[38] Their key concern is that the integration of development issues, including corruption, into human rights leads to a domination of the rule-based aspect of human rights (i.e. human rights as laid down in positive law) over the political aspect of human rights (i.e. their emancipatory, symbolic value). It was stated that 'in blunting the potential of human rights, anti-corruptionism is deeply harmful to the human rights discourse where one views the empowering potential as their greatest asset.'[39] Yet, it can be

---

33 David Nelken, 'Corruption and Human Rights: An Afterword', in Martine Boersma and Hans Nelen (eds.), *Corruption & Human Rights: Interdisciplinary Perspectives* (Maastricht Series in Human Rights: Antwerp: Intersentia 2010), p. 241–261 at p. 260.

34 Goodwin and Rose-Sender, 'Linking Corruption and Human Rights: An Unwelcome Addition to the Development Discourse', at p. 227–228. A similar argument is made by Joel M. Ngugi, 'Making the Link Between Corruption and Human Rights: Promises and Perils, *American Society of International Law Proceedings*, 104 (2010) p. 246–250 at p. 249.

35 *Ibid.* at p. 228–229.

36 *Ibid.* at p. 229.

37 Wambui Kimathi, 'Corruption: A Complex Phenomenon That Undermines Government's Capability of Working for the Poor', *Nguzo za Haki: a publication of the KNCHR*, 3 (February 2005), p. 3.

38 Goodwin and Rose-Sender, 'Linking Corruption and Human Rights: An Unwelcome Addition to the Development Discourse', at p. 229–230.

39 *Ibid.* at p. 231.

argued that using human rights mechanisms to tackle corruption *is* empowering, since it creates ways of action which are available if a human rights approach is not adopted. Goodwin and Rose-Sender point to the use of the criminal justice system to investigate and punish corruption, but more often than not, this system fails to do so in many countries with high levels of corruption. They doubted how the submission of a complaint about corruption to a treaty body in Geneva could help combating endemic corruption.[40] It is true that the views of a Committee on an individual complaint will not deter States as such to engage in corrupt practices, but the views do send strong signals towards States and the international community at large, and may offer relief in individual situations. The argument that 'there are perhaps more effective mechanisms for tackling corruption'[41] ignores that a combination of anti-corruption tactics is most warranted. Moreover, the argument that 'corruption does not lend itself well to capture by human rights language'[42] will be challenged in the present chapter. The human rights framework as set out by the ICCPR and the ICESCR is indeed very well capable of capturing corruption.

What should be added in light of the foregoing discussion on the allegedly neo-liberal character of the anti-corruption discourse, and the opposition to bringing anti-corruption within the human rights sphere altogether, is that in order to avoid 'monopolisation' of the anti-corruption discourse by players with a neo-liberal agenda, the human rights discourse should be used to address corruption. One needs the human rights discourse to guarantee that anti-corruption is placed in the light of human dignity, and anti-corruption can move beyond the sphere of the World Bank and other 'Western' institutions.

3. Corruption as a Violation of Civil and Political Rights

3.1. The Right to Equality and Non-Discrimination

3.1.1. Introduction

As pointed out by Nowak, 'along with liberty, equality is the most important principle imbuing and inspiring the concept of human rights.'[43] Given the importance of the principle of equality, it is enshrined in Article 7 UDHR, as well as in many, if not all, human rights treaties.[44] Equality and non-discrimination

---

40 *Ibid.* at p. 234.

41 *Ibid.*

42 *Ibid.* at p. 222.

43 Manfred Nowak, *UN Covenant on Civil and Political Rights: CCPR Commentary* (2nd edn.; Kehl: Engel, 2005) at p. 598, §1.

44 Article 14 ECHR, Article 24 ACHR, Articles 3(1) and (2) AfChHPR; Article 2 CRC. Furthermore, the ICERD and CEDAW are instruments that have the prevention of discrimination as their aim.

'run like a red thread throughout the ICCPR'.[45] First, Article 2(1) holds that States are required to respect and ensure the rights contained in the Covenant without discrimination to all individuals in their territory and subject to their jurisdiction.[46] Furthermore, Article 3 requires States to ensure the equal rights of men and women to the enjoyment of the rights in the Covenant, while Article 4(1) states that derogations from the Covenant in cases of public emergency may not be discriminatory. Moreover, Articles 23, 24 and 25 require equality of treatment and non-discrimination in respect of marriage, children and the exercise of political rights.[47] The Covenant's central provision on equality is Article 26.[48]

Nowak noted that Article 2(1) is accessory to the independent right to equality of Article 26.[49] The latter provision contains several elements: (i) the general right to equality before the law; (ii) the right to equal protection of the law; and (iii) a general prohibition of discrimination, directed at the legislature.[50] These elements, and their relationship to corruption, are discussed below.

It is a remarkable omission that the UN treaty bodies have failed to make the specific connection between corrupt acts and the rights to equality and non-discrimination. However, a number of scholars have paid some attention to this connection.[51] Moreover, as formulated by former UN Secretary-General Kofi Annan, 'corruption hurts the poor disproportionately – by diverting funds intended for development, undermining a government's ability to provide basic services, feeding inequality and injustice, and discouraging foreign investment and aid.'[52]

---

45 Nowak, *UN Covenant on Civil and Political Rights: CCPR Commentary* at p. 600, §6.

46 Note that Article 2(2) ICESCR contains a similar provision. For more on this provision, see Magdalena Sepúlveda, *The Nature of the Obligations under the International Covenant on Economic, Social and Cultural Rights* (School of Human Rights Research, 18; Antwerpen: Intersentia, 2003) at p. 391–404.

47 Nowak, *UN Covenant on Civil and Political Rights: CCPR Commentary* at p. 600, §6.

48 Article 26 ICCPR: 'All persons are equal before the law and are entitled without any discrimination to the equal protection of the law. In this respect, the law shall prohibit any discrimination and guarantee to all persons equal and effective protection against discrimination on any ground such as race, colour, sex, language, religion, political or other opinion, national or ethnic origin, property, birth or other status.'

49 Nowak, *UN Covenant on Civil and Political Rights: CCPR Commentary* at p. 604, §12. The Human Rights Committee also specifically held that Article 26 is an autonomous right, which does not merely duplicate the guarantee of Article 2(1). See Human Rights Committee, General Comment No. 18 on non-discrimination, thirty-seventh session (1989), §12.

50 *Ibid.* at p. 600, §6.

51 International Council on Human Rights Policy, *Corruption and Human Rights: Making the Connection* at p. 32–33; Julio Bacio Terracino, 'Corruption as a Violation of Human Rights', *Working paper* (Geneva: International Council on Human Rights Policy, 2008) at p. 29–31; Nihal Jayawickrama, 'Corruption – a Violation of Human Rights?' *Working Paper* (Sofia: Transparency International, 1–2 June1998) at p. 2–3.

52 Kofi Annan, Statement on the adoption of the UNCAC by the General Assembly.

3.1.2. *The Right to Equality Before the Law*

The right to equality before the law is not directed at legislation but at judges and administrative officials, who must ensure that in enforcing the law, they do not act in an arbitrary way. When a court or administrative decision is based on manifestly arbitrary considerations, meaning that these lack any objective justification, this violates the requirement of equal treatment. Whenever people are being discriminated against solely because of one of the criteria mentioned in Article 26, second sentence, a decision is arbitrary.[53] If courts are corrupt, they will apply the law in an arbitrary fashion, i.e. in favour of the bribing party, violating the right to equality.

3.1.3. *The Right to Equal Protection of the Law*

The right to equal protection of the law is directed at the national legislative power, which is obliged to protect the right to equality without discrimination. This entails both positive and negative aspects: the legislature may not discriminate in the enactment of laws (negative obligation); and the legislature must prohibit discrimination by passing special laws and by affording effective protection against discrimination (positive obligation).[54] According to Nowak, the right to equal protection of the law forms a unit together with the prohibition of discrimination and the right to protection against discrimination. They all concern the obligation of States to ensure substantive equality through legislation.[55] Corruption in politics can lead to a distorted legislative process, which does not respect the right to equal protection of the law. For instance, whenever Members of Parliament acquired their positions through unlawful means (i.e. through bribery in the election procedure, or close ties to those in power), law-making may not serve the purpose of offering equal protection without discrimination.

3.1.4. *The Prohibition of Discrimination*

'Discrimination' is defined in the Human Rights Committee's General Comment No. 18, which states that it implies:

> … any distinction, exclusion, restriction or preference which is based on any ground such as race, colour, sex, language, religion, political or other opinion, national or social origin, property, birth or other status, and which has the purpose or effect of nullifying or impairing the recognition, enjoyment or exercise by all persons, on an equal footing, of all rights and freedoms.[56]

---

53 Nowak, *UN Covenant on Civil and Political Rights: CCPR Commentary* at p. 605–606, §14–15.

54 *Ibid.* at p. 607, §17.

55 *Ibid.* at p. 608, §18.

56 General Comment No. 18, §7.

From the wording of this phrase, it becomes clear that both direct discrimination (a practice with a discriminatory purpose) as well as indirect discrimination (a practice with a discriminatory effect) are prohibited.[57]

Concerning the prohibited grounds of discrimination listed in Article 26 ICCPR, these are not exclusive, as can be seen by the wording 'or other status'. This includes citizenship, sexual orientation and marriage. If differential treatment is not justified by reasonable and objective grounds, any general distinction might qualify as discrimination.[58] Yet, there are certain differentiating practices which may not constitute discrimination. The Human Rights Committee noted that this is the case whenever the criteria for a differentiation of treatment are reasonable and objective and if the aim is to achieve a purpose which is legitimate under the Covenant.[59]

The question arises on what basis discrimination takes place in cases of corruption. Article 26 covers discrimination on the ground of 'other status'. It is reasonable to argue that the ability to pay bribes (depending on income), or the willingness to do so (depending on morality) is also covered by Article 26 ICCPR.

3.2. The Right to Equality Before Courts and Tribunals and the Right to a Fair Trial

3.2.1. Introduction

The preceding chapters showed that corruption in the judiciary is one of the topics drawing most attention from human rights supervisory bodies, as compared to corrupt practices in other parts of society or government. It is possible to elaborate upon the findings of the supervisory mechanisms in order to make the links between forms of corruption and the right to equality before courts and tribunals and the right to a fair trial, as enshrined in Article 14 ICCPR, more explicit.[60] At the outset it must be noted that there is a myriad of types of judicial corruption.

---

57 Richard Burchill, 'Equality and Non-Discrimination', in Alex Conte and Richard Burchill (eds.), *Defining Civil and Political Rights: The Jurisprudence of the United Nations Human Rights Committee* (2nd edn.; Surrey: Ashgate, 2009) at p. 290–292.

58 Nowak, *UN Covenant on Civil and Political Rights: CCPR Commentary* at p. 626, §47.

59 General Comment No. 18, §13.

60 A number of authors already elaborated upon the topic of corruption and the right to a fair trial, in particular Bacio Terracino, 'Corruption as a Violation of Human Rights', at p. 10–12, §38–50; Victoria Jennett, 'The Relationship between Human Rights and Corruption: The Impact of Corruption on the Rights to Equal Access to Justice and Effective Remedy', *Working Paper* (Geneva: International Council on Human Rights Policy, 2007); Zoe Pearson, 'An International Human Rights Approach to Corruption', in Peter Larmour & Nick Wolanin (ed.), *Corruption and Anti-Corruption* (Canberra: Asia Pacific Press, 2001), p. 30–61 at p. 55–56; Lyal S. Sunga and Ilaria Bottigliero, 'In-Depth Study on the Linkages between Anti-Corruption and Human Rights for the United Nations Development Program', (Raoul Wallenberg Institute, 15 January 2007) at p. 32–35. See also International Council on Human Rights Policy, *Corruption and Human Rights: Making the Connection* at p. 35–43.

While various classifications can be made, we can at least distinguish between the following basic forms.[61]

To begin with, there is the issue of political interference in judicial processes by the executive or legislature. Judges may be appointed on the basis of their loyalty to the ruling political party, or the executive may interfere with court cases, for example when the interests of powerful officials are at stake.[62]

Bribery is a mode of corruption rampant in the judicial branch in many countries. Bribery can take place at the level of court support staff or at the level of the judges and prosecutors. It is also possible to separate administrative bribery from operational bribery. In the first case, bribes are used to speed up the procedure (the outcome of the case may be just), while in the second case, the actual decision-making of the judge is influenced, leading to an unjust outcome of the case.[63] Furthermore, bribes may be offered by either the party, or the suspect in criminal cases, or may be extorted by the support staff or the judge.[64]

Embezzlement of funds intended for the judicial system also constitutes corruption. Funds may disappear at the central and/or at the local level.

Even without identifying all possible types of corruption in the judiciary, we can specifically connect cases of judicial corruption to the legal obligations incumbent upon States under Article 14 ICCPR. Particularly useful to this end are the concrete examples of corruption mentioned in the country studies of the TI's Global Corruption Report 2007, on corruption in judicial systems.[65]

---

61 In its Global Corruption Report, TI's main annual publication, the distinction is made between (i) political inference; and (ii) different forms of bribery. It does not explicitly mention embezzlement as a third category. Transparency International, 'Executive Summary: Key Judicial Corruption Problems', in Transparency International (ed.), *Global Corruption Report 2007: Corruption in Judicial Systems* (Cambridge: Cambridge University Press, 2007), p. xxi-xxviii at xxii-xxiv.

62 *Ibid.* at p. xxii-xxiii.

63 TI Ghana distinguishes between 'administrative corruption' and 'operational corruption'. See Dominic Ayine, Mechtild Ruenger, and Daniel Batidam, 'Computerised Courts Reduce Delays in Ghana', *Ibid.*, p. 208–210 at p. 209. Furthermore, Ford and Seng noted that in Cambodia, 'citizens distinguish between bribes that influence the outcome of a trial and bribes intended to facilitate service'. See Samantha Ford and Theary C. Seng, 'Corruption in the Judiciary of Cambodia', in Transparency International (ed.), *Global Corruption Report 2007: Corruption in Judicial Systems* (Cambridge: Cambridge University Press, 2007), 183–186 at p. 183–184. The distinction between 'just' and 'unjust' outcomes is made by Transparency International, 'Executive Summary: Key Judicial Corruption Problems', at p. xxii.

64 International Council on Human Rights Policy, *Corruption and Human Rights: Making the Connection* at p. 37–38.

65 Transparency International, *Global Corruption Report 2007: Corruption in Judicial Systems* (Cambridge: Cambridge University Press, 2007).

3.2.2. *The Right to Equality Before Courts and Tribunals*

The right to equality before courts and tribunals and the right to a fair trial, enshrined in Article 10 UDHR, are laid down in various human rights treaties,[66] including the regional instruments.[67] They can also be found in many domestic constitutions. The key provision on the international plane is Article 14 ICCPR.[68] The Human Rights Committee's General Comment No. 32 is the most authoritative interpretation of this provision to date,[69] in which the Committee stressed the crucial importance of the right to equality before the courts and tribunals and to a fair trial,[70] and acknowledged the complexity of Article 14.[71]

The first paragraph of Article 14 is composed of three sentences.[72] The first sentence of Article 14(1) is the general guarantee of *equality* before courts and tribunals that applies regardless of the nature of proceedings before such bodies.[73] According to Nowak, this right is a specific manifestation of the general right of equality in Article 26 ICCPR, which cannot be found in any other general human rights treaty.[74] The Committee held that, in addition to the principles laid down in the second sentence of Article 14(1), the right to equality guarantees equal access and equality of arms, and ensures the treatment of parties without discrimination.[75]

---

66 Article 5(a) ICERD; Article 15(2) CEDAW.

67 Article 6 ECHR; Article 8 ACHR; Article 7 AfCHPR.

68 For a more elaborate analysis of the fair trial provisions of the UDHR and the ICCPR, and their *travaux préparatoires* in particular, see David Weissbrodt, *The Right to a Fair Trial under the Universal Declaration of Human Rights and the International Covenant on Civil and Political Rights*, ed. Hurst Hannum (The Universal Declaration of Human Rights, 1; The Hague: Martinus Nijhoff Publishers, 2001).

69 Human Rights Committee, General Comment No. 32 on the right to equality before courts and tribunals and to a fair trial (Article 14), Ninetieth session (23 August 2007), UN Doc. CCPR/C/GC/32. This General Comment replaces General Comment No. 13 (Article 14), Twenty-first session (1984), UN Doc. HRI/GEN/1/Rev.1 at 14.

70 General Comment No. 32, §2.

71 *Ibid.* §3.

72 Article 14(1) ICCPR: 'All persons shall be equal before the courts and tribunals. In the determination of any criminal charge against him, or of his rights and obligations in a suit at law, everyone shall be entitled to a fair and public hearing by a competent, independent and impartial tribunal established by law. The Press and the public may be excluded from all or part of a trial for reasons of morals, public order (*ordre public*) or national security in a democratic society, or when the interest of the private lives of the parties so requires, or to the extent strictly necessary in the opinion of the court in special circumstances where publicity would prejudice the interests of justice; but any judgment rendered in a criminal case or in a suit at law shall be made public except where the interest of juvenile persons otherwise requires or the proceedings concern matrimonial disputes or the guardianship of children.'

73 General Comment No. 32, §3 and 7.

74 Nowak, *UN Covenant on Civil and Political Rights: CCPR Commentary* at p. 307, §5.

75 General Comment No. 32, §8.

The right of *access* to courts, a right of all individuals,[76] relates to access to first instance procedures.[77] It prohibits any distinctions regarding access to courts and tribunals which are not based on law and cannot be justified on objective and reasonable grounds. Whenever persons are barred from bringing a suit against another person because of race, colour, sex, language, religion, political or other opinion, national or social origin, property, birth or other status, the guarantee of access is violated.[78] The Committee noted the relevance of legal assistance in this respect.[79] Furthermore, the Committee found that imposing fees on the parties to the proceedings that would *de facto* prevent their access to justice might generate problems under Article 14(1).[80] *A fortiori*, it is apparent that the right of equal access is violated whenever persons are asked to pay bribes in order for their case to be processed or speeded up. For example, a Croatian judge was indicted for having accepted bribes worth up to US $4,000 from litigants to speed up court processes.[81] Furthermore, in a survey published by Transparency International Paraguay in 2005, 18.7 per cent of the respondents indicated that bribes had to be paid to receive a court service, with an average value of US $130.[82] It follows that persons, particularly the poor, who cannot pay these sums, do not have equal access to courts compared to those that can afford the bribes, which constitutes a violation of the right to equality as laid down in Article 14(1). The distinction is not based on law and cannot be justified on objective and reasonable grounds.

Equality of arms (*'audiatur et altera pars'*)[83] entails that the same procedural rights have to be provided to all the parties, unless distinctions are based on law and can be justified on objective and reasonable grounds, not entailing actual disadvantage or other unfairness to the defendant.[84] It also requires that similar cases are dealt with in similar proceedings.[85] Equality of arms may be violated by corruption. Where one party to a dispute is able to bribe the judge, this party has an unfair advantage compared to the other party. As a result of bribery, the bribing party might be given different procedural rights. According to the Paraguayan survey referred to above, 62 per cent of the respondents indicated that there were many ways to bribe a judge to secure a favourable outcome, while a mere 7 per cent

---

76 *Ibid.* §9.

77 *Ibid.* §12.

78 *Ibid.* §9.

79 *Ibid.* §10.

80 *Ibid.* §11.

81 For a concrete example of bribes paid to speed up court processes in Croatia, see: Transparency International Croatia, 'Croatia: Still in Transition', in Transparency International (ed.), *Global Corruption Report 2007: Corruption in Judicial Systems* (Cambridge: Cambridge University Press, 2007), p. 194–197 at p. 195.

82 Transparency International Paraguay, 'Politics and Nepotism Plague Paraguay's Courts', *Ibid.*, p. 255–258 at p. 257.

83 Nowak, *UN Covenant on Civil and Political Rights: CCPR Commentary* at p. 321, §29.

84 General Comment No. 32, §13.

85 *Ibid.* §14.

said it would be difficult or not possible to do so.[86] Hence, it follows that a corrupt judiciary ignores the principle of treatment without discrimination, and that judicial corruption can constitute a direct violation of the right to equality before courts and tribunals.

3.2.3. The Right to a Fair Trial

The second sentence of Article 14(1) gives individuals the right to a fair and public hearing by a competent, independent and impartial tribunal established by law, if they face criminal charges or if their rights and obligations are determined in a suit of law.[87] This is an absolute right, not subject to any exception.[88]

Independence refers in particular to the procedures and qualifications for the appointment of judges, and guarantees concerning their security of tenure, the conditions governing promotion, transfer, suspension and cessation, and the actual independence of the judiciary from political interference by the executive and the legislature.[89] On the topic of the dismissal of judges, the Committee noted, *inter alia*, that dismissal by the executive of allegedly corrupt judges without following any of the procedures provided for by the law, is incompatible with the independence of the judiciary.[90] Albeit a correct observation, it is remarkable that the Committee takes the opportunity to comment upon this aspect, while disregarding in this General Comment the influence of judicial corruption on the requirements of independence and impartiality. As seen in the concluding observations discussed *supra*in chapter III, corrupt acts are detrimental to the independence of judges. Whenever judges are appointed because of political loyalties, or family or friendship ties to those in power, their independence is clearly at stake.[91] For example, in respect of Bangladesh, it was noted that 'political clout is demonstrated in the appointment of junior judges to senior posts in defiance of a tradition of appointing judges on the basis of seniority and experience. Capability, efficiency, integrity, fearlessness and character have ceased to be the criteria for appointment, promotion and transfer.'[92] Moreover, it was reported that in Egypt, the Ministry of Justice gives generous bonuses to 'compliant' judges, and that judges must provide the

---

86 Transparency International Paraguay, 'Politics and Nepotism Plague Paraguay's Courts', in Transparency International (ed.), *Global Corruption Report 2007: Corruption in Judicial Systems* (Cambridge: Cambridge University Press, 2007), p. 255–258 at p. 257.

87 General Comment No. 32, §3.

88 *Ibid.* §19.

89 *Ibid.* §19.

90 *Ibid.* §20; Communication No. 933/2000, *Mundyo Busyo et al. v. Democratic Republic of Congo*, §5.2.

91 International Council on Human Rights Policy, *Corruption and Human Rights: Making the Connection* at p. 38.

92 S.I. Laskar, 'Bangladesh: Justice in Disarray', in Transparency International (ed.), *Global Corruption Report 2007: Corruption in Judicial Systems* (Cambridge: Cambridge University Press, 2007), p. 179–183 at p. 181–182.

Ministry with copies of civil or criminal lawsuits against important officials.[93] These practices clearly violate the requirement of judicial independence.

Impartiality consists of two aspects. In the first place, judges must not allow their judgment to be influenced by personal bias or prejudice and not have preconceptions about the case before them, nor behave in ways that improperly promote the interests of one of the parties to the disadvantage of the other party. In the second place, the tribunal must also appear to be impartial to a reasonable observer.[94] The requirement of independence relates to the appointment and impeachment of judges and other members of a tribunal. Impartiality however concerns the specific holding in a particular case. A biased judge, for example because of a personal interest in a given case, is not impartial. Furthermore, a judge may not be excessively guided by emotions or political motives or be influenced by 'media justice'. Impartiality is also closely related to the guarantees of a fair trial and equality before the courts as enshrined in Article 14(1). The Committee stated in *Karttunen v. Finland* that impartiality of the court implies that 'judges must not harbour preconceptions about the matter put before them, and that they must not act in ways that promote the interests of one of the parties.'[95] It is obvious that corrupt acts can constitute a direct violation of the guarantee of an impartial judge. Whenever a judge accepts a bribe from one of the parties in a court case, the judge is prejudiced. Transparency International Zambia reported about the conviction of a judge who solicited bribes to find in favour of a litigant.[96] In Azerbaijan, judges reportedly rule either on political grounds, or in favour of the highest bidder, as if it were a construction tender.[97] Bribe-taking or extortion of bribes by judges constitutes a direct violation of the right to a fair trial.

Regarding the *fairness* of the hearing, this entails the absence of any direct or indirect influence, pressure or intimidation or intrusion from whatever side and for whatever motive. As examples, the Committee observed that the guarantee to a fair hearing is violated when a defendant in a criminal case faces the expression of a hostile attitude from the public or support for one party in the courtroom that is tolerated by the court, thereby impinging on the right to defence, or when the defendant is exposed to other manifestations of hostility with similar effects.[98] In addition, the Committee held that Article 14 only guarantees procedural equality and fairness, and as such does not aim to ensure the absence of error on the part of the tribunal.[99] Furthermore, the expeditiousness of the hearing is an important

---

93 Hossam Baghat, 'Egypt's Judiciary Flexes Its Muscles', *Ibid.*, p. 201–204 at p. 201.

94 General Comment No. 32, §21.

95 Nowak, *UN Covenant on Civil and Political Rights: CCPR Commentary* at p. 321, §27.

96 Davies Chikalanga, Goodwell Lungu, and Ngoza Yezi, 'Zambian Judiciary Struggles to Modernise', in Transparency International (ed.), *Global Corruption Report 2007: Corruption in Judicial Systems* (Cambridge: Cambridge University Press, 2007), p. 287–290 at p. 288.

97 Rena Safaralieva, 'Azerbaijan's Yawning Gap between Reforms on Paper and in Practice', *Ibid.*, p. 175–178 at p. 175.

98 General Comment No. 32, §25.

99 *Ibid.* §26.

component of fairness.[100] Expeditiousness is infringed when a judge is bribed so as to the delay the proceedings.[101]

3.2.4. The Presumption of Innocence

Under the presumption of innocence of Article 14(2) ICCPR, no guilt may be presumed.[102] It is up to the prosecutor to prove guilt. In cases of judicial corruption, this fundamental principle may be violated. Amongst others, it is likely that a judge appointed by the ruling political party will not respect the presumption of innocence in cases where political opponents are standing trial. The same holds true if politically-appointed judges have to rule in cases brought against whistleblowers, such as critical journalists.

3.2.5. Rights of Persons Charged with a Criminal Offense

Article 14(3) ICCPR contains a number of minimum guarantees applicable in criminal cases.[103] Violations of the rights of persons charged with a criminal offense can be closely related to corruption. For example, it was reported that 71 per cent of the persons detained in Mexico City did not receive advice from a lawyer while being held in custody of the office of the public prosecutor. Of the 29 per cent who did receive legal assistance, 70 per cent were not allowed to communicate privately with the lawyer. Furthermore, when being brought before the judge, who determines whether the trial will proceed or whether the suspect will be released, 60 per cent of the detainees were not informed about the right to remain silent. One in four detainees was not assisted by a lawyer when making a preparatory statement before the judge. In these circumstances, it is possible that detainees cannot

---

100 *Ibid.* §27.

101 International Council on Human Rights Policy, *Corruption and Human Rights: Making the Connection* at p. 39.

102 Article 14(2) ICCPR: 'Everyone charged with a criminal offence shall have the right to be presumed innocent until proven guilty according to law.' See General Comment No. 32, §30.

103 Article 14(3) ICCPR: 'In the determination of any criminal charge against him, everyone shall be entitled to the following minimum guarantees, in full equality: (a) to be informed promptly and in detail in a language which he understands of the nature and cause of the charge against him; (b) to have adequate time and facilities for the preparation of his defence and to communicate with counsel of his own choosing; (c) to be tried without undue delay; (d) to be tried in his presence, and to defend himself in person or through legal assistance of his own choosing; to be informed, if he does not have legal assistance, of this right; and to have legal assistance, assigned to him, in any case where the interests of justice so require, and without payment by him in any such case if he does not have sufficient means to pay for it; (e) to examine, or to have examined, the witnesses against him and to obtain the attendance and examination of witnesses on his behalf under the same conditions as witnesses against him; (f) to have the free assistance of an interpreter if he cannot understand or speak the language used in court; (g) not to be compelled to testify against himself or to confess guilt.' See General Comment No. 32, §31–41.

withstand pressure from the police to offer money. 80 per cent of the detainees never spoke to the judge who condemned them, and in 71 per cent of the cases a judge was absent during the statement of the detainee at the judicial offices. Hence, it is probable that the police will pressure the detainee for money.[104]

3.2.6. The Right to a Remedy

In the view of the Committee, Article 14 has a relationship with the right to an effective remedy as enshrined in Article 2(3) ICCPR. This provision needs to be respected whenever there has been a violation of any of the guarantees of Article 14. However, Article 14(5) is a *lex specialis* in relation to Article 2(3) when invoking the right to access a tribunal at the appeals level. This provision accords persons who were criminally convicted the right to turn to a higher tribunal.[105]

As regards Article 2(3),[106] this provision may also be violated by a corrupt judiciary. When a person suffering from a violation of civil or political rights aims to obtain a remedy from a court, this might be impossible due to corruption. As noted by Bacio Terracino, 'corruption in the administration of justice has the double effect of infringing upon the right to a fair trial and the right to an effective remedy.'[107]

3.3. Rights of Political Participation

3.3.1. Introduction

Rights of political participation, laid down in Article 21 UDHR, can be found in many human rights instruments at both the international[108] and regional plane.[109]

104 Miguel Carbonell, 'Judicial Corruption and Impunity in Mexico', in Transparency International (ed.), *Global Corruption Report 2007: Corruption in Judicial Systems* (Cambridge: Cambridge University Press, 2007), p. 225–228 at p. 226.

105 Article 14(5) ICCPR: 'Everyone convicted of a crime shall have the right to his conviction and sentence being reviewed by a higher tribunal according to law.' See General Comment No. 32, §45–51.

106 Article 2(3) ICCPR: 'Each State Party to the present Covenant undertakes: (a) to ensure that any person whose rights or freedoms as herein recognized are violated shall have an effective remedy, notwithstanding that the violation has been committed by persons acting in an official capacity; (b) to ensure that any person claiming such a remedy shall have his right thereto determined by competent judicial, administrative or legislative authorities, or by any other competent authority provided for by the legal system of the State, and to develop the possibilities of judicial remedy; (c) to ensure that the competent authorities shall enforce such remedies when granted.'

107 Bacio Terracino, 'Corruption as a Violation of Human Rights', at p. 11–12, §50.

108 Article 5(c) CERD; Article 7 CEDAW.

109 Article 3 First Protocol to the ECHR contains the right to free elections; Article 23 ACHR; Article 13 AfCHPR.

The most important provision is Article 25 ICCPR,[110] guaranteeing a number of rights to every citizen (not to every individual[111]). Its content is clarified in the HRC's General Comment No. 25.[112] In addition to giving citizens the mentioned political rights, Article 25 provides that citizens have to be given the opportunity to exercise the rights concerned. According to Nowak, this means that State Parties are obliged to take positive measures to guarantee that citizens have the actual opportunity to exercise their political rights.[113] This is an example of the fact that first generation human rights can also impose positive obligations upon States.

It was pointed out in 2004 that:

> ... the General Comment [No. 25] fails to mention one of the biggest threats to the right of political participation: corruption. Corrupt political processes systematically deny persons the right, on a fair and equal basis, to take part in public affairs. In order fully to comply with Article 25, a State party must take measures to prevent and punish instances of corruption and bribery.[114]

The absence of the explicit mention of corruption in the General Comment is indeed remarkable, although it can perhaps be explained by the fact that this document was adopted already in 1996. It is also striking that not a single concluding observation of the treaty bodies touched upon the issue of corruption in relation to rights of political participation, and neither is the issue a main topic of concern in the work of the other monitoring bodies. Meanwhile, the detrimental effect of corruption on the rights of Article 25 was noted by a number of scholars.[115] The following

---

110 Article 25 ICCPR: 'Every citizen shall have the right and the opportunity, without any of the distinctions mentioned in Article 2 and without unreasonable restrictions:
(a) to take part in the conduct of public affairs, directly or through freely chosen representatives;
(b) to vote and to be elected at genuine periodic elections which shall be by universal and equal suffrage and shall be held by secret ballot, guaranteeing the free expression of the will of the electors;
(c) to have access, on general terms of equality, to public service in his country.'

111 General Comment No. 25, §3.

112 HUMAN RIGHTS COMMITTEE, General Comment No. 25 on the right to participate in public affairs, voting rights and the right of equal access to public service (Article 25), Fifty-seventh session (12 July 1996), UN Doc. CCPR/C/21/Rev.1/Add.7.

113 NOWAK, *UN Covenant on Civil and Political Rights: CCPR Commentary* at p. 569, §9. This is also stated in General Comment No. 25, §11 and 12.

114 SARAH JOSEPH, JENNY SCHULTZ, and MELISSA CASTAN, *The International Covenant on Civil and Political Rights: Cases, Materials and Commentary* (2nd edn.; Oxford: Oxford University Press, 2004) at §22.18.

115 BACIO TERRACINO, 'Corruption as a Violation of Human Rights', at p. 14–16, §65–72; MARKKU SUKSI, 'Good Governance in the Electoral Process', in Hans-Otto Sano and Gudmundur Alfredsson (eds.), *Human Rights and Good Governance. Building Bridges* (The Raoul Wallenberg Institute Human Rights Library, 9; The Hague: Kluwer Law International, 2002), p. 203–227 at p. 218; INTERNATIONAL COUNCIL ON HUMAN RIGHTS POLICY, *Corruption and Human Rights: Making the Connection* at p. 43–45; JAYAWICKRAMA, 'Corruption – a Violation of Human Rights?' at p. 5; PEARSON, 'An International Human Rights Approach to Corruption', at p. 54–55;

sections discuss each right contained in this provision, and consider how these may be violated by corrupt practices.

3.3.2. The Right to Take Part in the Conduct of Public Affairs

Article 25, section (a) ICCPR contains the right to take part in the conduct of public affairs. This means that the exercise of State authority must be based on the principle of sovereignty of the people.[116] The Committee stated that the conduct of public affairs is a broad concept, relating to the exercise of political power, particularly the exercise of legislative, executive and administrative powers, covering all aspects of public administration, and the formulation and implementation of policy at the international, national, regional and local level.[117] As specified in Article 25, citizens have the right and opportunity to participate directly, or through freely chosen representatives. Direct participation entails the exercise of power as a member of legislative bodies or by holding executive office; by deciding issues through a referendum or other electoral processes; or by taking part in popular assemblies or bodies established to represent citizens in consultation with government.[118] Participation through freely chosen representatives implies that these representatives exercise governmental power, for which they are accountable.[119] Furthermore, citizens can also participate in public affairs by engaging in public debate and dialogue with their representatives or by organising themselves. This has obvious links to the rights to freedom of expression, assembly and association.[120]

Corruption may violate the right to take part in the conduct of public affairs whenever citizens are being denied the right to participate. An example would be when the results of a referendum are rigged.[121]

3.3.3. The Right to Vote

The first right enshrined in section (b) of Article 25 ICCPR is the right to vote. Citizens have the right to vote themselves, a right that must be established by law, and may only be subjected to reasonable restrictions.[122] States are obliged to take effective measures to ensure that those citizens, entitled to vote, can actually exercise this right. Voter registration, whenever required, has to be facilitated and

Sunga and Bottigliero, 'In-Depth Study on the Linkages between Anti-Corruption and Human Rights for the United Nations Development Program', at p. 20–22.

116 Nowak, *UN Covenant on Civil and Political Rights: CCPR Commentary* at p. 570, §11.

117 General Comment No. 25, §5.

118 General Comment No. 25, §6.

119 *Ibid.* §7.

120 *Ibid.* §8.

121 See for example, 'Armenian Protesters: Referendum Rigged', *Journal of Turkish Weekly*, 29 November 2005.

122 General Comment No. 25, §10.

there should be no obstacles to registration. Abusive interference with registration or voting, as well as intimidation or coercion of voters should be prohibited by penal laws, and should be strictly enforced.[123] Yet, it is possible that election officials are bribed by politicians, so as to tamper with the registration of voters,[124] violating the right to vote.

In the view of the Committee, voters must be free to cast their votes, without undue influence or coercion of any kind which may distort or inhibit the free expression of his/her will. They should be able to form opinions independently, free from violence or the threat thereof, compulsion, inducement or manipulative interference of any kind.[125] Here lies a particular problem as regards corruption. The practice of bribing of voters by, or on behalf of, politicians is highly problematic.[126] In Nigeria, reportedly one out of five citizens is personally exposed to vote buying. In the majority of vote-buying transactions, voters were offered money (68 per cent), followed by commodities (e.g. food or clothing, 26 per cent), and jobs (6 per cent).[127]

Furthermore, elections must be held by secret ballot; they must be fair and free; and be held on a periodic basis.[128] Elections must be supervised by an independent electoral authority.[129] However, corruption can occur at the level of the electoral authority: election officials may be bribed by public officials to interfere with ballot boxes or with the counting of votes. This is a violation of the right to vote.[130]

Finally, elections have to conform to the requirement of universal suffrage, i.e. the right to vote may not be restricted to certain groups or classes.[131] In addition, each vote has to carry equal weight, i.e. the principle of equal suffrage.[132]

3.3.4. The Right to be Elected

The second right laid down in Article 25 section (b) ICCPR is the right and opportunity for citizens to stand for elective office. Restrictions to this right have to be objective and reasonable.[133] Conditions relating to nomination dates, fees or deposits also have to be reasonable and non-discriminatory.[134] Yet, corruption at

---

123 *Ibid.* §11.

124 Suksi, 'Good Governance in the Electoral Process', at p. 218.

125 General Comment No. 25, §19.

126 Bribing of voters is discussed by Bacio Terracino, 'Corruption as a Violation of Human Rights', at p. 15, §67; Jayawickrama, 'Corruption – a Violation of Human Rights?', at p. 5.

127 Michael Bratton, 'Vote Buying and Violence in Nigerian Election Campaigns', *Electoral Studies*, 27 (2008), p. 621–632.

128 General Comment No. 25, §19.

129 *Ibid.* §20.

130 Bacio Terracino, 'Corruption as a Violation of Human Rights', at p. 15, §67; Jayawickrama, 'Corruption – a Violation of Human Rights?', at p. 5.

131 Nowak, *UN Covenant on Civil and Political Rights: CCPR Commentary* at p. 576, §22.

132 General Comment No. 25, §21; *Ibid.* at p. 581, §31.

133 General Comment No. 25, §15.

134 *Ibid.* §16.

the level of an electoral commission may violate the right to be elected, for example when a certain candidate is not allowed to register because the commission was bribed by a political opponent of the candidate.[135] Also, members of an election commission may demand bribes from candidates, affecting those candidates with little resources. Moreover, it can be argued that the bribing of voters and/or election officials may also violate the right of candidates to stand for elective office.[136]

3.3.5. The Right of Equal Access to Public Service

The right of equal access to public service can be found in section (c) of Article 25. The right entails that the criteria and processes for appointment, promotion, suspension and dismissal of public service positions must be objective and reasonable. Those holding public service positions must be free from political interference or pressures.[137] Corruption might violate this right of equal access, since public service may only be accessible to those who manage to obtain access in a corrupt way, such as bribery.[138]

3.4. The Prohibition of Human Trafficking

3.4.1. Introduction

A number of concluding observations of the HRC, the CESCR, the CRC and CEDAW, as well as the reports of the Special Rapporteur on the sale of children, child prostitution and child pornography, and of the Special Rapporteur on trafficking in persons, point to the role played by corruption in the perpetration of human trafficking. The matter was also touched upon during the UPR. Moreover, a study evaluated the relative impact of both poverty and official corruption on human trafficking. Researchers found that per capita income, average life expectancy, infant mortality and access to primary education are not good predictors of trafficking problems within a country.[139] Rather, it was concluded that corruption is 'probably the most important factor in explaining human trafficking.'[140] At the same time, as argued by Kendall, there appears to be too little attention for the role of corruption in relation to trafficking,[141] hence the necessity of further elaboration of its human rights dimension.

---

135 Bacio Terracino, 'Corruption as a Violation of Human Rights', at p. 15, §69.

136 *Ibid.* at p. 15, §68.

137 General Comment No. 25, §23.

138 Bacio Terracino, 'Corruption as a Violation of Human Rights', at p. 15, §70–71.

139 Sheldon X. Zhang and Samuel L. Pineda, 'Corruption as a Causal Factor in Human Trafficking', in Dina Siegel and Hans Nelen (eds.), *Organized Crime: Culture, Markets and Policies* (Studies of Organized Crime: Springer, 2008), p. 41–55 at p. 48–52.

140 *Ibid.* at p. 52.

141 Virginia M. Kendall, 'Greasing the Palm: An Argument for an Increased Focus on Public Corruption in the Fight Against International Human Trafficking', 44 *Cornell International Law Journal*, p. 33–47 at p. 35, 36 *et seq.*

'Human trafficking' is defined in Article 3(a) of the Trafficking Protocol[142] stating that this practice consists of three elements: (i) the *act*: the recruitment, transportation, transfer, harbouring or receipt of persons; (i) the *means*: the threat or use of force or other forms of coercion, abduction, deception, the abuse of power or vulnerability, giving or receiving payments or benefits to achieve the consent of a person having control over another person; and (iii) the *purpose*: for exploitation. This includes, at a minimum, the exploitation of the prostitution of others or other forms of sexual exploitation, forced labour or services, slavery or practices similar to slavery, servitude or the removal of organs.[143] Whenever any of the listed means has been used, it is irrelevant whether or not the trafficking victim has consented to the exploitation.[144] Nevertheless, in the case of children (persons under eighteen)[145] it is not necessary for any of the listed means to be used. Whenever the elements of act and purpose are present, this shall be considered trafficking.[146]

Trafficking of human beings is usually committed by private individuals or groups, not by State actors.[147] The prohibition of trafficking thus has a horizontal effect. Yet, under the tripartite typology of human rights obligations, States have the obligation to protect rightholders against human rights violations committed by third parties, such as traffickers. It can be very well argued that States also have to provide protection against corrupt practices committed by private parties.

According to the United Nations Global Initiative to Fight Human Trafficking (hereafter: UN.GIFT)[148] there are four phases in trafficking: recruitment, transport, exploitation, and laundering of the proceeds.[149] In any of these phases, corruption can play a role. In source countries, along trafficking routes and in destination countries, public officials may be involved in facilitating trafficking, *inter alia*, by providing false travel documents, by turning a blind eye to prostitution in exchange for bribes, or even by abusing victims of trafficking themselves.[150]

---

142 Protocol to Prevent, Suppress and Punish Trafficking in Persons, Especially Women and Children, supplementing the United Nations Convention Against Transnational Organized Crime (UNCTOC, also known as the Palermo Convention).

143 United Nations Global Initiative to Fight Human Trafficking, 'Corruption and Human Trafficking: The Grease That Facilitates the Crime', *The Vienna Forum to fight Human Trafficking* (Austria Center Vienna, 13–15 February 2008) at p. 2.

144 Article 3(b) Trafficking Protocol.

145 Article 3(d) Trafficking Protocol.

146 Article 3(c) Trafficking Protocol.

147 Tom Obokata, *Trafficking in Human Beings from a Human Rights Perspective: Towards a Holistic Approach* (International Studies in Human Rights, 89; Leiden: Martinus Nijhoff Publishers, 2006) at p. 127.

148 UN.GIFT was established in March 2007 by the UNODC, see UN.GIFT, <www.ungift.org>.

149 United Nations Global Initiative to Fight Human Trafficking, 'Corruption and Human Trafficking: The Grease That Facilitates the Crime', at p. 2.

150 Kendall, 'Greasing the Palm: An Argument for an Increased Focus on Public Corruption in the Fight Against International Human Trafficking', at p. 35.

3.4.2. *State Obligations under the Trafficking Protocol*

The Trafficking Protocol imposes a number of obligations upon State Parties: (i) to criminalise trafficking at the national level;[151] (ii) to protect trafficking victims;[152] (iii) to take preventive measures;[153] (iv) to cooperate in the area of law enforcement and immigration by exchanging information aimed at identifying trafficking victims, and methods and means used by traffickers;[154] (v) to provide or strengthen training for law enforcement, immigration and other officials;[155] and (vi) to strengthen border controls.[156] It can very well be argued that these obligations also include fighting corruption. Criminalisation of trafficking cannot do without criminalising and prosecuting trafficking-related corruption. Preventive measures should also most certainly be aimed at preventing corruption. For instance, poorly paid officials may be easily tempted to 'ignore' trafficking. Also, training for law enforcement, immigration and other officials ought to have a strong anti-corruption component. Finally, in the area of border controls, preventing and punishing corruption are essential.

The Trafficking Protocol is a not human rights treaty (and neither is the UNCTOC, which it supplements); rather it aims to combat organised crime.[157] Yet the Protocol recognises trafficked persons as victims of human rights abuse. It preserves their rights under international law and suggests that States should meet victims' needs for care, support, and relief from deportation.[158]

3.4.3. *Article 8 ICCPR*

Apart from a number of soft law instruments,[159] a large number of human rights treaties deals with human trafficking. We can distinguish between human rights

151 Article 5 Trafficking Protocol.

152 Chapter II Trafficking Protocol.

153 Article 9 Trafficking Protocol. As accurately formulated by Gallagher, the Protocol's provisions on prevention of trafficking 'are phrased in the UN's best, programmatic, non-obligatory style.' Anne T. Gallagher, 'Human Rights and the New UN Protocols on Trafficking and Migrant Smuggling: A Preliminary Analysis', *Human Rights Quarterly*, 23 (2001), p. 975–1004 at p. 995.

154 Article 10(1) Trafficking Protocol.

155 Article 10(2) Trafficking Protocol.

156 Article 11 Trafficking Protocol.

157 Joan Fitzpatrick, 'Trafficking as a Human Rights Violation: The Complex Intersection of Legal Frameworks for Conceptualizing and Combating Trafficking', *Michigan Journal of International Law*, 24 (2003), p. 1143–1167 at p. 1151; Gallagher, 'Human Rights and the New UN Protocols on Trafficking and Migrant Smuggling: A Preliminary Analysis', at p. 1003.

158 Fitzpatrick, 'Trafficking as a Human Rights Violation: The Complex Intersection of Legal Frameworks for Conceptualizing and Combating Trafficking', at p. 1151.

159 The UNHCHR Recommended Principles and Guidelines on Human Rights and Human Trafficking and the UNICEF Guidelines for the Protection of the Rights of the Child Victims of Trafficking. For a further discussion of these instruments, see Silvia Scarpa, *Trafficking in Human Beings: Modern Slavery* (Oxford: Oxford University Press, 2008) at p. 73 *et seq.*

treaties which explicitly mention trafficking, and treaties which do not.[160] The second category is comprised of treaties containing the prohibition of slavery, servitude and forced or compulsory labour, most importantly Article 8 ICCPR.[161] This trichotomy was intentionally inserted into the ICCPR by its drafters, in order to emphasise the fundamental differences between the practices.[162] Article 8 itself does not define what is meant by the terms, and the Human Rights Committee has not released a General Comment on Article 8.[163]

The question arises which of the three practices contained in Article 8 covers human trafficking. Scarpa argued that trafficking in persons falls under the category of slavery when the domination and control of the victim are complete. Whenever

---

160 This distinction was made by Obokata, *Trafficking in Human Beings from a Human Rights Perspective: Towards a Holistic Approach*, at p. 33–34. Treaties explicitly mentioning trafficking: Article 6 CEDAW; Article 35 CRC and the Optional Protocol to the CRC; Article 5(3) Charter of Fundamental Rights of the EU; the COE Convention on Action Against Trafficking in Human Beings; Article 6(1) ACHR; the Inter-American Convention on International Trafficking in Minors; the 1949 Convention for the Suppression of the Traffic in Persons and of the Exploitation of the Prostitution of Others; the Convention on Preventing and Combating Trafficking in Women and Children for Prostitution of the South Asian Association for Regional Cooperation.

161 Article 8 ICCPR: 1. No one shall be held in slavery; slavery and the slave-trade in all their forms shall be prohibited.
2. No one shall be held in servitude.
3. (a) No one shall be required to perform forced or compulsory labour;
(b) Paragraph 3(a) shall not be held to preclude, in countries where imprisonment with hard labour may be imposed as a punishment for a crime, the performance of hard labour in pursuance of a sentence to such punishment by a competent court;
(c) For the purpose of this paragraph the term 'forced or compulsory labour' shall not include:
(i) any work or service, not referred to in subparagraph (b), normally required of a person who is under detention in consequence of a lawful order of a court, or of a person during conditional release from such detention;
(ii) any service of a military character and, in countries where conscientious objection is recognised, any national service required by law of conscientious objectors;
(iii) any service exacted in cases of emergency or calamity threatening the life or well-being of the community;
(iv) any work or service which forms part of normal civil obligations.
See also Article 4 UDHR; Article 11 ICPRMW; Article 4 ECHR; Article 6 ACHR; Article 5 AfCHPR; the 1926 Slavery Convention, the 1953 Protocol and the 1956 Supplementary Convention.

162 Nowak, *UN Covenant on Civil and Political Rights: CCPR Commentary* at p. 198, §9.

163 According to Hathaway, who is quite critical about the current fight against human trafficking as envisaged by the Trafficking Protocol, 'slavery in fact always has been something of an orphaned issue within the United Nations. [...] It is surely telling that despite the clear prohibition of slavery in Article 8 of the ICCPR, the generally well-regarded Human Rights Committee that oversees that treaty [...] has never engaged in the fight against slavery. Incredibly, the Human Rights Committee has referred to Article 8 of the Covenant in only three decisions [...] and has never issued a general comment on point.' James C. Hathaway, 'The Human Rights Quagmire Of "Human Trafficking"', *Virginia Journal of International Law,* 49 (2008), p. 1–59 at p. 19–20.

trafficking reveals dominance and degeneration, it is a type of servitude in its lighter forms, according to Scarpa.[164] Assuming that human trafficking can constitute slavery, we need to determine the content of this notion under Article 8(1). As regards the definitions of slavery and slave trade, it follows from the *travaux* that these are understood in their narrow, traditional sense, which is the destruction of one's juridical personality.[165] The 1926 Slavery Convention defines slavery as 'the status or condition of a person over whom any or all of the powers attaching to the right of ownership are exercised'.[166] Slave trade includes:

> ... all acts involved in the capture, acquisition or disposal of a person with intent to reduce him to slavery; all acts involved in the acquisition of a slave with a view to selling or exchanging him; all acts of disposal by sale or exchange of a slave acquired with a view to being sold or exchanged, and, in general, every act of trade or transport in slaves.[167]

Under Article 8(1), States are obliged to take positive measures to ensure the realisation of the prohibition of slavery: slavery and slave trade must be criminalised in national law; they are bound to undertake all measures to prevent slavery and slave trade; and they must consider a slave taking refuge on State territory to be legally free, and offer protection.[168] As pointed out by Nowak, the prohibition of slavery is *ius cogens* in the meaning of Article 53 of the VCLT.[169]

Partly contrary to Scarpa, Nowak held that traffic in women and children is a slavery-like practice (i.e. servitude), as laid down in the second paragraph of Article 8.[170] This stance seems to be supported by the HRC's General Comment No. 28:

> Having regard to their obligations under Article 8, State Parties should inform the Committee of measures taken to eliminate *trafficking* of women and children, within the country or across borders, and forced prostitution. They must also provide information on measures taken to protect women and children, including foreign women and children, from *slavery*, disguised, *inter alia*, as domestic or other kinds of personal service. States Parties where women and children are recruited, and from which they are taken, and States Parties where they are received should provide information on measures, national or international, which have been taken in order to prevent the violation of women's and children's rights. [emphasis added, MB][171]

---

164 Scarpa, *Trafficking in Human Beings: Modern Slavery* at p. 88.
165 Nowak, *UN Covenant on Civil and Political Rights: CCPR Commentary* at p. 198, §9.
166 Article 1(1) 1926 Slavery Convention.
167 Article 1(2) 1926 Slavery Convention.
168 Nowak, *UN Covenant on Civil and Political Rights: CCPR Commentary* at p. 199, §11.
169 *Ibid.* at p. 197, §7.
170 *Ibid.* at p. 200, §13.
171 Human Rights Committee, General Comment No. 28, Sixty-eighth session, Article 3: equality of rights between men and women, (2000) UN Doc. A/55/40, §12.

This wording distinguishes between trafficking and slavery. Hence, it is necessary to define 'servitude' as laid down in Article 8(2). The concept was introduced by the 1956 Supplementary Slavery Convention and it aimed to make a difference between a 'slave' (a victim of slavery) and a 'person of servile status' (a victim of slave-like practices). Thus, 'servitude' is a practice separate from and broader than slavery.[172] In Nowak's view, servitude is considered 'to be applicable to all conceivable forms of dominance and degradation of human beings by human beings'.[173] It covers serfdom; debt bondage; the compulsory betrothal of women to the brother or deceased husband; and child labour or prostitution.[174] Nowak set out that victims of these slavery-like practices are not merely economically exploited; rather, they may be totally dependent upon others.[175] Under Article 8(2), States have to adopt broad statutory and other positive measures to guarantee the prohibition of servitude.[176] This obligation should encompass the obligation to adopt a wide range of measures to prevent trafficking-related corruption.

It is important to determine which obligations rest upon States with regard to human trafficking committed by non-State actors. Obokata argued that these obligations are fourfold. First of all, States are under the obligation to prohibit trafficking and related acts. This is laid down in the existing human rights treaties as discussed *supra*[177] Second, there is an obligation to investigate, prosecute and punish traffickers with due diligence, as clarified, *inter alia*, by the Inter-American Court of Human Rights in *Velazquez Rodriguez v. Honduras*.[178] Public officials involved in trafficking should also be prosecuted. Third, there is the obligation to protect victims of trafficking. Several existing instruments provide for this obligation, such as the 1949 Convention; the Optional Protocol to the CRC; the Inter-American Convention on Trafficking in Minors; and the COE Convention on Trafficking.[179] Fourth and finally, States are under the obligation to address the causes and consequences of trafficking.[180] The latter obligation certainly comprises the obligation to address corrupt practices by public officials, since corruption is a main cause of trafficking.

---

172 Anne T. Gallagher, 'Human Rights and Human Trafficking: Quagmire or Firm Ground? A Response to James Hathaway', *Virginia Journal of International Law*, 49 (2009), p. 789–848 at p. 802.

173 Nowak, *UN Covenant on Civil and Political Rights: CCPR Commentary* at p. 199, §12.

174 *Ibid.* at p. 200. §13.

175 *Ibid.* at p. 200, §13.

176 *Ibid.* at p. 201, §14.

177 Obokata, *Trafficking in Human Beings from a Human Rights Perspective: Towards a Holistic Approach*, at p. 148–150.

178 *Ibid.* at p. 150–153.

179 *Ibid.* at p. 153–161.

180 *Ibid.* at p. 161–164.

3.5. The Rights of Detainees to be Treated with Humanity and Dignity

3.5.1. Introduction

The Human Rights Committee and the Committee Against Torture briefly touched upon the relationship between corruption and the rights of detainees. Yet, the specific link in legal terms was not yet made. An appropriate starting point is Article 10 ICCPR, containing a number of rights specifically accorded to detainees.[181] Other relevant provisions can be found in the American Convention on Human Rights,[182] and in the UN Convention Against Torture. Also important are the Standard Minimum Rules for the Treatment of Prisoners,[183] which are not binding however and do not have a formal relationship to the ICCPR. Nonetheless, General Assembly delegates specifically stressed that the Minimum Rules should be taken into account in the interpretation and application of Article 10.[184] The Committee held in General Comment No. 21 that States should indicate in their reports to what extent they apply the relevant UN standards applicable to the treatment of prisoners. These include, amongst others, the Minimum Rules.[185]

3.5.2. Article 10 ICCPR

The first paragraph of Article 10 contains the right of all persons deprived of their liberty to be treated with humanity and respect for their dignity. It applies to anyone deprived of his or her liberty under the laws and authority of the State who is held

---

181 Article 10 ICCPR: '1. All persons deprived of their liberty shall be treated with humanity and with respect for the inherent dignity of the human person.

2. (a) Accused persons shall, save in exceptional circumstances, be segregated from convicted persons and shall be subject to separate treatment appropriate to their status as unconvicted persons;

(b) Accused juvenile persons shall be separated from adults and brought as speedily as possible for adjudication.

3. The penitentiary system shall comprise treatment of prisoners the essential aim of which shall be their reformation and social rehabilitation. Juvenile offenders shall be segregated from adults and be accorded treatment appropriate to their age and legal status.'

For a more elaborate analysis of the various rules applicable to the treatment of prisoners, see Nigel Rodley and Matt Pollard, *The Treatment of Prisoners under International Law* (Oxford: Oxford University Press, 2009). and Jim Murdoch, *The Treatment of Prisoners: European Standards* (Strasbourg: Council of Europe Publishing, 2006).

182 Article 5 ACHR.

183 Adopted by the First UN Congress on the Prevention of Crime and the Treatment of Offenders (Geneva 1955), approved by the Economic and Social Council by its resolutions 663 C (XXIV) of 31 July 1957 and 2076 (LXII) of 13 May 1977. The Rules can be consulted through <www2.ohchr.org/english/law/treatmentprisoners.htm>.

184 Nowak, *UN Covenant on Civil and Political Rights: CCPR Commentary* at p. 243, §6.

185 Human Rights Committee, General Comment No. 21 concerning humane treatment of persons deprived of liberty (Article 10), Forty-fourth session (1992), UN Doc. HRI/GEN/1/Rev.6 at 153, §5. This General Comment replaced preceding General Comment No. 9.

in prisons, (psychiatric) hospitals, detention camps, correctional institutions or elsewhere.[186] Paragraph 1 imposes a positive obligation upon States towards these particularly vulnerable persons. For those persons, Article 10(1) complements Article 7 ICCPR, which contains the prohibition of torture or other cruel, inhuman or degrading treatment or punishment.[187] The Committee stressed that the right laid down in Article 10(1) is fundamental and universally applicable. Thus, its application cannot depend on a State's material resources, and the rule must be applied without distinction of any kind.[188] In the Committee's view, Article 10(1) forms the basis for the more specific State obligations in respect of criminal justice, as laid down in paragraph 2 and 3 of the Article.[189] The second paragraph provides for the separation of accused persons from convicted persons, and for the separation of juveniles from adults, while the third paragraph states that the treatment of prisoners in the penitentiary system should have the reformation and social rehabilitation of prisoners as the essential aim.

The rights laid down in Article 10 may be violated by corruption, which is a phenomenon tainting prison systems in both developing and developed countries. For instance, an investigation by the British authorities revealed that more than 1,000 prison officers were allegedly involved in corruption.[190] Furthermore, it must be kept in mind that 'prison corruption' is a very broad concept. The specific links to human rights violations can only be made whenever it is clear which forms prison corruption can take. Although this can be done in the abstract, it is illustrative to take an actual situation as a point of departure, such as the findings of the South African Jali Commission. This commission of inquiry was appointed in 2001 by President Mbeki to investigate corruption, maladministration, violence and intimidation in South African prisons.[191] In its work, the Commission also examined human rights, in particular the rights of prisoners and staff to dignity, fair and humane treatment, equality, race, sexual orientation and gender.[192] The Commission's report referred to the international standards of the treatment of

---

186 General Comment No. 21, §2.

187 *Ibid.* §3.

188 *Ibid.* §4.

189 General Comment No. 21, §8.

190 Examples of corruption mentioned in the report include prison officers accepting cash payments from inmates to have them transferred to less secure prisons, or to bring mobile phones and drugs into prisons. Lee Glendinning, 'Corruption 'Rife' among Prison Staff, Report Claims', *The Times*, 31 July 2006.

191 The official name of the Jali Commission is the Judicial Commission of Inquiry into Allegations of Corruption, Maladministration, Violence or Intimidation in the Department of Correctional Services. The Jali Commission's final report consists of 500 pages, laid down in five volumes: Jali Commission, 'Final Report', <www.info.gov.za/otherdocs/2006/jali/index.html>, accessed 14 July 2009. The present thesis makes use of the Commissions official executive summary of this report: Jali Commission, 'Executive Summary of Final Report', <www.pmg.org.za/docs/2006/061017jali.pdf>, accessed 14 July 2009.

192 Jali Commission, 'Executive Summary of Final Report', p. 3.

prisoners, and mentioned Article 10 of the ICCPR.[193] Amongst other serious misconduct, the Commission found large-scale corruption in the country's penitentiary facilities. It was observed that prison employees were primarily driven by greed and the need to make easy money.[194] A wide range of corrupt acts were listed, including, but not limited to, the following:

(i) prisoners were only allowed to receive visitors whenever they paid bribes to prison staff, while the prisoners were entitled to these visits;[195]
(ii) prisoners bribed prison staff in exchange for private contact of the prisoners with their wives or girlfriends, while this contact was not allowed;[196]
(iii) prison staff stole or ate the food intended for prisoners (i.e. embezzlement);[197]
(iv) prison staff sold young prisoners as sex slaves within the prison to the highest bidder;[198]
(v) prisoners had to bribe prison officials to be released on parole or to be transferred, while they are entitled to this;[199]
(vi) prisoners who paid bribes to prison staff in order to escape from prison;[200]
(vii) prison staff smuggled drugs, alcohol, weapons and other items such as electronic equipment into prison in exchange for bribes;[201]
(viii) prisoners had to pay bribes to use the telephone or to buy food;[202]

From this selection, it becomes clear that there is a divide between, on the one hand, the extortion of bribes by prison staff for goods and services the prisoners were already entitled to without payment; and, on the other hand, the acceptance of bribes by prison staff, who then supply prisoners with goods or treatment they are not entitled to. It is the first group of corrupt acts that clearly violates the rights of detainees to be treated with humanity and dignity, and is contrary to Article 10 ICCPR.

3.6. The Right to Freedom of Movement

3.6.1. Introduction

A few concluding observations of the Human Rights Committee and the Committee on the Elimination of Racial Discrimination indicated that corrupt practices may

193 *Ibid.* p. 25.
194 *Ibid.* p. 5.
195 *Ibid.* p. 27.
196 *Ibid.* p. 27.
197 *Ibid.* p. 28, 63, 72.
198 *Ibid.* p. 29, 75–76.
199 *Ibid.* p. 32.
200 *Ibid.* p. 49.
201 *Ibid.* p. 16–17, 63, 72, 76.
202 *Ibid.* p. 72.

pose problems in respect of the right to freedom of movement. However, this right is rarely discussed in the existing literature, such as the ICHRP report. Hence, the topic merits further analysis. The starting point is the right to freedom of movement as enshrined in Article 12 ICCPR.[203] The right can also be found in other international[204] and regional human rights instruments.[205] The Human Rights Committee's General Comment No. 27 clarifies the content of Article 12 ICCPR.[206] From this document we can learn that States have to protect the rights in this provision from both public as well as private interference.[207]

3.6.2. The Right to Liberty of Movement and Freedom to Choose Residence

The first paragraph of Article 12 lays down the right to liberty of movement and freedom to choose residence in a State, which applies to citizens of a State, and to aliens who are lawfully within the territory of a State. The latter issue is subject to domestic law.[208] The right applies to a State's entire territory, including all parts of federal States.[209] Article 12(1) protects the rightholders against all forms of forced internal displacement and prohibits preventing the entry or stay of persons in a defined part of State territory.[210] The right to liberty of movement, as laid down in Article 12(1) can be violated by corruption. For example, it was reported that in Ghana, bribes need to be paid to public officials on the stops of the Tema-Ouagadougou trade corridor, which goes from Ghana to Burkina Faso.[211] A Ghanaian human rights NGO pointed out that this practice violates the right to freedom of movement.[212] The same holds true for corruption at roadblocks or checkpoints, which is a common practice in many countries, such as Nigeria. Police

---

203 Article 12 ICCPR: '1. Everyone lawfully within the territory of a State shall, within that territory, have the right to liberty of movement and freedom to choose his residence.
2. Everyone shall be free to leave any country, including his own.
3. The above-mentioned rights shall not be subject to any restrictions except those which are provided by law, are necessary to protect national security, public order (ordre public), public health or morals or the rights and freedoms of others, and are consistent with the other rights recognised in the present Covenant.
4. No one shall be arbitrarily deprived of the right to enter his own country.'

204 Article 13 UDHR; Article 5(d)(i) and (ii) ICERD.

205 Article 2 Protocol No. 4 to the ECHR; Article 12 AfCHPR; Article 22 ACHR.

206 Human Rights Committee, General Comment No. 27 on freedom of movement (Article 12), sixty-seventh session (18 October 1999), UN Doc. CCPR/C/21/Rev.1/Add.9.

207 General Comment No. 27, §6.

208 *Ibid.* §4.

209 *Ibid.* §5.

210 *Ibid.* §7.

211 Bribes also have to be paid during stops at checkpoints in Ghana, so not just to cross the border with Burkina Faso.

212 Legal Resources Centre, 'Freedom of Movement under Siege! Urgent Need to Address Widespread Corruption on the Tema-Ouagadougou Trade Corridor.' <http://ghanaweb.com/GhanaHomePage/economy/artikel.php?ID=170597>, accessed 6 July 2011.

officers stop car drivers in order to extort bribes from them, often under the threat of violence. No service is rendered in these situations.[213]

Corrupt practices in relation to free movement cannot be justified under the third paragraph of Article 12, which allows for restrictions to the rights laid down in the first and second paragraph. These rights can only be restricted when a number of conditions are fulfilled.[214] First, restrictions may only serve a limited number of purposes: the protection of national security; public order; public health or morals; or the rights and freedoms of others.[215] Second, these restrictions must be provided for by law. In adopting national legislation on this issue, States should be guided by the principle that restrictions must not impair the essence of the right; the relation between right and restriction must not be reversed. National legislation should use precise criteria and may not confer unfettered discretion on the persons charged with the execution of the law concerned.[216] Third, restrictions are subject to the requirements of necessity and proportionality.[217] Fourth and finally, the restrictions must be consistent with the other rights in the ICCPR and with the fundamental principles of equality and non-discrimination.[218] Corrupt practices do not meet any one of these conditions. Moreover, the Committee noted that the multiple legal and bureaucratic barriers which unnecessarily affect the full enjoyment of Article 12 constitute a major source of concern. Concerning the right to movement within a country, the Committee criticised provisions obliging individuals to ask for permission to change their residence or to ask for approval of the place of destination, and delays in the processing of these written applications.[219]

3.6.3. The Freedom to Leave a Country and Liberty of Emigration

The second paragraph of Article 12 contains the freedom to leave any country, including one's own. This guarantee applies to both citizens and aliens alike and covers both foreign travel and departure for permanent emigration. The individual concerned is free to decide to which State to go.[220] Furthermore, in the Committee's view, the right to leave a country must include the right to obtain the necessary travel documents.[221] The Committee noted that, often, legal rules and

---

213 Daniel Jordan Smith, *A Culture of Corruption. Everyday Deception and Popular Discontent in Nigeria* (Princeton: Princeton University Press, 2007) at p. 61–63.

214 For an elaborate discussion of the four criteria listed, see: Nowak, *UN Covenant on Civil and Political Rights: CCPR Commentary* at p. 271, §26.

215 General Comment No. 27, §11.

216 *Ibid.* §12–13.

217 *Ibid.* §14–16.

218 *Ibid.* §18.

219 *Ibid.* §17.

220 *Ibid.* §8.

221 *Ibid.* §9.

administrative measures adversely affect the right to leave, particularly one's own country.[222]

As noted *supra* the right to leave a country can only be restricted if the conditions set out in Article 12(3) are met. In respect of the restrictions on the right to leave a country, the Committee held that many obstacles are present in State practice which make it difficult to leave a country. Examples are: applicants' lack of access to the competent authorities and lack of information about requirements; the requirement to apply for special forms to obtain the proper application document for the issuance of a passport; the need for statements from employers or family; the need for the precise description of the travel route; disproportionally high fees that have to be paid to get a passport; unreasonable delays in obtaining travel documents; restrictions on family members travelling together; the requirement to have a repatriation deposit or return ticket; the requirement of an invitation from the State of destination or from persons living there; harassment of applicants; and refusal of a passport because the applicant supposedly harms the country's good name.[223] The Committee did not specifically denounce acts of corruption, although this could perhaps be categorised under the disproportionate amount of money that needs to be paid to obtain a passport. It does follow from this overview of obstacles, as provided by the Committee, that leaving a country, including the process of obtaining travel documents, can be a process vulnerable to corruption. It involves contacts between citizens and lower level public officials and requires paperwork. As a result, bribes may be offered or demanded to speed up the process, or to obtain the required documents. For example, a Zimbabwean NGO reported that in Zimbabwe, an artificial shortage of passports is created, so that the applicants are forced to bribe the official who is in charge of issuing the documents.[224] Furthermore, the Vice-President of Malawi brought forward that the Immigration Department is one of the most corrupt in the country, and denounced bribery in respect of the issuance of passports.[225] It is fair to say that corruption, such as the demand for a bribe by a public official in exchange for the issuance of travel documents, constitutes a restriction of this right. This restriction does not fall under the scope of Article 12(3) ICCPR, since the demanded bribe does not meet one of the purposes listed; it is not provided for by law; it will not meet the requirements of necessity and proportionality; and it is certainly not consistent with the principles of equality and non-discrimination. Moreover, the Human Rights Committee held that 'restrictions which are not provided for in the law, or are not in conformity with the requirements of Article 12(3) would violate the rights guaranteed by paragraph

222 *Ibid.* §10.

223 *Ibid.* §17.

224 Sokwanele, 'Corruption in the Passport Office', <www.sokwanele.com/thisiszimbabwe/archives/591>, accessed 6 July 2011.

225 Nyasa Times, 'Veep Launches Malawi Passport, Denounce Corruption at Immigration', <www.nyasatimes.com/national/veep-launches-malawi-new-passport-denounce-corruption-at-immigration.html>, accessed 6 July 2011.

1 and 2.'[226] In sum: corrupt acts such as the demand for bribes in the issuance of travel documents can constitute a violation of the right to leave a country and should be treated as such.

3.6.4. The Right to Enter One's Own Country

The fourth paragraph of Article 12 contains the right to enter one's own country. This also implies the right to remain in one's own country; and includes the right to return after having left and the right to come to one's own country for the first time if the person was born outside the country.[227] In these situations, corrupt practices may also occur, for example in the processing of administrative requirements. Again, such practices may violate Article 12.

4. Corruption as a Violation of Economic, Social and Cultural Rights

4.1. State Party Obligations under Article 2(1) ICESCR

4.1.1. Introduction

The concluding observations of the CESCR and the CRC, as well as the reports of the Special Rapporteur on corruption and human rights, demonstrate that corruption has a negative impact upon a State's resources available for the realisation of economic, social and cultural rights. This was also acknowledged by the Office of the United Nations High Commissioner for Human Rights, whose website notes that 'corruption leads to violation of the government's obligation "to take steps… to the maximum of its available resources, with a view to achieving progressively the full realization of the rights recognized in the [International] Covenant [on Economic, Social and Cultural Rights]".'[228] This is a clause from Article 2(1) ICESCR, which contains State obligations relevant in respect of all substantive rights listed in part III of the Covenant.[229]

Nevertheless, the precise ways in which corruption may violate Article 2(1) ICESCR were not yet examined by human rights monitoring bodies in great detail.

---

226 General Comment No. 27, §12.

227 *Ibid.* §19.

228 Office of the United Nations High Commissioner for Human Rights, 'Website 'Development – Good Governance', Subsection 'Corruption and Human Rights'', <www2.ohchr.org/english/issues/development/governance/anti_corruption.htm>, accessed 14 April 2010.

229 Article 2(1) ICESCR: 'Each State party to the present Covenant undertakes to take steps, individually and through international assistance and co-operation, especially economic and technical, to the maximum of its available resources, with a view to achieving progressively the full realisation of the rights recognised in the present Covenant by all appropriate means, including particularly the adoption of legislative measures.'

The present section therefore links forms of corruption to the obligations under Article 2(1), a provision that was extensively analysed in recent years. The CESCR has released several General Comments on the matter, most notably General Comment No. 3.[230] Scholarly efforts have also contributed to a better understanding of the above-mentioned provision, including the Limburg Principles[231] and the Maastricht Guidelines.[232] Furthermore, a comprehensive study by Sepúlveda held that it is possible to distill several legal obligations from the Committee's work on Article 2(1). In her view, these distinct obligations form the 'hard core' of the Article and apply to all State Parties to the ICESCR in a uniform manner, regardless of their level of development or available resources. Moreover, the obligations are of an immediate character.[233] The following overview takes the text of Article 2(1) as a starting point, in order to clarify the precise meaning of each of the five phrases of which this provision consists. Moreover, it discusses the seven 'hard core' obligations distinguished by Sepúlveda, and how these may be violated by corruption. Contemporary research on the topic is also taken into account.[234]

4.1.2. 'Undertakes To Take Steps'

The obligation 'to take steps and to devote the maximum available resources' is the first 'hard core' obligation.[235] The CESCR noted that this obligation is of immediate effect,[236] which was also pointed out in the Limburg Principles.[237] States must take steps towards the goal of progressive realisation within a reasonably short time after becoming Party to the Covenant. These steps should be 'deliberate, concrete and targeted as clearly as possible towards meeting the obligations recognised in the Covenant.'[238] It can be argued that the steps that need

230 Committee on Economic, Social and Cultural Rights, General Comment No. 3 on the nature of States Parties' obligations (Art. 2, par. 1 of the Covenant), fifth session (1990).

231 The Limburg Principles were drafted in 1986 by a group of 29 international law experts who unanimously agreed upon a number of principles which, in their view, reflected the state of international law at that time. 'The Limburg Principles on the Implementation of the International Covenant on Economic, Social and Cultural Rights (1986)', *Human Rights Quarterly*, 9 (1987), p. 122–135.

232 The Maastricht Guidelines came into being in 1997 when a group of experts elaborated upon the Limburg Principles as regards the nature and scope of violations of economic, social and cultural rights and appropriate responses and remedies. 'The Maastricht Guidelines on Violations of Economic, Social and Cultural Rights (1997)', *Human Rights Quarterly*, 20 (1998), p. 691–704.

233 Sepúlveda, *The Nature of the Obligations under the International Covenant on Economic, Social and Cultural Rights* at p. 426.

234 Including Bacio Terracino, 'Corruption as a Violation of Human Rights'; Jayawickrama, 'Corruption – a Violation of Human Rights?'

235 Sepúlveda, *The Nature of the Obligations under the International Covenant on Economic, Social and Cultural Rights* at p. 313–319.

236 General Comment No. 3, §1 and 2.

237 Limburg Principles, §16.

238 General Comment No. 3, §2. This was later repeated in General Comment No. 13, §43.

to be taken should include the removal of impediments in the realisation of economic, social and cultural rights. Since corruption is such an impediment, States are obliged to take anti-corruption actions.[239]

The obligation to take steps includes the obligation to take an active role to prevent and to protect individuals against violations by private actors, including multinational corporations. If a State remains passive when a private entity violates economic, social or cultural rights, this may entail a violation of the Covenant.[240] In this light, States should put safeguards in place to minimise corruption by corporate actors, such as bribery of labour inspectors in sweatshop factories.

Another 'hard core' obligation is the obligation to monitor the realisation of the rights and the obligation to devise strategies and programmes for their implementation, which are in Sepúlveda's view, independent, implied obligations.[241] The Maastricht Guidelines also indicate that the failure to do so constitutes a violation of the Covenant.[242] In the context of monitoring the realisation of economic, social, and cultural rights, it was already found that the Inter-American Commission on Human Rights prepared guidelines for the preparation of progress indicators, which can be used to monitor progressive realisation. Among these indicators, anti-corruption indicators were also present.[243] This shows that monitoring progress in realising economic, social and cultural rights ought also to include the monitoring of anti-corruption efforts.

4.1.3. 'Individually and Through International Assistance and Co-operation, Especially Economic and Technical'

This is another 'hard core' obligation. International co-operation, as laid down in Articles 55 and 56 of the UN Charter, must be directed, as a matter of priority, to the realisation of all human rights.[244] The Limburg Principles also recognise that there is a duty for States to cooperate.[245] This obligation can be linked to the UNCAC, which also provides that State Parties shall cooperate in criminal matters related to corruption.[246] In any case, whenever States provide international assistance and co-operation to other States under Article 2(1) ICESCR, they should ensure that anti-corruption safeguards are put in place, so as to avoid embezzlement

239 As argued by C Raj Kumar, 'Corruption and Human Rights: Promoting Transparency in Governance and the Fundamental Right to Corruption-Free Service in India', *Columbia Journal of Asian Law*, 17 (2003), p. 31–72 at p. 59.

240 Sepúlveda, *The Nature of the Obligations under the International Covenant on Economic, Social and Cultural Rights* at p. 314–315.

241 *Ibid.* at p. 360–365.

242 Maastricht Guidelines, §15 (f).

243 See chapter V, §3.2.3 *supra.*

244 Sepúlveda, *The Nature of the Obligations under the International Covenant on Economic, Social and Cultural Rights* at p. 370–376. General Comment No. 3, §14.

245 Limburg Principles, §29–34.

246 Chapter IV of the UNCAC.

of funds at any stage. Development aid is vulnerable to corruption, and in order to contribute to the realisation of economic, social and cultural rights, aid flows need to be monitored throughout the entire process.[247]

4.1.4. 'To the Maximum of Its Available Resources'

As noted *supra* this phrase forms part of the first 'hard core' obligation, and is indeed of major significance. While it does not mean that States have to devote *all* their resources to the realisation of economic, social and cultural rights, it does limit the freedom of a State to allocate resources.[248] It is crucial to note that the obligation to use the maximum available resources implies the duty to use the allocated resources in an effective and efficient manner.[249] This is also stated in the Limburg Principles.[250] Furthermore, there is a prohibition on the diversion of resources devoted to the rights in the ICESCR.[251] The CESCR's concluding observations stress the importance of combating corruption that negatively affects the implementation of the rights.[252] Moreover, the CESCR held that violation of the obligation to devote the maximum available resources 'may be indicated when the State has not spent funds allocated to certain Covenant-related activities due to inefficient administration or corruption.'[253] The Maastricht Guidelines also state that the failure to utilise the maximum of available resources towards the full realisation of the Covenant constitutes a violation.[254]

Whenever public funds are misappropriated, and money intended for the realisation of economic, social and cultural rights ends up in the private pockets of public officials, this constitutes a violation of the obligation to devote the maximum available resources.[255] A perfect example is the planned purchase by Teodorin Obiang of one of the world's most expensive yachts, worth US $380 million. Teodorin is the Minister of Agriculture and Forestry of Equatorial Guinea, and son of Teodoro Obiang, the country's ruler since 1979. Earlier reports already

---

247 On this topic, see Georg Cremer, *Corruption and Development Aid: Confronting the Challenges* (Freiburg: Lambertus Verlag, 2008).

248 Sepúlveda, *The Nature of the Obligations under the International Covenant on Economic, Social and Cultural Rights* at p. 315.

249 *Ibid.*

250 Limburg Principles, §27: 'In determining whether adequate measures have been taken for the realisation of rights recognised in the Covenant attention shall be paid to equitable and effective use of and access to the available resources.'

251 Sepúlveda, *The Nature of the Obligations under the International Covenant on Economic, Social and Cultural Rights* at p. 315.

252 *Ibid.*

253 *Ibid.* at p. 317.

254 Maastricht Guidelines, §15 (e).

255 Also argued by Jayawickrama, 'Corruption – a Violation of Human Rights?' at p. 3–4. Bacio Terracino, 'Corruption as a Violation of Human Rights', at p. 7 and p. 28, §131 and International Council on Human Rights Policy, *Corruption and Human Rights: Making the Connection* at p. 46.

demonstrated large-scale self-enrichment by Teodorin, who owns *inter alia* a mansion in Malibu worth US $35 million, a fleet of luxury cars and a private jet. Meanwhile, 77 per cent of Equatorial Guinea's population falls below the poverty line, 35 per cent dies before age 40, and 58 per cent lacks access to safe water.[256] Assuming these figures are accurate, it needs no further evidence that Equatorial Guinea, a State Party to the Covenant, grossly violates its obligations under Article 2(1).

In addition, whenever corruption causes an inefficient use of allocated resources, this also constitutes a violation. This can be seen for example when public funds are spent on large, unnecessary infrastructural or defense projects (which offer opportunities for personal enrichment of public officials through misappropriation or bribery), or on goods or services of inferior quality (because kickbacks were obtained during the procurement process).

4.1.5. 'With a View to Achieving Progressively the Full Realisation of the Rights Recognised in the Covenant'

According to the CESCR, the term 'progressive realisation' recognises that full implementation of all economic, social and cultural rights can generally not be achieved in a short period of time.[257] The phrase above encompasses two hard core obligations.

The first obligation consists of two elements, as identified in General Comment No. 3:[258] the obligation to continuously improve conditions and the prohibition of taking deliberately retrogressive measures.[259] The adoption of deliberately retrogressive measures constitutes a violation of the Covenant, which is also recognised in the Maastricht Guidelines.[260] An example of such a measure is an unjustified reduction by a State Party in public expenditures devoted to the implementation of economic, social and cultural rights, in the absence of adequate compensation for the injured individuals.[261] Embezzlement of public funds is such an unjustified reduction, and hence constitutes a violation of Article 2(1).

The second 'hard core' obligation that can be grouped under this phrase is the obligation to accord a degree of priority to human rights in the allocation of

---

256 Global Witness, 'Son of Equatorial Guinea's dictator plans one of world's most expensive yachts', 28th February 2011, <www.globalwitness.org/library/son-equatorial-guineas-dictator-plans-one-worlds-most-expensive-yachts>, accessed 2 March 2011.

257 General Comment No. 3, §9.

258 *Ibid.* §9.

259 Sepúlveda, *The Nature of the Obligations under the International Covenant on Economic, Social and Cultural Rights* at p. 319.

260 Maastricht Guidelines, §14 (e). See also International Council on Human Rights Policy, *Corruption and Human Rights: Making the Connection* at p. 47.

261 Sepúlveda, *The Nature of the Obligations under the International Covenant on Economic, Social and Cultural Rights* at p. 324.

resources,[262] also found in the Limburg Principles.[263] High-level embezzlement of public money constitutes a violation of this obligation, since, in such a case, the financing of the lifestyle of a country's officials enjoys priority over the realisation of economic, social and cultural rights. Where the private interests of public officials prevail over the realisation of human rights, Article 2(1) is violated. A flagrant violation of the obligation to accord priority to human rights in resource allocation can be found in the shopping sprees of Grace Mugabe, the First Lady of Zimbabwe, also known as 'Gucci Grace'. While the country's population is suffering tremendous hardship and food shortages, she reportedly spent £75,000 in two hours, while shopping in Paris.[264] Violations also occur when priority is given to projects that offer opportunities for corruption (e.g. large infrastructural prestige projects), instead of projects devoted to the realisation of economic, social and cultural rights.

4.1.6. 'By all Appropriate Means, Including Particularly the Adoption of Legislative Measures'

This constitutes another 'hard core' obligation.[265] The CESCR held that not only legislative measures should be taken, but that judicial remedies ought to be provided, and that administrative, financial, educational and social measures should be taken.[266] This is also noted in the Limburg Principles.[267] Concerning the adoption of legislation, Toebes observed that under Article 2(1), States are obliged to adopt anti-corruption legislation to ensure that Covenant-rights are realised in a transparent and efficient manner.[268] Moreover, it can be argued that this hard core obligation includes the obligation to ratify anti-corruption treaties, and to launch domestic anti-corruption campaigns and set up preventive policies, for example in the health and education sector.

Furthermore, the seventh and final 'hard core' obligation is to ensure the minimum core level of each right[269] stated in General Comment No. 3. States have 'to ensure the satisfaction of, at the very least, minimum essential levels of each of the rights'. Therefore, 'a State Party in which any of significant number of individuals is deprived of essential foodstuffs, of essential primary health care, of

---

262 *Ibid.* at p. 332–335.

263 Limburg Principles, §28.

264 The New Zimbabwean, 11 December 2009, 'Spend it like Grace', <www.newzimbabwe.com/pages/shopper6.11592.html>, accessed 7 January 2012.

265 Sepúlveda, *The Nature of the Obligations under the International Covenant on Economic, Social and Cultural Rights* at p. 335–360.

266 General Comment No. 3, §4, 5, 7.

267 Limburg Principles, §17.

268 Brigit Toebes, 'The Impact of Acts of Corruption on the Enjoyment of the Right to Health', *Working Paper* (Geneva: International Council on Human Rights Policy, 2007) at §16.

269 Sepúlveda, *The Nature of the Obligations under the International Covenant on Economic, Social and Cultural Rights* at p. 365–370.

basic shelter and housing, or of the most basic forms of education is, prima facie, failing to discharge its obligations under the Covenant.'[270] This is the 'core obligations approach'.[271] Anti-corruption measures will contribute to meeting the obligation to ensure the minimum core level of economic, social and cultural rights.

4.2. The Right to Food

4.2.1. Introduction

While possible causes of food insecurity can be numerous – think of natural disasters and armed conflict – the impact of corruption on (the right to) food is not cited very often.[272] An exception to this is found in the Voluntary Guidelines of the Food and Agriculture Organization (hereafter: FAO), which do mention corruption.[273] Also, it emerged from the analysis in chapter IV that the Special Rapporteur on the right to food paid attention to corruption as a factor impacting upon this right. Amongst other things, it was held that the obligation to protect the right to food imposes a number of duties upon States, including the duty to combat corruption.[274] Yet, on only one occasion did the CESCR discuss corruption in relation to the right to food, i.e. in its 2008 concluding observations on India, stating that corruption hampers access to food.[275] The current section therefore develops the links between corruption and the right to food, starting with an analysis of the normative content of the right. Subsequently, State obligations under the ICESCR are discussed, as well as possible violations of the right to food by corruption.

---

270 General Comment No. 3, §10.

271 See Audrey R. Chapman and Sage Russell (eds.), *Core Obligations: Building a Framework for Economic, Social and Cultural Rights* (Antwerp: Intersentia, 2002).

272 Heidelberg-based NGO FIAN, working on the right to food, does not seem to dedicate a great deal of systematic attention to the role of corruption.

273 Voluntary Guidelines to support the progressive realisation of the right to adequate food in the context of national food security, adopted by the 127th session of the FAO Council (November 2004). Guideline 5.5: 'States should take measures, where and if necessary, to develop, strengthen, implement and maintain effective anticorruption legislation and policies, including in the food sector and in the management of emergency food aid.' Guideline 13.3: 'States should establish transparent, non-discriminatory eligibility criteria in order to ensure effective targeting of assistance, so that no one who is in need is excluded, or that those not in need are included. Effective accountability and administrative systems are essential to prevent leakages and corruption. Factors to take into account include household and individual assets and income, nutrition and health status, as well as existing coping mechanisms.'

274 Report of the Special Rapporteur on the right to food, CHR 57th session, 7 February 2001, UN Doc. E/CN.4/2001/53, §28.

275 CESCR CO India May 2008, UN Doc. E/C.12/IND/CO/5, §25.

4.2.2. Content

The right to food is a component of the right to an adequate standard of living, as laid down in Article 25(1) UDHR and Article 11 ICESCR.[276] Relevant provisions can also be found in other instruments.[277] When examining the content of the right to food at the international level, the CESCR's General Comment No. 12 is one of the most important interpretative documents.[278] According to the Committee, 'the right to adequate food is realised when every man, woman and child, alone or in community with others, has physical and economic access at all times to adequate food or means for its procurement.'[279] Indeed, it is not the lack of food itself that causes many people worldwide to suffer from hunger and malnutrition, but rather the lack of access to available food.[280]

The Committee stressed the importance of the concepts of 'adequacy' and 'sustainability' of food availability and access. The notion of *adequacy* highlights a number of factors (e.g. social, economic, cultural, climatic and ecological) which must be considered in determining whether particular foods or diets that are accessible can be considered the most appropriate under the given circumstances for the purpose of Article 11.[281] The notion of *sustainability* is linked to adequate

---

[276] Article 11 ICESCR: '1. The States parties to the present Covenant recognise the right of everyone to an adequate standard of living for himself and his family, including adequate food, clothing and housing, and to the continuous improvement of his living conditions. The States parties will take appropriate steps to ensure the realisation of this right, recognising to this effect the essential importance of international co-operation based on free consent.
2. The States parties to the present Covenant, recognising the fundamental right of everyone to be free from hunger, shall take, individually and through international co-operation, the measures, including specific programmes, which are needed:
(a) to improve methods of production, conservation and distribution of food by making full use of technical and scientific knowledge, by disseminating knowledge of the principles of nutrition and by developing or reforming agrarian systems in such a way as to achieve the most efficient development and utilisation of natural resources;
(b) taking into account the problems of both food-importing and food-exporting countries, to ensure an equitable distribution of world food supplies in relation to need.'

[277] Article 24(1) and (2), 27(3) UN Convention on the Rights of the Child; Article 12 Protocol of San Salvador. For more on the latter topic, see Héctor Faúndez Ledesma, 'The Right to Food in the Inter-American System', in Marco Borghi and Letizia Postiglione Blommestein (eds.), *The Right to Adequate Food and Access to Justice* (Collection Interdisciplinaire, 31; Brussels: Bruylant, Geneva: Schulthess, 2006), p. 91–113.

[278] Committee on Economic, Social and Cultural Rights, General Comment No. 12 on the right to adequate food (Article 11), Twentieth session (1999), UN Doc. E/C.12/1999/5. For more on the right to food, see also Wenche Barth Eide and Uwe Kracht, 'The Right to Adequate Food in Human Rights Instruments: Legal Norms and Interpretations', in Wenche Barth Eide (ed.), *Food and Human Rights in Development (Volume I): Legal and Institutional Dimensions and Selected Topics.* (Antwerp: Intersentia, 2005), p. 99–118.

[279] General Comment No. 12, §6.

[280] *Ibid.* §5.

[281] *Ibid.* §7.

food or food security, which means that food should be accessible for present and future generations, incorporating availability and accessibility in the long run.[282]

According to the Committee, 'the core content of the right to adequate food implies: the availability of food in a quantity and quality sufficient to satisfy the dietary needs of individuals, free from adverse substances, and acceptable within a given culture' as well as 'the accessibility of such food in ways that are sustainable and that do not interfere with the enjoyment of other human rights.'[283] This core content consists of several elements.

Availability refers to a person's possibilities to feed him/herself directly from productive land or other natural resources, or to the possibilities for well functioning distribution, processing and market systems that can move food from the production site to the place of demand.[284] In cases of corruption in the supply of humanitarian food aid, when food is embezzled by public officials, the availability element is clearly violated by such an act of corruption. *Dietary needs* refers to the nutritional value of the food.[285] *Free from adverse substances* means that the food must be safe, uncontaminated and non-toxic.[286] Corruption in the food production chain may affect this requirement, for instance when food inspectors are bribed to turn a blind eye to unsafe products. *Cultural or consumer acceptability* stresses the need to take 'non nutrient-based values' into account.[287] For example, pork meat would generally not be culturally acceptable in societies with a large Muslim population.

Accessibility includes economic as well as physical accessibility. *Economic access* entails that food has to be affordable, so that the costs of food do not constitute a disproportionate part of the household income. Corrupt practices in the food chain may lead to an increase in the price of foods, impeding economic accessibility. *Physical access* implies that food should be accessible to everyone, including vulnerable and disadvantaged groups.[288]

4.2.3. State Obligations and Violations

Regarding State Parties' obligations that flow from the right to food, the Committee acknowledged that this right will have to be realised progressively.[289] However, a State has 'a *core obligation* to take the necessary action to mitigate and alleviate hunger as provided for in paragraph 2 of Article 11, even in times of natural or other

282 *Ibid.* §7.

283 General Comment No. 12, §8. For more on the minimum core content of the right to adequate food, see: ROLF KÜNNEMANN, 'The Right to Adequate Food: Violations Related to Its Minimum Core Content', in Audrey R. Chapman and Sage Russell (eds.), *Core Obligations: Building a Framework for Economic, Social and Cultural Rights* (Antwerp: Intersentia, 2002), p. 161–183.

284 General Comment No. 12, §12.

285 *Ibid.* §9.

286 *Ibid.* §10.

287 *Ibid.* §11.

288 *Ibid.* §13.

289 *Ibid.* §6 and 14.

disasters.'[290] States have to ensure the minimum essential level required to be free from hunger.[291] Whenever this is not met due to unwillingness (rather than inability) of a State Party, this constitutes a violation of the Covenant.[292] This is the so-called core obligations approach.[293] Several countries, where a large number of people suffer from undernourishment and malnutrition, rank among the most corrupt. For those States, it will be hard to demonstrate that they are actually unable, instead of unwilling, to meet their core obligations. Take for example the Philippines, a State Party to the ICESCR. Looking at the country's recent history, we can see a notoriously corrupt leadership. During the reign of Ferdinand Marcos (1972–1986), the State's assets were plundered. Transparency International estimated that Marcos embezzled somewhere between $5 and 10 billion.[294] Still today, in the CPI 2011, the country ranks 129 out of 183 countries.[295] Meanwhile, statistics reveal massive poverty in the Philippines. The Asian Development Bank identified governance concerns including corruption as one of the seven major causes of poverty.[296] A country in which the political leadership misappropriated such large amounts of money while the population is suffering clearly does not meet its obligation of devoting the 'maximum available resources' as required by Article 2(1) ICESCR.

Furthermore, the tripartite typology is relevant. The obligation *to respect* the right to food requires States not to prevent existing access to adequate food.[297] This obligation has a negative character: States may not interfere. It is also an immediate obligation which involves little costs.[298] As pointed out by the CESCR in its concluding observations on India (2008), corruption prevents access to food. Thus, it constitutes a breach of the obligation to respect the right to food. Both economic accessibility and physical accessibility may be at stake due to corruption.

Under the obligation *to protect*, States must take measures to ensure that corporations or individuals do not deprive citizens of their access to adequate food. By engaging in corrupt practices, a State may breach this obligation to protect.

290 *Ibid.* §6.
291 *Ibid.* §14.
292 *Ibid.* §17.
293 For more on the minimum core obligations resulting from the right to adequate food, see Künnemann, 'The Right to Adequate Food: Violations Related to Its Minimum Core Content.'
294 Robin Hodess, 'Introduction to Political Corruption', in Transparency International (ed.), *Global Corruption Report* (2004), p. 11–18 at p. 13.
295 See <http://cpi.transparency.org/cpi2011> accessed 7 January 2012.
296 The Asian Development Bank identifies governance concerns including corruption as one of the seven major causes of poverty. See Asian Development Bank, 'Poverty in the Philippines: Income, Assets, and Access', (2005).
297 General Comment No. 12, §15.
298 Christophe Golay, 'The Right to Food and Access to Justice: The International Covenant on Economic, Social and Cultural Rights before National Jurisdictions', in Marco Borghi and Letizia Postiglione Blommestein (eds.), *The Right to Adequate Food and Access to Justice* (Collection Interdisciplinaire, 31; Brussels: Bruylant, Geneva: Schulthess, 2006), 117–149 at 129–130.

Imagine an international oil corporation, eager to obtain the concession to drill for oil. The corporation may offer bribes to the public officials in charge of the relevant area, or the public officials may demand bribes from the corporation. Such bribery may lead to the situation in which environmental regulations are disrespected, with pollution of water and soil as a result. This pollution may violate various rights, such as the right to life, health and food. The latter is true if the area concerned was used for food production by its inhabitants. While it is ultimately the corporation polluting the area, this is the result of the act of bribery, which was an inducement for the public official to ignore environmental regulations. The acceptance or extortion of the bribe and the subsequent pollution constitutes a direct violation of the State obligation to protect the right to food. Moreover, even if no contamination is involved, the right to food can be violated, for example by forced relocation of indigenous peoples inhabiting an area where valuable natural resources can be found. As a result of relocation, these peoples will no longer have access to their food production sites (element of physical accessibility).[299] Another example is the bribing by a food corporation of public officials who are in charge of food safety regulations. Where food producers subsequently bring unsafe food on the market to maximise profits, the obligation to protect the right to food is also violated. In such a case, the food is no longer free from adverse substances, as required by Article 11.[300]

The obligation *to fulfil* includes the obligation to facilitate and to provide the right to adequate food. *To facilitate* means that States must productively engage in activities which strengthen people's access to and use of resources and means to ensure their livelihood, including food security. The obligation *to provide* applies when individuals or groups are unable, for reasons beyond their control, to enjoy the right to adequate food by the means at their disposal (including those who have fallen victim of natural or other disasters).[301] Misappropriation by public officials of foodstuffs or of funds intended for food aid constitutes a violation of the obligation to fulfil the right to food. An Indian study revealed that within a food subsidy programme for the poor, more than 50 per cent of the food grain did not reach the poor due to embezzlement.[302] In such cases, the obligation to provide is not met.

Concerning violations of the right to adequate food, the Committee noted that it constitutes a violation of the ICESCR when a State discriminates in access to food, as well as to means and entitlements of its procurement.[303] Corruption is an inherently discriminatory act. Hence, forms of corruption may constitute a violation

---

299 Example of indigenous peoples mentioned in: International Council on Human Rights Policy, *Corruption and Human Rights: Making the Connection* at p. 44.

300 Example mentioned in *Ibid.*

301 General Comment No. 12, §15.

302 George Cheriyan, 'Enforcing the Right to Food in India: Bottlenecks in Delivering the Expected Outcome', *UNI-WIDER Research Paper No. 2006/132*, (November 2006) at p. 11.

303 General Comment No. 12, §18.

of the right to food because they discriminate in access to food, for example, where money has to be paid to obtain access to food aid, this discriminates against those who do not have the financial means to pay the bribes. Also, whenever food aid in relief situations is diverted by officials for private purposes, this is discriminatory. The previously mentioned Indian study argued that subsidized wheat intended for tribal populations was siphoned off by workers of the ruling political party.[304]

As regards the implementation of the right to food at the national level, the Committee stressed that:

> … the formulation and implementation of national strategies for the right to food requires full compliance with the principles of accountability, transparency, people's participation, decentralisation, legislative capacity and the independence of the judiciary. Good governance is essential to the realisation of all human rights, including the elimination of poverty and ensuring a satisfactory livelihood for all.[305]

This clear reference to transparency and good governance implies that in order to realise the right to food, corruption should also be combated.

4.2. The Right to Adequate Housing

4.3.1. Introduction

Corruption and its impact upon the right to housing was touched upon by the treaty bodies on only a few occasions. In 2010, the CESCR made remarks about corruption in relation to housing loans in Kazakhstan,[306] and in land allocation schemes in Afghanistan.[307] Furthermore, the reports of the Special Rapporteur on the right to adequate housing, while containing comments on corruption, unfortunately lack an in-depth analysis of the topic. Yet, there is evidence that corruption and the right to housing are closely linked. A report of the South African Human Rights Commission on the right of access to adequate housing identified corruption as one of the challenges for the realisation of the right.[308] It emerged that in one of South Africa's housing departments, under-expenditure on housing was, amongst others, a result of 'mismanagement, incompetence, corruption, political intervention and nepotism at the municipal level' which 'also impede the delivery of adequate and quality housing and related infrastructure.'[309] Hence, the present section discusses

---

304 Cheriyan, 'Enforcing the Right to Food in India: Bottlenecks in Delivering the Expected Outcome', at p. 11–12.

305 General Comment No. 12, §23.

306 CESCR CO Kazakhstan 7 June 2010, UN Doc. E/C.12/KAZ/CO/1, §30.

307 CESCR CO Afghanistan 7 June 2010, UN Doc. E/C.12/AFG/CO/2–4, §36.

308 South African Human Rights Commission, 'The Right of Access to Adequate Housing', *5th Economic and Social Rights Report Series, 2002/2003 Financial Year* (21 June 2004) at p. 45–46.

309 *Ibid.* at p. 36.

how the various aspects of the right to adequate housing may be violated by corrupt practices.

4.3.2. Content

The right to adequate housing is a component of the right to an adequate standard of living as enshrined in Article 25(1) UDHR and Article 11(1) ICESCR, and is also laid down in several other international instruments.[310] As pointed out by Westendorp, these provisions lack sufficient clarity for normative objectives and control.[311] The CESCR elucidated the content of the right to housing in its General Comments No. 4[312] and No. 7,[313] which are considered to be the most authoritative interpretations of this right.

While the CESCR found that 'adequacy' is partly determined by social, economic, cultural, climatic, ecological and other factors, it is generally acknowledged that the right to adequate housing consists of a number of components.[314] *Legal security of tenure* entails that persons should be legally protected against forced eviction, harassment and other threats.[315] The ICHRP noted that security of tenure is undermined by corruption: i) companies may bribe officials to grant leases on land that is already occupied; ii) officials or businesses may bribe homeowners directly to sell up, often throwing poor tenants on the street; and iii) village leaders may be bribed so as to sign blank contracts with the local land administration, which then sells the land to developers.[316] Moreover, the Centre on Housing Rights and Evictions (hereafter: COHRE)[317] reported on forced evictions and land rights in Burma, and noted the role of corruption in this respect.[318] In certain areas of the country, policies of the Burmese government and military deployments have encouraged ethnic villagers to flee. As a result, these people often had to abandon their land and their property, or their traditional customary land practices. At the same time, military families started moving onto confiscated lands, where they often built permanent housing, which they later sold

310 Article 5(e)(iii) CERD; Article 27(3) CRC; Article 43(1) ICMW; Article 14(2) Women's Convention.

311 Ingrid Westendorp, *Women and Housing: Gender Makes a Difference* (School of Human Rights Research Series, 23; (Antwerp: Intersentia, 2007) at p. 33.

312 General Comment No. 4 on the right to housing (Art. 11(1)), Sixth session, 1991.

313 General Comment No. 7 on the right to adequate housing (Article 11(1)): forced evictions, Sixteenth session, 1997.

314 General Comment No. 4, §8.

315 *Ibid.* §8(a).

316 International Council on Human Rights Policy, *Corruption and Human Rights: Making the Connection* at p. 51.

317 COHRE is a Geneva-based NGO campaigning for the protection of housing rights and the prevention of forced evictions.

318 Burma is not a party to the ICCPR or to the ICESCR. However, it has acceded to the Women's Convention and the CRC.

to third parties.[319] Hence, government policies are employed for private benefit, violating the right to housing. Furthermore, military officers and government officials have used confiscated lands from resettlement areas to build modern, luxurious houses in valuable locations. Since the government subsidised land ownership for its employees, officials can easily acquire land. In addition, land and other property are sometimes forcibly sold to powerful officers and other officials, who coerce the sale by the threat of force. The officials subsequently pay prices below the market level. Concomitantly, the land and housing officials are corrupt, since they change ownership documents in exchange for bribes. Even though the State owns all the land and leases it to farmers, leases can be passed on with the agreement of local state authorities. While, in theory, land cannot be sold, in practice the land record officials are willing to transfer ownership titles in return for bribes.[320] These examples demonstrate the central role of corruption in relation to land rights. Where ownership documents are changed by a corrupt official who has accepted bribes, this act of bribery is a violation of the right to adequate housing, since it violates legal security of tenure.

Availability of services, materials, facilities, and infrastructure: adequate housing includes facilities that are essential for health, security, comfort and nutrition. Therefore, persons should have sustainable access to natural and common resources; potable drinking water; energy to cook, heat and light; sanitation and washing facilities; food storage; waste disposal; site drainage and emergency services.[321] Corruption can impact upon water supply and energy facilities, impeding the availability component of the right to adequate housing.

Affordability entails that the costs of housing should be at such a level that the fulfillment of other basic needs (consider food and health) is not threatened or compromised. States have to ensure that housing costs are proportionate to the income level, and establish housing subsidies and housing finance for those who need this.[322] Where bribes have to be paid to obtain access to housing or to land, this directly hampers the affordability component of the right to housing. For instance, in Cambodia land titles are difficult to obtain due to corruption, since an application for such a title can cost between \$200 and \$700 in informal payments to government officials.[323]

Habitability requires that housing must be habitable, i.e. it must provide enough space and protect the inhabitants from weather conditions, health threats, structural hazards and disease vectors. Also, physical safety must be safeguarded.[324] As argued by the ICHRP, embezzlement of funds in a programme for the construction

---

319 The Centre on Housing Rights and Evictions (COHRE), 'Displacement and Dispossession: Forced Migration and Land Rights in Burma', *COHRE Country Report* (November 2007) at p. 48.

320 *Ibid.* at p. 49.

321 General Comment No. 4, §8(b).

322 *Ibid.* §8(c).

323 Joanne Pawlowski, 'Forced Evictions of Cambodia's Poor', *Human Rights Tribune* 11/3 (2005).

324 General Comment No. 4, §8(d).

of housing units or bribery in the selection of contractors, may lead to construction works of substandard quality, which may impair habitability.[325]

Accessibility means that those entitled to housing must be able to access housing, which is particularly relevant for disadvantaged groups such as the elderly, children, and sick or disabled people and victims of natural disasters. Relevant in this respect is access to land for landless or poor segments of society.[326] Accessibility of housing can be affected by corruption, for example when a bribe is demanded in order to obtain a house.[327] This is indeed especially harmful to the poorest segments of society.

The aspect of *location* requires that housing must be in a location with access to employment options, health care, education and other social facilities. The location must also be safe, i.e. not in polluted areas or close to sources of pollution that threaten the right to health.[328] It is possible however that due to corruption in the process of procurement, that the location component is compromised, and housing is realised in unsafe areas, in order to embezzle the money that was saved.

Finally, *cultural adequacy* demands that the cultural aspects of construction, building materials and policies are also taken into account.[329]

In addition to the seven components discussed above, the aspect of non-discrimination is crucial. Pursuant to Article 2(2) ICESCR, enjoyment of the right to adequate housing must not be subject to any form of discrimination.[330] As the examples in the present section have illustrated, corruption is inherently discriminatory, since the poor are discriminated against *vis-à-vis* the rich.

4.3.3. State Obligations and Violations

Concerning State obligations related to the right to housing, the CESCR held that there are steps which must be taken immediately, irrespective of a country's level of development. Many measures only require State abstention (negative obligations) and a commitment to facilitate self-help by affected groups.[331] Furthermore, States must give priority to social groups living in unfavourable conditions.[332] Also, a general decline in living and housing conditions which can be directly attributed to a State's policy and legislative decisions, while there are no compensatory measures, would be inconsistent with the obligations under the Covenant.[333] The CESCR

---

325 International Council on Human Rights Policy, *Corruption and Human Rights: Making the Connection* at p. 51.
326 General Comment No. 4, §8(e).
327 International Council on Human Rights Policy, *Corruption and Human Rights: Making the Connection* at p. 51.
328 General Comment No. 4, §8(f).
329 General Comment No. 4, §8(g).
330 *Ibid.* §6 and 9.
331 *Ibid.* §10.
332 *Ibid.* §11.
333 *Ibid.* §11.

noted that it will vary from one State to another what will be the most appropriate means of achieving the full realisation of the right to adequate housing. However, States have to take whatever steps are necessary to this end. This will almost invariably include the adoption of a national housing strategy.[334] In the author's view, such a housing strategy ought to contain a strong anti-corruption component, with attention for the prevention of corruption in relation to housing and land. Another obligation of immediate effect is the effective monitoring of the housing situation.[335] Furthermore, the CESCR opined that States can use whatever mix of public and private sector measures in order to comply with their obligations.[336] Finally, the CESCR considered that instances of forced eviction are *prima facie* incompatible with the Covenant, and can only be justified in the most exceptional circumstances, and in accordance with the relevant principles of international law.[337] The issue of forced evictions is further elaborated upon in the CESCR's General Comment No. 7. As noted *supra*in the case of Burma, forced evictions can be motivated by the pursuit of personal profit of public officials. Such conduct violates the right to adequate housing.

As noted in General Comment No. 3, there is a minimum core obligation in respect of the right to housing: 'a State Party in which any significant number of individuals is deprived of [...] basic shelter and housing [...] is, *prima facie*, failing to discharge its obligations under the Covenant.'[338] Beyond this core obligation, there are five levels of obligations incumbent on States regarding the right to adequate housing: the obligation to recognise, to respect, to protect, to promote and to fulfil, as identified by Sachar, former Special Rapporteur on the right to adequate housing.[339]

The obligation *to recognise* the right to adequate housing consists of three key areas. First, States must recognise the human rights dimensions of housing and abstain from taking measures intended to erode the legal status of the right.[340] States must also take legislative measures and appropriate policies in order to realise housing rights progressively. Incompatible existing legislation or policies have to be repealed or amended.[341] Finally, States must determine to what extent

334 *Ibid.* §12.
335 *Ibid.* §13.
336 *Ibid.* §14.
337 *Ibid.* §18.
338 General Comment No. 3, §10.
339 Report of the SR on the right to adequate housing, CHR 45th session, 22 June 2003, UN Doc. E/CN.4/Sub.2/1993/15, §61. See also Office of the United Nations High Commissioner for Human Rights, 'Fact Sheet No. 21, the Human Right to Adequate Housing', <www.ohchr.org/Documents/Publications/FactSheet21en.pdf>, accessed 7 April 2009. This document appears to be based on the report of the Special Rapporteur and the General Comments of the CESCR. See also Westendorp, *Women and Housing: Gender Makes a Difference* at p. 37–39, for a discussion of the four-layer typology.
340 Report of the SR on the right to adequate housing, CHR 45th session, 22 June 2003, UN Doc.E/CN.4/Sub.2/1993/15, §62.
341 *Ibid.* §63.

the right to adequate housing is already enjoyed, and the degree to which the right is not enjoyed.[342]

The obligation *to respect* stands for the negative duty upon the State to refrain from action which prevents people from exercising the right to housing themselves when they are capable of doing so. Moreover, States are not allowed to forcibly evict people.[343] It can be very well argued that the obligation to respect includes the obligation to abstain from corrupt practices within the housing sector.

The obligation *to protect* entails that States have to prevent violations of housing rights by third parties (e.g. landlords or property developers). Where violations do take place, the State has to act to prevent any further deprivations and assure access to legal remedies or redress to those affected. Furthermore, States have to take immediate measures to grant legal security or tenure to those who are presently not protected. In addition, States have to ensure that housing costs are reasonable and they have to establish a system of subsidies whenever housing costs threaten other basic needs.[344] The author finds that under the obligation to protect, State Parties must prevent and combat corrupt practices in the housing sector committed by third parties.

The obligation *to promote* means that States have to emphasise the relevance of the realisation of the right to adequate housing, and take measures in this respect.[345]

Under the obligation *to fulfil,* States have to realise the right to housing for those who are not capable of achieving adequate housing themselves.[346] While meeting this obligation, States must make sure that relevant funds intended for housing are spent appropriately, and anti-corruption safeguards need to be put in place. Embezzlement of funds constitutes a violation of the obligation to fulfil.

4.4. The Right to Education

4.4.1. Introduction

The CRC made clear in its concluding observations that corruption negatively impacts upon the resources available for the realisation of children's rights, including the right to education. Such was the case in the observations on Benin (2006),[347] Congo (2006),[348] Bulgaria (2008),[349] the Philippines (2009),[350] Sri Lanka

342 *Ibid.* §64.
343 *Ibid.* §66–68.
344 *Ibid.* §69–72.
345 *Ibid.* §73.
346 *Ibid.* §74–79.
347 CRC CO Benin 20 October 2006, UN Doc. CRC/C/BEN/CO/2, §17.
348 CRC CO Congo 20 October 2006, UN Doc. CRC/C/COG/CO/1, §14.
349 CRC CO Bulgaria 23 June 2008, UN Doc. CRC/C/BGR/CO/2, §16–17.
350 CRC CO Philippines 22 October 2009, UN Doc. CRC/C/COG/CO/1, §19.

(2010)[351] and Afghanistan (2011).[352] The right to education was also addressed in the observations on Mozambique (2002), expressing the concern that 'there is alleged corruption and sexual abuse and economic exploitation of pupils by professionals, including teachers, in the school system', and recommending that Mozambique ends these practices.[353] Unfortunately, the Committee CESCR did not address educational corruption, and also the Special Rapporteur on the right to education did not take the opportunity to address the matter in a comprehensive fashion.

At the same time, it is clear that the absence of discussions on educational corruption in the work of the CESCR and the Special Rapporteur does not reflect reality, since corruption in the education sector is a rampant global phenomenon. Research indicates that it is widespread in South and South East Asia, and endemic in the Balkans, the former Soviet Union and Africa.[354] However, the destructive practice also occurs in other parts of the world.[355] In 2009, a corruption scandal shook German academia. It has been reported that over 100 professors throughout Germany awarded doctoral titles to PhD candidates in exchange for bribes.[356] This demonstrates that even in an advanced educational system, corruption can be difficult to wipe out.

In order to place discussions about educational corruption within the human rights framework, the present section first elaborates upon the normative content of the right to education, and argues how corruption may run counter to these various features. Then it goes on to discuss specific State obligations and violations. As noted by the CESCR:

> ... when the normative content of Article 13 is applied to the general and specific obligations of States Parties, a dynamic process is set in motion which facilitates identification of violations of the right to education. Violations of Article 13 may occur through the direct action of States Parties (acts of commission) or through their failure to take steps required by the Covenant (acts of omission).[357]

---

351 CRC CO Sri Lanka 19 October 2010, UN Doc. CRC/C/LKA/CO/3–4, §16(c).

352 CRC CO Afghanistan 8 April 2011, UN Doc. CRC/C/AFG/CO/1, §17.

353 CRC CO Mozambique 3 April 2002, UN Doc. CRC/C/15/Add.172, §56 and 57.

354 U4 Anti-Corruption Resource Centre, 'Corruption in the Education Sector', *U4 Issue* (Bergen: Chr. Michelsen Institute, 2006) at p. 3.

355 For numerous examples of educational corruption, see Jacques Hallak and Muriel Poisson, 'Corrupt Schools, Corrupt Universities: What Can Be Done?' (Paris: International Institute for Educational Planning (UNESCO), 2007); Vincent R. Johnson, 'Corruption in Education: A Global Legal Challenge', <http://works.bepress.com/vincent_johnson/1>, accessed 12 April 2010.

356 Jochen Leffers, 'Germany Rocked by Allegations of Ph.D Bribes (24 August 2009)', *Der Spiegel*, <www.spiegel.de/international/germany/0,1518,644639,00.html>, accessed 12 April 2009.

357 General Comment No. 13, §58.

It is indeed precisely the aim of the present piece to identify how corruption can violate the right to education in various ways.[358]

4.4.2. Content

The right to education is enshrined in Articles 13 and 14 ICESCR,[359] as well as in other international[360] and regional human rights instruments.[361] The CESCR's General Comment No. 13 is the most reliable source of interpretation.[362] While Article 13(1) sets out the aims and objectives of education,[363] Article 13(2) is the

358 Also touching upon corruption and the right to education are SUNGA and BOTTIGLIERO, 'In-Depth Study on the Linkages between Anti-Corruption and Human Rights for the United Nations Development Program', at p. 28–29.

359 Article 13 ICESCR: '1. The States parties to the present Covenant recognise the right of everyone to education. They agree that education shall be directed to the full development of the human personality and the sense of its dignity, and shall strengthen the respect for human rights and fundamental freedoms. They further agree that education shall enable all persons to participate effectively in a free society, promote understanding, tolerance and friendship among all nations and all racial, ethnic or religious groups, and further the activities of the United Nations for the maintenance of peace.

2. The States parties to the present Covenant recognise that, with a view to achieving the full realisation of this right:
   (a) primary education shall be compulsory and available free to all;
   (b) secondary education in its different forms, including technical and vocational secondary education, shall be made generally available and accessible to all by every appropriate means, and in particular by the progressive introduction of free education;
   (c) higher education shall be made equally accessible to all, on the basis of capacity, by every appropriate means, and in particular by the progressive introduction of free education;
   (d) fundamental education shall be encouraged or intensified as far as possible for those persons who have not received or completed the whole period of their primary education;
   (e) the development of a systems of schools at all levels shall be actively pursued, an adequate fellowship system shall be established, and the material conditions of teaching staff shall be continuously improved.
3. The States parties to the present Covenant undertake to have respect for the liberty of parents and, when applicable, legal guardians to choose for their children schools, other than those established by the public authorities, which conform to such minimum educational standards as may be laid down or approved by the State and to ensure the religious and moral education of their children in conformity with their own convictions.
4. No part of this Article shall be construed so as to interfere with the liberty of individuals and bodies to establish and direct educational institutions, subject always to the observance of the principles set forth in paragraph 1 of this article and to the requirement that the education given in such institutions shall conform to such minimum standards as may be laid down by the State.'

360 Article 26 UDHR; Article 28 CRC.

361 Article 2 First Protocol ECHR; Article 13 Protocol of San Salvador; Article 17(1) AfChHPR.

362 COMMITTEE ON ECONOMIC, SOCIAL AND CULTURAL RIGHTS, General Comment No. 13 on the right to education (Art. 13), twenty-first session (1999), UN Doc. E/C.12/1999/10.

363 General Comment No. 13, §4 and 5.

actual right to receive an education, distinguishing between various levels: primary, secondary, higher and fundamental education. States have different obligations in respect of these levels.[364] Importantly, under Article 13(2)(a), primary education has to be both compulsory and free of charge. This aspect is further developed in General Comment No. 11,[365] which concerns Article 14 ICESCR on plans of action for primary education, and is complementary to General Comment No. 13.[366] Moreover, Article 13(3) and 13(4) contain the right to educational freedom. Under Article 13(3), States have to respect the freedom of parents and guardians to ensure the religious and moral education of their children in conformity with their own convictions.[367] In addition, parents and guardians are free to choose schools other than public schools for their children.[368] Under Article 13(4), everyone, also non-nationals, has the liberty to establish and direct educational institutions.[369]

According to the Committee, the right to education encompasses four interrelated and essential features, the AAAA or four-A framework.[370] In the application of these four features, the student's best interests shall be a primary consideration.[371] This is also the core principle of the UN Convention of the Rights of the Child.[372] State Parties have to respect, protect, and fulfil each of these features (see *infra* for a further discussion of this typology).[373]

(i) Availability

Availability entails that there has to be a sufficient number of functioning educational institutions and programmes within a State Party. These institutions and programmes need a number of things to function well, for example: buildings; sanitation facilities; safe potable water; trained teachers with domestically competitive salaries; teaching materials; libraries and computers.[374] Many corrupt practices run counter to the availability dimension of education, such as the embezzlement of public funds intended for teaching materials and school

---

364 *Ibid.* §8–24.

365 Committee on Economic, Social and Cultural Rights, General Comment No. 11 on plans of action for primary education (Art. 14), twentieth session (1999) UN Doc. E/C.12/1999/4.

366 General Comment No. 13, §2.

367 *Ibid.* §28.

368 General Comment No. 13, §29.

369 *Ibid.* §30.

370 For an elaborate discussion of the four-A framework, the reader is referred to Katarina Tomasevski, *Human Rights Obligations in Education: The 4-a Scheme* (Nijmegen: Wolf Legal Publishers, 2006).

371 General Comment No. 13, §7.

372 Fons Coomans, 'In Search of the Core Content of the Right to Education', in Audrey R. Chapman and Sage Russell (eds.), *Core Obligations: Building a Framework for Economic, Social and Cultural Rights* (Antwerp: Intersentia, 2002), p. 217–246 at p. 223.

373 General Comment No. 13, §50.

374 *Ibid.* §6(a).

buildings,[375] the diversion of school textbooks and their subsequent sale at local markets.[376] Also hindering the availability feature of the right to education is corruption in procurement for, for example, school buildings or maintenance, or for teaching materials or school meals. This can result in substandard quality of goods and services and higher prices.[377] The outcomes of procurement can be influenced by the bribes paid to the responsible decision maker in the public sector. Although this concerns the delivery of goods and services by third parties, it is the State which has the obligation to protect against infringements of the right to education by third parties. Thus, whenever bribes are accepted or demanded by public officials in the procurement process, this violates the obligation to protect the availability feature of the right to education.[378]

(ii) Accessibility

Accessibility includes the overlapping dimensions of non-discrimination, economic accessibility and physical accessibility.[379] *Non-discrimination* is an important component of accessibility. According to the Committee, there is a *minimum core obligation* of States to ensure the most basic forms of education.[380] This includes the obligation to ensure the right of access to public educational institutions and programmes on a non-discriminatory basis.[381] Moreover, the Committee expressly stated that a State's failure to take measures which address *de facto* educational discrimination constitutes a violation of the right to education.[382] A large number of corrupt practices within the educational system constitute discrimination, and thus directly violate the right to education. Not taking anti-corruption measures in the education sector therefore violates the right to education. A clear example of how corruption constitutes discrimination is the practice of bribery within the public school system. Bribes can be demanded for a wide range of possible purposes such as: for admission to educational institutions; for good grades; for exam passes; and for the release of examination results. It has also been reported that children from certain communities were favoured for admission to schools, while others were subjected to extra payments. Another practice is that children have to pay for private tutoring in order to pass.[383] The demand for bribes by teachers and/or other

---

375 U4 Anti-Corruption Resource Centre, 'Corruption in the Education Sector', at p. 3; Pearson, 'An International Human Rights Approach to Corruption', at p. 57.

376 U4 Anti-Corruption Resource Centre, 'Corruption in the Education Sector', at p. 4.

377 *Ibid.* at p. 3, 5.

378 The ICHRP also argued that embezzlement in the education sector affects the availability component of the right to education. International Council on Human Rights Policy, *Corruption and Human Rights: Making the Connection* at p. 56 and 59.

379 General Comment No. 13, §6(b).

380 General Comment No. 3, §10.

381 General Comment No. 13, §57.

382 *Ibid.* §59.

383 U4 Anti-Corruption Resource Centre, 'Corruption in the Education Sector', at p. 3, 5.

school staff violates the principle of non-discrimination, as enshrined in Article 2(2) ICESCR because students who cannot afford these bribes are being denied access to the normal features of educational life. Discrimination takes place on the basis of property, or 'other status'.

Moreover, discrimination resulting from corrupt practices in schools has a clear gender dimension. The demand for bribes by teachers is particularly harmful to school girls in developing countries, since they might be forced to pay bribes by granting sexual favours. Needless to say this is highly problematic, and contributes to the spread of HIV/AIDS. In case of pregnancy, there is also a high chance that girls will quit their education.[384] Also, whenever monetary bribes are required to obtain school admission, parents might be more willing to pay bribes for their male children rather than for their female children, since the education of boys is still considered to be more important in certain parts of the world.[385]

What are the legal consequences of discrimination in the educational system on the basis of corruption? Nowak noted that:

> ... any unreasonable distinction [based on the prohibited grounds of Article 26 ICCPR] relating to the law and/or practice of education (access to education, dismissal, tuition and fees, subsidies, contents and quality of education etc.) constitutes a violation of Article 26 of the CCPR, and the victims of such discrimination have a right to submit a complaint to the Human Rights Committee provided the State concerned has ratified the First Optional Protocol to that Covenant.[386]

This offers victims of educational corruption, or their parents, a concrete opportunity to vindicate their rights.

Economic accessibility, or affordability, is another dimension of accessibility. It can overlap with other dimensions, such as non-discrimination.[387] As a result, a large number of corrupt practices identified above as a violation of the principle of non-discrimination also constitute impediments to the economic accessibility of education. The most striking example is of course the demand for bribes, which can

---

384 Namawu Alhassan Alolo, *Corruption, Human Rights and Gender: An Empirical Investigation Ghana* (Working Paper Geneva: International Council on Human Rights Policy, 2007) at §78 *et seq*; Nordic Consulting Group, *A Gender Analysis of Corruption – Forms, Effects and Eradication Strategies* (Study prepared for the Royal Danish Embassy in Uganda, September 2009) at p. 14; Maaria Seppänen and Pekka Virtanen, *Corruption, Poverty and Gender. With Case Studies of Nicaragua and Tanzania* (Finland Ministry for Foreign Affairs, 2008) at p. 138–139.

385 Alolo, *Corruption, Human Rights and Gender: An Empirical Investigation Ghana* at §81; Seppänen and Virtanen, *Corruption, Poverty and Gender. With Case Studies of Nicaragua and Tanzania* at p. 32.

386 Manfred Nowak, 'The Right to Education', in Asbjørn Eide, Catarina Krause, and Allan Rosas (eds.), *Economic, Social and Cultural Rights: A Textbook* (2nd edn.; Dordrecht: Martinus Nijhoff Publishers, 2001), 245–271 at p. 258.

387 General Comment No. 13, §6(b).

keep children out of school, and is contrary to the obligation of States to provide free and compulsory primary education.

Physical accessibility requires that education is within safe physical reach.[388] This feature may also be violated by corruption. Corruption in the procurement of school buildings can lead to distorted decision-making. Real educational needs may be neglected, resulting in the construction of school buildings at unsuitable locations, far from the target population. In these cases, the opportunities for self-enrichment of public officials prevail over the actual realisation of the right to education.

(iii) Acceptability

Acceptability means that education has to be acceptable to students and parents. For example, education has to be relevant, culturally appropriate and of good quality.[389] Due to corruption, education may no longer be acceptable. If educational funds are embezzled, and there are no resources left to pay proper teacher salaries, the quality of education may reach a substandard level.

(iv) Adaptability

Adaptability requires that education is flexible, in order to adapt to the needs of changing societies and communities and to respond to the need of students within diverse social and cultural settings.[390]

Other important principles in respect of the right to education are those of non-discrimination and equal treatment. These principles, which are immediately applicable to all aspects of education, are enshrined in Article 2(2) ICESCR.[391] In the Committee's view, States are bound to closely monitor education, including all relevant policies, institutions, programmes, spending patterns and other practices, in order to identify and take measures to redress any *de facto* discrimination.[392]

4.4.3. State Obligations and Violations

On a general note, the Committee stressed the duty of progressive realisation under the ICESCR, as well as the obligations of immediate effect. First, States have the obligation of non-discrimination (Article 2(2)). According to the Committee, the right to education is violated if a State fails to take measures to address *de facto* educational discrimination.[393] Since corrupt practices may constitute such

388 *Ibid.* §6(b).
389 *Ibid.* §6(c).
390 *Ibid.* §6(d).
391 *Ibid.* §31.
392 *Ibid.* §37.
393 *Ibid.* §59.

discrimination, the failure to take anti-corruption measures in education constitutes a violation of Article 13. Second, States have the immediate obligation to take deliberate, concrete and targeted steps (Article 2(1)).[394] The failure to take such steps towards the progressive realisation of secondary, higher and fundamental education in accordance with Article 13(2)(b)-(d) constitutes a violation of Article 13.[395] As elaborated upon earlier in the present chapter, retrogressive measures are presumed to be impermissible.[396]

In respect of the tripartite typology of the right to education, it is clear that States have to respect, protect and fulfil each of the AAAA-features of the right to education. The obligation *to respect* obliges States to avoid measures that hinder or prevent the enjoyment of the right to education.[397]

The obligation *to protect* requires States to take measures to prevent third parties from interfering with the enjoyment of the right.[398]

Under the obligation *to fulfil* (*facilitate*), States have to take positive measures to enable and assist individuals and communities to enjoy the right to education. The obligation *to fulfil* (*provide*) the right exists whenever individuals or groups are unable to realise the right themselves, for reasons beyond their control.[399] Under Article 13, States have the principal responsibility for the direct provision of education in most circumstances. However, the parameters of State obligations to fulfil (provide) are different for the respective levels of education.[400] *Inter alia*, the Committee clearly expressed that States have the legal obligation to fulfil (provide) the availability of education by actively developing a school system, building classrooms, delivering programmes, providing teaching materials, training teachers and paying them domestically competitive salaries.[401] However, as mentioned *supra* various corrupt practices constitute clear breaches of these obligations, violating the right to education.

As noted earlier, the Committee found that there is a minimum core obligation of States to ensure the most basic forms of education. Not only does this mean that States have to ensure the right of access to public education on a non-discriminatory basis, it also entails that States are obliged to provide primary education for all in accordance with Article 13(2).[402] Hence, whenever entrenched corruption leads to a State not meeting this obligation, there is a violation of the Covenant.

394 *Ibid.* §43 and 52.
395 *Ibid.* §59.
396 *Ibid.* §45.
397 *Ibid.* §47.
398 *Ibid.* §47.
399 *Ibid.* §47.
400 *Ibid.* §48 and 51.
401 *Ibid.* §50.
402 *Ibid.* §57.

4.5. The Right to Health

4.5.1. Introduction

The treaty bodies' concluding observations revealed the following about the connection between corruption and the right to health. The CRC paid attention to this topic on a number of occasions. For example, the observations on Pakistan (2003) stated that the Committee was 'extremely concerned' about the very poor health situation of children and the unavailability of children's health care services. As a particular matter of concern, the CRC listed, *inter alia*, 'the poor provision of health care, particularly in rural areas, owing to lack of necessary support structures such as education, communication, transport and other facilities, as well as reports of corruption within the framework of projects supported by international organizations.'[403] Moreover, in the observations on Kenya (2007), the CRC '*recommends* that the State party step-up anti-corruption measures relating to the management of funds for the health sector' [emphasis added, MB].[404] The observations on Benin (2006) also mentioned the impact of corruption on the resources available for children's health,[405] as did the observations on Congo (2006),[406] Bulgaria (2008),[407] and the Philippines (2009).[408] While one would have also expected some critical words from the CESCR, this body did not pay attention to the ways in which corruption affects the right to health. Hence, a further analysis of corruption in the light of Article 12 ICESCR is desirable.

From the reports of the Special Rapporteur on the right to health, we can learn that corruption and its impact upon the right to health is clearly on the agenda of this mandate. Amongst other things, it was stated that 'a right-to-health policy is also an anti-corruption policy',[409] and that the obligation to respect and to protect the right to health prompts States 'to take all appropriate action to combat corruption in the health sector'.[410]

Further exploration of the topic is desired since corruption is a major problem in health care. It is believed that the health sector is particularly vulnerable to corruption, since health sectors are complex in character, health markets are uncertain, and there is an asymmetry of information in the health sector (e.g.

---

403 CRC CO Pakistan 27 October 2003, UN Doc. CRC/C/15/Add.217, §52(e).
404 CRC CO Kenya 19 June 2007, UN Doc. CRC/C/KEN/CO/2, §48 (g).
405 CRC CO Benin 20 October 2006, UN Doc. CRC/C/BEN/CO/2, §17.
406 CRC CO Congo 20 October 2006, UN Doc. CRC/C/COG/CO/1, §14.
407 CRC CO Bulgaria 23 June 2008, UN Doc. CRC/C/BGR/CO/2, §16–17.
408 CRC CO Philippines 22 October 2009, UN Doc. CRC/C/PHL/CO/3–4, §19.
409 Report of the Special Rapporteur on the right to health, Mission to Mozambique, CHR 61st session, 4 January 2005, UN Doc. E/CN.4/2005/51/Add.2, §69.
410 *Ibid.* §70.

medical professionals *vis-à-vis* patients).[411] Meanwhile, the human rights aspects of health sector corruption are not yet fully acknowledged. In the foreword of the 2006 Global Corruption Report on corruption and health, Mary Robinson stated that 'the human rights community needs to pay even more attention to corruption. [...] Corruption – alongside poverty, inequity, civil conflict, discrimination and violence – is a major issue that has not been adequately addressed within the framework of [Article 12 ICESCR].'[412]

A number of scholars noted that 'in the health sector, corruption is literally a matter of life and death, if hospitals crumble because of embezzled construction funds, if doctors extort under-the-table payments from patients who cannot afford to pay, and if corrupt regulators allow fake drugs to flood markets.'[413]

Health sector corruption is receiving a growing deal of attention by anti-corruption researchers and practitioners,[414] but academic human rights research on corrupt practices and the right to health is more scarce. Yet, particularly valuable is the work done by Toebes, who also contributed to the ICHRP project.[415] The present section draws from, and elaborates upon, her analysis.

---

411 Brigit Toebes, 'Health Sector Corruption and Human Rights: A Case Study', in Martine Boersma and Hans Nelen (eds.), *Corruption and Human Rights: Interdisciplinary Perspectives* (Maastricht Series in Human Rights; Antwerp: Intersentia, 2010), p. 91–123 at p. 96–97.

412 Mary Robinson, 'Foreword', in Transparency International (ed.), *Global Corruption Report 2006: Corruption and Health* (London – Ann Arbor, Michigan: Pluto Press, 2006).

413 Taryn Vian, William D. Savedoff, and Harald Mathisen, 'Introduction: Closing Opportunities for Corruption in the Health Sector', in Taryn Vian, William D. Savedoff, and Harald Mathisen (eds.), *Anticorruption in the Health Sector: Strategies for Transparency and Accountability* (Sterling, VA: Kumarian Press, 2010), p. 3–15 at p. 4.

414 For more on corruption in the health sector, the following works are particularly recommended: Taryn Vian, William D. Savedoff, and Harald Mathisen (eds.), *Anticorruption in the Health Sector: Strategies for Transparency and Accountability* (Sterling, VA: Kumarian Press, 2010). Transparency International, *Global Corruption Report 2006: Corruption and Health* (London – Ann Arbor, Michigan: Pluto Press, 2006). U4 Anti-Corruption Resource Centre, 'Corruption in the Health Sector', *U4 Brief* (Bergen: Chr. Michelsen Institute, 2008).

415 Relevant publications include Brigit Toebes, 'Human Rights, Health Sector Abuse and Corruption', *Human Rights & Human Welfare working papers, no. 64* (1 April 2011); Toebes, 'Health Sector Corruption and Human Rights: A Case Study'; Toebes, 'The Impact of Acts of Corruption on the Enjoyment of the Right to Health'. Based on Toebes' work, the 2009 report of the ICHRP contains a section on the right to health, see International Council on Human Rights Policy, *Corruption and Human Rights: Making the Connection* at p. 51–55. Another report dealing with corruption and the right to health is Sunga and Bottigliero, 'In-Depth Study on the Linkages between Anti-Corruption and Human Rights for the United Nations Development Program', at p. 26–27.

4.5.2. Content

The right to health can be found in Article 12 ICESCR,[416] as well as in other international[417] and regional human rights treaties.[418] The CESCR's General Comment No. 14 is the most authoritative interpretation of Article 12 ICESCR to date.[419] Rather than a right to be healthy, the right to health consists of both freedoms and entitlements.[420] The concept of 'the highest attainable standard of health' takes into consideration a person's biological and socio-economic preconditions, as well as the resources available within a State. Therefore, the right to health is a right to the enjoyment of a variety of facilities, goods, services and conditions necessary for the realisation of the highest attainable standard of health.[421]

According to the Committee, both timely and appropriate *health care* is relevant, as well as *the underlying determinants of health.* Examples of such determinants are food and nutrition; housing; access to safe and potable water; adequate sanitation; safe and healthy working conditions; a healthy environment; access to health-related information and education; hospitals, clinics and other health-related buildings; trained medical and professional personnel receiving domestically competitive salaries; and essential drugs.[422] Toebes suggested that when looking at corruption in relation to the right to health, it is important to scrutinise not only the health care sector, but also other sectors such as water provision and the occupational and environmental health sectors.[423] Moreover, in the Committee's view, the population's participation in all health-related decision making at the community, national and international level is also important.[424]

---

416 Article 12 ICESCR: '1. The States parties to the present Covenant recognise the right of everyone to the enjoyment of the highest attainable standard of physical and mental health.
2. The steps to be taken by the States parties to the present Covenant to achieve the full realisation of this right shall include those necessary for:
(a) the provision for the reduction of the still-birth rate and of infant mortality and for the healthy development of the child;
(b) the improvement of all aspects of environmental and industrial hygiene;
(c) the prevention, treatment and control of epidemic, endemic, occupational and other diseases;
(d) the creation of conditions which would assure to all medical service and medical attention in the event of sickness.'

417 Article 25(1) UDHR; Article 24 CRC; Article 5(e)(iv) CERD; Article 11(1)(f) CEDAW.

418 Article 11 ESC; Article 10 Protocol of San Salvador; Article 16 AfChHPR.

419 Committtee on Economic, Social and Cultural Rights, General Comment No. 14 on the right to the highest attainable standard of health (Art. 12), twenty-second session (2000), UN Doc. E/C.12/2000/4. For a comprehensive discussion of the right to health, pre-dating the General Comment, see: Brigit Toebes, *The Right to Health as a Human Right in International Law* (School of Human Rights Research Series, 1; Antwerp: Intersentia, 1999).

420 General Comment No. 14, §8.

421 *Ibid.* §9.

422 *Ibid.* §4, 11 and 12(a).

423 Toebes, 'Health Sector Corruption and Human Rights: A Case Study', at p. 103.

424 General Comment No. 14, §11.

The CESCR set out four interrelated and essential elements of the right to health (also known as the 'AAAQ' framework), while the precise application of these elements will depend on the specific conditions in a State party.[425] As demonstrated below, each element of the right to health may be impaired by corrupt practices.

(i) Availability

Availability entails that States need to have a sufficient number of functioning public health and health-care facilities, goods, services and programmes, the exact nature of which will depend on various factors, such as a State's level of development. Nevertheless, they comprise the underlying determinants of health.[426] Availability is impaired by corruption in various ways. Embezzlement of funds intended for health care is an obvious example. Because of this practice, less resources are available, for example for salaries of medical staff, maintenance of hospitals, and the purchase of hospital equipment.[427] Whenever funds 'disappear' at the central level, this constitutes a violation of the obligation to devote the maximum available resources to the progressive realisation of the right to health, under Article 2(1) ICESCR. If resources are embezzled at the local level, States are under an obligation to combat corruption at this level. Also hampering availability is the diversion of drug supplies.[428]

(ii) Accessibility

Accessibility, requiring that health facilities, goods and services are accessible to all without discrimination, has four overlapping dimensions: non-discrimination, physical accessibility, economic accessibility (affordability), and information accessibility.[429]

Non-discrimination entails that health facilities, goods and services have to be accessible to all, particularly to the most vulnerable and marginalised groups.[430] In many cases this principle is legally enforceable at the domestic level.[431] Moreover, the guarantee of non-discrimination is a State obligation with immediate effect

---

425 *Ibid.* §12.

426 *Ibid.* §12(a).

427 Vian, Savedoff, and Mathisen, 'Introduction: Closing Opportunities for Corruption in the Health Sector', at p. 6. Toebes also noted that corruption affects the availability element. Toebes, 'Health Sector Corruption and Human Rights: A Case Study', at p. 6.

428 For more on drug diversion, and the prevention thereof, see Taryn Vian, William D. Savedoff, and Harald Mathisen, 'Preventing Drug Diversion through Supply Chain Management', in Taryn Vian, William D. Savedoff, and Harald Mathisen (eds.), *Anticorruption in the Health Sector: Strategies for Transparency and Accountability* (Sterling, VA: Kumarian Press, 2010), p. 77–84.

429 General Comment No. 14, §12(b).

430 *Ibid.* §12(b).

431 *Ibid.* §1 and endnote 1.

under Article 2(2) ICESCR.[432] As acknowledged by Special Rapporteur Paul Hunt, the poor are disproportionately affected by corruption, since they are less able to pay bribes for services that ought to be free, or to pay for private health care when corruption has depleted public health care.[433] Therefore, in the words of Hunt, corruption is inconsistent with the principles of non-discrimination and equality.[434] Similar arguments were made by Toebes, adding *inter alia* that women are also particularly vulnerable to corruption in health care, because of their reproductive functions.[435]

Physical accessibility requires that health facilities, goods and services are within safe physical reach for everyone, including vulnerable or marginalised groups.[436] According to Toebes, corruption in the health sector can lead to choices that are less favourable to the community (for example hospitals built in a cheaper, more distant area of the city, or rather in wealthy areas).[437]

Economic accessibility or *affordability* demands that health facilities, goods and services must be affordable to everyone.[438] Nevertheless, research shows that in many instances, bribes (or informal user fees or payments) have to be paid to health workers.[439] Underlying reasons for these bribes can be various: to gain access to health services which are supposed to be free of charge; to reduce waiting time; to receive drugs, treatment or hospital means; to ensure better attention and improved quality of treatment.[440] As demonstrated by the studies by the Special Rapporteur, the illicit charging of user fees hinders the economic accessibility of the right to health.[441] Demanding payments from patients for services that ought to be free impedes the affordability dimension of the right to health.[442]

---

432 *Ibid.* §30.

433 For example see Report of the Special Rapporteur on the right to health, GA 61st session, 13 September 2006, UN Doc. A/61/338, §79.

434 Report of the Special Rapporteur on the right to health, Mission to Romania, CHR 61st session, 4 February 2005, UN Doc. E/CN.4/2005/51/Add.4, §34.

435 Toebes, 'Health Sector Corruption and Human Rights: A Case Study', at p. 106–107.

436 General Comment No. 14, §12(b).

437 Toebes, 'Health Sector Corruption and Human Rights: A Case Study', at p. 107.

438 General Comment No. 14, §12(b).

439 For more on informal payments for health services, see Ottar Maestad and Aziza Mwisongo, 'Informal Pay and the Quality of Health Care: Lessons from Tanzania', in Taryn Vian, William D. Savedoff, and Harald Mathisen (eds.), *Anticorruption in the Health Sector: Strategies for Transparency and Accountability* (Sterling, VA: Kumarian Press, 2010), p. 45–53. and Kelly Miller and Taryn Vian, 'Strategies for Reducing Informal Payments', in Taryn Vian, William D. Savedoff, and Harald Mathisen (eds.), *Anticorruption in the Health Sector: Strategies for Transparency and Accountability* (Sterling, VA: Kumarian Press, 2010), p. 55–66.

440 U4 Anti-Corruption Resource Centre, 'Corruption in the Health Sector', at p. 12.

441 Report of the Special Rapporteur on the right to health, mission to Mozambique, CHR 61st session, 4 January 2005, UN Doc. E/CN.4/2005/51/Add.2, §45–52.

442 Report of the Special Rapporteur on the right to health, mission to India, HRC 14th session, 15 April 2010, UN Doc. A/HRC/14/20/Add.2, §52. Toebes also discussed the impact of corruption upon affordability: Toebes, 'Health Sector Corruption and Human Rights: A Case Study', at p. 107.

Access to information is the right to seek, receive and impart information and ideas about health issues.[443] According to the Special Rapporteur, health information enables individuals and communities to expose corruption.[444] Health care is prone to corruption because of the asymmetry in information: for example between doctors *vis-à-vis* patients.[445]

(ii) Acceptability

Acceptability requires that health facilities, goods and services respect medical ethics and are culturally appropriate. In addition, they must respect confidentiality and improve the health of the persons involved.[446] Toebes noted that, because of the asymmetry of information, the health sector professional has a stronger position than the patient. This could lead to a situation in which a health professional, being influenced by a pharmaceutical company, prescribes drugs which are not ethically appropriate.[447]

(iv) Quality

Quality means that health facilities, goods and services must be scientifically and medically appropriate and of good quality, requiring skilled medical personnel; scientifically approved and unexpired drugs and hospital equipment; safe and potable water and adequate sanitation.[448] The second paragraph of Article 12 ICESCR (which is non-exhaustive) provides guidance in defining the action that should be taken by States.[449]

Regarding the demand for bribes (informal payments) by health workers, researchers have found that this practice negatively affects the quality of health care. Amongst other things, health workers may be tempted to create artificial drug and supply shortages or queues in order to extort bribes from patients. Also, the quality of health care may be deliberately reduced by health workers (e.g. nurses), so as to induce their colleagues (e.g. doctors) to share their bribes with them.[450]

The issue of drug supply is an important topic in the discussion about corruption and the quality dimension of the right to health. The Special Rapporteur found that States have a legal obligation to ensure a reliable, efficient and transparent system for the supply of quality affordable medicines, and this supply system must avoid

---

443 General Comment No. 14, §12(b).

444 Report of the Special Rapporteur on the right to health, HRC 7th session, 31 January 2008, UN Doc. A/HRC/7/11, §40.

445 Toebes, 'Health Sector Corruption and Human Rights: A Case Study', at p. 108.

446 General Comment No. 14, §12(c).

447 Toebes, 'Health Sector Corruption and Human Rights: A Case Study', at p. 108.

448 General Comment No. 14, §12(d).

449 *Ibid.* §13.

450 Maestad and Mwisongo, 'Informal Pay and the Quality of Health Care: Lessons from Tanzania', at p. 48–50.

corruption.[451] The Rapporteur also pointed to endemic corruption in some medicine supply systems: products are diverted, 'fees' are required for customs clearance, and counterfeit medicines are permitted to circulate.[452] While diversion of drugs and the demand for fees are contrary to availability and accessibility, the problem of counterfeit or otherwise unsafe medicines clearly affects the quality dimension of the right to health. When regulators are bribed to allow these drugs to circulate, quality is impaired.[453]

(v) Accountability

While General Comment No. 14 does not extensively deal with the principles of accountability and participation, Toebes suggested that these principles are also relevant in the context of anti-corruption and the right to health.[454] As regards accountability, this comprises (i) monitoring; (ii) accountability mechanisms; (iii) remedies; and (iv) participation. Toebes suggested that the concept is closely linked to the State obligation to protect the right to health.[455]

(vi) Participation

The principle of participation requires that the public participates in the process of decision making in the health sector. This may improve transparency and reduce corruption vulnerabilities.[456]

4.5.3. State Obligations and Violations

(i) Immediate Obligations and Core Obligations

In defining the obligations of State parties, the CESCR recognised the difficulties States may have in progressively realising the right to health because of limited available resources. Nonetheless, there are various obligations with immediate effect: the principle of non-discrimination of Article 2(2) ICESCR and the obligation to take deliberate, concrete and targeted steps as required by Article 2(1)

---

451 Report of the Special Rapporteur on the right to health, GA 61st session, 13 September 2006, UN Doc. A/61/338, §68.

452 *Ibid.* §78.

453 Also noted by Toebes, 'Health Sector Corruption and Human Rights: A Case Study', at p. 109.

454 *Ibid.* at p. 106.

455 *Ibid.* at p. 109. For a further discussion of accountability in relation to health, see William D. Savedoff and Ethan Joselow, 'Budget Transparency, Civil Society and Public Expenditure Tracking Surveys', in Taryn Vian, William D. Savedoff, and Harald Mathisen (eds.), *Anticorruption in the Health Sector: Strategies for Transparency and Accountability* (Sterling, VA: Kumarian Press, 2010), p. 123–136.

456 Toebes, 'Health Sector Corruption and Human Rights: A Case Study', at p. 109–110.

ICESCR.[457] Moreover, deliberate retrogressive measures are, in general, not permitted.[458]

The Committee formulated a number of *core obligations* in relation to the right to health,[459] and a number of obligations of comparable priority.[460] Non-compliance with the non-derogable core obligations cannot be justified under any circumstance whatsoever.[461] According to the Committee, the core obligations include at least the obligations: (a) to ensure the right of access to health facilities, goods and services on a non-discriminatory basis, especially for vulnerable or marginalized groups; (b) to ensure access to the minimum essential food which is nutritionally adequate and safe, to ensure freedom from hunger to everyone; (c) to ensure access to basic shelter, housing and sanitation, and an adequate supply of safe and potable water; (d) to provide essential drugs, as defined under the WHO Action Programme on Essential Drugs; (e) to ensure equitable distribution of all health facilities, goods and services; and (f) to adopt and implement a national public health strategy and plan of action, on the basis of epidemiological evidence, addressing the health concerns of the whole population; the strategy and plan of action shall be devised, and periodically reviewed, on the basis of a participatory and transparent process; they shall include methods, such as right to health indicators and benchmarks, by which progress can be closely monitored; the process by which the strategy and plan of action are devised, as well as their content, shall give particular attention to all vulnerable or marginalized groups.[462] As already touched upon *supra* various corrupt practices may violate precisely these core obligations. For example, whenever States allow corruption to flourish in public hospitals, this directly violates the right of non-discriminatory access under (a). Amongst other things, the demand for bribes for medical services in public hospitals denies particular groups, i.e. the poor, access to treatment or to medicines. If corrupt practices occur in the drug supply chain, this may be contrary to (d).

Obligations of comparable priority are the obligations (a) to ensure reproductive, maternal (pre-natal as well as post-natal) and child health care; (b) to provide immunisation against the major infectious diseases occurring in the community; (c) to take measures to prevent, treat and control epidemic and endemic diseases; (d) to provide education and access to information concerning the main health problems in the community, including methods of preventing and controlling them;

457 General Comment No. 14, §30.

458 *Ibid.* §32.

459 General Comment No. 14, §43. For a more elaborate discussion of the core obligations of the right to health, see: Audrey R. Chapman, 'Core Obligations Related to the Right to Health', in Audrey R. Chapman and Sage Russell (eds.), *Core Obligations: Building a Framework for Economic, Social and Cultural Rights*, (Antwerp: Intersentia, 2002), 185–215.

460 General Comment No. 14, §44.

461 *Ibid.* §47.

462 *Ibid.* §43.

and (e) to provide appropriate training for health personnel, including education on health and human rights.[463] Again, corruption may violate these obligations.

As for the other rights enshrined in the ICESCR, the Committee elaborated upon the obligation to respect, to protect and to fulfil the right to health,[464] and provided illustrations of violations these obligations.[465] In the latter respect, the distinction between a State's inability or unwillingness to comply with its obligations should again be kept in mind. It is up to States to prove that they are unable, instead of unwilling, to comply with their obligations under Article 12 ICESCR.[466] Furthermore, violations can occur through direct action or through omission.[467] The following sub-sections discuss the obligations to respect, protect and fulfil, and how corruption may violate them.

(ii) The Obligation to Respect

Under the obligation to respect, States have to refrain from interfering (in)directly with the enjoyment of the right to health.[468] The General Comment contains a non-exhaustive list of twelve acts from which States ought to refrain.[469] In addition, examples are given of possible violations of the obligation to respect.[470] These are those State actions, policies or laws that contravene the standards of Article 12 and are likely to result in bodily harm, unnecessary morbity and preventable mortality.[471]

---

463 *Ibid.* §44.

464 *Ibid.* §33–37.

465 *Ibid.* §50–52.

466 *Ibid.* §47.

467 *Ibid.* §48–49.

468 *Ibid.* §33.

469 *Ibid.* §34. States are not allowed (i) to deny or limit equal access for everybody to preventive, curative and palliative health services; (ii) to enforce discriminatory practices as State policy; (iii) to impose discriminatory practices relating to women's health status and needs; (iv) to prohibit or impede traditional preventive care, healing practices and medicines; (v) to market unsafe drugs; (vi) to apply coercive medical treatments (unless in exceptional circumstances); (vii) to limit access to contraceptives and other means of maintaining sexual and reproductive health; (viii) to censor, withhold or intentionally misrepresent health-related information, including sexual education and information; (ix) to prevent people's participation in health-related matters; (x) to unlawfully pollute air, water and soil; (xi) to use or test nuclear, biological or chemical weapons if this results in the release of harmful substances; or (xii) to limit access to health services as a punitive measure.

470 General Comment No. 14, §50. Examples of violations of the right to health are (i) the denial of access to health facilities, goods and services to particular individuals or groups as a result of *de jure* or *de facto* discrimination; (ii) the deliberate withholding or misrepresentation of information vital to health protection or treatment; (iii) the suspension of legislation or the adoption of laws or policies that interfere with the enjoyment of any of the components of the right to health; and (iv) the failure of the State to take into account its legal obligations regarding the right to health when entering into bilateral or multilateral agreements with other States, international organisations and other entities, such as multinational corporations.

471 General Comment No. 14, §50.

Particularly relevant in the context of health sector corruption is that the Committee found that States have the obligation to refrain from denying or limiting equal access for all persons (including prisoners or detainees, minorities, asylum seekers and illegal immigrants) to preventive, curative and palliative health services.[472] In the Committee's view, States violate the obligation to respect the right to health, *inter alia*, when they deny access to health facilities, goods and services to certain individuals or groups as a result of *de jure* or *de facto* discrimination.[473] Since, for example, the demand for bribes in the public health care system is a form of unjustified discrimination in the access to health services, this form of corruption constitutes a violation of the obligation to respect the right to health.

Moreover, the Committee held that States should abstain from marketing unsafe drugs.[474] As shown above, corruption can have this effect. As elaborated upon in the reports of the Special Rapporteur on the right to health, corrupt acts can result in the entering on the market of unsafe or counterfeit medicines. Whenever this occurs due to corrupt public officials, this violates the obligation to respect. One a final note, it must be kept in mind that there are many more possible examples of corruption violating the obligation to respect the right to health.[475] Corrupt acts leading to a denial of the underlying determinants of health are also prohibited.

(iii) The Obligation to Protect

The obligation to protect the right to health entails that States have to take measures to prevent third parties from interfering with the guarantees of Article 12.[476] The General Comment lists a number of duties falling under the obligation to protect.[477] Violations of the obligation to protect occur whenever States fail to take all necessary measures to safeguard persons within their jurisdiction from

---

472 *Ibid.* §34.
473 *Ibid.* §50.
474 *Ibid.* §34.
475 For a useful overview, see Toebes, 'Health Sector Corruption and Human Rights: A Case Study', at p. 111.
476 General Comment No. 14, §33.
477 General Comment No. 14, §35. States are required (i) to adopt legislation or take other measures to ensure equal access to health care and health-related services provided by third parties; (ii) to ensure that privatisation of the health sector does not threaten the availability, accessibility, acceptability and quality of health facilities, goods and services; (iii) to control the marketing of medical equipment and medicines by third parties; (iv) to ensure that medical practitioners and other health professionals meet appropriate standards of education, skill and ethical codes of conduct; (v) to ensure that harmful social or traditional practices do not interfere with access to pre- and post-natal care and family planning; (vi) to prevent third parties from coercing women to undergo traditional practices; (vii) to take measures to protect all vulnerable or marginalised societal groups; and (viii) to ensure that third parties do not limit people's access to information and services related to health.

infringements of the right to health by third parties. A number of examples are also given.[478]

The Committee held that the obligation to protect obliges States, amongst others, to adopt legislation or take other measures to ensure equal access to health care and health-related services provided by third parties.[479] The failure to do so constitutes a violation.[480] One can argue that this encompasses the obligation for States to adopt legislation which criminalises corruption, including corruption in health care provided by non-State actors.

Another duty falling under the obligation to protect is the obligation to control the marketing of medical equipment and medicines by third parties.[481] Whenever third parties are *de facto* allowed to market unsafe drugs (e.g. in exchange for bribes to the responsible public officials), this obligation is violated.

Furthermore, States have to ensure that medical practitioners and other health professionals meet appropriate standards of education, skill and ethical codes of conduct.[482] It is obvious that health professionals do not act in accordance with medical ethical standards whenever they demand bribes from their patients. Thus, States ought to combat the demand for bribes by medical staff through legal and practical means. For example, the belief is regularly expressed that very low salaries in the health care sector bring about the necessity for medical staff to demand bribes.[483] Thus, in order to combat bribery, States ought to ensure adequate remuneration to those working in the medical profession.

Moreover, the obligation to protect the right to health is violated when States fail to enact or enforce laws to prevent the pollution of water, air and soil by extractive and manufacturing industries.[484] Pollution by extractive industries can be the result of the lax enforcement of environmental regulations, which can have its roots in the bribery of public officials by corporations. In return for personal gain, public officials can turn a blind eye to pollution. As discussed previously, access to safe and potable water and a healthy environment are underlying determinants of health, upon which pollution can have an impact. Whenever public officials practically allow third parties to pollute because of bribery, this constitutes a violation of the obligation to protect the right to health.

---

478 General Comment No. 14, §51. Examples of violations of the obligation to protect are the failure (i) to protect consumers and workers from practices detrimental to health, e.g. by employers and manufacturers of medicines or food; (ii) to discourage production, marketing and consumption of tobacco, narcotics and other harmful substances; (iii) to protect women against violence or to prosecute perpetrators; (iv) to discourage the continued observance of harmful traditional or cultural practices; (v) to enact or enforce laws to prevent the pollution of water, air and soil by extractive and manufacturing industries.

479 General Comment No. 14, §35.

480 *Ibid.* §51.

481 *Ibid.* §35.

482 *Ibid.* §35.

483 U4 Anti-Corruption Resource Centre, 'Corruption in the Health Sector', at p. 27. For further discussion of the role of salaries in relation to corruption, see Chapter 7 of this report.

484 General Comment No. 14, §51.

Again, many more examples are possible of how corruption may violate the State obligation to protect. Toebes argued that the obligation to protect obliges States to regulate, to monitor, to provide for accountability mechanisms, to provide for remedies, and to enable the public to participate.[485] She also specified particular obligations to protect the right to health, in relation to hospitals and in relation to healthworkers.[486]

(iv) The Obligation to Fulfil

The obligation to fulfil requires States to recognise the right to health in the national political and legal systems, preferably by way of legislative implementation, and to adopt a national health policy with a detailed plan for realising the right to health.[487] In the view of Toebes, this should also include an anti-corruption policy.[488] Furthermore, the General Comment lists a range of duties in respect of the obligation to fulfil.[489] Whenever States fail to take all necessary steps to ensure the realisation of the right to health, the obligation to fulfil is violated.[490] The Committee listed a range of possible violations.[491]

---

485 Toebes, 'Health Sector Corruption and Human Rights: A Case Study', at p. 112.

486 *Ibid.* at p. 113–114.

487 General Comment No. 14, §36.

488 Toebes, 'Health Sector Corruption and Human Rights: A Case Study', at p. 114.

489 General Comment No. 14, §36. Duties which are obligatory to be fulfilled include the duty (i) to ensure the provision of health care (including immunisation programmes against the major infectious diseases); (ii) to ensure equal access for all to the underlying determinants of health; (iii) to provide for sexual and reproductive health services, including safe motherhood, especially in rural areas; (iv) to ensure the appropriate training of doctors and other medical personnel; (v) to provide a sufficient number of hospitals, clinics and other health-related facilities; (vi) to ensure the promotion and support of the establishment of institutions providing counselling and mental health services, with due regard to equitable distribution throughout the country; (vii) to provide a public, private or mixed health insurance system affordable to all; (viii) to promote medical research and health education, as well as information campaigns, in particular with respect to HIV/AIDS, sexual and reproductive health, traditional practices, domestic violence, alcohol abuse and the use of cigarettes, drugs and other harmful substances; (ix) to adopt measures against environmental and occupational health hazards and against any other threat as demonstrated by epidemiological data; (x) to formulate, implement and periodically review a coherent national policy to minimize the risk of occupational accidents and diseases; and (xi) to provide a coherent national policy on occupational safety and health services.

490 General Comment No. 14, §52.

491 *Ibid.* §52. Examples of violations of the obligation to fulfil are the failure (i) to adopt or implement a national health policy designed to ensure the right to health to everyone; (ii) to have insufficient health expenditure or misallocation of public resources which results in the non-enjoyment of the right to health by individuals or groups, particularly the vulnerable or the marginalised; (iii) to monitor the realisation of the right to health at the national level (e.g. through the use of health indicators and benchmarks); (iv) to take measures to reduce the inequitable distribution of health facilities, goods and services; (v) to adopt a gender-sensitive approach to health; (vi) to lower infant and maternal mortality rates.

Furthermore, the distinction is made between the obligation to facilitate, to provide, and to promote. Under the obligation to fulfil (*facilitate*), States have to take positive measures to enable and assist individuals and communities to enjoy the right to health. They also have to fulfil (*provide*) a specific economic, social or cultural right whenever individuals or groups are themselves, for reasons beyond their control, unable to realise this by the means at their disposal. Under the obligation to fulfil (*promote*), States have to take actions that create, maintain and restore the health of the population. This includes (i) fostering recognition of factors that favour positive health results, such as research and information provision; (ii) ensuring that health services are culturally appropriate and that health care staff are trained to recognise and respond to the specific needs of vulnerable or marginalized groups; (iii) ensuring that the State meets its obligations in the supply of appropriate information relating to healthy lifestyles and nutrition, harmful traditional practices and the availability of services; and (iv) supporting people in making informed choices about their health.[492]

Violations of the obligation to fulfil occur, *inter alia*, whenever States fail to have insufficient health expenditure or misallocation of public resources which results in the non-enjoyment of the right to health by individuals or groups, particularly the marginalised.[493] Thus, embezzlement of financial or other resources intended for the realisation of the right to health (health budgets; medical supplies) clearly constitutes a violation of the right to health.

5. Towards a New Human Right to a Corruption-Free Society?

As touched upon *supra*in the General Introduction, a small number of authors argued in favour of a new human right to a corruption-free society. Questions can be raised (i) whether claims about the existence of such a right are legally valid; and (ii) whether such a separate right is both necessary and feasible, taking the analysis of the previous sections into account. Both questions will be addressed hereafter.

The proposal for a new human right to a corruption-free society was advanced by Kofele-Kale, and later supported in the work of Raj Kumar.[494] Kofele-Kale argued that:

> ... there is sufficient State practice to support a claim for an emerging international customary law prohibiting corruption in all societies. That is, a case can be made for the right to a corruption-free society as a fundamental human right; a right that should be recognized as a component part of the right to economic self-

492 General Comment No. 14, §37.

493 *Ibid.* §52.

494 See *inter alia* Raj Kumar, 'Corruption and Human Rights: Promoting Transparency in Governance and the Fundamental Right to Corruption-Free Service in India.'

> determination and the right to development. Alternatively, the right to a corruption-free environment can be viewed as a freestanding, autonomous right, if you will, a right in its own right.[495]

Kofele-Kale also made a case for 'treating a breach of this right as a crime under international law.'[496] Furthermore, he argued that 'the right to a society free of corruption is inherently a basic human right because life, dignity, and other important human values depend on this right. That is, it is a right without which these essential values lose their meaning.'[497] These are bold claims, deserving careful scrutiny.

As regards the assertion that the prohibition of corruption in all societies may be 'emerging customary law', this should be rejected. To begin with, a number of scholars argued that:

> … a device that is all too often used to blur the lines between *lex lata* and *lex ferenda* is that of 'emerging' human rights or 'emerging' interpretations of such rights. The term 'emerging' in this context may provide a smokescreen for wishful thinking and should be employed only sparingly.[498]

Likewise, claims about 'emerging customary law' ought to be critically analysed. The formation of a norm of customary law requires both State practice as well as *opinio juris*. State practice includes actual State activity (acts and omissions), statements made in concrete situations or disputes, statements of legal principle made in the abstract, domestic legislation and the practice of international organisations.[499] State practice needs to be constant and uniform, i.e. reasonably consistent.[500] Moreover, the practice must be fairly general, i.e. common to a significant number of States.[501] While there may be a wide range of global and regional anti-corruption treaties,[502] as well as domestic anti-corruption laws, it is

---

495 Ndiva Kofele-Kale, 'The Right to a Corruption-Free Society as an Individual and Collective Human Right: Elevating Official Corruption to a Crime under International Law', *The International Lawyer*, 34 (2000), p. 149–178 at p. 152.

496 Ndiva Kofele-Kale, 'The Right to a Corruption-Free Society as an Individual and Collective Human Right: Elevating Official Corruption to a Crime under International Law', *The International Lawyer*, 34 (2000), p. 149–178 at p. 152. Note that the claim about corruption as an international crime is further discussed in Part C *infra.*

497 *Ibid.* at p. 163.

498 Fons Coomans, Fred Grünfeld, and Menno T. Kamminga, 'A Primer', in Fons Coomans, Fred Grünfeld, and Menno Kamminga (eds.), *Methods of Human Rights Research* (Maastricht Series in Human Rights; Antwerp: Intersentia, 2009), p. 11–17 at p. 16.

499 Martin Dixon, *Textbook on International Law* (6th edn.; Oxford: Oxford University Press, 2007) at p. 31.

500 Permanent Court of International Justice, *Lotus Case* (1927), PCIJ Ser. A No. 10. See *Ibid.* at p. 31–32.

501 International Court of Justice, *Anglo-Norwegian Fisheries Case* (1951), ICJ Rep 116. See *Ibid.* at p. 32 *et seq.*

502 As discussed *supra*in chapter II.

by no means self-evident that these constitute enough general, uniform and consistent State practice to argue that corruption is prohibited all over the world. Moreover, it is unlikely that the required *opinio juris* is present. This requires that States act the way they do because they believe that the practice concerned is required by law.[503] Since most anti-corruption treaties contain non-binding, aspirational provisions and proper enforcement mechanisms are largely lacking, there is no reason to assume that States believe that corruption is prohibited. Moreover, there is no universal agreement on the content of the term 'corruption'. In order for a norm to be customary law, its content needs to be clear.

As noted, Kofele-Kale based the right to a corruption-free society on the right of people to exercise sovereignty over their natural resources and wealth (the right to economic self-determination), as laid down in common Article 1 ICCPR and ICESCR, and on the right to development. As regards the first aspect, it was argued that economic self-determination can be violated (i) when a State alienates the people's patrimony in its resources by granting corrupt or unwise concessions to foreign companies; and (ii) when it corruptly transfers the ownership of national wealth to a select number of powerful individuals.[504] Secondly, his claim is grounded in the right to development.[505] Yet, the existence of this right and its precise content is in itself a contended issue.

With respect to the argument that the right to a corruption-free society is inherently a basic human right because life, dignity, and other important human values depend on this right, this is most certainly an exaggerated statement. It is highly unlikely that life, dignity and other values are, in all cases, immediately affected by every instance of corruption. Such far-fetched claims do not help the anti-corruption discourse.

In sum, on the basis of the preceding legal analysis, Kofele-Kale's and Raj Kumar's claim to the existence, *de lege lata*, of a separate right to a corruption-free society can be dismissed. The question must now be addressed whether such a right ought to exist, *de lege ferenda*. These are the questions of necessity and feasibility. As regards necessity, it should be noted that adding new norms to the already elaborate human rights framework does not automatically lead to improved human rights protection. Already in 1984, Alston called for quality control in the conjuring up of new human rights, so as to avoid 'a serious devaluation of the human rights currency.'[506] As demonstrated in the previous sections of the present chapter, corruption can already be addressed in a proper manner by the existing human rights framework. Making use of internationally recognised human rights is much more sensible than drawing attention to corruption with a newly constructed right.

---

503 Dixon, *Textbook on International Law* at p. 34–36.

504 Kofele-Kale, 'The Right to a Corruption-Free Society as an Individual and Collective Human Right: Elevating Official Corruption to a Crime under International Law', at p. 165.

505 *Ibid.*

506 Philip Alston, 'Conjuring up New Human Rights: A Proposal for Quality Control', *American Journal of International Law*, 78 (1984), p. 607–621 at p. 614.

Moreover, as regards the element of feasibility, it is likely that such a new anti-corruption right will meet fierce opposition from States. Since there is not even international agreement on binding monitoring mechanisms to accompany anti-corruption treaties, the construction of a new human right to fight corruption (which has a legal as well as a strong moral component) will not be easily accepted by the community of States.

6. Concluding Remarks: The Merits and Limits of the Human Rights Approach to Corruption

6.1. General Conclusions

The study of the practice of the global and regional human rights monitoring mechanisms revealed that these bodies made the connection between corruption and human rights. Yet, since the precise links were far from clear, the current chapter aimed to demonstrate exactly *how* corrupt acts may violate specific human rights, both civil and political rights, as well as economic, social and cultural rights. By elaborating upon the specific content of human rights provisions enshrined in the ICCPR and the ICESCR, and by pointing out clear State obligations under these provisions, it was shown that corrupt practices may violate these obligations and hence constitute a violation of a number of rights: (i) the right to equality and non-discrimination; (ii) the right to equality before courts and tribunals and to a fair trial; (iii) rights of political participation; (iv) the prohibition of human trafficking; (v) the right of detainees to be treated with humanity and dignity; (vi) the right to freedom of movement; (vii) the right to food; (viii) the right to housing; (ix) the right to education; and (x) the right to health. Moreover, it was shown that corruption breaches several of the obligations captured in Article 2(1) ICESCR. Two disclaimers are necessary at this point. First, the study does not claim exhaustiveness: corrupt acts may also violate other rights. Also, generalisations ought to be avoided. Each case of corruption should be examined individually to ascertain whether there is a violation of a certain right. Hopefully the mentioned examples and the accompanying legal reasoning in this chapter may offer inspiration to those working in the field.

In the examination of a concrete case of corruption, it should be ascertained whether corruption violates State obligations to respect, to protect, or to fulfil human rights. Particularly in the field of economic, social and cultural rights this is the commonly used framework. Also, in respect of this category of rights the various components such as availability, accessibility, adaptability, acceptability, and quality should, whenever applicable, be tested in order to determine how corruption violates any of these components. From the examples given, it can be concluded that corruption severely hampers the mentioned aspects.

Now, one may ask what the added value is of framing corruption as a human rights violation. This is a legitimate question, deserving proper consideration. To begin with, it was mentioned that a clear advantage of showing that corruption can violate human rights is that this can influence public attitudes. Bringing in the moral dimension of human rights may lead to a wider support for anti-corruption initiatives, also among public officials, the judicial branch, the business sector, the media and the public at large.[507] Furthermore, the use of a human rights approach to corruption also offers a number of additional avenues from a legal and practical point of view. These are discussed below. Yet, while rejecting the main line of reasoning of Goodwin and Rose-Sender, who argued that corruption should be kept out of the human rights sphere altogether, one should acknowledge that the human rights approach to corruption does indeed have a number of important limitations, which are also dealt with below.

While it is recommended that the current human rights framework is employed to address corruption, the establishment of a new right to a corruption-free society should be rejected. There is not sufficient legal ground to argue that such a right already exists, and there is also no need to be in favour of this right. The present human rights provisions are very well capable of covering corrupt practices, and a new anti-corruption human right will not be met with enthusiasm by the community of States.

Article 35 UNCAC provides that States have to take measures to ensure that entities or persons who have suffered damage as a result of an act of corruption have the right to initiate legal proceedings against those responsible for that damage in order to obtain compensation.[508] In the spirit of this provision, the following sub-sections are devoted to possibilities to challenge corrupt acts by making use of human rights law.

6.2. Employing the UN Treaty Bodies

Since the present chapter argued that many cases of corruption may be clear-cut human rights violations, the human rights monitoring procedures available before the UN treaty bodies can be used to address corruption.[509] These are a welcome addition to the use of domestic criminal law to this end.

---

[507] International Council on Human Rights Policy, *Corruption and Human Rights: Making the Connection* at p. 5. and John Hatchard, 'Adopting a Human Rights Approach Towards Combating Corruption', in Martine Boersma and Hans Nelen (eds.), *Corruption & Human Rights: Interdisciplinary Perspectives* (Maastricht Series in Human Rights; Antwerp: Intersentia, 2010), p. 7–23 at p. 16. Also argued by Sunga and Bottigliero, 'In-Depth Study on the Linkages between Anti-Corruption and Human Rights for the United Nations Development Program', at p. 2.

[508] Also pointed out by International Council on Human Rights Policy, *Integrating Human Rights in the Anti-Corruption Agenda: Challenges, Possibilities and Opportunities* at p. 37.

[509] Also argued by International Council on Human Rights Policy, *Corruption and Human Rights: Making the Connection* at p. 5–6 and p. 72.

In the reporting procedure, the Committees should monitor how corrupt practices in the State concerned are affecting the human rights situation in the country, and whether States are making serious efforts to address corrupt practices. The individual complaints procedure, as available before the HRC, CEDAW, CAT, CERD, CMW and CRPD, offers opportunities for victims of corruption to complain about a specific violation of their rights as brought about by corrupt practices. The legal reasoning developed in this chapter may benefit the work of the Committees. Annex II to the present work contains a proposal for a draft General Comment on corruption and human rights. Since corruption affects the subject matter of all Committees, it is recommended for them to adopt a joint General Comment, something that has not been done before, but which will certainly prove to be useful. Particularly the Human Rights Committee and the Committee on Economic, Social and Cultural Rights should join forces to address corruption in a systematic and coherent fashion.

At the same time, an important issue of concern is the capacity of the treaty bodies to deal with corruption, *inter alia*, in the reporting procedure. As convincingly shown by Dowell-Jones in her 2004 study of the summary records of the CESCR on corruption, the Committee lacks the economic expertise that is required to properly consider complex economic problems such as corruption.[510] This is a concern that should be taken seriously, and which will not only apply to the CESCR, but also to the other treaty bodies. In part, this could be remedied by the supply of high-quality external information on corruption. Also the limited time for the examination of a State report may be a hindrance to in-depth discussions of corruption,[511] as well as the political sensitivity of the topic.[512]

As regards the possibility to submit an individual complaint about corruption to the treaty bodies, the requirement of the exhaustion of domestic remedies applies. While this protects the Committees against being overburdened, it does constitute a considerable practical and financial barrier to those affected by corruption. The poor will not easily challenge corrupt practices in court – although public interest litigation as discussed *infra* may offer a remedy in a number of instances.

6.3. The Role of the Human Rights Council: UPR and Special Procedures

As is the case to date, the UPR can be used by the State under review to provide other States with information about how it is dealing with problems of corruption. Other States can ask questions and formulate recommendations. Yet, we must bear in mind the political nature of the UPR mechanism. Furthermore, the Special Procedures are very well equipped to monitor the situation in countries over a

---

510 Mary Dowell-Jones, *Contextualising the International Covenant on Economic, Social and Cultural Rights: Assessing the Economic Deficit* (International Studies in Human Rights, 80; Leiden Martinus Nijhoff Publishers, 2004) at p. 81–96.

511 *Ibid.* at p. 93.

512 *Ibid.* at p. 83.

longer period of time, and to address recommendations to the State concerned. Nonetheless, as is the case with the treaty bodies, the mandate holders also need to be supplied with reliable third-party information on corruption.

6.4. Bringing Corruption Before Regional Human Rights Instances

The regional human rights instances, particularly the European Court of Human Rights, the Inter-American Commission on Human Rights, and the African Commission on Human Rights may examine complaints from individuals, alleging that corrupt practices constitute a violation of their rights under the applicable regional instrument. Given the content of the European Convention on Human Rights, complaints before the ECtHR can only concern violations of civil and political rights. What comes to mind first are cases in which the complainant holds that he or she did not receive a fair trial due to corruption in the judiciary. In addition, as is already the case, the regional human rights instances can rule about cases in which whistleblowers claim that their rights were violated, such as the right to freedom of expression.

An example of the successful use of a regional human rights court to address corruption is *SERAP v. Nigeria*, a case brought by Nigerian human rights NGO SERAP before the Community Court of Justice of West African States in Lagos, Nigeria (hereafter: ECOWAS CCJ). Citizens of ECOWAS member States can complain to the ECOWAS CCJ about human rights violations by State actors. Interestingly, there is no requirement of the exhaustion of local remedies.[513] In *SERAP v. Nigeria*, the complaint brought by SERAP concerned the embezzlement of funds for basic education by high-level Nigerian government authorities.[514] As evidence, a report by Nigeria's Independent Corrupt Practices Commission (ICPC) was submitted. SERAP argued that the embezzlement of educational funds infringed the right to education. According to the ECOWAS CCJ, the right to education is justiciable under the African Charter on Human and Peoples' Rights. Moreover, the Court held that the embezzlement of education funds has a negative impact on the right to education, since less money is available for the provision of education.[515] Therefore, the Court ordered Nigeria to 'take the necessary steps to provide the money to cover the shortfall to ensure a smooth implementation of the education programme, lest a section of the people should be denied a right to education.'[516]

---

513 For more on the ECOWAS CCJ, see <www.courtecowas.org>, accessed 2 August 2011.

514 ECOWAS Community Court of Justice, Judgment *The Registered Trustees of the Socio-Economic Rights and Accountability Project (SERAP) v. The Federal Republic of Nigeria and Universal Basic Education Commission (UBEC)*, 30 November 2010, ECW/CCJ/APP/12/07; ECW/CCJ/JUD/07/10. The judgment can be found at <www.worldcourts.com/ecowasccj/eng/decisions/2010.11.30_SERAP_v_Nigeria.htm>, accessed 2 August 2011.

515 *Ibid.* §19.

516 *Ibid.* §28.

6.5. Domestic Human Rights Litigation

Also at the national level, there are several possibilities to combat corruption by making use of human rights. Domestic human rights litigation is an important route. One option is the use of the human rights provisions contained in domestic constitutions, which – in many countries – can be enforced by Courts. As argued by Hatchard, if a judge is bribed by one of the parties in a dispute, the other party may submit a complaint to, for example, the Constitutional Court to complain about a violation of his right to a fair trial, as enshrined in the constitution. Hatchard found that such an approach has a number of benefits: (i) because the claimant controls the development of the constitutional case and the government cannot lawfully prevent the matter from being brought before the court, the chance of political interference (at least in the open) is reduced; (ii) since constitutional cases are generally dealt with by the Constitutional Court or another high-level court, there may be a lower chance of corruption at that instance, since these courts are occupied by the most senior and experienced judges; (iii) the rules of evidence in constitutional cases are less tight than in criminal law cases; (iv) in many constitutional cases, there is assistance available for persons who want to bring such a case, and a wider range of persons may bring a case, possibly allowing for NGOs to bring a case, and offering opportunities for public interest litigation; and (v) significant damages may be awarded, since the case is brought against the State.[517]

As noted above, the possibility of public interest litigation (hereafter: PIL) should be emphasised. PIL entails that the court itself or a private party other than the victim may bring a case. This is for instance possible before the Supreme Court in India. Victims of corrupt practices may want to bring a case but are often unable to do so when they are poor. Civil society organisations working in the field of anti-corruption and/or human rights could then bring the case to court. Moreover, under PIL in India, the Supreme Court deals with good governance and accountability of public officials. For example, in *Vineet Narain vs. Union of India*, journalist Narain and three other persons filed a petition, arguing that the country's Central Bureau of Investigation should have proceeded with a case concerning bribes given to a number of high-ranking politicians and bureaucrats, in return for favours in the award of government contracts. The case resulted in directions given by the Supreme Court to the Central Bureau of Investigation, holding that it should continue with investigating the high-level corruption case. This resulted in 34 charge sheets filed against 54 persons.[518]

Nonetheless, there are also a number of considerable difficulties when it comes to domestic human rights litigation in general. For a successful case, high quality

---

517 Hatchard, 'Adopting a Human Rights Approach Towards Combating Corruption', at p. 17–18.

518 Ashok H. Desai and S. Muralidhar, 'Public Interest Litigation: Potential and Problem', in B.N. Kirpal (ed.), *Supreme but Not Infallible: Essays in Honour of the Supreme Court of India* (New Delhi: Oxford University Press, 2000), p. 159. Version available online <http:www.ielrc.org/content/a0003.pdf>, p. 11–12, accessed 19 July 2011.

evidence is required, as well as good cooperation between victims, lawyers and human rights advocates. Also, a professional legal team is necessary, for which financial means are needed. In addition, the legislation on which the victim relies may be poorly drafted, and the court itself may be corrupt. Procedures may take a considerable period of time. Moreover, the persons who are most urgently in need of protection are often those who have the least access to expensive and time-consuming procedures.[519]

Another problem when it comes to domestic human rights litigation is the possible non-justiciability of economic, social, and cultural rights. While a number of constitutions and other legislation do include this category of rights, this is not the case in all countries. Moreover, even if socio-economic rights are included, they may be considered non-justiciable before national courts.[520]

As regards both domestic human rights litigation, as well as the submission of individual complaints to the treaty bodies, the issue of causality should not be overlooked. In concrete cases, mainly if petty corruption is involved, it may be comparatively easy to link a specific corrupt act to a human rights violation, for instance in those cases where bribes are demanded by judges, school teachers and hospital doctors. Yet, it will be very difficult for an individual to prove that his or her right was violated by an act of grand corruption. While, for example, the embezzlement of funds at a country's Ministry of Education may indeed have resulted in a lack of school equipment and the non-payment of teacher salaries, an individual student can usually not bring such a case to court, stating that his right to education is violated. The causal link between the act of grand corruption and the human rights violation is in most cases impossible to prove.[521] Hence, individual human rights claims flowing from grand corruption are not likely to be successful, also because hard evidence of high-level corruption is generally covered up and almost impossible to obtain for an individual citizen.

6.6. National Human Rights Institutions (NHRIs)

Another possibility for addressing corruption at the national level is the use of National Human Rights Institutions (hereafter: NHRIs).[522] Council of Europe

519 International Council on Human Rights Policy, *Corruption and Human Rights: Making the Connection* at p. 74; International Council on Human Rights Policy, *Integrating Human Rights in the Anti-Corruption Agenda: Challenges, Possibilities and Opportunities* at p. 38.

520 For more on this topic, see Fons Coomans (ed.), *Justiciability of Economic and Social Rights. Experiences from Domestic Systems* (Maastricht Series in Human Rights, Antwerp: Intersentia, 2006). Also interesting is Obiajulu Nnamuchi, 'Kleptocracy and Its Many Faces: The Challenges of Justiciability of the Right to Health Care in Nigeria', *Journal of African Law*, 52 (2008), p. 1–42.

521 This was also noted by Toebes, 'Health Sector Corruption and Human Rights: A Case Study', at p. 122–123.

522 The suggestion to use NHRIs in the fight against corruption was also brought forward by International Council on Human Rights Policy, *Corruption and Human Rights: Making the*

Commissioner for Human Rights Hammarberg, recognising that corruption is major human rights problem, sees a role for ombudsmen and other independent national human rights structures, and noted that this is already the case in Georgia, Armenia and Latvia.[523] Moreover, some NHRIs, such as the Commission on Human Rights and Administrative Justice in Ghana, even have a specific mandate on anti-corruption.[524] Even if that is not the case, victims of corruption may complain to such a Commission about a violation of their rights. For many people, this will be a much more accessible option than complaining at the regional or international level.[525] Hatchard argued that the investigative and remedial powers of the Commissions can offer great benefits to those complaining about corruption.[526]

Apart from dealing with individual complaints, many NHRIs issue reports on human rights matters, which can also include corruption. For example, the Kenyan National Commission on Human Rights (hereafter: KNCHR) released thematic reports on corruption,[527] one of which was written in cooperation with Transparency International Kenya,[528] and another one together with the Kenya Land Alliance.[529] Interestingly, the KNCHR noted that its 'involvement in advocacy on issues of corruption has been met with criticism because corruption is not seen as a human rights issue. The issue was precipitated by the need to enlighten society on the nexus between corruption and human rights.'[530] The KNHRC is clearly of the view that corruption is a violation of human rights, and takes an interest in working in this area.[531] Other NHRIs may also take up the issue, and cooperate with national anti-corruption bodies.

Connection at p. 70 and by MORTEN KJAERUM, 'Breaking the Vicious Cycle: Corruption and Poverty; Obstacles to Social and Economic Rights. A Human Rights Based Bottom-up Approach.' *12th International Anti-Corruption Conference* (Guatemala City and Antigua, Guatemala, 2006) at p. 2–3. For more on NHRIs in general, see INTERNATIONAL COUNCIL ON HUMAN RIGHTS POLICY, *Performance & Legitimacy: National Human Rights Institutions* (2nd edn.; Versoix, Switzerland, 2004).

523 THOMAS HAMMARBERG, 'Corruption Is a Major Human Rights Problem', *CommDH/Speech(2009)9* (Strasbourg, 5 October 2009).

524 HATCHARD, 'Adopting a Human Rights Approach Towards Combating Corruption', at p. 19.

525 Note that for a complaint to be lodged at the regional or international level, usually the requirement of exhaustion of domestic remedies also applies, posing another practical and financial barriers for those who are victims of corrupt practices.

526 HATCHARD, 'Adopting a Human Rights Approach Towards Combating Corruption', at p. 20–22.

527 The first was a thematic issue on corruption and human rights of the KNCHR's journal, see KENYA NATIONAL COMMISSION ON HUMAN RIGHTS, *Nguzo za Haki: a publication of the KNCHR*, 3 (February 2005).

528 KENYA NATIONAL COMMISSION ON HUMAN RIGHTS and TRANSPARENCY INTERNATIONAL KENYA, 'Living Large: Counting the Cost of Official Extravagance in Kenya', (2005).

529 KENYA NATIONAL COMMISSION ON HUMAN RIGHTS and KENYA LAND ALLIANCE, 'Unjust Enrichment: The Making of Land Grabbing Millionares', (2006).

530 As noted on its website <www.knchr.org/index.php?Itemid=85&id=73&option=com_content&task=view>, accessed 19 July 2011.

531 MAINA KIAI, 'Corruption Is a Violation of Human Rights', *Nguzo za Haki: a publication of the KNCHR*, 3 (February 2005), p. 4–7.

6.7. Cooperation between Human Rights Actors and Anti-Corruption Organisations

Cooperation between human rights institutions and organisations (including treaty bodies and Special Rapporteurs as well as NHRIs) and anti-corruption organisations (such as TI and the World Bank) may be fruitful.[532] One the one hand, corruption is becoming a concern of human rights advocates (which is the main argument of the present thesis), whose fight for the protection of these rights is strengthened if corruption is addressed. Yet, in order to do so effectively, they will need the knowledge of anti-corruption specialists. On the other hand, anti-corruption organisations can make use of human rights language and actions in their work.[533] The ICHRP pointed to various ways in which cooperation between the two may be useful. *Inter alia*, collaboration could raise awareness; it could help to enforce existing legislation and to advocate for new laws and codes of conduct; budget analysis could be conducted; public contracting and international aid can be monitored; and litigation may be conducted together.[534]

532 Dowell-Jones, *Contextualising the International Covenant on Economic, Social and Cultural Rights: Assessing the Economic Deficit,* at p. 95.

533 For more on this topic, see International Council on Human Rights Policy, *Integrating Human Rights in the Anti-Corruption Agenda: Challenges, Possibilities and Opportunities.* See also Sunga and Bottigliero, 'In-Depth Study on the Linkages between Anti-Corruption and Human Rights for the United Nations Development Program', at p. 36–39.

534 International Council on Human Rights Policy, *Corruption and Human Rights: Making the Connection* at p. 69–76.

Part C

Individual Responsibility: Corruption as a Crime under International Law?

CHAPTER VII
SITUATING CORRUPTION WITHIN INTERNATIONAL CRIMINAL LAW

1. INTRODUCTION

While Part B focused on *State* responsibility for corruption by examining the human rights dimension, Part C is concerned with *individual* responsibility for acts of corruption, i.e. the possibilities to hold those who commit corrupt acts accountable under international criminal law. The objects of study are persons belonging to the State apparatus, i.e. public officials, not private individuals or companies.[1]

Before looking into several specific offences codified in the Rome Statute, it is of primary importance to consider first whether or not international criminal law is an appropriate and desirable mechanism to combat corruption and, if so, which forms of corruption would qualify for such an approach.

A first step that needs to be taken is clarifying the notions of 'international criminal law' (*largo sensu* and *stricto sensu*) and 'transnational criminal law', and of the concepts of 'international crimes', 'crimes under international law', and 'transnational crimes' (section 2).

Furthermore, a concise study of the historical roots of international criminal law is needed, so as to ascertain whether attention has been paid to corruption in this area of law. The various stepping stones in the development of international criminal law are discussed, including the developments before and after the First World War, after the Second World War, and in the final decade of the twentieth century. Most importantly, the developments leading up to the establishment of the International Criminal Court (hereafter: ICC) are analysed, as well as the *travaux préparatoires* of the Rome Statute. This may reveal whether or not the inclusion of economic crimes such as corruption was at any point considered by the drafters (section 3).

Moreover, one should pay attention to the underlying rationales of international criminalisation, in order to determine whether it would make proper sense to criminalise corrupt offences at the international plane, even if this is not self-evident from the preceding historical analysis (section 4).

In addition, the objectives of punishment in international criminal law have to be considered, so as to reflect on whether these objectives can be met by criminalising forms of corruption at the international plane (section 5).

If one arrives at the conclusion that combating corruption would indeed fit within the system of international criminal law, it has to be determined which forms of corruption – as identified *supra* in chapter I of Part A – qualify for criminalisation at the international level (section 6). Finally, section 7 draws conclusions from the foregoing, providing the foundation for subsequent chapters.

---

1 This does not imply that the private sector – especially multinational corporations – should be exempt from scrutiny. However, this matter falls outside of the scope of the present research.

2. Key Concepts

2.1. ICL *largo sensu*: ICL *stricto sensu* and Transnational Criminal Law

Since various scholars have defined 'international criminal law' differently, the terminology used in the present Part C has to be clarified at the outset, in order to avoid any conceptual confusion. Central to the discussion is the fact that the notion of 'international criminal law' can be defined in either a broad or a narrow manner: *largo sensu* or *stricto sensu.*

To begin with, Bassiouni employed a rather broad definition: in his view 'international criminal law' includes the criminal law aspects of international law, as well as the international aspects of national criminal law.[2] This can be labelled international criminal law *largo sensu*, covering both direct and indirect systems of enforcement: prosecutions of crimes by international tribunals, and by domestic authorities based on treaties.[3] Hence, Bassiouni lists ten penal characteristics of international criminal law. In his view, the existence of any of the following characteristics in a certain international convention makes the proscribed conduct part of international criminal law in the broad sense: (i) explicit recognition of proscribed conduct as constituting an international crime, or a crime under international law, or a crime; (ii) implicit recognition of the penal nature of the act by establishing a duty to prohibit, prevent, prosecute, punish, or the like; (iii) criminalisation of the proscribed conduct; (iv) duty or right to prosecute; (v) duty or right to punish the proscribed conduct; (vi) duty or right to extradite; (vii) duty or right to cooperate in prosecution, punishment (including judicial assistance in penal proceedings); (viii) establishment of a criminal jurisdictional basis (or theory of criminal jurisdiction or priority in criminal jurisdiction); (ix) reference to the establishment of an international criminal court or an international tribunal with penal characteristics (or prerogatives); and (x) elimination of the defence of superior orders.[4]

However, other scholars, such as Werle and Cryer, used a more narrow definition of 'international criminal law', also known as *Völkerstrafrecht*, *droit international pénal*, or *derecho internacional penal*. In this view, international criminal law *stricto sensu* 'encompasses all norms that establish, exclude, or otherwise regulate responsibility for crimes under international law.'[5] It does not cover the international

---

2 M. Cherif Bassiouni, 'The Sources and Content of International Criminal Law: A Theoretical Framework', in M. Cherif Bassiouni (ed.), *International Criminal Law: Crimes* (2nd edn., I; Ardsley, New York: Transnational Publishers, 1999), p. 3–125 at p. 8–9.

3 Obviously, the Rome Statute itself is also a treaty. Whenever the expression 'treaty (based) crime' is used, this refers to a treaty which obliges States to criminalise certain conduct at the domestic level. See section 2.2 hereafter.

4 M. Cherif Bassiouni, *Introduction to International Criminal Law*, ed. M. Cherif Bassiouni (International and Comparative Criminal Law Series; Ardsley, New York: Transnational Publishers, 2003) at p. 115. See also Bassiouni, 'The Sources and Content of International Criminal Law: A Theoretical Framework', at p. 46–48.

5 Gerhard Werle, *Principles of International Criminal Law* (The Hague: TMC Asser Press, 2009) at p. 29, §83; Robert Cryer *et al.*, *An Introduction to International Criminal Law and Procedure* (Cambridge: Cambridge University Press, 2007) at p. 3.

aspects of national criminal law, thus limiting itself to the direct enforcement mechanisms at the international level.

The international aspects of national criminal law are captured in the notion of 'transnational criminal law', or *Internationales Strafrecht, droit pénal international,* or *derecho penal internacional,* referring to 'those parts of a State's domestic criminal law which deal with transnational crimes, that is, crimes with actual or potential transborder effects'.[6] When using the term transnational criminal law, this refers to the treaty-based crimes which do not necessarily fall under the ICC's jurisdiction. Thus, international criminal law *largo sensu* covers both international criminal law *stricto sensu*, and transnational criminal law.[7]

As elaborated upon in chapter II *supra* it is clear that corruption forms part of transnational criminal law, since various international and regional treaties impose obligations on States to, *inter alia*, criminalise corruption at the national level and to offer mutual legal assistance. However, the main question here is whether international criminal law *stricto sensu* also offers avenues to combat corruption. The present work therefore uses the narrow definition of international criminal law, as employed amongst others by Werle and Cryer. The typical feature of this branch of law, as compared to traditional public international law, is that individuals can be held responsible at the international plane, instead of States. This constitutes a shift away from the sole focus on State conduct.[8]

2.2. International Crimes: Crimes under International Law and Transnational Crimes

The concepts of 'international crimes' and 'crimes under international law' should also be defined, because sometimes these terms are used interchangeably, while in other instances they are considered to be distinct concepts. The present work adopts the latter view, as explained hereafter.

'Crimes under international law' are the crimes which involve direct individual criminal responsibility under international law. Thus, they are directly punishable under international law, notably by the ICC. This differs from the broader notion of 'international crimes'. 'International crimes' also include so-called 'treaty-based crimes' or 'transnational crimes': crimes that have to be criminalised by States at the domestic level, pursuant to an obligation laid down in an international treaty (e.g. the UNCAC). Hence, both 'crimes under international law' and 'treaty-based crimes' are part of the concept of 'international crimes', as demonstrated by figure 4 below.[9]

---

6 Cryer *et al.*, *An Introduction to International Criminal Law and Procedure*, at p. 4.

7 See also Neil Boister, ''Transnational Criminal Law'?' *European Journal of International Law*, 14 (2003), p. 953–976. for more on the distinction between international criminal law *stricto sensu* and transnational criminal law.

8 Werle, *Principles of International Criminal Law*, at p. 3, §2.

9 *Ibid.* at p. 42, §114. See also Robert Cryer, 'The Doctrinal Foundations of International Criminalization', in M. Cherif Bassiouni (ed.), *International Criminal Law: Sources, Subjects,*

Interestingly, on the basis of the previously discussed list of the ten penal characteristics of international criminal law, Bassiouni has drawn up an inventory of twenty-eight offences which he considers to be international crimes. Given his broad view on international criminal law, this list includes both crimes under international law as well as treaty-based crimes. These are: (1) aggression; (2) genocide; (3) crimes against humanity; (4) war crimes; (5) unlawful possession and/or use of weapons; (6) theft of nuclear materials; (7) mercenarism; (8) apartheid; (9) slavery and slave-related practices; (10) torture and other forms of cruel, inhuman or degrading treatment; (11) unlawful human experimentation; (12) piracy; (13) aircraft hijacking and unlawful acts against international air safety; (14) unlawful acts against the safety of maritime navigation and the safety of platforms on the high seas; (15) threat and use of force against internationally protected persons; (16) crimes against UN and associated personnel; (17) taking of civilian hostages; (18) unlawful use of the mail; (19) attacks with explosives; (20) financing of terrorism; (21) unlawful traffic in drugs and related drug offences; (22) organised crime; (23) destruction and/or theft of national treasures; (24) unlawful acts against certain internationally protected elements of the environment; (25) international traffic in obscene materials; (26) falsification and counterfeiting; (27) unlawful interference with international submarine cables; and (28) bribery of foreign public officials.[10]

On the basis of his five criteria for international criminalisation (see section 4.2 hereafter), Bassiouni placed the twenty-eight offences into three hierarchical categories. To this end, he also drew a parallel with domestic criminal law systems, which have established a hierarchy of crimes on the basis of: (i) the social interest to be protected; (ii) the harm which has to be averted; (iii) the intrinsic seriousness of the violation; (iv) the dangerousness of the transgressor manifested by the commission of a given transgression; (v) the degree of general deterrence sought to be manifested; (vi) the policy of criminalisation; and (vii) the policy choices reflected in the opportunity of criminal prosecution. By taking these factors into account, it is possible to categorise each of the 28 international crimes in one of three groups: international crimes; international delicts; and international infractions.[11]

International crimes are the crimes listed under (1) to (11): the present thesis labels these offences as 'crimes under international law'. They are 'those international criminal law normative proscriptions whose violation is likely to affect the peace and security of humankind or is contrary to fundamental humanitarian values, or which is the product of State actions or a State-favouring policy.'[12]

---

and Contents (3rd edn., I; Leiden: Martinus Nijhoff, 2008), p. 107–128 at p. 108–109. For a clear discussion of the difference between 'core' crimes and transnational crimes.

10 Bassiouni, *Introduction to International Criminal Law*, at p. 116–117. See also Bassiouni, 'The Sources and Content of International Criminal Law: A Theoretical Framework', at p. 48 *et seq.* which contains a list of 25 international crimes. Bassiouni has recently added the crimes of attacks with explosives, financing of terrorism, and organised crime.

11 Bassiouni, *Introduction to International Criminal Law*, at p. 120.

12 *Ibid.* at p. 121.

International delicts, which are lower in the hierarchy, are the crimes numbered (12) to (24), and can be defined as 'those international criminal law normative proscriptions that affect an international protected interest, and whose commission involves more than one State or harms victims from more than one State.'[13]

International infractions, which we find at the bottom of the hierarchy, are the crimes (25) to (28). These are simply 'those international criminal law normative violations not included in the categories of 'international crimes' and 'international delicts''.[14]

In the author's opinion, Bassiouni's list of 28 international crimes, based on the ten penal characteristics, needs to be brought up to date. The only type of corruption that is seen by Bassiouni as a crime in conventional international criminal law is bribery of foreign public officials. However, several of the ten penal characteristics also apply to other types of corruption. As demonstrated in chapter II, there are many treaties, most notably the UNCAC, which fulfil a number of the mentioned characteristics: for example, there is a duty to prohibit, prevent, prosecute and punish corruption (i.e. characteristic no. (ii)); and there are provisions on international cooperation (i.e. characteristic no. (vii)). Hence, other types of corruption should be added to the list of international crimes, since they are treaty-based crimes.

Furthermore, concerning the nature of the offences that are on Bassiouni's list of international crimes it can be observed that, in his view, a number of crimes, i.e. (21), (23), (24), (25), (26) and (28) affect social, cultural and economic interests, and also have a human rights dimension.[15] Still, it was noted that:

> … instruments of an economic nature, or those concerning economic and social matters, such as bribery of foreign public officials, falsification or counterfeiting and international traffic in obscene materials, seem to be the least in number, and contain the least number of penal provisions. The international harm from these crimes may well be perceived as being of a lesser qualitative level than that from other crimes, and the drafters may be wary of the limits of international enforcement in this area.[16]

Furthermore, in the ranking of international crimes, offences against life and personal safety and well-being precede those affecting social, economic, cultural, and other interests.[17] Moreover, it was stated that economic interests are perceived as the least important of the international interests that international criminal law aims to protect, and for this reason, protection of economic interests, with respect to crimes that are not part of *ius cogens*, has the lowest rank on the list of international crimes. They are considered as being merely international infractions.[18]

---

13 *Ibid.* at p. 122–123.

14 *Ibid.* at p. 123–124.

15 Bassiouni, 'The Sources and Content of International Criminal Law: A Theoretical Framework', at p. 46.

16 *Ibid.* at p. 54.

17 *Ibid.* at p. 58.

18 Bassiouni, *Introduction to International Criminal Law*, at p. 133.

These observations deserve further scrutiny. Is it actually true that crimes affecting economic and social interests are by their nature less harmful than the other crimes on Bassiouni's list? When comparing the crime of falsification or counterfeiting with, for example, genocide or crimes against humanity, it does indeed make sense that the harm resulting from the latter crimes is far more serious than the harm caused by the first. However, we should not underestimate the harm done by economic crimes such as corruption. As elaborated upon in chapter I *supra* the political, economic, social and environmental consequences of corrupt practices are severe in many respects. Moreover, as shown in Part B, corruption can violate both civil and political, as well as economic, social and cultural human rights. The notion of 'harm' in international criminal law is discussed further in section 4.2 hereafter.

In sum, corruption clearly is a treaty-based or transnational crime, forming part of transnational criminal law. However, the present piece aims to examine whether it can also be conceptualised as a crime under international law, thus falling under international criminal law *stricto sensu*. To this end, the current chapter takes account of the history of international criminal law, its rationales for criminalisation, and its objectives of punishment.

Figure 4. The system of international criminal law largo sensu and international crimes

3. Corruption in International Criminal Law from a Historical Perspective

The question whether corruption would fit within the framework of international criminal law can be considered from a historical perspective. Rather than providing an extensive overview of the evolution of this area of law, which has already been done by others, it is more useful for the present purpose to analyse on which occasions attention has been paid to economic crimes, such as corruption, throughout the history of international criminal law.

3.1. Developments until World War I

International criminal law norms have a number of early precedents. Certain rules, mostly on warfare, were already present in the systems of ancient civilisations of the Middle East, China, India, and Greece, and were further developed during the Middle Ages and beyond.[19] Much later, the first treaty obliging States to punish individuals who have committed 'unnecessary cruelty and acts of barbarism against the enemy' was the final Protocol produced by the 1874 Brussels Conference.[20] In the field of norm development, the Geneva Conventions of 1864, 1906 and 1929 deserve to be mentioned,[21] as well as the Hague Conventions of 1899 and 1907.[22] However, these instruments are directed towards States and do not place direct criminal responsibility upon individuals under international law.

As regards the enforcement of rules on warfare, several trials are noteworthy, such as the prosecution of Sir William Wallace by an English court in 1305, which is the earliest recorded trial of an individual for war crimes. However, Peter von

19 *Ibid.* at p. 25–29; Robert Cryer, *Prosecuting International Crimes: Selectivity and the International Criminal Law Regime* (Cambridge: Cambridge University Press, 2005) at p. 11–17. See also Timothy L.H. McCormack, 'From Sun Tzu to the Sixth Committee: The Evolution of an International Criminal Law Regime', in Timothy L.H. Mccormack and Gerry J. Simpson (eds.), *The Law of War Crimes: National and International Approaches* (The Hague: Kluwer Law International, 1997), p. 31–63.

20 This document was signed by 15 European States, but never ratified. Ronald C. Slye and Beth van Schaack, *International Criminal Law: The Essentials* (New York: Aspen Publishers, 2009) at p. 19. Paragraph III of the Protocol of the Brussels Conference stated: 'The laws and customs of war not only forbid unnecessary cruelty and acts of barbarism committed against the enemy; they demand also, on the part of the appropriate authorities, the immediate punishment of these persons who are guilty of these acts, if they are not caused by an absolute necessity.'

21 First Geneva Convention for the Amelioration of the Condition of the Wounded and Sick in Armed Forces in the Field (1864); Second Geneva Convention for the Amelioration of the Condition of the Wounded, Sick and Shipwrecked Members of Armed Forces at Sea (1906); Third Geneva Convention relative to the Treatment of Prisoners of War (1929).

22 Hague Convention of 1899; Hague Convention of 1907.

Hagenbach's trial in Austria in 1474 is often mentioned in this respect.[23] Furthermore, the trial of Conradin von Hohenstaufen in 1268 is another historic prosecution for international war crimes.[24] Henry Wirz' trial in 1865 is also a well-known example of an early prosecution for violations of the laws and customs of war.[25]

From this quick glance into early norm development and enforcement,[26] we can learn that the origins of international criminal law are rooted in situations of armed conflict and focus upon the punishment of individuals for their misbehaviour during such conflicts.

3.2. Post-World War I

After the first World War, the Paris Peace Conference aimed to peacefully settle the disputes arising out of the war, and to this end, the Conference appointed the 1919 Commission on the Responsibility of the Authors of the War and on Enforcement of Penalties (hereafter: the Commission), in order to inquire into the causes of and responsibilities for the war. The Commission, which was the first modern international investigative body of its kind, reported to the Conference about its findings.[27]

Inter alia, the Commission compiled a list of (groups of) crimes as a basis for the future collection of information about these crimes. The list specified offences in violation of the laws and customs of war. For the purpose of the present study, it is interesting to note that this list, consisting of 32 offences, also included offences that do not inherently consist of physical violence, but are rather of an economic or property nature: pillage; confiscation of property; exaction of illegitimate or exorbitant contributions and requisitions; and debasement of currency[28] Particularly

---

23 Slye and Schaack, *International Criminal Law: The Essentials,* at p. 18–19. For example, Greppi refers to Von Hagenbach's trial as the earliest trial for war crimes, see Edoardo Greppi, 'The Evolution of Individual Criminal Responsibility under International Law', *International Review of the Red Cross*, no. 835 (1999), p. 531–553. For more on the Von Hagenbach trial, see Cryer, *Prosecuting International Crimes: Selectivity and the International Criminal Law Regime* at p. 17–21.

24 Bassiouni, *Introduction to International Criminal Law*, at p. 24, footnote 91.

25 Slye and Schaack, *International Criminal Law: The Essentials*, at p. 19–20.

26 When describing the development of international criminal law, a distinction can be made between norm development and the development of the direct enforcement system. Bassiouni, *Introduction to International Criminal Law*, at p. 25.

27 M. Cherif Bassiouni, 'World War I: "The War to End All Wars" And the Birth of a Handicapped International Criminal Justice System', *Denver Journal of International Law and Policy*, 30 (2002), p. 244–291 at p. 253–254.

28 Commission on the Responsibility of the Authors of the War and on Enforcement of Penalties, 'Report Presented to the Preliminary Peace Conference, March 29, 1919', *American Journal of International Law*, 14 (1920), 95–154. See also Remigiusz Bierzanek, 'War Crimes: History and Definition', in M. Cherif Bassiouni (ed.), *International Criminal Law: Enforcement* (2nd edn., III; Ardsley, New York: Transnational Publishers, 1999), 87–108 at p. 90.

the offence of 'exaction' bears resemblance to corruption. It is not a violent offence which one would normally associate with war, but an economic crime.[29] Nonetheless, it is categorised by the Commission as a war crime. Moreover, the crimes listed by the Commission fall within the meaning of war crimes under law and custom and the 1907 Hague Convention.[30] However, Sandoz noted that 'although the list is somewhat interesting historically, it cannot be viewed as the result of a serious and systematic work of scholarship carried out to show established doctrine or State practice'. This can be explained by the fact that the process of the identification of war crimes was driven by facts first, and after that legal labels were given to practices of specific concern.[31]

As a result of the Paris Peace Conference, the Treaty of Versailles came into being, which provided for prosecution of the German emperor Wilhelm II before an ad hoc international criminal tribunal, and for the prosecution by the Allied military courts of other Germans accused of war crimes.[32]

Concluding, it is obvious that the post-World War I efforts in the field of international criminal law were the result of the atrocities committed during the war. Hence, the focus is on war crimes, which may also include the 'exaction of illegitimate or exorbitant contributions and requisitions', as stated in the list compiled by the 1919 Commission. This may support the idea that ICL does leave some room for the inclusion of economic crimes, albeit related to war.

3.3. Post-World War II

Following the horrors of the Second World War, the United Nations War Crimes Commission (hereafter: UNWCC) was established by the Allied Powers in 1942 to investigate and obtain evidence of war crimes.[33] Subsequently, the London Agreement was concluded in 1945, which contained as an annex the Charter of the

---

29 See James W. Garner, 'Contributions, Requisitions, and Compulsory Service in Occupied Territory', *American Journal of International Law*, 11 (1917), p. 74–112.

30 Bassiouni, 'World War I: "The War to End All Wars" And the Birth of a Handicapped International Criminal Justice System', at p. 261.

31 Yves Sandoz, 'The History of the Grave Breaches Regime', *Journal of International Criminal Justice*, 7 (2009), p. 657–682 at p. 668–669.

32 Articles 227, 228 and 229 of the Treaty of Peace Between the Allied and Associated Powers and Germany, concluded at Versailles, June 28, 1919. Reprinted in M. Cherif Bassiouni (ed.), *International Criminal Law: Enforcement* (2nd edn., III; Ardsley, New York: Transnational Publishers, 1999) at p. 66 (Appendix 1). For more on the background of these provisions, see Bassiouni, 'World War I: "The War to End All Wars" And the Birth of a Handicapped International Criminal Justice System', at p. 268–274. However, the German emperor fled to the Netherlands, which refused to extradite him, and as a result, he was never prosecuted and the international tribunal was never set up. Moreover, the prosecution of other German war criminals by the Allied Powers never took place. Rather, the Germans themselves carried out a limited number of prosecutions before the Supreme Court in Leipzig.

33 M. Cherif Bassiouni, 'International Criminal Investigations and Prosecutions: From Versailles to Rwanda', in M.Cherif Bassiouni (ed.), *International Criminal Law: Enforcement* (2nd edn.,

International Military Tribunal at Nuremberg (hereafter: Nuremberg Charter).[34] The relevance of this instrument, whose principles are now considered to be customary law, cannot be overstated easily: it has been labelled 'the birth certificate of international criminal law'.[35] Under Article 6 of the Nuremberg Charter, crimes against peace, war crimes, and crimes against humanity were criminalised, entailing *individual* responsibility under international law. The definitions of these crimes in Article 6 do not include any offences resembling corruption.

Furthermore, the Allied Control Council Law No. 10 (hereafter: CCL 10) permitted the Allies to prosecute Germans in their respective occupational zones. This was similar to the Nuremberg Charter, except for crimes against humanity: the connection to the initiation of war or to war crimes was removed.[36]

Also set up in 1945 was the Far Eastern Commission (hereafter: FEC), a political body which aimed to establish a policy of occupation for Japan and to coordinate the policies of the Allies in the Far East. The Supreme Commander for the Allied Powers in Japan, General MacArthur, who controlled occupational matters, promulgated an order which established the International Military Tribunal for the Far East: the Tokyo Tribunal. Dissimilar from the Nuremberg Tribunal, it was not set up by a treaty.[37] The Tokyo Tribunal had jurisdiction to prosecute Far Eastern war criminals for crimes against peace, conventional war crimes, or crimes against humanity (Article 5).[38]

Again, in the aftermath of another world war, international criminal law was directed towards the atrocities committed during armed conflict, and there is no clear evidence of attention paid to economic crimes. The same is true for the Statutes of the International Criminal Tribunal for the Former Yugoslavia (hereafter: ICTY)[39] and the International Criminal Tribunal for Rwanda (hereafter: ICTR).[40] The ICTY has jurisdiction over grave breaches of the 1949 Geneva Conventions; violations of the laws or customs of war, genocide, and crimes against humanity (Articles 2–5 ICTY Statute).[41] All of these crimes within the jurisdiction of the ICTY, except genocide, have to be committed in the context of an armed

III; Ardsley, New York: Transnational Publishers, 1999), p. 31–86 at p. 39. As noted by Bassiouni, the UNWCC was not related to the United Nations, the organisation founded in 1945.

34 Charter of the International Military Tribunal, Annexed to the London Agreement, 1945.

35 Werle, *Principles of International Criminal Law*, at p. 7, §15–16.

36 Bassiouni, 'International Criminal Investigations and Prosecutions: From Versailles to Rwanda', at p. 45–46.

37 *Ibid.* at p. 47.

38 See R. John Pritchard, 'The International Military Tribunal for the Far East and the Allied National War Crimes Trials in Asia', in M. Cherif Bassiouni (ed.), *Ibid.*, p. 109–146.

39 The ICTY was set up by SC Resolution 808, UN SCOR, 48th session, UN Doc. S/RES/808 (1993).

40 The ICTR was set up by SC Resolution 955, UN SCOR, 49th session, UN Doc.S/RES/955 (1994).

41 Bassiouni, 'International Criminal Investigations and Prosecutions: From Versailles to Rwanda', at p. 56.

conflict.[42] Furthermore, the ICTR has jurisdiction over genocide,[43] crimes against humanity,[44] and violations of common Article 3 of the 1949 Geneva Conventions and of Additional Protocol 2.[45] These crimes have to have been committed between January 1 and December 31, 1994.[46] Hence, the jurisdiction of both the ICTY and the ICTR is limited to violent crimes, committed during conflict situations. *Prima facie*, crimes of an economic nature do not seem to be covered by the Statutes.

Apart from the ad hoc ICTY and ICTR and the permanent ICC (see section 3.4 hereafter), the post-World War II era witnessed the establishment of a number of other institutions dealing with crimes under international law. These are the so-called 'hybrid' courts and other internationalised domestic courts and tribunals: the Special Court for Sierra Leone; the Extraordinary Chambers of Cambodia; Kosovo Regulation 64 Panels; East Timor Special Panels for Serious Crimes; the Bosnia War Crimes Chamber; the Special Tribunal for Lebanon; the Iraqi High Tribunal; and the Serbian War Crimes Chamber.[47] These institutions all aim to respond to extraordinary situations of armed conflict, dealing with violent crimes. Economic crimes are not considered as such.

3.4. The International Criminal Court

3.4.1. Developments Leading to the ICC's Establishment

Even though the setting up of the ICTY and the ICTR in the 1990s has provided an important impetus for the ultimate establishment of the ICC,[48] initiatives to create a permanent international criminal court were launched much earlier. The idea for the development of an international criminal court was already expressed by the 1919 Commission. Also, in 1920 the Committee of Jurists, meeting in The Hague for the preparation of a draft Statute for the Permanent Court of International Justice, adopted a *voeu* which recommended the creation of a separate High Court of International Justice 'competent to try crimes constituting a breach of international public order or against the universal law of nations.' However, the Council of the League of Nations was not enthusiastic about this idea. Subsequently,

42 Bartram S. Brown, 'The International Criminal Tribunal for the Former Yugoslavia', in M. Cherif Bassiouni (ed.), *Ibid.*, p. 489–518 at p. 493 *et seq.*

43 Article 2 ICTR Statute.

44 Article 3 ICTR Statute.

45 Article 4 ICTR Statute.

46 Article 7 ICTR Statute. See Larry D. Johnson, 'The International Criminal Tribunal for Rwanda', in M. Cherif Bassiouni (ed.), *International Criminal Law: Enforcement* (2nd edn., III; Ardsley, New York: Transnational Publishers, 1999), p. 549–565.

47 Malcolm N. Shaw, *International Law* (6th edn.; Cambridge: Cambridge University Press, 2008) at p. 417–430; Werle, *Principles of International Criminal Law*, at p. 26, §76–78.

48 M. Cherif Bassiouni, 'Historical Survey: 1919–1998', in M. Cherif Bassiouni (ed.), *International Criminal Law: Enforcement* (2nd edn., III; Ardsley, New York: Transnational Publishers, 1999), p. 597–635 at p. 617.

in 1922, the International Law Association favoured the creation of an international criminal court, and drafted a proposed statute for such an institution. Furthermore, in 1925 the Interparliamentary Union also considered a proposal to bestow criminal jurisdiction upon the Permanent Court of International Justice. Additionally, an International Congress of Penal Law in 1926 adopted a resolution which favoured the exercise of criminal jurisdiction by an international court. Moreover, the 1920s saw a number of publications on the topic of an international criminal court.[49]

In 1937, the Convention for the Creation of an International Criminal Court saw the light of day within the context of the League of Nations.[50] This Court would solely have jurisdiction over the enforcement of the 1937 Terrorism Convention. The Convention was signed by 13 countries, but it never entered into force because India was the only country to ratify it.[51] The initiative again reveals the focus upon violent crime such as terrorism.

After the Second World War, the newly established United Nations aimed to set up a permanent international criminal court. In this respect, it is important to distinguish two sets of efforts: (i) to draw up a code of international crimes; and (ii) to draft a statute for an international criminal court. As noted by Bassiouni, these efforts remained separated because of a lack of political will to join them.[52] The following paragraphs briefly describe both developments.

In the area of codification of international criminal law (ad (i)), the Committee on the Codification of International Law (the predecessor to the International Law Commission, hereafter: ILC) was mandated in 1947 by the General Assembly (hereafter: GA) to formulate the principles of international law recognised in the Nuremberg Charter and in the judgments of the Nuremberg Tribunal, and to prepare a Draft Code of Offences Against the Peace and Security of Mankind.[53] To this end, a subcommittee was formed, and a Special Rapporteur was appointed.[54] In 1954, the ILC submitted its Draft Code of Offences to the GA.[55]

The 1954 Draft Code of Offences Against the Peace and Security of Mankind stated in Article 1 that offences against the peace and security of mankind are crimes under international law, for which the responsible individuals shall be punished. When analysing the nature of the offences laid down in the Draft Code, listed in Article 2,[56] we find that the first nine acts all concern action by State

---

49 Manley O. Hudson, 'The Proposed International Criminal Court', *American Journal of International Law*, 32 (1938), p. 549–554 at p. 549–551.

50 Convention for the Creation of an International Criminal Court, 16 November 1937, League of Nations Doc. C.547(I).M.384(I).1937.v (1938).

51 For more on the 1937 Convention, see Hudson, 'The Proposed International Criminal Court',.

52 Bassiouni, 'Historical Survey: 1919–1998', at p. 608.

53 GA Res. 174, UN GAOR, 2nd session, UN Doc. A/519 (1947).

54 First report completed in 1950, Report of the International Law Commission, UN GAOR, 5th session, UN Doc. A/CN.4/25 (1950). Bassiouni, 'Historical Survey: 1919–1998', at p. 608–609.

55 GA Res. 898 (IX), UN GAOR, 9th session, Supp. No. 21, at 50, UN Doc. A/2890 (1954).

56 Article 2 of the 1954 Draft Code of Offences lists: (1) aggression; (2) the threat to resort to aggression; (3) the preparation by State authorities of the employment of armed force against

authorities. The crimes listed all infringe classic rules on international peace and security. The acts listed under (10), (11) and (12) can also be committed by individuals. These acts, which are now known as genocide, crimes against humanity, and war crimes, are all violent crimes. Crimes of an economic nature are not included in the 1954 Draft Code.

Concerning the drafting of a statute for an international criminal court (ad (ii)), the GA mandated a Special Rapporteur to formulate a draft statute for the establishment of an international criminal court, who concluded that a substantive criminal code and such a statute should complement each other. As noted above, this did not happen. In 1950, the GA appointed another Special Rapporteur on the matter, and set up a Special Committee, consisting of 17 State representatives, to draft a convention for the establishment of an international criminal court. This Special Committee finished its task in 1951, but after an extension of the Committee's mandate, a revised Draft Statute was submitted to the GA in 1953. However, because at that time, the Draft Code of Offences was not yet finished, the GA wanted to wait for that document, which was completed in 1954 (as described *supra*. But the 1954 Draft Code was tabled because the offence of 'aggression' could not be defined. The GA took the task of defining aggression away from the ILC, and gave it to a Special Committee of the GA. The latter Committee eventually defined aggression much later, in 1974.[57]

In 1978, NGOs put pressure on the GA to take up the issue of a Draft Code again. In 1980, the GA mandated the ILC to work on the matter. In 1982, the first report on the Draft Code of Offences was produced by a new ILC rapporteur, and in 1991 an intended final text came into being. After criticisms on this report by governments and scholars, the text was revised and adopted by the ILC in 1996.[58]

---

another State; (4) (the encouragement of) the organisation by State authorities of armed bands within its territory or any other territory for incursions into the territory of another State; (5) the undertaking or encouragement by State authorities of activities calculated to foment civil strife in another State, or the toleration by States of organised activities to this end; (6) the undertaking or encouragement by State authorities of terrorist activities in another State, or the toleration by States of organised activities to this end; (7) violations of treaty obligations designed to ensure international peace and security by means of restrictions or limitations on armaments, or on military training, or on fortifications, or of other restrictions of the same character; (8) the annexation by a State authorities of territory of another State; (9) the intervention by State authorities in the internal or external affairs of another State, by means of coercive measures of an economic or political character in order to force its will and thereby obtain advantages of any kind; (10) genocide committed by State authorities or by private individiduals; (11) inhuman acts committed by State authorities or by private individuals; (12) acts in violation of the laws or customs of war; (13) conspiracy, incitement, complicity and attempt to commit any of the offences in the preceding sections of Article 2.

57 Bassiouni, 'Historical Survey: 1919–1998', at p. 609–611.

58 *Ibid.* at p. 611–612. For a further explanation of the Draft Code of Crimes, see M. Cherif Bassiouni, 'The Draft Code of Crimes against the Peace and Security of Mankind', in M.Cherif Bassiouni (ed.), *International Criminal Law: Crimes* (2nd edn., I; Ardsley, New York: Transnational Publishers, 1999), 293–310.

This 1996 Draft Code of Crimes of Against the Peace and Security of Mankind[59] contained a number of crimes against the peace and security of mankind, which are, according to Article 1, crimes under international law. These crimes are aggression (Article 16); genocide (Article 17); crimes against humanity (Article 18); crimes against United Nations and associated personnel (Article 19); and war crimes (Article 20). Article 20(e)(v) states that plunder of public or private property, whenever committed in a systematic manner or on a large scale, is a war crime, if committed in violation of the laws and customs of war. Under Article 20(f)(vi), pillage is also a war crime, if committed in a systematic manner or on a large scale, and in violation of international humanitarian law applicable in non-international armed conflict.

The efforts for the establishment of an international criminal court were renewed in 1989, when the GA held a special session on the topic of drug trafficking. Sixteen Caribbean and Latin American countries, led by Trinidad and Tobago, spoke out in favour of establishing a specialised international criminal court on this matter. Subsequently, the ILC was requested by the GA to prepare a report on setting up an international criminal court for the prosecution of persons engaged in drug trafficking.[60] This is interesting because drug trafficking is an offence which does not have to be related to armed conflict, and is in itself not a violent crime. As demonstrated by the historical overview in the present section, and as noted by Starr, international criminal law is primarily focused upon armed conflict. The fact that the GA has placed the issue of drug trafficking within the context of possibly setting up an international criminal court reveals that international criminal law can serve much broader purposes than responding to conflict and violence.[61]

It is also noteworthy that in 1990, an NGO expert committee, chaired by Bassiouni, prepared a draft statute for an international criminal tribunal with jurisdiction over all international crimes.[62] These international crimes are listed in the Code of Offences which is annexed to the expert committee's draft statute. In the view of the expert committee, the international criminal tribunal should also have jurisdiction over treaty-based crimes (transnational crimes). The unofficial text of the draft statute was submitted to the Eighth UN Congress on Crime Prevention and the Treatment of Offenders, which recognised the need for such a court and recommended that the ILC take up the matter.[63] Although this is in itself

---

59 Draft Code of Crimes Against the Peace and Security of Mankind: Titles and Articles on the Draft Code of Crimes Against the Peace and Security of Mankind, adopted by the International Law Commission on its forty-eight session, UN GAOR, 51st session, UN Doc. A/CN.4L.532, rev'd by UN Doc. A/CN.4L.532/Corr.1 and UN Doc. A/CN.4L/532/Corr.3.

60 Bassiouni, 'Historical Survey: 1919–1998', at p. 613.

61 Sonja Starr, 'Extraordinary Crimes at Ordinary Times: International Justice Beyond Crisis Situations', *Northwestern University Law Review,* 101 (2007), p. 1257–1314 at p. 1270.

62 UN Doc. A/Conf.144/NGO.7, Draft Statute: International Criminal Tribunal (1990), item 5, reprinted in 15 *Nova Law Review*, p. 375 (1991).

63 M. Cherif Bassiouni, 'Historical Survey: 1919–1998', in M. Cherif Bassiouni (ed.), *International Criminal Law: Enforcement* (2nd edn., III; Ardsley, New York: Transnational Publishers, 1999),

not related to the efforts of Bassiouni's expert committee, it is interesting to observe that the Eighth UN Congress – already in 1990 – adopted a resolution on corruption in government,[64] and also developed a manual on practical measures against corruption.[65]

In 1990, the ILC completed its report on the establishment of an international criminal court, which was not limited to drug trafficking, and submitted this to the GA. The GA encouraged the ILC to continue, and the ILC started with a preliminary report in 1992, a comprehensive text in 1993, and a modified text in 1994. The latter document was submitted to the 49th session of the GA, which set up the 1995 Ad Hoc Committee for the Establishment of an International Criminal Court, to discuss the proposal. The report of the Ad Hoc Committee became the basis for the establishment of the 1996 Preparatory Committee (hereafter: PrepCom), which also relied on the ILC's 1994 Draft Statute, and modified this. Subsequently, the Prepcom had to prepare a consolidated text for an international criminal court for the diplomatic conference to be held in Rome, June 15 – July 17, 1998.[66] Ultimately, the Rome Statute of the International Criminal Court was adopted on 17 July 1998, and it entered into force on 1 July 2002.[67] Currently, 116 countries are Party to the Rome Statute.[68]

3.4.2. Travaux Préparatoires of the Rome Statute

(i) UN Compilation

At this point, it is interesting to examine whether offences of an economic nature, such as corruption, were at any point taken into consideration during the Rome

597–635 at p. 614; Michael P. Scharf, 'The Draft Statute for an International Criminal Court', in M. Cherif Bassiouni (ed.), *International Criminal Law: Enforcement* (2nd edn., III; Ardsley, New York: Transnational Publishers, 1999), p. 637–653 at p. 639.

64 Eight United Nations Congress on the Prevention of Crime and the Treatment of Offenders, Havana, 27 August – 7 September 1990, UN Doc. A/CONF.144/28/Rev.1. The resolution on corruption in government can be found on p. 136 *et seq.*

65 Eight United Nations Congress on the Prevention of Crime and the Treatment of Offenders, Practical measures against corruption; manual prepared by the Secretariat. UN Doc. A/CONF.144/8, 29 May 1990.

66 Bassiouni, 'Historical Survey: 1919–1998', at p. 614–616. For more on the Rome Conference, see Cherif Bassiouni, 'Historical Survey: 1919–1998', at p. 625–633. For a compilation of the most important documents of *inter alia* the International Law Commission, the PrepCom, and the Ad Hoc Committee, see M. Cherif Bassiouni, *The Statute of the International Criminal Court: A Documentary History* (Ardsley, New York: Transnational Publishers, 1998).

67 Rome Statute for the International Criminal Court, adopted by the United Nations Diplomatic Conference of Plenipotentiaries on the Establishment of an International Criminal Court on 17 July 1998.

68 United Nations Treaty Collection, Status of Treaties Database, <http://treaties.un.org/Pages/ViewDetails.aspx?src=IND&mtdsg_no=XVIII-10&chapter=18&lang=en>, accessed 26 July 2011.

Conference of 1998, either by State Parties or by NGOs. To this end, it is imperative to study the *travaux préparatoires* of the Conference, i.e. the official records of the negotiations on the Rome Statute, which resulted in the following information.[69]

Upon examination of the summary records, as contained in Volume II of the *travaux*, we find the following remark by the Libyan delegate:

> In addition to so-called aggression and so-called terrorism, the Court might deal with drug trafficking, insults to religion, violation of humanitarian values, forbidding of religious rites, white slavery, organized crime, involvement of children in war, violence and prostitution, *economic and financial crimes*, aggression against the environment and other threats' [emphasis added, MB].[70]

The summary records reveal no further discussion on the matter of economic or financial crimes.

Furthermore, the *travaux* reveal that Cuba has made a proposal to include as a crime against humanity 'other inhumane acts, such as economic, financial and commercial blockades intentionally causing great suffering or seriously injuring physical integrity or mental or physical health.'[71] Like corruption, the topic of economic embargoes has an economic nature. As shown by the summary records, the Cuban proposal was discussed by a number of countries. Syria,[72] Iran,[73] Iraq,[74] Burundi,[75] Vietnam,[76] and Libya[77] were in favour of including economic embargoes as a crime against humanity. However, Belgium,[78] Japan,[79] and Brazil[80] were opposed to the inclusion of economic embargoes. As pointed out by Brazil, the Rome Statute deals with criminal acts on a personal and individual basis, not with State acts.

In addition, Nigeria stated that 'crimes related to [...] money laundering should come under the jurisdiction of the Court. Those are of as much concern to the

---

69 The adopted research methodology is discussed in the General Introduction to this work.

70 United Nations Diplomatic Conference of Plenipotentiaries on the Establishment of an International Criminal Court, Rome, 15 June – 17 July 1998. Official Records, Volume II: Summary records of the plenary meetings and of the meetings of the Committee of the Whole, p. 102, para. 82. (Hereafter: Official Records, Volume II).

71 Document A/CONF.183/C.1/L.17, included in United Nations Diplomatic Conference of Plenipotentiaries on the Establishment of an International Criminal Court, Rome, 15 June – 17 July 1998. Official Records, Volume III: Reports and other documents, p. 240. (Hereafter: Official Records, Volume III).

72 Official Records, Volume II, p. 271, §46.

73 *Ibid.* p. 280, §100.

74 *Ibid.* p. 282, §2; and p. 341, §64.

75 *Ibid.* p. 285, §46; and p. 336, §19.

76 *Ibid.* p. 287, §64.

77 *Ibid.* p. 344, §6.

78 *Ibid.* p. 269, §22.

79 *Ibid.* p. 269, §27.

80 *Ibid.* p. 277, §48.

international community as the four core crimes.'[81] No further debate took place on the matter.

Also, a proposal was made by Barbados, Jamaica, and Trinidad and Tobago on crimes involving the illicit trafficking in narcotic drugs and psychotropic substances. This proposal states that:

> For the purposes of the present Statute, crimes involving the illicit traffic in narcotic drugs and psychotropic substances are those crimes set out in article 3, sections 1 and 2, of the United Nations Convention against the Illicit Traffic in Narcotic Drugs and Psychotropic Substances of 1988 when committed: [...] (d) in a context in which corrupt influence is exerted over the public, the media, and public institutions.'[82]

Here, drug trafficking is linked to corruption.

(ii) ICC Legal Tools

In addition to the *travaux* compiled by the UN, the ICC Legal Tools project of the ICC Office of the Prosecutor includes a database of the ICC preparatory works.[83] The search in the ICC Legal Tools however generated very few results. Apart from the information that was already obtained by using the UN documents described above, little was found. The only relevant result is a document from 1996 of the Prepcom's Informal Group on Penalties.[84] This is a proposal relating to the draft Article 47 of the Rome Statute, which concerned the penalties that could be imposed by the ICC.[85] The Prepcom document states that:

> ... a delegation observed that the inclusion of the penalty of forfeiture in Article 47 will provide effective enforcement mechanism for the economic crime resulting in international social problems such as crime of drug trafficking which may fall under the definition of serious crimes of international concern under Article 20(e) of the ILC Draft. Should in the future these crimes be listed in the Annex of Article 20(e), there will be no need to amend the Statute to incorporate such penalty to govern the said crimes.

---

81 *Ibid.* p. 111, §86.

82 Document A/CONF.183/C.1/L.48, included in Official Records, Volume III at p. 246.

83 The adopted research method is discussed in the General Introduction to this work.

84 Preparatory Committee on the Establishment of an International Criminal Court, Informal Group on Penalties, Proposals relating to Article 47 of the Statute of an International Criminal Court, 27 August 1996, A/AC.249/CRP.13/Add.1.

85 The draft Article reads as follows: 'The Court may impose on a person convicted of a crime under this Statute one or more of the following penalties:
(a) a term of life imprisonment, or of imprisonment for a specified number of years;
(b) a fine;
[(c) a disfranchisement in the modality and to the extent such penalty could be imposed in accordance with the laws mentioned in section 2.] or [(c) a forfeiture]).'

However, drug trafficking was not included in the Rome Statute after all.

3.5. Findings

From the analysis carried out in the present section, it has become clear that very little attention has been paid to corruption in the system of international criminal law *stricto sensu*. We find some reference to economic crimes in the list of offences compiled by the 1919 Commission, as well as in the 1996 Draft Code of Crimes. However, specific reference to (types of) corruption as such is absent. Moreover, the *travaux préparatoires* of the Rome Statute reveal that the issue of economic crime has hardly been considered. This deficiency can possibly be explained by three main features of international criminal law as it currently stands.

First of all, as noted by Starr, international criminal law has a 'crisis focus': it principally deals with crimes committed during crisis situations, mostly wars. Crimes committed during peacetime – such as corruption – remain unpunished at the international level.[86]

Second, international criminal law emphasises crimes involving severe and/or massive acts of physical violence. Cassese noted that 'international crimes are very often linked to, or produced by, war-like violence. In most cases they are perpetrated during an international or internal armed conflict, when personal aggressiveness is triggered or enhanced by war.'[87] Davidsson therefore argued that individuals who engage in economic oppression should also be punished.[88]

Third, international criminal law privileges civil and political rights over economic and social rights.[89] Skogly pointed out that the existing concept of crimes against humanity solely focuses upon violations of civil and political rights. For this reason, she argued that certain violations of economic and social rights, such as deliberate starvation (violating the right to food) or forced evictions (violating the right to housing), should also be seen as crimes against humanity.[90]

Hence, from the historical perspective, it will be rather difficult to argue that economic crimes such as corruption belong within the system of international criminal law *stricto sensu*, since they were never given much consideration. Nevertheless, as the example of drug trafficking demonstrates, there do not seem to be any theoretical arguments that would impede paying attention to non-violent

---

86 Starr, 'Extraordinary Crimes at Ordinary Times: International Justice Beyond Crisis Situations',.

87 Antonio Cassese, 'The Rationale for International Criminal Justice', in Antonio Cassese (ed.), *The Oxford Companion to International Criminal Justice* (Oxford: Oxford University Press, 2009), p. 123–130 at p. 124.

88 Elias Davidsson, 'Economic Oppression as an International Wrong or as a Crime against Humanity', *Netherlands Quarterly of Human Rights,* 23 (2005), p. 213–241.

89 Paul D. Ocheje, 'Refocusing International Law on the Quest for Accountability in Africa: The Case against The "Other" Impunity', *Leiden Journal of International Law,* 15 (2002), p. 749–779 at p. 777–778.

90 S Skogly, 'Crimes against Humanity – Revisited: Is There a Role for Economic, Social and Cultural Rights?' *The International Journal of Human Rights,* 5 (2001), p. 58–80.

crimes committed during peacetime, especially since corruption does form part of transnational criminal law. This discrepancy can possibly be explained by the fact that international criminal law *stricto sensu* started to develop much earlier than the international efforts to eradicate corruption (as described in Part A, chapter II). The international treaties which oblige States to criminalise corruption domestically (most notably the UNCAC) are all from a rather recent date.

4. Rationales for the International Criminalisation of Corruption

4.1. Introduction: Developing a Model for International Criminalisation

Having discussed the international criminalisation of corruption (or rather: the lack thereof within ICL *stricto sensu*) from a historical perspective, we must now consider its rationales: why does certain conduct deserve to be criminalised at the *international* plane, and not merely at the national level? And taking into consideration these rationales for international criminalisation, is it possible to conclude that certain forms of corruption ought to be criminalised at the international level, so that corruption will fall within the scope of international criminal law *stricto sensu*?

Before these questions can be answered, it is imperative to determine why certain behaviour should be criminalised at all, by the domestic legislator. To this end, the model developed by De Roos will be discussed and applied. This is a normative model of criminal policy which can be used to describe and evaluate (domestic) legislative decision-making on criminalisation.[91] The model aims to determine what considerations should apply to criminalisation, and formulates six principles that should be met: (i) feasibility and motivation of harm; (ii) tolerance; (iii) subsidiarity; (iv) proportionality; (v) legality; and (vi) practical applicability and effectivity.[92] Interestingly, De Roos has applied this model to the criminalisation of economic crime in the Netherlands.[93]

---

91 In Dutch: 'crimineel-politiek toetsingsschema voor de primaire criminalisering'. De Roos uses the Dutch term 'criminalisering', and the English term 'penalisation'. Given the fact that the present work employs the term 'criminalisation', this is the notion that will be used here. De Th. A. Roos, *Strafbaarstelling Van Economische Delicten: Een Crimineel-Politieke Studie* (Arnhem: Gouda Quint, 1987) at English summary on p. 237–239. The English terms used in the present section 4 for the six principles are the translations employed by De Roos himself in his English summary.

92 *Ibid.* at p. 239.

93 It is important to note in this respect that De Roos' study concerns economic offences committed by corporate actors, not by public officials. See *Ibid.* at p. 1–3. The examples of De Roos are unfair competition, non-official corruption, insider trading, the Act on Supplying Labour, the Act on Foreign Labour, the Act on Minimum Wages, the Bill of Law on equal treatment, as well

Moreover, the model of De Roos on *domestic* criminalisation can be combined with the framework developed by Bassiouni, who formulated a number of criteria for *international* criminalisation. The application of the De Roos-Bassiouni scheme will enable answering the question: what considerations should apply to the international criminalisation of forms of corruption?

4.2. Feasibility and Motivation of Harm

4.2.1. Content

The first relevant principle is the principle of feasibility and motivation of harm, also known as *in dubio pro libertate* (i.e. 'if in doubt favour liberty'). This entails that the conduct concerned must have harmful effects on third persons, or on society, and that the legislator must carefully specify and prove the existence of this harm.[94] A number of issues have to be clarified in this respect: (i) the structural background of the conduct; (ii) a clear identification of the conduct and its relation to the aforementioned background; (iii) identification of the consequences of the conduct (i.e. the harm), as much as possible in 'hard facts'; this enables identification of the victims, or the violated interests; (iv) gain an insight into the way in which the persons directly involved (perpetrators, victims, third parties) assess the conduct; (v) identify the legal or extra-legal mechanisms that already apply to the conduct, and their effects, as well as the (in)consistencies in relevant legislation; (vi) the frequency of the conduct; and (vii) possible comparative information on legislation, case law, etcetera from other countries.[95]

4.2.2. Defining 'Harm' at the International Level: Bassiouni's Criteria for International Criminalisation

The question arises how 'harm' can be defined in the international context. In this respect it is interesting to take note of the five criteria for international criminalisation, as identified by Bassiouni and elaborated upon by Yarnold. These criteria aim to clarify when certain conduct should be criminalised at the international level, and most of them are related to the requirement of harm.

At the outset it should be noted once more that Bassiouni employs a broad definition of international criminal law and international crimes (see section 2 *supra*. Whenever he discusses 'international criminalisation', he refers to both crimes under international law (which can be directly enforced under international

as other equality legislation. See Roos, *Strafbaarstelling Van Economische Delicten: Een Crimineel-Politieke Studie* at p. 238–239.

94 Dutch expression: 'beginsel van aannemelijkheid en motivering van de schade'. Roos, *Strafbaarstelling Van Economische Delicten: Een Crimineel-Politieke Studie*, at p. 54, 57.

95 *Ibid.* at p. 56.

law) as well as transnational or treaty-based crimes (which are enforced indirectly, i.e. by States at the domestic level). Hence, a number of the five criteria concern treaty-based crimes rather than crimes under international law.

(i) 'Significant international interest: threat to international peace and security'

First, international criminalisation should take place if the conduct concerned affects a significant international interest, particularly if it constitutes a threat to international peace and security.[96] In the words of Yarnold, this first category of conduct contains an international element.[97] Since Bassiouni labels such an offence as 'a truly international crime', this criterion corresponds to the category of 'crimes under international law' as employed by the present research. Hence, the deciding factor is harm to an international interest, in particular international peace and security. In Bassiouni's terminology, such conduct is an 'international crime' (see section 2.2 *supra*.

(ii) 'Conduct offending the commonly shared values of the world community, including conduct shocking the conscience of humanity'

Second, if the conduct constitutes egregious conduct deemed offensive to the commonly shared values of the world community, including what has historically been referred to as conduct shocking the conscience of humanity, international criminalisation is justified.[98] Again, whenever this condition is fulfilled, there is a crime under international law, or a truly international crime.[99] Within Yarnold's classification, this is once more the criterion of an international element, and a crime fulfilling such an element is criminalised out of considerations of principle, instead of policy.[100] Furthermore, Cryer points out that 'what is 'shocking to the conscience of mankind' is by no means a given.'[101]

(iii) 'Transnational implications' (transnational element)

Third, if the conduct has transnational implications because it involves or affects more than one State in its planning, preparation, or commission, either through the diversity of nationality of its perpetrators or victims, or because the means

---

96 Bassiouni, *Introduction to International Criminal Law*, at p. 114–115.

97 Barbara M. Yarnold, 'The Doctrinal Basis for the International Criminalisation Process', in M. Cherif Bassiouni (ed.), *International Criminal Law: Crimes* (2nd edn., I; Ardsley, New York: Transnational Publishers, 1999), p. 127–152 at p. 131.

98 Bassiouni, *Introduction to International Criminal Law*, at p. 115.

99 *Ibid.* at p. 119–120.

100 Yarnold, 'The Doctrinal Basis for the International Criminalisation Process', at p. 146.

101 Cryer, 'The Doctrinal Foundations of International Criminalization', at p. 126.

employed transcend national boundaries, criminalisation is justified.[102] This is what Yarnold calls the transnational element.[103] A crime which is criminalised for this reason is not a crime under international law, but a treaty-based crime or transnational crime.[104] Bassiouni labels such an offence an 'international delict'. Such a crime is criminalised out of policy considerations, instead of principle.[105]

(iv) 'Harm to an internationally protected person or interest'

Fourth, if the conduct is harmful to an internationally protected person or interest, criminalisation should take place.[106] In the view of Bassiouni, this is a partly international or transnational crime.[107] This is again a so-called international delict.[108]

(v) 'Violation of an internationally protected interest'

Fifth, if the conduct violates an internationally protected interest but it does not rise to the level required by (i) or (ii), however, because of its nature, it can best be prevented and suppressed by international criminalisation.[109] In the words of Yarnold, such an offence contains an element of 'international necessity'.[110] These crimes are also treaty-based crimes. This criterion corresponds to the category of international infractions, which can be found at the bottom of the hierarchy.[111]

When discussing each of the above-mentioned criteria, it is important to consider the degree of State involvement in the commission of the crimes. An offence is either: the product of State action; the product of a State-favouring policy; or the product of individual conduct.[112] According to Yarnold, crimes containing an international element (i.e. those under (i) and (ii)) are, as a general rule, State-sponsored or involve State activity. Crimes containing a transnational element or the element of international necessity (i.e. the crimes under (iii), (iv) and (v)) are usually conducted by individuals acting in their own capacity, without the involvement of the State.[113]

---

102 Bassiouni, *Introduction to International Criminal Law*, at p. 115.
103 Yarnold, 'The Doctrinal Basis for the International Criminalisation Process', at p. 131.
104 Bassiouni, *Introduction to International Criminal Law*, at p. 119–120.
105 Yarnold, 'The Doctrinal Basis for the International Criminalisation Process', at p. 146.
106 Bassiouni, *Introduction to International Criminal Law*, at p. 115.
107 *Ibid.* at p. 119–120.
108 *Ibid.* at p. 122–123.
109 *Ibid.* at p. 114–115 and 19.
110 Yarnold, 'The Doctrinal Basis for the International Criminalisation Process', at p. 131.
111 Bassiouni, *Introduction to International Criminal Law*, at p. 123–124.
112 *Ibid.* at p. 119.
113 Yarnold, 'The Doctrinal Basis for the International Criminalisation Process', at p. 147–148.

4.2.3. Application

It is now imperative to apply the first criterion, feasibility and motivation of harm, to corruption. This criterion makes clear that the legislator, be it the domestic legislative bodies or the Conference of State Parties to the Rome Statute, must specify and prove that corruption is harmful. When testing the seven criteria listed by De Roos, we find that, in the case of corruption, most of these will be met. In Part A of the present work, corrupt conduct and its background have been clearly identified (ad (i) and (ii)), as well as its consequences (ad (iii)). Also, attention has been paid to the international legal regime that already applies to corruption (ad (v)), and to the frequency of corruption as measured by the CPI (ad (vi)). The criterion that might deserve some further consideration in the case of corruption is the fourth one (ad (iv)), which requires an insight into the way in which the persons directly involved in corruption assess the conduct. It not unlikely that some perpetrators of corruption will not consider their behaviour to be harmful.

Now, it is important to establish what 'harm' means at the international level. Here we can apply Bassiouni's five criteria. As elaborated upon above, the three main rationales for criminalising certain conduct at the international level are the presence of either: an international element (which can take two possible forms); a transnational element; or an element of international necessity.

Can corruption meet these criteria? In the view of Ocheje, this is indeed the case. He argued that:

> ... looting of public treasuries satisfies all of the listed criteria. It is a violation of the internationally guaranteed rights of people to use their national wealth for their own welfare. That it cannot be successfully accomplished without a collaborating financial institution abroad means that such collaboration is part of the delict. Looting of public funds impoverishes millions and sets the context for the despair and hopelessness which breed violence in societies. Poverty also provides the context for social upheavals, setting in motion waves of displacement, refugee flows, and unplanned migration. Given the current knowledge about the emergence of terrorist networks, and the difficulties relating to the management of refugee flows and the patterns of migration, it is fair to conclude that political corruption is a threat to the peace and security of the international community. The magnitude of theft by African leaders and the living conditions of most Africans would undoubtedly shock the collective conscience of the world. The mode of stealing, which involves the transfer of stolen funds from Africa to offshore banks, is obviously transnational, and the use of State power to perpetrate the theft clearly implicates State action or policy. International co-operation is fundamental to effectively preventing, suppressing or controlling this phenomenon.[114]

---

[114] Ocheje, 'Refocusing International Law on the Quest for Accountability in Africa: The Case against The "Other" Impunity', at p. 776.

These claims have to be critically examined.

First, the first type of international element: the threat to international peace and security. Could certain forms of corruption be perceived in this way? Clearly, petty corruption does not constitute such a threat, since its consequences will be felt first and foremost within the country where the corrupt act takes place. Yet, in exceptional circumstances, grand corruption can indeed threaten international peace and security. As shown above in chapter I, section 5.2.2, corruption can fuel armed conflict, which may disturb an entire region.

Second, the second type of international element: the conduct offends the commonly shared values of the world community. Conduct fulfilling this criterion is conduct in which State activity is involved. It does not require much imagination to understand that certain forms of large-scale corruption are offensive to the common values of the world community. Large-scale looting of a developing country's public funds by its own high-level public officials, often involving millions or billions of dollars, leaves a country crippled. The foreseeable result: massive poverty. An example is the conduct of Mobutu Sese-Seko, the late president of Zaire (the Democratic Republic of Congo), who allegedly embezzled approximately $5 billion, earning him the number three spot on the list of the world's most corrupt leaders.[115] Meanwhile, the population of the Congo is still poor: UNDP statistics show that 59.2 per cent of the population lives below $1.25 a day, while the average life expectancy is 47.6 years.[116] Such conduct does indeed receive the condemnation of the international community, and is no less shocking than atrocities committed during armed conflict. Hence, international criminalisation of corruption should take place because it offends the values of world community.

Third, a transnational element can be present whenever (a) the conduct affects interests of more than one State; (b) the conduct includes citizens of more than one State; or (c) the conduct involves means or methods transcending national boundaries.[117] Clearly, many forms of corruption do contain such a transnational element. Yarnold already noted that bribery of foreign public officials, i.e. only the supply side of bribery, contains a transnational element, since citizens of more than one State are involved. In her opinion, supply-side bribery does not contain an international element, while she does not consider the element of international necessity. Hence, the transnational dimension is beyond doubt, meaning that corruption is a transnational or treaty-based crime, which is confirmed by several treaties (see chapter II *supra*.

115 Robin Hodess, 'Introduction to Political Corruption', in Transparency International (ed.), *Global Corruption Report* (2004), p. 11–18 at p. 13.

116 United Nations Development Programme, *Human Development Report 2009*, 'Democratic Republic of the Congo', <http://hdrstats.undp.org/en/countries/data_sheets/cty_ds_COD.html>, accessed 19 April 2010.

117 Yarnold, 'The Doctrinal Basis for the International Criminalisation Process', at p. 131.

Fourth, the element of international necessity is present whenever there is recognition by the world community that certain conduct must be criminalised at the international level for effective control. The prohibition of certain conduct must be enforced by joint efforts and cooperation of more than one State because one single State will not succeed in doing so.[118] In essence, corruption meets the element of international necessity, since it can only be effectively combated if there is a consistent international approach. This is demonstrated by the wide range of global and international anti-corruption treaties, as discussed in chapter II *supra* At the same time, it must be recognised that not all ratifying States are seriously convinced that corruption should be addressed, and hence the political will to act upon the various treaty provisions may be absent.

In sum, the conclusion is justified that corruption meets the criterion of feasibility and motivation of harm, also at the international level. We have seen that grand corruption is a crime containing a so-called international element, since (i) it may constitute a threat to international peace and security in certain circumstances; and (ii) it is conduct offending the commonly shared values of the world community. Moreover, as argued by Yarnold, crimes with such an international element are generally State-sponsored or involve State activity. This is also the case with grand corruption, since it is precisely the power of the State that is abused by high-level officials. Hence, grand corruption deserves to be criminalised at the international level, and the prohibition should also be directly enforced at the international level.

As regards the transnational element and the element of international necessity, these are also met in the case of corruption, meaning that corruption forms part of transnational criminal law, which is enforced indirectly, at the national level.

4.3. Tolerance

4.3.1. Content

The second criterion, the principle of tolerance, entails that even if certain conduct is found to be harmful, it should nevertheless not be criminalised whenever it falls within a citizen's personal liberty. De Roos mentions the examples of pornography and auto-mutilation. Even though these practices may be harmful, they should be legally allowed because of the importance of individual liberty. Governments can use other methods than criminalisation to address the matter, for example by campaigns to raise awareness about a certain problem.[119]

---

118 *Ibid.* at p. 131–132.

119 Roos, *Strafbaarstelling van Economische Delicten: Een Crimineel-Politieke Studie*, at p. 58–60.

4.3.2. Application

When considering the principle of tolerance, we can conclude that corruption in the public sector does not fall within the sphere of individual liberty. The fact that public officials are entrusted with the responsibility of ensuring benefit for citizens places their conduct within the public sphere, where the personal liberty of officials is limited.

4.4. Subsidiarity

4.4.1. Content

The principle of subsidiarity is the third relevant principle identified by De Roos. It signifies that the legislator has to abstain from criminalising certain conduct, whenever other means can also guarantee that the social norm in question is upheld. Criminal law should be the final resort, an *ultimum remedium*. Generally, there are two alternatives to criminal law: legal means and other means. The latter consists, for example, of educational programmes, and crime prevention programmes by the police or other societal institutions. The legal alternatives to the use of criminal law at the national level are the use of civil law and administrative law.[120] For instance, the use of domestic oversight mechanisms in domestic administrative law and accompanying administrative sanctions (including fines) may be an alternative to the use of criminal law, also in the case of corruption.

4.4.2. Application

There are several alternatives to the international criminalisation of corrupt offences, the most important of which is the criminalisation of corrupt practices in domestic legislation. Pursuant to the various international treaties discussed in chapter II, this obligation is already incumbent upon many States. However, it remains to be seen whether all 152 State parties to the UNCAC have proper anti-corruption legislation put in place, or will do so in the future. Since the convention is not complemented with an *adequate* monitoring mechanism, there is a serious risk of non-compliance, which is particularly present in respect of grand corruption. Governments with a high level of corruption are not likely to enforce anti-corruption legislation against themselves.[121] This problem can be partially remedied by international criminalisation and enforcement by an international tribunal. Furthermore, the UNCAC's provisions on prevention, international cooperation, and asset recovery remain important, but will probably not suffice to

120 *Ibid.* at p. 60–70.

121 See chapter II *supra*for a discussion of UNCAC, and the problems of monitoring.

curb corruption by themselves. This is of course not to underrate the important role of corruption prevention.

Other alternatives to the use of international criminal law are (i) amnesties;[122] (ii) truth commissions;[123] (iii) lustration;[124] and (iv) reparations and civil claims.[125] Let us now consider these possibilities.

As regards amnesties, Carranza noted that 'while amnesty-for-truth mechanisms have often immediately (and justifiably) triggered concerns that they encourage impunity with respect to human rights violations, a similar approach with respect to large-scale corruption and economic crimes may not be as controversial, especially if it results in the recovery of assets amassed through those crimes.'[126] In this respect, Carranza referred to Article 37(3) UNCAC, which sets out that 'Each State Party shall consider providing for the possibility, in accordance with fundamental principles of its domestic law, of granting immunity from prosecution to a person who provides substantial cooperation in the investigation or prosecution of an offence established in accordance with this Convention.' This is an important observation, given the fact that often large amounts of money are involved in high-level corruption. Hence, in some cases amnesties might be appropriate in order to recover the assets. However, Starr argues otherwise. She concludes that there is no reason to believe that amnesties will be a desirable option in most corruption cases.[127]

Concerning truth commissions, both Carranza and Schabas argued that these institutions can play an important role in addressing the economic aspects of armed conflict, including corruption.[128] Nevertheless, Carranza stated that 'only a handful of more than 30 past truth commissions incorporated economic crimes into their

---

122 Cryer, *Prosecuting International Crimes: Selectivity and the International Criminal Law Regime*, at p. 31–33; Slye and Schaack, *International Criminal Law: The Essentials*, at p. 254–263 and 309–310.

123 Cryer, *Prosecuting International Crimes: Selectivity and the International Criminal Law Regime*, at p. 33–35; Slye and Schaack, *International Criminal Law: The Essentials*, at p. 310–312.

124 Cryer, *Prosecuting International Crimes: Selectivity and the International Criminal Law Regime*, at p. 35; Slye and Schaack, *International Criminal Law: The Essentials*, at p. 312.

125 Cryer, *Prosecuting International Crimes: Selectivity and the International Criminal Law Regime*, at p. 35–36; Slye and Schaack, *International Criminal Law: The Essentials*, at p. 312–313.

126 Ruben Carranza, 'Plunder and Pain: Should Transitional Justice Engage with Corruption and Economic Crimes?' *The International Journal of Transitional Justice,* 2 (2008), p. 310–330 at p. 325–326.

127 Starr, 'Extraordinary Crimes at Ordinary Times: International Justice Beyond Crisis Situations', at p. 1290–1291.

128 Carranza, 'Plunder and Pain: Should Transitional Justice Engage with Corruption and Economic Crimes?' at p. 435–437; William A. Schabas, 'War Economies, Economic Actors, and International Criminal Law', in Karen Ballentine and Heiko Nitzschke (eds.), *Profiting from Peace: Managing the Resource Dimension of Civil War* (Boulder: Lynne Rienner Publishers 2005), p. 425–443.

truth-seeking work'.[129] One of the few commissions which actually took on this task is the Sierra Leone Truth and Reconciliation Commission. The Commission condemned the successive Sierra Leonean governments for endemic corruption, mismanagement of natural resources, which contributed to the conflict, and widespread looting.[130]

Furthermore, lustration, to be understood as the removal of public officials who are thought to be responsible for international crimes, is also interesting. Lustration, as a form of punishment, could be applied to corrupt governmental officials. For example, the Sierra Leone Truth and Reconciliation Commission stated that it:

> ... seriously considered whether to recommend lustration in the public service and security forces. Lustration would involve the purging from these institutions of all public officials, soldiers and police members tainted by the fact that they committed human rights violations or engaged in corrupt acts in the past. After much reflection, the Commission decided not to recommend lustration.[131]

This was decided because:

> ... the Commission is of the view that lustration, in the context of post-conflict Sierra Leone, has the potential to be enormously divisive. Besides being unworkable at a practical level, there is the real potential that the process will be abused for political ends and used for purposes of settling scores and pursuing vendettas. This would seriously undermine the prospects for national reconciliation.[132]

Finally, reparations and civil claims brought by victims of corrupt practices could, in certain cases, provide additional opportunities to combat corruption.[133] However, in the case of grand corruption, this can be problematic because these cases might lack a clearly defined victim.

4.5. Proportionality

4.5.1. Content

The fourth principle is that of proportionality, which means that criminalisation should not go further than strictly necessary. In other words, the penalty has to be

---

129 Carranza, 'Plunder and Pain: Should Transitional Justice Engage with Corruption and Economic Crimes?' at p. 321.

130 See Schabas, 'War Economies, Economic Actors, and International Criminal Law', at p. 436.

131 Sierra Leone Truth & Reconciliation Commission, 'Witness to Truth: Volume 2', (2004) at p. 159, §259.

132 *Ibid.* at p. 159, para. 261.

133 For more on this topic, see Abiola O. Makinwa, 'Researching Civil Remedies for International Corruption: The Choice of the Functional Comparative Method', *Erasmus Law Review,* 2 (2009), p. 331–351.

proportional to the harm that is caused by the criminal offence. 'Harm' includes both a financial and economic component, as well as an ethical-normative component.[134]

4.5.2. Application

For the purpose of the present work, the principle of proportionality demands that the punishment that can possibly be imposed by the International Criminal Court is proportional to the corrupt offence that is committed. The Rome Statute leaves ample room for differentiation in penalties. Pursuant to Article 77, imprisonment can either be temporary with a maximum of 30 years, or life imprisonment. Furthermore, the Court may order the imposition of a fine, and the forfeiture of proceeds, property and assets derived (in)directly from the crime committed. Further rules on sentencing are laid down in Chapter 7 of the Courts's Rules of Procedure and Evidence.

4.6. Legality

4.6.1. Content

The principle of legality, *nullum crimen, nulla poena sine lege*, is one of the cornerstones of both national and international criminal law. Under this principle, there is no crime without prior criminalisation of the offence, and no punishment can be imposed. Hence, retroactive application of criminal law is not possible, nor is it possible to apply criminal law by analogy. Moreover, the principle of legality demands that the criminal law provision is formulated as clearly as possible. Vague provisions are not allowed.[135] The Rome Statute contains the various aspects of the principle of legality in Articles 22, 23 and 24.[136]

4.6.2. Application

The legality principle necessitates that corruption must be brought under one of the existing provisions of the Rome Statute (*de lege lata*), or that any anti-corruption provision which can possibly be inserted into the Statute in the future clearly spells out the corrupt conduct in detail (*de lege ferenda*). See section 6 hereafter on the types of corruption that could possibly fall within the scope of international criminal law.

---

134 Roos, *Strafbaarstelling van Economische Delicten: Een Crimineel-Politieke Studie*, at p. 70–72.

135 *Ibid.* at p. 73–75.

136 Article 22: *nullum crimen sine lege*; Article 23: *nulla poena sine lege*; Article 24: non-retroactivity *ratione personae*.

4.7. Practical Applicability and Effectivity

4.7.1. Content

When the principles of feasibility and motivation of harm; tolerance; subsidiarity; proportionality; and legality are met, it is important to determine (i) whether the application of the criminal provision is possible in practice; (ii) whether this application can be guaranteed when considering the capacity of the criminal justice system; and (iii) whether the general preventive function of the criminal provision can be expected.[137]

The first requirement is of a legal-technical nature. It entails that the provision concerned must provide sufficient grip for the investigative, prosecuting and judicial authorities. Also, the components of the criminal provision should not pose insurmountable problems in terms of evidence.[138] The second requirement is organisational: it concerns the capacity and the organisational structure of the criminal justice system to actually address the conduct concerned. When it is clear beforehand that there is no capacity to enforce the provision, one can question whether criminalisation is desirable.[139] The third requirement concerns the necessity of gathering and assessing empirical data about the general preventive quality of the criminal provision. This relates to the idea that criminalisation of conduct itself will prevent citizens from committing the crime concerned. However, the Roos mentions that the prevention will come from the chance of being caught, rather than from criminalisation. Nevertheless, he also acknowledges the 'value expressive' function of criminalisation.[140]

4.7.2. Application

The three requirements set out above make clear that any provision criminalising corruption, also at the international level, should be sufficiently clear and precise for the authorities who investigate, prosecute and adjudicate corruption cases. Also, the provision should be feasible when it comes to evidence matters. Moreover, the criminal justice system, i.e. the ICC, should have the organisational and financial capacity to deal with corruption cases. In this area there may be problems. The Court already has a relatively limited capacity: it can only deal with a fraction of all crimes under international law that are being committed worldwide. Hence, given the probably complex nature of investigating corruption, only few cases against corrupt public officials could be brought before the ICC. However, the same is true for the crimes already laid down in the Rome Statute. Whenever crimes against humanity are committed, the Court can only try a small number of all perpetrators.

---

137 Roos, *Strafbaarstelling van Economische Delicten: Een Crimineel-Politieke Studie*, at p. 76.
138 *Ibid.* at p. 76–77.
139 *Ibid.* at p. 77–78.
140 *Ibid.* at p. 78–79.

Hence, this should not deter us from arguing that prosecuting corrupt public officials can fall within the tasks of the ICC, also because of the expressive function of punishment (see section 5.4 *infra*).

Worth mentioning in the context of the principle of practical applicability and effectivity are the ICC's potential powers in respect of asset recovery.[141] In cases of grand corruption, embezzled funds are often channelled away from developing countries to foreign bank accounts, complicating the recovery of assets, for example, after the collapse of a certain corrupt regime. It was held that 'the amount of money extorted and stolen each year from developing countries is over 10 times the approximately $100 billion in foreign assistance being provided by all governments and civil organizations in the world.'[142] Moreover, as stated earlier, it is estimated that Africa loses approximately $148 billion each year due to corruption, which is 25 per cent of the GDP of the continent.[143] Hence, it would be a major improvement if asset recovery could be achieved by ICC prosecution of high-level corrupt officials. Under Article 86, State Parties have a general obligation to cooperate with the Court in its investigation and prosecution of crimes. Article 87 further sets out provisions on the requests for cooperation. In addition, Article 93(1)(k) provides that State Parties shall comply with requests by the ICC to provide assistance in relation to investigations and prosecutions, including the identification, tracing and freezing or seizure of proceeds, property and assets and instrumentalities of crimes for the purpose of eventual forfeiture. Hence, by bringing corruption under the Rome Statute, the proceeds of corruption can be more easily traced because State Parties have to cooperate with ICC in this respect. Meanwhile, it is also possible to apply the above-mentioned provisions of the Statute in case other ICC crimes are committed. For instance, when a (corrupt) high-level official is indicted for crimes against humanity or war crimes, asset recovery is also an option.

A related issue is that of the penalties that can be imposed by the ICC on perpetrators. Article 77(2) of the Rome Statute provides that, in addition to imprisonment, the Court may order the following penalties: (a) the imposition of a fine; (b) a forfeiture of proceeds, property and assets derived directly or indirectly from the crime. Under Article 109, States have to enforce fines and forfeiture measures. Moreover, Article 78 creates a Trust Fund for the benefit of victims and their families. Money and other property collected through fines or forfeiture may be transferred to such a Trust Fund. Also, as stated in Article 110(4)(b), the ICC may reduce a sentence if the person voluntarily assists in enabling the enforcement

---

141 As mentioned by Starr, 'Extraordinary Crimes at Ordinary Times: International Justice Beyond Crisis Situations', (at p. 1259, 87, 88–89. and briefly noted by Ocheje, 'Refocusing International Law on the Quest for Accountability in Africa: The Case against The "Other" Impunity', at p. 776–777.

142 Jack Smith, Mark Pieth, and Guillermo Jorge, 'The Recovery of Stolen Assets: A Fundamental Principle of the UN Convention against Corruption', *U4 Brief* (Bergen, Norway: Chr. Michelsen Institute, February 2007) at p. 1.

143 *Ibid.*

of the judgments and orders of the Court in other cases, and in particular in providing assistance in locating assets subject to orders of fine, forfeiture or reparation which may be used for the benefit of victims.

4.8. Findings

When applying De Roos' framework for criminalisation to corruption in the public sector, it can be argued that all six principles are met: (i) feasibility and motivation of harm; (ii) tolerance; (iii) subsidiarity; (iv) proportionality; (v) legality; and (vi) practical applicability and effectivity. In respect of the first criterion, i.e. harm, it is possible to apply the structure developed by Bassiouni concerning international criminalisation. When examining his key rationales for international criminalisation, the conclusion can be drawn that instances of grand corruption involving State actors contain an *international element*: their commission shocks the commonly shared values of the international community, and may even constitute a threat to international peace and security. Therefore grand corruption deserves to be criminalised at the international level, and should be seen as a crime under international law, not merely as a treaty-based crime (which it already is since the transnational element and the element of international necessity are also met). From this point of view, international criminal law, as enforced by an international tribunal, should therefore be used to combat grand corruption.

5. Objectives of Punishment in International Criminal Law

5.1. Introduction

In addition to clarifying the rationales of international criminalisation, we must also take due account of the objectives of punishment in international criminal law, in order to determine whether – given these objectives – corruption can be approached from the perspective of international criminal law. Which goals of punishment at the international level can be achieved by criminalising corruption at that level?

The question arises whether or not the objectives of punishment at the national level can simply be transferred to the international level. It has been brought forward, amongst others by Tallgren, that there are different justifications for punishment in international criminal law than in national criminal law.[144] However, Cryer holds that it is questionable whether the objectives of punishment ought to differ significantly between international and municipal criminal law.[145]

144 Immi Tallgren, 'The Sensibility and Sense of International Criminal Law', *European Journal of International Law*, 13 (2002), p. 561–595.

145 Cryer *et al.*, *An Introduction to International Criminal Law and Procedure*, at p. 17.

In general, there are three approaches to justifying punishment. First, the consequentialist approach (i.e. deterrence, incapacitation and rehabilitation) which is forward-looking or teleological. Second, the non-consequentialist approach, also known as retributivism, is backward-looking because it focuses on the crime committed and is therefore known as deontological. Third, in the expressivist approach, which is forward-looking, punishment aims to achieve communication and education. Furthermore, there are a number of remaining goals of punishment which are typical for international criminal law.[146] The following section will further elaborate upon these objectives of punishment, in the context of international criminal law.

5.2. Retributivism

Retribution is the first main goal of punishment in international criminal law: a perpetrator of a crime under international law *deserves* to be punished for his or her actions.[147] Retributive theories, originating from Immanuel Kant, are repeatedly stated in the case law of the ad hoc tribunals.[148] Moreover, SC Resolutions 827 (1993) and 955 (1994), which establish the ICTY and the ICTR, also refer to retribution, since they state that the Tribunals shall 'bring to justice the persons who are responsible' for the crimes laid down in the Statutes and that the Tribunals were established 'for the sole purpose of prosecuting persons responsible'.[149] Garland argues that since the 1970s, a clear trend can be detected, i.e. the decline of consequentialism (including the ideal of rehabilitation of offenders), and the emphasis on retribution as a goal of punishment.[150]

For offences of corruption, retribution is an adequate justification for punishment. Given the harmful consequences of the conduct, as described in chapter I, the general public will hold the opinion that public officials engaging in

---

146 *Ibid.* at p. 18 *et seq*; Antony Duff, 'Legal Punishment', *Stanford Encyclopedia of Philosophy* (Stanford, 2008); R.A. Duff and David Garland, 'Introduction: Thinking About Punishment', in R.A. Duff and David Garland (eds.), *A Reader on Punishment* (Oxford: Oxford University Press, 1994), p. 1–43 at p. 6–8.

147 Mark A. Drumbl, *Atrocity, Punishment and International Law* (Cambridge: Cambridge University Press, 2007) at p. 150–169; Cryer *et al.*, *An Introduction to International Criminal Law and Procedure* at p. 19–20; Slye and Schaack, *International Criminal Law: The Essentials*, at p. 297–298. For a criticism of retribution as a justification for punishment in international criminal law, see Robert D. Sloane, 'The Expressive Capacity of International Punishment: The Limits of the National Law Analogy and the Potential of International Criminal Law', *Stanford Journal of International Law*, 43 (2007), 39–94 at p. 77–81.

148 Drumbl, *Atrocity, Punishment and International Law*, at p. 60–61.

149 Elies van Sliedregt, 'Criminal Responsibility in International Law: Liability Shaped by Policy Goals and Moral Outrage', *European Journal of Crime, Criminal Law and Criminal Justice*, 14 (2006), p. 81–114 at p. 100.

150 David Garland, *The Culture of Control* (Oxford: Oxford University Press, 2001) at p. 8–9; R.A. Duff and David Garland (eds.), *A Reader on Punishment* (Oxford: Oxford University Press, 1994) at p. 8–16.

grand corruption deserve to receive a punishment which is proportionate to the crime committed.

5.3. Consequentialism

5.3.1. Deterrence

Another central aim of punishment in international criminal law is deterrence, which is oriented towards future conduct. Here, we can make the distinction between general deterrence and particular deterrence. General deterrence entails that persons other than the perpetrator will be deterred from engaging in criminal behaviour. Particular or specific deterrence means that the perpetrator him- or herself will refrain from repetition of the criminal behaviour, because of his or her punishment.[151]

In the case law of the ad hoc criminal tribunals, general deterrence is often said to be an important justification for punishment.[152] It can also be found in the SC Resolution establishing the ICTY and the ICTR: these tribunals have to 'put an end to such crimes' and ensure 'that such violations are halted.'[153] Moreover, the Rome Statute acknowledges the importance of deterrence, by stating in section 5 of the Preamble that State Parties are 'determined to put an end to impunity for the perpetrators of these crimes and thus to contribute to the prevention of such crimes.'[154]

The question is whether the general deterrent function of international criminal law can be of use in the fight against corruption. Will corrupt high-level officials proceed with caution because other officials are prosecuted by the ICC for corrupt practices? According to classical deterrence theory, as developed by Beccaria, three key factors should be taken into account: the swiftness of the punishment, the certainty of punishment (how likely punishment is to occur) and the severity of punishment. It has been argued that the element of certainty is more relevant than the severity of punishment.[155]

At the international level, it is fair to say that the chance of being brought before the ICC for the commission of a crime currently listed in the Rome Statute, is not very high. However, it has been brought forward that the deterrent function of

---

151 Cryer *et al.*, *An Introduction to International Criminal Law and Procedure*, at p. 20–22; Slye and Schaack, *International Criminal Law: The Essentials*, at p. 298–300.

152 Drumbl, *Atrocity, Punishment and International Law*, at p. 60–63 and 169–173.

153 Sliedregt, 'Criminal Responsibility in International Law: Liability Shaped by Policy Goals and Moral Outrage', at p. 100–101.

154 Cryer *et al.*, *An Introduction to International Criminal Law and Procedure*, at p. 20–22.

155 C. Beccaria, 1767/1995), *On Crimes and Punishments and Other Writings* (translated by Richard Bellamy) (Cambridge: Cambridge University Press 1995). See also Drumbl, *Atrocity, Punishment and International Law* at p. 169–170; Slye and Schaack, *International Criminal Law: The Essentials*, at p. 299–300.

punishment may be most effective at the level of regime elites: the persons who make the deliberate choice to sponsor international crimes for reasons of power consolidation. Because the international criminal tribunals more and more focus on the prosecution of leaders, rather than lower-level followers, political and military elites may take the possibility of ICC prosecution into account in their cost-benefit analysis.[156] In the words of Sloane, 'the power of international criminal law to disempower elites through stigma and reputational injury should not be underestimated.'[157] Hence, the general deterrent function of international criminal law may be able to play a role in the fight against corruption where it concerns high-level public officials.

5.3.2. Incapacitation

Incapacitation can be linked to specific deterrence: crimes are prevented because the person concerned is detained. The influence of this theory on international criminal law has been quite limited. Also, the theory is controversial because it is difficult to determine in general whether a person will or will not commit another crime.[158] In the context of corruption, the value of incapacitation is likely to be limited, since systems of widespread corruption may continue, even if one perpetrator is kept in detention.

5.3.3. Rehabilitation

Rehabilitation entails that through punishment, perpetrators can be reformed. This is not a theory with wide support in international criminal law because the main perpetrators of crimes under international law are not thought to be the appropriate beneficiaries of rehabilitation. However, international tribunals have mentioned rehabilitation in respect of lower level offenders.[159] When considering corruption, this theory may be useful only where it concerns petty corruption, since perpetrators of grand corruption will generally not be rehabilitated.

5.4. Expressivism

In the theory of expressivism, criminal procedures and punishment are an opportunity to communicate the nature of the wrongdoing to the offender, the victims, and the wider society. This aims to engage offenders, and to let them know what was wrong with their behaviour. In addition, the norm is reaffirmed in

---

156 Slye and Schaack, *International Criminal Law: The Essentials*, at p. 299–300.

157 Sloane, 'The Expressive Capacity of International Punishment: The Limits of the National Law Analogy and the Potential of International Criminal Law', at p. 73–74.

158 Cryer *et al.*, *An Introduction to International Criminal Law and Procedure*, at p. 22.

159 *Ibid.*; Slye and Schaack, *International Criminal Law: The Essentials*, at p. 300–302.

the community, and society is educated about the unacceptable nature of the offence.[160]

This is what Feinberg labels 'the expressive function of punishment': 'punishment is a conventional device for the expression of attitudes of resentment and indignation, and of judgments of disapproval and reprobation, on the part either of the punishing authority himself or of those 'in whose name' the punishment is inflicted. Punishment, in short, has a *symbolic significance* largely missing from other kinds of penalties.' [original emphasis][161] Moreover, according to Sloane, this expressive function is essential in international criminal law:

> … the principal value of ICL punishment lies in its expressive dimensions, which more accurately capture the nature of international sentencing and ICL's realistic institutional capacity to contribute to the ambitious objectives ascribed to it. International criminal tribunals can contribute most effectively to world public order as self-consciously expressive penal institutions: publicly condemning acts deplored by international law, acting as an engine of jurisprudential development at the local level, and encouraging the legal and normative internalization of human rights and humanitarian law.[162]

It is interesting to observe that Drumbl finds that the ICTY has a tendency at times to understand retribution as 'the expression of condemnation and outrage of the international community'. As correctly pointed out by Drumbl, this statement is actually of an expressivist nature, which, in his view, is a currently subordinate justification for punishment.[163]

In the context of anti-corruption, the expressive function of punishment in international criminal law is certainly the most interesting one. Prosecution of corrupt high-level officials before the ICC has symbolic value because it can demonstrate to the international community that corrupt practices are no longer tolerated, even in societies where corruption may be deeply rooted in the political and social fabric. The ICTY has phrased this feature of punishment as follows: 'Another relevant sentencing purpose is to show the people of not only the former Yugoslavia, but of the world in general, that there is no impunity for these types of crimes'.[164]

---

160 Cryer *et al.*, *An Introduction to International Criminal Law and Procedure*, at p. 23.

161 Joel Feinberg, 'The Expressive Function of Punishment', *Doing and Deserving: Essays in the Theory of Responsibility* (Princeton, New Jersey: Princeton University Press, 1970), 95–118 at p. 98.

162 Sloane, 'The Expressive Capacity of International Punishment: The Limits of the National Law Analogy and the Potential of International Criminal Law', at p. 44.

163 Drumbl, *Atrocity, Punishment and International Law*, at p. 61 and 173–179.

164 ICTY Prosecutor v. Kupreskic *et al*, Judgment Case No. IT–95–16, 14 January 2000, para. 48 as mentioned by Sliedregt, 'Criminal Responsibility in International Law: Liability Shaped by Policy Goals and Moral Outrage', at p. 101.

5.5. Other Goals

In addition to the five aims of punishment in international criminal law set out above, there are a number of broader goals. Cryer *et al.* lists: (i) justice for victims; (ii) recording history; (iii) post-conflict reconciliation; and (iv) further benefits of international trials.[165]

In respect of the first goal, i.e. justice for victims, prosecution of corrupt high-level officials may very well serve this purpose. Whenever citizens are living under a highly corrupt government, this can pervade their daily lives to a large extent. Seeing the responsible leaders facing trial can provide these citizens with a feeling that justice is being done. This is particularly important because the citizens concerned may not have any other avenue to challenge corruption by government officials. Many instances of grand corruption will lack a clear individualised victim, especially whenever funds 'disappear' at the level of ministries, before even reaching the beneficiaries.

The objective of recording history – truth telling – can also be served by bringing perpetrators of grand corruption to justice. A trial before the ICC is likely to reveal the specifics about a certain corrupt practice in which a public official is involved, and will disclose information which would otherwise be kept secret.

Post-conflict reconciliation could possibly be served by punishing corruption, whenever corruption occurs within the context of armed conflict.

As regards the benefits of international trials, as compared to domestic trials, these certainly apply to trials about grand corruption. *Inter alia*, it has been noted that international trials do not suffer so much from political manipulation or influence, nor from unconsciously biased judges.[166] Indeed, conducting an anti-corruption trial in the public official's own country can pose many of these problems. Furthermore, it has been observed that international tribunals are better equipped for the prosecution of offences which cross State borders.[167] In fact, it is probable that grand corruption cases do possess such a transboundary dimension, especially whenever funds are transferred abroad.

5.6. Findings

It is fair to conclude that punishing corruption at the international level could possibly serve several objectives of punishment in international criminal law, particularly retribution, general deterrence, expressivism, justice for victims, and truth telling. The expressivist function of punishment, however, is central.

---

165 Cryer *et al.*, *An Introduction to International Criminal Law and Procedure*, at p. 23–26.

166 Cryer, *Prosecuting International Crimes: Selectivity and the International Criminal Law Regime*, at p. 25; Antonio Cassese, 'Reflections on International Criminal Justice', *Modern Law Review*, 61 (1998), 1–10 at p. 7.

167 Cryer, *Prosecuting International Crimes: Selectivity and the International Criminal Law Regime*, at p. 25.

6. Types of Corruption Eligible for International Criminalisation *de lege ferenda*

Chapter I of part A discussed the various types of corruption that are commonly identified, most importantly by the UNCAC. It is not self-evident that all of these forms can be brought within the scope of international criminal law, on the contrary.

6.1. Demand-side Corruption: Tackling the Public Sector

As noted in chapter I, several types of corruption, including bribery, involve both public and private actors. International criminal law should focus on addressing the demand side of corruption: public officials. The responsibility of the private sector (notably corporations) is governed by international treaties, obliging States to criminalise, *inter alia*, (foreign) bribery of public officials in their domestic legislation.[168] Another reason not to include the role of the private sector in the present study is the fact that, pursuant to Article 25(1) of the Rome Statute, the ICC only has jurisdiction over natural persons, not over legal persons. The possibilities of corporate criminal liability in international law are only beginning to be examined quite recently.[169]

6.2. Focus on Grand Corruption

Most certainly, petty corruption would not fall within the realm of international criminal law. The mere thought of criminalisation, at the international level, of the acceptance or demand of small bribes for minor public services is unappealing. International criminal law as a system should focus on the 'big fish'. In the context of corruption this means those who commit acts of grand corruption. As elaborated upon earlier, grand corruption is committed by public actors at the policy formulation end of politics. Hence, the term 'grand' refers to the level where corruption takes place.

Acts of grand corruption deserve to be criminalised for several reasons. The seriousness of these acts, as demonstrated in chapter I, is the main reason. Corrupt conduct of high-level public officials affects countries politically, economically, socially, and environmentally. This is particularly grave because the persons concerned have been given the most wide-ranging responsibilities over the welfare of the citizens, and therefore serious abuse of these public tasks for private benefit deserves to be punished. Yet, the argument that international criminal law should

---

168 See chapter II *supra*for an overview of the treaty regime.

169 See Desislava Stoitchkova, *Towards Corporate Liability in International Criminal Law* (School of Human Rights Research Series, 38; Antwerp: Intersentia, 2010).

focus on grand corruption does not intend to trivialise the harmfulness of petty corruption, which can also have destabilising effects. Rather, since grand corruption generally tends to trickle down, combating high-level corruption can also play an influential role in diminishing petty corruption.

Also, the officials working in the highest echelons of the nation State should be held accountable at the international level because it is likely that they will enjoy *de facto* immunity in their own country: for political reasons, those persons belonging to the government will probably escape prosecution at the domestic level. Moreover, under national legislation, certain State officials may also enjoy *de jure* immunity from the jurisdiction of their own national courts. This is particularly true for Heads of State and Government, and members of Cabinet and Parliament.[170]

Moreover, high level officials also enjoy immunity in foreign courts. Because of this *de facto* and *de jure* immunity, the responsibility for certain corrupt acts as described below, should be raised to the international level. The Rome Statute provides in Article 27 that neither immunities *ratione materiae* (functional immunities), nor immunities *ratione personae* (personal immunities) can be invoked before the ICC.[171]

The difficulty, however, lies in determining where to draw the actual line between petty and grand corruption, i.e. the conduct of which officials constitutes grand corruption? From a factual perspective, this can be troublesome, and anti-corruption treaties are also not useful when it comes to determining the dividing line between the two levels of corruption. Therefore, it is proposed to use the reasoning above as a guideline: the persons who enjoy immunity of prosecution before their own national courts should come under ICC jurisdiction. As a general rule, these are heads of State, heads of government, cabinet ministers and members of parliament.[172] Corrupt acts committed by these officials can be qualified as grand corruption, and should be addressed by international criminal law, with direct enforcement mechanisms at the international level. Inevitably, this limitation of actors will exclude other high-level officials not falling within the categories mentioned above, which may come across as arbitrary. Yet, at this moment, priority

---

170 Paola Gaeta, 'Official Capacity and Immunities', in Antonio Cassese, Paola Gaeta, and John R.W.D. Jones (eds.), *The Rome Statute of the International Criminal Court: A Commentary* (1; Oxford: Oxford University Press, 2002), 975–1002 at p. 977–978; Micaela Frulli, 'Immunities of Persons from Jurisdiction', in Antonio Cassese (ed.), *The Oxford Companion to International Criminal Justice* (Oxford: Oxford University Press, 2009), p. 368–369 at p. 368.

171 Article 27 of the Rome Statute: 1. This Statute shall apply equally to all persons without any distinction based on official capacity. In particular, official capacity as a Head of State or Government, a member of a Government or parliament, an elected representative or a government official shall in no case exempt a person from criminal responsibility under this Statute, nor shall it, in and of itself, constitute a ground for reduction of sentence.
2. Immunities or special procedural rules which may attach to the official capacity of a person, whether under national or international law, shall not bar the Court from exercising its jurisdiction over such a person.

172 Gaeta, 'Official Capacity and Immunities', at p. 977–978; Frulli, 'Immunities of Persons from Jurisdiction', at p. 368.

should be given to setting clear boundaries for the purpose of international criminalisation.

6.3. Types of Corruption – UNCAC

When searching for a listing of corrupt offences, the UNCAC should be used.[173] Given the fact that currently 152 States are Party to this treaty, the definitions of the various types of corruption it contains are supported by a large majority of States. The UNCAC lists the following types of corruption: active and passive bribery; active and passive trading in influence; embezzlement; abuse of functions; and illicit enrichment.[174]

For the purposes of international criminal law, emphasis should be put on passive bribery and embezzlement. Passive bribery is defined by Article 15 UNCAC as 'the solicitation or acceptance by a public official, directly or indirectly, of an undue advantage, for the official him-or herself or another person or entity, in order that the official act or refrain from acting in the exercise of his or her official duties.' Embezzlement is defined by Article 17 UNCAC as:

> … the embezzlement, misappropriation or other diversion by a public official for his or her benefit or the benefit of another person or entity, of any property, public or private funds or securities or any other thing of value entrusted to the public official by virtue of his or her position.

Focus on passive bribery and embezzlement is justified because, under the UNCAC, it is mandatory for State Parties to criminalise these offences in their national legislation, unlike a number of other corruption offences, which are merely optional to criminalise. As noted above, active bribery and active trading influence fall outside of the realm of the present work because these offences focus upon the supply side, a role fulfilled by private persons or institutions.

Furthermore, the offences of passive trading in influence, abuse of functions, and illicit enrichment should be kept, for the time being, outside of the debate on international criminalisation. Passive trading in influence is too vague an offence to be criminalised at the international level. The same is true for abuse of functions. It is also relevant that the UNCAC does not demand compulsory criminalisation of these offences; rather, it is stated that States 'shall consider adopting' legislation on these matters. Moreover, the concepts are likely to be problematic in terms of their compliance with the principle of legality, *nullum crimen sine lege*, which requires that the conduct concerned must be defined as clearly as possible in the definition of the crime.[175] For abuse of functions and illicit enrichment, this is not the case. Also,

[173] See chapter II, §3.6.2 *supra*for an extensive discussion of the content of the UNCAC.

[174] See chapter I, section 3 *supra*for an elaborate discussion of these five types of corruption.

[175] Werle, *Principles of International Criminal Law*, at p. 37, para. 104.

from a practical point of view (i.e. international prosecution) these offences are troublesome because evidence gathering will be difficult. Furthermore, the offence of illicit enrichment also poses problems because it reverses the burden of proof: the accused public official has to demonstrate that his increase in income is a result of legal means.

Consequently, the focus of the present Part C is on passive bribery and embezzlement, as committed by heads of State, heads of government, cabinet ministers and members of parliament.

7. Concluding Remarks

The present chapter aimed to determine whether the system of international criminal law leaves any room for tackling corruption. To this end, a historical analysis was conducted, as well as a study into the underlying rationales for international criminalisation, and an inquiry into the objectives of punishment in international criminal law.

From the historical analysis, it followed that, thus far, little attention was paid to economic crimes. International criminal law was, and is, mainly seen as a response to crimes committed during conflict situations, instead of crimes committed during peacetime. Furthermore, international criminal law primarily focuses upon violent crimes, and accords preferential treatment to civil and political rights as compared to economic and social rights. In the words of Bantekas, 'from a criminal policy perspective, prosecutors, judges and academic commentators in the West are accustomed to exorcizing international crimes that involve the spilling of blood.'[176] Hence, it is difficult to argue that economic crimes would fit within the system from a historical point of view. Only on a small number of occasions have economic crimes been discussed. On the other hand, there seem to be few convincing arguments to support the conclusion that non-violent crimes such as corruption should *not* be included in international criminal law. History shows that the establishment of the Rome Statute has its roots, *inter alia*, in proposals to combat drug trafficking, which is not necessarily a violent crime. Moreover, it is clear that corruption does form part of transnational criminal law since many treaties exist that oblige States to criminalise a variety of forms of corruption at the national level.

The study into the rationales for international criminalisation demonstrated that all six principles for criminalisation, as identified by De Roos, can be met. One of the main criteria for international criminalisation, as noted by Bassiouni, is the presence of an international element, consisting of conduct which offends the commonly shared values of the world community. It can be argued that large-scale

176 Ilias Bantekas, 'Corruption as an International Crime and a Crime against Humanity: An Outline of Supplementary Criminal Justice Policies', *Journal of International Criminal Justice*, 4 (2006), p. 466–484 at p. 473.

corruption, such as embezzlement of public funds which leaves developing countries crippled, does indeed constitute such conduct. Furthermore, it is also possible that corruption poses a threat to international peace and security. Moreover, crimes under international law containing an international element are State-sponsored or involve State activity. Corruption meets this standard, since (especially high-level) corrupt officials perceive of State institutions as mere vehicles to obtain access to the wealth of a country for personal gain. In such instances, international criminal law is an appropriate mechanism to curb the greed of officials.

Examination of the objectives of punishment in international criminal law supports the view that international criminalisation of corruption is merited. Punishment of corrupt public officials at the international level may serve several objectives, in particular retribution, general deterrence, expressivism, justice for victims, and truth telling. The expressivist goal is crucial in this respect: punishing grand corruption in the public sector at the international level will communicate the universal disapproval of corruption to the general public and to the offender.

If one concludes that corruption should indeed be addressed by employing international criminal law, it is important to determine which types of corruption qualify for this approach. As argued, emphasis should be put on two out of five types of corruption included in the UNCAC: passive bribery and embezzlement, because the UNCAC provides for mandatory criminalisation of these offences. Furthermore, these offences have to be committed at the highest levels of the State: by heads of State, heads of government, cabinet ministers and members of parliament, since these officials are likely to escape prosecution before domestic courts.

The question now arises how international criminal law, as it currently stands, should specifically address corrupt acts committed by the above-mentioned actors. It is interesting to examine whether corruption can constitute a crime under international law, as codified in the Rome Statute. What comes to mind first is the concept of crimes against humanity, since these crimes do not have to be committed during armed conflict.[177] The possibilities of conceptualising corruption as a crime against humanity are studied in the following chapter VIII. Furthermore, chapter IX considers the possibilities for inclusion of a new provision into the Rome Statute, criminalising forms of corruption (*de lege ferenda* perspective), as well as other options for using international criminal law to combat corruption.

---

177 ICTY *Prosecutor v. Tadić*, IT–94–1-AR72, Appeals Chamber Judgment 2 October 1995, §141.

Chapter VIII
Corruption as a Crime Against Humanity under International Law *de lege lata*?

1. Introduction

In 2008, the Socio-Economic Rights and Accountability Project (hereafter: SERAP), a Nigerian NGO, petitioned the ICC Prosecutor to request the Court to use its position and powers 'to examine and investigate whether the systemic/grand corruption in Nigeria amounts to a crime against humanity within the jurisdiction of the International Criminal Court, and to prevail on the Nigerian government to fulfil its obligations to effectively and fairly investigate and prosecute all allegations of grand corruption since 1985.' SERAP argued that:

> ... the nature and scale of official/grand corruption in Nigeria amounts to an 'international' crime – that is, conduct that is in breach of 'peremptory norms' and for which universal jurisdiction is appropriate. Systemic/official corruption at the highest level of government has had a catastrophic effect on the lives of millions of Nigerians, akin to crimes against humanity as a contemplated under the Rome Statute and within the jurisdiction of the Court. [...] The common denominator of those crimes against humanity is that they are grave affronts to human security and dignity. As demonstrated above, the scale and magnitude of grand corruption in Nigeria creates just these consequences. Crimes against humanity are not only physical violence; rampant corruption holds a comparable gravity, which the Prosecutor should example and investigate.[1]

In a similar vein, the present chapter examines whether certain forms of corruption can be conceptualised as a crime against humanity *de lege lata*. Focus is on passive bribery and embezzlement, committed by heads of State, heads of government, cabinet ministers and members of parliament. The provisions of the Rome Statute are taken as a starting point.

To begin with, the concept of crimes against humanity is explored by examining its components *actus reus*, *mens rea*, and the contextual element. These components are shared by all crimes under international law, as codified in the Rome Statute. *Actus reus* (*Lat*: guilty act; criminal conduct) is the material or objective element of the crime, which is comprised of all elements in the definition of the crime, with the exception of the mental element of the accused.[2] This mental or subjective element is *mens rea* (*Lat*: guilty mind), which entails the state of mind of the accused at the

---

1 SERAP Nigeria, <www.serap-nigeria.org/cases-in-court>.

2 Liu Daqun, 'Actus Reus', in Antonio Cassese (ed.), *The Oxford Companion to International Criminal Justice* (Oxford: Oxford University Press, 2009), p. 229–230.

time of the offence.[3] The third common feature of crimes under international law is the existence of a contextual element. This is crucial because it separates a crime under international law from an ordinary crime under national law.[4] Section 2 elaborates upon the *actus reus*, *mens rea*, and contextual element of crimes against humanity.

Thereafter, a number of crimes against humanity that are currently criminalised in the Rome Statute are considered, in order to determine whether these crimes can possibly cover corrupt practices. Scholarly claims arguing that corruption can be seen as either extermination (section 3) or as another inhumane act (section 4) are carefully scrutinised.

Finally, section 5 provides conclusions, and argues that the classification of corruption as a crime against humanity under the current Rome Statute is highly unlikely.

2. Elements of Crimes Against Humanity: General Framework

2.1. Article 7 Rome Statute

Crimes against humanity were first codified in the Nuremberg Charter (Article 6 (c)), and were later included in the Tokyo Charter and in Control Council Law No. 10. Subsequently, the Statutes of the ICTY (Article 5) and the ICTR (Article 3) provide for the prosecution of this type of crimes.[5] The present section concentrates on the Rome Statute, which contains a definition of crimes against humanity in Article 7(1):

> For the purpose of this Statute, "crime against humanity" means any of the following acts when committed as part of a widespread or systematic attack directed against any civilian population, with knowledge of the attack:
>
> (a) Murder;
> (b) Extermination;
> (c) Enslavement;
> (d) Deportation or forcible transfer of population;

---

3 Antonio Vallini, 'Mens Rea', in Antonio Cassese (ed.), *The Oxford Companion to International Criminal Justice* (Oxford: Oxford University Press, 2009), p. 412–415.

4 Gerhard Werle, *Principles of International Criminal Law* (The Hague: TMC Asser Press, 2009) at p. 141, §375.

5 For more on the historical background of crimes against humanity, see M. Cherif Bassiouni, 'Crimes against Humanity', in M. Cherif Bassiouni (ed.), *International Criminal Law* (3rd edn., Volume I: Sources, subjects and contents Leiden: Martinus Nijhoff Publishers, 2008), p. 437–492.

(e) Imprisonment or other severe deprivation of physical liberty in violation of fundamental rules of international law;
(f) Torture;
(g) Rape, sexual slavery, enforced prostitution, forced pregnancy, enforced sterilisation, or any other form of sexual violence of comparable gravity;
(h) Persecution against any identifiable group or collectivity on political, racial, national, ethnic, cultural, religious, gender as defined in paragraph 3, or other grounds that are universally recognised as impermissible under international law, in connection with any act referred to in this paragraph or any crime within the jurisdiction of the Court;
(i) Enforced disappearance of persons;
(j) The crime of apartheid;
(k) Other inhumane acts of a similar character intentionally causing great suffering, or serious injury to body or to mental or physical health.

It is imperative to carefully analyse each component of the definition contained in the *chapeau* of Article 7(1), before defining a number of the specific crimes listed under (a) – (k). In this respect the Elements of Crimes should be consulted.[6]

An important observation can be found in the introduction to the Elements of crimes against humanity, which states that:

> Since article 7 pertains to international criminal law, its provisions, consistent with article 22, *must be strictly construed*, taking into account that crimes against humanity as defined in article 7 are among the most serious crimes of concern to the international community as a whole, warrant and entail individual criminal responsibility, and require conduct which is impermissible under generally applicable international law, as recognized by the principal legal systems of the world [emphasis added, MB].[7]

Article 22 provides in its second paragraph that 'the definition of a crime shall be strictly construed and shall not be extended by analogy. In case of ambiguity, the definition shall be interpreted in favour of the person being investigated, prosecuted or convicted.' Hence, crimes codified in the Rome Statute, including crimes against humanity, may not be interpreted broadly.

---

6 The Elements of Crimes, to which Article 9 of the Rome Statute refers, were written by the Preparatory Commission for the ICC, and adopted in December 2002 by the Assembly of States Parties. The Elements contain detailed explanations of the components of Article 6, 7 and 8 of the Rome Statute, and thus provide guidance for the ICC. See Robert Cryer, 'Elements of Crimes', in Antonio Cassese (ed.), *The Oxford Companion to International Criminal Justice* (Oxford: Oxford University Press, 2009), p. 308–309; Roy S. Lee (ed.), *The International Criminal Court: Elements of Crimes and Rules of Procedure and Evidence* (Ardsley: Transnational Publishers, 2001) at Part One; Mauro Politi, 'Elements of Crimes', in Antonio Cassese, Paola Gaeta, and John R.W.D. Jones (eds.), *The Rome Statute of the International Criminal Court: A Commentary* (1; Oxford: Oxford University Press, 2002), p. 443–473.

7 Elements of Crimes, Article 7 Introduction §1.

2.2. *Actus Reus*

The material element of crimes against humanity, the *actus reus*, consists of three components: conduct, consequence and circumstance. This can be inferred from Article 30 of the Rome Statute, which itself deals with the mental elements of crimes. 'Conduct' (Article 30(2)(a)) simply means that the crime must consist of an action or omission. While most crimes in the Rome Statute can only be committed through an act, some crimes can also be committed by an omission. 'Consequence' (Article 30(2)(b)) entails that the consequence of the crime must actually occur. However, certain crimes can also include the risk that a certain consequence occurs. In this case, it is not necessary that the consequence of the crime actually takes place. 'Circumstance' (Article 30(3)) concerns the factual circumstances of the crime (e.g. the age of the victim) or its legal circumstances (e.g. the fact that the victim is protected under the Geneva Conventions). Moreover, the contextual element is a special type of circumstantial element, which is discussed *infra* in section 2.4.[8]

2.3. *Mens Rea*

As noted, Article 30 of the Rome Statute contains the mental elements of crimes under international law. Pursuant to the first paragraph of this Article, the two components of *mens rea* are intent and knowledge.[9] Their existence can be inferred from relevant facts and circumstances.[10] Article 30 applies by default to the crimes laid down in the Rome Statute, unless the Elements of Crimes provide otherwise. Whenever there are deviations from Article 30, there is nearly always a reduction of the standard of Article 30.[11]

---

8 Maria Kelt and Herman von Hebel, 'The Making of the Elements of Crimes – IV. What Are Elements of Crimes?' in Roy S. Lee (ed.), *The International Criminal Court: Elements of Crimes and Rules of Procedure and Evidence* (Ardsley: Transnational Publishers, 2001), p. 13–18 at p. 14–15; Maria Kelt and Herman von Hebel, 'General Principles of Criminal Law and the Elements of Crimes', in Roy S. Lee (ed.), *The International Criminal Court: Elements of Crimes and Rules of Procedure and Evidence* (Ardsley: Transnational Publishers, 2001), p. 19–40 at p. 26–28. See also Erkin Gadirov and revised by Roger S. Clark, 'Article 9: Elements of Crimes', in Otto Triffterer (ed.), *Commentary on the Rome Statute of the International Criminal Court. Observers' Notes, Article by Article* (2nd edn.; München: C.H. Beck, 2008), p. 505–529 at p. 515–522, §13–24.

9 Article 30(1) Rome Statute: Unless otherwise provided, a person shall be criminally responsible and liable for punishment for a crime within the jurisdiction of the Court only if the material elements are committed with intent and knowledge.

10 Elements of Crimes, General Introduction §3.

11 Elements of Crimes, General Introduction §2. Kelt and Hebel, 'General Principles of Criminal Law and the Elements of Crimes', at p. 29–30; Donald K. Piragoff and Darryl Robinson, 'Article 30: Mental Element', in Otto Triffterer (ed.), *Commentary on the Rome Statute of the International Criminal Court. Observers' Notes, Article by Article* (2nd edn.; München: C.H. Beck, 2008), p. 849–961 at p. 856–858, §14–15.

2.3.1. *'Intent'*

From the second paragraph of Article 30, we can learn that 'intent' relates to both conduct and consequence. Intent in relation to conduct signifies that the person means to engage in the conduct, i.e. the perpetrator must act voluntary and with some degree of knowledge.[12]

Intent in relation to a consequence is present when the person means to cause that consequence or is aware that it will occur in the ordinary course of events. The latter phrase deserves further consideration. When can we conclude that a person is 'aware' that a consequence will occur in the ordinary course of events, in other words: what degree of awareness is required? Here, we must distinguish between the notions *dolus directus* (in the first and second degree) and *dolus eventualis*. *Dolus directus* in the first degree entails that the perpetrator knows of, and wants to achieve, the consequence of the criminal action. *Dolus directus* in the second degree signifies that the perpetrator is aware of the inevitability of the consequence of the criminal action. *Dolus eventualis* however is present:

> ... when a person, who is going to do something that will cause an event, is fully aware of the possible outcome as a side-effect to such behaviour, but nevertheless decides to continue with the conduct, recognizing and approving the result as a possible cost of attaining the aimed goal. Approval of an evil result, though not directly pursued by the actor ('side effect'), is the subjective attitude that underpins the criminal conviction.[13]

It is crucial to determine whether or not Article 30 allows for *dolus eventualis* as a type of intent. This is a contentious issue.[14] Van Sliedregt found that *dolus eventualis* is not part of the mental element of Article 30 because this provision explicitly requires awareness that the consequence '*will* occur'.[15] Moreover, Werle noted that the *mens rea* standard of Article 30 is stricter than the standards applied by national courts and international courts such as the ICTY and the ICTR (which do accept *dolus eventualis* as a type of intent), and questioned this contradiction.[16]

---

12 Piragoff and Robinson, 'Article 30: Mental Element', at p. 859, §19.

13 Alberto di Martino, 'Dolus Eventualis', in Antonio Cassese (ed.), *The Oxford Companion to International Criminal Justice* (Oxford: Oxford University Press, 2009), p. 302–304 at p. 302., see also Piragoff and Robinson, 'Article 30: Mental Element', at p. 860, §22.

14 Martino, 'Dolus Eventualis', at p. 303. Gerhard Werle and Florian Jessberger, ''Unless Otherwise Provided': Article 30 of the ICC Statute and the Mental Element of Crimes under International Criminal Law', *Journal of International Criminal Justice*, 3 (2005), p. 35–55 at p. 52. See footnote 95 of their contribution for an overview of scholarly opinions on the question whether or not *dolus eventualis* comes under the scope of Article 30.

15 E. van Sliedregt, *The Criminal Responsibility of Individuals for Violations of International Humanitarian Law* (The Hague: TMC Asser Press, 2003) at p. 51–52.

16 Werle, *Principles of International Criminal Law* at p. 153–154, §409. Werle and Jessberger, ''Unless Otherwise Provided': Article 30 of the ICC Statute and the Mental Element of Crimes under International Criminal Law', at p. 41–42 and 51–54.

However, there are a number of new developments. Werle referred to the decision of the ICC Pre-Trial Chamber in *Lubanga*, which set out that apart from first and second degree *dolus directus*, Article 30 also encompasses 'situations in which the suspect is aware that the risk of the objective elements of the crime may result from his or her actions or omissions and accepts such an outcome by reconciling himself or herself with it or consenting to it (also known as *dolus eventualis*).' Hence, this judgment interprets Article 30 in a more extensive matter, with the phrase 'in the *ordinary* course of events' as a starting point.[17] Nonetheless, Werle noted that such an interpretation is contrary to the wording of Article 30 and criticised the Pre-Trial Chamber for flaws in its line of reasoning.[18] Instead, in order to solve the problem of the narrowly worded Article 30, Werle referred to the phrase 'unless otherwise provided', which may cover provisions from the Rome Statute, from the Elements of Crimes, and from other sources of international law under Article 21 of the Statute, particularly customary international law.[19] In the same line of reasoning, Di Martino pointed out that, while the text of Article 30(2)(b) does not leave room for *dolus eventualis*, it can however be sufficient as a mental element for some crimes, because of the phrase 'unless otherwise provided'. General principles of criminal law do allow for *dolus eventualis* as a form of *mens rea*.[20]

Nevertheless, the ICC Pre-Trial Chamber II decision in *Bemba* clearly deviates from *Lubanga*, by making clear that *dolus eventualis* is *not* covered by Article 30. The Chamber stated: 'With respect to *dolus eventualis* as the third form of *dolus*, recklessness or any lower form of culpability, the Chamber is of the view that such concepts are not captured by Article 30 of the Statute. This conclusion is supported by the express language of the phrase 'will occur in the ordinary course of events', which does not accommodate a lower standard than the one required by *dolus directus in the second degree* (oblique intention).'[21] Furthermore, the Chamber stated that this finding 'ensures that the Chamber is not substituting the concept of *de lege lata* with the concept of *de lege ferenda* only for the sake of widening the scope of Article 30 of the Statute and capturing a broader range of perpetrators.'[22]

---

17 ICC *Prosecutor v. Lubanga Dyilo*, Decision Pre-Trial Chamber I, 29 January 2007, ICC–01/04–01/06–803, §349 *et seq.* and especially §352. WERLE, *Principles of International Criminal Law* at p. 154, §410–411.

18 *Ibid.* at p. 155, §412.

19 *Ibid.* at p. 155, §413 and p. 156, §416. WERLE and JESSBERGER, ''Unless Otherwise Provided': Article 30 of the ICC Statute and the Mental Element of Crimes under International Criminal Law', at p. 51–54.

20 MARTINO, 'Dolus Eventualis', at p. 303–304.

21 ICC *Prosecutor v. Jean-Pierre Bemba Gombo*, Decision Pre-Trial Chamber 15 June 2009, ICC–01/05–01/08, §360. For criticism on the Pre-Trial Chamber's reasoning, see KAI AMBOS, 'Critical Issues in the Bemba Confirmation Decision', *Leiden Journal of International Law*, 22 (2009), p. 715–726 at p. 717–719 and MOHAMED ELEWA BADAR, 'Dolus Eventualis and the Rome Statute without It?' *New Criminal Law Review*, 12 (2009), p. 433–467.

22 *Prosecutor v. Bemba*, §369.

This view is upheld by the ICC Trial Chamber in its first trial judgment, *Lubanga*.[23] In this judgment, the ICC rejects the views on *dolus eventualis* of the Pre-Trial Chamber in *Lubanga*. The Trial Chamber sets out that:

> The drafting history of the Statute suggests that the notion of *dolus eventualis*, along with the concept of recklessness, was deliberately excluded from the framework of the Statute (e.g. see the use of the words "unless otherwise provided" in the first sentence of Article 30). The plain language of the Statute, and most particularly the use of the words "will occur" in Article 30(2)(b) as opposed to "may occur", excludes the concept of *dolus eventualis.* The Chamber accepts the approach of Pre-Trial Chamber II on this issue.[24]

2.3.2. 'Knowledge'

According to the third paragraph of Article 30, 'knowledge' relates to circumstance and consequence. 'Knowledge' means awareness that a circumstance exists or a consequence will occur in the ordinary course of events.

As indicated in the *chapeau* of Article 7(1), the perpetrator must have knowledge of the widespread or systematic attack, i.e. knowledge of the contextual element of a crime against humanity. According to the Elements of Crimes, all crimes against humanity require that 'the perpetrator knew that the conduct was part of or intended the conduct to be part of a widespread or systematic attack against a civilian population.' Nevertheless, it is also stated that this:

> '... should not be interpreted as requiring proof that the perpetrator had knowledge of *all* characteristics of the attack or the precise details of the plan or policy of the State or organization. In case of an emerging widespread or systematic attack against a civilian population, the intent clause of the last element indicates that this mental element is satisfied if the perpetrator intended to further such an attack.[25]

In sum, the mental element for a crime against humanity consists of both (i) the knowledge of the contextual element; and (ii) the *mens rea* required for the specific criminal act.[26] These and other matters are elaborated upon in further detail in

---

23 ICC *Prosecutor v. Thomas Lubanga Dyilo*, Judgment Pursuant to Article 74 of the Statute, Trial Chamber 14 March 2012, ICC–01/04–01/06.

24 *Ibid.* at §1011. For a further elaboration of this topic, see THOMAS R. LIEFLÄNDER, 'The Lubanga Judgment of the ICC: More than Just the First Step?', *Cambridge Journal of International and Comparative Law*, (2012), p. 191–212, section 3.

25 Elements of Crimes, Article 7 Introduction §2. See also RODNEY DIXON and REVISED BY CHRISTOPHER K. HALL, 'Article 7: Crimes against Humanity', in Otto Triffterer (ed.), *Commentary on the Rome Statute of the International Criminal Court. Observers' Notes, Article by Article* (2nd edn.; München: C.H. Beck, 2008), p. 168–183 at p. 181–182, §15.

26 SIMON CHESTERMAN, 'An Altogether Different Order: Defining the Elements of Crimes against Humanity', *Duke Journal of Comparative and International Law*, 10 (2000), p. 307–343 at p. 314.

section 3, hereafter, when discussing the material and mental elements of various crimes against humanity listed in Article 7.

2.4. Contextual Element: 'Widespread or Systematic Attack Directed Against Any Civilian Population'

As previously noted, crimes under international law all contain a contextual element. For crimes against humanity, this is the requirement of 'a widespread or systematic attack directed against any civilian population', as stated in the *chapeau* of Article 7(1) and further elaborated upon in Article 7(2)(a) and in the Elements of Crimes, Introduction to Article 7.

2.4.1. 'Widespread'

First, there must be either a widespread attack, *or* a systematic attack.[27] The notion of 'widespread' refers to a quantitative element, i.e. the number of victims or the broad geographical extension.[28] It was defined by the ICTR in *Akayesu,* its first trial, as 'massive, frequent, large scale action, carried out collectively with considerable seriousness and directed against a multiplicity of victims.'[29] However, both Dixon and Cryer argued that this imposes an excessively high threshold, and note that recent ICTR and ICTY case law is more expansive; it is now understood that 'widespread' refers to 'the large-scale nature of the attack and the number of targeted persons.'[30] It will depend on the factual circumstances whether an attack is widespread.[31]

2.4.2. 'Systematic'

The notion of a 'systematic' attack, which is qualitative in nature,[32] has been defined in various ways, *inter alia,* by the ICTR in *Akayesu:* 'the concept of

---

27 Note that only the *attack* has to be widespread *or* systematic, not the individual act itself: DIXON and REVISED BY CHRISTOPHER K. HALL, 'Article 7: Crimes against Humanity', at p. 179, §11.

28 WERLE, *Principles of International Criminal Law* at p. 298, §804.

29 ICTR *Prosecutor v. Akayesu* ICTR–96–4-T, Trial Chamber Judgment 2 September 1998, §580. CHESTERMAN, 'An Altogether Different Order: Defining the Elements of Crimes against Humanity', at p. 315. For more on the Akayesu trial, see AMIR ČENGIĆ, 'Akayesu', in Antonio Cassese (ed.), *The Oxford Companion to International Criminal Justice* (Oxford: Oxford University Press, 2009), p. 577–580.

30 DIXON and REVISED BY CHRISTOPHER K. HALL, 'Article 7: Crimes against Humanity', at p. 178, §11. ROBERT CRYER *et al., An Introduction to International Criminal Law and Procedure* (Cambridge: Cambridge University Press, 2007) at p. 194–195 and footnote 39. For an overview of later ICTR, ICTY and ICC case law on the criterion of a 'widespread attack', see also WERLE, *Principles of International Criminal Law* at p. 298, footnote 61–62.

31 CRYER *et al., An Introduction to International Criminal Law and Procedure* at p. 194–195.

32 WERLE, *Principles of International Criminal Law* at p. 298, §805.

'systematic' may be defined as thoroughly organised and following a regular pattern on the basis of a common policy involving substantial public or private resources.'[33]Again, it is noted that this judgment sets too high a standard, and that later case law adopts a broader definition: 'systematic' refers to 'the organised nature of the acts of violence and the improbability of their random occurrence.' Moreover, 'patterns of crimes, in the sense of the non-accidental repetition of similar criminal conduct on a regular basis, are a common expression of such systematic occurrence.'[34] In sum, according to Cryer, the key characteristic of 'systematic' is the high degree of organisation. Important factors are components such as patterns, continuous commission, use of resources, planning, and political objectives.[35]

2.4.3. 'Attack'

Article 7(2)(a) of the Rome Statute provides that '"attack directed against any civilian population" means a course of conduct involving the multiple commission of acts referred to in paragraph 1 against any civilian population, pursuant to or in furtherance of a State or organisational policy to commit such an attack.' This is reiterated in the Elements of Crimes.[36]

As regards the nature of the attack, the Elements set out that 'the acts need not constitute a military attack.'[37] Furthermore, as confirmed by the ICTY in *Tadić*, an act does not require a nexus to a situation of armed conflict in order to qualify as a crime against humanity.[38] Moreover, an attack does not have to involve the use of armed force: it can consist of any mistreatment of the civilian population. Violence is not required. For example, the crimes against humanity of apartheid and imprisonment can be non-violent.[39]

---

33 ICTR *Prosecutor v. Akayesu*, ICTR–96–4-T, Trial Chamber Judgment 2 September 1998, §580. Chesterman, 'An Altogether Different Order: Defining the Elements of Crimes against Humanity', at p. 315.

34 Dixon and revised by Christopher K. Hall, 'Article 7: Crimes against Humanity', at p. 179, §11.

35 Cryer *et al.*, *An Introduction to International Criminal Law and Procedure* at p. 195.

36 Elements of Crimes, Article 7 Introduction §3.

37 *Ibid.*

38 ICTY *Prosecutor v. Tadić,* IT–94–1-AR72, Appeals Chamber Judgment 2 October 1995, §141. The ICTY stated that 'it is by now a settled rule of customary international law that crimes against humanity do not require a connection to international armed conflict. Indeed, as the Prosecutor points out, customary international law may not require a connection between crimes against humanity and any conflict at all. Thus, by requiring that crimes against humanity be committed in either internal or international armed conflict, the Security Council may have defined the crime in Article 5 more narrowly than necessary under customary international law. There is no question, however, that the definition of crimes against humanity adopted by the Security Council in Article 5 comports with the principle of *nullum crimen sine lege*.' See also Yoram Dinstein, 'Crimes against Humanity after Tadić', *Leiden Journal of International Law*, 13 (2000), p. 373–393.

39 Dixon and revised by Christopher K. Hall, 'Article 7: Crimes against Humanity', at p. 175, §8–9. Cryer *et al.*, *An Introduction to International Criminal Law and Procedure* at p. 195.

In respect of the policy to commit an attack against any civilian population, the Elements set out that such a policy 'requires that the State or organization actively promote or encourage such an attack against a civilian population.'[40] Furthermore, a policy which has a civilian population as the object of the attack would be implemented by State or organisational action. Such a policy may, in exceptional circumstances, be implemented by a deliberate failure to take action, which is consciously aimed at encouraging such an attack. The existence of such a policy cannot be inferred solely from the absence of governmental or organisational action.[41] This policy element is what separates an isolated crime under domestic law from a crime under international law.[42] Overall, as noted by Bassiouni, crimes against humanity demand that (i) there is a State policy; (ii) this policy must be to commit specific crimes listed in Article 7(1); and (iii) that the commission of these crimes is either widespread or systematic.[43] Nonetheless, it was noted by Dixon that the policy requirement is not in conformity with customary international law.[44]

2.4.4. 'Directed Against Any Civilian Population'

The term 'any' civilian population reveals that crimes against humanity can also be committed against a country's own citizens, not merely against foreign citizens.[45] The notion 'population' entails that 'a larger body of victims is visualised', and that 'single or isolated acts against individuals' are not covered by the concept. But it is not necessary that the entire population of a State, entity or territory is subject to the attack.[46] For the existence of an 'attack against any civilian population', there must be at least multiple acts or multiple victims. The acts can all be of the same type, or of different types, i.e. a combination of various crimes against humanity listed in Article 7(1).[47]

2.5. Individual Criminal Responsibility

After the establishment of the material, mental, and contextual elements of the crime, the grounds for individual criminal responsibility have to be considered.

CHESTERMAN, 'An Altogether Different Order: Defining the Elements of Crimes against Humanity', at p. 315–316.

40 Elements of Crimes, Article 7 Introduction §3.

41 *Ibid.* footnote 6.

42 CHESTERMAN, 'An Altogether Different Order: Defining the Elements of Crimes against Humanity', at p. 316–317.

43 BASSIOUNI, 'Crimes against Humanity', at p. 462.

44 DIXON and REVISED BY CHRISTOPHER K. HALL, 'Article 7: Crimes against Humanity', at p. 236, §91.

45 CRYER *et al.*, *An Introduction to International Criminal Law and Procedure* at p. 188 and 92. DIXON and REVISED BY CHRISTOPHER K. HALL, 'Article 7: Crimes against Humanity', at p. 181, §13.

46 CRYER *et al.*, *An Introduction to International Criminal Law and Procedure* at p. 192. DIXON and REVISED BY CHRISTOPHER K. HALL, 'Article 7: Crimes against Humanity', at p. 180, §13.

47 CRYER *et al.*, *An Introduction to International Criminal Law and Procedure* at p. 195.

Article 25 of the Rome Statute lays down several modes of participation: (i) commission as an individual, joint commission, commission through another person (Article 25(3)(a)); (ii) encouragement in the form of ordering or instigation (Article 25(3)(b); (iii) assistance of the (primary) perpetrator, of the commission of a crime by a group (Article 25(3)(c) and (d).[48] Article 28 lays down the responsibility of commanders and other superiors.[49]

Sections 3 and 4 hereafter concern the first mode of participation (i.e. commission as an individual or jointly with another person) and employ the structure indicated in the Elements of Crimes:

> The elements of crimes are generally structured in accordance with the following principles:
>
> – As the elements of crimes focus on the conduct, consequences and circumstances associated with each crime, they are generally listed in that order;
> – When required, a particular mental element is listed after the affected conduct, consequence or circumstance;
> – Contextual elements are listed last.[50]

3. Corruption as 'Extermination'?

3.1. Introduction

The time has now come to critically assess the validity of a number of claims made by several scholars, all directed at conceptualising corruption as a crime against humanity. For example, Bantekas argued that corruption can be regarded a crime against humanity, namely as extermination.[51] In his view, this approach has a number of benefits: (i) it covers misappropriation of foreign aid and State resources by the government, which results in deprivation of food and medical care; (ii) corruption as a crime against humanity would become subject to universal jurisdiction and would fall within the jurisdiction of the ICC; and (iii) corruption as a crime against humanity would become subject to a stricter regime of sanctions.[52] This, in itself sympathetic, argumentation deserves to be examined carefully, while it should also be noted that Bantekas did not intend 'to offer an exhaustive analysis, but rather to give rise to an academic debate by sketching out the parameters of

48 Gerhard Werle, *Principles of International Criminal Law* (The Hague: TMC Asser Press, 2005) at p. 120–128, §345–366.
49 *Ibid.* at p. 128–137, §367–400.
50 Elements of Crimes, General Introduction §7.
51 Ilias Bantekas, 'Corruption as an International Crime and a Crime against Humanity: An Outline of Supplementary Criminal Justice Policies', *Journal of International Criminal Justice*, 4 (2006), p. 466–484.
52 *Ibid.* at p. 475, 484.

corruption as a possible crime against humanity'.[53] Likewise, Davidsson discussed the possibility of framing 'economic oppression' as extermination.[54] Hence, it is now essential to further develop upon the reasoning of both authors, and to test whether corruption can indeed be conceptualised as extermination.

3.2. Elements of Extermination

Extermination, listed in Article 7(1)(b) of the Rome Statute as a crime against humanity, can be defined as 'an act or combination of acts which contributes to the killing of a large number of individuals', either directly or indirectly.[55] It is further specified in Article 7(2)(b), which provides that this offence 'includes the intentional infliction of conditions of life, *inter alia* the deprivation of access to food and medicine, calculated to bring about the destruction of part of a population'.[56]

The Elements of Crimes state that extermination entails that the perpetrator killed one or more persons, including by inflicting conditions of life calculated to bring about the destruction of part of a population.[57] This conduct can be committed by different methods of killing, either directly or indirectly.[58] Furthermore, the infliction of the conditions of life can include the deprivation of access to food and medicine.[59] As examples of such indirect killings, the ICTR mentions the imprisonment of a large group of people while depriving them of necessities; or the infection of a large group of people with a deadly virus, while withholding medical care from them.[60] The above-mentioned constitutes the conduct element of the *actus reus* of extermination. The *mens rea* requirements that apply to this conduct

---

53 *Ibid.* at p. 474.

54 Elias Davidsson, 'Economic Oppression as an International Wrong or as a Crime against Humanity', *Netherlands Quarterly of Human Rights*, 23 (2005), p. 173–212 at p. 193–196. Davidsson defines economic oppression as a crime against humanity as 'deliberate measures adopted with the intent or knowledge that they will subject a civilian population to inhumane conditions of existence or perpetuate such conditions.' Davidsson, 'Economic Oppression as an International Wrong or as a Crime against Humanity', at p. 185.

55 Guénaël Mettraux, 'Extermination', in Antonio Cassese (ed.), *The Oxford Companion to International Criminal Justice* (Oxford: Oxford University Press, 2009), p. 320–322 at p. 320.

56 Extermination is also included in Article 6(c) of the Nuremberg Charter, Article 5(c) of the Tokyo Charter, Article II(1)(c) of the Control Council Law No. 10, Article 5(b) of the ICTY Statute and Article 3(b) of the ICTR Statute. The phrase 'includes [...] population' stems from the 1948 Genocide Convention. Darryl Robinson, 'The Elements of Crimes against Humanity – Iii. Elements of the Specific Forms of Crime against Humanity: Article 7(1)(a)-Article 7(G)', in Roy S. Lee (ed.), *The International Criminal Court: Elements of Crimes and Rules of Procedure and Evidence* (Ardsley: Transnational Publishers, 2001), p. 80–93 at p. 81–82.

57 Elements of Crimes, Article 7(1)(b), §1.

58 Elements of Crimes, Article 7(1)(b), §1 footnote 8.

59 Elements of Crimes, Article 7(1)(b), §1 footnote 9.

60 Werle, *Principles of International Criminal Law* at p. 308, §830.

element are those laid down in Article 30, which applies by default.[61] Hence, the perpetrator must have intended to kill a large number of individuals, or to inflict grievous bodily harm, or serious injury, in the reasonable knowledge that such an act or omission was likely to cause death as in the case of murder. In the view of Mettraux, recklessness or gross negligence are not sufficient.[62]

The *actus reus* also consists of a circumstance element. This is laid down in the Elements of Crimes: 'the conduct constituted, or took place as part of, a mass killing of members of a civilian population'.[63] The term 'as part of' would include the initial conduct in a mass killing.[64] The circumstance of mass killing is what distinguishes extermination from murder.[65] In the view of Hall, it is not completely clear how many victims are required for the crime of extermination to occur.[66] Concerning the *mens rea* required for the circumstance element, it is held that the perpetrator needs to be aware that the conduct was part of the mass killing.[67]

Finally, like all crimes against humanity, extermination requires a contextual element: there must be a 'widespread or systematic attack directed against any civilian population', of which the perpetrator must have knowledge.[68]

When comparing extermination to murder, the difference lies in the fact that, as noted, extermination requires the circumstance of mass killing. Furthermore, extermination also includes indirect means of killing. Extermination is different from genocide, because genocide requires the special intent to destroy a group as such. In addition, genocide can only be targeted at either a national, ethnical, racial or religious group. Such requirements do not exist for extermination.[69]

3.3. Application

Can acts of corruption fulfil the criteria for extermination as stated above? When considering the conduct element of the *actus reus,* it seems that corruption can meet the standard of 'the infliction of conditions of life, *inter alia* the deprivation of

---

61 Robinson, 'The Elements of Crimes against Humanity – III. Elements of the Specific Forms of Crime against Humanity: Article 7(1)(a)–Article 7(G)', at p. 83.

62 Mettraux, 'Extermination', at p. 321. However, Hall notes that the case law of the Chambers of the ICTY and the ICTR is not consistent on the *mens rea* required for extermination. See Christopher K. Hall, 'Article 7: Crimes against Humanity; (B) Extermination', in Otto Triffterer (ed.), *Commentary on the Rome Statute of the International Criminal Court. Observers' Notes, Article by Article* (2nd edn.; München: C.H. Beck, 2008), p. 237–243 at p. 241–242, §94.

63 Elements of Crimes, Article 7(1)(b), §2.

64 *Ibid.* footnote 10.

65 Werle, *Principles of International Criminal Law* at p. 307, §828.

66 Hall, 'Article 7: Crimes against Humanity; (B) Extermination', at p. 238–239, §94.

67 Robinson, 'The Elements of Crimes against Humanity – III. Elements of the Specific Forms of Crime against Humanity: Article 7(1)(a)–Article 7(G)', at p. 84. Mettraux, 'Extermination', at p. 320.

68 Elements of Crimes, Article 7(1)(b), §3–4.

69 Cryer *et al.*, *An Introduction to International Criminal Law and Procedure* at p. 202–203.

access to food and medicine.' It is possible that by embezzling State resources, high-level public officials deprive their citizens of basic necessities, leading to deaths. This is particularly true in situations of humanitarian disasters. Whenever funds or goods intended for relief do not reach their beneficiaries, this can cause starvation of civilians.

However, when we consider the *mens rea* that is required in this respect, i.e. standard of intent and knowledge as laid down in Article 30, this raises a problem. As discussed *supra*in section 2.3, the ICC Pre-Trial Chamber in *Bemba* found that Article 30 does not cover *dolus eventualis*. This was confirmed by the ICC Trial Chamber in *Lubanga*. Rather, Article 30 is limited to *dolus directus* in the first and second degree. In this case, it is highly unlikely that officials actually *intend* to kill a large number of people by means of their corrupt practices. Rather, the possible deaths resulting from a corrupt transaction will be a side effect of the corrupt conduct, i.e. *dolus eventualis*. Hence, Bantekas and Nash, arguing in favour of conceptualising corruption as a crime against humanity, are incorrect when they state that Article 30(2)(b) does include *dolus eventualis*, which 'suffices to hold members of government responsible for crimes against humanity perpetrated against their own people in peacetime by placing them in conditions of life, which in the ordinary course of events would deprive them of access to sufficient food and medical care.'[70] Also Davidsson does not properly develop the *mens rea* requirement. In sum, under *lex lata*, it is not possible for corruption to meet the *mens rea* standard for extermination under the Rome Statute because *dolus eventualis* does not fall under the scope of Article 30.

As regards the circumstance element of the *actus reus*, i.e. the mass killing, this could be fulfilled by a large-scale practice of looting of State resources. The *mens rea* for this circumstance will be fulfilled whenever the perpetrator has knowledge about this practice.

The contextual element, i.e. the widespread or systematic attack against any civilian population can be satisfied in cases of grand corruption. As elaborated upon earlier, an attack does not have to be violent. Furthermore, corruption can constitute a widespread attack when there is a large number of victims. Also, the attack can be systematic when the corrupt practice possesses a high degree of organisation. Given the complexity of grand corruption, this systematic element is likely to be present. As noted by Ocheje, 'the theft of public funds and pillage of the economy are a carefully planned and meticulously executed enterprise.' Examples mentioned are the looting by Mobutu Sese Seko of Zaire and by Babangida and Abacha of Nigeria.[71] Concerning the policy element, this will also be satisfied. The rationale of kleptocracies is self-enrichment, and grand corruption is the *modus operandus*.

---

70 Ilias Bantekas and Susan Nash, *International Criminal Law* (3rd edn.; London/New York: Routledge-Cavendish, 2007) at p. 474–475.

71 Paul D. Ocheje, 'Refocusing International Law on the Quest for Accountability in Africa: The Case against The "Other" Impunity', *Leiden Journal of International Law,* 15 (2002), p. 749–779 at p. 754.

Finally, the civilian population will be the victim of the attack. As far as the *mens rea* for the contextual element is concerned, knowledge of the widespread or systematic attack is required. This knowledge will be present with the perpetrators of grand corruption.[72]

Another aspect that deserves to be considered here is causality: how can one prove the causal link between the corrupt acts and the death of the civilians concerned? In many instances, there might be a wider range of factors which impact upon the conditions of life of citizens. It will be hard to obtain evidence for the proposition that corrupt act A (e.g. the embezzlement of a specific aid fund at the governmental level) directly brought about the death of persons B, C and D.

Also, it deserves to be mentioned that the 'corruption as extermination' hypothesis can only be of use in a relatively limited number of cases, since corrupt practices will not always cause the death of civilians. Thus, even if it were possible to bring corruption under the scope of Article 7(1)(b), this would not solve the various instances in which corruption does not lead to fatal casualties, but rather causes non-lethal poverty.

4. Corruption as 'an Other Inhumane Act'?

4.1. Introduction

Starr argued that in certain instances, grand corruption can fall within the scope of 'an other inhumane act', as codified in Article 7(1)(k) of the Rome Statute.[73] Davidsson also considered that economic oppression can fall under this provision, 'when imposed against a civilian population with the awareness that it will, in the ordinary course of events, cause great suffering, or serious injury to body or to mental or physical health.'[74] A similar argument was made by Acquaah-Gaisie, by stating 'let us classify serious corruption as a crime against humanity. The Rome Statute of the ICC 1998 proscribes atrocities. Corruption by Third World political leaders and other elites holds a comparable gravity. Large-scale corruption causes the death of infants, devastation by diseases such as aids and malaria, denial of a decent education, results as serious as the repercussions of armed conflict.' Acquaah-Gaisie then referred to Article 7(1)(k). Hence, he noted that 'at the first review of the International Criminal Court in 2009 we should add serious corruption to the Court's universal jurisdiction [*sic*]'.[75] Claims such as these merit

---

72 For a further discussion of the application of the contextual element on grand corruption, see Sonja Starr, 'Extraordinary Crimes at Ordinary Times: International Justice Beyond Crisis Situations', *Northwestern University Law Review*, 101 (2007), p. 1257–1314 at p. 1304–1305.

73 *Ibid.*

74 Davidsson, 'Economic Oppression as an International Wrong or as a Crime against Humanity', at p. 196–198.

75 Gerald Acquaah-Gaisie, 'Grand Corruption – a Crime against Humanity.' *The Global Business and Technology Association International Conference* (Lisbon, 2005) at p. 1, 5–6. and Gerald

careful scrutiny. It should not be easily assumed that certain conduct is a crime against humanity under Article 7(1)(k), particularly because of Article 22 of the Rome Statute.[76]

4.2. Elements of an Other Inhumane Act

It was deemed impossible during the negotiations on the Rome Statute to list all possible crimes against humanity.[77] Hence, Article 7(1)(k) of the Rome Statute provides that 'other inhumane acts of a similar character intentionally causing great suffering, or serious injury to body or to mental or physical health' are also crimes against humanity.[78] In *Prosecutor v. Katanga and Ngudjolo Chui*, the ICC's Pre-Trial Chamber I defined inhumane acts as 'serious violations of international customary law and the basic rights pertaining to human beings, drawn from the norms of international human rights law, which are of a similar nature and gravity to the acts referred to in article 7(1)'.[79]

The *actus reus* consists of the fact that the perpetrator inflicted great suffering, or serious injury to body or to mental or physical health, by means of an inhumane act.[80] Such an act needs to be of a character similar to any other act referred to in Article 7(1).[81] This 'character' refers to the nature and gravity of the act.[82] Hence, there is a two-fold test: (i) the consequences of the crime (i.e. great suffering or serious injury); and (ii) the character of the crime (i.e. nature and gravity).[83]

As regards (i) the consequences of the act, it has been established by the ICTY's Trial Chamber in *Prosecutor v. Delalic* that the mentioned suffering also encompasses moral suffering, and can thus be both physical and mental.[84]

Acquaah-Gaisie, 'Curbing Financial Crime among Third World Elites', *Journal of Money Laundering Control,* 8 (2005), p. 371–381 at p. 379. Note that the jurisdiction of the ICC is laid down in Article 12 of the Rome Statute, which does not provide for universality.

76 See section 2.1 *supra.*

77 Werle, *Principles of International Criminal Law* at p. 339, §920.

78 Similar provisions are present in Article 6(c) of the Nuremberg Charter, the Nuremberg Principles, Article 5(c) of the Tokyo Charter, Article 2 para. 1(c) of Control Council Law No. 10, Article 5(i) of the ICTY Statute and Article 3(i) of the ICTR Statute.

79 ICC *Prosecutor v. Katanga and Ngudjolo Chui*, Decision Pre-Trial Chamber 30 September 2008, ICC–01/04–01/07, §448 as noted by Werle, *Principles of International Criminal Law* at p. 340, §921.

80 Elements of Crimes, Article 7(1)(k), §1.

81 *Ibid.* at §2.

82 *Ibid.* footnote 30.

83 As noted by Boot: 'the inhumanity of the act must both be judged by its consequences and by the (inhumane) nature of the act as such.' Machteld Boot and revised by Christopher K. Hall, 'Article 7: Crimes against Humanity (K); 'Other Inhumane Acts'', in Otto Triffterer (ed.), *Commentary on the Rome Statute of the International Criminal Court. Observers' Notes, Article by Article* (2nd edn.; München: C.H. Beck, 2008), p. 230–234 at p. 232, §82.

84 ICTY *Prosecutor v. Delalic* (aka *Celebici* Trial Chamber Judgment), IT–96–21-T, Trial Chamber Judgment 16 November 1998, §509 as noted by *Ibid.* at p. 233, §85.

Concerning (ii) the character of the crime, Werle noted that according to established case law, a comparison of severity must not be conducted in a schematic way; rather the circumstances of the individual case must always be considered.[85] Furthermore, Boot pointed out that persecution and apartheid do not amount to great suffering, or serious injury to body or to mental or physical health *per se*. Rather, these crimes are considered to be inhumane in and of themselves, e.g. the enactment of discriminatory legislation.[86] Boot also noted that deprivation of means of sustenance might be covered by Article 7(1)(k).[87]

As noted by Davidsson, the crimes listed in Article 7 are very diverse, and the suffering experienced by victims, or the effects of the crime may vary.[88] The ICTY and ICTR opined that the following acts are crimes against humanity: forcible transfer of population; serious physical or mental injury; biological, medical or scientific experiments; enforced prostitution; other acts of sexual violence; acts of sexual violence to and mutilation of a dead body that caused mental suffering to eye-witnesses; and enforced disappearances.[89] Interestingly, the Special Court for Sierra Leone also held that forced marriages can be seen as another inhumane act.[90] This is also a non-violent crime.[91]

The required *mens rea* is contained in the standard Article 30. The Elements of Crime again state that the perpetrator must be aware of the factual circumstances that established the character of the act.[92] Also, the text of Article 7(1)(k), includes the term 'intentionally'. Boot noted that Article 7(1)(k) 'excludes inhumane acts which cause the enumerated consequences without intent.'[93]

As for all crimes against humanity, the contextual element is that the conduct must be committed as part of a widespread or systematic attack directed against a

---

85 Werle, *Principles of International Criminal Law* at p. 340–341, §922. See also Boot and revised by Christopher K. Hall, 'Article 7: Crimes against Humanity (K); 'Other Inhumane Acts'', at p. 231, §81.

86 Boot and revised by Christopher K. Hall, 'Article 7: Crimes against Humanity (K); 'Other Inhumane Acts'', at p. 231, §81.

87 *Ibid.* at p. 230, §79. Boot referred to *The Charter and Judgment of the Nürnberg Tribunal: History and Analysis,* Memorandum submitted by the Secretary-General, p. 67, which states that 'the phrase "and other inhumane acts" indicates that the list of explicitly named activities is not exhaustive. It could be asked, for instance, whether deprivation of means of sustenance might not be considered as an "inhumane act".'

88 Davidsson, 'Economic Oppression as an International Wrong or as a Crime against Humanity', at p. 196.

89 Boot and revised by Christopher K. Hall, 'Article 7: Crimes against Humanity (K); 'Other Inhumane Acts'', at p. 231, §81.

90 *Prosecutor v. Brima et al.*, SCSL (Appeals Chamber), Judgment of 22 February 2008, §181 *et seq.*

91 See Micaela Frulli, 'Advancing International Criminal Law: The Special Court for Sierra Leone Recognizes Forced Marriage as a 'New' Crime against Humanity', *Journal of International Criminal Justice,* 6 (2008), p. 1033–1042.

92 Elements of Crimes, Article 7(1)(k), §3.

93 Boot and revised by Christopher K. Hall, 'Article 7: Crimes against Humanity (K); 'Other Inhumane Acts'', at p. 232, §83.

civilian population.[94] The *mens rea* required in this respect is that the perpetrator knew that the conduct was part of or intended the conduct to be part of a widespread or systematic attack against a civilian population.[95]

4.3. Application

In the analysis of whether acts of corruption can be qualified as an other inhumane act, two issues are crucial to determine at the outset. First, what are the consequences of corruption? Can great suffering or serious injury to body or to mental or physical health be inflicted? Second, what is the character (i.e. nature and gravity) of a corrupt act?

In respect of the consequences of corruption, it is necessary that great suffering *or* serious injury to body or to mental or physical health is inflicted. Corrupt acts can meet this standard. In the case of embezzlement of funds or goods (e.g. food or medicines), this can immediately cause suffering, bodily injury or injury to mental or physical health. It is argued by Starr that:

> ... there is no requirement that the suffering or injury be an *immediate* consequence of the crime, with no intervening causes, as in an act of violence. Likewise, it is not necessary to identify the individual victims of crimes causing collective harm; thus, the prosecution need not prove that any particular act of corruption caused any particular victim to suffer.[96]

Hence, the consequence requirement seems to be met.

As regards the question of whether corruption is of a character similar to the other crimes listed in Article 7, it must be noted that this provision also includes crimes that do not necessarily involve physical violence, such as apartheid, imprisonment and persecution. The fact that corruption does not involve physical violence does therefore not constitute a barrier in this respect. Moreover, Starr argued that:

> ... the worst acts of grand corruption share significant similarities with other listed acts. Like all of the listed acts, they are gross violations of human rights. Like murder and extermination, they kill people, often in large numbers. Like deportation, forcible transfer, and economic persecution, they inflict severe deprivation affecting the fundamental conditions of life. Like apartheid, kleptocracy is a governmental regime that systematically oppresses part of the population in order to benefit those

---

94 Elements of Crimes, Article 7(1)(k), §4.

95 *Ibid.* §5.

96 Starr, 'Extraordinary Crimes at Ordinary Times: International Justice Beyond Crisis Situations', at p. 1301–1302.

> imposing the system. Moreover, no categorical dissimilarity distinguishes grand corruption from all of the other acts.[97]

Thus, it is legitimate to conclude that grand corruption does not fundamentally differ from the other crimes listed in Article 7.

It is also necessary to establish the necessary *mens rea* for an 'other inhumane act'. As stated earlier, Article 30 applies, which does not allow for *dolus eventualis*. Hence, the mental element for an 'other inhumane act' cannot be met, because the great suffering or the serious injury to body or to mental or physical health will be a mere side effect of the corrupt act, which was not as such intended, but of which the perpetrator was fully aware and accepts as one of the consequences of the corrupt practice. This is the case because the perpetrator of grand corruption does not intend to inflict great suffering or serious injury to body or to mental or physical health. Rather, the corrupt high-level official will act out of the desire to enrich him- or herself, or family, friends, political party or ethnic group. The fact that great suffering or serious injury to body or to mental or physical health is inflicted upon (part of) a population, is a side effect of the corrupt practice. The official will recognise and accept this consequence as a result of the corrupt behaviour.[98] *Dolus directus* is not present in such a case. In conclusion: grand corruption cannot meet the *mens rea* standard for an 'other inhumane act', because Article 30 is limited to first and second degree *dolus directus*.

Moreover, the contextual element (i.e. a widespread or systematic attack directed against any civilian population) and the corresponding *mens rea* must also be present: As stated *supra* in section 3.3, the contextual element is likely to be satisfied in cases of grand corruption.

In the view of Starr, 'there is thus a fairly strong case that the worst cases of grand corruption will satisfy each of these seven requirements[99] and can be prosecuted as crimes against humanity, even with no link to crises situations'.[100] In view of the recent ICC Pre-Trial Chamber decision in *Bemba,* as well as the ICC Trial Chamber judgment in *Lubanga*, this statement cannot be upheld, because Article 30 does not allow for *dolus eventualis*.

---

97 *Ibid.* at p. 1301.

98 The reasoning of Starr in respect of the *mens rea* requirement is not clear, and can probably not be upheld. *Ibid.* at p. 1302–1304.

99 Starr distinguishes between: (i) an inhumane act; (ii) of a similar character to any of the other crimes listed in Article 7(1); (iii) the act caused great suffering, or serious injury to body or to mental or physical health; (iv) the consequences were intentional; (v) the act was part of an attack direct against any civilian population; (vi) the attack was widespread or systematic; and (vii) the accused knew that his act was connected to this attack. *Ibid.* at p. 1299.

100 *Ibid.* at p. 1305.

5. Concluding Remarks

The current chapter attempted to examine whether corruption could possibly be classified as a crime against humanity under Article 7 of the Rome Statute. Two conclusions can be drawn from this analysis. First, upon consideration of the crime of extermination (Article 7(1)(b)), it emerged that scholarly claims conceptualising corruption as such an offense are not valid. Particularly the *mens rea* requirement poses problems since the applicable standard of Article 30 does not cover *dolus eventualis*. Rather, the provision is limited to *dolus directus* in the first and second degree.

Second, the category of 'other inhumane acts' was considered. Grand corruption can possibly result in great suffering or serious injury to body or to mental or physical health, and can be said to be of a similar character as the other crimes listed in Article 7. The requirements for the contextual element can also be met. However, what poses a barrier once more is the *mens rea* demanded by Article 30. In cases of grand corruption, the degree of intent required by *dolus directus* will not be present in most cases, since corrupt high-level officials will not primarily intend to harm the persons, but rather aim to enrich themselves.

In sum, under the Rome Statute, corruption cannot be conceptualised as extermination or as an other inhumane act. However, there might be possibilities to view corruption as such an offence in customary international law, which might allow for a broader *mens rea*, which does include *dolus eventualis*. Moreover, the ICC has not yet given its last judgment about the doctrine of *dolus eventualis*; on the contrary: it is not completely elucidated. Future case law may differ from the current status quo, and therefore the possibility that the *mens rea* element does cover *dolus eventualis* should not be ruled out altogether.

Chapter IX
Possibilities of Combating Corruption under International Criminal Law *de lege ferenda*?

1. Introduction

As noted by Starr:

> Grand corruption cannot be prosecuted internationally without some legal basis. The ideal option would be widespread ratification of a new treaty, or an amendment to the ICC's Rome Statute, spelling out the elements of the crime. This would remove any doctrinal doubt and would send a clear and loud signal as to what conduct is prohibited – valuable in terms of fairness to defendants as well as potential deterrent and norm-shaping effects.[1]

A similar argument is made by Eboe-Osuji[2] and Kofele-Kale.[3] Moreover, a member of Belgian Parliament submitted a proposal to the government, in order to induce the government to lobby for the inclusion of 'serious economic crimes' into Article 5 of the Rome Statute.[4]

While the preceding chapter viewed corruption from the angle of current international law, the present chapter deals with the matter from a *lege ferenda* perspective, i.e. the law as it ought to be in the opinion of the author. In line with the proposals by the authors mentioned *supra* it is examined how international criminal law may possibly be used to address corruption. Various options are explored, such

---

1 Sonja Starr, 'Extraordinary Crimes at Ordinary Times: International Justice Beyond Crisis Situations', *Northwestern University Law Review,* 101 (2007), p. 1257–1314 at p. 1297. Note that she does not discuss this idea in depth, because she follows the approach of trying to bring grand corruption under the scope of existing Article 7. See chapter VII on this matter.

2 Chile Eboe-Osuji, 'Kleptocracy: A Desired Subject of International Criminal Law That is in Dire Need of Prosecution by Universal Jurisdiction', in Evelyn A. Ankumah and Edward K. Kwakwa (eds.), *African Perspectives on International Criminal Justice* (Special Series, 3; Accra-Maastricht-Pretoria: Africa Legal Aid, 2005), p. 121–132.

3 Ndiva Kofele-Kale, 'Patrimonicide: The International Economic Crime of Indigenous Spoliation', *Vanderbilt Journal of Transnational Law,* 28 (1995), p. 45–118; Ndiva Kofele-Kale, 'The Right to a Corruption-Free Society as an Individual and Collective Human Right: Elevating Official Corruption to a Crime under International Law', *The International Lawyer,* 34 (2000), p. 149–178; Ndiva Kofele-Kale, *The International Law of Responsibility for Economic Crimes: Holding State Officials Individually Liable for Acts of Fraudulent Enrichment* (2nd edn.; Aldershot: Ashgate, 2006).

4 Belgische Kamer van Volksvertegenwoordigers 27 April 2000, Voorstel van Resolutie betreffende de uitbreiding van de rechtsmacht van het Internationaal Strafgerechtshof tot andere ernstige internationale delicten, inzonderheid economische delicten (ingediend door de heer Mark Eyskens). Doc 50 0607/001. The proposal aimed to include *inter alia* active and passive corruption of foreign public officials, international money laundering, and cross-border fraud into Article 5 of the Rome Statute. It is not clear what happened to the proposal.

as the inclusion of a new anti-corruption provision into the Rome Statute (section 2), as well as the practical challenges and political feasibility of such a provision (sections 3 and 4). Attention is also paid to the ways in which grand corruption can possibly be addressed in present cases before the ICC (section 5), and to the possible establishment of a permanent or ad hoc anti-corruption tribunal (section 6). By doing so, the chapter aims to explore a number of novel approaches from which grand corruption can be considered, but does not intend to deal with the matter in an exhaustive fashion. Finally, conclusions are provided in section 7.

2. Possible Content of an Anti-Corruption Provision in the Rome Statute

2.1. Inclusion of a Separate Anti-Corruption Provision?

2.1.1. Introduction

The first option for criminalisation would be the inclusion of a new provision into the Rome Statute, which entails that corruption becomes a separate offence next to genocide, crimes against humanity, war crimes and aggression. An advantage of express codification of corruption flows from the principle of complementarity, enshrined in Articles 1 and 17(1)(a) of the Rome Statute. Complementarity entails that the Court has jurisdiction over the crime concerned, if the State which has jurisdiction is either unwilling or unable to investigate or prosecute.[5] Hence, should grand corruption be included into the Statute, this entails that State Parties are obliged to tackle it domestically. If not, they run the risk that the ICC takes up the case. Criminalisation into the Rome Statute of grand corruption is thus an incentive for States to prosecute corruption domestically.

What should be included in a provision on corruption? First, it has to be determined how petty corruption can be excluded. As set out earlier, international criminal law should focus on grand corruption: acts committed by heads of State, heads of government, cabinet ministers and members of Parliament. These are the persons who tend to enjoy immunity before their own national courts.[6]

Second, it must be clarified what conduct ought to be prohibited. As explained earlier, the focus of international criminal law should be on passive bribery and embezzlement, when committed by a person in the above-mentioned list of high-level officials.[7]

---

5 Article 1 of the Rome Statute provides that ICC's jurisdiction is complementary to national criminal jurisdictions. Article 17(1)(a) of the Rome Statute sets out that a case before the ICC is admissible if the State which has jurisdiction is unwilling or unable to carry out the investigation or prosecution.

6 See chapter VII, §6.2.

7 See chapter VII, §6.3.

2.1.2. Passive Bribery

The definition of passive bribery provided by Article 15 UNCAC is 'the solicitation or acceptance by a public official, directly or indirectly, of an undue advantage, for the official him- or herself or another person or entity, in order that the official act or refrain from acting in the exercise of his or her official duties.' It can be doubted whether this provision is specific enough to be incorporated directly into international criminal law. If not, the principle of legality is at stake. Hence, it is necessary to turn to other provisions that can serve as possible candidates for the purpose of international criminalisation of passive bribery.

As a starting point, reference may be made to the anti-corruption provisions in the Dutch Criminal Code (hereafter: DCC). Legislation on corruption was amended in 2001 in order to comply with international treaty obligations, including the UNCAC.[8] The provisions on passive bribery by public servants are laid down in Articles 362 and 363 DCC. Since these Articles comply with the leading treaty on anti-corruption, they are an interesting point of departure for the current analysis.

The provisions make a distinction between instances of bribe-taking where the public servant does not breach his/her official duty (Article 362), and instances of bribe-taking where the public servant does breach his/her official duty (Article 363). Article 362 reads as follows:

> 1. Punished by a prison sentence of not more than two years or a fine of the fifth category shall be a public servant:
>   1° who accepts a gift, promise or service, knowing or reasonably suspecting that this was given, promised or rendered in order to induce him to do or not to do something in the discharge of his current duties, without violating these duties;
>   2° who accepts a gift, promise or service, knowing or reasonable suspecting that this was given, promised or rendered as a result of or in reply of something he has done or not done in the discharge of his current or former duties, without violating these duties;
>   3° who requests a gift, promise or service, in order to induce him to do or not to something in the discharge of his current duties, without violating these duties;
>   4° who requests a gift, promise or service as a result of or in reply of something he has done or not done in the discharge of his current or former duties, without violating these duties.
> 2. Punished with the same sentence will be the person who, under the prospect of his appointment as a public servant, commits an offence as described in the first section, under 1° and 3°.
> 3. The person who commits an offence as described in the first section in the capacity of minister, secretary of State, King's Commissioner, deputy, mayor,

8 E. Sikkema, 'De Strafrechtelijke Corruptiewetgeving; Opmerkingen Naar Aanleiding van Wetsvoorstel 31 391', *Strafblad*, 7/1 (20 February 2009), p. 5–13 at p. 9.

> municipal executive or member of a general representative organ, shall be punished by a prison sentence of not more than four years or a fine of the fifth category.

Hence, Article 362 makes a distinction between cases where the bribe-taking was initiated by the bribe-giver (section 1 under 1° and 2°), and cases where the bribe-taking was initiated by the public servant (section 1 under 3° and 4°). Furthermore, the provision distinguishes between bribery before a certain favour is granted to the bribe-giver (section 1 under 1° and 3°), and bribery after a certain favour is granted (section 1 under 2° and 4°). In addition, punishment for higher-level officials as listed in section 3 can be twice as high as punishment for lower-level officials.

Article 363, nearly identical to Article 362, criminalises passive bribery of civil servants, in cases where the public servant does violate his/her duty:

> 1. Punished by a prison sentence of not more than four years or a fine of the fifth category shall be a public servant:
>   1° who accepts a gift, promise or service, knowing or reasonably suspecting that this was given, promised or rendered in order to induce him to do or not to do something in violation with the discharge of his current duties;
>   2° who accepts a gift, promise or service, knowing or reasonable suspecting that this was given, promised or rendered as a result of or in reply of something he has done or not done in violation with the discharge of his current or former duties;
>   3° who requests a gift, promise or service, in order to induce him to do or not to something in violation with the discharge of his current duties;
>   4° who requests a gift, promise or service as a result of or in reply of something he has done or not done in violation with the discharge of his current or former duties;
> 2. Punished with the same sentence will be the person who, under the prospect of his appointment as a public servant, commits an offence as described in the first section, under 1° and 3°.
> 3. The person who commits an offence as described in the first section in the capacity of minister, secretary of State, King's Commissioner, deputy, mayor, municipal executive or member of a general representative organ, shall be punished by a prison sentence of not more than six years or a fine of the fifth category.

The same distinctions apply: (i) between bribery initiated by the bribe-give, and bribery initiated by the public servant; and (ii) between bribery before and after a favour is granted to the bribe-giver. Furthermore, Article 364 provides a special provision for passive bribery committed by judges.

Having looked at the content of the Dutch criminal law provisions on passive bribery, it is now important to ascertain whether Articles 362 and 363 comply with the requirements of a crime under the Rome Statute. First of all, the *actus reus* of passive bribery must be clear. This is not likely to pose any problems, since

Articles 362 and 363 clearly set out the objective elements of the crime. A Rome Statute provision should cover both bribery initiated by the bribe-giver, and bribery initiated by the public servant. Also, both bribery before and after the favour should be covered. However, the question arises whether the distinction between bribery in violation of the official's duty and bribery not in violation of the official's duty should be maintained at the international level. Perhaps it is more appropriate to leave the distinction out of the Rome Statute, since it can be hard to determine whether the official acted in violation of his duty or not. Furthermore, the Rome Statute provision should be limited to covering passive bribery by high-level officials.

Second, the provisions have to meet the *mens rea* standard required by the Statute. As discussed in the previous chapter, this is captured in Article 30 of the Rome Statute. This applies by default to the crimes laid down in the Statute, although the Elements of Crimes can provide otherwise. The first element of *mens rea* is intent, the second element is knowledge. Articles 362 and 363 provide that the public servant should 'know or reasonably suspect' ('*wetende of redelijkerwijs vermoedende*') that the gift, promise or service was given, promised or rendered to influence the public servant's decision-making. The question arises how this phrase should be interpreted. According to the Dutch Supreme Court, the phrase 'know that' includes '*voorwaardelijk opzet*', i.e. *dolus eventualis*.[9] Such a requirement does not meet the standard of Article 30, which excludes *dolus eventualis*. Nevertheless, this does obviously not bind the ICC. It is very well possible to insert a provision such as 362 or 363 into the Rome Statute without the wording 'reasonably suspect', and maintain the threshold of Article 30. However, the consequence is that the threshold for the *mens rea* aspect of passive bribery is higher. The better option would be to deviate in the Elements of Crimes from the threshold in Article 30, to allow for *dolus eventualis* in cases of passive bribery.

Third, all crimes under the Rome Statute possess a certain contextual element. This distinguishes ordinary crimes from crimes under international law. What should such a contextual element consist of in cases of passive bribery? A new provision on corruption does not have to meet the contextual element of genocide, war crimes, or crimes against humanity. Rather, it is possible to codify a new type of contextual element. For example, the requirement of large-scale corruption, as opposed to single incidents would be suitable. Instances of widespread bribery at the level of the State tend to be embedded into larger systems of corruption and looting of State property.

---

9 Hoge Raad 30 May 2008, NJ 2008/318, LJN BC8673. The term 'voorwaardelijk opzet' is translated by Foster as '*dolus eventualis*'. See Tony Foster, *Dutch Legal Terminology in English* (3rd edn.: Kluwer, 2009) at p. 132.

2.1.3. *Embezzlement*

The definition of embezzlement laid down in Article 17 UNCAC is 'the embezzlement, misappropriation or other diversion by a public official for his or her benefit or the benefit of another person or entity, of any property, public or private funds or securities or any other thing of value entrusted to the public official by virtue of his or her position.' Again, this provision might not be suitable for inclusion into the Rome Statute, because it does not properly specify the elements of the crime. Article 359 of the Dutch Criminal Code also contains a provision on embezzlement:

> A public servant or any other person charged, either on a permanent or temporary basis, with any public office, who intentionally embezzles money or paper of monetary value which is in his control in the execution of his duties, or allows another person to remove or to embezzle such, or as an accessory assists that other person in such act, is liable to a term of imprisonment of not more than six years or a fine of the fifth category.[10]

In respect of the *actus reus* and *mens rea* element, such a provision is not likely to cause many problems in terms of compliance with the Rome Statute. The contextual element can possibly consist of the large-scale diversion of State funds. What should be added to the provision is the scope of persons covered by it, i.e. only high-level officials.

2.2. Inclusion of New Crimes Against Humanity?

The second option for criminalisation would be the inclusion of two new categories of crimes against humanity, i.e. passive bribery and embezzlement. Hence, an amendment to Article 7 of the Rome Statute would be necessary. Any new crime against humanity would consist of an *actus reus* and *mens rea*, as well as a contextual element. The first two elements have been discussed *supra* What is particularly important here is the contextual element in crimes against humanity, which is the presence of 'a widespread or systematic attack directed against any civilian population'. It was noted earlier that such an attack does not have to be violent. Corruption can constitute a widespread attack because corrupt government can produce many victims. Moreover, it can be systematic when the corrupt practice possesses a high degree of organisation. Hence, this requirement can in principle be met.[11]

However, from a systematic point of view, it would be less desirable to include forms of corruption as new crimes against humanity. Article 30 would apply by default, which is problematic in respect of passive bribery since *dolus eventualis*

10 Translation by Louise Rayar and Stafford Wadsworth, *The Dutch Penal Code* (The American Series of Foreign Penal Codes, 30; Littleton, Colorado: Rothman & Co, 1997).

11 See more extensively chapter VII, §3.3.

would be excluded. A separate provision on corruption, which awards economic crimes the attention it deserves, and is able to make clear its specificities, would be more desirable. In the Elements of Crimes, tailor-made provisions can be included, instead of applying the current Elements of crimes against humanity.

3. Practical Challenges of International Prosecution Before the ICC

Prosecution of high-level officials for corruption before the ICC may pose a number of practical challenges. Corrupt practices may not leave a paper trail. In the wake of the announcement that a case is brought against a corrupt high-level official, or after the issuance of an arrest warrant, evidence may be destroyed. On the other hand, some domestic cases such as the one against the former President of Peru, Alberto Fujimori, demonstrate that there may be a great deal of evidence to make a strong case against high-level political corruption.[12]

Moreover, while with regard to war crimes, crimes against humanity and genocide there may be victims who can testify as witnesses, grand corruption is not likely to produce such concrete, individualised victims. Unlike other ICC crimes, it not possible to reveal physical harm. Witness evidence would have to be provided by insiders involved in corrupt networks themselves.

There are also other problematic aspects of investigations into corruption, which also exist at the domestic level. Often it remains unclear whether something was exchanged between parties in a corrupt transaction, and if so: what was exchanged. None of the parties has an interest in disclosing the specificities, and therefore the investigating authorities have to rely on the presence of witnesses and their willingness to testify. Yet, these witnesses may be reluctant to do so because of their loyalty towards persons in their social environment, fear of expulsion from society as well as repercussions, including threats, harassment and physical violence. Adequate whistleblower protection should therefore be put in place, yet this may not always be sufficient.[13] In previous chapters, the dangers to which whistleblowers may be exposed were already touched upon.

What should also be noted is that frequently quite some time will elapse between the moment when rumours of corruption first emerge, and the start of the actual investigation (in this case by the ICC prosecutor). The investigating authorities then have to deal with situations that occurred a few years ago, which may negatively affect the quality of witness testimony. Moreover, hearing suspects in cases of grand corruption requires special skills on the part of the interrogator.[14]

---

12 BBC News, 'Fujimori Sentenced for Corruption', <http://news.bbc.co.uk/2/hi/americas/8283844.stm>, accessed 1 August 2011.

13 J.M. Nelen, De Strafrechtelijke afdoening van ambtelijke corruptie, *Justitiële Verkenningen* (2005), p. 41–42.

14 *Ibid.*

A positive aspect is that State Parties have to cooperate with the Court in its investigation and prosecution of Rome Statute crimes,[15] and the Court can request State Parties to cooperate.[16] Moreover, States have to comply with ICC requests to provide assistance regarding the identification, tracing and freezing or seizure of proceeds, property and assets and instrumentalities of crimes for the purpose of eventual forfeiture.[17]

4. Feasibility of Including an Anti-Corruption Provision into the Rome Statute

While the inclusion of grand corruption into the Rome Statute may be both desirable and theoretically possible, one has to consider whether this is also feasible. The first Review Conference of the Rome Statute took place in Kampala, Uganda, between 31 May and 11 June 2010. During this meeting, economic crimes were not on the agenda. Corruption is a topic which is still highly politically sensitive. On the one hand, developed States are often reluctant to criticise corrupt leadership in developing countries, because of complicity of their own corporations and officials in corrupt transactions abroad. Moreover, in the Cold War era, both the East and the West supported corrupt dictators in developing countries, because of their alliance with either communist or capitalist ideology. Furthermore, the proceeds of corruption in developing nations are often kept in Western banks, and States are not keen on giving up bank secrecy laws. On the other hand, developing States may face serious corruption problems themselves – as shown by their CPI score – and therefore they will not be supportive of including corruption into the Statute. Not only is corruption a political issue, it is also argued that the ICC is 'a complex institution whose political dimension needs to be understood as a constructive (albeit formative) component of global politics.'[18] In addition, many States will feel that the ICC has not delivered a great deal of output yet. Therefore, countries will argue that the Court should do its work first, before already changing the rules of the game by adding more crimes to its jurisdiction.

Pursuant to Article 121(3) of the Rome Statute, amendments to the Statute have to be adopted by a two-thirds majority of State Parties. It is improbable that such a majority can be reached. Furthermore, Article 121(4) states that an amendment enters into force *for all State Parties* one year after ratification or acceptance by seven-eights of all State Parties. Again, it cannot be expected that such a high threshold will be met. Also, any State Party which does not accept the amendment

15 Article 86 Rome Statute.

16 Article 87 Rome Statute.

17 Article 93 (1)(k) Rome Statute.

18 Steven R. Roach, *Politicizing the International Criminal Court: The Convergence of Politics, Ethics, and Law* (Lanham: Rowman & Littlefield Publishers, 2006) at p. 1.

can withdraw from the Rome Statute with immediate effect, as provided in Article 121(6).

Moreover, Article 121(5) provides that amendments to Articles 5, 6, 7 and 8 will enter into force *for those State Parties which have accepted the amendment*, one year after ratification or acceptance. If a State does not accept the amendment, the ICC will not exercise its jurisdiction regarding a crime covered by the amendment when committed by that State Party's nationals or on its territory. Article 121(5) entails that including corruption into Article 7 is a more difficult enterprise than including a new anti-corruption provision.

Hence, in the words of Starr, 'express codification [of an anti-corruption provision] is extremely unlikely for the indefinite future. Even if enough States could be convinced to put an amendment or a new treaty into effect, many of the most crucial States – kleptocracies and money-laundering havens – would probably refuse to sign on [for political reasons].'[19] On the other hand, in 1977, when the Foreign Corrupt Practices Act came into being in the US, corruption was still a taboo subject, and at the time no one would have guessed that, 30 years later, a wide range of anti-corruption treaties would exist. While currently international criminalisation of corruption and enforcement at the international level will seem far-fetched, perhaps 30 years later, these ideas may be put in practice. Only time will tell.

5. Addressing Grand Corruption in Present Cases before the ICC

While it is at the moment not possible to bring high-level officials before the ICC because of corruption charges, the current cases before the Court may allow the Court to deal with corruption in relation to other crimes. While the charge itself cannot mention corruption, the trial may show the links between the commission of crimes against humanity or war crimes, and corrupt practices. For instance, ICC cases can offer insights into the ways in which violent conflict is financed. An example would be the case against Omar Al Bashir, President of Sudan. Arrest warrants have been issued against him for crimes against humanity, war crimes and genocide. Interestingly, US diplomatic cables on WikiLeaks contain conversations between US officials and ICC Prosecutor Luis Moreno-Ocampo, revealing that Al Bashir has embezzled US $9 billion, most of which is generated by Sudan's oil industry. Moreno-Ocampo hinted that a majority of the money was siphoned off to London banks. It remains yet unclear how Moreno-Ocampo intends to use this information. As pointed out by Human Rights Watch, the embezzled billions could serve as a source of reparation for the victims of Al Bashir's crimes in Darfur.[20]

---

19 Starr, 'Extraordinary Crimes at Ordinary Times: International Justice Beyond Crisis Situations', at p. 1297.

20 Afua Hirsch, 'WikiLeaks Cables: Sudanese President 'stashed $9bn in UK Banks'', *The Guardian* 17 December 2010.

6. Establishing an Anti-Corruption Tribunal: A Possible Alternative?

6.1. A Permanent Anti-Corruption Court?

Since amendment of the Rome Statute is not likely in the near future, we might as well explore other options. One of them would be the establishment of a separate anti-corruption tribunal, competent to deal with the prosecution of corruption. Interestingly, Dutch political party D66 recently argued in favour of establishment of a permanent international anti-corruption court in The Hague.[21]

An advantage of such a separate instance would be its specific expertise on corruption. Ideally, such a court should be based on the United Nations Convention Against Corruption, so as to enforce its provisions. In the establishment of such an institution, lessons can be learned from the experiences of the various national anti-corruption tribunals that currently operate, such as those in Kenya and the Philippines.[22]

Yet, taking into account that the recently established review mechanism to the UNCAC is rather 'soft', it is not likely that States will agree on setting up such a criminal tribunal in the near future. An alternative would be the setting up of an anti-corruption commission within the framework of UNCAC. Such a commission should ideally consist of independent experts on anti-corruption. Among the experts should not just be lawyers, but also economists and political scientists. Their task could, *inter alia*, consist of monitoring State compliance with the UNCAC, by considering periodic reports from all State Parties to the Convention. To make their work truly meaningful, the experts should have the power to conduct country visits and to obtain information from third parties. Most importantly, the findings of the commission should be binding upon State Parties.

6.2. An Ad Hoc Anti-Corruption Tribunal?

In recent years, a number of mixed or internationalised ad hoc criminal tribunals (hybrid tribunals) were established, including those dealing with crimes committed in East Timor, Lebanon, Cambodia and Sierra Leone. Such tribunals are generally established in response to atrocities committed during armed conflict in the respective territories. The way in which such tribunals are set up may differ. For example, the Special Court for Sierra Leone was established by a bilateral treaty between the UN and the Sierra Leonean government,[23] while the Special Tribunal

21 D66, 'D66 Pleit voor Financieel Strafhof in Den Haag', 21 April 2012, <http://site.d66.nl/d66nl/nieuws/20120421/d66_pleit_voor_financieel_strafhof> accessed 3 July 2012.

22 See U4 Anti-Corruption Resource Centre, 'Special Courts for Corruption Cases', *U4 Helpdesk Query* <www.u4.no/helpdesk/helpdesk/query.cfm?id=19>, accessed 10 June 2011.

23 Luc Côté, 'Special Court for Sierra Leone', in Antonio Cassese (ed.), *The Oxford Companion to International Criminal Justice* (Oxford: Oxford University Press, 2009), p. 515–517 at p. 515.

for Lebanon was set up by a resolution of the UN Security Council.[24] In any case, it is likely that there will be a prominent role for the Security Council. Ad hoc tribunals are attractive if the State itself cannot deal with the crimes on its own, while setting up an ICTY or ICTR-type of court is not possible due to cost and capacity.[25]

Establishment of ad hoc anti-corruption tribunals might be an appropriate option. Hybrid tribunals can be established in the State where the offences were committed.[26] This would be a clear advantage in the case of an ad hoc anti-corruption tribunal, competent to examine corrupt practices of a country's leadership, where it concerns evidence gathering and the questioning of witnesses.

The uprisings during the Arab Spring in 2011 were partly fueled by public disgruntlement about corruption.[27] Moreover, regime changes also led to domestic prosecutions of high-level officials for corruption, including the prosecution of former Presidents Hosni Mubarak in Egypt[28] and Ben Ali in Tunisia.[29] Such domestic prosecutions are certainly to be welcomed. Yet, if the country cannot manage such trials on its own, a mixed tribunal could be an option. Both domestic as well as internationalised proceedings are of course most likely should there be a change in regime.

7. Concluding Remarks

Inclusion of grand corruption into the Rome Statute is theoretically possible either by inserting a new, separate provision on corruption, or by including a new crime against humanity into the present Article 7. The first option is the most desirable one. Furthermore, from the viewpoint of the principle of legality, it is recommended not to use the provisions of the UNCAC, but rather to take domestic legislation on passive bribery and embezzlement as a starting point. The present chapter examined Articles 362–363 and 359 of the Dutch Criminal Code, since this legislation complies with the UNCAC. Of course, this is merely a starting point.

Should the international prosecution of grand corruption become possible, this poses a number of practical challenges. Moreover, at the present moment,

---

24 Marieke Wierda, 'Special Tribunal for Lebanon', in Antonio Cassese (ed.), *The Oxford Companion to International Criminal Justice* (Oxford: Oxford University Press, 2009), p. 519–520 at p. 519.

25 Florian Jessberger, 'International v. National Prosecution of International Crimes', in Antonio Cassese (ed.), *The Oxford Companion to International Criminal Justice* (Oxford: Oxford University Press, 2009), p. 208–215 at p. 210–211.

26 *Ibid.* at p. 210.

27 Stuart Levey, 'Fighting Corruption after the Arab Spring', *Foreign Affairs* (16 June 2011).

28 CNN, 'Mubarak Trial to Open Next Week, Egypt Says', <http://edition.cnn.com/2011/WORLD/meast/07/28/egypt.mubarak/>, accessed 29 July 2011.

29 Reuters Africa, 'Tunisian Court Sentences Ben Ali for Corruption', <http://af.reuters.com/article/topNews/idAFJOE76S02V20110729>, accessed 29 July 2011.

amendment of the Rome Statute to accommodate an inclusion of corruption is highly unlikely, if not impossible. Corruption is still a highly politicised topic and many developing and developed States will oppose the inclusion of corruption into the Statute – even though future geo-political developments cannot be predicted. A reasonable option at this moment would be for the ICC to pay attention to corrupt practices in the cases it is currently dealing with, including the trial of Al Bashir. Moreover, the UNCAC may be complemented with an anti-corruption tribunal, or more likely, with an anti-corruption commission comprised of experts. Finally, an option would be the establishment of an ad hoc criminal tribunal to try corrupt public officials.

Part D

Summary, Reflections and Recommendations

Chapter X
Summary

1. Introduction

The aim of the present study was to explore new avenues to fighting the global social evil of corruption, making use of international human rights law, as well as international criminal law. While good governance and anti-corruption became popular buzzwords during the second half of the 1990s, it is only very recently that efforts are also being made to view corruption through the lens of human rights law. Even less attention is being paid by international criminal law scholars, largely keeping corruption out of the debate on international criminalisation. The present thesis therefore hopes to provide new insights, food for thought and new discussions to those working in the field of human rights and international criminal law. Yet, it also accepts that many specificities yet have to be tested in practice.

The current chapter X aims to summarise the main findings of the study, and hence provide answers to the research questions posed in the General Introduction. Recommendations and further reflections on the topic can be found in the final chapter XI.

2. Part A: The Phenomenon of Corruption: An Introductory Analysis

2.1. Defining and Measuring Corruption

Before the links between corruption, on the one hand, and human rights and international criminal law, on the other hand, could be dealt with, it was deemed imperative to develop a useful working definition of corruption. This is not as easy as it may seem, since even the large majority of the existing anti-corruption treaties do not define the notion. Therefore, chapter I of Part A compared the definitions employed by anti-corruption NGO Transparency International and by the World Bank, which has become a major player in the field of anti-corruption. While TI's definition captures both corruption in the public sector as well as the private sector, the World Bank's description is limited to public sector corruption: 'the abuse of public office for private gain.' Since the present thesis is primarily concerned with State conduct, rather than behaviour of non-State actors, the definition of the Bank was taken as a starting point. This, however, does not necessarily imply that the thesis supports the views or policies of the Bank. In addition, it was acknowledged that corrupt practices do not necessarily have to benefit the public official his- or herself: the conduct can also benefit friends, family or political relations.

Furthermore, corruption may not be perpetrated merely for private gain, but also for political gain. Hence, the definition used in this work is 'the abuse of public office for private or political gain'.

Public sector corruption, as defined above, can be divided into grand corruption and petty corruption. The former occurs at the policy formulation end of politics, involving public officials at the highest levels of the State. The latter takes place at the policy implementation end of politics, and is committed by lower-level officials. Hence, in labelling something as 'grand' or 'petty', it is not the size of the resources involved that is decisive, but rather the level where the conduct takes place.

Corruption is often linked to concepts such as economic crime, white collar crime, fraud, and collusion. While there are many overlaps and links, corruption is not a synonym for any of these phenomena. What one should also bear in mind is that corruption is a topic with a strong cultural undertone. One should outright reject justifications for corruption based on culture. Yet, in studying corruption and in developing policies against it, the larger cultural and societal context needs to be taken into account, to avoid one-size-fits-all solutions.

With the above-mentioned definition as a starting point, various types of corruption were identified, since one 'umbrella definition' does not properly suit those studying corruption from a legal point of view. Taking the United Nations Convention Against Corruption as a starting point, it is possible to distinguish between (i) active and passive bribery; (ii) embezzlement; (iii) trading in influence; (iv) abuse of functions (which in the author's view includes patronage and nepotism); and (v) illicit enrichment.

Bearing in mind the various types of corruption, one may wonder how these practices can be measured. This is indeed a difficult task, since corruption, by its nature, is a secretive practice. Yet, there is a need for data on the occurrence of corruption, because without it, progress cannot be measured, and countries cannot be compared. Therefore, a number of instruments were developed in recent years. Transparency International's Corruption Perceptions Index (CPI) is one of the best known instruments, measuring perceptions of corruption and ranking countries from 1 (perceived as least corrupt) to 178 (perceived as most corrupt). The Index shows that throughout the world, corruption is rather the rule than the exception. Among other measurement tools, we find the Bribe Payers Index, the European Fraud Survey, the Global Corruption Barometer, and the International Crime Victims Survey. While there is an obvious need for tools such as the CPI, it must be acknowledged that these are not without flaws, and criticisms can also be heard on the underlying research methodologies. This must be kept in mind, also when the present thesis makes use of the CPI and other data from Transparency International.

2.2. Harmful Consequences of Corruption

Efforts aimed at combating corruption rest on the premise that corruption is harmful. Indeed, extensive research in various disciplines offers insights into why corruption ought to be addressed. The consequences of corruption can be felt politically, economically, socially, and environmentally. In the political sphere, corruption erodes democracy and legitimacy. Corrupt rulers are likely to disregard the real needs of the people, and as a result, citizens lose their confidence in the system. Moreover, corruption may be related to the occurrence and duration of armed conflict. Both practices can also have a strong relation with the presence of natural resource wealth. As regards the economic effects of corruption, research points to various ways in which corruption may lower economic growth. It is believed that corruption leads to fewer investments; misallocation of talent of well-educated people, who are likely to engage in rent-seeking behaviour; reduced effectiveness of aid flows due to embezzlement; a loss of tax revenue; inferior quality of public infrastructure and service; as well as a distorted composition of government expenditure. Furthermore, corruption not only hampers economic growth, it also increases income inequalities and poverty. With poverty come poor living conditions, low life-expectancy, high infant-mortality and high illiteracy rates, also severely affecting the lives of future generations. Moreover, corruption has adverse effects on the natural environment. Corrupt practices lead to the unsustainable exploitation of natural resources, for instance by illegal logging and polluting oil exploitation. Wildlife conservation is also at risk due to corruption, such as the facilitation by public officials of poaching and the illegal trade in animals or their 'products', and the embezzlement of conservation funds. All in all, corruption affects the very fabric of society, and therefore measures against it are warranted.

2.3. Global and Regional Legal Framework

In chapter II, research question (1) was answered: *What international and regional legal framework currently exists to curb corruption, and how does it function?* The study shows that there is a wide range of treaties applicable to various corrupt practices: the Inter-American Convention Against Corruption, the Convention on the Protection of the European Communities' Financial Interests and its two Protocols, the OECD Anti-Bribery Convention, the Council of Europe's Criminal and Civil Law Conventions on Corruption, the SADC Protocol Against Corruption, the ECOWAS Protocol on the Fight Against Corruption, the African Union Convention on Preventing and Combating Corruption, the UN Convention Against Transnational Organized Crime, and the UN Convention Against Corruption.

While none of the instruments provides an all-encompassing definition of corruption or a set list of corrupt acts, the instruments do list what may be seen as corruption for the purpose of the treaty. The scope of some treaties remains limited to forms of bribery (e.g. the OECD Anti-Bribery Convention), while others are much more comprehensive and cover a wider range of corrupt practices. The main focus of all treaties is on tackling corruption at the national level, by criminalisation and prevention, as well as international cooperation.

A number of provisions in some treaties are worded in a non-obligatory fashion. Either they leave it up to States to decide whether they criminalise certain conduct (as is the case with the preventive measures and some acts of corruption in the UNCAC), or they contain safeguard clauses, allowing States to make certain treaty provisions dependent upon national legislation.

With respect to the monitoring of the treaties, we find that the main method that is adopted is non-binding peer or expert review. The Inter-American Convention is monitored by MESICIC, the OECD Anti-Bribery Convention by the Working Group on Bribery, the Council of Europe's Conventions by GRECO, the SADC Protocol by the Committee of State Parties, and the AU Convention by the Advisory Board on Corruption. Finally, the UNCAC is supplemented by a peer review process, the oversight of which is in the hands of the Implementation Review Group, consisting of State Party representatives. While these 'soft' mechanisms may contribute to a better understanding of State obligations and the implementation thereof, it is by no means certain that State Parties will comply with the various treaties, and since the monitoring mechanisms lack teeth, forcing States into compliance is not possible.

As stated, the treaties mainly oblige States to take measures at the national level. However, it can be severely doubted whether States with high-level corruption have the political will to combat corruption. Oftentimes, anti-corruption efforts in such countries remain limited to dealing with political opponents or catching the 'small fish'. For this reason, anti-corruption should be raised to the international level, by considering international obligations of States, *inter alia*, in the field of international human rights law and international criminal law.

3. Part B: Responsibility of States: Corruption as a Violation of Human Rights?

Part B explored research question (2): *Is it possible to conceptualise (certain forms of) public sector corruption as a violation of human rights?*

3.1. Human Rights Practice

A first component of the question posed above is *(a) What does the practice of the global and regional human rights supervisory bodies reveal about the link between corruption and human rights violations?* To answer this question, the study examined (i) the concluding observations and views of the UN Human Rights treaty bodies; (ii) the Universal Periodic Review of the Human Rights Council; (iii) a selected number of Special Procedures of the Human Rights Council; and (iv) regional mechanisms for human rights protection in Europe, the Americas, and Africa. The main findings are set out below.

3.1.1. UN Human Rights Treaty Bodies

The present study analysed the practice of the so-called treaty-based system of human rights monitoring: the output of the UN human rights treaty bodies, composed of independent human rights experts. In order to supervise State compliance with the core human rights treaties at the international level (i) all treaty bodies examine State reports under the reporting procedure, resulting in concluding observations; and (ii) a number of treaty bodies may be competent to consider complaints from individuals and issue so-called 'views'. Neither concluding observations nor views on individual complaints are legally binding upon States, but they are nevertheless regarded as authoritative.

In respect of the concluding observations of the treaty bodies which discuss corruption, the following can be said. A total number of 131 concluding observations discussing corruption were found. Annex 1 contains an overview of all observations, organised alphabetically per country and including the country's score on the 2011 Corruption Perceptions Index of Transparency International. A total number of 67 States was scrutinised by the treaty bodies on the matter of corruption, the majority of which were developing countries, with Sub-Saharan African countries in the lead (23). Other observations were made on States located in: Eastern Europe (11), Central Asia (8) and Latin America (8), South-East Asia (6), other Asian countries (3), and South-Asia (2). Much less attention was paid to the Caribbean (2), North Africa (1), the Middle East (1), Southern Europe (1) and Western Europe (1). The large majority of the 67 States does indeed occupy the lower places of the CPI, since there are high levels of perceived corruption in these countries. Thus, the concluding observations of the Committees largely seem to reflect actual perceptions about corruption. But meanwhile, it is unclear why some countries are scrutinised on corruption, while other equally corrupt States avoid scrutiny. Late or non-submission of State reports, as well as the fact that some States are not a Party to all human rights treaties, may play a role.

The Committee on the Rights of the Child is the treaty body that has thus far paid most attention to corruption (50 observations), followed by the Committee on Economic, Social and Cultural Rights (31), the Human Rights Committee (28), the Committee Against Torture (12), the Committee on the Elimination of all forms of Racial Discrimination (7), and the Committee on the Elimination of all forms of Discrimination against Women (3). The fact that CEDAW issued very few observations on the topic is worrisome. Women, especially in developing nations, are disproportionately affected by corrupt practices, particularly by petty corruption which they may encounter due to their role as caretakers.

The civil and political rights that are, in the view of the Committees, affected by corruption are first and foremost the right to equality before courts and tribunals and to a fair trial. The HRC, as well as the CESCR and CAT, pay a great deal of attention to corruption in the judiciary. Other civil and political rights discussed by the HRC, CESCR and CAT in the context of corruption are the prohibition of human trafficking, the right to freedom of movement and the rights of detainees. It is noteworthy that the HRC failed to address the impact of corruption upon political rights (Article 25 ICCPR), since, *inter alia*, corruption in elections is an important topic worldwide. Perhaps this is still deemed to be too politically sensitive?

In respect of economic, social and cultural rights, we found that the CESCR rarely connected corruption to State obligations under a *particular* right enshrined in the ICESCR. This was only done in respect of the right to food, and the right to social security. Also, while the Committee made clear that corruption has a negative impact upon the equal enjoyment/implementation/realisation/exercise of economic social and cultural rights, and that corruption affects a State's resources available for social programmes, this issue could be developed much further by analysing the specific obligations under Article 2(1) ICESCR. The CRC did pay quite some attention to the impact of corruption on the maximum available resources. This Committee, on a number of occasions, also referred to the rights to health and education. Among the other issues discussed by the CRC was the role of corruption in adoption procedures and in trafficking in children.

Considering the language used by the Committees to condemn corruption, it can be observed that this does not significantly differ from the language used to discuss other human rights problems. Observations are usually worded in a very general way. While none of the observations specified that corruption violates a human right, it follows from the wording used that this is actually the case. In respect of Kenya, the HRC stated that 'allegations of judicial corruption 'seriously undermine' the independence and impartiality of the judiciary', which are components of the right to a fair trial. Also, the fact that for example the CESCR 'urges' Congo (2009) to take a clear set of anti-corruption measures[1] may show that, in such a case, the State Party does not meet its obligations under the ICESCR, although it does remain unclear what provision of the treaty is at stake here.

Interestingly, most observations on corruption, especially those which are more elaborately worded, were adopted rather recently. Greater scrutiny of corruption is therefore a trend among the treaty bodies, which can be considered a positive development. This trend follows the growing attention for corruption in wider society and among international players such as the World Bank.

Regarding the views on individual complaints, very few complaints were found where corruption played a substantial role. The HRC dealt with a number of complaints concerning maltreatment of persons exposing corrupt practices (whistleblowers), most notably *Philip Afuson Njaru v. Cameroon*.[2] Other complaints concerned allegations that the applicant did not receive a fair trial due to judicial corruption. Furthermore, it flows from the HRC's views in *Michael and Brian Hill v. Spain* that misappropriation of funds for food or drinks for prisoners can lead to a

1 CESCR CO Congo 20 November 2009, UN Doc. E/C.12/COD/CO/4, §11.

2 Communication no. 1353/2005, *Philip Afuson Njaru v. Cameroon*, views of 19 March 2007, UN Doc. CCPR/C/89/D/1353/2005.

violation of Article 10 ICCPR, containing detainees' rights.[3] In addition, a small number of complaints brought before the Committee Against Torture showed that persons exposing corruption may face torture or inhumane treatment and therefore request asylum abroad. Finally, neither CERD nor CEDAW issued any relevant views on corruption.

3.1.2. Universal Periodic Review

Under the Universal Periodic Review, established by the General Assembly in 2006, the human rights record of all 192 UN Member States is periodically reviewed by other Member States every four years, within the context of the Human Rights Council. Advantage of this peer review system is that it does not matter whether the State concerned has ratified a certain human rights treaty or not.

The study analysed all 128 outcome reports of the first eight UPR sessions. In respect of 77 countries, corruption was discussed. The large majority of these States are developing countries with high levels of perceived corruption according to the CPI. Some countries ranking in the middle of the CPI were also scrutinised. Only few comments about corruption were made in respect of States not generally known for pervasive corruption, such as Germany. The countries that made comments, asked questions, or formulated recommendations about corruption to States under review were sometimes the countries located in the same region as the State under review. Nevertheless, discussions on corruption crossed regional boundaries, with both developed and developing nations involved in the discussion. A number of developed States such as Canada and the US were rather actively involved in giving their views. On the other hand, African States (often found at lower levels of the CPI) rarely criticised countries for corruption.

It can be concluded that States under review did report to the Council themselves in their national reports about problems they experience with corruption. States also discussed the actions taken to combat corruption, including becoming a Party to anti-corruption treaties; adopting domestic anti-corruption legislation; establishing domestic anti-corruption bodies; and prosecuting corrupt officials. Furthermore, many reviewing States made comments about corruption, asked questions, and formulated recommendations. Among the topics discussed were judicial corruption, corruption in the police and the military, the vulnerable position of whistleblowers, and the role of corrupt officials in human trafficking. Reviewing States often recommended that States under review should ratify anti-corruption treaties such as the UNCAC, and that they should adopt anti-corruption laws and set up anti-corruption bodies at the national level. A small number of recommendations were more specific, which is to be applauded. States under review benefit most from more specific recommendations.

---

3 Communication no. 526/1993, Michael and Brian Hill v. Spain, views of 22 June 1997, UN Doc. CCPR/C/59/D/526/1993.

As regards the relation between corruption and human rights violations, the outcome reports rarely found that corruption in itself is a human rights violation. Yet, it follows from the statements by the States under review, as well as from the questions, comments, and recommendations by reviewing States, that corruption is discussed among 'classic' human rights issues, demonstrating that corruption clearly is a human rights topic, on the agenda of the UPR. While prior to the mid–1990s, corruption was still a taboo subject, it is promising that States put corruption on the agenda within the UN Human Rights Council.

3.1.3. Special Procedures of the Human Rights Council

A wide range of Special Procedures exist under the Human Rights Council. Currently, 33 thematic mandates and 8 country mandates are in place. These are carried out by either one person (Special Rapporteur, Special Representative of the Secretary-General, or Independent Expert), or by a group of five persons (Working Group). All are independent and impartial experts. The current study examined ten selected thematic mandates, as well as all eight country mandates, so as to determine how corruption was dealt with in these mechanisms. Related resolutions of the current Human Rights Council, the former Human Rights Commission, and the General Assembly were also taken into account.

The most important thematic mandate for this study is that of the former Special Rapporteur on corruption and its impact on the full enjoyment of human rights, in particular economic, social and cultural rights. Mandate-holder Mbonu was appointed in 2003 by the former Sub-Commission on the Promotion and Protection of Human Rights, and her mandate already ended in 2006. In this period, a working paper, a preliminary report, a progress report, and a final report were published. In itself, the establishment of a Special Procedure on corruption and economic, social and cultural rights offered an excellent opportunity to examine the matter. Regrettably, the output of the mandate was scant. Rather than examining the particularities of the linkages between corruption and human rights, the reports were descriptive and lacked the desired quality. Mbonu's analysis remained limited to concluding, *inter alia*, that 'the enjoyment of all regimes of rights, be they economic, social and cultural or civil and political, is seriously undermined by the phenomenon of corruption.'[4] The Special Rapporteur also held that 'corruption, whether systemic, endemic or petty, violates citizens' enjoyment of all the rights contained in all the international instruments.'[5] Argumentation supporting such a bold claim is absent. Mbonu did mention rights of political participation, the right to equality and non-discrimination, and the right to a fair trial, and found that

4 Working paper submitted by Ms. Christy Mbonu in accordance with Sub-Commission decision 2002/106, 14 May 2003, UN Doc. E/CN.4/Sub.2/2003/18, §3.

5 Preliminary report of the Special Rapporteur on corruption and its impact on the full enjoyment of human rights, in particular economic, social and cultural rights, Sub-Cion 56th session, 7 July 2004, UN Doc. E/CN.4/Sub.2/2004/23, §57.

embezzlement of public funds leads to the denial of economic, social and cultural rights. Yet, a proper legal analysis could not be detected. It is therefore not a surprise that the mandate was discontinued.

The study considered a number of thematic mandates on civil and political rights. To begin with, the Special Rapporteur on the independence of judges and lawyers paid substantial attention to judicial corruption in his/her reports. Corruption was found, *inter alia*, to be 'one of the most serious obstacles to the promotion and protection of human rights', having 'a detrimental impact on human rights'.[6] Importantly, the Rapporteur also provided a number of concrete recommendations to combat corruption.[7] In contrast to this Rapporteur, the Special Rapporteur on trafficking in persons, especially in women and children, paid little attention in the annual reports to the role of corrupt public officials in the perpetration of human trafficking. While the SR found in 2009 that corruption is one of the root causes of trafficking,[8] a proper analysis is not present. A few country reports did mention the problem. Furthermore, the Special Rapporteur on the sale of children, child prostitution and child pornography did discuss corruption in many annual reports. The role of corrupt officials was repeatedly emphasised, and many of the country reports also addressed the matter. This active attitude is certainly laudable.

Regarding the thematic mandates on economic, social and cultural rights, the output of the Special Procedures on housing, education, food, and health was analysed. The Special Rapporteur on the right to adequate housing paid some attention to corruption in the annual reports, as well as in the country reports. However, any proper problem analysis and the specific links to the various components of the right to housing is lacking. Furthermore, the same holds true for the Special Rapporteur on the right to education, whose annual reports hardly mentioned corruption. The country reports are largely limited to stating that corruption results in less available resources for education. Nevertheless, a different, more positive, picture emerges in respect of the mandates on the right to food and education. As demonstrated in his annual reports and country reports, the Special Rapporteur on the right to food is clearly aware of the problems posed by corruption in the realisation of this right. *Inter alia*, the Rapporteur argued that the obligation to protect the right to food imposed the duty on States to combat corruption. Also, corruption was considered to be one of the seven problem areas directly affecting the right to food. Likewise, the Special Rapporteur on the right to health was also actively involved in discussing corrupt practices in the health sector,

6 Report of the Special Rapporteur on the independence of judges and lawyers, HRC 14th session, 25 March 2010, UN Doc. A/HRC/14/26, §73–74.

7 Report of the Special Rapporteur on the independence of judges and lawyers, GA 65th session, 10 August 2010, UN Doc. A/65/274, §44–45.

8 Report of the Special Rapporteur on trafficking in persons, especially women and children, HRC 10th session, 20 February 2009, UN Doc. A/HRC/10/16, section Conclusions and Recommendations.

both in his annual reports and in the country reports. It was repeatedly stated that a right-to-health policy is also an anti-corruption policy,[9] and that corruption is a major obstacle to the enjoyment of the right to health, including access to medicines.[10] The country reports demonstrated how corruption hinders the economic accessibility (affordability) of the right to health, by the illicit charging of user fees.[11] Moreover, a country report urged the government to take all appropriate action to combat health sector corruption, which is, in the view of the Rapporteur, in line with State obligation to respect and to protect the right to health.[12] To conclude, the Special Rapporteur on the right to health is, to date, the best example of how corruption can and should be addressed in the thematic Special Procedures.

The study also looked into the thematic mandates of the Independent Expert on the question of human rights and extreme poverty, and of the Special Representative of the Secretary-General on the issue of human rights and transnational corporations and other business enterprises. The first mandate, on human rights and extreme poverty, showed that mandate-holders are in an appropriate position to provide detailed anti-corruption recommendations in a country report.[13] This is certainly the way forward. However, this cannot be said of the way in which the Special Representative on human rights and business, John Ruggie, has dealt with corruption. While he did find, *inter alia*, that corruption is a significant impediment to the realisation of human rights, his reports offered little novel insights – even though the topic of the mandate did offer the opportunity to discuss the matter in greater detail.

When looking at the resolutions of the Human Rights Council, the former Commission and the General Assembly on the topics of the thematic Procedures, we find little reference to corruption, not even in those cases where the mandate-holders did report about the problems posed by corrupt practices. Yet, one should admit that this discrepancy is a broader concern within the UN context, not limited to discussion about corruption.

Considering the eight country mandates that currently exist, we find great differences as to the extent in which corruption was discussed. While the CPI 2011 indicates that the countries under scrutiny have extremely high levels of perceived corruption (i.e. Haïti, Cambodia, Burundi, Sudan, Myanmar and Somalia), this is

---

9 Report of the Special Rapporteur on the right to health, GA 61st session, 13 September 2006, UN Doc.A/61/338, §80.

10 Report of the Special Rapporteur on the right to health, GA 63rd session, 11 August 2008, UN Doc. A/63/263.

11 Report of the Special Rapporteur on the right to health, Mission to Mozambique, CHR 61st session, 4 January 2005, UN Doc. E/CN.4/2005/51/Add.2, §45–52, 69 and Report of the Special Rapporteur on the right to health, Mission to India, HRC 14th session, 15 April 2010, UN Doc. A/HRC/14/20/Add.2, §52.

12 Report of the Special Rapporteur on the right to health, Mission to Mozambique, CHR 61st session, 4 January 2005, UN Doc. E/CN.4/2005/51/Add.2, §70.

13 Report of the Independent Expert on the question of human rights and extreme poverty, HRC 14th session, 11 May 2010, UN Doc. A/HRC/14/31/Add.1, §112.

not adequately reflected in the reports of the mandate-holders. Good examples of how corruption can be dealt with by the Special Procedures can be found in the reports of the Independent Expert on Burundi, the Independent Expert on Haïti, and the Special Representative on Cambodia. While the reports of these mandates do not show how corrupt practices may violate human rights, they make clear that the mandate-holders are in the position to discuss corruption, to formulate recommendations, and to monitor the situation in the long run. Particularly encouraging are the remarks by the Expert on Burundi on the problem of grand corruption.[14] Other topics discussed in the three procedures were judicial corruption and police corruption. Especially the mandate on Cambodia discussed a wider variety of corruption- related topics. Contrary to these three procedures, the mandates on Somalia, Sudan, Northern Korea, Myanmar, and the Occupied Palestinian Territories do not properly address corruption.

When analysing the outcomes of the Special Procedures about corruption, one should keep an eye on a number of general weaknesses of the system of these Procedures, including the selection process of mandate-holders, the lack of financial and staff support, the restricted maximum length of reports, the possibly non-cooperative attitudes of governments concerned, as well as the lack of a thorough follow-up procedure.

3.1.4. Regional Human Rights Mechanisms

The core of the European system of human rights protection is the European Convention on Human Rights, supervised by the European Court of Human Rights. Its case law on corruption centers around the right of whistleblowers to freedom of expression under Article 10 ECHR; as well as the rights of persons accused of corruption, *inter alia*, under Articles 5, 6 and 8 ECHR.

The Court's case law on the rights of whistleblowers can be divided into cases on civil servants blowing the whistle, and cases about journalists exposing corruption. As regards civil servants, the Grand Chamber set out a framework for testing whether whistleblowing is allowed in *Guja v. Moldova*.[15] Restrictions on the right to freedom of expression under Article 10 need to be 'necessary in a democratic society', pursuant to 10(2). For civil servants, the Court formulated six criteria: (i) the availability and use of alternative channels; (ii) the public interest in the disclosed information; (iii) the authenticity of the disclosed information; (iv) weighing the damage suffered by the public authority against the public interest; (v) the motive of the whistleblower; and (vi) the penalty imposed on the

14 Report of the Independent Expert on the situation of human rights in Burundi, GA 62nd session, 8 August 2007, UN Doc. A/62/213, §49. Similar concerns about high-level corruption were also expressed in: Interim report of the Independent Expert on the situation of human rights in Burundi, HRC 4th session, 26 February 2007, UN Doc. A/HRC/4/5, §70.

15 ECtHR Grand Chamber Judgment *Guja v. Moldova*, 12 February 2008, Application no. 14277/04.

whistleblower and its consequences. In respect of Guja, the Court found a violation of Article 10 since his dismissal after disclosure of documents to a newspaper was not necessary in a democratic society. Regarding journalists, there is a larger body of case law concerning journalists or newspaper editors who published accusations of corruption and were prosecuted as a result. In the large majority of these cases, the Court found a violation of Article 10. For example, in *Cumpana and Mazare v. Romania*[16] the Court had to decide whether the conviction of journalists for publishing allegations of corruption – restricting the right to freedom of expression – was necessary in a democratic society. In order to meet this standard, the restriction had to meet a pressing social need. In this respect, the Court emphasised the vital role of the press as public watchdog. Also, the imposed sanction (the conviction) needed to be proportional. In the present case, the Court ruled that while there was a pressing social need for restricting the right to freedom of expression, the sanction imposed was disproportional.

Apart from the case law on whistleblowers, the Court has ruled in cases where the rights of persons accused of corruption were allegedly violated by anti-corruption measures. It concerned, *inter alia*, a violation of the right to a fair trial under Article 6 by the use of undercover agents (*Ramanauskas v. Lithuania*);[17] a violation of the right to private life under Article 8 by the use of intercepted phone calls (*Craxi v. Italy*);[18] as well as the violation of Article 5(4) by restricting defence rights during a corruption investigation (*Lietzow v. Germany*).[19]

In the American context, the American Convention on the Protection of Human Rights (containing civil and political rights) and the Protocol of San Salvador (containing economic, social and cultural rights) are at the heart of the regional system of human rights protection in the Americas. Supervision with these instruments is in the hands of the Inter-American Commission on Human Rights, and the Inter-American Court of Human Rights. In the practice of the Commission, only a small number of petitions from individuals address corruption. Yet, in many country reports, the matter is addressed with increasing vigour. The thematic reports and other publication also addressed corruption every now and then, but few resolutions are concerned with the matter. When looking at the themes that were discussed, we find some petitions about judicial corruption in which individuals complain that, due to corruption in the judiciary, they did not receive a fair trial under Article 8 ACHR. Also, many of the country reports discuss judicial corruption. Interestingly, the report on Paraguay unequivocally stated that corruption by a judge may constitute a violation of the right to a fair trial.[20] Other topics discussed by the Commission in relation to corruption include the rights of

---

16 ECtHR Grand Chamber Judgment *Cumpana and Mazare v. Romania*, 17 December 2004, Application no. 33348/96.

17 ECtHR Judgment *Ramanauskas v. Lithuania*, 5 February 2008, Application no. 74420/01.

18 ECtHR Judgment *Craxi v. Italy* (No. 2), 17 July 2003, Application no. 25337/94.

19 ECtHR Judgment *Lietzow v. Germany*, 13 February 2001, Application no. 24479/94.

20 IACionHR, Third report on the situation of human rights in Paraguay, 9 March 2001, OEA/Ser.L/V/II.110, chapter II, §47.

whistleblowers; economic, social and cultural rights; police corruption; and corruption in prisons.

Regarding the practice of the Inter-American Court of Human Rights, it can be concluded that in only a small number of cases, corruption was discussed. The case law is centered around the rights of whistleblowers, particularly their right to freedom of expression of Article 13 ACHR. Illustrative cases are *Ivcher Bronstein v. Peru*[21] and *Ricardo Canese v. Paraguay.*[22]

The African system of human rights protection consists of the African Charter on Human and Peoples' Rights, supervised by the African Commission on Human and People's Rights and the (not yet functioning) African Court on Human and Peoples' Rights. Except for one corruption-related individual complaint (which was declared inadmissible), no relevant statements on corruption could be found. This is a pity, given the fact that corruption is large problem in many African countries. For corruption to be addressed in the Commission's individual complaint procedure, it is obviously necessary for individuals to submit complaints, which may be difficult in practical terms for the most vulnerable groups. The admissibility requirement of exhaustion of domestic remedies may also be a barrier, as well as the requirement that communications must not be written in disparaging or insulting language directed to the State. Unfortunately, the Commission held in *Ilesanmi v. Nigeria* that an individual complaint on corruption was indeed inadmissible because of such language.[23] It is recommended that the Commission will loosely apply this requirement in future cases about corruption.

3.2. Further Links

3.2.1. General Conclusions

The second component (b) of research question (2) is *What further links can be established between corruption and human rights violations, and what are the merits of such an approach?* To begin with, the study argued that there are five so-called 'dimensions' of the connection between corruption and human rights: (i) corruption and human rights violations often exist in the same environment; (ii) human rights, including the rights to freedom of expression, assembly, and association, are necessary tools to fight corruption, and these rights are often violated by State authorities wishing to silence whistleblowers; (iii) human rights, including the right to a fair trial, may be violated by anti-corruption measures; (iv) nti-corruption reforms may negatively impact upon the human rights of vulnerable groups; and (v) corruption may in itself constitute a violation of human

21 Inter-American Court of Human Rights, *Ivcher Bronstein v. Peru,* Judgment of 6 Februari 2001.

22 Inter-American Court of Human Rights, *Ricardo Canese v. Paraguay*, Judgment of 31 August 2004.

23 African Commission on Human and Peoples'Rights, *Ilesanmi v. Nigeria,* Communication 268/2003.

rights. It is this latter dimension that was extensively dealt with, both in respect of civil and political rights, as well economic, social and cultural rights.

Also discussed was the opposition voiced by a number of authors against anti-corruptionism in general, and against linking corruption to human rights more specifically. Largely dismissing these claims, it was argued, *inter alia*, that while anti-corruption may be on the agenda of those pursuing neo-liberal economic policies, there are also strong and sincere calls from citizens in developing countries to combat corruption, as well as acknowledgements that linking corruption to human rights may be useful to that end. Moreover, to avoid that the theme of anti-corruption will be monopolised by players such as the World Bank, the use of human rights language and monitoring mechanisms will be particularly helpful.

Moreover, some argued in favour of a new human right to a corruption-free society. Yet, the present work rejected this claim. There is insufficient evidence for the existence of such a right in current human rights law, nor is there a need for this right. The present framework of human rights protection is very well capable of addressing corrupt practices, while the international community of States will most likely oppose a new anti-corruption human right.

Hence, the way forward lies in linking specific acts of corruption to State obligations under the ICCPR and the ICESCR. The present dissertation demonstrated exactly how corrupt acts may violate, *inter alia*, (i) the right to equality and non-discrimination; (ii) the right to equality before courts and tribunals and to a fair trial; (iii) rights of political participation; (iv) the prohibition of human trafficking; (v) rights of detainees to be treated with humanity and dignity; (vi) the right to freedom of movement; (vii) the right to food; (viii) the right to housing; (ix) the right to education; and (x) the right to health. In the context of economic, social and cultural rights, it was also demonstrated that corruption violates the obligations of States under Article 2(1) ICESCR.

In the examination of a concrete case of corruption, one should determine whether corruption violates any of the State obligations to respect, to protect or to fulfil human rights, particularly in the field of economic, social and cultural rights. Moreover, in relation to these type of rights, the various components including availability, accessibility, adaptability, acceptability and quality should be tested, so as to find out how these are violated by corruption.

3.2.2. Merits and Limits of the Human Rights Approach to Corruption

Although conceptualising corruption as a violation of human rights is most certainly not a cure for all illnesses, this approach has a number of advantages. To begin with, showing that corruption may violate human rights can influence public attitudes: the moral dimension of human rights can lead to a wider support for anti-corruption initiatives, also among public officials, the judiciary, business, media, and the public at large.

Furthermore, perceiving corruption as a human rights violation entails that the UN treaty bodies, the UPR and the Special Procedures of the Human Rights Council can be used to address the practice. Particularly the treaty bodies have a role to play in discussing corruption in the State reporting procedure, and by examining complaints about corruption from individuals. Yet, we must also recognise that the treaty bodies may lack the economic expertise to consider complex economic problems such as corruption. For this, the Committees have to rely on accurate third party information. NGOs such as Transparency International certainly have a role to play in this respect. Also affecting the ability of the Committees to deal with corruption is the limited time for the examination of State reports, as well as the political sensitivity of the topic. Moreover, regional human rights instances such as the European Court of Human Rights, the Inter-American Commission on Human Rights, as well as the African Commission on Human Rights, may consider cases from individuals who allege that their rights have been violated by corruption.

Also, possibilities exist at the national level. Domestic human rights litigation is an important route, especially if one aims to rely on human rights provisions enshrined in domestic constitutions. In addition, public interest litigation may offer advantages. At the same time, difficulties may be posed by the fact that high quality evidence is required, as well as professional legal representation, and that domestic courts may be corrupt themselves. Procedures are also very costly and time-consuming. Another problem that should not be overlooked is the matter of causality, which also applies to the individual complaints procedure before the treaty bodies as well as before regional human rights instances. At the heart of human rights complaints about corruption lies that corruption itself may constitute a violation of legally guaranteed human rights. (Semi) judicial human rights bodies obviously require evidence of the corrupt act, and evidence that the harm done to the victim is indeed caused by that very act. In cases of petty corruption, this may be easier to establish than in cases of grand corruption. For instance, embezzlement at the Ministry of Health, resulting in a violation of the right to health, will not be proper material for domestic human rights litigation, since causality is hard to demonstrate, and proper evidence can usually not be produced by the victims. Finally, the lack of justiciability of economic, social and cultural rights at the national level may pose problems.

4. Part C: Individual Responsibility: Corruption as a Crime under International Law?

In Part C, research question (3) was addressed: *Is it possible to conceptualise (certain forms of) public sector corruption as a crime under international law?* This question was divided into three sub-questions.

4.1. Theoretical Considerations

Sub-question 3(a) asked *Should the system of international criminal law be used to fight corruption and, if so, which forms of corruption would qualify for this approach?*

Answering this question requires a clear definition of the term 'international criminal law' (hereafter: ICL). It was argued that ICL *largo sensu* differs from ICL *stricto sensu.* ICL *largo sensu* is comprised of both the criminal law aspects of international law (i.e. ICL *stricto sensu,* with direct enforcement at the international level) and the international aspects of national criminal law (i.e. transnational criminal law, with indirect enforcement at by domestic authorities based on international treaty obligations). Furthermore, crimes which involve direct individual criminal responsibility under international law, directly punishable at the international level, are crimes under international law. These crimes differ from so-called treaty-based or transnational crimes, which have to be criminalised and enforced at the national level. Both categories of crimes are 'international crimes'.

As elaborated upon earlier, corruption is clearly part of transnational criminal law, since there are many anti-corruption treaties obliging State Parties to criminalise and prosecute forms of corruption at the national level. Hence, corruption is a treaty-based or transnational crime. The question arises whether corruption is also part of ICL *stricto sensu,* a system which can hold individuals accountable at the international, rather than the domestic, level. This concerns the matter whether corruption is also a crime under international law. To answer this question, ICL's history, its rationales for criminalisation, as well as its objectives of punishment were taken into account.

In respect of the history of international criminal law (*stricto sensu*), the study showed that this area of law paid little attention to economic crimes. ICL has its origins in situations of armed conflict, and is very much focused on the occurrence of physical violence. Yet, we find that the 1919 Commission on the Responsibility of the Authors of the War and on Enforcement of Penalties (appointed by the Paris Peace Conference after the First World War), listed 32 offences which constituted war crimes, including offences which do not consist of physical violence, but are rather of an economic or property nature. Yet, economic crimes were not considered as such in the aftermath of Second World War, nor by the ICTY, the ICTR or the various hybrid courts and other internationalised domestic courts and tribunals. However, efforts for the establishment of the International Criminal Court partly resulted from a proposal by sixteen Caribbean and Latin American States to set up an international tribunal to combat drug trafficking, which is not a violent crime per se, and which is often committed outside of armed conflict situations. The *travaux préparatoires* of the Rome Statute do however show little reference to economic crimes, except from some remarks by a Libyan and a Nigerian delegate, which were not acted upon. All in all, current ICL *stricto sensu* has a strong focus on crisis situations, places emphasis on violent crimes, and favours civil and political rights over economic, social and cultural rights. Yet, this does not mean that, theoretically, ICL should not or cannot be used to address non-violent crimes committed during peacetime, such as corruption. The example of drug trafficking demonstrates this. The reason why ICL *stricto sensu* does not deal with economic crimes, while transnational criminal does cover these crimes, is probably that ICL *stricto sensu* started to develop earlier than efforts to combat economic offences. These type of crimes simply missed the boat of international criminalisation.

When looking into the rationales for international criminalisation, it was argued that the normative model for criminal policy developed by Theo De Roos for national criminalisation can also be largely applied in the international context. This model formulates six criteria that should be met in order for criminalisation of conduct to take place: (i) feasibility and motivation of harm; (ii) tolerance; (iii) subsidiarity; (iv) proportionality; (v) legality; and (vi) practical applicability and effectivity. When testing these principles, it was found that corruption meets all of them. As regards (i) the harm done by corrupt conduct, this requirement was further developed by applying a number of criteria developed by Cherif Bassiouni and Barbara Yarnold. They argued that there are five criteria, setting out when certain conduct should be treated as a crime under international law or as a treaty-based crime: (i) in the case of a significant international interest: a threat to international peace and security (crime under international law); (ii) should the conduct offend the commonly shared values of the world community, including if the conduct shocks the conscience of humanity (crime under international law); (iii) if there are transnational implications (treaty-based crime); (iv) if there is harm to an internationally protected person or interest (treaty-based crime); or (v) if there is a violation of an internationally protected interest (treaty-based crime). In the case of (i) and (ii), the conduct is generally State-sponsored or involves State activity, while in the case of (iii), (iv) and (v), State involvement is usually lacking. Since corruption is already a treaty-based crime, it was examined whether criterion (i) and/or (ii) also apply. This is indeed the case. First, corruption can threaten international peace and security. Corruption erodes democracy and legitimacy, and may fuel armed conflict. Such conflict may disturb an entire region, which makes corruption much more than an internal affair. Second, corruption is offensive to the commonly shared values of the world community. Large-scale looters of a developing country's public funds, by its own high-level public officials, leaves the people of a nation with little, often with unimaginable poverty as a result. Such situations are condemned by the international community, and are as shocking as the atrocities committed during armed conflict. For these reasons, corruption deserves to be treated as a crime under international law, and not just as a treaty-based crime. Moreover, corruption can be distinguished from other harmful practices such as drug trafficking, human trafficking or terrorism, because, in cases of corruption, it is the State that is acting. State power is abused, and therefore it meets the criteria for international criminalisation formulated by Bassiouni and Yarnold.

The objectives of punishment at the international level also point to international criminalisation of corruption. To begin with, retribution is an adequate justification for corruption, since public officials deserve to be punished given the harmful consequences of their conduct. The general deterrent function of punishment may also play a role: by prosecuting a corrupt high-level official, other officials may be deterred from engaging in corruption. Important in this respect are the speed with which punishment will take place, the predictability of punishment, as well as its severity. Since it was argued that the general deterrent function is particularly effective when the perpetrators are regime elites, this function may be of use in the context of grand corruption. Most importantly, the expressivist function of punishment is highly valuable in the context of corruption. This function concerns the symbolic significance of punishment. Punishment of corruption demonstrates to the public officials, a country's citizens and to the international community at large that corruption is unacceptable. Furthermore, other goals that may be served by punishing corruption are justice for victims, recording history, and post-conflict reconciliation. Finally, international trials have a number of advantages: they do not suffer so much from political manipulation or influence, or biased judges.

It is fair to argue that given the rationales for international criminalisation and the objectives of punishment in international law, corruption should be criminalised at the international level as a crime under international law, and not just as a treaty-based crime. Hence, it should be made clear which forms of corruption are eligible for such treatment. First, only grand corruption can fall within ICL's scope. More specifically, ICL should focus on those persons able to escape domestic prosecution due to *de jure* or *de facto* immunity. These are heads of State, heads of government, cabinet ministers and members of parliament. Corrupt acts committed by these officials can be qualified as grand corruption. Moreover, ICL *stricto sensu* should focus on passive bribery and embezzlement. Trading in influence, abuse of functions, and illicit enrichment should be kept, for the time being, outside of the debate on international criminalisation.

4.2. *De lege lata* Perspective

4.2.1. Introductory Remarks

Subsequently, sub-question 3(b) asked *Can certain forms of corruption be conceptualised under the Rome Statute as a crime against humanity* de lege lata? To answer this question, the general elements of all crimes against humanity listed in Article 7(1) of the Rome Statute were considered, starting with the *actus reus*. This is the material element of the crime, consisting of conduct, consequence, and circumstance. The *mens rea* is the mental element of the crime, i.e. the state of mind of the accused at the time of the crime. This requirement consists of the components intent and knowledge. Finally, the contextual element must be present. For crimes against humanity, it is required that there is a widespread or systematic attack directed against any civilian population. The next step consisted of looking into two specific crimes against humanity, i.e. extermination and other inhumane acts, since some authors have argued that corruption can be qualified as one of these crimes.

4.2.2. Corruption as Extermination (Article 7(1)(b) Rome Statute)?

Extermination is listed in Article 7(1)(b) of the Rome Statute. It is defined as 'an act or combination of acts which contribute to the killing of a large number of individuals, either directly or indirectly. Moreover, it includes the intentional infliction of conditions of life, *inter alia*, the deprivation of access to food and medicine, calculated to bring about the destruction of part of a population.

The *actus reus* of extermination consists of the killing of one or more persons by the perpetrator, which can also take place by inflicting the mentioned conditions of life. This element can be met by corruption, since it can constitute an infliction of conditions of life, including the deprivation of access to food and medicine. By embezzling State resources, high-level public officials deprive their citizens of basic necessities, leading to deaths. This is particularly true in situations of humanitarian disasters. If funds or good intended for relief do not reach their beneficiaries, starvation of civilians can be the result.

The *mens rea* required for extermination, laid down in Article 30 of the Rome Statute, requires that the perpetrator has the intent to kill a large number of individuals, or to inflict grievous bodily harm, or serious injury, in the reasonable knowledge that such an act or omission was likely to cause death as in the case of murder. This element cannot be met by corruption. The ICC Pre-Trial Chamber II in the *Bemba* case held that Article 30 is limited to *dolus directus* in the first and the second degree. This entails that either (i) the perpetrator knows of, and wants to achieve the consequence of the criminal offence; or (ii) the perpetrator is aware that the consequence of the criminal action is inevitable. These two types of *dolus directus* must be separated from *dolus eventualis*, which, according to the Pre-Trial Chamber in *Bemba*, is not covered by Article 30.[24] This was confirmed by the ICC Trial Chamber in its judgment in *Lubanga* in March 2012.[25] *Dolus eventualis* is present when the perpetrator is fully aware of the possible outcome as a side effect of his act, but still decides to continue with the conduct, and therefore recognises and approves the result as a possible cost of achieving his goal. In cases of grand corruption, it is not likely that the public official engages in corruption in order to kill civilians. Rather, the deaths will be a side effect of the corrupt practices. Hence, the mental element in cases of corruption will be *dolus eventualis*, rather than first

24 ICC *Prosecutor v. Jean-Pierre Bemba Gombo*, Decision Pre-Trial Chamber 15 June 2009, ICC–01/05–01/08.

25 ICC *Prosecutor v. Thomas Lubanga Dyilo*, Judgment Pursuant to Article 74 of the Statute, Trial Chamber 14 March 2012, ICC–01/04–01/06.

or second degree *dolus directus*. Since Article 30 does not include the first type of intent, corruption cannot constitute extermination.

While the claim about 'corruption as extermination' will fail given the fact that the required *mens rea* standard cannot be met, it should be noted that the contextual element of extermination can however be met. As noted above, there must be a widespread or systematic attack against any civilian population. 'Widespread' is a quantitative notion, referring to the number of victims or the broad geographical extension. 'Systematic' is a qualitative notion, referring to a high degree of organisation. Furthermore, the attack does not have to be violent, nor does the act require a nexus to armed conflict. Whenever there are many victims, corruption meets the requirement of a widespread attack. In any case, there will be a systematic attack in cases of grand corruption, since high-level corruption will usually possess a high degree of organisation. In addition, looting of State assets requires some sort of 'policy' in order for it to be carried out. It is also necessary that the perpetrators of extermination have knowledge about the widespread or systematic attack. In cases of grand corruption, this knowledge of a widespread looting of State property will be present with the perpetrators.

What is problematic about the 'corruption as extermination' hypothesis, apart from the lack of *mens rea*, is the difficulty of having to prove causality between a specific corrupt act and the death of civilians (e.g. by starvation). More often than not, there are many more factors that play a role. Finally, the hypothesis does not offer possibilities if corruption does not lead to (immediate) deaths. In sum, the conceptualisation of grand corruption as extermination under Article 7(1)(b) of the Rome Statute is not legally possible.

4.2.3. Corruption as an Other Inhumane Act (Article 7(1)(k) Rome Statute)?

Article 7(1)(k) of the Rome Statute provides that, in addition to the crimes listed under (1)(a) to (j), a crime against humanity can also consist of another inhumane act of a similar character intentionally causing great suffering, or serious injury to body or to mental or physical health. These are, in the words of the ICC Pre-Trial Chamber I in *Katanga and Ngudjolo Chui*, 'serious violations of international customary law and the basic rights pertaining to human beings, drawn from the norms of international human rights law, which are of a similar nature and gravity to the acts referred to in Article 7(1).'[26]

The *actus reus* of another inhumane act is two-fold: (i) the consequences of the crime (great suffering, or serious injury to body or to mental or physical health); and (ii) the character of the crime (i.e. the act must be of similar nature and gravity as other crimes against humanity). As regards (i) the consequences of corruption, it is possible that great suffering or serious injury to body or to mental or physical

26 ICC *Prosecutor v. Katanga and Ngudjolo Chui*, Decision Pre-Trial Chamber 30 September 2008, ICC–01/04–01/07.

health is the result of corrupt practices, for example in cases of embezzlement of funds intended for food or medical care. Concerning (ii) the nature and gravity of corruption as compared to the other crimes in Article 7(1), it must be noted that this provision also includes crimes that do not necessarily involve physical violence. Hence, absence of physical violence is not an obstacle to labelling grand corruption as an other inhumane act.

As regards the required *mens rea*, Article 30 applies, covering *dolus directus* in the first and in the second degree. Also, Article 7(1)(k) contains the word 'intentionally', which makes clear that the consequences have to be caused with intent. As is the case with extermination, grand corruption will not meet the standard of *dolus directus*, and, hence, it cannot be conceptualised as another inhumane act under the Rome Statute.

The contextual element can however be fulfilled by grand corruption. As argued *supra* the requirement of a widespread or systematic attack can be met by corruption.

In sum, research question 3(b) must be answered in the negative: neither Article 7(1)(b) nor Article 7(1)(k) of the Rome Statute allows for the inclusion of grand corruption.

4.3. *De Lege Ferenda* Perspective

The answer to 3(b) brings us to sub-question 3(c), which inquired *What possibilities does international criminal law* de lege ferenda *offer to combat corruption at the international level?* To begin with, it was advocated that the Rome Statute should be amended so as to include a new, anti-corruption provision, covering both passive bribery and embezzlement by high-level public officials. Such codification is advantageous because, in addition to direct enforcement by the ICC, it may lead to prosecutions at the national level due to the principle of complementarity. In case States are unable or unwilling to prosecute grand corruption, the ICC may step in. Codification could take the form of either a new category of crimes against humanity under Article 7 of the Rome Statute, or of a separate provision. The latter is the most desirable option, since it offers room to set out the specificities of this type of crime, and to complement the Article with a new provision in the Elements of Crime. As a possible starting point for international criminalisation, the UNCAC may not be appropriate, since the provisions are not specific enough. Hence, the thesis offered a brief analysis of Articles 362–362 and 359 of the Dutch Criminal Code. This legislation was amended in 2001 so as to comply with the UNCAC. Needless to state other legislation can also be used as a point of departure. To a large extent, the mentioned provisions would be suitable for use at the international level. Yet, the offence of passive bribery in Dutch law includes *dolus eventualis* as a form of intent. To be able to transpose this to the Rome Statute, the Elements of Crimes ought to deviate from Article 30 of the Statute, which applies by default.

With regard to the required contextual element, in case of grand corruption this should consist of the requirement that there is a broader context of corruption.

Prosecution of grand corruption, be it passive bribery or embezzlement may be problematic in terms of evidence: a paper trail may be destroyed, while it is difficult to identify individualised victims. Witnesses should be guaranteed whistleblower protection. At the same time, the Court requires State Parties to cooperate in the investigation and prosecution of crimes, and States have to comply with ICC requests to provide assistance in respect of the identification, tracing and freezing or seizure of proceeds, property and assets and instrumentalities of crimes for the purpose of eventual forfeiture.

Politically, inclusion of grand corruption into the Rome Statute is highly sensitive, to say the least. Apart from the high threshold that is required to amend the Statute, both developed and developing States alike will not easily support proposals to include passive bribery and embezzlement. Moreover, since the ICC has not yet produced a large amount of outcome, States will be hesitant to extent the Court's jurisdiction.

Thus, instead of codification in the Rome Statute, it would be more feasible to complement the United Nations Convention Against Corruption with a better monitoring mechanism. Ideally, this could take the form of a separate anti-corruption criminal tribunal, competent to investigate and prosecute. Yet, an expert commission that can monitor State compliance with the treaty, and that can give binding recommendations, would already be a great improvement from the current system of secretive peer review that supplements the UNCAC to date. Furthermore, another option would be the establishment of an ad hoc anti-corruption tribunal, such as the internationalised or mixed tribunals on East Timor, Lebanon and Sierra Leone. The current domestic prosecutions of corrupt leaders such as Hosni Mubarak and Ben Ali show that the establishment of such a tribunal is not an impossible option.

Finally, it was argued that grand corruption may be implicitly addressed in current cases before the ICC. Current trials, with indictments for crimes against humanity or war crimes, may shed light on the role of corrupt practices in the financing of armed conflict. Furthermore, asset freezing and recovery procedures may be initiated.

Chapter XI
Reflections and Recommendations

'Repression takes many forms, and too many nations are plagued by problems that condemn their people to poverty. No country is going to create wealth if its leaders exploit the economy to enrich themselves, or police can be bought off by drug traffickers. No business wants to invest in a place where the government skims 20 percent off the top, or the head of the Port Authority is corrupt. No person wants to live in a society where the rule of law gives way to the rule of brutality and bribery. That is not democracy, that is tyranny, and now is the time for it to end.'

~ US President Barack Obama, Speech to the Parliament of Ghana, 11 July 2009 ~

1. Introduction

After having summarised the main findings of the present study in the previous chapter, this chapter formulates recommendations to relevant actors in the field of corruption, human rights and international criminal law. Moreover, it provides further reflections on the topic, and aims to be the starting point for both academic and practical work in the areas of human rights and international criminal law. Hopefully, the present thesis is by no means the end of discussions on corruption in the aforementioned areas, but rather the beginning. Perhaps it is even possible to draw a cautious parallel between the devastating effects of corruption and the crisis that is currently suffered by the global financial system. Both are living proof that a greed-driven society does more harm than good, and that limits ought to be imposed.

2. Corruption and International Human Rights Law

2.1. Paradigm Shift: Corruption as a Violation of Human Rights

As noted elsewhere, there are five dimensions in the connection between corruption and human rights: (i) corruption and human rights violations often exist in the same environment; (ii) human rights, including the rights to freedom of expression, assembly, and association, are necessary tools to fight corruption, and these rights are often violated by State authorities wishing to silence whistleblowers; (iii) human rights, including the right to a fair trial, may be violated by anti-corruption measures; (iv) anti-corruption reforms may negatively impact upon the human rights of vulnerable groups; and (v) corruption may in itself constitute a violation of human rights.

The value of the present study primarily lies in developing the final dimension. It demonstrated that corruption in itself may constitute a *violation* of internationally recognised human rights. Acceptance of a bribe by a judge violates the right to a fair trial; demand for bribes by a doctor in a public hospital violates the right to health; embezzlement of funds for school books at public schools violates the right to education, and so forth. The study made clear that recent years have seen a growing attention for corruption by human rights supervisory bodies at the global and regional level, which is to be applauded. It can no longer be denied that anti-corruption measures and human rights are two different areas. Rather, they are, to put it in human rights language, interrelated, interdependent, and indivisible. Combating corruption is likely to be beneficial for human rights,[1] and human rights work can no longer do without an anti-corruption component. Yet, the recognition – perhaps present implicitly – that corruption is a violation of human rights, is not often articulated loudly and clearly. It is the objective of this thesis to turn this into common practice within the human rights monitoring bodies and beyond. This line of reasoning transforms a corrupt act into a possible starting point for legal action, be it at the national level by invoking domestic constitutional provisions, or at the international level by submitting a complaint to a regional or global human rights monitoring body.[2] It is this paradigm shift in looking at corruption which this thesis hopes to contribute to.

2.2. Human Rights Treaty Bodies of the United Nations

While an increasing number of concluding observations are dedicated to corruption, the following recommendations can be addressed to the UN human rights treaty bodies:

(i) Corruption should consistently be on the agenda of all treaty bodies, including CEDAW;

(ii) Corrupt practices worldwide should be scrutinised, not merely in those countries with alarmingly high levels of corruption;

(iii) The list of indicators that is annexed to the harmonised reporting guidelines should be amended so as to include corruption. This obliges States to provide the treaty bodies with facts and figures about corruption in their territory, and makes it easier for these bodies to evaluate progress. Yet, it must be acknowledged that the reliability of the information provided by States will inevitably vary;

(iv) Whenever there are indications that the State concerned has serious corruption problems, the list of issues should ask the State to provide

1 Although tensions may arise in respect of dimension (iii) and (iv) mentioned above.

2 Yet, it must be acknowledged that the intrinsic secretive nature of corrupt acts may hinder legal action.

information, also about anti-corruption measures taken. The constructive dialogue should, as a general rule, cover corruption;

(v) The concluding observations should clearly indicate how corrupt practices affect the various components of human rights. Use should be made of the various typologies developed in the Committees' General Comments/ General Recommendations;

(vi) Whenever corruption violates one of the components of the rights laid down in one of the core human rights treaties, the treaty body should identify this as a violation;

(vii) The CESCR should elaborate upon the links between corruption and the various State obligations under Article 2(1) ICESCR;

(viii) The HRC should pay attention to corruption in relation to the exercise of political rights;

(ix) Whenever a violation is found, the treaty body should make specific recommendations to the State concerned on what measures ought to be taken. The treaty body should abstain from making general observations that are of little use to the State;

(x) The treaty bodies, especially the Committee on Economic, Social, and Cultural Rights, should devote a general day of discussion to the issue of corruption and its relationship to human rights violations;

(xi) The treaty bodies should adopt a joint General Comment on Corruption and Human Rights. A draft proposal for such a document can be found in Annex 2;

(xii) Since they strongly rely on high quality information provided by NGOs, the treaty bodies should closely cooperate with anti-corruption organisations, particularly Transparency International. The National Chapters of this organisation, as well as the Secretariat in Berlin are very well able to supply the treaty bodies with country specific data and case studies, that can be used in the reporting procedure, as a counterbalance to State-supplied information.

Yet, one must maintain a realist view on what the reporting procedure of the treaty bodies can achieve. As pointed out by one author, 'unfortunately, given the relatively short time that the treaty bodies can dedicate to each country, the concluding observations remain often at a rather general level, and their jurisprudential impact is marginal and exceptional.'[3] Still, the condemnation of corrupt practices by the treaty bodies will send a strong signal towards States with high levels of corruption, and concluding observations on the matter will provide States with guidance on how to fulfil their obligations under the human rights treaties. The study conducted in the present thesis demonstrated that corruption already is on the agenda of the treaty bodies, and that attention for the topic is

3 Kerstin Mechlem, 'Treaty Bodies and the Interpretation of Human Rights', *Vanderbilt Journal of Transnational Law*, 42 (2009), p. 905–947 at p. 923.

increasing. The number of observations on corruption appears to be growing steadily. This may very well indicate the beginning of an era in which corruption is considered a fully-fledged human rights topic, and will be treated as such by States.

2.3. Universal Periodic Review of the Human Rights Council

It is a positive development that the UPR is employed to address corruption, and it is desirable that States translate their comments and questions, whenever necessary, into recommendations. In particular, it is important that these recommendations are clearly formulated, so as to provide tangible guidance to the State concerned. As noted by NGO Info, the recommendations are the cornerstones of the UPR process, since they are the roadmap of the State under review for the next four years to improve human rights.[4]

Also, the relevance of NGO input should be underscored. Whenever the stakeholder summary contains adequate information about corruption, this is a welcome contribution, on the basis of which the reviewing States can ask questions. There might be a role for the National Chapters of Transparency International in this respect, to submit country-specific information to the UPR process.

Regardless of the fact that it would be beneficial if recommendations about corruption in the UPR were formulated in a more detailed way, the reality is that corruption is currently being discussed by States themselves within the highly politicised context of the Human Rights Council. This entails that States view corruption as a legitimate human rights topic, which marks a major shift from the position taken by the international community before the 1990s, when corruption was still considered a taboo subject. In a relatively short period of time, corruption as a human rights concern has entered the international arena, and is hopefully there to stay.

2.4. Special Procedures of the Human Rights Council

A number of specific recommendations can be addressed to the various Special Procedures of the Human Rights Council:

(i) Establishment of a mandate for a Special Rapporteur on Corruption & Human Rights Violations. This mandate should concentrate on formulating the precise links between corruption and human rights violations, which should not be limited to violations of economic, social and cultural rights, but also cover civil and political rights. In this context, country visits should be conducted to deal with specific instances of corruption;

(ii) Other thematic mandates, including the Special Rapporteur on trafficking in persons, as well as Special Rapporteurs on housing and education, should

[4] UPR Info, 'Analytical Assessment of the Universal Periodic Review', at p. 9.

integrate the problem of corruption into their future reports, and monitor progress over longer periods of time;

(iii) Given the high levels of perceived corruption as indicated by the CPI 2011, the country mandates on Somalia, Sudan, Myanmar, North Korea, and the Occupied Palestinian Territories should devote serious attention to the ways in which corrupt practices in these countries affect the enjoyment of human rights;

(iv) Like the country mandate on Burundi, the Special Procedures should not shy away from discussing grand corruption when necessary, although it will depend on the political climate whether this is possible during country visits;

(v) Anti-corruption NGOs should familiarise themselves with the work of the Special Procedures, and if possible supply the mandate-holders with accurate country-specific information, as well as information about corruption in relation to a certain area such as health, education, the justice system, or elections. A wealth of information is already available, *inter alia*, in TI's Global Corruption Reports, but this has yet to reach the mandate-holders of the Special Procedures;

(vi) Whenever the Special Procedures discuss corruption in their reports, these concerns should return in the resolutions of the Human Rights Council and the General Assembly.

2.5. Regional Human Rights Mechanisms

As regards the European Court of Human Rights, this institution is dependent upon the cases brought before it. However, the work of the Inter-American Commission involves much more than examining individual petitions. Particularly the country reports offer an excellent opportunity to address corruption, especially since country visits are also conducted. These visits might be well suited to discuss both progress and problems in the fight against corruption, and to link corrupt practices to the obligations of State Parties under various provisions of the ACHR. Also, cross-fertilisation between the Commission and anti-corruption NGOs is highly recommended. As regards the Commission's thematic reports and other publications, it was concluded that these pay relatively little attention to corruption. Hence, a future thematic report solely dedicated to corruption and its links to human rights is a good idea, especially given the high levels of perceived corruption in many OAS countries. Moreover, the topic ought to return in the Commission's resolutions.

As regards the African system, the present study found that until now, very few decisions of the African Commission in the individual complaint procedure are concerned with corruption. The relative newness of the mechanism might be an explanation for the absence of corruption-related cases, as well as the probability that many Africans will not have practical access to the Commission. In theory, the individual complaint mechanism of the Commission (and the practice of the future

Court) can provide a mechanism for redress in cases of corruption, especially since the African Charter contains both civil and political rights, and economic, social and cultural rights. In order for this to be possible, the quality of the Commission's decisions ought to be improved. The admissibility requirement that communications must not be written in disparaging or insulting language should not hinder the Commission from dealing with complaints about corruption. Finally, it may be possible to address corruption through the Commission's Special Mechanisms, which include a number of Special Rapporteurs and Working Groups.[5]

All in all, regional systems for human rights protection may contribute significantly to legal protection against corrupt practices that violate human rights, and may offer redress in those cases where whistleblowers are confronted with violations of their rights.

3. Corruption and International Criminal Law

From the study into the human rights dimensions of corruption, it followed that no new right to a corruption-free society is feasible, or necessary. International human rights law as it currently stands is able to address corruption by making use of the existing framework of internationally recognised rights. This is different however for international criminal law under the Rome Statute. The International Criminal Court has only recently begun its work, and many concepts have to be tested in practice. Also, current provisions from the Rome Statute will most likely not suffice to cover corrupt practices. Therefore, suggestions were made for amendments to the Statute. One should not think lightly about such changes to the Statute. Yet, the saying that 'Rome wasn't built in a day' certainly applies here. What is rejected at this very moment as far-fetched may become a reality somewhere in the decades to come. Meanwhile, those who follow the work of the ICC should keep a close eye on the ways in which corrupt practices somehow play a role in the indictments for crimes against humanity or war crimes. Without financial backing, few crimes would be committed. The role corruption plays in this respect should be emphasised and further dealt with. Also, alternatives such as the establishment of a permanent anti-corruption court, or anti-corruption commission to monitor compliance with the United Nations Convention Against Corruption should be kept in mind, as well as the possibility of setting up ad hoc anti-corruption tribunals.

To end on a positive note, Cryer is correct when pointing out that:

> Even though international criminal law is not always the answer, and has developed spasmodically, in a reactive, politicised fashion, scholars should engage in discussion about how to improve the law. The criminalization process will continue whether academics are involved or not. It is by attempting to provide critique on rational bases of proposals, or existing law, that academic international criminal lawyers

---

[5] Viljoen, *International Human Rights Law in Africa*, at p. 392–401.

may seek to improve the law. Crime and politics may be linked, and interdependent, but that is no reason not to enter the ethical/political debate about what international criminal law ought to be, and, indeed through that, contribute something to the discussion about what the international society/community ought to, and might, become.[6]

4. Final Remarks

Full eradication of corruption around the globe amounts to wishful thinking. Both the use of human rights law and international criminal law will not offer miracle cures in the fight against corruption. Moreover, the law alone is not sufficient to make lasting changes in a society's social fabric. Anti-corruption measures cannot be imposed from the outside, they have to be firmly rooted in society. Leaders of developing countries should take their responsibility, and so should the West. Governments, transnational corporations and financial institutions have a strong responsibility to tackle corruption, and not merely out of self-interest or reparation of the wrongs of the colonial past. A sound combination of anti-corruption strategies, both preventive and punitive, may alleviate the plight of the many John and Jane Doe's of this world. The use of human rights law gives a face to the victims of corruption, while using international criminal law gives a face to its perpetrators, and as such, can contribute to a gradual decline in global corruption levels. By approaching corruption from the angle of human rights and international criminal law, corruption may be awarded the attention it deserves. Anti-corruption efforts can no longer be downgraded as a neo-colonialist endeavour, since universal norms accepted by the large community of States are applicable. *'All this will not be finished in the first 100 days. Nor will it be finished in the first 1,000 days, nor in the life of this administration, nor even perhaps in our lifetime on this planet. But let us begin.'*[7]

---

6 Robert Cryer, 'The Doctrinal Foundations of International Criminalization', in M. Cherif Bassiouni (ed.), *International Criminal Law: Sources, Subjects, and Contents* (3rd edn., I; Leiden: Martinus Nijhoff, 2008), p. 107–128 at p. 128.

7 John F. Kennedy, Inaugural Address 1961.

Samenvatting
Corruptie: een schending van mensenrechten en een misdrijf in het internationale recht?

1. Introductie

Het doel van de onderhavige studie is het verkennen van nieuwe – aanvullende – wegen om corruptie te bestrijden, met gebruikmaking van het systeem van internationaal erkende mensenrechten en internationaal strafrecht. Terwijl *good governance* en anti-corruptie populaire begrippen werden in de tweede helft van de jaren negentig van de twintigste eeuw, is het pas sinds kort dat corruptie ook als een mensenrechtelijk thema wordt gezien. Nog minder aandacht is er voor corruptie vanuit het perspectief van internationaal strafrecht, waardoor corruptie grotendeels buiten beschouwing blijft in het debat over de internationale strafbaarstelling van misdrijven. Dit proefschrift hoopt derhalve nieuwe inzichten te verschaffen en *food for thought* te leveren aan degenen die zich bezighouden met mensenrechten dan wel met internationaal strafrecht. Erkend moet echter ook worden dat een aantal hypothesen in de praktijk zal moeten worden getoetst.

2. Deel A: Het Fenomeen Corruptie: een Inleidende Analyse

2.1. Definities en Meetinstrumenten

Voordat de verbanden tussen enerzijds corruptie en anderzijds mensenrechten en internationaal strafrecht kunnen worden gelegd, is het essentieel om een bruikbare definitie van corruptie te formuleren. Dit is echter makkelijker gezegd dan gedaan, te meer nu de overgrote meerderheid van de bestaande anti-corruptieverdragen geen definitie bevatten. Om die reden vergelijkt hoofdstuk I van deel A de definities van de non-gouvernementele anti-corruptieorganisatie Transparency International (hierna: TI) en de Wereldbank. Laatstgenoemde is een belangrijke speler geworden op anti-corruptiegebied. Terwijl de definitie van TI zowel corruptie in de publieke als in de private sector omvat, is de definitie van de Wereldbank beperkt tot corruptie in de publieke sector: 'misbruik van een publieke functie voor privaat gewin'. Gelet op het feit dat dit proefschrift zich voornamelijk richt op gedragingen van statelijke actoren, en niet zozeer op het handelen van niet-statelijke actoren, wordt de definitie van de Wereldbank als uitgangspunt genomen. Hierbij moet worden opgemerkt dat het proefschrift niet noodzakelijkerwijs de opvattingen of het beleid van de Wereldbank onderschrijft. Ook moet worden erkend dat corrupte praktijken niet alleen de publieke persoon zelf hoeven te bevoordelen. Immers, ook vrienden, familie of politieke relaties kunnen voordeel behalen bij corruptie. Ook wordt corruptie niet alleen voor privaat gewin aangewend, maar ook voor politiek gewin. Derhalve gaat dit proefschrift uit van corruptie als 'misbruik van een publieke functie voor privaat of politiek gewin.'

Corruptie in de publieke sector, zoals hierboven gedefinieerd, kan worden opgesplitst in zogeheten *grand* corruptie en *petty* corruptie. De eerste vorm vindt plaats op het niveau van de politiek waar beleid wordt gemaakt, en betreft ambtenaren in de hoogste regionen van de staat. De tweede vorm speelt zich af op lager niveau, waar het beleid wordt geïmplementeerd door ambtenaren lager in rang. Het is derhalve niet het bedrag aan geld dat beslissend is voor het onderscheid tussen *grand* en *petty*, maar het niveau waar de gedragingen zich afspelen.

Begrippen zoals economische misdaad, witteboordencriminaliteit, fraude en collusie worden vaak in verband gebracht met corruptie. Hoewel er beslist overlap is en verbanden zijn, is corruptie geen synoniem voor voornoemde praktijken. Voorts moet worden bedacht dat corruptie een fenomeen is met een sterke culturele ondertoon. Rechtvaardigingen van corruptie op basis van culturele argumenten dienen te worden verworpen. Tegelijkertijd dient de bredere culturele en maatschappelijke context in aanmerking te worden genomen bij het bestuderen van corruptie en het ontwikkelen van beleid ertegen. Alleen dan kunnen eenvormige oplossingen worden voorkómen.

Met de eerder geformuleerde definitie als vertrekpunt zijn er verschillende typen corruptie te onderscheiden. Immers, één containerbegrip volstaat niet in een juridische context. Het VN Verdrag tegen Corruptie maakt een onderscheid tussen (i) actieve en passieve omkoping; (ii) verduistering; (iii) ongeoorloofde beïnvloeding; (iv) misbruik van functies (hetgeen patronage en nepotisme omvat) en (iv) ongerechtvaardigde verrijking.

Gelet op de grote verscheidenheid in corrupte praktijken, rijst de vraag hoe deze kunnen worden gemeten. Dit is beslist een lastige taak, aangezien corruptie zich doorgaans in het geheim afspeelt. Tegelijkertijd is er behoefte aan statistische gegevens over het vóórkomen van corruptie teneinde vooruitgang te kunnen meten en landen te kunnen vergelijken. Er is dan ook een aantal instrumenten ontwikkeld in de afgelopen jaren, waarvan de *Corruption Perceptions Index* (hierna: CPI) van TI veruit de bekendste is. Dit instrument meet de perceptie van corruptie en rangschikt landen van 1 (zijnde het land dat gezien wordt als het minst corrupt) tot 178 (zijnde het land dat gezien wordt als het meest corrupt). De Index laat helaas zien dat corruptie wereldwijd meer regel is dan uitzondering. Andere instrumenten zijn de *Bribe Payers Index*, de *European Fraud Survey*, de *Global Corruption Barometer*, en de *International Crime Victims Survey*. Deze instrumenten zijn weliswaar zeer nuttig, maar ook niet zonder gebreken. De onderliggende onderzoeksmethoden zijn geregeld onderworpen aan kritiek, hetgeen ook in aanmerking moet worden genomen wanneer dit proefschrift gebruikmaakt van met name de gegevens uit de CPI.

2.2. Schadelijke Gevolgen van Corruptie

Inspanningen gericht op het bestrijden van corruptie zijn gebaseerd op de premisse dat corruptie schadelijk is. Uitgebreid onderzoek in diverse disciplines geeft inderdaad weer waarom corruptie het verdient te worden aangepakt. De gevolgen van corruptie zijn voelbaar op politiek, economisch, sociaal en milieugebied. In de politiek tast corruptie de beginselen van democratie en legitimiteit aan. Corrupte gezagsdragers zullen naar alle waarschijnlijkheid de werkelijke behoeften van de bevolking negeren, als gevolg waarvan het vertrouwen in het politieke systeem aan de kant van de burger zal afnemen. Corruptie wordt ook in verband gebracht met het vóórkomen en de duur van gewapend conflict. Zowel corruptie als gewapend conflict kunnen bovendien gelieerd zijn aan de aanwezigheid van natuurlijke hulpbronnen zoals olie en diamanten.

Wat betreft de economische effecten van corruptie, toont onderzoek aan dat corruptie op verschillende wijzen leidt tot een vermindering van economische groei. Aangenomen wordt dat corruptie leidt tot: minder investeringen; het niet goed benutten van talent van hoogopgeleiden (die immers voor lucratieve loopbanen zullen kiezen); verminderde effectiviteit van hulpstromen door verduistering; verlies van belastinginkomsten; inferieure kwaliteit van publieke infrastructuur en publieke diensten; en een verstoorde samenstelling van overheidsuitgaven. Bovendien vergroot corruptie ongelijkheid en armoede. Armoede is intrinsiek verbonden met slechte leefomstandigheden, lage levensverwachting, hoge kindersterfte en een hoog niveau van analfabetisme. Op die manier tast corruptie niet alleen de huidige maar ook de toekomstige generaties aan.

Ook de natuurlijke omgeving wordt sterk negatief beïnvloed door corrupte praktijken, nu deze leiden tot niet-duurzame exploitatie van natuurlijke hulpbronnen. Voorbeelden zijn illegale houtkap en vervuilende oliewinning. Ook bedreigde diersoorten komen in gevaar, met name wanneer corrupte ambtenaren stropers en illegale handelaars te hulp schieten, en wanneer er fondsen voor natuurbescherming worden verduisterd. Al met al tast corruptie het fundament van de samenleving op vele manieren aan, hetgeen reden te meer is waarom anti-corruptiemaatregelen noodzakelijk zijn.

2.3. Internationaal en Regionaal Juridisch Kader

In hoofdstuk II wordt onderzoeksvraag (1) beantwoord: *Welk internationaal en regionaal juridisch kader bestaat er om corruptie te bestrijden, en hoe functioneert dit thans?* De studie laat zien dat er een groot aantal anti-corruptieverdragen bestaat: (i) de *Inter-American Convention Against Corruption*; (ii) de *Convention on the Protection of the European Communities' Financial Interests* en de twee Protocollen; (iii) de *OECD Anti-Bribery Convention*; (iv) de *Council of Europe's Criminal Law Convention on Corruption*; (v) de *Council of Europe's Civil Law Convention on Corruption*; (vi) het *SADC Protocol Against Corruption*; (vii) het

ECOWAS Protocol on the Fight Against Corruption; (viii) de *African Union Convention on Preventing and Combating Corruption*; (ix) de *UN Convention Against Transnational Organized Crime*; en (x) de *UN Convention Against Corruption.*

Geen van deze verdragen voorziet in een allesomvattende definitie van corruptie of in een lijst van corrupte praktijken. Echter, de verdragen bepalen wel welke corrupte gedragingen er vallen onder de werkingssfeer van het verdrag. Sommige verdragen hebben een beperkter bereik en zijn enkel van toepassing op omkoping (bijvoorbeeld de *OECD Anti-Bribery Convention*), terwijl andere verdragen veel uitgebreider zijn en een breder kader van corrupte praktijken omvatten. Het belangrijkste oogmerk van de verdragen is het bestrijden van corruptie op nationaal niveau door middel van nationale strafbaarstelling en preventie, alsmede door internationale samenwerking.

Een aantal verdragen bevat bepalingen die op niet-dwingende wijze zijn geformuleerd. Dergelijke bepalingen laten het aan staten zelf over of zij bepaalde gedragingen al dan niet strafbaar stellen. Dit is bijvoorbeeld het geval met de preventieve maatregelen en sommige vormen van corruptie in het VN Verdrag tegen Corruptie. Ook zijn er verdragsbepalingen die zogeheten *safeguard clauses* bevatten, op basis waarvan verdragsbepalingen afhankelijk worden van nationale wetgeving.

Ten aanzien van het toezicht op de naleving van de verdragen, kan worden geconstateerd dat de voornaamste methode bestaat uit niet-bindende *peer review* of toezicht door experts. De *Inter-American Convention* wordt gemonitord door MESICIC, de *OECD Anti-Bribery Convention* door de *Working Group on Bribery*, de *Council of Europe's Conventions* door GRECO, het *SADC Protocol door het Committee of State Parties*, en de *AU Convention door de Advisory Board on Corruption.* Het VN Verdrag tegen Corruptie wordt gecomplementeerd door een *peer review* mechanisme, met het toezicht daarop in handen van de *Implementation Review Group*, bestaande uit vertegenwoordigers van verdragspartijen. Dergelijke 'zachte' mechanismen kunnen bijdragen aan een beter begrip van verdragsbepalingen en de implementatie ervan. Echter, het is geenszins zeker dat verdragspartijen zich daadwerkelijk zullen houden aan de diverse verdragen. Nu de toezichtmechanismen nagenoeg tandeloos zijn, is het niet mogelijk om naleving door af te dwingen.

Zoals gezegd verplichten de verdragen staten vooral om op nationaal niveau maatregelen te nemen. Het kan echter sterk worden betwijfeld of staten met een aanzienlijke hoeveelheid corruptie op hoog niveau wel de politieke wil hebben om corruptie aan te pakken. Vaak blijven anti-corruptiemaatregelen in dergelijke landen beperkt tot het bestrijden van politieke tegenstanders of het vangen van 'kleine vissen' bij wijze van symboolpolitiek. Om deze reden dient anti-corruptie niet beperkt te blijven tot maatregelen op nationaal niveau, maar is het ook zinvol om de verplichtingen van staten op internationaal niveau te benadrukken, met name op het gebied van mensenrechten en internationaal strafrecht.

3. Deel B: Verantwoordelijkheid van Staten: Corruptie als een Mensenrechtenschending?

Deel B behandelt onderzoeksvraag (2): *Is het mogelijk om (bepaalde typen) corruptie in de publieke sector te kwalificeren als een mensenrechtenschending?*

3.1. De Mensenrechtenpraktijk

Het eerste onderdeel van de hierboven gestelde vraag is *(a) Wat laat de praktijk van de internationale en regionale toezichtmechanismen op het gebied van mensenrechten zien over het verband tussen corruptie en mensenrechtenschendingen?* Teneinde deze vraag te beantwoorden, wordt het volgende bestudeerd: (i) de *concluding observations* en de *views* van de VN Verdragscomités die toezicht houden op de diverse mensenrechtenverdragen; (ii) de *Universal Periodic Review* van de VN Mensenrechtenraad; (iii) een geselecteerd aantal Speciale Procedures van de VN Mensenrechtenraad; en (iv) de regionale mensenrechtenmechanismen in Europa, Amerika en Afrika. De belangrijkste bevindingen zijn als volgt.

3.1.1. VN Verdragscomités

Hoofdstuk III van de onderhavige studie analyseert de praktijk van de VN Verdragscomités op het gebied van mensenrechten, bestaande uit onafhankelijke experts. Naleving van de kernverdragen op internationaal niveau wordt bewerkstelligd door (i) het beoordelen van statenrapporten in de rapportage-procedure, hetgeen uitmondt in de zogeheten *concluding observations*; en (ii) het behandelen van klachten van individuen, een bevoegdheid die een aantal verdragscomités heeft en uitmondt in de zogeheten *views*. Noch *concluding observations* noch *views* zijn bindend voor staten, maar zij worden wel als zeer gezaghebbend beschouwd.

Wat betreft de *concluding observations* van de verdragscomités die betrekking hebben op corruptie, heeft het volgende te gelden. In totaal zijn er 131 *concluding observations* over corruptie, zoals weergegeven in Annex 1. Er zijn 67 staten onder de loep genomen, en het merendeel hiervan zijn ontwikkelingslanden, met name in Sub-Sahara Afrika (23). Andere *observations* betreffen landen in Oost-Europa (11), Centraal-Azië (8) en Latijns-Amerika (8), Zuid-Oost-Azië (6), andere Aziatische landen (3), en Zuid-Azië (2). Veel minder aandacht is er voor corruptie in het Caraïbische gebied (2), Noord-Afrika (1), het Midden-Oosten (1), Zuid-Europa (1) en West-Europa (1). De grote meerderheid van de 67 landen bezet inderdaad de lagere regionen van de *Corruption Perceptions Index*, nu er in de betreffende landen een hoge perceptie van corruptie is. Het lijkt er dan ook op dat de concluding observations een afspiegeling zijn van de daadwerkelijke perceptie van corruptie. Maar tegelijkertijd is het onduidelijk waarom sommige landen bekritiseerd worden met betrekking tot corruptie, terwijl landen met gelijke corruptieniveaus de dans ontspringen. Wat mogelijk een rol speelt is dat statenrapporten vaak te laat of niet worden ingediend in de rapportageprocedure, en dat sommige landen geen partij zijn bij een aantal mensenrechtenverdragen.

Het Kinderrechtencomité besteed tot dusver de meeste aandacht aan corruptie (50 *observations*), gevolgd door het Comité inzake Economische, Sociale en Culturele Rechten (31), het Mensenrechtencomité (28), het Comité tegen Foltering (12), het Comité tegen Rassendiscriminatie (7), en het Comité dat toezicht houdt op het Vrouwenverdrag (3). Het feit dat laatstgenoemd Comité amper *observations* over corruptie heeft aangenomen is verontrustend. Het zijn immers vaak vrouwen, met name in ontwikkelingslanden, die met kleine corruptie worden geconfronteerd (bijvoorbeeld op scholen en ziekenhuizen), zulks gelet op hun taak als zorgdragers.

De burger- en politieke rechten die volgens de Comités worden aangetast door corruptie zijn het recht op gelijkheid voor de rechter en het recht op een eerlijk proces. Het Mensenrechtencomité, het Comité inzake Economisch, Sociale en Culturele Rechten en het Comité tegen Foltering besteden veel aandacht aan corruptie in de rechterlijke macht. Andere burger- en politieke rechten die door de drie genoemde Comités worden besproken in de context van corruptie zijn het verbod op mensenhandel, het recht op vrijheid van beweging en de rechten van gedetineerden. Het verdient vermelding dat het Mensenrechtencomité tot op heden niet aan de orde heeft gesteld welke invloed corruptie heeft op de politieke rechten van artikel 25 van het Internationaal Verdrag inzake Burger- en Politieke Rechten (hierna: IVBPR). Corruptie bij verkiezingen is immers een belangrijk thema. Wellicht acht het Comité dit onderwerp politiek gezien nog te gevoelig?

Wat betreft economische, sociale en culturele rechten, kan worden opgemerkt dat het Comité inzake Economische, Sociale en Culturele Rechten corruptie zelden in verband brengt met de verplichtingen van staten onder een *specifiek* recht zoals vastgelegd in het Internationaal Verdrag inzake Economische Sociale en Culturele Rechten (hierna: IVESCR). Dit is enkel gebeurd met betrekking tot het recht op voedsel en het recht op sociale zekerheid. Het Comité maakt duidelijk dat corruptie een negatieve invloed heeft op de gelijke implementatie/realisatie/uitoefening van economische, sociale en culturele rechten en dat corruptie de middelen van staten beschikbaar voor sociale voorzieningen aantast. Het Comité kan echter veel verder op dit onderwerp ingaan dan zij tot op heden heeft gedaan, door de specifieke verplichtingen onder artikel 2(1) IVESCR te analyseren. Het Kinderrechtencomité heeft wel aandacht besteed aan de invloed van corruptie op de maximaal beschikbare middelen. Dit Comité verwijst, bij een aantal gelegenheden, naar het recht op gezondheid en het recht op onderwijs. Ook bespreekt dit Comité de rol van corruptie in adoptieprocedures en bij kinderhandel

Wanneer het taalgebruik van de Verdragscomités wordt bestudeerd, dan kan worden geconcludeerd dat de *observations* over corruptie op dit punt niet significant afwijken van de *observations* over andere onderwerpen. *Observations* zijn immers meestal zeer algemeen verwoord. Terwijl geen *observation* expliciet stelt dat corruptie een bepaald recht heeft geschonden, volgt het wel uit de bewoordingen dat dit het geval is. Met betrekking tot Kenia bepaalde het Mensenrechtencomité dat 'beschuldigingen van corruptie in de rechterlijke macht de onafhankelijkheid en onpartijdigheid van de rechterlijke macht 'serieus ondermijnen'. Een ander voorbeeld is het Comité inzake Economische, Sociale en Culturele Rechten, dat in 2009 Congo 'urges' om duidelijke anti-corruptiemaatregelen te treffen. Dit illustreert dat in een dergelijk geval een verdragspartij haar verplichtingen onder het IVESCR niet nakomt.

Vermeldenswaardig is dat de meeste *observations* over corruptie, vooral de meest scherp geformuleerde, tamelijk recent zijn. Het is derhalve gerechtvaardigd om te spreken van een trend bij de Verdragscomités, hetgeen een positieve ontwikkeling is. Deze tendens volgt op de toenemende aandacht voor corruptie in de samenleving als geheel en bij internationale actoren zoals de Wereldbank.

Wat betreft de *views* naar aanleiding van klachten van individuen, kan worden opgemerkt dat er weinig views zijn waarin corruptie een substantiële rol speelt. Het Mensenrechtencomité handelde een aantal klachten of over de slechte behandeling van klokkenluiders; een prominent voorbeeld is *Philip Afuson Njaru v. Cameroon.*[1] Andere klachten betreffen aantijgingen dat de klager geen eerlijk proces heeft gekregen door corruptie binnen de rechterlijke macht. Ook vloeit het voort uit de views van het Mensenrechtencomité inzake *Michael and Brian Hill v. Spain* dat verduistering van gelden bestemd voor voedsel en drank voor gevangen kan leiden tot een schending van artikel 10 IVBPR.[2] Ook toont een klein aantal klachten voor het Comité tegen Foltering aan dat personen die corruptie aan het licht brengen een risico lopen om blootgesteld te worden aan foltering, en derhalve in het buitenland asiel aanvragen. Het Comité tegen Rassendiscriminatie en het Comité dat toezicht houdt op het Vrouwenverdrag hebben geen *views* gegeven over corruptie.

3.1.2. Universal Periodic Review

Het Universal Periodic Review systeem is in 2006 door de Algemene Vergadering van de Verenigde Naties in het leven geroepen, en houdt in dat de mensenrechtensituatie in alle 192 VN lidstaten elke vier jaar wordt getoetst door andere lidstaten, binnen de context van de VN Mensenrechtenraad. Voordeel van dit systeem is dat het irrelevant is of een land een bepaald mensenrechtenverdrag al dan niet geratificeerd heeft.

Hoofdstuk IV studie analyseert alle 128 *outcome reports* van de eerste acht sessies van de UPR. Met betrekking tot 77 landen is corruptie besproken. Het overgrote deel hiervan zijn ontwikkelingslanden met hoge niveaus van corruptieperceptie volgens de CPI. Sommige landen in de middenmoot van de CPI

1 Communication no. 1353/2005, *Philip Afuson Njaru v. Cameroon*, views of 19 March 2007, UN Doc. CCPR/C/89/D/1353/2005.

2 Communication no. 526/1993, *Michael and Brian Hill v. Spain*, views of 22 June 1997, UN Doc. CCPR/C/59/D/526/1993.

mandaten en alle 8 landenmandaten omgaan met corruptie. De betreffende resoluties van de Mensenrechtenraad, de voormalige Mensenrechtencommissie en de Algemene Vergadering worden hier ook in meegenomen.

Het thematische mandaat dat voor deze studie het belangrijkste is, is dat van de voormalige Speciale Rapporteur inzake corruptie en de gevolgen daarvan voor mensenrechten, met name economische, sociale en culturele rechten. Mandaathouder Mbonu werd in 2003 benoemd door de voormalige Subcommissie, en haar mandaat is in 2006 geëindigd. In de tussenliggende periode publiceerde Mbonu een *working paper*, een eerste rapport, een vervolgrapport en een eindrapport. Op zichzelf bood het instellen van een Speciale Procedure op het gebied van corruptie en economische, sociale en culturele rechten dé gelegenheid bij uitstek om het thema te onderzoeken. Helaas heeft deze Procedure weinig opgeleverd. In plaats van het bestuderen van de precieze verbanden tussen corruptie en mensenrechten zijn de rapporten van Mbonu vrij beschrijvend en ontberen zij de vereiste kwaliteit. Mbonu's analyse blijft beperkt tot de conclusie dat 'het genot van alle rechten, zowel economisch, sociaal en cultureel als burger- en politiek, ernstig wordt ondermijnd door het fenomeen van corruptie.'[3] Ook werd vermeld dat 'corruptie, of dit nu wijdverbreid is of niet, schendt de uitoefening van de rechten van burgers zoals opgenomen in alle internationale instrumenten'.[4] Onderbouwing van een dergelijke claim blijft uit. Mbonu noemt politieke rechten, het recht op gelijkheid en non-discriminatie, en het recht op een eerlijk proces, en stelt dat verduistering van publieke gelden leidt tot een ontzegging van economische, sociale en culturele rechten. Een degelijke juridische analyse ontbreekt echter. Het is dan ook niet verbazingwekkend te noemen dat het mandaat niet werd verlengd.

Vervolgens komen een aantal thematische mandaten op het gebied van burger- en politieke rechten aan de orde. De rapporten van de Speciale Rapporteur op het gebied van de onafhankelijkheid van rechters en advocaten besteden substantiële aandacht aan corruptie binnen de rechterlijke macht. Corruptie wordt benoemd als zijnde één van de meest serieuze obstakels van de promotie en bescherming van mensenrechten, en heeft een vernietigende invloed op mensenrechten.[5] Ook heeft deze Rapporteur een aantal concrete aanbevelingen geformuleerd om corruptie te bestrijden.[6] De Speciale Rapporteur inzake mensenhandel in de jaarrapporten heeft echter weinig aandacht besteed aan de rol van corrupte ambtenaren bij mensenhandel. Terwijl deze Rapporteur in 2009 concludeerde dat corruptie één van

3 Working paper submitted by Ms. Christy Mbonu in accordance with Sub-Commission decision 2002/106, 14 May 2003, UN Doc. E/CN.4/Sub.2/2003/18, § 3.

4 Preliminary report of the Special Rapporteur on corruption and its impact on the full enjoyment of human rights, in particular economic, social and cultural rights, Sub-Cion 56th session, 7 July 2004, UN Doc. E/CN.4/Sub.2/2004/23, § 57.

5 Report of the Special Rapporteur on the independence of judges and lawyers, HRC 14th session, 25 March 2010, UN Doc. A/HRC/14/26, § 73-74.

6 Report of the Special Rapporteur on the independence of judges and lawyers, GA 65th session, 10 August 2010, UN Doc. A/65/274, § 44-45.

de kernoorzaken van mensenhandel is[7], ontbreekt een gefundeerde analyse. Een aantal landenrapporten vermeldt het probleem wel. De Speciale Rapporteur inzake kinderhandel, kinderprostitutie, en kinderporno bespreekt corruptie wel in veel jaarlijkse rapporten. De rol van corrupte ambtenaren wordt herhaaldelijk benadrukt, en ook veel landenrapporten bespreken de kwestie. De actieve houding van deze Rapporteur verdient navolging.

Wat betreft de thematische mandaten op het gebied van economische, sociale en culturele rechten, worden de bevindingen van de Speciale Procedures inzake huisvesting, onderwijs, voedsel en gezondheid geanalyseerd. De Speciale Rapporteur inzake het recht op huisvesting besteedt her en der aandacht aan corruptie in de jaarlijkse rapporten en in de landenrapporten. Een solide probleemanalyse ontbreekt, en de link naar de verschillende componenten van het recht op huisvesting wordt niet gelegd. Hetzelfde geldt voor de rapporten van de Speciale Rapporteur inzake het recht op onderwijs. De jaarlijkse rapporten bespreken corruptie amper, en de landenrapporten beperken zich tot de opmerking dat corruptie ertoe leidt dat er minder middelen beschikbaar zijn voor onderwijs. Een heel ander, meer positief beeld komt naar voren wat betreft de mandaten inzake het recht op voedsel en het recht op gezondheid. De Speciale Rapporteur inzake het recht op voedsel is zich duidelijk bewust van de problemen veroorzaakt door corruptie bij het verwezenlijken van voornoemd recht. Vermeld wordt onder andere dat de verplichting tot bescherming van het recht op voedsel (*obligation to protect*) Staten verplicht om corruptie te bestrijden. Ook wordt corruptie genoemd als één van de 7 problemen die direct het recht op voedsel beïnvloeden. De Speciale Rapporteur inzake het recht op gezondheid is ook actief betrokken bij het bespreken van corrupte praktijken in de gezondheidszorg, zowel in de jaarlijkse rapporten als in de landenrapporten. Herhaaldelijk wordt gesteld dat een beleid inzake het recht op gezondheid ook een anti-corruptiebeleid is[8], en dat corruptie een grote belemmering is voor het genot van het recht op gezondheid, waaronder toegang tot medicijnen.[9] De landenrapporten tonen aan hoe corruptie de economische toegankelijkheid (betaalbaarheid) van het recht op gezondheid aantast, door de oneigenlijke heffing van tarieven aan patiënten.[10] Een landenrapport roept de regering op om alle passende actie te nemen om corruptie in de gezondheidssector te bestrijden, hetgeen volgens de Special Rapporteur in overeenstemming is met de

---

7 Report of the Special Rapporteur on trafficking in persons, especially women and children, HRC 10th session, 20 February 2009, UN Doc. A/HRC/10/16, section Conclusions and Recommendations.

8 Report of the Special Rapporteur on the right to health, GA 61st session, 13 September 2006, UN Doc.A/61/338, § 80.

9 Report of the Special Rapporteur on the right to health, GA 63rd session, 11 August 2008, UN Doc. A/63/263.

10 Report of the Special Rapporteur on the right to health, Mission to Mozambique, CHR 61st session, 4 January 2005, UN Doc. E/CN.4/2005/51/Add.2, § 45-52, 69 and Report of the Special Rapporteur on the right to health, Mission to India, HRC 14th session, 15 April 2010, UN Doc. A/HRC/14/20/Add.2, § 52.

werden ook bekritiseerd. Slechts enkele opmerkingen werden gemaakt over corruptie in landen die niet algemeen bekend staan om wijdverspreide corruptie, zoals Duitsland. De landen die de opmerkingen maken, vragen stellen, of aanbevelingen formuleren zijn soms gelegen in de regio van het land dat verantwoording moet afleggen. Desalniettemin overschrijden de discussies over corruptie ook regionale grenzen, en zijn zowel ontwikkelde landen als ontwikkelingslanden hierbij betrokken. Een aantal ontwikkelde landen zoals Canada en de Verenigde Staten zijn vrij actief in het geven van hun opvattingen. Afrikaanse landen, die zelf vaak onderaan de CPI genoteerd staan, geven zelden kritiek op landen wat betreft corruptie.

Staten rapporteren ook zelf in hun landenrapporten aan de Mensenrechtenraad over de problemen die zij ondervinden met betrekking tot corruptie. Hierin vermelden ze de actie die zij ondernemen om corruptie tegen te gaan, waaronder het ratificeren van anti-corruptieverdragen, het aannemen van nationale wetgeving, het opzetten van nationale anticorruptie-instellingen, en het vervolgen van corrupte ambtenaren. Ook zijn er veel *reviewing* landen die opmerkingen maken over corruptie, vragen stellen en aanbevelingen formuleren. De besproken onderwerpen zijn corruptie binnen de rechterlijke macht, corruptie bij de politie en het leger, de kwetsbare positie van klokkenluiders, en de rol van corrupte ambtenaren bij mensenhandel. *Reviewing* landen bevelen dikwijls aan dat landen onder review anti-corruptieverdragen zoals het VN Verdrag tegen Corruptie zouden moeten ratificeren, en dat er op nationaal niveau anti-corruptiewetgeving en instellingen zouden moeten komen. Een klein aantal aanbevelingen zijn meer specifiek geformuleerd, en dit verdient lof.

Wat betreft de relatie tussen corruptie en mensenrechtenschendingen, kan worden geconstateerd dat de *outcome reports* zelden benoemen dat corruptie zelf een mensenrechtenschending is. Het volgt echter uit de uitspraken van de landen onder *review*, alsook uit de vragen, opmerkingen en aanbevelingen van reviewing landen dat corruptie wordt besproken zij aan zij met klassieke mensenrechtenthema's. Dit illustreert dat corruptie duidelijk ook een mensenrechtelijk onderwerp is, dat op de agenda staat van de UPR. Terwijl corruptie vóór het midden van de jaren negentig van de twintigste eeuw corruptie als taboe-onderwerp werd beschouwd, is het thans veelbelovend dat landen corruptie zelf op de agenda zetten binnen de VN Mensenrechtenraad.

3.1.3. Speciale Procedures van de VN Mensenrechtenraad

Er bestaat een breed spectrum van zogeheten Speciale Procedures van de VN Mensenrechtenraad. Op dit moment zijn er 33 thematische mandaten en 8 landenmandaten, die worden uitgevoerd door één persoon (Speciaal Rapporteur, Speciale Vertegenwoordiger van de Secretaris-Generaal, of Onafhankelijk Expert), dan wel door een team van vijf personen (Werkgroep). Allen zijn onafhankelijke en onpartijdige experts. Hoofdstuk IV onderzoekt hoe 10 geselecteerde thematische verplichting om het recht op gezondheid te eerbiedigen en te beschermen (*to respect and to protect*).[11] Tot op heden is het mandaat van de Speciale Rapporteur inzake het recht op gezondheid het beste voorbeeld van hoe corruptie kan worden belicht in de thematische mandaten.

Ook het mandaat van de Onafhankelijke Expert inzake het vraagstuk van mensenrechten en extreme armoede, en het mandaat van de Speciale Vertegenwoordiger van de Secretaris-Generaal inzake mensenrechten en transnationale ondernemingen worden besproken. Het eerste mandaat toont aan dat degenen die het mandaat uitoefenen in een geschikte positie zijn om vrij gedetailleerde aanbevelingen op het gebied van corruptie te verwerken in landenrapporten.[12] Dit verdient beslist navolging, hetgeen niet kan worden gezegd van de manier waarop er in het tweede genoemde mandaat, vervuld door John Ruggie, is omgegaan met corruptie. Hoewel corruptie wordt genoemd als een significante barrière voor de verwezenlijking van mensenrechten, geven de rapporten weinig nieuwe inzichten, terwijl het onderwerp van het mandaat zich daarvoor wel bij uitstek zou hebben geleend. Met name de rol van het bedrijfsleven in corrupte handelingen had uitgediept kunnen worden.

De resoluties van de VN Mensenrechtenraad, de voormalige Mensenrechtencommissie en de Algemene Vergadering ter zake van de thematische procedures maken weinig melding van corruptie, zelfs niet in die gevallen waarin de mandaathouders wel verslag deden van corruptie. Men moet echter in het oog houden dat deze discrepantie wijder verspreid is in de context van de VN, en niet beperkt is tot corruptie.

De studie van de 8 landenmandaten laat zien dat er grote verschillen zijn voor wat betreft de aandacht die aan corruptie wordt besteed. De CPI 2011 geeft aan dat de betreffende landen (te weten Haïti, Cambodja, Burundi, Sudan, Myanmar en Somalië)[13] zeer hoge niveaus van corruptieperceptie hebben, doch dit komt niet als zodanig naar voren in de rapporten. Goede voorbeelden van hoe corruptie kan worden behandeld zijn de mandaten inzake Burundi, Haïti en Cambodja. De betreffende rapporten laten weliswaar niet zien hoe corruptie mensenrechten kan schenden, maar maken wel duidelijk dat de mandaathouders in de positie zijn om corruptie aan de kaak te stellen, aanbevelingen te formuleren, en de situatie op langere termijn te monitoren. Vooral bemoedigend zijn de opmerkingen van de Onafhankelijke Expert inzake Burundi aangaande het probleem van *grand* corruptie.[14] Andere onderwerpen die besproken worden in de procedures inzake

---

11 Report of the Special Rapporteur on the right to health, Mission to Mozambique, CHR 61st session, 4 January 2005, UN Doc. E/CN.4/2005/51/Add.2, § 70.

12 Report of the Independent Expert on the question of human rights and extreme poverty, HRC 14th session, 11 May 2010, UN Doc. A/HRC/14/31/Add.1, § 112.

13 Noord-Korea en de Bezette Palestijnse Gebieden zijn niet opgenomen in de CPI 2011.

14 Report of the Independent Expert on the situation of human rights in Burundi, GA 62nd session, 8 August 2007, UN Doc. A/62/213, § 49. Similar concerns about high-level corruption were also expressed in: Interim report of the Independent Expert on the situation of human rights in Burundi, HRC 4th session, 26 February 2007, UN Doc. A/HRC/4/5, § 70.

Burundi, Haïti en Cambodja zijn corruptie in de rechterlijke macht en in het politieapparaat. Vooral het mandaat inzake Cambodja bespreekt een breder scala corruptie-gerelateerde onderwerpen. De mandaten inzake Somalië, Sudan, Noord-Korea, Myanmar, and de Bezette Palestijnse Gebieden bespreken corruptie echter niet naar behoren.

Wanneer de uitkomsten van de Speciale Procedures worden bekeken, dient in het oog te worden gehouden dat het systeem van deze Procedures een aantal, meer algemene, zwakke punten kent, waaronder het selectieproces van de mandaathouders, het gebrek aan financiële middelen en personeel, de gemaximeerde lengte van rapporten, de mogelijke onwil van regeringen om mee te werken, en het gebrek aan een follow-up procedure.

3.1.4. Regionale Systemen van Mensenrechtenbescherming

Hoofdstuk V bespreekt op welke wijze er op regionaal niveau verbanden worden gelegd tussen corruptie en mensenrechten. Kern van het Europese systeem van mensenrechtenbescherming vormt het Europese Verdrag voor de Rechten van de Mens (hierna: EVRM), waarop toezicht wordt uitgeoefend door het Europees Hof voor de Rechten van de Mens (hierna: EHRM). De jurisprudentie van het EHRM inzake corruptie betreft voornamelijk de rechten van klokkenluiders op vrijheid van meningsuiting onder artikel 10 EVRM, en de rechten van degenen die beticht worden van corruptie, onder meer onder artikelen 5, 6 en 8 EVRM.

De jurisprudentie van het Hof inzake de rechten van klokkenluiders kan worden onderverdeeld in zaken over ambtenaren, en zaken over journalisten. Wat betreft ambtenaren heeft de Grote Kamer van het Hof in *Guja v. Moldova*[15] een kader uiteengezet dat kan worden gebruikt om te bezien of klokkenluiden toegestaan is. Beperkingen van het recht op vrijheid van meningsuiting dienen 'noodzakelijk te zijn in een democratische samenleving', volgens artikel 10 lid 2 EVRM. Ten aanzien van ambtenaren heeft het Hof zes criteria geformuleerd: (i) de beschikbaarheid en het gebruik van alternatieve wegen; (ii) het publieke belang bij de onthulde informatie; (iii) de authenticiteit van de onthulde informatie; (iv) het afwegen van de schade geleden door de overheid tegen het publieke belang; (v) het motief van de klokkenluider; en (vi) de straf die aan de klokkenluider wordt opgelegd, en de consequenties daarvan. In onderhavige zaak werd wel een schending van artikel 10 EVRM aangenomen. Wat betreft journalisten is er een groter aantal zaken betreffende journalisten of redacteuren die vervolgd werden nadat zij beschuldigingen van corruptie publiceerden. In de grote meerderheid van zaken acht het Hof een schending van artikel 10 EVRM aanwezig. In *Cumpana and Mazare v. Romania*[16] beoordeelde het Hof of de veroordeling van journalisten nadat

15 ECtHR Grand Chamber Judgment *Guja v. Moldova*, 12 February 2008, Application no. 14277/04.

16 ECtHR Grand Chamber Judgment *Cumpana and Mazare v. Romania*, 17 December 2004, Application no. 33348/96.

zij aantijgingen van corruptie hadden gepubliceerd 'noodzakelijk is in een democratische samenleving'. Om laatstgenoemd criterium te vervullen, moet er sprake zijn van een 'pressing social need'. Het Hof benadrukt de belangrijke rol van de pers als publieke waakhond. Ook dient de opgelegde straf proportioneel te zijn. In onderhavige zaak oordeelde het Hof dat er wel een 'pressing social need' aanwezig was, maar dat de opgelegde straf niet proportioneel was.

Naast de jurisprudentie over klokkenluiders, zijn er zaken waarin het Hof heeft geoordeeld over de beweerdelijke schending van de rechten van degenen die beschuldigd zijn van corruptie. Het betreft onder andere een schending van het recht op een eerlijk proces ex artikel 6 EVRM door het gebruik van undercover-agenten (*Ramanauskas v. Lithuania*)[17]; een schending van het recht op privéleven ex artikel 18 EVRM door het gebruik van getapte telefoons (*Craxi v. Italy*)[18]; en de schending van artikel 5(4) EVRM door beperking van de rechten van de verdediging gedurende een onderzoek naar corruptie (*Lietzow v. Germany*).[19]

In de Amerikaanse context zijn het Amerikaans Verdrag voor de Rechten van de Mens (inhoudende burger- en politieke rechten) en het Protocol van San Salvador (dat economische, sociale en culturele rechten bevat) de kern van het regionale systeem van mensenbescherming. Supervisie is in handen van de Inter-Amerikaanse Commissie voor de Rechten van de Mens en het Inter-Amerikaans Hof voor de Rechten van de Mens. In de praktijk van de Commissie zijn er slechts een klein aantal petities van individuen te vinden die corruptie betreffen. Daarentegen wordt corruptie in toenemende mate besproken in de landenrapporten van de Commissie. Ook de thematische rapporten en andere publicaties bespreken her en der corruptie, doch er zijn maar weinig resoluties over het onderwerp. Aangaande de thema's die worden besproken, heeft te gelden dat er een aantal petities zijn over corruptie in de rechterlijke macht, waarin individuen klagen dat zij geen eerlijk proces ex artikel 8 ACHR hebben gehad door corruptie. Ook veel landenrapporten bespreken corruptie in de rechterlijke macht. Het rapport inzake Paraguay vermeldt zelfs duidelijk dat corruptie door een rechter een schending kan opleveren van het recht op een eerlijk proces.[20] Andere corruptie-gerelateerde onderwerpen besproken door de Commissie zijn de rechten van klokkenluiders, economische, sociale en culturele rechten, corruptie bij de politie en in gevangenissen.

De praktijk van het Inter-Amerikaanse Hof voor de Rechten van de Mens toont aan dat corruptie slechts in een klein aantal zaken aan de orde komt. De jurisprudentie betreft vooral de rechten van klokkenluiders, voornamelijk hun recht

17 ECtHR Judgment *Ramanauskas v. Lithuania*, 5 February 2008, Application no. 74420/01.

18 ECtHR Judgment *Craxi v. Italy* (No. 2), 17 July 2003, Application no. 25337/94.

19 ECtHR Judgment *Lietzow v. Germany*, 13 February 2001, Application no. 24479/94.

20 IACionHR, Third report on the situation of human rights in Paraguay, 9 March 2001, OEA/Ser.L/V/II.110, chapter II, § 47.

op vrijheid van meningsuiting ex artikel 13 ACHR, zoals het geval was in *Ivcher Bronstein v. Peru*[21] en *Ricardo Canese v. Paraguay*.[22]

Het Afrikaanse systeem van mensenrechtenbescherming bestaat uit het Afrikaans Handvest voor de Rechten van de Mens en Volken, waarover de Afrikaanse Commissie voor de Rechten van de Mens en Volken en het Afrikaans Hof voor de Rechten van de Mens en Volken (nog niet in werking) toezicht oefenen. Met uitzondering van één corruptie-gerelateerde klacht van een individu (die niet-ontvankelijk werd verklaard), zijn er geen relevante zaken over corruptie gevonden. Dit is jammer, gelet op de schaal van de corruptie-problematiek in veel Afrikaanse landen. Wil corruptie kunnen worden aangekaart in de individuele klachtenprocedure, dan is het natuurlijk noodzakelijk dat individuen ook daadwerkelijk een klacht indienen. In de praktijk is dit voor kwetsbare groepen niet eenvoudig. Het vereiste van uitputting van nationale rechtsmiddelen is ook een hindernis, evenals het vereiste dat klachten geen taalgebruik mogen bevatten dat grievend of beledigend is voor de betreffende staat. De Commissie heeft inzake *Ilesanmi v. Nigeria* geoordeeld dat een klacht over corruptie niet-ontvankelijk is door zulk taalgebruik.[23] Het verdient dan ook aanbeveling dat de Commissie dit vereiste minder rigide toepast in toekomstige zaken over corruptie.

3.2. Verdere Verbanden

3.2.1. Algemene Conclusies

Het tweede onderdeel (b) van onderzoeksvraag (2) luidt als volgt: *Welke verdere verbanden kunnen er worden gelegd tussen corruptie en mensenrechten-schendingen, en wat is de waarde van een dergelijke benadering?* Om te beginnen stelt hoofdstuk VI dat er vijf zogeheten 'dimensies' zijn van het verband tussen corruptie en mensenrechten: (i) corruptie en mensenrechtenschendingen bestaan vaak in dezelfde omgeving; (ii) mensenrechten, waaronder het recht op vrijheid van meningsuiting en het recht op vrijheid van vergadering, zijn noodzakelijke instrumenten om corruptie te bestrijden, en deze rechten worden derhalve vaak geschonden door autoriteiten die klokkenluiders de mond wensen te snoeren; (iii) mensenrechten, waaronder het recht op een eerlijk proces, kunnen worden geschonden door anti-corruptiemaatregelen; (iv) anti-corruptiemaatregelen kunnen de mensenrechten van degenen behorende tot kwetsbare groepen negatief beïnvloeden; (v) corruptie kan zelf een mensenrechtenschending opleveren. Het is deze laatste dimensie die uitvoering besproken wordt in hoofdstuk VI.

---

21 Inter-American Court of Human Rights, *Ivcher Bronstein v. Peru*, Judgment of 6 February 2001.

22 Inter-American Court of Human Rights, *Ricardo Canese v. Paraguay*, Judgment of 31 August 2004.

23 African Commission on Human and Peoples' Rights, *Ilesanmi v. Nigeria*, Communication 268/2003.

Opgemerkt dient te worden dat er ook weerstand is tegen het zogeheten 'anti-corruptionisme' in het algemeen, en meer specifiek tegen het plaatsen van corruptie binnen het mensenrechtenkader. De onderhavige studie erkent dat anti-corruptie als thema weliswaar op de agenda staat van Westerse instellingen die een neo-liberaal economisch beleid voorstaan, maar beargumenteert dat er ook vanuit ontwikkelingslanden een sterke en oprechte roep klinkt om corruptie tegen te gaan, mede met gebruik van het mensenrechtenkader. Juist om te voorkómen dat anti-corruptie gemonopoliseerd wordt door spelers zoals de Wereldbank, is het bruikbaar om de taal van de mensenrechten en de bijbehorende toezichtmechanismen in te zetten.

Andere auteurs gaan juist verder, en zijn voorstander van een nieuw mensenrecht op een corruptievrije samenleving. Dit proefschrift verwerpt dergelijke stellingen. Er is thans onvoldoende bewijs voor het bestaan van een dergelijk nieuw recht, en evenmin is er daadwerkelijk behoefte aan. Het huidige kader van bestaande mensenrechtenverdragen is zeer wel in staat om corrupte praktijken aan te pakken, en bovendien zal de internationale gemeenschap geen voorstander zijn van een nieuw anti-corruptie mensenrecht.

De manier waarop corruptie kan worden bestreden – als aanvulling op bestaande methoden – bestaat uit het leggen van verbanden tussen enerzijds een specifieke corrupte handeling en anderzijds de verplichtingen van staten zoals neergelegd in onder meer het IVBPR en het IVESCR. Hoofdstuk V beschrijft hoe corrupte handelingen een schending kunnen opleveren van de volgende rechten: (i) het recht op gelijkheid en non-discriminatie; (ii) het recht op gelijkheid voor de rechter en het recht op een eerlijk proces; (iii) politieke rechten; (iv) het verbod van mensenhandel; (v) rechten van gedetineerden; (vi) het recht op vrijheid van beweging; (vii) het recht op voedsel; (viii) het recht op huisvesting; (ix) het recht op onderwijs; en (x) het recht op gezondheid. In het kader van economische, sociale en culturele rechten wordt ook aangetoond dat corruptie een schending kan opleveren van de verplichtingen van staten onder artikel 2 lid 1 IVESCR.

Wanneer een concreet geval van corruptie wordt bestudeerd, dient men de vraag te stellen of corruptie één of meer van de verplichtingen van staten schendt: om mensenrechten te eerbiedigen, te beschermen, en te realiseren. Dit is vooral van belang voor economische, sociale en culturele rechten. Ook de diverse componenten van beschikbaarheid, toegankelijkheid, aanpassing, accepteerbaarheid en kwaliteit moeten worden getoetst, om vast te stellen of, en zo ja: hoe, deze worden geschonden door corruptie.

3.2.2. *Voordelen en Beperkingen van de Mensenrechtelijke Benadering van Corruptie*

Hoewel het kwalificeren van corruptie als een mensenrechtenschending zeer zeker geen wondermiddel is, kleven er desalniettemin een aantal voordelen aan deze benadering. Om te beginnen kan het de publieke opinie beïnvloeden zodra corruptie als een mensenrechtenschending wordt neergezet. Deze morele dimensie kan ertoe leiden dat er een breder draagvlak komt voor anti-corruptie initiatieven, ook bij de ambtenaren zelf, de rechterlijke macht, het bedrijfsleven, de media en het publiek in zijn algemeenheid.

Ook kunnen de mensenrechtenmechanismen van de VN worden ingezet wanneer corruptie een schending oplevert: de VN Verdragscomités, de UPR en de Speciale Procedures van de Mensenrechtenraad. Met name de Verdragscomités kunnen hier een belangrijke rol vervullen wanneer zij statenrapporten bestuderen, en wanneer zij klachten van individuen behandelen. Echter, het dient erkend te worden dat de Verdragscomités wellicht de economische expertise missen om complexe economische problemen te bestuderen. De Comités zijn dan ook afhankelijk van betrouwbare informatie verstrekt door derden. Non-gouvernementele organisaties zoals Transparency International kunnen hier een nuttige rol vervullen. Het vermogen van de Verdragscomités om corruptie te bespreken wordt ook beïnvloed door de beperkte tijd die er beschikbaar is voor het bestuderen van statenrapporten, en de politieke gevoeligheid van het thema. Regionale mensenrechteninstellingen zoals het ECHR, de Inter-Amerikaanse Commissie en de Afrikaanse Commissie kunnen klachten in behandeling nemen die zijn ingediend door individuen die stellen dat hun rechten zijn geschonden door corruptie.

Op nationaal niveau zijn er ook mogelijkheden. Voor de nationale rechter procederen is een belangrijke route, vooral wanneer men gebruik maakt van de grondrechten die in de nationale grondwet zijn opgenomen. Zogeheten *public interest litigation* kan ook voordelen bieden. Tegelijkertijd wordt procederen bemoeilijkt door het feit dat er kwalitatief goed bewijs voorhanden dient te zijn, alsmede professionele juridische bijstand, en wellicht corrupte praktijken op nationaal niveau. Procederen is bovendien duur en tijdrovend. Een ander probleem dat niet uit het oog mag worden verloren is het aspect van causaal verband, dat zowel van belang is in de individuele klachtprocedures van de Verdragscomités als in de procedures op regionaal of nationaal niveau. Kern van een mensenrechtelijke klacht over corruptie is dat corruptie zelf een schending oplevert van een erkend mensenrecht. (Semi) gerechtelijke instanties vereisen dat er bewijs wordt geleverd van de corrupte handeling, en van het feit dat de schade ook daadwerkelijk hierdoor is ontstaan. Bij *petty* corruptie is dit bewijs waarschijnlijk makkelijker te leveren dan bij *grand* corruptie. Bijvoorbeeld, wanneer er bij het Ministerie voor Gezondheidszorg gelden achterover zijn gedrukt, dan levert dit een schending op van het recht op gezondheid. Dit zal echter geen geschikte zaak zijn om op nationaal niveau over te procederen, aangezien causaal verband moeilijk aan te tonen is, en de slachtoffers bezwaarlijk bewijs kunnen leveren. Ten slotte kan het ontbreken van de afdwingbaarheid van economische, sociale en culturele rechten op nationaal niveau moeilijkheden veroorzaken.

4. Part C: Individuele Verantwoordelijkheid: Corruptie als Misdrijf in het Internationale Recht?

In Deel C komt onderzoeksvraag (3) aan de orde: *Is het mogelijk om (bepaalde vormen van) corruptie in de publieke sector te kwalificeren als een misdrijf in het internationale recht?* Deze vraag is onderverdeeld in drie deelvragen.

4.1. Theoretische Beschouwingen

Deelvraag 3(a) luidt: *Dient het systeem van internationaal strafrecht te worden gebruikt om corruptie te bestrijden, en zo ja, welke typen corruptie komen voor deze benadering in aanmerking?*

Vooraleer deze vraag kan worden beantwoord, moet helder zijn wat er bedoeld wordt met de term 'internationaal strafrecht'. Dit wordt besproken in hoofdstuk VII. Over het algemeen maakt men een onderscheid tussen internationaal strafrecht *largo sensu* en internationaal strafrecht *stricto sensu*. Internationaal strafrecht *largo sensu* bestaat uit zowel de strafrechtelijke aspecten van internationaal recht (te weten internationaal strafrecht *stricto sensu*, direct afdwingbaar op internationaal niveau), en uit de internationale aspecten van nationaal strafrecht (te weten transnationaal strafrecht, indirect afdwingbaar op nationaal niveau op basis van verdragsbepalingen). Misdrijven die directe individuele strafrechtelijke verantwoordelijkheid onder het internationale recht met zich meebrengen, en die derhalve op internationaal niveau strafbaar zijn gesteld, zijn 'misdrijven onder het internationale recht'. Deze verschillen van de zogeheten 'transnationale misdrijven', die op nationaal niveau strafbaar gesteld zijn. Beide typen zijn 'internationale misdrijven'

Zoals in hoofdstuk II aan de orde kwam, is corruptie duidelijk onderdeel van het transnationaal strafrecht, nu er een veelvoud aan anticorruptieverdragen bestaat, op basis waarvan verdragsluitende staten verplicht zijn om vormen van corruptie op nationaal niveau strafbaar te stellen en te vervolgen. Corruptie is derhalve een transnationaal misdrijf. De vraag rijst of corruptie echter óók onderdeel uitmaakt van internationaal strafrecht *stricto sensu*, een systeem waarin individuen direct op internationaal niveau verantwoordelijk kunnen worden gehouden. Met andere woorden, is corruptie ook een misdrijf onder het internationale recht? Deze vraag wordt beantwoord aan de hand van de geschiedenis van het internationale strafrecht, de achterliggende gedachten van strafbaarstelling, en de doeleinden van straffen.

Wat betreft de geschiedenis van internationaal strafrecht *stricto sensu*, toont hoofdstuk VII aan dat dit rechtsgebied traditioneel weinig aandacht heeft voor economische misdrijven. De oorsprong van internationaal strafrecht ligt in situaties van gewapend conflict, en is zeer gericht op situaties waarin fysiek geweld voorkomt. Opmerkelijk genoeg heeft de *1919 Commission on the Responsibility of the Authors of the War and on Enforcement of Penalties* (benoemd door de

Vredesconferentie van Parijs na de Eerste Wereldoorlog) een lijst opgesteld van 32 delicten die als oorlogsmisdaden werden gezien, waaronder ook delicten die niet bestaan uit het gebruik van fysiek geweld, maar die handelingen van economische aard inhouden. Echter, na de Tweede Wereldoorlog zijn economische misdrijven niet veel in ogenschouw genomen, noch door het Joegoslavië Tribunaal, door het Rwanda Tribunaal of door de verschillende hybride tribunalen of andere geïnternationaliseerde nationale tribunalen. Wat wel vermeldenswaardig is, is dat de inspanningen om te komen tot oprichting van het Internationaal Strafhof gedeeltelijk voortvloeien uit een voorstel van zestien Caraïbische en Latijns-Amerikaanse staten om een internationaal tribunaal op te richten ter bestrijding van drugshandel – een misdrijf dat niet noodzakelijkerwijs gewelddadig is, en dikwijls gepleegd wordt buiten situaties van gewapend conflict. De *travaux préparatoires* van het Statuut van Rome laten echter weinig verwijzingen zien naar economische misdrijven, met uitzonderingen van enkele opmerkingen van een Libische en Nigeriaanse afgevaardigde, waarop overigens geen actie is ondernomen. Kortom, internationaal strafrecht *stricto sensu* is sterk gericht op crisissituaties, en benadrukt gewelddadige misdrijven, waarmee schendingen van burger- en politieke rechten meer aandacht krijgen dan schendingen van economische, sociale en culturele rechten. Dit wil echter níet zeggen dat in theorie internationaal strafrecht niet gebruikt zou moeten of kunnen worden om niet-gewelddadige misdrijven aan te pakken die bovendien gepleegd zijn gedurende vredestijd, zoals corruptie. Het voorbeeld van drugshandel demonstreert dit. De reden waarom internationaal strafrecht *stricto sensu* zich tot op heden niet zozeer richt op economische misdrijven, terwijl transnationaal strafrecht dat wel doet, is waarschijnlijk gelegen in het feit dat internationaal strafrecht *stricto sensu* zich veel eerder ontwikkeld heeft dan inspanningen om economische misdaad te bestrijden.

Wanneer de achterliggende gedachten van internationale strafbaarstelling bezien worden, past hoofdstuk VII het model zoals ontwikkeld door Theo de Roos toe in de internationale context. Dit model bestaat uit zes criteria waaraan voldaan moet zijn voordat strafbaarstelling plaats dient te vinden: (i) het beginsel van aannemelijkheid en motivering van schade; (ii) het beginsel van tolerantie; (iii) het subsidiariteitsbeginsel; (iv) het proportionaliteitsbeginsel; (v) het legaliteitsbeginsel; en (vi) het beginsel van praktische toepasbaarheid en effectiviteit. Hoofdstuk VII concludeert dat corruptie aan alle zes criteria kan voldoen. Wat betreft het eerste criterium, te weten de schade die wordt berokkend door corruptie, past deze studie de criteria toe zoals ontwikkeld door Cherif Bassiouni and Barbara Yarnold. Zij stellen dat er vijf toetsingsgronden zijn, die uiteenzetten wanneer bepaalde gedragingen zouden moeten worden behandeld als een internationaal misdrijf: (i) in geval van een groot internationaal belang: een bedreiging van internationale vrede en veiligheid (misdrijf onder het internationale recht) (ii) als de gedraging strijdig is met de gedeelde waarden van de internationale gemeenschap, waaronder de situatie dat de gedraging het geweten van de mensheid schokt (misdrijf onder het internationale recht) (iii) als er transnationale implicaties zijn (transnationaal misdrijf); (iv) als er schade is aan een internationaal beschermd persoon of belang (transnationaal misdrijf); of (v) als er schending is van een internationaal beschermd belang (transnationaal misdrijf). In situatie (i) en (ii) wordt de gedraging doorgaans gesteund door de staat, of houdt deze activiteiten van staten in, terwijl in situatie (iii), (iv) en (v), de bemoeienis van de staat meestal uitblijft. Nu corruptie reeds een transnationaal misdrijf is, wordt de vraag beantwoord of criteria (i) en/of (ii) ook van toepassing zijn. Dit is inderdaad het geval. Ten eerste kan corruptie een bedreiging vormen voor internationale vrede en veiligheid. Corruptie holt democratie en legitimiteit uit, en kan gewapend conflict aanwakkeren. Een dergelijk conflict heeft de potentie om een gehele regio te ontwrichten, hetgeen corruptie maakt tot veel méér dan een interne aangelegenheid. Ten tweede is corruptie strijdig met de gedeelde waarden van de internationale gemeenschap. Plundering van publieke gelden door hoge functionarissen van een ontwikkelingsland dikwijls direct leidt tot abjecte armoede bij de eigen bevolking. De internationale gemeenschap veroordeelt dit, en gesteld kan worden dat flagrante corruptie onder omstandigheden even schokkend kan zijn als de gruwelijkheden gepleegd gedurende gewapend conflict. Derhalve verdient corruptie het om behandeld te worden als een misdrijf onder het internationale recht, en niet enkel als een transnationaal misdrijf. Corruptie kan bovendien duidelijk worden onderscheiden van praktijken zoals drugshandel, mensenhandel en terrorisme, nu het in geval van corruptie gaat om handelen met staatsbemoeienis. Publiekrechtelijke macht wordt misbruikt, en derhalve wordt voldaan aan de voorwaarden voor internationale strafbaarstelling zoals geformuleerd door Bassiouni and Yarnold.

De doeleinden van straffen op internationaal niveau wijzen er ook op dat corruptie geschikt is om internationaal strafbaar gesteld te worden. Om te beginnen is vergelding een rechtvaardiging voor strafbaarstelling van corruptie, nu ambtenaren gestraft dienen te worden voor de schadelijke gevolgen van hun handelen. Ook de algemene afschrikwekkende functie van straffen kan een rol spelen. Vervolging van corrupte hoge ambtenaren kan mogelijk anderen afschrikken. Van belang in dit verband zijn met name de snelheid waarmee gestraft wordt, de voorspelbaarheid van de straf, en de hoogte ervan. Nu wordt beargumenteerd dat de algemene afschrikwekkende functie van straffen voornamelijk effectief kan zijn wanneer het gaat om elites van een regime, kan deze functie van groot belang zijn in het kader van *grand* corruptie. Nog belangrijker is de expressieve functie van straffen. Deze betreft de symbolische waarde van straffen. Het bestraffen van corruptie laat zien aan ambtenaren, aan burgers, en aan de internationale gemeenschap dat corruptie onacceptabel is. Andere doelen die gediend kunnen worden zijn het bereiken van gerechtigheid voor slachtoffers, het adequaat weergeven van de geschiedenis, alsmede verzoening na conflicten. Internationale tribunalen hebben bovendien als voordeel dat zij doorgaans niet zo gevoelig zijn voor politieke manipulatie of bevooroordeelde rechters.

Geconcludeerd kan worden dat gelet op de achterliggende gedachten van internationale strafbaarstelling en de doeleinden van bestraffing in het internationale recht, corruptie op internationaal niveau strafbaar gesteld dient te worden als misdrijf onder het internationale recht, en niet slechts als transnationaal misdrijf.

De verschijningsvormen van corruptie die voor internationale strafbaarstelling in aanmerking komen, zijn vormen van *grand* corruptie. Het internationale strafrecht zou zich bovendien moeten richten op vervolging van diegenen die op nationaal niveau de dans ontspringen door *de jure* of *de facto* immuniteit. Dit zijn met name staatshoofden, regeringsleiders, ministers en parlementsleden. Corruptie gepleegd door deze personen is *grand* corruptie. Voorts dient het internationale strafrecht zich te richten op passieve omkoping en verduistering. Ongeoorloofde beïnvloeding, misbruik van functie en ongerechtvaardigde verrijking dienen – althans voorlopig – buiten het debat over internationale strafbaarstelling te worden gehouden.

4.2. *De Lege Lata* Perspectief

4.2.1. Inleidende Opmerkingen

Deelvraag 3(b) luidt als volgt: *Kunnen bepaalde typen corruptie onder het huidige recht gekwalificeerd worden als een misdaad tegen de menselijkheid in de zin van het Statuut van Rome?* Teneinde deze vraag te beantwoorden worden allereerst de algemene elementen van alle misdaden tegen de menselijkheid besproken in hoofdstuk VIII, te beginnen met *actus reus*, zijnde het materiële element van een misdrijf bestaande uit de handeling, het gevolg, en de omstandigheid. Het mentale element van een misdrijf is *mens rea*, zijnde de gemoedstoestand van de dader op het moment van de het misdrijf, bestaande uit opzet en kennis. Tot slot moet het contextuele element aanwezig zijn. Misdaden tegen de menselijkheid vereisen dat er een wijdverbreide dan wel stelselmatige aanval is, gericht tegen een burgerbevolking. Voorts bespreekt hoofdstuk VIII twee specifieke misdaden tegen de menselijkheid, te weten uitroeiing en ander onmenselijk handelen, nu sommige auteurs hebben bepleit dat corruptie als één van deze delicten kan worden gekwalificeerd.

4.2.2. Corruptie als Uitroeiing (artikel 7(1)(b) Statuut van Rome)?

Uitroeiing is opgenomen in artikel 7(1)(b) van het Statuut van Rome, en wordt gedefinieerd als 'inzonderheid het opzettelijk opleggen van levensvoorwaarden, onder andere de onthouding van toegang tot voedsel en geneesmiddelen, bedoeld om de vernietiging van een deel van een bevolking te bewerkstelligen'.

De *actus reus* bestaat uit het doden van één of meer personen door de dader, hetgeen ook kan plaatsvinden door het opleggen van levensvoorwaarden. Corruptie voldoet aan dit element wanneer het ertoe leidt dat levensvoorwaarden worden opgelegd, waaronder het onthouden van toegang tot voedsel en medicijnen.

Wanneer publieke middelen worden weggesluisd, onthouden (hoge) ambtenaren de bevolking basisvoorzieningen, waardoor burgers kunnen omkomen. Dit is vooral het geval wanneer noodfondsen in geval van humanitaire rampen worden geplunderd.

De *mens rea* vereist voor uitroeiing, zoals opgenomen in artikel 30 van het Statuut van Rome, vereist dat de dader de opzet heeft om een groot aantal personen te doden, of om ernstig lichamelijk letsel toe te brengen, met de redelijke kennis dat zijn handelen of nalaten waarschijnlijk dit gevolg heeft. Aan dit criterium voldoet corruptie niet. De Pre-Trial Chamber II van het Internationaal Strafhof heeft in haar beslissing inzake *Bemba* besloten dat artikel 30 zich slechts uitstrekt tot *dolus directus* in de eerste en tweede graad.[24] Dit betekent dat oftewel (i) de dader weet van het gevolg van het misdrijf, en wil dit ook bereiken; oftewel (ii) de dader weet dat het gevolg van het misdrijf onvermijdelijk is. Deze twee vormen moeten worden onderscheiden van *dolus eventualis*, dat niet onder artikel 30 valt. Dit is bevestigd door de Trial Chamber van het Internationaal Strafhof inzake *Lubanga*.[25] *Dolus eventualis* is aanwezig wanneer de dader zich volledig bewust is van de mogelijke uitkomst als bijgevolg van zijn handelen, maar hij toch zijn handelingen doorzet, en daarmee de mogelijke uitkomst erkent en goedkeurt als zijnde mogelijke kosten die zijn verbonden aan het bereiken van zijn doel. In geval van *grand* corruptie is het niet waarschijnlijk dat de hoge ambtenaren in kwestie corrupte handelingen verrichten met het oogmerk om burgers te doden. Dodelijke burgerslachtoffers door corruptie is een mogelijk neveneffect van de corrupte handeling. Bij corruptie zal het mentale element beperkt zijn tot *dolus eventualis*, en niet *dolus directus* in de eerste of tweede graad omvatten. Nu artikel 30 *dolus eventualis* niet omvat, kan corruptie onder het huidige recht dan ook niet als uitroeiing worden gekwalificeerd.

Opgemerkt dient te worden dat corruptie wel kan voldoen aan het contextuele element van uitroeiing. Zoals eerder besproken moet er sprake zijn van een wijdverbreide dan wel stelselmatige aanval gericht tegen een burgerbevolking. 'Wijdverbreid' is een kwantitatief begrip, dat verwijst naar het aantal slachtoffers of het brede geografische bereik van de aanval. 'Stelselmatig' is een kwalitatief begrip dat ziet op een hoge mate van organisatie. De aanval hoeft niet gewelddadig te zijn, noch is een verband met een gewapend conflict vereist. Wanneer er veel slachtoffers zijn, is er voldaan aan het vereiste van een wijdverbreide aanval. In geval van grand corruptie zal er in ieder geval sprake zijn van een stelselmatige aanval, aangezien corruptie op hoog niveau doorgaans een grote mate van organisatie bezit. Bovendien vereist het plunderen van de staatskas een zekere mate van 'beleid'. Voorts is het noodzakelijk dat de plegers van uitroeiing kennis hebben van de wijdverbreide dan wel stelselmatige aanval. Bij *grand* corruptie zal de kennis van de grootschalige verduistering van staatsgelden veelal aanwezig zijn bij de plegers.

---

24 ICC *Prosecutor v. Jean-Pierre Bemba Gombo*, Decision Pre-Trial Chamber 15 June 2009, ICC–01/05-01/08.

25 ICC *Prosecutor v. Thomas Lubanga Dyilo*, Judgment Pursuant to Article 74 of the Statute, Trial Chamber 14 March 2012, ICC–01/04-01/06.

Afgezien van het gebrek aan het vereist *mens rea*, is er nog een ander problematisch aspect verbonden aan de stelling dat corruptie kan worden gekwalificeerd als uitroeiing. Dit heeft te maken met de moeilijkheid om het oorzakelijk verband aan te tonen tussen een specifieke corrupte handeling en het omkomen van burgers (bijvoorbeeld door honger). Er zullen in de meeste gevallen veel meer factoren zijn die een rol hierin spelen. Ten slotte biedt de stelling geen mogelijkheden wanneer corruptie niet leidt tot dodelijke slachtoffers. De kwalificering van grand corruptie als uitroeiing in de zin van artikel 7(1)(b) van het Statuut van Rome is dan ook niet mogelijk.

4.2.3. Corruptie als 'ander onmenselijk handelen' (artikel 7(1)(k) Statuut van Rome)?

Artikel 7(1)(k) van het Statuut van Rome bepaalt dat, in aanvulling op de misdrijven genoemd onder (1)(a) tot (j), een misdaad tegen de menselijkheid ook kan bestaan uit ander onmenselijk handelen van vergelijkbare aard waardoor opzettelijk ernstig lijden of ernstig lichamelijk letsel of schade aan de geestelijke of lichamelijke gezondheid wordt veroorzaakt. Zoals geformuleerd door Pre-Trial Chamber I van het Strafhof in *Katanga and Ngudjolo Chui*, gaat het hier om 'ernstige schendingen van internationaal gewoonterecht en de basisrechten die aan alle mensen toekomen, voortvloeiend uit de normen van internationaal humanitair recht, die hetzelfde karakter en dezelfde ernst bezitten als de andere misdaden van artikel 7(1).'[26]

De *actus reus* van een ander onmenselijk handelen bestaat uit twee componenten: (i) de gevolgen van het misdrijf (te weten ernstig lijden of ernstig lichamelijk letsel of schade aan de geestelijke of lichamelijke gezondheid); en (ii) het karakter van het misdrijf (te weten dat de handeling hetzelfde karakter en dezelfde ernst dient te bezitten als de andere misdaden tegen de menselijkheid). Wat betreft (i) is het mogelijk dat ernstig lijden of ernstig lichamelijk letsel of schade aan de geestelijke of lichamelijke gezondheid kan worden veroorzaakt door corruptie, bijvoorbeeld wanneer fondsen voor voedsel of medische zorg worden verduisterd. Met betrekking tot (ii) heeft te gelden dat 'ander onmenselijk handelen' ook misdrijven omvat die niet noodzakelijkerwijs fysiek geweld inhouden. Het ontbreken van fysiek geweld is dan ook geen obstakel voor het kwalificeren van *grand* corruptie als ander onmenselijk handelen.

Met betrekking tot het vereiste *mens rea* is wederom artikel 30 van het Statuut van Rome van toepassing, hetgeen zich enkel uitstrekt tot *dolus directus* in de eerste en de tweede graad.

Artikel 7(1)(k) bevat ook het woord 'opzettelijk', hetgeen duidelijk maakt dat de gevolgen van het handelen met opzet veroorzaakt dienen te zijn. Zoals het geval is met uitroeiing, zal *grand* corruptie niet voldoen aan de vereiste *dolus directus*, en

---

[26] ICC *Prosecutor v. Katanga and Ngudjolo Chui*, Decision Pre-Trial Chamber 30 September 2008, ICC–01/04-01/07.

kan het niet worden gekwalificeerd als ander onmenselijk handelen onder het Statuut van Rome. Aan het contextuele element kan wel worden voldaan, nu corruptie wel een wijdverbreide of stelselmatige aanval kan inhouden.

Het antwoord op onderzoeksvraag 3(b) luidt derhalve dat noch artikel 7(1)(b) noch artikel 7(1)(k) van het Statuut van Rome van toepassing kunnen zijn op *grand* corruptie.

4.3. *De Lege Ferenda* Perspectief

Het voorgaande leidt tot deelvraag 3(b): *Welke mogelijkheden biedt internationaal strafrecht de lege ferenda om corruptie op internationaal niveau te bestrijden?* Om te beginnen stelt hoofdstuk IX dat het Statuut van Rome gewijzigd dient te worden teneinde een nieuwe anti-corruptiebepaling op te nemen, die zich uitstrekt tot passieve omkoping en verduistering wanneer gepleegd door hooggeplaatste ambtenaren. Een dergelijke codificatie biedt voordelen, aangezien het kan niet alleen kan leiden tot directe naleving door het Internationaal Strafhof, maar ook tot vervolging op nationaal niveau gelet op het beginsel van complementariteit. Wanneer staten niet in staat zijn om grand corruptie te vervolgen, dan wel indien zij onwillig zijn om tot vervolging over te gaan, dan kan het Strafhof in actie komen. Codificatie kan de vorm aannemen van het opnemen van een nieuwe categorie misdaden tegen de menselijkheid onder artikel 7, of van een nieuwe bepaling. Dit laatste verdient de voorkeur, nu dit ruimte laat voor het uitwerken van de specifieke eigenschappen van corruptie, en het completeren van de toekomstige bepaling met een nieuwe bepaling in de Elements of Crime. Als mogelijk vertrekpunt voor codificatie is het VN Verdrag tegen Corruptie waarschijnlijk niet geschikt, nu de bepalingen daarin niet gedetailleerd genoeg zijn geformuleerd.

Derhalve neemt hoofdstuk IX de artikelen 362, 363 en 359 van het Nederlandse Wetboek van Strafboek als mogelijk uitgangspunt. Deze wetgeving is in 2001 aangepast teneinde te voldoen aan de eisen van het VN Verdrag tegen Corruptie. De genoemde artikelen zijn tot op zekere hoogte geschikt om op internationaal niveau te gebruiken. Opgemerkt moet wel worden dat passieve omkoping in het Nederlands recht wel *dolus eventualis* omvat. De Elements of Crimes zouden derhalve moeten afwijken van de standaardregel dat artikel 30 van het Statuut van toepassing is. Het vereiste contextuele element in geval van grand corruptie zou moeten bestaan uit het vereiste dat een corrupte handeling niet op zichzelf staat, maar zich voordoet in een breder systeem van corrupte praktijken.

Bewijstechnisch kan vervolging van grand corruptie, zowel passieve omkoping als verduistering, problematisch zijn: papieren sporen kunnen zijn gewist, en geïndividualiseerde slachtoffers kunnen ontbreken. Getuigen dienen beschermd te worden als klokkenluider. Tegelijkertijd is er wel de verplichting voor staten om mee te werken aan onderzoek en vervolging van misdrijven, en moeten zij voldoen aan verzoeken van het Strafhof om assistentie te verlenen bij het achterhalen, bevriezen en in beslag nemen van middelen en opbrengsten gerelateerd aan de misdrijven.

Politiek gezien ligt het opnemen van *grand* corruptie in het Statuut van Rome zeer gevoelig. Nog afgezien van de hoge technische eisen die worden gesteld aan wijzigingen van het Statuut, zullen zowel ontwikkelde landen als ontwikkelingslanden zeer kritisch zijn ten aanzien van uitbreiding van de rechtsmacht van het Strafhof, met name omdat het Strafhof tot op heden nog niet veel zaken tot een einde heeft gebracht.

In plaats van codificatie ligt het meer voor de hand om het VN Verdrag tegen Corruptie aan te vullen met een beter toezichtmechanisme. Idealiter dient dit de vorm aan te nemen van een apart anti-corruptietribunaal, bevoegd tot het instellen van onderzoek en vervolging. Een afgezwakte vorm, namelijk een commissie bestaande uit experts, zou ook al een grote verbetering zijn ten opzichte van het huidige systeem van *peer review*. Een andere mogelijkheid is het instellen van een ad hoc anti-corruptietribunaal. De huidige vervolging op nationaal niveau van leiders zoals Hosni Mubarak en Ben Ali laten zien dat dit niet ondenkbaar is.

Tot slot wordt beargumenteerd dat grand corruptie impliciet aan de orde kan komen in huidige zaken die door het Strafhof worden behandeld. Met name de zaken betreffende misdaden tegen de menselijkheid of oorlogsmisdaden kunnen de rol van corruptie bij het financieren van gewapend conflict inzichtelijk maken. Ook de ter beschikking staande middelen inzake het bevriezen van tegoeden en *asset recovery* kunnen behulpzaam zijn.

5. Part D: Samenvatting, Nadere Beschouwingen en Aanbevelingen

Tot slot geeft hoofdstuk X een samenvatting van de voornaamste bevindingen, en formuleert hoofdstuk XI een aantal concrete aanbevelingen. Het proefschrift sluit af met een concept *General Comment*, die behulpzaam kan zijn voor met name het Mensenrechtencomité en het Comité inzake Economische, Sociale en Culturele Rechten.

ANNEX 1
OVERVIEW OF CONCLUDING OBSERVATIONS ON CORRUPTION

Country	Region	Treaty Body and Year	UN Doc.	CPI 2011 ranking
1) Afghanistan	Central Asia	CESCR 2010 CRC 2011	E/C.12/AFG/CO/2–4 CRC/C/AFG/CO/1	180
2) Albania	Eastern Europe	HRC 2004 CERD 2003 CRC 2005 CESCR 2006	CCPR/CO/82/ALB CERD/C/63/CO/1 CRC/C/15/Add.249 E/C.12/ALB/CO/1	95
3) Algeria	North-Africa	HRC 1998 CESCR 2010	CCPR/C/79/Add.95 E/C.12/DZA/CO/4	112
4) Angola	Sub-Saharan Africa	CRC 2004 CESCR 2008	CRC/C/15/Add.246 E/C.12/AGO/CO/3	168
5) Argentina	Latin America	HRC 2000	CCPR/CO/70/ARG	100
6) Austria	Western Europe	CAT 2010	CAT/C/AUT/CO/4–5	16
7) Azerbaijan	Central Asia	CESCR 1997 CESCR 2004 HRC 2009 CERD 2009	E/C.12/1/Add.20 E/C.12/1/Add.104 CCPR/C/AZE/CO/3 CERD /C/AZE/CO/6	143
8) Bangladesh	Southeast Asia	CRC 2009	CRC/C/BGD/CO/4	120
9) Benin	Sub-Saharan Africa	HRC 2004 CRC 2006 CAT 2007	CCPR/CO/82/BEN CRC/C/BEN/CO/2 CAT/C/BEN/CO/2	100
10) Bolivia	Latin-America	CESCR 2001	E/C.12/1/Add.60	118
11) Bosnia and Herzegovina	Eastern Europe	HRC 2006	CCPR/C/BIH/CO/1	91
12) Brazil	Latin-America	HRC 2005	CCPR/C/BRA/CO/2	73
13) Bulgaria	Eastern Europe	CRC 2008 CRC 2008 CERD 2009	CRC/C/OPSC/BGR/CO/1 CRC/C/BGR/CO/2 CERD/C/BGR/CO/19	86
14) Burkina Faso	Sub-Saharan Africa	CRC 2010	CRC/C/BFA/CO/3–4	100
15) Burundi	Sub-Saharan Africa	CRC 2010	CRC/C/BDI/CO/2	172
16) Cambodia	Southeast Asia	HRC 1999 CRC 2000 CAT 2003 CESCR 2009 CERD 2010 CAT 2011	CCPR/C/79/Add.108 CRC/C/15/Add.128 CAT/C/ECU/CO/3 E/C.12/KHM/CO/1 CERD/C/KHM/CO/8–13 CAT/C/KHM/CO/2	164

Country	Region	Treaty Body and Year	UN Doc.	CPI 2011 ranking
17) Cameroon	Sub-Saharan Africa	CRC 2001 CRC 2010 CAT 2010	CRC/C/15/Add.164 CRC/C/CMR/CO/2 CAT/C/CMR/CO/4	134
18) Central African Republic	Sub-Saharan Africa	HRC 2006	CCPR/C/CAF/CO/2	154
19) Chad	Sub-Saharan Africa	CESCR 2009 CERD 2009 HRC 2009 CAT 2009	E/C.12/TCD/CO/3 CERD/C/TCD/15 CCPR/C/TCD/CO/1 CAT/C/TCD/CO/1	168
20) China	Asia	CEDAW 1999	CEDAW/C/1999/I/L.1/ Add.7	75
21) Colombia	Latin-America	CESCR 2010	E/C.12/COL/CO/5	80
22) Congo	Sub-Saharan Africa	HRC 2006 CRC 2006 CESCR 2009	CCPR/C/COD/CO/3 CRC/C/COG/CO/1 E/C.12/COD/CO/4	168
23) Dominican Republic	Caribbean	CESCR 1996 CESCR 1997	E/C.12/1/Add.6 E/C.12/1/Add.16	129
24) Ecuador	Latin America	CAT 2005	CAT/C/ECU/CO/3	120
25) El Salvador	Latin-America	CRC 2010	CRC/C/SLV/CO/3–4	80
26) Gabon	Sub- Saharan Africa	CRC 2002	CRC/C/15/Add.171	100
27) Georgia	Eastern Europe	HRC 1997 CRC 2000 CESCR 2002 CRC 2003 HRC 2002 HRC 2007	CCPR/C/79/Add.75 CRC/C/15/Add.124 E/C.12/1/Add.83 CRC/C/15/Add.222 CCPR/CO/74/GEO CCPR/C/GEO/CO/3	64
28) Guatemala	Latin America	CESCR 2003 CRC 2010	E/C.12/1/Add.93 CRC/C/GTM/CO/3–4	120
29) India	Asia	CESCR 2008	E/C.12/IND/CO/5	95
30) Indonesia	South-East Asia	CAT 2008	CAT/C/IDN/CO/2	100
31) Italy	Southern Europe	HRC 1994 CAT 1995	CCPR/C/79/Add.37 A/50/44 paras 146–158	69
32) Kazakhstan	Central Asia	CRC 2006 CESCR 2010	CRC/C/OPSC/KAZ/CO/1 E/C.12/KAZ/CO/1	120
33) Kenya	Sub-Saharan Africa	CRC 2001 HRC 2005 CRC 2007 CESCR 2008 CAT 2008	CRC/C/15/Add.160 CCPR/CO/83/KEN CRC/C/KEN/CO/2 E/C.12/KEN/CO/1 CAT/C/KEN/CO/1	154

Country	Region	Treaty Body and Year	UN Doc.	CPI 2011 ranking
34) Kosovo (UNMIK)	Eastern Europe	HRC 2006	CCPR/C/UNK/CO/1	112
35) Kyrgyzstan	Central Asia	HRC 2000 CRC 2004 CRC 2007	CCPR/CO/69/KGZ CRC/C/15/Add.249 CRC/C/OPSC/KGZ/CO/1	164
36) Latvia	Eastern Europe	CESCR 2007	E/C.12/LVA/CO/1	61
37) Liberia	Sub-Saharan Africa	CRC 2004	CRC/C/15/Add.236	91
38) Macau	Asia	HRC 1997 HRC 1999	CCPR/C/79/Add.77 CCPR/C/79/Add.115	46
39) Macedonia	Eastern Europe	HRC 2008	CCPR/C/MKD/CO/2	69
40) Madagascar	Sub-Saharan Africa	CERD 2004 CESCR 2009	CERD/C/65/CO/4 E/C.12/MDG/CO/2	100
41) Malawi	Sub-Saharan Africa	CRC 2002	CRC/C/15/Add.174	100
42) Mauritius	Sub-Saharan Africa	CESCR 2010	E/C.12/MUS/CO/4	46
43) Mexico	Latin America	CESCR 1999 CRC 2011	E/C.12/1/Add.41 CRC/C/OPSC/MEX/CO/1	100
44) Moldova	Eastern Europe	CESCR 2003 CRC 2009 HRC 2009	E/C.12/1/Add.91 CRC/C/MDA/CO/3 CCPR/C/MDA/CO/2	112
45) Mongolia	Central Asia	CRC 2005 CRC 2010 HRC 2011	CRC/C/15/Add.264 CRC/C/MNG/CO/3–4 CCPR/C/MNG/CO/5	120
46) Mozambique	Sub-Saharan Africa	CRC 2002 CRC 2009	CRC/C/15/Add.172 CRC/C/MOZ/CO/2	120
47) Nepal	South Asia	CAT 2007	CAT/C/NPL/CO/2	154
48) Niger	Sub-Saharan Africa	CRC 2009	CRC/C/NER/CO/2	134
49) Nigeria	Sub-Saharan Africa	CESCR 1998 CRC 2005 CRC 2010	E/C.12/1/Add.23 CRC/C/15/Add.257 CRC/C/NGA/CO3–4	143
50) Pakistan	South Asia	CRC 2003	CRC/C/15/Add.217	134
51) Philippines	Southeast Asia	CESCR 2008 CRC 2009	E/C.12/PHL/CO/4 CRC/C/PHL/CO/3–4	129
52) Romania	Eastern Europe	CRC 2009	CRC/C/ROM/CO/4	75
53) Russia	Central Asia	CESCR 1997 CRC 2005 HRC 2009 CESCR 2011	E/C.12/1/Add.13 CRC/C/RUS/CO/3 CCPR/C/RUS/CO/6 E/C.12/RUS/CO/5	143
54) Rwanda	Sub-Saharan Africa	HRC 2009	CCPR/C/RWA/CO/3	49
55) Sao Tome and Principe	Sub-Saharan Africa	CRC 2004	CRC/C/15/Add.235	100

Country	Region	Treaty Body and Year	UN Doc.	CPI 2011 ranking
56) Sierra Leone	Sub-Saharan Africa	CRC 2008 CRC 2010	CRC/C/SLE/CO/2 CRC/C/OPSC/SLE/CO/1	134
57) Serbia and Montenegro	Eastern Europe	CESCR 2005	E/C.12/1/Add.108	86 and 66
58) Sri Lanka	South-East Asia	CESCR 2010 CRC 2010	E/C.12/LKA/CO/2–4 CRC/C/LKA/CO/3–4	86
59) Tajikistan	Central Asia	CRC 2000 CESCR 2006 CAT 2006 CRC 2010	CRC/C/TJK/CO/2 E/C.12/TJK/CO/1 CAT/C/TJK/CO/1 CRC/C/15/Add.136	152
60) Thailand	Southeast Asia	CRC 1998 CEDAW 2006	CRC/C/15/Add.97	80
61) Togo	Sub-Saharan Africa	CRC 2005	CRC/C/15/Add.255	143
62) Trinidad and Tobago	Caribbean	HRC 2000	CCPR/CO/70/TTO	91
63)Uganda	Sub-Saharan Africa	CEDAW 2010	CEDAW/C/UGA/CO/7	143
64) Ukraine	Eastern Europe	HRC 2006 CRC 2007 CRC 2011	CCPR/C/UKR/CO/6 CRC/C/OPSC/UKR/CO/1 CRC/C/UKR/CO/3–4	152
65) Uzbekistan	Central Asia	CERD 2006 CRC 2006 HRC 2010	CERD/C/UZB/CO/5 CRC/C/UZB/CO/2 CCPR/C/UZB/CO/3	177
66) Yemen	Middle East	CESCR 2011	E/C.12/YEM/CO/2	164
67) Zambia	Sub-Saharan Africa	CRC 2003	CRC/C/15/Add.206	91

ANNEX 2
GENERAL COMMENT ON CORRUPTION AND HUMAN RIGHTS: A DRAFT PROPOSAL

JOINT GENERAL COMMENT No. 1 BY THE HUMAN RIGHTS COMMITTEE AND THE COMMITTEE ON ECONOMIC, SOCIAL AND CULTURAL RIGHTS

Corruption as a Human Rights Violation

Introduction

1. While corruption remained a taboo issue until the relatively recent past, it is now beyond dispute that it has detrimental consequences on the political, economic, social and environmental plane, and that these consequences are often intertwined. From a political point of view, corruption erodes democracy and legitimacy, and may have a strong relation to the the occurrence and duration of armed conflict, particularly in countries with an abundance of natural resources (the 'resource curse'). At the economic level, research shows that corruption lowers economic growth in various ways. This is detrimental to the realisation of particularly economic, social and cultural rights in developing countries. Moreover, the African Union estimates that corruption costs African economies more than US $148 billion every year, leading to a loss of 50 per cent in tax revenue, increasing the costs of African goods by 20 per cent and eating away 25 per cent of Africa's GDP.[1] Corruption also affects the way in which wealth is distributed: it has a considerable impact on income inequality and poverty, disproportionately affecting the poor. Lower economic growth is linked to poverty, and with poverty come poor living conditions, low life-expectancy, high infant-mortality and high illiteracy rates. In addition, corruption has a severe negative impact upon the natural environment, since corrupt exploitation of natural resources will be unsustainable, leading to illegal logging and resulting deforestation, as well as to pollution by extractive industries. These factors will also negatively affect the standard of living of the persons inhabiting the relevant areas, especially indigenous groups.

2. Although corruption has been studied for some time by experts and organisations from various disciplines, the phenomenon has rarely been analysed from the angle of international human rights law. There is however a growing body of literature on the subject-matter.[2]

---

1 WILLIAM DE MARIA, 'Cross Cultural Trespass: Assessing African Anti-Corruption Capacity', *International Journal of Cross Cultural Management*, 8/3 (2008), p. 317–341 at p. 317. These figures are also mentioned by Transparency International, see TRANSPARENCY INTERNATIONAL, 'Frequently Asked Questions on Corruption and Africa', <www.transparency.org/news_room/in_focus/2005/g8_summit/faq>, accessed 23 May 2011.

2 See for example INTERNATIONAL COUNCIL ON HUMAN RIGHTS POLICY, *Corruption and Human Rights: Making the Connection* (Versoix, Switzerland, 2009); INTERNATIONAL COUNCIL ON HUMAN RIGHTS POLICY, *Integrating Human Rights in the Anti-Corruption Agenda: Challenges, Possibilities and Opportunities* (Geneva, Switzerland, 2010); ZOE PEARSON, 'An International Human Rights Approach to Corruption', in Peter Larmour & Nick Wolanin (ed.), *Corruption and Anti-Corruption* (Canberra: Asia Pacific Press, 2001), p. 30–61; MARTINE BOERSMA and

Even though the various human rights Committees are devoting a growing amount of attention to the connection between corruption and human rights in their concluding observations, an in-depth analysis of this connection is not yet available. The present Joint General Comment aims to fill this gap by setting out how corruption may violate human rights, and by clearly specifying State obligations in combating corruption. Focus of this General Comment is on corruption in the public sector, both in developed and developing countries alike.

3. A first necessary step towards a better understanding of corruption is formulating a definition. While the content of the term 'corruption' may be subject to various interpretations, the definition of 'the abuse of public power for private gain' is often employed. Yet, we must acknowledge that apart from private gain, political gain may also be a motivation for corrupt behaviour. The present Comment therefore covers both the abuse of public power for private and for political gain. Also, benefits may accrue not only to the public official him- or herself, but also to family and friends. Hence, in order for an act to be considered corrupt, the following elements ought to be present: (i) an entrusted power in the public sector; (ii) an abuse of this power; and (iii) a private or political benefit obtained by the public official or his or her family or friends.

4. Corruption can take place at the policy formulation end of politics, involving public officials in the highest levels of the State, which is termed 'grand corruption'. When corruption occurs at the implementation end of politics, involving lower level public officials, this is 'petty corruption'. Both forms of corruption may have a grave human rights impact, and States ought to devote serious efforts to combating both types. To this end, political will is essential.

5. For legal purposes, it is important to distinguish further between various forms of corruption. In 2003, the United Nations Convention Against Corruption (hereafter: UNCAC) entered into force. Although there are various anti-corruption treaties at the international[3] and regional level, such as in Europe,[4] the Americas[5] and Africa,[6] the UNCAC is the only truly global anti-corruption convention to date, and it is ratified by the large majority of States. The treaty bodies strongly urge that States which have not already ratified the UNCAC, to do so, and calls upon the many countries which are already a Party, to meet their obligations under the treaty. While the UNCAC refrains from defining corruption, it does distinguish between: (i) active and passive bribery (Article 15 UNCAC);

HANS NELEN (eds.), *Corruption & Human Rights: Interdisciplinary Perspectives* (Maastricht Series in Human Rights Antwerp: Intersentia, 2010).

3 OECD Convention on Combating Bribery of Foreign Public Officials in International Business Transactions.

4 Council of Europe Criminal Law Criminal Law Convention on Corruption; Council of Europe Civil Law Convention on Corruption; Convention on the Protection of the European Communities' Financial Interests and its two Protocols; Convention on the Fight Against Corruption Involving Officials of the European Communities or Officials of EU Member States.

5 Inter-American Convention Against Corruption.

6 SADC Protocol Against Corruption; ECOWAS Protocol on the Fight Against Corruption; African Union Convention on Preventing and Combating Corruption.

(ii) embezzlement (Article 16 UNCAC); (iii) trading in influence (Article 18 UNCAC); (iv) abuse of functions (Article 19 UNCAC); and (v) illicit enrichment (Article 20 UNCAC).

Dimensions of the Corruption & Human Rights Connection

6. In the discourse on corruption and its linkages to human rights, **five dimensions** can be identified.

(a) Corruption and human rights violations often exist in the same environment. A country with a corrupt leadership is not likely to respect human rights, and a State with a poor human rights record is rarely devoid of corruption.Both corruption and human rights are examples of abuse of power, which are particularly harmful to the most vulnerable segments of society.

(b) Human rights are necessary tools to fight corruption. The importance of the right to freedom of expression, including the right to seek, receive and impart information (Article 19(2) ICCPR), the right of peaceful assembly (Article 21 ICCPR), and the right to freedom of association (Article 22 ICCPR) should be underscored. Unfortunately, these rights are too often violated whenever they are exercised by whistleblowers, including those working in the journalist profession.

(c) Care must be taken to respect the human rights of persons accused of corruption, including the right to privacy and the right to a fair trial. Particularly special investigative techniques should respect human rights norms.

(d) Anti-corruption reforms should pay due regard to the human rights of vulnerable groups. Measures taken by States to address corruption should also focus on improving the situation of the poor, and not solely on improving the position of (foreign) investors.

(e) Corrupt practices may violate human rights. This dimension is central in the remainder of this General Comment.

Equality and Non-discrimination

7. **Equality and non-discrimination** are, *inter alia*, enshrined in Article 26 ICCPR, providing for an independent right to equality, consisting of (i) the right to equality before the law; (ii) the right to equal protection of the law; and (iii) the prohibition of discrimination.[7] These components are grossly violated by corruption, which is an inherently discriminatory practice. Equality before the law is absent if judges and administrative officials are corrupt. Equal protection of the law is hampered if corruption distorts the legislative process, resulting in discrimination in the enactment of laws. Finally, the prohibition of discrimination can be violated by corruption. Article 26 provides that

7 See Human Rights Committee, General Comment No. 18 on non-discrimination, thirty-seventh session (1989), §12.

discrimination on the basis of 'other status' is in principle prohibited. If persons are denied their rights, for example, because they cannot afford to pay bribes, this constitutes such discrimination.

Civil and Political Rights

8. Since corruption may violate a wide range of **civil and political rights,** the Committees request State Parties to provide information in their State reports about (i) the problems they encounter with corruption in relation to these rights; (ii) the steps they are taking to remedy corruption in these areas, including – but not limited to – the ratification of anti-corruption treaties, the adoption of domestic legislation, the establishment of preventive measures, and the prosecution of corrupt public officials and private entities.

9. **The right to equality before courts and tribunals and to a fair trial** is enshrined in Article 14 ICCPR.[8] Various concluding observations have already touched upon the detrimental impact of corruption upon these rights.[9] The following overview demonstrates more specifically how corruption may violate the component rights of Article 14.0

---

8 See Human Rights Committee, General Comment No. 32 on the right to equality before courts and tribunals and to a fair trial (Article 14), Ninetieth session (23 August 2007), UN Doc. CCPR/C/GC/32.

9 **HRC**: *Cambodia* 27 July 1999, UN Doc. CCPR/C/79/Add.108, §. 8 and 10; *Kyrgyzstan* 24 July 2000, UN Doc. CCPR/CO/69/KGZ, §. 15; *Georgia* 19 April 2002, UN Doc. CCPR/CO/74/GEO, §12 and *Georgia* 15 November 2007, UN Doc. CCPR/C/GEO/CO/3, §13; *Benin* 1 December 2004, UN Doc. CCPR/CO/82/BEN, §18; *Albania* 2 December 2004, UN Doc. CCPR/CO/82/ALB, §18; *Kenya* 29 April 2005, UN Doc. CCPR/CO/83/KEN, §9 and 20; *Brazil* 1 December 2005, UN Doc. CCPR/C/BRA/CO/2, §17; *Congo* 26 April 2006, UN Doc. CCPR/C/COD/CO/3, §21; *Central African Republic* 27 July 2006, UN Doc. CCPR/C/CAF/CO/2, §16; *Kosovo* 14 August 2006, UN Doc. CCPR/C/UNK/CO/1, §20; *Ukraine* 28 November 2006, UN Doc. CCPR/C/UKR/CO/6, §17; *Rwanda* 31 March 2009, UN Doc. CCPR/C/RWA/CO/3, §17; *Chad* 11 August 2009, UN Doc. CCPR/C/TCD/CO/1, §26; *Azerbaijan* 13 August 2009 UN Doc. CCPR/C/AZE/CO/3, §12; *Moldova* 4 November 2009, UN Doc. CCPR/C/MDA/CO/2, §23; *Russia* 24 November 2009, UN Doc. CCPR/C/RUS/CO/6, §21; *Mongolia* 2 May 2011, UN Doc. CCPR/C/MNG/CO/5, §17.
CESCR: *Dominican Republic* 3 December 1996, UN Doc. E/C.12/1/Add.6, §16; *Dominican Republic* 12 December 1997, UN Doc. E/C.12/1/Add.16, §4 and 29; *Bolivia* 21 May 2001, UN Doc. E/C.12/1/Add.60, §12; *Moldova* 12 December 2003, UN Doc. E/C.12/1/Add.91, §12 and 33; *Azerbaijan* 14 December 2004, UN Doc. E/C.12/1/Add.104, §6, 13 and 38; *Latvia* 7 January 2008, UN Doc. E/C.12/LVA/CO/1, §9 and 35; *Angola* 1 December 2008, UN Doc. E/C.12/AGO/CO/3, §10 and 12; *Cambodia* 22 May 2009, UN Doc. E/C.12/KHM/CO/1, §14; *Congo* 20 November 2009, UN Doc. E/C.12/COD/CO/4, §10–11; *Kazakhstan* 7 June 2010, UN Doc. E/C.12/KAZ/CO/1, §11; *Afghanistan* 7 June 2010, UN Doc. E/C.12/AFG/CO/2–4, §15.
CERD: *Chad* 21 September 2009, UN Doc. CERD/C/TCD/15, §11; *Cambodia* 16 March 2010, UN Doc. CERD/C/KHM/CO/8–13.
CAT (on corruption in the police/judiciary): *Cambodia* 5 February 2004, UN Doc. CAT/C/CR/31/7, §6(e); *Nepal* 13 April 2007, UN Doc. CAT/C/NPL/CO/2, §16; *Benin* 19 February 2008, UN Doc. CAT/C/BEN/CO/2, §13, 29; *Indonesia* 2 July 2008, UN Doc. CAT/C/IDN/CO/2, §22; *Kenya* 19 January 2009, UN Doc. CAT/C/KEN/CO/1, §12; *Chad* 19 May 2009, UN Doc. CAT/C/TCD/CO/1, §24; *Cambodia* 20 January 2011, UN Doc. CAT/C/KHM/CO/2, §13.

(a) *The right to equality before courts and tribunals* of Article 14(1), is composed of (i) the general guarantee of equality before courts and tribunals, applicable regardless of the nature of the proceedings; (ii) the right of access to courts; and (iii) equality of arms. As regards the second element, access to courts may be denied if bribes need to be paid in the judicial sector, either to court support staff, or to judges, in order for their case to be processed or speeded up. Persons who cannot afford to pay bribes, are denied access to court, which constitutes a violation of Article 14(1) ICCPR. Concerning the third element, equality of arms, this requires that all parties are granted the same procedural rights. If one party to a dispute bribes the judge, this constitutes an unfair advantage compared to the other party, as a result of which the bribing party may be given different procedural rights. Again, such a practice violates Article 14(1) ICCPR.

(b) *The right to a fair trial* (second sentence of Article 14(1)) contains the requirements of judicial independence, judicial impartiality, and fairness. Independence is severely affected by corruption, for instance when judges are appointed because of political loyalties, or family or friendship ties to those in power. Impartiality is lacking in cases of bribery of judges. Bribe-taking or extortion of bribes by judges is a violation of the right to a fair trial. Fairness may also be compromised in cases of bribery, for example when the expeditiousness of a hearing is infringed as a result.

(c) *The presumption of innocence* under Article 14(2) requires that no guilt may be presumed. Judicial corruption may violate this principle. For instance, a judge appointed by the ruling political party will not respect the presumption of innocence in cases where political opponents are standing trial. The same holds true if politically-appointed judges have to rule in cases brought against whistleblowers, such as critical journalists.

(d) *Rights of persons charged with a criminal offence* are enshrined in Article 14(3), constituting minimum guarantees in criminal cases. These rights may be closely related to corruption. If they are not respected, it is very well possible that pressure is put on them by court staff or police officers to pay bribes.

(e) *The right to a remedy* can be found in Article 2(3) ICCPR. Whenever any of the guarantees of Article 14 is violated, the right to a remedy needs to be protected. Yet, Article 2(3) may be violated by a corrupt judiciary. Whenever a person, suffering from a violation of civil or political rights, aims to obtain a remedy from a court, this may be impossible due to corruption. Hence, judicial corruption may violate both the right to a fair trial as well as the right to an effective remedy.

10. **Rights of political participation** (Article 25 ICCPR)[10] are often violated by corrupt practices:

---

10 See Human Rights Committee, General Comment No. 25 on the right to participate in public affairs, voting rights and the right of equal access to public service (Article 25), Fifty-seventh session (12 July 1996), UN Doc. CCPR/C/21/Rev.1/Add.7.

(a) *The right to take part in the conduct of public affairs*, in Article 25 section (a), is violated whenever citizens are being denied the right to participate, for instance when the results of a referendum are rigged.

(b) *The right to vote*, in Article 25 section (b), requires that there are no obstacles to the exercise of this right, for example with regard to voter registration. Whenever election officials are bribed to tamper with the registration of voters, the right to vote is violated. Furthermore, the right to vote demands that voters must be free to cast their votes, without undue influence or coercion of any kind which may distort or inhibited the free expression of his or her will. Hence, the bribing of voters by, or on behalf of, politicians is highly problematic, and violates Article 25(b). Moreover, elections must be held by secret ballot, they must be fair and free, and be held on a periodic basis. They must also be supervised by an independent electoral authority. If corruption takes place at such an authority, for example if election officials are bribed by candidates to interfere with ballot boxes or vote counting, this violates the right to vote.

(c) *The right to be elected,* contained in Article 25 section (b), is the right and opportunity for citizens to stand for elective office, and restrictions of this right have to be objective and reasonable. Conditions relating to nomination dates, fees or deposits have to be reasonable and non-discriminatory. Corruption at the level of an electoral commission may violate the right to be elected: a candidate may not be allowed to register because the commission was bribed by the candidate's political opponent. It is also possible that members of the electoral commission demand bribes from candidates, which negatively affects poorer candidates. Hence, the acceptance or demand of bribes by election officials constitutes a violation of the right to stand for elective office.

(d) *The right of equal access to public service*, Article 25 section (c), entails that the criteria and processes for appointment, promotion, suspension and dismissal of public service positions must be objective and reasonable. Persons holding such positions must be free from political interference or pressures. This right is violated if public service is only accessible to those who manage to obtain access in a corrupt way, such as bribery.

11. **The prohibition of human trafficking** forms part of Article 8 ICCPR. The connection between corruption and the occurrence of human trafficking is a very strong one. Without the involvement of corrupt public officials, who may be actively engaged in trafficking or who often turn a blind eye to these practices, traffickers would face many more difficulties. Policies to combat human trafficking cannot do without specific anti-corruption measures, in the areas of prevention, cooperation, and the imposition of sanctions.

12. **The rights of detainees to be treated with humanity and respect for their human dignity** (Article 10 ICCPR)[11] may be violated by corruption. Some links were already made

[11] See Human Rights Committee, General Comment No. 21 concerning humane treatment of persons deprived of liberty (Article 10), Forty-fourth session (1992), UN Doc. HRI/GEN/1/Rev.6 at 153, §5.

by the Human Rights Committee[12] and the Committee Against Torture[13] between corruption and Article 10. An example is the requirement that prisoners have to pay bribes to receive visitors, to be released on parole, to use the telephone or to buy food. Another example is the embezzlement by prison staff of food that was intended for the prisoners.

13. Corruption may violate **the right to freedom of movement** (Article 12 ICCPR),[14] a matter already touched upon by the Human Rights Committee[15] and the Committee on the Elimination of Racial Discrimination.[16] For instance, the right to liberty of movement and freedom to choose residence is violated, *inter alia*, by the demand of bribes, to be paid to police officers at road stops, without any service being rendered. Such practice cannot be justified under Article 12(3). Moreover, the freedom to leave any country and the liberty of immigration includes the right to obtain the necessary travel documents. It is particularly in this area in which corruption often occurs, especially when bribes have to be paid to obtain a passport. Such practice violates Article 12(2) and does not fall under the scope of the third paragraph of Article 12. Finally, the right to enter one's own country may also be affected by corruption, for example in the processing of administrative requirements, violating Article 12.

Economic, Social and Cultural Rights

14. A wide spectrum of **economic, social and cultural rights** can be violated by corruption. By means of example, the following sections deal with the rights to food, adequate housing, education, and health. Future State Reports to the Committee on Economic, Social and Cultural Rights should devote attention to (i) the problems States encounter with corruption in relation to these rights; (ii) the steps they are taking to remedy corruption in these areas, including – but not limited to – the ratification of anti-corruption treaties, the adoption of domestic legislation, the establishment of preventive measures, and the prosecution of corrupt public officials.

15. **Article 2(1)** ICESCR, applies to all substantive rights of the Covenant.[17] The various phrases of this provision capture a number of State obligations, all of which may be violated by corrupt practices.

(a) *'Undertakes to take steps'*. The obligation to take steps towards the progressive realisation of economic, social and cultural rights is an immediate obligation.[18] Steps should

---

12 Communication no. 526/1993, *Michael and Brian Hill v. Spain*, views of 22 June 1997, UN Doc. CCPR/C/59/D/526/1993.

13 *Ecuador* 8 February 2006, UN Doc. CAT/C/ECU/CO/3, §24.

14 See Human Rights Committee, General Comment No. 27 on freedom of movement (Article 12), sixty-seventh session (18 October 1999), UN Doc. CCPR/C/21/Rev.1/Add.9.

15 *Georgia* 5 May 1997, UN Doc. CCPR/C/79/Add.75,§6 and 19; *Azerbaijan* 13 August 2009, UN Doc. CCPR/C/AZE/CO/3, §18; *Uzbekistan* 7 April 2010, UN Doc. CCPR/C/UZB/CO/3, §18;.

16 *Uzbekistan* 4 April 2006, UN Doc. CERD/C/UZB/CO/5, §16.

17 See Committee on Economic, Social and Cultural Rights, General Comment No. 3.

18 General Comment No. 3, §1 and 2.

be deliberate, concrete, and targeted as clearly as possible towards meeting the obligations recognised in the ICESCR.[19] Since corruption impedes the realisation of economic, social and cultural rights, the steps taken should include anti-corruption measures. Furthermore, the obligation to take steps includes the obligation to take an active role to prevent and to protect individuals against violations by private actors such as multinational corporations. When a State remains passive when MNCs engage in corruption that violates economic, social and cultural rights, this entails a violation of the Covenant. Moreover, States have the obligation to monitor the realisation of rights and to devise strategies and programmes for their implementation. This includes the obligation to monitor progress in the fight against corruption.

(b) *'Individually and through international assistance and co-operation, especially economic and technical'*. International cooperation must be directed to the realisation of all human rights. Whenever States provide international assistance and cooperation to other States, they should ensure that anti-corruption safeguards are put in place, so as to avoid embezzlement or misuse of funds or goods at any stage. Aid flows are vulnerable to corruption, and in order to contribute to the realisation of economic, social and cultural rights, they need to be monitored throughout the entire process.

(c) *'To the maximum of its available resources'*. While State Parties do not have to devote all their resources to the realisation of economic, social and cultural rights, there is an obligation to use the allocated resources in an effective and efficient manner.[20] Corruption violates this obligation. The concluding observations of the CESCR and the CRC[21] point to the fact that corruption has a negative impact upon a State's resources available for the realisation of economic, social and cultural rights.[22] Indeed, whenever public funds are

---

19 General Comment No. 3, §2.

20 See also 'The Limburg Principles on the Implementation of the International Covenant on Economic, Social and Cultural Rights (1986)', *Human Rights Quarterly*, 9 (1987), p. 122–135. §27.

21 Article 4 of the Convention on the Rights of the Child provides that 'States Parties shall undertake all appropriate legislative, administrative, and other measures for the implementation of the rights recognised in the present Convention. With regard to economic, social and cultural rights, State Parties shall undertake such measures to the maximum extent of their available resources and, where needed, within the framework of international co-operation.'

22 **CESCR:** see, *inter alia*, *Yemen* 1 June 2011, UN Doc. E/C.12/YEM/CO/2, §4.
CRC: see *Georgia* 28 June 2000, UN Doc. CRC/C/15/Add.124, §18–19; *Malawi* 2 April 2002, UN Doc. CRC/C/15/Add.174, §5, 14–15; *Zambia* 2 July 2003, UN Doc. CRC/C/15/Add.206, §4, 15–16; *Georgia* 27 October 2003, UN Doc. CRC/C/15/Add.222, §13–14, 54; *Sao Tome and Principe* 1 July 2004, UN Doc. CRC/C/15/Add.235, §15; *Angola* 3 November 2004, UN Doc. CRC/C/15/Add.246, §14; *Liberia* 4 June 2004, UN Doc. CRC/C/15/Add.236, §14; *Albania* 31 March 2005, UN Doc. CRC/C/15/Add.249, §15–16; *Togo* 31 March 2005, UN Doc. CRC/C/15/Add.255, §17; *Nigeria* 13 April 2005, UN Doc. CRC/C/15/Add.257, §21–22; *Russia* 23 November 2005, UN Doc. CRC/C/RUS/CO/3, §19–20; *Uzbekistan* 2 June 2006, UN Doc. CRC/C/UZB/CO/2, §52–53(c); *Benin* 20 October 2006, UN Doc. CRC/C/BEN/CO/2, §17–18; *Congo* 20 October 2006, UN Doc. CRC/C/COG/CO/1, §14–15; *Sierra Leone* 20 June 2008, UN Doc. CRC/C/SLE/CO/2, §18; *Bulgaria* 23 June 2008, UN Doc. CRC/C/BGR/CO/2, §16–17; *Bangladesh* 12 June 2009, UN Doc. CRC/C/BGD/CO/4, §22–23; *Niger* 12 June 2009, UN Doc.

embezzled, and public money intended for the realisation of these rights ends up in the private pockets of officials, this constitutes a violation of the obligation to devote the maximum available resources. In addition, whenever corruption causes an inefficient use of allocated resources, this also constitutes a violation. An example is the spending of public funds on large, unnecessary infrastructural or defense projects (offering opportunities for personal enrichment of public officials through embezzlement or bribery), or on goods or services of inferior quality (because bribes where obtained during the procurement process).

(d) *'With a view to achieving progressively the full realisation of the rights recognised in the Covenant'.* 'Progressive realisation' entails that full implementation of all economic, social and cultural rights can generally not be achieved in a short period of time.[23] Yet, States have the obligation to continuously improve conditions, and they are under the prohibition of taking deliberately retrogressive measures. An example of such a measure is an unjustified reduction by the State of public expenditures devoted to the implementation of economic, social and cultural rights, in the absence of adequate compensation.[24] Embezzlement of public funds constitutes such an unjustified reduction, and violates Article 2(1). Moreover, States have to accord a degree of priority to human rights in the allocation of resources.[25] High-level embezzlement of public money violates this obligation since, in such a case, the financing of the lifestyle of a country's officials enjoys priority over the realisation of economic, social and cultural rights. The same is true where priority is given to projects that offer opportunities for corruption, instead of projects devoted to the realisation of economic, social and cultural rights.

(e) *'By all appropriate means, including particularly the adoption of legislative measures'.* To realise economic, social and cultural rights, States need to adopt legislative measures, provide judicial remedies, and take administrative, financial, educational and social measures.[26] This includes the ratification of anti-corruption treaties, the adoption of anti-corruption legislation, the launch of domestic anti-corruption campaigns and the setting up of preventive policies. Also, anti-corruption measures will contribute to meeting the obligation of ensuring the minimum core level of each right laid down in the ICESCR.[27]

CRC/C/NER/CO/2, §17–18(f); *Romania* 12 June 2009, UN Doc. CRC/C/ROM/CO/4, §15–16; *Philippines* 22 October 2009, UN Doc. CRC/C/PHL/CO/3–4, §19–20(d); *Mozambique* 4 November 2009, UN Doc. CRC/C/MOZ/CO/2, §17–18(f); *Burkina Faso* 9 February 2010, UN Doc. CRC/C/BFA/CO/3–4, §16–17(e); *Mongolia* 29 January 2010, UN Doc. CRC/C/MNG/CO/3–4, §17–18(e); Cameroon 18 February 2010, UN Doc. CRC/C/CMR/CO/2, §17–18(f); *Tajikistan* 5 February 2010, UN Doc. CRC/C/CMR/CO/2, §17(e); *El Salvador* 17 February 2010, UN Doc. CRC/C/SLV/CO/3–4, §18(f); *Nigeria* 11 June 2010, UN Doc. CRC/C/NGA/CO3–4, §16–17(a); *Sri Lanka* 19 October 2010, UN Doc. CRC/C/LKA/CO/3–4, §16(c) and 17(f); *Afghanistan* 8 April 2011, UN Doc. CRC/C/AFG/CO/1, §17–18.

23 General Comment No. 3, §9.

24 The Maastricht Guidelines on Violations of Economic, Social and Cultural Rights (1997)', *Human Rights Quarterly*, 20 (1998), p. 691–704. §14 (e).

25 Limburg Principles, §28.

26 General Comment No. 3, §4, 5, 7.

27 General Comment No. 3, §10.

16. **The right to food: content.** This right is a component of the right to an adequate standard of living (Article 11 ICESCR). Important concepts are *adequacy*[28] and *sustainability*[29] of food availability and access. The core content of the right to food implies: the availability of food in a quantity and quality sufficient to satisfy the dietary needs of individuals, free from adverse substances, and acceptable within a given culture, as well as the accessibility of such food in ways that are sustainable and that do not interfere with the enjoyment of other human rights.[30]

(a) *Availability*[31] is violated by corruption if food aid for humanitarian disasters is embezzled by public officials. The element of *dietary needs*[32] and the requirement that food ought to be *free from adverse substances*[33] may be affected by corruption in the food production chain, for instance when food inspectors are bribed to turn a blind eye to unsafe products, or to products with little nutritional value.

(b) *Accessibility* includes economic as well as physical accessibility. *Economic access* entails that food has to be affordable, so that the costs of food do not constitute a disproportionate part of the household income. Corrupt practices in the food chain may lead to an increase in the price of foods, impeding economic accessibility. *Physical access* implies that food should be accessible to everyone, including vulnerable and disadvantaged groups.[34]

17. **The right to food: State obligations and violations.**

(a) While the right to food has to be realised progressively,[35] State Parties have a core obligation to take the necessary action to mitigate and alleviate hunger as provided for in Article 11(2) ICESCR, even in times of natural or other disasters.[36] States have to ensure the minimum essential level required to be free from hunger.[37] Whenever this is not met due to unwillingness – rather than inability – of a State Party, this constitutes a violation of the ICESCR.[38] Several countries where a large number of people suffer from undernourishment and malnutrition rank among the most corrupt. For those States, it will be hard to demonstrate that they are actually unable, instead of unwilling, to meet their core obligations. A country in which the political leadership misappropriates large amounts of money while the population is suffering clearly does not meet its obligation of devoting the 'maximum available resources' as required by Article 2(1) ICESCR.

---

28 Committee on Economic, Social and Cultural Rights, General Comment No. 12 on the right to adequate food (Article 11), Twentieth session (1999), UN Doc. E/C.12/1999/5, §7.

29 *Ibid.* §7.

30 *Ibid.* §8.

31 *Ibid.* §12.

32 *Ibid.* §9.

33 *Ibid.* §10.

34 *Ibid.* §13.

35 General Comment No. 12, §6 and 14.

36 *Ibid.* §6.

37 *Ibid.* §14.

38 *Ibid.* §17.

(b) Under the obligation *to respect* the right to food, States are required not to prevent existing access to adequate food.[39] States may not interfere. As pointed out by the CESCR in its concluding observations on India (2008), corruption prevents access to food.[40] Thus, it constitutes a violation of the obligation to respect the right to food. Both economic accessibility and physical accessibility may be at stake due to corruption.

(c) The obligation *to protect* obliges States to take measures to ensure that corporations or individuals do not deprive citizens of their access to adequate food. By engaging in corrupt practices, a State may breach this obligation to protect. Imagine an international oil corporation, eager to obtain the concession to drill for oil. The corporation might offer bribes to the public officials in charge of the relevant area, or the public officials might demand bribes from the corporation. Such bribery might lead to the situation in which environmental regulations are disrespected, with pollution of water and soil as a result. This pollution may violate various rights, such as the right to life, health and food. The latter is true if the area concerned was used for food production by its inhabitants. While it is ultimately the corporation which pollutes the area, this is the result of the act of bribery, which was an inducement for the public official to ignore environmental regulations. The acceptance or extortion of the bribe and the subsequent pollution constitutes a direct violation of the State obligation to protect the right to food. Moreover, even if no contamination is involved, the right to food can be violated, for example by forced relocation of indigenous peoples inhabiting an area where valuable natural resources can be found. As a result of relocation, these peoples will no longer have access to their food production sites (element of physical accessibility). A second illustration may be the bribing by a food corporation of public officials who are in charge of food safety regulations. Where food producers subsequently bring unsafe food onto the market, this also constitutes a breach of the obligation to protect the right to food. In such a case, the food is no longer free from adverse substances, as required by Article 11.

(d) The obligation *to fulfil* includes the obligation to facilitate and the obligation to provide the right to adequate food. The obligation *to facilitate* means that States must productively engage in activities which strengthen people's access to and use of resources and means to ensure their livelihood, including food security. The obligation *to provide* applies when individuals or groups are unable, for reasons beyond their control, to enjoy the right to adequate food by the means at their disposal (including those who have fallen victim of natural or other disasters).[41] Misappropriation by public officials of funds intended for food aid or of the foodstuffs constitutes a breach of the obligation to fulfil the right to food. An Indian study revealed that within a food subsidy programme for the poor, more than 50 per cent of the food grain did not reach the poor due to embezzlement.[42] In such cases, the obligation to provide is not met.

---

39 *Ibid.* §15.

40 Committee on Economic, Social and Cultural Rights, Concluding observations on India, May 2008, UN Doc. E/C.12/IND/CO/5, §25.

41 General Comment No. 12, §15.

42 George Cheriyan, 'Enforcing the Right to Food in India: Bottlenecks in Delivering the Expected Outcome', *UNI-WIDER Research Paper No. 2006/132*, (November 2006) at p. 11.

(e) Violations of the right to food take place, *inter alia*, when a State discriminates in access to food, as well as to means and entitlements of its procurement.[43] Since corruption is an inherently discriminatory act, forms of corruption may constitute a violation of the right to food because they discriminate in access to food. An example would be where money has to be paid to obtain access to food aid, discriminating against those who do not have the financial means to pay the bribes. Also, whenever food aid in relief situations is diverted by officials for private purposes, this is discriminatory. The previously mentioned Indian study argued that subsidised wheat intended for tribal populations was siphoned off by workers of the ruling political party.[44]

(f) As regards the implementation of the right to food at the national level, it should be emphasised once more that the formulation and implementation of national strategies for the right to food requires full compliance with the principles of accountability, transparency, people's participation, decentralisation, legislative capacity and the independence of the judiciary. Good governance is essential to the realisation of all human rights, including the elimination of poverty and ensuring a satisfactory livelihood for all.[45] Hence, in order to realise the right to food, corruption should also be combated.

18. **The right to adequate housing: content.** This right is also a component of the right to an adequate standard of living of Article 11 ESCR. The CESCR recently pointed to the negative impact of corruption in relation to housing.[46]

(a) *Legal security of tenure*[47] may be undermined by corruption: i) companies may bribe officials to grant leases on land that is already occupied; ii) officials or businesses may bribe homeowners directly to sell up, often throwing poor tenants on the street; and iii) village leaders may be bribed so as to sign blank contracts with the local land administration, which then sells the land to developers.[48] Moreover, the Centre on Housing Rights and Evictions (hereafter: COHRE)[49] reported on forced evictions and land rights in Burma, and pointed to the role of corruption in this respect.[50]

---

43 General Comment No. 12, §18.

44 Cheriyan, 'Enforcing the Right to Food in India: Bottlenecks in Delivering the Expected Outcome', at p. 11–12.

45 General Comment No. 12, §23.

46 CESCR CO Kazakhstan 7 June 2010, UN Doc. E/C.12/KAZ/CO/1, §30; CESCR CO Afghanistan 7 June 2010, UN Doc. E/C.12/AFG/CO/2–4, §36.

47 *Ibid.* §8(a).

48 International Council on Human Rights Policy, *Corruption and Human Rights: Making the Connection* at p. 51.

49 The Centre on Housing Rights and Evictions (COHRE), 'Displacement and Dispossession: Forced Migration and Land Rights in Burma', *COHRE Country Report* (November 2007) at p. 48.

50 Burma is not a party to the ICCPR or to the ICESCR. It has however acceded to the Women's Convention and the CRC.

(b) *Availability* of services, materials, facilities, and infrastructure: adequate housing includes facilities that are essential for health, security, comfort and nutrition.[51] Corruption can impact upon water supply and energy facilities, impeding the availability component of the right to adequate housing.

(c) *Affordability*[52] is directly hampered where bribes have to be paid to obtain access to housing or to land titles.

(d) *Habitability*[53] Is impaired by the embezzlement of funds in a programme for the construction of housing units or bribery in the selection of contractors, which may lead to construction works of substandard quality[54]

(e) *Accessibility*[55] can be affected by corruption, for example when bribes are demanded in order to obtain a house.[56] This is indeed especially harmful to the poorest segments of society.

(f) The component of *location*[57] may be compromised due to corruption in the process of procurement, when this leads to housing that is realised in unsafe areas.

(g) Aspects of *cultural adequacy*[58] may be ignored when corrupt motives are leading in constructing and building housing.

(h) The aspect of non-discrimination should be emphasised once more. Pursuant to Article 2(2) ICESCR, enjoyment of the right to adequate housing must not be subject to any form of discrimination.[59] As the examples in the present section have illustrated, corruption is inherently discriminatory, since the poor are discriminated against *vis-à-vis* the rich.

19. **The right to housing: State obligations and violations.**

(a) Certain steps must be taken immediately by States, irrespective of a country's level of development. Many measures only require State abstention (negative obligations) and a commitment to facilitate self-help by affected groups.[60] Furthermore, States must give priority to social groups living in unfavourable conditions.[61] Also, a general decline in

---

51 General Comment No. 4, §8(b).
52 *Ibid.* §8(c).
53 General Comment No. 4, §8(d).
54 International Council on Human Rights Policy, *Corruption and Human Rights: Making the Connection* at p. 51.
55 General Comment No. 4, §8(e).
56 International Council on Human Rights Policy, *Corruption and Human Rights: Making the Connection* at p. 51.
57 General Comment No. 4, §8(f).
58 General Comment No. 4, §8(g).
59 *Ibid.* §6 and 9.
60 *Ibid.* §10.
61 *Ibid.* §11.

living and housing conditions which can be directly attributed to a State's policy and legislative decisions, while there are no compensatory measures, would be inconsistent with the obligations under the Covenant.[62] It will vary from one State to another what will be the most appropriate means of achieving the full realisation of the right to adequate housing. However, States have to take whatever steps necessary to this end. This will almost invariably include the adoption of a national housing strategy.[63] Such a housing strategy ought to contain a strong anti-corruption component. Another obligation of immediate effect is the effective monitoring of the housing situation.[64] States can use whatever mix of public and private sector measures in order to comply with their obligations.[65] Finally, instances of forced eviction are *prima facie* incompatible with the Covenant, and can only be justified in the most exceptional circumstances, and in accordance with the relevant principles of international law.[66] Forced evictions can be motivated by the pursuit of personal profit by public officials. Such conduct violates the right to adequate housing.

(b) The minimum core obligation in respect of the right to housing entails that a State Party in which any significant number of individuals are deprived of basic shelter and housing is, *prima facie*, failing to discharge its obligations under the Covenant.[67] Beyond this core obligation, there are five levels of obligations incumbent on States regarding the right to adequate housing: the obligation to recognise, to respect, to protect, to promote and to fulfil.[68]

(c) The obligation *to recognise* the right to adequate housing consists of three key areas. First, States must recognise the human rights dimensions of housing and abstain from taking measures intended to erode the legal status of the right.[69] Second, States must take legislative measures and appropriate policies in order to realise housing rights progressively. Incompatible existing legislation or policies have to be repealed or amended.[70] Third, States must determine to what extent the right to adequate housing is already enjoyed, and the degree to which the right is not enjoyed.[71]

---

62 *Ibid.* §11.
63 *Ibid.* §12.
64 *Ibid.* §13.
65 *Ibid.* §14.
66 *Ibid.* §18.
67 General Comment No. 3, §10. On forced eviction, see Committee on Economic, Social and Cultural Rights, General Comment No. 7.
68 Report of the SR on the right to adequate housing, CHR 45th session, 22 June 2003, UN Doc. E/CN.4/Sub.2/1993/15, §61. See also: Office of the United Nations High Commissioner for Human Rights, 'Fact Sheet No. 21, the Human Right to Adequate Housing', <www.ohchr.org/Documents/Publications/FactSheet21en.pdf>, accessed 7 April 2009. This document appears to be based on the report of the Special Rapporteur and the General Comments of the CESCR. See also Ingrid Westendorp, *Women and Housing: Gender Makes a Difference* (School of Human Rights Research Series, 23; Antwerp: Intersentia, 2007) at p. 37–39 for a discussion of the four-layer typology.
69 Report of the SR on the right to adequate housing, CHR 45th session, 22 June 2003, UN Doc.E/CN.4/Sub.2/1993/15, §62.
70 *Ibid.* §63.
71 *Ibid.* §64.

(d) The obligation *to respect* stands for the negative duty upon the State to refrain from action which prevents people from exercising the right to housing themselves when they are able of doing so. Moreover, States are not allowed to forcibly evict people.[72] The obligation to respect includes the obligation to abstain from corrupt practices within the housing sector.

(e) The obligation *to protect* entails that States have to prevent violations of housing rights by third parties (e.g. landlords or property developers). Where violations do take place, the State has to act to prevent any further deprivations and assure access to legal remedies or redress to those affected. Furthermore, States have to take immediate measures to grant legal security or tenure to those who are presently not protected. In addition, States have to ensure that housing costs are reasonable and they have to establish a system of subsidies whenever housing costs threaten other basic needs.[73] Under the obligation to protect, State Parties must prevent and combat corrupt practices in the housing sector, committed by third parties.

(f) The obligation *to promote* means that States have to emphasise the relevance of the realisation of the right to adequate housing, and take measures in this respect.[74]

(g) Under the obligation *to fulfil,* States have to realise the right to housing for those who are not capable of achieving adequate housing themselves.[75] While meeting this obligation, States must make sure that relevant funds intended for housing are spent appropriately, and anti-corruption safeguards need to be put in place. Embezzlement of funds constitutes a breach of the obligation to fulfil.

20. **The right to education: content.** This right is laid down in Articles 13 and 14 ICESCR, and in Article 28 CRC. It encompasses four interrelated and essential features, the AAAA or four-A framework. In the application of these four features, the student's best interests shall be a primary consideration. State Parties have to respect, protect, and fulfil each of these features.

(a) *Availability*[76] is severely affected by corrupt practices, such as embezzlement of public funds intended for teaching materials and school buildings,[77] diversion of school textbooks and their subsequent sale at local markets.[78] The same holds true for corruption in procurement for, for example, school buildings or maintenance, or for teaching materials or

72 *Ibid.* §66–68.
73 *Ibid.* §69–72.
74 *Ibid.* §73.
75 *Ibid.* §74–79.
76 Committee on Economic, Social and Cultural Rights, General Comment No. 13 on the right to education (Art. 13), twenty-first session (1999), UN Doc. E/C.12/1999/10, §6(a).
77 U4 Anti-Corruption Resource Centre, 'Corruption in the Education Sector', *U4 Issue* (Bergen: Chr. Michelsen Institute, 2006) at p. 3; Pearson, 'An International Human Rights Approach to Corruption', at p. 57.
78 U4 Anti-Corruption Resource Centre, 'Corruption in the Education Sector', at p. 4.

school meals, resulting in substandard quality of goods and services and higher prices.[79] The outcomes of procurement can be influenced by the bribes paid to the responsible decision maker in the public sector. Although this concerns the delivery of goods and services by third parties, it is the State which has the obligation to protect against infringements of the right to education by third parties. Thus, whenever bribes are accepted or demanded by public officials in the procurement process, this violates the obligation to protect the availability feature of the right to education.[80]

(b) *Accessibility* includes the overlapping dimensions of non-discrimination, economic accessibility and physical accessibility.[81]

(ii) *Non-discrimination* is an important component of accessibility. According to the Committee, there is a *minimum core obligation* of States to ensure the most basic forms of education.[82] This includes the obligation to ensure the right of access to public educational institutions and programmes on a non-discriminatory basis.[83] Moreover, a State's failure to take measures which address *de facto* educational discrimination constitutes a violation of the right to education.[84] A large number of corrupt practices within the educational system constitute discrimination, and thus directly violate the right to education. Not taking anti-corruption measures in the education sector therefore violates the right to education. A clear example of how corruption constitutes discrimination is the practice of bribery within the public school system. Bribes can be demanded for a wide range of possible purposes such as: for admission to educational institutions; for good grades; for exam passes; and for the release of examination results. It has also been reported that children from certain communities were favoured for admission to schools, while other were subjected to extra payments. Another practice is that children have to pay for private tutoring in order to pass.[85] The demand for bribes by teachers and/or other school staff violates the principle of non-discrimination, as enshrined in Article 2(2) ICESCR because students who cannot afford these bribes are being denied access to the normal features of educational life. Discrimination takes place on the basis of property, or 'other status'.

Discrimination resulting from corrupt practices in schools has a clear gender dimension. The demand for bribes by teachers is particularly harmful to school girls in developing countries, since they might be forced to pay bribes by granting sexual favours. This is highly problematic, and contributes to the spread of HIV/AIDS. In case of pregnancy, there is also a high chance that girls will quit their education.[86] Also, whenever monetary bribes

---

79 *Ibid.* at p. 3, 5.

80 The ICHRP also argued that embezzlement in the education sector affects the availability component of the right to education. International Council on Human Rights Policy, *Corruption and Human Rights: Making the Connection* at p. 56 and 59.

81 General Comment No. 13, §6(b).

82 General Comment No. 3, §10.

83 General Comment No. 13, §57.

84 *Ibid.* §59.

85 U4 Anti-Corruption Resource Centre, 'Corruption in the Education Sector', at p. 3, 5.

86 Namawu Alhassan Alolo, *Corruption, Human Rights and Gender: An Empirical Investigation Ghana* (Working Paper Geneva: International Council on Human Rights Policy, 2007) at §78 *et*

are required to obtain school admission, parents may be more willing to pay bribes for their male children rather than for their female children, since the education of boys is still considered to be more important in certain parts of the world.[87]

(ii) *Economic accessibility*, or affordability, can overlap other dimensions of accessibility, such as non-discrimination.[88] As a result, a large number of corrupt practices identified above as a violation of the principle of non-discrimination, also constitute impediments to the economic accessibility of education. The most striking example is of course the demand for bribes, which can keep children out of school, and is contrary to the obligation of States to provide free and compulsory primary education.

(iii) *Physical accessibility* requires that education is within safe physical reach.[89] This feature may also be violated by corruption. Corruption in the procurement of school buildings can lead to distorted decision-making. Real educational needs may be neglected, resulting in the construction of school buildings at unsuited locations, far from the target population. In these cases, the opportunities for self-enrichment of public officials prevail over the actual realisation of the right to education.

(b) *Acceptability*[90] May not be present because of corruption. For instance if educational funds are embezzled, there may be no resources left to pay proper teacher salaries, and as a result, the quality of education may reach a substandard level, so that it is no longer acceptable.

(c) *Adaptability* requires that education is flexible, in order to adapt to the needs of changing societies and communities and to respond to the need of students within diverse social and cultural settings.[91]

(d) Other important principles in respect of the right to education are those of non-discrimination and equal treatment. These principles, which are immediately applicable to all aspects of education, are enshrined in Article 2(2) ICESCR.[92] States are bound to closely monitor education, including all relevant policies, institutions, programmes, spending patterns and other practices, in order to identify and take measures to redress any *de facto* discrimination.[93]

---

seq; NORDIC CONSULTING GROUP, *A Gender Analysis of Corruption – Forms, Effects and Eradication Strategies* (Study prepared for the Royal Danish Embassy in Uganda, September 2009) at p. 14; MAARIA SEPPÄNEN and PEKKA VIRTANEN, *Corruption, Poverty and Gender. With Case Studies of Nicaragua and Tanzania* (Finland Ministry for Foreign Affairs, 2008) at p. 138–139.

87 ALOLO, *Corruption, Human Rights and Gender: An Empirical Investigation Ghana*, at §81; SEPPÄNEN and VIRTANEN, *Corruption, Poverty and Gender. With Case Studies of Nicaragua and Tanzania*, at p. 132.

88 General Comment No. 13, §6(b).

89 *Ibid.* §6(b).

90 *Ibid.* §6(c).

91 *Ibid.* §6(d).

92 *Ibid.* §31.

93 *Ibid.* §37.

21. **The right to education: State obligations and violations.**

(a) The duty of progressive realisation under the ICESCR should be stressed once more, as well as the obligations of immediate effect. First, States have the obligation of non-discrimination (Article 2(2)). The right to education is violated if a State fails to take measures to address *de facto* educational discrimination.[94] Since corrupt practices may constitute such discrimination, the failure to take anti-corruption measures in education constitutes a violation of Article 13. Second, States have the immediate obligation to take deliberate, concrete and targeted steps (Article 2(1)).[95] The failure to take such steps towards the progressive realisation of secondary, higher and fundamental education in accordance with Article 13(2)(b)-(d) constitutes a violation of Article 13.[96] As elaborated upon earlier in the present chapter, retrogressive measures are presumed to be impermissible.[97] In respect of the tripartite typology of the right to education, it is clear that States have to respect, protect and fulfil each of the AAAA-features of the right to education.

(b) The obligation *to respect* obliges States to avoid measures that hinder or prevent the enjoyment of the right to education.[98] Corruption can hinder access to education, thus violating this obligation.

(c) The obligation *to protect* requires States to take measures to prevent third parties from interfering with the enjoyment of the right.[99]

(d) Under the obligation *to fulfil* (*facilitate*), States have to take positive measures to enable and assist individuals and communities to enjoy the right to education. The obligation *to fulfil* (*provide*) the right exists whenever individuals or groups are unable to realise the right themselves, for reasons beyond their control.[100] Under Article 13, States have the principal responsibility for the direct provision of education in most circumstances. However, the parameters of State obligations to fulfil (provide) are different for the respective levels of education.[101] *Inter alia*, States have the legal obligation to fulfil (provide) the availability of education, by actively developing a school system, building classrooms, delivering programmes, providing teaching materials, training teachers and paying them domestically competitive salaries.[102] However, as mentioned *supra* various corrupt practices constitute clear breaches of these obligations, violating the right to education.

(e) There is a minimum core obligation of States to ensure the most basic forms of education. Not only does this mean that States have to ensure the right of access to public education on

---

94 *Ibid.* §59.
95 *Ibid.* §43 and 52.
96 *Ibid.* §59.
97 *Ibid.* §45.
98 *Ibid.* §47.
99 *Ibid.* §47.
100 *Ibid.* §47.
101 *Ibid.* §48 and 51.
102 *Ibid.* §50.

a non-discriminatory basis, it also entails that States are obliged to provide primary education for all in accordance with Article 13(2).[103] Hence, whenever entrenched corruption leads to a State not meeting this obligation, there is a violation of the Covenant.

22. **The right to health: content.** This right is enshrined in Article 12 ICESCR, Article 24 CRC, Article 5(e)(iv) CERD, and Article 11(1)(f) CEDAW.

(a) Rather than a right to be healthy, the right to health consists of both freedoms and entitlements.[104] The concept of 'the highest attainable standard of health' takes into consideration a person's biological and socio-economic preconditions, as well as the resources available within a State. Therefore, the right to health is a right to the enjoyment of a variety of facilities, goods, services and conditions necessary for the realisation of the highest attainable standard of health.[105] Both timely and appropriate *health care* is relevant, as well as *the underlying determinants of health.*[106] When considering corruption in relation to the right to health, it is important to scrutinise not only the health care sector, but also other sectors such as water provision and the occupational and environmental health sectors.[107] Moreover, the population's participation in all health-related decision making at the community, national and international level is also important.[108]

The right to health consists of four interrelated and essential elements (also known as the 'AAAQ' framework), while the precise application of these elements will depend on the specific conditions in a State party.[109] Each element of the right to health may be impaired by corrupt practices.

(b) *Availability*[110] is impaired by corruption in various ways. Embezzlement of funds intended for health care is an obvious example. Because of this practice, less resources are available, for example, for salaries of medical staff, maintenance of hospitals, and the purchase of hospital equipment.[111] Whenever funds 'disappear' at the central level, this constitutes a breach of the obligation to devote the maximum available resources to the

---

103 *Ibid.* §57.

104 Committtee on Economic, Social and Cultural Rights, General Comment No. 14 on the right to the highest attainable standard of health (Art. 12), twenty-second session (2000), UN Doc. E/C.12/2000/4. §8.

105 *Ibid.* §9.

106 *Ibid.* §4, 11 and 12(a).

107 Brigit Toebes, 'Health Sector Corruption and Human Rights: A Case Study', in Martine Boersma and Hans Nelen (eds.), *Corruption and Human Rights: Interdisciplinary Perspectives* (Maastricht Series in Human Rights; Antwerp: Intersentia, 2010), p. 91–123 at p. 103.

108 General Comment No. 14, §11.

109 *Ibid.* §12.

110 *Ibid.* §12(a).

111 Taryn Vian, William D. Savedoff, and Harald Mathisen, 'Introduction: Closing Opportunities for Corruption in the Health Sector', in Taryn Vian, William D. Savedoff, and Harald Mathisen (eds.), *Anticorruption in the Health Sector: Strategies for Transparency and Accountability* (Sterling, VA: Kumarian Press, 2010), p. 3–15 at p. 6. Toebes also noted that corruption affects the availability element. Toebes, 'Health Sector Corruption and Human Rights: A Case Study', at p. 6.

progressive realisation of the right to health, under Article 2(1) ICESCR. If resources are embezzled at the local level, States are under an obligation to combat corruption at this level. Also hampering availability is the diversion of drug supplies.[112]

(c) *Accessibility*, requiring that health facilities, goods and services are accessible to all without discrimination, has four overlapping dimensions: non-discrimination, physical accessibility, economic accessibility (affordability), and information accessibility.[113]

(i) *Non-discrimination*[114] is in many cases is legally enforceable at the domestic level.[115] Moreover, the guarantee of non-discrimination is a State obligation of immediate effect under Article 2(2) ICESCR.[116] As acknowledged by former Special Rapporteur Paul Hunt, the poor are disproportionately affected by corruption, since they are less able to pay bribes for services that ought to be free, or to pay for private health care when corruption has depleted public health care.[117] Therefore, corruption is inconsistent with the principles of non-discrimination and equality.[118] Moreover, women are also particularly vulnerable to corruption in health care, because of their reproductive functions.[119]

(ii) *Physical accessibility*[120] is affected by corruption in the health sector, which often leads to choices that are less favourable to the community (e.g. hospitals built in a cheaper, more distant area of the city, or rather in wealthy areas).[121]

(iii) *Economic accessibility* or *affordability*[122] is often at stake. Research shows that in many instances, bribes (or informal user fees or payments) have to be paid to health workers.[123]

---

112 For more on drug diversion, and the prevention thereof, see Taryn Vian, William D. Savedoff, and Harald Mathisen, 'Preventing Drug Diversion through Supply Chain Management', in Taryn Vian, William D. Savedoff, and Harald Mathisen (eds.), *Anticorruption in the Health Sector: Strategies for Transparency and Accountability* (Sterling, VA: Kumarian Press, 2010), p. 77–84.

113 General Comment No. 14, §12(b).

114 *Ibid.* §12(b).

115 *Ibid.* §1 and endnote 1.

116 *Ibid.* §30.

117 For example see Report of the Special Rapporteur on the right to health, GA 61st session, 13 September 2006, UN Doc. A/61/338, §79.

118 Report of the Special Rapporteur on the right to health, Mission to Romania, CHR 61st session, 4 February 2005, UN Doc. E/CN.4/2005/51/Add.4, §34.

119 Toebes, 'Health Sector Corruption and Human Rights: A Case Study', at p. 106–107.

120 General Comment No. 14, §12(b).

121 Toebes, 'Health Sector Corruption and Human Rights: A Case Study', at p. 107.

122 General Comment No. 14, §12(b).

123 For more on informal payments for health services, see Ottar Maestad and Aziza Mwisongo, 'Informal Pay and the Quality of Health Care: Lessons from Tanzania', in Taryn Vian, William D. Savedoff, and Harald Mathisen (eds.), *Anticorruption in the Health Sector: Strategies for Transparency and Accountability* (Sterling, VA: Kumarian Press, 2010), p. 45–53 and Kelly Miller and Taryn Vian, 'Strategies for Reducing Informal Payments', in Taryn Vian, William D. Savedoff, and Harald Mathisen (eds.), *Anticorruption in the Health Sector: Strategies for Transparency and Accountability* (Sterling, VA: Kumarian Press, 2010), p. 55–66.

Underlying reasons for these bribes can be various: to gain access to health services which are supposed to be free of charge; to reduce waiting time; to receive drugs, treatment or hospital means; to ensure better attention and improved quality of treatment.[124] As demonstrated by the studies by the Special Rapporteur, the illicit charging of user fees hinders the economic accessibility of the right to health.[125] Demanding payments from patients for services that ought to be free impedes the affordability dimension of the right to health.[126]

(iv) *Access to information*[127] enables, according to the Special Rapporteur, individuals and communities to expose corruption.[128] Health care is prone to corruption because of the asymmetry in information: e.g. doctors *vis-à-vis* patients.[129]

(d) *Acceptability* may also be affected by corruption.[130] Because of the asymmetry of information, the health sector professional has a stronger position than the patient. This could lead to a situation in which a health professional, being influenced by a pharmaceutical company, prescribes drugs which are not ethically appropriate.[131]

(e) *Quality*[132] is often violated by corruption. Regarding the demand for bribes (informal payments) by health workers, researchers have found that this practice negatively affects the quality of health care. Amongst other things, health workers may be tempted to create artificial drug and supply shortages or queues in order to extort bribes from patients. Also, the quality of health care may be deliberately reduced by health workers (e.g. nurses), so as to induce their colleagues (e.g. doctors) to share their bribes with them.[133]

The issue of drug supply is another important topic in the discussion about corruption and the quality dimension of the right to health. The Special Rapporteur found that States have a legal obligation to ensure a reliable, efficient and transparent system for the supply of quality affordable medicines, and this supply system must avoid corruption.[134] The Rapporteur also pointed to endemic corruption in some medicine supply systems: products

124 U4 Anti-Corruption Resource Centre, 'Corruption in the Health Sector', *U4 Brief* (Bergen: Chr. Michelsen Institute, 2008) at p. 12.

125 Report of the Special Rapporteur on the right to health, mission to Mozambique, CHR 61st session, 4 January 2005, UN Doc. E/CN.4/2005/51/Add.2, §45–52.

126 Report of the Special Rapporteur on the right to health, mission to India, HRC 14th session, 15 April 2010, UN Doc. A/HRC/14/20/Add.2, §52. Toebes also discussed the impact of corruption upon affordability: Toebes, 'Health Sector Corruption and Human Rights: A Case Study', at p. 107.

127 General Comment No. 14, §12(b).

128 Report of the Special Rapporteur on the right to health, HRC 7th session, 31 January 2008, UN Doc. A/HRC/7/11, §40.

129 Toebes, 'Health Sector Corruption and Human Rights: A Case Study', at p. 108.

130 General Comment No. 14, §12(c).

131 Toebes, 'Health Sector Corruption and Human Rights: A Case Study', at p. 108.

132 General Comment No. 14, §12(d).

133 Maestad and Mwisongo, 'Informal Pay and the Quality of Health Care: Lessons from Tanzania', at p. 48–50.

134 Report of the Special Rapporteur on the right to health, GA 61st session, 13 September 2006, UN Doc. A/61/338, §68.

are diverted, 'fees' are required for customs clearance, and counterfeit medicines are permitted to circulate.[135] While diversion of drugs and the demand for fees are contrary to availability and accessibility, the problem of counterfeit or otherwise unsafe medicines clearly affects the quality dimension of the right to health. When regulators are bribed to allow these drugs to circulate, quality is impaired.[136]

(f) *Accountability:* the principles of accountability and participation are relevant in the context of anti-corruption and the right to health.[137] As regards accountability, this comprises (i) monitoring; (ii) accountability mechanisms; (iii) remedies; and (iv) participation. The concept is closely linked to the State obligation to protect the right to health.[138]

(g) *Participation*

The principle of participation requires that the public participates in the process of decision making in the health sector. This may improve transparency and reduce corruption vulnerabilities.[139]

23. **The right to health: State obligations and violations.**

(a) While States may experience difficulties in progressively realising the right to health due to limited available resources, there are various obligations of immediate effect: the principle of non-discrimination of Article 2(2) ICESCR and the obligation to take deliberate, concrete and targeted steps as required by Article 2(1) ICESCR.[140] Deliberate retrogressive measures are in general not permitted.[141]

(b) There are a number of core obligations in relation to the right to health,[142] and a number of obligations of comparable priority.[143] Non-compliance with the non-derogable core obligations cannot be justified under any circumstance whatsoever.[144] Various corrupt practices may violate precisely these core obligations. Whenever States allow corruption to flourish in public hospitals, this directly violates the right of non-discriminatory access. Amongst other things, the demand for bribes for medical services in public hospitals denies particular groups, i.e. the poor, access to treatment or to medicines. If corrupt practices

---

135 *Ibid.* §78.

136 Also noted by Toebes, 'Health Sector Corruption and Human Rights: A Case Study', at p. 109.

137 *Ibid.* at p. 106.

138 *Ibid.* at p. 109. For a further discussion of accountability in relation to health, see William D. Savedoff and Ethan Joselow, 'Budget Transparency, Civil Society and Public Expenditure Tracking Surveys', in Taryn Vian, William D. Savedoff, and Harald Mathisen (eds.), *Anticorruption in the Health Sector: Strategies for Transparency and Accountability* (Sterling, VA: Kumarian Press, 2010), p. 123–136.

139 Toebes, 'Health Sector Corruption and Human Rights: A Case Study', at p. 109–110.

140 General Comment No. 14, §30.

141 *Ibid.* §32.

142 *Ibid.* §43.

143 *Ibid.* §44.

144 *Ibid.* §47.

occur in the drug supply chain, this may be contrary to the core obligation to provide essential drugs. Likewise, corruption may run counter to the obligations of comparable priority.

(c) State Parties are under the obligation to respect, to protect and to fulfil the right to health.[145] With regard to violations of these obligations, the distinction between a State's inability or unwillingness to comply with its obligations must be kept in mind. States must prove that they are unable, instead of unwilling, to comply with their obligations under Article 12 ICESCR.[146] Violations can occur through direct action or through omission.[147]

(d) Under the obligation *to respect*, States have to refrain from interfering (in)directly with the enjoyment of the right to health.[148] Particularly relevant in the context of health sector corruption, is that States have the obligation to refrain from denying or limiting equal access for all persons (including prisoners or detainees, minorities, asylum seekers and illegal immigrants) to preventive, curative and palliative health services.[149] States violate the obligation to respect the right to health. *inter alia*, by denying access to health facilities, goods and services to certain individuals or groups as a result of *de jure* or *de facto* discrimination.[150] Since the demand for bribes in the public health care systems is a form of unjustified discrimination in the access to health services, this form of corruption constitutes a violation of the obligation to respect the right to health. Furthermore, States should abstain from marketing unsafe drugs.[151] As shown above, corruption can have this effect. As elaborated upon in the reports of the Special Rapporteur on the right to health, corrupt acts can result in the entering onto the market of unsafe or counterfeit medicines. Whenever this occurs due to corrupt public officials, this violates the obligation to respect the right to health. There are many more possible examples of corruption violating the obligation to respect the right to health,[152] and corrupt acts leading to a denial of the underlying determinants of health are also prohibited.

(e) The obligation *to protect* the right to health entails that States have to take measures to prevent third parties from interfering with the guarantees of Article 12.[153] Violations of this obligation occur whenever States fail to take all necessary measures to safeguard persons within their jurisdiction from infringements of the right to health by third parties.[154] The

145 *Ibid.* §33–37.
146 *Ibid.* §47.
147 *Ibid.* §48–49.
148 *Ibid.* §33, 34.
149 *Ibid.* §34.
150 *Ibid.* §50.
151 *Ibid.* §34.
152 For a useful overview, see TOEBES, 'Health Sector Corruption and Human Rights: A Case Study', at p. 111.
153 General Comment No. 14, §33.
154 General Comment No. 14, §51. Examples of violations of the obligation to protect are the failure (i) to protect consumers and workers from practices detrimental to health, e.g. by employers and manufacturers of medicines or food; (ii) to discourage production, marketing and consumption of tobacco, narcotics and other harmful substances; (iii) to protect women against violence or to

obligation to protect obliges States, amongst other things, to adopt legislation or take other measures to ensure equal access to health care and health-related services provided by third parties.[155] The failure to do so constitutes a violation.[156] This encompasses the obligation for States to adopt legislation which criminalises corruption, including corruption in health care provided by non-State actors.

Another duty falling under the obligation to protect is the obligation to control the marketing of medical equipment and medicines by third parties.[157] Whenever third parties are *de facto* allowed to market unsafe drugs (e.g. in exchange for bribes to the responsible public officials), this obligation is violated.

Furthermore, States have to ensure that medical practitioners and other health professionals meet appropriate standards of education, skill and ethical codes of conduct.[158] It is obvious that health professionals do not act in accordance with medical ethical standards whenever they demand bribes from their patients. States ought to combat the demand for bribes by medical staff through legal and practical means. For example, the belief is regularly expressed that very low salaries in the health care sector bring about the necessity for medical staff to demand bribes.[159] Thus, in order to combat bribery, States ought to ensure adequate remuneration to those working in the medical profession.

Moreover, the obligation to protect the right to health is violated when States fail to enact or enforce laws to prevent the pollution of water, air and soil by extractive and manufacturing industries.[160] Pollution by extractive industries can be the result of the lax enforcement of environmental regulations, which can have its roots in the bribery of public officials by corporations. In return for personal gain, public officials can turn a blind eye to pollution. Access to safe and potable water and a healthy environment are the underlying determinants of health, upon which pollution can have an impact. Whenever public officials practically allow third parties to pollute because of bribery, this constitutes a violation of the obligation to protect the right to health. The obligation to protect obliges States to regulate, to monitor, to provide for accountability mechanisms, to provide for remedies, and to enable the public to participate.[161]

(f) The obligation *to fulfil* requires States to recognise the right to health in the national political and legal systems, preferably by way of legislative implementation, and to adopt a national health policy with a detailed plan for realising the right to health.[162] This also includes an anti-corruption policy.[163] Furthermore, States have a wide range of duties in

---

prosecute perpetrators; (iv) to discourage the continued observance of harmful traditional or cultural practices; (v) to enact or enforce laws to prevent the pollution of water, air and soil by extractive and manufacturing industries.

155 General Comment No. 14, §35.

156 *Ibid.* §51.

157 *Ibid.* §35.

158 *Ibid.* §35.

159 U4 Anti-Corruption Resource Centre, 'Corruption in the Health Sector', at p. 27. For further discussion of the role of salaries in relation to corruption, see Chapter 7 of this report.

160 General Comment No. 14, §51.

161 Toebes, 'Health Sector Corruption and Human Rights: A Case Study', at p. 112.

162 General Comment No. 14, §36.

163 Toebes, 'Health Sector Corruption and Human Rights: A Case Study', at p. 114.

respect of the obligation to fulfil.[164] Whenever States fail to take all necessary steps to ensure the realisation of the right to health, the obligation to fulfil is violated.[165]

Furthermore, there is a distinction between the obligation to facilitate, to provide, and to promote. Under the obligation to fulfil (*facilitate*), States have to take positive measures to enable and assist individuals and communities to enjoy the right to health. They also have to fulfil (*provide*) a specific economic, social or cultural right whenever individuals or groups are themselves, for reasons beyond their control, unable to realise this by the means at their disposal. Under the obligation to fulfil (*promote*), States have to take actions that create, maintain and restore the health of the population. This includes (i) fostering recognition of factors that favour positive health results, such as research and information provision; (ii) ensuring that health services are culturally appropriate and that health care staff are trained to recognise and respond to the specific needs of vulnerable or marginalised groups; (iii) ensuring that the State meets its obligations in the supply of appropriate information relating to healthy lifestyles and nutrition, harmful traditional practices and the availability of services; and (iv) supporting people in making informed choices about their health.[166]

Violations of the obligation to fulfil occur, *inter alia*, whenever States fail to have insufficient health expenditure or misallocation of public resources which results in the non-enjoyment of the right to health by individuals or groups, particularly the marginalised.[167] Hence, embezzlement of financial or other resources intended for the realisation of the right to health (health budgets; medical supplies) clearly constitutes a violation of the right to health.

24. To conclude, the Committees again emphasise that States should pay appropriate attention to the linkages between corruption and human rights, and urge them to adopt preventive measures, to ratify anti-corruption treaties, to establish domestic anti-corruption legislation and to prosecute those responsible. These obligations are inherently part of State obligations under the ICCPR and the ICESCR, and therefore periodic State reports should, as a general rule, deal with these matters.

164 General Comment No. 14, §36.
165 *Ibid.* §52.
166 *Ibid.* §37.
167 *Ibid.* §52.

Bibliography

Acheampong, Kenneth Asamoa, 'Combating Grand Corruption: The Potential Impact of a United Nations Convention on the Prevention and Punishment of the Crime of Economic Genocide', *Revue Africaine des Droits de l'Homme,* 7 (1998), p. 38–55.

Acquaah-Gaisie, Gerald, 'Curbing Financial Crime among Third World Elites', *Journal of Money Laundering Control,* 8 (2005), p. 371–381.

Acquaah-Gaisie, Gerald, 'Grand Corruption – a Crime against Humanity', *The Global Business and Technology Association International Conference* (Lisbon, 2005).

African Commission on Human and Peoples' Rights, Decisions on Individual Communications, <www.achpr.org/english/_info/List_Decision_Communications.html>.

African Union, Ratification Status of the African Charter on Human and Peoples' Rights, <www.achpr.org/english/ratifications/ratification_african%20charter.pdf>.

Aidt, Toke S., 'Corruption, Institutions and Economic Development', *Oxford Review of Economic Policy,* 25 (2009), p. 271–291.

Akre, Jennifer L., 'Overcoming Chad's Oil Curse: The African Union Convention on Preventing and Combating Corruption as a Framework for Securing Foreign Investments', <http://works.bepress.com/cgi/viewcontent.cgi?article=1000&context=jennifer_akre>, accessed 10 November 2008.

Alatas, Syed Hussein, *Corruption: Its Nature, Causes and Functions* (Aldershot; Brookfield, Vt., USA: Avebury, 1990).

Alolo, Namawu Alhassan, *Corruption, Human Rights and Gender: An Empirical Investigation Ghana* (Working Paper Geneva: International Council on Human Rights Policy, 2007).

Alston, Philip, 'Conjuring up New Human Rights: A Proposal for Quality Control', *American Journal of International Law,* 78 (1984), p. 607–621.

Alston, Philip and Crawford, James (eds.), *The Future of UN Human Rights Treaty Monitoring* (Cambridge: Cambridge University Press, 2000).

Altamirano, Giorleny D., 'The Impact of the Inter-American Convention against Corruption', *The University of Miami Inter-American Law Review,* 38 (2007), p. 487–547.

Ambos, Kai, 'Critical Issues in the Bemba Confirmation Decision', *Leiden Journal of International Law,* 22 (2009), p. 715–726.

Amundsen, Inge, 'Political Corruption: An Introduction to the Issues', *Working Paper, 1999:7* (Bergen: Chr. Michelsen Institute, 1999).

Amundsen, Inge, 'Political Corruption', *U4 Issue, 6:2006* (Bergen: Chr. Michelsen Institute, 2006).

Andvig, Jens Chr. *et al.*, 'Research on Corruption. A Policy Oriented Survey', (Bergen/Oslo: Chr. Michelsen Institute (CMI) & Norwegian Institute of International Affairs (NUPI), 2000).

ANDVIG, JENS CHR., *et al.*, 'Corruption: A Review of Contemporary Research', *CMI Report, R 2001:7* (Bergen: Chr. Michelsen Institute 2001).

ANGELES, LUIS and NEANIDIS, KYRIAKOS C., 'Colonialism, Elite Formation and Corruption', *Discussion Paper Series no. 144* (Centre for Growth & Business Cycle – University of Manchester, June 2010).

ASIAN DEVELOPMENT BANK, 'Poverty in the Philippines: Income, Assets, and Access', (2005).

AYINE, DOMINIC, RUENGER, MECHTILD, and BATIDAM, DANIEL, 'Computerised Courts Reduce Delays in Ghana', in Transparency International (ed.), *Global Corruption Report 2007: Corruption in Judicial Systems* (Cambridge: Cambridge University Press, 2007), p. 208–210.

BACIO TERRACINO, JULIO, 'Hard Law Connections between Corruption and Human Rights', *Working Paper* (Geneva: International Council on Human Rights Policy, 2007).

BACIO TERRACINO, JULIO, 'Corruption as a Violation of Human Rights', *Working paper* (Geneva: International Council on Human Rights Policy, 2008).

BADAR, MOHAMED ELEWA, 'Dolus Eventualis and the Rome Statute without It?' *New Criminal Law Review,* 12 (2009), p. 433–467.

BAGHAT, HOSSAM, 'Egypt's Judiciary Flexes Its Muscles', in Transparency International (ed.), *Global Corruption Report 2007: Corruption in Judicial Systems* (Cambridge: Cambridge University Press, 2007), p. 201–204.

BAKER HUGHES, <www.aboutus.org/BakerHughes.com>, accessed 24 May 2011.

BALLENTINE, KAREN, 'Beyond Greed and Grievance: Reconsidering the Economic Dynamics of Armed Conflict', in Karen Ballentine and Jake Sherman (eds.), *The Political Economy of Armed Conflict: Beyond Greed and Grievance* (A Project of the International Peace Academy; Boulder: Lynne Rienner Publishers, 2003), p. 259–283.

BALLENTINE, KAREN and NITZSCHKE, HEIKO, 'Introduction', in Karen Ballentine and Heiko Nitzschke (eds.), *Profiting from Peace: Managing the Resource Dimension of Civil War* (Boulder: Lynne Rienner Publishers 2005), p. 1–24.

BALLENTINE, KAREN and SHERMAN, JAKE, 'Introduction', in Karen Ballentine and Jake Sherman (eds.), *The Political Economy of Armed Conflict: Beyond Greed and Grievance* (A Project of the International Peace Academy; Boulder: Lynne Rienner Publishers, 2003), p. 1–15.

BANTEKAS, ILIAS, 'Corruption as an International Crime and a Crime against Humanity: An Outline of Supplementary Criminal Justice Policies', *Journal of International Criminal Justice,* 4 (2006), p. 466–484.

BANTON, MICHAEL, 'Decision-Taking in the Committee on the Elimination of Racial Discrimination', in Philip Alston and James Crawford (eds.), *The Future of UN Human Rights Treaty Monitoring* (Cambridge: Cambridge University Press, 2000), p. 55–78.

BANTEKAS, ILIAS and NASH, SUSAN, *International Criminal Law* (3rd edn.; London/New York: Routledge-Cavendish, 2007).

BARTH EIDE, WENCHE and KRACHT, UWE, 'The Right to Adequate Food in Human Rights Instruments: Legal Norms and Interpretations', in Wenche Barth Eide (ed.), *Food and Human Rights in Development (Volume I): Legal and Institutional Dimensions and Selected Topics.* (Antwerp: Intersentia, 2005), p. 99–118.

Bassiouni, M. Cherif, *The Statute of the International Criminal Court: a Documentary History* (Ardsley, New York: Transnational Publishers, 1998).

Bassiouni, M. Cherif, 'The Draft Code of Crimes Against the Peace and Security of Mankind', in M.Cherif Bassiouni (ed.), *International Criminal Law: Crimes* (2nd edn., I; Ardsley, New York: Transnational Publishers, 1999), p. 293–310.

Bassiouni, M. Cherif, 'Historical Survey: 1919–1998', in M. Cherif Bassiouni (ed.), *International criminal law: enforcement* (2nd edn., III; Ardsley, New York: Transnational Publishers, 1999), p. 597–635.

Bassiouni, M. Cherif, 'The Sources and Content of International Criminal Law: a Theoretical Framework', in M. Cherif Bassiouni (ed.), *International Criminal Law: Crimes* (2nd edn., I; Ardsley, New York: Transnational Publishers, 1999), p. 3–125.

Bassiouni, M. Cherif 'International Criminal Investigations and Prosecutions: from Versailles to Rwanda', in M.Cherif Bassiouni (ed.), *International Criminal Law: Enforcement* (2nd edn., III; Ardsley, New York: Transnational Publishers, 1999), p. 31–86.

Bassiouni, M. Cherif (ed.), *International Criminal Law: Enforcement* (2nd edn., III; Ardsley, New York: Transnational Publishers, 1999).

Bassiouni, M. Cherif, 'World War I: "the War to End All Wars" and the Birth of a Handicapped International Criminal Justice System', *Denver Journal of International Law and Policy,* 30 (2002), p. 244–291.

Bassiouni, M. Cherif, *Introduction to International Criminal Law*, ed. M. Cherif Bassiouni (International and Comparative Criminal Law Series; Ardsley, New York: Transnational Publishers, 2003).

Bassiouni, M. Cherif, 'Historical Survey: 1919–1998', in M. Cherif Bassiouni (ed.), *International criminal law: enforcement* (2nd edn., III; Ardsley, New York: Transnational Publishers, 1999), p. 597–635.

Bassiouni, M. Cherif, 'Crimes against Humanity', in M. Cherif Bassiouni (ed.), *International Criminal Law* (3rd edn., Volume I: Sources, Subjects and Contents, Leiden: Martinus Nijhoff Publishers, 2008), p. 437–492.

Bayefsky, Anne F. (ed.), *The UN Human Rights Treaty System in the 21st Century* (The Hague: Kluwer Law International, 2000).

Bayefsky, Anne F., *The UN Human Rights Treaty System: Universality at the Crossroads* (Ardsley, NY: Transnational Publishers, 2001).

Bayley, David H., 'The Effects of Corruption in a Developing Nation', in Arnold J. Heidenheimer, Michael Johnston, and Victor T. LeVine (eds.), *Political Corruption: A Handbook* (New Brunswick: Transaction, 1989), p. 935–952.

BBC News Online, 'Monsanto Fined $1.5m for Bribery', <http://news.bbc.co.uk/2/hi/business/4153635.stm>, accessed 8 January 2009.

BBC News, 'Fujimori Sentenced for Corruption', <http://news.bbc.co.uk/2/hi/americas/8283844.stm>, accessed 1 August 2011.

Beccaria, C., *On Crimes and Punishments and Other Writings* (translated by Richard Bellamy) (Cambridge: Cambridge University Press 1995).

Berkman, Steve, *The World Bank and the Gods of Lending* (Sterling, VA: Kumarian Press, 2008).

BIERZANEK, REMIGIUSZ, 'War Crimes: History and Definition', in M. Cherif Bassiouni (ed.), *International Criminal Law: Enforcement* (2nd edn., III; Ardsley, New York: Transnational Publishers, 1999), p. 87–108.

BILLON, PHILIPPE LE, 'Buying Peace or Fuelling War: The Role of Corruption in Armed Conflicts', *Journal of International Development,* 15 (2003), p. 413–426.

BLUNDO, GEORGIO and OLIVIER DE SARDAN, J.P. (eds.), *Everyday Corruption and the State. Citizens and Public Officials in Africa* (Cape Town: David Philip, 2006).

BOEREFIJN, INEKE, *The Reporting Procedure under the Covenant on Civil and Political Rights: Practice and Procedure of the Human Rights Committee* (School of Human Rights Research Series, 2; Antwerp: Intersentia, 1999).

BOERSMA, MARTINE and NELEN, HANS (eds.), *Corruption & Human Rights: Interdisciplinary Perspectives* (Maastricht Series in Human Rights Antwerp: Intersentia, 2010).

BOERSMA, MARTINE, 'The Impact of Corruption Upon Women's Rights: A Neglected Area?' in: Ingrid Westendorp (ed.), *The Women's Convention Turned 30: Achievements, Setbacks and Prospects* (Antwerp: Intersentia, forthcoming).

BOISTER, NEIL, ''Transnational Criminal Law'?' *European Journal of International Law,* 14 (2003), p. 953–976.

BONUCCI, NICOLA, 'Article 12. Monitoring and Follow-Up', in Mark Pieth, Lucinda A. Low, and Peter J. Cullen (eds.), *The OECD Convention on Bribery: A Commentary* (Cambridge: Cambridge University Press, 2007), p. 445–475.

BOOT, MACHTELD and revised by CHRISTOPHER K. HALL, 'Article 7: Crimes against Humanity (K); "Other Inhumane Acts", in Otto Triffterer (ed.), *Commentary on the Rome Statute of the International Criminal Court. Observers' Notes, Article by Article* (2nd edn.; München: C.H. Beck, 2008), p. 230–234.

BRATTON, MICHAEL, 'Vote Buying and Violence in Nigerian Election Campaigns', *Electoral Studies,* 27 (2008), p. 621–632.

BRETT, RACHEL, 'State Reporting: An NGO Perspective', in Anne F. Bayefsky (ed.), *The UN Human Rights Treaty System in the 21st Century* (The Hague: Kluwer Law International, 2000), p. 57–62.

BRIBE PAYERS INDEX 2008, <www.transparency.org/policy_research/surveys_indices/bpi/bpi_2008>, accessed 18 May 2011.

BROWN, A.J., 'What Are We Trying to Measure? Reviewing the Basics of Corruption Definition', in Charles Sampford, *et al.* (eds.), *Measuring Corruption* (Aldershot: Ashgate, 2006), p. 57–79.

BROWN, BARTRAM S., 'The International Criminal Tribunal for the Former Yugoslavia', in M. Cherif Bassiouni (ed.), *International criminal law: enforcement* (2nd edn., III; Ardsley, New York: Transnational Publishers, 1999), p. 489–518.

BRUCH, GREGORY S. and ADKINS, AKITA N., 'Article 8. Accounting', in Mark Pieth, Lucinda A. Low, and Peter J. Cullen (eds.), *The OECD Convention on Bribery: A Commentary* (Cambridge: Cambridge University Press, 2007), p. 377–405.

BUCKLEY, MARELLA, 'Anti-Corruption Initiatives and Human Rights: The Potentials', in Hans-Otto Sano and Gudmundur Alfredsson (eds.), *Human Rights and Good Governance. Building Bridges* (The Raoul Wallenberg Institute Human Rights Library, 9; The Hague: Kluwer Law International, 2002), p. 173–201.

BUITENEN, PAUL VAN, *Strijd Voor Europa* (Baarn: Ten Have, 1999).

Burchill, Richard, 'Equality and Non-Discrimination', in Alex Conte and Richard Burchill (eds.), *Defining Civil and Political Rights: The Jurisprudence of the United Nations Human Rights Committee* (2nd edn.; Surrey: Ashgate, 2009).

Bustelo, Mara R., 'The Committee on the Elimination of Discrimination against Women at the Crossroads', in Philip Alston and James Crawford (eds.), *The Future of UN Human Rights Treaty Monitoring* (Cambridge: Cambridge University Press, 2000), p. 79–111.

Byrnes, Andrew, 'An Effective Complaints Procedure in the Context of International Human Rights Law', in Anne F. Bayefsky (ed.), *The UN Human Rights Treaty System in the 21st Century* (The Hague: Kluwer Law International, 2000), p. 139–162.

Campos, J. Edgardo, Lien, Donald, and Pradhan, Sanjay, 'The Impact of Corruption on Investment: Predictability Matters', *World Development,* 27 (1999), p. 1059–1067.

Carbonell, Miguel, 'Judicial Corruption and Impunity in Mexico', in Transparency International (ed.), *Global Corruption Report 2007: Corruption in Judicial Systems* (Cambridge: Cambridge University Press, 2007), p. 225–228.

Carlberg, Christopher K., 'A Truly Level Playing Field for International Business: Improving the OECD Convention on Combating Bribery Using Clear Standards', *Boston College International and Comparative Law Review,* 26 (2003), p. 95–112.

Carr, Indira, 'The United Nations Convention on Corruption: Making a Real Difference to the Quality of Life of Millions?' *Manchester Journal of International Economic Law,* 3 (2006), p. 3–44.

Carr, Indira, 'Corruption in Africa: Is the African Union Convention on Combating Corruption the Answer?' *Journal of Business Law,* March (2007), p. 111–136.

Carranza, Ruben, 'Plunder and Pain: Should Transitional Justice Engage with Corruption and Economic Crimes?' *The International Journal of Transitional Justice,* 2 (2008), p. 310–330.

Cassese, Antonio, 'Reflections on International Criminal Justice', *Modern Law Review,* 61 (1998), p. 1–10.

Cassese, Antonio, 'The Rationale for International Criminal Justice', in Antonio Cassese (ed.), *The Oxford Companion to International Criminal Justice* (Oxford: Oxford University Press, 2009), p. 123–130.

Čengić, Amir, 'Akayesu', in Antonio Cassese (ed.), *The Oxford Companion to International Criminal Justice* (Oxford: Oxford University Press, 2009), p. 577–580.

Centre on Housing Rights and Evictions (COHRE), 'Displacement and Dispossession: Forced Migration and Land Rights in Burma', *COHRE Country Report* (November 2007).

Chaikin, David, 'Extraterritoriality and the Criminalization of Foreign Bribes', in Barry Rider (ed.), *Corruption: The Enemy Within* (The Hague/London/Boston: Kluwer Law International 1997), p. 285–301.

Chapman, Audrey R., 'A "Violations Approach" For Monitoring the International Covenant on Economic, Social and Cultural Rights', *Human Rights Quarterly,* 18 (1996), p. 23–66.

Chapman, Audrey R. and Russell, Sage (eds.), *Core Obligations: Building a Framework for Economic, Social and Cultural Rights* (Antwerp: Intersentia, 2002).

Chapman, Audrey R., 'Core Obligations Related to the Right to Health', in Audrey R. Chapman and Sage Russell (eds.), *Core Obligations: Building a Framework for Economic, Social and Cultural Rights* (Antwerp: Intersentia, 2002), p. 185–215.

Chapman, Audrey R., 'The Status of Efforts to Monitor Economic, Social and Cultural Rights', in Shareen Hertel and Lanse Minkler (eds.), *Economic Rights: Conceptual, Measurement and Policy Issues* (Cambridge University Press, 2007), p. 143–164.

Cherian Huskins, Priya, 'FCPA Prosecutions: Liability Trend to Watch', *Stanford Law Review,* 60 (2008), p. 1447–1457.

Cheriyan, George, 'Enforcing the Right to Food in India: Bottlenecks in Delivering the Expected Outcome', *UNI-WIDER Research Paper No. 2006/132,* (November 2006).

Chesterman, Simon, 'An Altogether Different Order: Defining the Elements of Crimes against Humanity', *Duke Journal of Comparative and International Law,* 10 (2000), p. 307–343.

Chetwynd, Eric, Chetwynd, Frances, and Spector, Bertram 'Corruption and Poverty: A Review of Recent Literature', (Washington, DC: Management Systems International, January 2003).

Chikalanga, Davies, Lungu, Goodwell, and Yezi, Ngoza, 'Zambian Judiciary Struggles to Modernise', in Transparency International (ed.), *Global Corruption Report 2007: Corruption in Judicial Systems* (Cambridge: Cambridge University Press, 2007), 287–290.

Chun, Liu, 'The Control of Corruption and Protection of Human Rights', in Errol P. Mendes and Anik Lalonde-Roussy (eds.), *Bridging the Global Divide on Human Rights: A Canada-China Dialogue* (Aldershot: Ashgate, 2003), p. 305–327.

Clapham, Andrew, 'Defining the Role of Non-Governmental Organizations with Regard to the UN Human Rights Treaty Bodies', in: Anne F. Bayefsky (ed.), *The UN Human Rights Treaty System in the 21st Century* (The Hague: Kluwer Law International, 2000), p. 183–194.

CNN, 'Mubarak Trial to Open Next Week, Egypt Says', <http://edition.cnn.com/2011/WORLD/meast/07/28/egypt.mubarak/>, accessed 29 July 2011.

Cockroft, Laurence, 'Corruption and Human Rights: A Crucial Link', *Working Paper* (Berlin: Transparency International, 19 October 1998).

Cockroft, Laurence, 'Implementation of the OECD Convention: The Conditions for Success', *Seminar Corruption and Bribery in Foreign Business Transactions: New Global and Canadian Standards* (Vancouver, Canada 4–5 February 1999).

Commission on the Responsibility of the Authors of the War and on Enforcement of Penalties, 'Report Presented to the Preliminary Peace Conference, March 29, 1919', *American Journal of International Law,* 14 (1920), p. 95–154.

Commonwealth Secretariat & Chatham House, 'Anti-Corruption Conference: The UN Convention against Corruption. Implementation and Enforcement: Meeting the Challenges', (Chatham House, London, 24–25 April 2006).

Conference, 'The Experts Roundtable: A Hemispheric Approach to Combating Corruption', *American University International Law Review,* 15 (2000), p. 768–780.

Coomans, Fons, 'Schendingen van Economische, Sociale en Culturele Rechten', in Fons Coomans, A.W. Heringa, and Ingrid Westendorp (eds.), *De Toenemende Betekenis van Economische, Sociale en Culturele Mensenrechten* (Leiden: Stichting NJCM-Boekerij, 1994), p. 59–73.

Coomans, Fons, 'In Search of the Core Content of the Right to Education', in Audrey R. Chapman and Sage Russell (eds.), *Core Obligations: Building a Framework for Economic, Social and Cultural Rights* (Antwerp: Intersentia, 2002), p. 217–246.

Coomans, Fons (ed.), *Justiciability of Economic and Social Rights. Experiences from Domestic Systems* (Maastricht Series in Human Rights, Antwerp: Intersentia, 2006).

Coomans, Fons, Grünfeld, Fred, and Kamminga, Menno T., 'A Primer', in Fons Coomans, Fred Grünfeld, and Menno Kamminga (eds.), *Methods of Human Rights Research* (Maastricht Series in Human Rights; Antwerp: Intersentia, 2009), p. 11–17.

Corr, Christopher F. and Lawler, Judd, 'Damned If You Do, Damned If You Don't? The OECD Convention and the Globalization of Anti-Bribery Measures.' *Vanderbilt Journal of Transnational Law,* 32 (1999), p. 1249–1344.

Corruption Perceptions Index 2011, <http://cpi.transparency.org/cpi2011/result>, accessed 10 December 2011.

Côté, Luc, 'Special Court for Sierra Leone', in Antonio Cassese (ed.), *The Oxford Companion to International Criminal Justice* (Oxford: Oxford University Press, 2009), p. 515–517.

Council of Europe, Additional Protocol to the Criminal Law Convention on Corruption – Signatures and Ratifications, <http://conventions.coe.int/Treaty/Commun/ChercheSig.asp?NT=191&CM=1&DF=6/4/2008&CL=ENG>, accessed 7 October 2008.

Council of Europe, Civil Law Convention on Corruption – Signatures and Ratifications, <http://conventions.coe.int/Treaty/Commun/ChercheSig.asp?NT=174&CM=7&DF=10/7/2008&CL=ENG>, accessed 24 May 2011.

Council of Europe, Criminal Law Convention on Corruption – Signatures and Ratifications, <http://conventions.coe.int/Treaty/Commun/ChercheSig.asp?NT=173&CM=7&DF=10/7/2008&CL=ENG>, accessed 24 May 2011.

Cragg, Wesley and Woof, William, 'The US Foreign Corrupt Practices Act: A Study of Its Effectiveness', *Business and Society Review,* 107 (2002), p. 98–144.

Cremer, Georg, *Corruption and Development Aid: Confronting the Challenges* (Freiburg: Lambertus Verlag, 2008).

Crutchfield George, Barbara and Lacey, Kathleen A., 'A Coalition of Industrialized Nations, Developing Nations, Multilateral Development Banks, and Non-Governmental Organizations: A Pivotal Complement to Current Anti-Corruption Initiatives', *Cornell International Law Journal,* 33 (2000), p. 547–592.

Crutchfield George, Barbara, Lacey, Kathleen A., and Birmele, Jutta, 'On the Treshold of the Adoption of Global Antibribery Legislation: A Critical Analysis of Current Domestic and International Efforts toward the Reduction of Business Corruption', *Vanderbilt Journal of Transnational Law,* 32 (1999), p. 1–48.

Cryer, Robert, *Prosecuting International Crimes: Selectivity and the International Criminal Law Regime* (Cambridge: Cambridge University Press, 2005).

Cryer, Robert, *et al., An Introduction to International Criminal Law and Procedure* (Cambridge: Cambridge University Press, 2007).

CRYER, ROBERT, 'The Doctrinal Foundations of International Criminalization', in M. Cherif Bassiouni (ed.), *International Criminal Law: Sources, Subjects, and Contents* (3rd edn., I; Leiden: Martinus Nijhoff, 2008), p. 107–128.

CRYER, ROBERT, 'Elements of Crimes', in Antonio Cassese (ed.), *The Oxford Companion to International Criminal Justice* (Oxford: Oxford University Press, 2009), p. 308–309.

CSONKA, PETER, 'Corruption: The Council of Europe's Approach', in Barry Rider (ed.), *Corruption: The Enemy Within* (The Hague – London – Boston: Kluwer Law International, 1997), p. 343–353.

CULLEN, PETER J., 'Article 3. Sanctions', in Mark Pieth, Lucinda A. Low, and Peter J. Cullen (eds.), *The OECD Convention on Bribery: A Commentary* (Cambridge: Cambridge University Press, 2007), p. 207–266.

DANDAN, VIRGINIA, 'The Committee on Economic, Social and Cultural Rights and Non-Governmental Organizations', in Anne F. Bayefsky (ed.), *The UN Human Rights Treaty System in the 21st Century* (The Hague: Kluwer Law International, 2000), p. 227–230.

DAVIDSSON, ELIAS, 'Economic Oppression as an International Wrong or as a Crime against Humanity', *Netherlands Quarterly of Human Rights,* 23 (2005), p. 173–212.

DELL, GILLIAN, 'Anti-Corruption Conventions in the Americas. What Civil Society Can Do to Make Them Work', (Berlin: Transparency International 2006).

DELMAS-MARTY, MIREILLE, 'The European Union and Penal Law', *European Law Journal* 4(1998), p. 87–115.

DEMING, STUART H., *The Foreign Corrupt Practices Act and the New International Norms* (International Practitioner's Deskbook Series; Chicago: Section of International Law and Practice, American Bar Association, 2005).

DESAI, ASHOK H. and MURALIDHAR, S., 'Public Interest Litigation: Potential and Problem', in B.N. Kirpal (ed.), *Supreme but Not Infallible: Essays in Honour of the Supreme Court of India* (New Delhi: Oxford University Press, 2000), p. 159.

DIJK, JAN VAN, *The World of Crime. Breaking the Silence on Problems of Security, Justice and Development across the World* (Thousand Oaks, CA: Sage, 2008).

DINSTEIN, YORAM, 'Crimes against Humanity after Tadić', *Leiden Journal of International Law,* 13 (2000), p. 373–393.

DIXON, MARTIN, *Textbook on International Law* (6th edn.; Oxford: Oxford University Press, 2007).

DIXON, RODNEY and REVISED BY CHRISTOPHER K. HALL, 'Article 7: Crimes against Humanity', in Otto Triffterer (ed.), *Commentary on the Rome Statute of the International Criminal Court. Observers' Notes, Article by Article* (2nd edn.; München: C.H. Beck, 2008), p. 168–183.

DOWELL-JONES, MARY *Contextualising the International Covenant on Economic, Social and Cultural Rights: Assessing the Economic Deficit* (International Studies in Human Rights, 80; Leiden Martinus Nijhoff Publishers, 2004).

DRESLER, CAROLYN and MARKS, STEPHEN P., 'The Emerging Human Right to Tobacco Control', *Human Rights Quarterly,* 28 (2006), p. 599–651.

DRUMBL, MARK A., *Atrocity, punishment and international law* (Cambridge: Cambridge University Press, 2007).

DUFF, ANTONY, 'Legal Punishment', *Stanford Encyclopedia of Philosophy* (Stanford, 2008).

Duff, R.A. and Garland, David, 'Introduction: Thinking About Punishment', in R.A. Duff and David Garland (eds.), *A Reader on Punishment* (Oxford: Oxford University Press, 1994), p. 1–43.

Durojaye, Ebenezer, 'Corruption as a Threat to Human Security in Africa', in Ademola Abass (ed.), *Protecting Human Security in Africa* (Oxford: Oxford University Press, 2010), p. 217–243.

D66, 'D66 Pleit voor Financieel Strafhof in Den Haag', 21 April 2012, <http://site.d66.nl/d66nl/nieuws/20120421/d66_pleit_voor_financieel_strafhof> accessed 3 July 2012.

Earle, Beverly, 'The United States' Foreign Corrupt Practices Act and the OECD Anti-Bribery Recommendation: When Moral Suasion Won't Work, Try the Money Argument', *Dickinson Journal of International Law,* 14 (1996), p. 207–242.

Eboe-Osuji, Chile, 'Kleptocracy: A Desired Subject of International Criminal Law That Is in Dire Need of Prosecution by Universal Jurisdiction', in Evelyn A. Ankumah and Edward K. Kwakwa (eds.), *African Perspectives on International Criminal Justice* (Special Series, 3; Accra-Maastricht-Pretoria: Africa Legal Aid, 2005), p. 121–132.

ECOWAS Community Court of Justice, <www.courtecowas.org>, accessed 2 August 2011.

Effeh, Ubong E., 'Sub-Saharan Africa: A Case Study on How Not to Realize Economic, Social and Cultural Rights, and a Proposal for Change', *Northwestern Journal of International Human Rights,* 3 (2005).

Eigen, Peter, 'Corruption in a Globalized World', *SAIS Review,* 22 (2002), p. 45–59.

Elliott, Kimberley Ann, 'Corruption as an International Policy Problem: Overview and Recommendations', in Kimberley Ann Elliott (ed.), *Corruption and the Global Economy* (Washington, D.C.: Institute for International Economics, 1997), p. 175–233.

Environmental Science and Policy Workshop, 'Corruption & the Environment. A Project for Transparency International', (Columbia University, School of International and Public Affairs, April 2006).

Ernst & Young, *European Fraud Survey 2011: Recovery, Regulation and Integrity* (2011).

Ernst & Young, 'Corruption or Compliance – Weighing the Costs: 10th Global Fraud Survey', (2008).

European Court of Human Rights, HUDOC Database <www.echr.coe.int/ECHR/EN/Header/Case-Law/Hudoc/Hudoc+database/>.

Evans Webster, Mary, 'Fifteen Minutes of Shame: The Growing Notoriety of Grand Corruption', *Hastings International and Comparative Law Review,* 31 (2008), p. 807–826.

Faúndez Ledesma, Héctor, 'The Right to Food in the Inter-American System', in Marco Borghi and Letizia Postiglione Blommestein (eds.), *The Right to Adequate Food and Access to Justice* (Collection Interdisciplinaire, 31; Brussels: Bruylant, Geneva: Schulthess, 2006), p. 91–113.

Feinberg, Joel, 'The expressive function of punishment', *Doing and deserving: essays in the theory of responsibility* (Princeton, New Jersey: Princeton University Press, 1970), p. 95–118.

Ferola, Laura, 'Anti-Bribery Measures in the European Union: A Comparison with the Italian Legal Order', *International Journal of Legal Info,* 28 (2000), p. 512–557.

FITZPATRICK, JOAN, 'Trafficking as a Human Rights Violation: The Complex Intersection of Legal Frameworks for Conceptualizing and Combating Trafficking', *Michigan Journal of International Law,* 24 (2003), p. 1143–1167.

FORD, SAMANTHA and SENG, THEARY C., 'Corruption in the Judiciary of Cambodia', in Transparency International (ed.), *Global Corruption Report 2007: Corruption in Judicial Systems* (Cambridge: Cambridge University Press, 2007), p. 183–186.

FOSTER, TONY, *Dutch Legal Terminology in English* (3rd edn.: Kluwer, 2009).

FRULLI, MICAELA, 'Immunities of persons from jurisdiction', in Antonio Cassese (ed.), *The Oxford companion to international criminal justice* (Oxford: Oxford University Press, 2009), p. 368–369.

FRULLI, MICAELA, 'Advancing International Criminal Law: The Special Court for Sierra Leone Recognizes Forced Marriage as a 'New' Crime against Humanity', *Journal of International Criminal Justice,* 6 (2008), p. 1033–1042.

GADIROV, ERKIN and REVISED BY ROGER S. CLARK, 'Article 9: Elements of Crimes', in Otto Triffterer (ed.), *Commentary on the Rome Statute of the International Criminal Court. Observers' Notes, Article by Article* (2nd edn.; München: C.H. Beck, 2008), p. 505–529.

GAETA, PAOLA, 'Official Capacity and Immunities', in Antonio Cassese, Paola Gaeta, and John R.W.D. Jones (eds.), *The Rome Statute of the International Criminal Court: a commentary* (1; Oxford: Oxford University Press, 2002), p. 975–1002.

GALLAGHER, ANNE T., 'Human Rights and the New UN Protocols on Trafficking and Migrant Smuggling: A Preliminary Analysis', *Human Rights Quarterly,* 23 (2001), p. 975–1004.

GALLAGHER, ANNE T., 'Human Rights and Human Trafficking: Quagmire or Firm Ground? A Response to James Hathaway', *Virginia Journal of International Law,* 49 (2009), p. 789–848.

GALTUNG, FREDRIK, 'Measuring the Immeasurable: Boundaries and Functions of (Macro) Corruption Indices', in Charles Sampford, *et al.* (eds.), *Measuring Corruption* (Aldershot: Ashgate, 2006), p. 102–130.

GANTZ, DAVID A., 'Globalizing Sanctions against Foreign Bribery: The Emergence of a New International Legal Consensus', *Northwestern Journal of International Law & Business,* 18 (1998), p. 457–497.

GATHII, JAMES THUO, 'Defining the Relationship between Human Rights and Corruption', *University of Pennsylvania Journal of International Law,* 31 (2009), p. 125–202.

GARDINER, JOHN, 'Defining Corruption', in Arnold J. Heidenheimer and Michael Johnston (eds.), *Political Corruption: Concepts and Contexts.* (New Brunswick: Transaction, 2002), p. 25–40.

GARLAND, DAVID, *The Culture of Control* (Oxford: Oxford University Press, 2001).

GARNER, JAMES W., 'Contributions, Requisitions, and Compulsory Service in Occupied Territory', *American Journal of International Law,* 11 (1917), p. 74–112.

GETZ, KATHLEEN A., 'The Effectiveness of Global Prohibition Regimes: Corruption and the Antibribery Convention', *Business & Society,* 45 (2006), p. 254–281.

GEWIRTZ, PAUL, 'On "I Know It When I See It"', *Yale Law Journal,* 105 (1996), p. 1023–1047.

Gibbons, Kenneth M., 'Variations in Attitudes Towards Corruption in Canada', in Arnold J. Heidenheimer, Michael Johnston, and Victor T. LeVine (eds.), *Political Corruption: A Handbook* (New Brunswick: Transaction, 1989), p. 763–780.

Githongo, John, 'Inequality, Ethnicity and the Fight against Corruption in Africa: A Kenyan Perspective', *Economic Affairs,* 26/4 (2006), p. 19–23.

Glendinning, Lee, 'Corruption 'Rife' among Prison Staff, Report Claims', *The Times,* 31 July 2006.

Global Corruption Barometer 2010, <www.transparency.org/policy_research/surveys_indices/gcb/2010>, accessed 18 May 2011.

Global Witness, 'The Sinews of War – Eliminating the Trade in Conflict Resources', (Washington DC, November 2006).

Global Witness, 'Son of Equitorial Guinea's Dictator Plans One of the World's Most Expensive Yachts', 28 February 2011, <www.globalwitness.org/library/son-equatorial-guineas-dictator-plans-one-worlds-most-expensive-yachts>, accessed 2 March 2011.

Glynn, Patrick, Kobrin, Stephen J., and Naím, Moisés, 'The Globalization of Corruption', in Kimberley Ann Elliott (ed.), *Corruption and the Global Economy* (Washington, D.C.: Institute for International Economics, 1997), p. 7–27.

Golay, Christophe, 'The Right to Food and Access to Justice: The International Covenant on Economic, Social and Cultural Rights before National Jurisdictions', in Marco Borghi and Letizia Postiglione Blommestein (eds.), *The Right to Adequate Food and Access to Justice* (Collection Interdisciplinaire, 31; Brussels: Bruylant, Geneva: Schulthess, 2006), p. 117–149.

Goodwin, Morag and Rose-Sender, Kate, 'Linking Corruption and Human Rights: An Unwelcome Addition to the Development Discourse', in Martine Boersma and Hans Nelen (eds.), *Corruption & Human Rights: Interdisciplinary Perspectives* (Maastricht Series in Human Rights Antwerp: Intersentia, 2010), p. 221–240.

Gorta, Angela, 'Research. A Tool for Building Corruption Resistance', in Peter Larmour and Nick Wolanin (eds.), *Corruption and Anti-Corruption* (Canberra: Asia Pacific Press, 2001), p. 11–29.

Gounari, Zoe, 'The OECD Convention on Combating Bribery of Foreign Public Officials in International Business Transactions: Theory and Practice'; <www.dundee.ac.uk/cepmlp/car/html/CAR9_ARTICLE2.pdf>.

Grant, Stefanie, 'The NGO Role: Implementation, Expanding Protection and Monitoring the Monitors', in Anne F. Bayefsky (ed.), *The UN Human Rights Treaty System in the 21st Century* (The Hague: Kluwer Law International, 2000), p. 209–217.

GRECO, How Does GRECO Work? <www.coe.int/t/dg1/greco/general/4.%20How%20does%20GRECO%20work_en.asp>, accessed 7 October 2008.

Greenpeace, 'Monsanto Pays Up', <www.greenpeace.org/international/news/monsanto-pays-fine-for-bribery>, accessed 12 January 2009.

Greppi, Edoardo, 'The evolution of individual criminal responsibility under international law', *International Review of the Red Cross,* no. 835 (1999), p. 531–553.

Gupta, Akhil, 'Blurred Boundaries: The Discourse of Corruption, the Culture of Politics, and the Imagined State', *American Ethnologist,* 22/2 (1995), p. 375–402.

GUPTA, SANJEEV, DAVOODI, HAMID R., and ALONSO-TERME, ROSA, 'Does Corruption Affect Income Inequality and Poverty?' in George T. Abed and Sanjeev Gupta (eds.), *Governance, Corruption & Economic Performance* (Washington, DC: International Monetary Fund, 2002), p. 458–486.

GUTTER, JEROEN, 'Special Procedures and the Human Rights Council: achievements and challenges ahead', *Human Rights Law Review,* 7 (2007), p. 93–107.

HALL, CHRISTOPHER L., 'The Foreign Corrupt Practices Act: A Competitive Disadvantage, but for How Long?' *Tulane Journal of International and Comparative Law,* 2 (1994), p. 289–316.

HALL, CHRISTOPHER K., 'Article 7: Crimes against Humanity; (B) Extermination', in Otto Triffterer (ed.), *Commentary on the Rome Statute of the International Criminal Court. Observers' Notes, Article by Article* (2nd edn.; München: C.H. Beck, 2008), p. 237–243.

HALLAK, JACQUES and POISSON, MURIEL, 'Corrupt Schools, Corrupt Universities: What Can Be Done?' (Paris: International Institute for Educational Planning (UNESCO), 2007).

HALLER, DIETER and SHORE, CRIS (eds.), *Corruption: Anthropological Perspectives*, eds. Thomas Hylland Eriksen and Jon P. Mitchell (Anthropology, Culture and Society, London, Ann Arbor, MI: Pluto Press, 2005).

HAMMARBERG, THOMAS, 'Corruption Is a Major Human Rights Problem', *CommDH/Speech(2009)9* (Strassbourg, 5 October 2009).

HAMMERGREN, LINN, 'Fighting judicial corruption: a comparative perspective from Latin America', in Transparency International (ed.), *Global Corruption Report 2007: Corruption in Judicial Systems* (Cambridge: Cambridge University Press, 2007), p. 138–146.

HARARI, MAURICE and JULEN BERTHOD, ANNE VALÉRIE, 'Articles 9, 10 and 11. International Co-Operation', in Mark Pieth, Lucinda A. Low, and Peter J. Cullen (eds.), *The OECD Convention on Bribery: A Commentary* (Cambridge: Cambridge University Press, 2007), p. 406–444.

HARRIS, DAVID JOHN, O'BOYLE, MICHAEL, and WARBRICK, COLIN, *Law of the European Convention on Human Rights* (2nd edn.; Oxford: Oxford University Press, 2009).

HATCHARD, JOHN, 'Adopting a Human Rights Approach Towards Combating Corruption', in Martine Boersma and Hans Nelen (eds.), *Corruption & Human Rights: Interdisciplinary Perspectives* (Maastricht Series in Human Rights; Antwerp: Intersentia, 2010), p. 7–23.

HATHAWAY, JAMES C., 'The Human Rights Quagmire Of "Human Trafficking"', *Virginia Journal of International Law,* 49 (2008), p. 1–59.

HEIDENHEIMER, A.J., JOHNSTON, M., and (EDS.), V. LE VINE, *Political Corruption: A Handbook* (New Brunswick: Transaction, 1989).

HEIDENHEIMER, ARNOLD J. and JOHNSTON, MICHAEL (eds.), *Political Corruption: Concepts and Contexts* (3rd edn., New Brunswick: Transaction, 2002).

HEIMANN, FRITZ, 'Will the OECD Convention Stop Foreign Bribery?' in Transparency International (ed.), *Global Corruption Report 2004. Political Corruption* (2004).

HEIMANN, FRITZ and DELL, GILLIAN, 'Progress Report 2007. Enforcement of the OECD Convention on Combating Bribery of Foreign Public Officials', (Berlin: Transparency International 2007).

HEIMANN, FRITZ and POORTMAN, CHRISTIAAN, 'TI Comments on OECD Consultation Paper', (Berlin: Transparency International, 5 March 2008).

HEIN ONLINE, <www.heinonline.org>

HEUVEL, GRAT VAN DEN, 'The Parliamentary Enquiry on Fraud in the Dutch Construction Industry: Collusion as Concept between Corruption and State-Corporate Crime', *Crime, Law & Social Change,* 44 (2005), p. 133–151.

HODESS, ROBIN, 'Introduction to Political Corruption', in Transparency International (ed.), *Global Corruption Report* (2004), p. 11–18.

HUDSON, MANLEY O., 'The proposed International Criminal Court', *American Journal of International Law,* 32 (1938), p. 549–554.

HULTEN, MICHEL VAN, 'Hier Geen Corruptie? Dat Lijkt Maar Zo.'*NRC Handelsblad,* 26 September 2007.

HUMAN RIGHTS WATCH, 'Chop Fine. The Human Rights Impact of Local Government Corruption and Mismanagement in Rivers State, Nigeria.' *Report, Volume 19, No. 2(A)* (New York, January 2007).

HUMAN RIGHTS WATCH, 'Curing the Selectivity Syndrome: the 2011 Review of the Human Rights Council', (New York, June 2010).

HUMBORG, CHRISTIAN, 'In the Fight Against Corruption, Germany Falls Behind', <http://blog.transparency.org/2011/05/16/in-the-fight-against-corruption-germany-falls-behind/>, accessed 26 May 2011

HUMPHREYS, MACARTAN, 'Natural Resources and Armed Conflicts: Issues and Options', in Karen Ballentine and Heiko Nitzschke (eds.), *Profiting from Peace: Managing the Resource Dimension of Civil War* (Boulder: Lynne Rienner Publishers 2005), p. 25–44.

HUNTINGTON, SAMUEL P., 'Modernization and Corruption', in Arnold J. Heidenheimer and Michael Johnston (eds.), *Political Corruption: Concepts and Contexts* (3rd edn.; New Brunswick: Transaction, 2002), p. 253–263.

ICC COMMISSION ON ANTI-CORRUPTION, 'Responses to the Consultation Paper on the Review of the OECD Anti-Bribery Instruments', (International Chamber of Commerce, 2008).

ICC LEGAL TOOLS, <www.legal-tools.org/en/go-to-database/ltfolder/0_3960/#results>, accessed 11 January 2010.

INTERNATIONAL CHAMBER OF COMMERCE, 'ICC Note On "The Most Important Obstacle to the Effective Enforcement of the OECD Anti-Bribery Convention"', (11 June 2007); <www.iccwbo.org/uploadedFiles/ICC/policy/anticorruption/Statements/ICC%20note%20on%20OECD%20Convention%20effective%20enforcement%2011%20June%202007.pdf>.

INTER-AMERICAN COMMISSION ON HUMAN RIGHTS, Annual Reports, <www.cidh.oas.org/annual.eng.htm>, accessed 12 January 2011.

INTER-AMERICAN COMMISSION ON HUMAN RIGHTS, <www.cidh.org/search/advcidh.asp>

INTER-AMERICAN COMMISSION ON HUMAN RIGHTS, Official Publications, < www.cidh.oas.org/publi.eng.htm>.

INTER-AMERICAN COURT OF HUMAN RIGHTS, <www.corteidh.or.cr/buscadores.cfm>.

INTERNATIONAL COUNCIL ON HUMAN RIGHTS POLICY, *Performance & Legitimacy: National Human Rights Institutions* (2nd edn.; Versoix, Switzerland, 2004).

International Council on Human Rights Policy, *Corruption and Human Rights: Making the Connection* (Versoix, Switzerland, 2009).

International Council on Human Rights Policy, *Integrating Human Rights in the Anti-Corruption Agenda: Challenges, Possibilities and Opportunities* (Geneva, Switzerland, 2010).

International Criminal Court, <www.icc-cpi.int/Menus/ICC/Situations+and+Cases/Cases>

International Criminal Tribunal for the Former Yugoslavia, <www.icty.org/action/cases/4>.

International Criminal Tribunal for Rwanda: <www.ictrcaselaw.org>

International Monetary Fund, 'OECD Convention on Combating Bribery of Foreign Public Officials in International Business Transactions', (2001).

Jali Commission, 'Executive Summary of Final Report', <www.pmg.org.za/docs/2006/061017jali.pdf>, accessed 14 July 2009.

Jali Commission, 'Final Report', <www.info.gov.za/otherdocs/2006/jali/index.html>, accessed 14 July 2009.

Jayawickrama, Nihal, 'Corruption – a Violation of Human Rights?' *Working Paper* (Sofia: Transparency International, 1–2 June 1998).

Jennett, Victoria, 'The Relationship between Human Rights and Corruption: The Impact of Corruption on the Rights to Equal Access to Justice and Effective Remedy', *Working Paper* (Geneva: International Council on Human Rights Policy, 2007).

Jessberger, Florian, 'International V. National Prosecution of International Crimes', in Antonio Cassese (ed.), *The Oxford Companion to International Criminal Justice* (Oxford: Oxford University Press, 2009), p. 208–215.

Johnson, Vincent R., 'Corruption in Education: A Global Legal Challenge', <http://works.bepress.com/vincent_johnson/1 >, accessed 12 April 2010.

Johnson, O. Thomas and Ridings, Donald J., 'The OECD Convention and the Emergence of an International Anti-Bribery Regime', in Carol J. Holgren and Anita M. Stover (eds.), *Private Investors Abroad: Problems and Solutions in International Business in 1998* (New York: Matthew Bender, 1998), 6.1–6.21.

Johnson, Larry D., 'The International Criminal Tribunal for Rwanda', in M. Cherif Bassiouni (ed.), *International Criminal Law: Enforcement* (2nd edn., III; Ardsley, New York: Transnational Publishers, 1999), p. 549–565.

Johnston, Michael, 'Public Officials, Private Interests, and Sustainable Democracy: When Politics and Corruption Meet', in Kimberley Ann Elliott (ed.), *Corruption and the Global Economy* (Washington, D.C.: Institute for International Economics, 1997), p. 61–82.

Joseph, Sarah, Schultz, Jenny, and Castan, Melissa, *The International Covenant on Civil and Political Rights: Cases, Materials and Commentary* (2nd edn.; Oxford: Oxford University Press, 2004).

'Armenian Protesters: Referendum Rigged', *Journal of Turkish Weekly,* 29 November 2005.

Karp, Judith, 'Reporting and the Committee on the Rights of the Child', in Anne F. Bayefsky (ed.), *The UN Human Rights Treaty System in the 21st Century* (The Hague: Kluwer Law International, 2000), p. 35–44.

KAUFMANN, DANIEL, 'Human Rights and Governance: The Empirical Challenge', in Philip Alston and Mary Robinson (eds.), *Human Rights and Development: Towards Mutual Reinforcement* (Oxford: Oxford University Press, 2005), p. 352–402.

KAUFMANN, DANIEL, KRAAY, AART, and MASTRUZZI, MASSIMO, 'Measuring Corruption: Myths and Realities', in Transparency International (ed.), *Global Corruption Report 2007: Corruption in Judicial Systems* (Cambridge: Cambridge University Press, 2007), p. 318–323.

KELT, MARIA and HEBEL, HERMAN VON, 'General Principles of Criminal Law and the Elements of Crimes', in Roy S. Lee (ed.), *The International Criminal Court: Elements of Crimes and Rules of Procedure and Evidence* (Ardsley: Transnational Publishers, 2001), p. 19–40.

KELT, MARIA and HEBEL, HERMAN VON, 'The Making of the Elements of Crimes – IV. What Are Elements of Crimes?' in Roy S. Lee (ed.), *The International Criminal Court: Elements of Crimes and Rules of Procedure and Evidence* (Ardsley: Transnational Publishers, 2001), p. 13–18.

KENNEDY, DAVID, 'The International Anti-Corruption Campaign', *Connecticut Journal of International Law,* 14 (1999), p. 455–465.

KENYA NATIONAL COMMISSION ON HUMAN RIGHTS, *Nguzo za Haki: a Publication of the KNCHR,* 3 (February 2005).

KENYA NATIONAL COMMISSION ON HUMAN RIGHTS and KENYA LAND ALLIANCE, 'Unjust Enrichment: The Making of Land Grabbing Millionares', (2006).

KENYA NATIONAL COMMISSION ON HUMAN RIGHTS and TRANSPARENCY INTERNATIONAL KENYA, 'Living Large: Counting the Cost of Official Extravagance in Kenya', (2005).

KIAI, MAINA, 'Corruption Is a Violation of Human Rights', *Nguzo za Haki: a publication of the KNCHR,* 3 (February 2005), p. 4–7.

KIMATHI, WAMBUI, 'Corruption: A Complex Phenomenon That Undermines Government's Capability of Working for the Poor', *Nguzo za Haki: a publication of the KNCHR,* 3 (February 2005), p. 3.

KJAERUM, MORTEN, 'Breaking the Vicious Cycle: Corruption and Poverty; Obstacles to Social and Economic Rights. A Human Rights Based Bottom-up Approach', *12th International Anti-Corruption Conference* (Guatemala City and Antigua, Guatemala, 2006), <www.12iacc.org/archivos/KJAERUM.pdf>, accessed 8 August 2011.

KLICH, AGNIESZKA, 'Bribery in Economies in Transition: The Foreign Corrupt Practices Act', *Stanford Journal of International Law,* 32 (1996), p. 121–147.

KOBONBAEV, MAKS and EICHER, SHARON, 'Quantifying the Immeasurable', in Sharon Eicher (ed.), *Corruption in International Business: The Challenge of Cultural and Legal Diversity* (Corporate Social Responsibility Series: Gower, 2009), p. 61–79.

KOBONBAEV, MAKS, JACOBSEN, DONALD, and EICHER, SHARON, 'Critiquing the Indicators of Corruption and Government', in Sharon Eicher (ed.), *Corruption in International Business: The Challenge of Cultural and Legal Diversity* (Corporate Social Responsibility Series: Gower, 2009), p. 81–89.

KOEHLER, MIKE, 'Compliance Lessons from an Active Year in FCPA Enforcement', *White Collar Crime Report,* 3 (15 February 2008).

KOFELE-KALE, NDIVA, 'Patrimonicide: The International Economic Crime of Indigenous Spoliation', *Vanderbilt Journal of Transnational Law,* 28 (1995), p. 45–118.

KOFELE-KALE, NDIVA, 'The Right to a Corruption-Free Society as an Individual and Collective Human Right: Elevating Official Corruption to a Crime under International Law', *The International Lawyer,* 34 (2000), p. 149–178.

KOFELE-KALE, NDIVA, 'Change or the Illusion of Change: The War against Official Corruption in Africa', *George Washington International Law Review,* 38/4 (2006), p. 697–747.

KOFELE-KALE, NDIVA, *The International Law of Responsibility for Economic Crimes: Holding State Officials Individually Liable for Acts of Fraudulent Enrichment* (2 edn.; Aldershot: Ashgate, 2006).

KOLTHOFF, EMILE, *Integriteit, Mensenrechten en de Veiligheidsmythe* (Den Haag: Boom Juridische Uitgevers 2010).

KRETZMER, DAVID and BURNS, PETER, 'Commentary on Complaint Processes by Human Rights Committee and Torture Committee Members', in Anne F. Bayefsky (ed.), *The UN Human Rights Treaty System in the 21st Century* (The Hague: Kluwer Law International, 2000), p. 163–167.

KREVER, TOR, 'Curbing Corruption? The Efficacy of the Foreign Corrupt Practices Act', *North Carolina Journal of International Law & Commercial Regulation,* 33 (2007), p. 83–102.

KÜNNEMANN, ROLF, 'The Right to Adequate Food: Violations Related to Its Minimum Core Content', in Audrey R. Chapman and Sage Russell (eds.), *Core Obligations: Building a Framework for Economic, Social and Cultural Rights* (Antwerp: Intersentia, 2002), p. 161–183.

KUTUTWA, NOEL, 'How to Combat Corruption While Respecting Human Rights', *Working Paper International Council on Human Rights Policy* (2007).

LAMBSDORFF, JOHANN GRAF, 'Measuring Corruption – the Validity and Precision of Subjective Indicators (CPI)', in Charles Sampford, *et al.* (eds.), *Measuring Corruption* (Aldershot: Ashgate, 2006), p. 81–99.

LANDMAN, TODD and SCHUDEL, C.J.W., 'Corruption and Human Rights: Empirical Relationships and Policy Advice', *Working Paper International Council on Human Rights Policy* (Geneva, 2007).

LANSDOWN, GERISON, 'The Reporting Process under the Convention on the Rights of the Child', in Philip Alston and James Crawford (eds.), *The Future of UN Human Rights Treaty Monitoring* (Cambridge: Cambridge University Press, 2000), p. 113–128.

LASHBROOKE, E.C., 'The Foreign Corrupt Practices Act of 1977: A Unilateral Solution to an International Problem', *Cornell International Law Journal,* 12 (1979), p. 227–243.

LASKAR, S.I., 'Bangladesh: Justice in Disarray', in Transparency International (ed.), *Global Corruption Report 2007: Corruption in Judicial Systems* (Cambridge: Cambridge University Press, 2007), p. 179–183.

LECKIE, SCOTT, 'Another Step Towards Indivisibility: Identifying the Key Features of Violations of Economic, Social and Cultural Rights', *Human Rights Quarterly,* 20 (1998), p. 81–124.

LEE, ROY S. (ed.), *The International Criminal Court: Elements of Crimes and Rules of Procedure and Evidence* (Ardsley: Transnational Publishers, 2001).

Leff, Nathaniel H., 'Economic Development through Bureaucratic Corruption', in Arnold J. Heidenheimer and Michael Johnston (eds.), *Political Corruption: Concepts and Contexts* (3 edn.; New Brunswick: Transaction, 2002), p. 307–320.

Leffers, Jochen, 'Germany Rocked by Allegations of Ph.D Bribes (24 August 2009)', *Der Spiegel* <www.spiegel.de/international/germany/0,1518,644639,00.html>, accessed 12 April 2009.

Legal Resources Centre, 'Freedom of Movement under Siege! Urgent Need to Address Widespread Corruption on the Tema-Ouagadougou Trade Corridor.' <http://ghanaweb.com/GhanaHomePage/economy/artikel.php?ID=170597>, accessed 6 July 2011.

Lempinen, Miko, *Challenges Facing the System of Special Procedures of the United Nations Commission on Human Rights* (Turku/Abo: Institute for Human Rights, Abo Akademi University, 2001).

Levey, Stuart, 'Fighting Corruption after the Arab Spring', *Foreign Affairs*, (16 June 2011).

Liefländer, Thomas R., 'The Lubanga Judgment of the ICC: More than Just the First Step?', *Cambridge Journal of International and Comparative Law*, (2012), p. 191–212.

Limburg Principles on the Implementation of the International Covenant on Economic, Social and Cultural Rights (1986), *Human Rights Quarterly*, 9 (1987), p. 122–135.

Linderfalk, Ulf, 'Is the Hierarchical Structure of Articles 31 and 32 of the Vienna Convention on the Law of Treaties Real or Not? Interpreting the Rules of Interpretation', *Netherlands International Law Review*, 54 (2007), p. 133–154.

Linderfalk, Ulf, *On the Interpretation of Treaties: The Modern International Law as Expressed in the 1969 Vienna Convention on the Law of Treaties* (Dordrecht: Springer, 2007).

Liu Daqun, 'Actus Reus', in Antonio Cassese (ed.), *The Oxford Companion to International Criminal Justice* (Oxford: Oxford University Press, 2009), p. 229–230.

Longobardi, Laura E., 'Reviewing the Situation: What Is to Be Done with the Foreign Corrupt Practices Act?' *Vanderbilt Journal of Transnational Law*, 20 (1987), p. 431–494.

Lovgren, Stefan, 'Corruption Top Threat to African Animals, Study Says', (National Geographic News, 5 November 2003).

Low, Lucinda A., 'The United Nations Convention against Corruption: The Globalization of Anticorruption Standards', *Conference of the International Bar Association, International Chamber of Commerce & Organization for Economic Cooperation and Development: The Awakening Giant of Anticorruption Enforcement* (London, England, 4–5 May 2006).

Maastricht Guidelines on Violations of Economic, Social and Cultural Rights (1997), *Human Rights Quarterly*, 20 (1998), p. 691–704.

Maestad, Ottar and Mwisongo, Aziza, 'Informal Pay and the Quality of Health Care: Lessons from Tanzania', in Taryn Vian, William D. Savedoff, and Harald Mathisen (eds.), *Anticorruption in the Health Sector: Strategies for Transparency and Accountability* (Sterling, VA: Kumarian Press, 2010), p. 45–53.

Makinwa, Abiola O., 'Researching Civil Remedies for International Corruption: the Choice of the Functional Comparative Method', *Erasmus Law Review*, 2 (2009), p. 331–351.

Manfroni, Carlos A., updated by Richard S. Werksman, *The Inter-American Convention against Corruption*, trans. Michael Ford (Lanham: Lexington Books, 2003).

Marquette, Heather, *Corruption, Politics and Development: The Role of the World Bank* (Hampshire: Palgrave Macmillan, 2003).

Maria, William De, 'Cross Cultural Trespass: Assessing African Anti-Corruption Capacity', *International Journal of Cross Cultural Management,* 8/3 (2008), p. 317–341.

Marquette, Heather, *Corruption, Politics and Development: The Role of the World Bank* (Hampshire: Palgrave Macmillan, 2003).

Martino, Alberto di, 'Dolus Eventualis', in Antonio Cassese (ed.), *The Oxford Companion to International Criminal Justice* (Oxford: Oxford University Press, 2009), p. 302–304.

Mauro, Paolo, 'Corruption and Growth', *The Quarterly Journal of Economics,* 110 (1995), p. 681–712.

Mauro, Paolo, 'The Effects of Corruption on Growth and Public Expenditure', in Arnold J. Heidenheimer and Michael Johnston (eds.), *Political Corruption: Concepts and Contexts* (3 edn.; New Brunswick: Transaction, 2002), p. 339–352.

Mbaku, John Mukum, *Corruption in Africa: Causes, Consequences and Cleanups* (Plymouth: Lexington Books, 2007).

McCormack, Timothy L.H., 'From Sun Tzu to the Sixth Committee: the evolution of an international criminal law regime', in Timothy L.H. McCormack and Gerry J. Simpson (eds.), *The law of war crimes: national and international approaches* (The Hague: Kluwer Law International, 1997), p. 31–63.

Mechlem, Kerstin, 'Treaty Bodies and the Interpretation of Human Rights', *Vanderbilt Journal of Transnational Law,* 42 (2009), p. 905–947.

Medina, Cecilia, 'The role of country reports in the Inter-American system of human rights', in David J. Harris and Stephen Livingstone (eds.), *The Inter-American system of human rights* (Oxford: Clarendon Press, 1998), p. 115–132.

Mendes, Errol P., 'Corruption: The Cancer of the International Bill of Rights – Democracy and Freedom of Expression, the Main Treatments?' in Errol P. Mendes and Anik Lalonde-Roussy (eds.), *Bridging the Global Divide on Human Rights: A Canada-China Dialogue* (Aldershot: Ashgate, 2003), p. 287–302.

Mettraux, Guénaël, 'Extermination', in Antonio Cassese (ed.), *The Oxford Companion to International Criminal Justice* (Oxford: Oxford University Press, 2009), p. 320–322.

Michele, Roberto de, 'The Follow-up Mechanism of the Inter-American Convention against Corruption: A Preliminary Assessment: Is the Glass Half Empty?' *Southwestern Journal of Law and Trade in the Americas,* 10 (2004), p. 295–318.

Milledge, Simon A.H., Gelvas, Ised K, and Ahrends, Antje, 'Forestry, Governance and National Development: Lessons Learned from a Logging Boom in Southern Tanzania', (Dar es Salaam: TRAFFIC East/Southern Africa / Tanzania Development Partners Group / Ministry of Natural Resources and Tourism, 2007).

Miller, Kelly and Vian, Taryn, 'Strategies for Reducing Informal Payments', in Taryn Vian, William D. Savedoff, and Harald Mathisen (eds.), *Anticorruption in the Health Sector: Strategies for Transparency and Accountability* (Sterling, VA: Kumarian Press, 2010), p. 55–66.

MOODY-STUART, GEORGE, *Grand Corruption in Third World Development* (Oxford: WorldView Publishing, 1997).

MORGAN, AMANDA L., 'Corruption: Causes, Consequences and Policy Implications. A Literature Review', *Working Paper nr. 9* (Asia Foundation, October 1998).

MUNA, AKERE, 'The African Union Convention against Corruption', in Transparency International (ed.), *Global Corruption Report 2004. Political Corruption* (2004), p. 116–121.

MURDOCH, JIM, *The Treatment of Prisoners: European Standards* (Strasbourg: Council of Europe Publishing, 2006).

MURPHY, KEVIN M., SHLEIFER, ANDREI, and VISHNY, ROBERT W., 'The Allocation of Talent: Implications for Growth', *The Quarterly Journal of Economics,* 106 (1991), p. 503–530.

MYRDAL, GUNNAR, 'Corruption: Its Causes and Effects', in Arnold J. Heidenheimer, Michael Johnston, and Victor T. LeVine (eds.), *Political Corruption: A Handbook* (New Brunswick Transaction, 1989), 953–962.

NAPLES-MITCHELL, JOANNA, 'Perspectives of UN Special Rapporteurs on Their Role: Inherent Tensions and Unique Contributions to Human Rights', *The International Journal of Human Rights,* 15/2 (2011), p. 232–248.

NELKEN, DAVID, 'White-Collar and Corporate Crime', in Mike Maguire, Rod Morgan, and Robert Reiner (eds.), *The Oxford Handbook of Criminology* (4th edn.; Oxford: Oxford University Press 2007), p. 733–770.

NELKEN, DAVID 'Corruption and Human Rights: An Afterword', in Martine Boersma and Hans Nelen (eds.), *Corruption & Human Rights: Interdisciplinary Perspectives* (Maastricht Series in Human Rights: Antwerp: Intersentia 2010), p. 241–261

NETHERLANDS INSTITUTE OF HUMAN RIGHTS (SIM), Documentation Site, <http://sim.law.uu.nl/sim/Dochome.nsf>.

NEWCOMB, DANFORTH and UROFSKY, PHILIP, 'FCPA Digest of Cases and Review Releases Relating to Bribes to Foreign Officials under the Foreign Corrupt Practices Act of 1977', (New York: Shearman & Sterling LLP, 2008).

NICHOLS, PHILIP M., 'Regulating Transnational Bribery in Times of Globalization and Fragmentation', *Yale Journal of International Law,* 24 (1999), p. 257–303.

NIFOSI, INGRID, *The UN Special Procedures in the Field of Human Rights* (Antwerp: Intersentia, 2005).

NNAMUCHI, OBIAJULU, 'Kleptocracy and Its Many Faces: The Challenges of Justiciability of the Right to Health Care in Nigeria', *Journal of African Law,* 52 (2008), p. 1–42.

NOONAN JR., JOHN T., *Bribes* (New York: Macmillan Publishing Company, 1984).

NORDIC CONSULTING GROUP, *A Gender Analysis of Corruption – Forms, Effects and Eradication Strategies* (Study prepared for the Royal Danish Embassy in Uganda, September 2009).

NOWAK, MANFRED, 'The Right to Education', in Asbjørn Eide, Catarina Krause, and Allan Rosas (eds.), *Economic, Social and Cultural Rights: A Textbook* (2nd edn.; Dordrecht: Martinus Nijhoff Publishers, 2001), p. 245–271.

NOWAK, MANFRED, *UN Covenant on Civil and Political Rights: CCPR Commentary* (2nd edn.; Kehl: Engel, 2005).

Nyasa Times, 'Veep Launches Malawi Passport, Denounce Corruption at Immigration', <www.nyasatimes.com/national/veep-launches-malawi-new-passport-denounce-corruption-at-immigration.html>, accessed 6 July 2011.

Nye, Joseph S., 'Corruption and Political Development: A Cost-Benefit Analysis', in Arnold J. Heidenheimer and Michael Johnston (eds.), *Political Corruption: Concepts and Contexts* (New Brunswick: Transaction, 2002), p. 281–300.

Obokata, Tom, *Trafficking in Human Beings from a Human Rights Perspective: Towards a Holistic Approach* (International Studies in Human Rights, 89; Leiden: Martinus Nijhoff Publishers, 2006).

Ocheje, Paul D., 'Refocusing international law on the quest for accountability in Africa: the case against the "other" impunity', *Leiden Journal of International Law,* 15 (2002), p. 749–779.

OECD, List of Ratifying Countries (Non-Member Countries), <www.oecd.org/infobycountry/0,3380,en_2649_34859_1_1_1_3_37447,00.html>, accessed 24 May 2011.

OECD, List of Ratifying Countries (OECD Member Countries), <www.oecd.org/infobycountry/0,3380,en_2649_34859_1_1_1_2_37447,00.html>, accessed 24 May 2011.

OECD, OECD Anti-Bribery Convention: Procedure of Self- and Mutual Evaluation – Phase 1, <www.oecd.org/document/21/0,3343,en_2649_37447_2022613_1_1_1_37447,00.html>, accessed 15 October 2008.

OECD, OECD Anti-Bribery Convention: Procedure of Self- and Mutual Evaluation – Phase 2, <www.oecd.org/document/27/0,3343,en_2649_37447_2022939_1_1_1_37447,00.html>, accessed 15 October 2008

OECD, 'Fighting Bribery and Corruption: Frequently Asked Questions' (2007); <www.oecd.org/documentprint/0,3455,en_2649_34859_35430226_1_1_1_1,00.html>.

OECD, 'Review of the OECD Anti-Bribery Instruments. Compilation of Responses to Consultation Paper', (OECD, 2008).

OECD Working Group on Bribery in International Business Transactions, 'Consultation Paper. Review of the OECD Instruments on Combating Bribery of Foreign Public Officials in International Business Transactions Ten Years after Adoption', <www.oecd.org/dataoecd/18/25/39882963.pdf>, accessed 15 October 2008

O'Flaherty, Michael, *Human Rights and the UN: Practice before the Treaty Bodies* (2nd edn., Nijhoff Law Specials, 54; The Hague: Kluwer Law International, 2002).

O'Flaherty, Michael, 'The Concluding Observations of the United Nations Human Rights Treaty Bodies', *Human Rights Law Review,* 6 (2006), p. 27–52.

Ocheje, Paul D., 'Refocusing International Law on the Quest for Accountability in Africa: The Case against The "Other" Impunity', *Leiden Journal of International Law,* 15 (2002), p. 749–779.

OHCHR, Human Rights Bodies – General Comments, <www2.ohchr.org/english/bodies/treaty/comments.htm>.

OHCHR, Introduction to the Special Procedures of the Human Rights Council, <www2.ohchr.org/english/bodies/chr/special/index.htm>, accessed 25 June 2011.

OHCHR, Special Procedures Assumed by the Human Rights Council – Country Mandates, <www2.ohchr.org/english/bodies/chr/special/countries.htm>, accessed 10 February 2011.

OHCHR, Special Procedures Assumed by the Human Rights Council – Thematic Mandates, <www2.ohchr.org/english/bodies/chr/special/themes.htm>, accessed 2 December 2010.
OHCHR, Treaty Body Document Search, <http://tb.ohchr.org/default.aspx>
OHCHR, Good Governance Practices for the Protection of Human Rights, (Geneva, 2007), <www.ohchr.org/Documents/Publications/GoodGovernance.pdf> accessed 8 August 2011.
OHCHR, Fact Sheet No. 21, the Human Right to Adequate Housing, <www.ohchr.org/Documents/Publications/FactSheet21en.pdf>, accessed 7 April 2009.
OHCHR, Website Development – Good Governance, Subsection 'Corruption and Human Rights', <www2.ohchr.org/english/issues/development/governance/anti_corruption.htm>, accessed 14 April 2010.
OHCHR, The Reporting Cycle under the Human Rights Treaties, <www2.ohchr.org/english/bodies/docs/ReportingCycle.gif>.
OHCHR, The United Nations Human Rights Treaty System: An Introduction to the Core Human Rights Treaties and the Treaty Bodies, *Fact sheet No. 30* <www2.ohchr.org/english/bodies/docs/OHCHR-FactSheet30.pdf>, accessed 20 June 2011.
OHCHR, Special Rapporteur on the independence of judges and lawyers – Issues in focus, <www2.ohchr.org/english/issues/judiciary/issues.htm>, accessed 15 September 2010.
OHCHR, Special Rapporteur on the independence of judges and lawyers – Annual reports, <www2.ohchr.org/english/issues/judiciary/annual.htm>, accessed 15 September 2010.
OHCHR, Special Rapporteur on the independence of judges and lawyers – Country visits, <www2.ohchr.org/english/issues/judiciary/visits.htm>, accessed 15 September 2010.
OHCHR, Special Rapporteur on trafficking in persons, especially in women and children – Annual reports, <www2.ohchr.org/english/issues/trafficking/annual.htm>, accessed 11 January 2011.
OHCHR, Special Rapporteur on trafficking in persons, especially in women and children – Communications, <www2.ohchr.org/english/issues/trafficking/communications.htm>, accessed 11 January 2011.
OHCHR, Special Rapporteur on the sale of children, child prostitution and child pornography – Annual Reports, <www2.ohchr.org/english/issues/children/rapporteur/annual.htm>, accessed 10 January 2011.
OHCHR, Special Rapporteur on the sale of children, child prostitution and child pornography – Country visits, <www2.ohchr.org/english/issues/children/rapporteur/visits.htm>, accessed 4 October 2010.
OHCHR, Special Rapporteur on the sale of children, child prostitution and child pornography – International Standards, <www2.ohchr.org/english/issues/children/rapporteur/standards.htm>, accessed 10 January 2011
OHCHR, Special Rapporteur on the right to adequate housing – Annual reports, <www2.ohchr.org/english/issues/housing/annual.htm>, accessed 6 January 2011
OHCHR, Special Rapporteur on the right to adequate housing – Country visits, <www2.ohchr.org/english/issues/housing/visits.htm>, accessed 6 January 2011
OHCHR, Special Rapporteur on the right to education – Annual reports, <www2.ohchr.org/english/issues/education/rapporteur/annual.htm>, accessed 7 January 2011.

OHCHR, Special Rapporteur on the right to education – Country visits, <www2.ohchr.org/english/issues/education/rapporteur/visits.htm>, accessed 7 January 2011.

OHCHR, Special Rapporteur on the right to education – Overview of the mandate, <www2.ohchr.org/english/issues/education/rapporteur/overview.htm>, accessed 14 April 2010.

OHCHR, Special Rapporteur on the right to food – Annual reports, <www2.ohchr.org/english/issues/food/annual.htm>, accessed 7 January 2011.

OHCHR, Special Rapporteur on the right to food – Country visits, <www2.ohchr.org/english/issues/food/visits.htm>, accessed 7 January 2011.

OHCHR, Special Rapporteur on the right to health – Annual reports, <www2.ohchr.org/english/issues/health/right/annual.htm>, accessed 7 January 2011.

OHCHR, Special Rapporteur on the right to health – Country visits, <www2.ohchr.org/english/issues/health/right/visits.htm>, accessed 7 January 2011.

OHCHR, Special Rapporteur on the right to health – Resolutions, <www2.ohchr.org/english/issues/health/right/overview.htm>, accessed 10 January 2011.

OHCHR, Independent Expert on the question of human rights and extreme poverty – Annual reports, <www.ohchr.org/EN/Issues/Poverty/Pages/AnnualReports.aspx>, accessed 5 January 2011.

OHCHR, Independent Expert on the question of human rights and extreme poverty – Country reports, <www.ohchr.org/EN/Issues/Poverty/Pages/CountryVisits.aspx>, accessed 5 January 2011.

OHCHR, Independent Expert on the situation of human rights in Haiti, <http://ap.ohchr.org/documents/dpage_e.aspx?m=47>, accessed 3 December 2010.

OHCHR, Resolutions and decisions on human rights and extreme poverty, <www.ohchr.org/EN/Issues/Poverty/Pages/Resolutions.aspx >, accessed 7 January 2011.

OHCHR, Special Representative of the S-G on the issue of human rights and transnational corporations and other business enterprises – Reports, <www.ohchr.org/EN/Issues/TransnationalCorporations/Pages/Reports.aspx>, accessed 5 January 2011.

OHCHR, Manual of the United Nations Human Rights Special Procedures, (August 2008).

OHCHR, Human Rights Committee <www2.ohchr.org/english/bodies/hrc/index.htm>, accessed 15 June 2011.

OHCHR, Committee on Economic, Social and Cultural Rights, <www2.ohchr.org/english/bodies/cescr/index.htm>, accessed 20 June 2011.

OHCHR, Committee on the Rights of the Child, <www2.ohchr.org/english/bodies/crc/index.htm>, accessed 15 June 2011.

OHCHR, Committee on the Elimination of All Forms of Discrimination Against Women, <www2.ohchr.org/english/bodies/cedaw/index.htm>, accessed 20 June 2011.

OHCHR, Committee on the Elimination of Racial Discrimination, <www2.ohchr.org/english/bodies/cerd/index.htm>, accessed 15 June 2011.

OHCHR, Committee Against Torture, <www2.ohchr.org/english/bodies/cat/index.htm>, accessed 15 June 2011.

OHCHR, Universal Periodic Review System, <www.ohchr.org/EN/HRBodies/UPR/Pages/UPRMain.aspx>, accessed 21 June 2011.

OHCHR, Universal Periodic Review System, All Sessions, <www.ohchr.org/EN/HRBodies/UPR/Pages/UPRSessions.aspx>, accessed 21 June 2011.

OHCHR, Universal Periodic Review System, Basic Facts, <www.ohchr.org/EN/HRBodies/UPR/Pages/BasicFacts.aspx>, accessed 21 June 2011.

OLAF website, <http://ec.europa.eu/anti_fraud/index_en.html>, accessed 8 August 2011.

Olaniyan, Kolawole, 'The African Union Convention on Preventing and Combating Corruption: A Critical Appraisal', *African Human Rights Law Journal,* 4 (2004), 74–92.

Open Society Institute's EU Monitoring and Advocacy Program (EUMAP), 'Corruption and Anti-Corruption Policy', <www.eumap.org/topics/corruption>, accessed 6 March 2008.

Organisation of American States, Signatures and Ratifications of the Inter-American Convention against Corruption, <www.oas.org/juridico/english/Sigs/b–58.html>, accessed 24 May 2011.

Organisation of American States, Rules of Procedure of the Conference of States Parties to the Mechanism for Follow-up on Implementation of the Inter-American Convention against Corruption, (2 April 2004).

Organisation of American States, Report of Buenos Aires on the Mechanism for Follow-up on the Implementation of the Inter-American Convention against Corruption, (4 May 2001).

Organisation of American States, Rules of Procedure of the Committee of Experts and Other Provisions, (29 June 2007).

Oxford English Dictionary <www.oed.com>.

Parker, Norma *et al.*, 'Corruption in Latin America: A Desk Assessment', *Americas' Accountability Anti-Corruption Project* (Alexandria, Virginia: Casals & Associates, 2004).

Pasqualucci, Jo M., *The practice and procedure of the Inter-American Court of Human Rights* (Cambridge: Cambridge University Press 2003).

Pawlowski, Joanne, 'Forced Evictions of Cambodia's Poor', *Human Rights Tribune* 11/3 (2005).

Pearson, Zoe, 'An International Human Rights Approach to Corruption', in Peter Larmour & Nick Wolanin (ed.), *Corruption and Anti-Corruption* (Canberra: Asia Pacific Press, 2001), p. 30–61.

Pendergast, William F., 'Foreign Corrupt Practices Act: An Overview of Almost Twenty Years of Foreign Bribery Prosecution', *International Quarterly,* 7 (1995), p. 187.

Philp, Mark, 'Corruption Definition and Measurement', in Charles Sampford, *et al.* (eds.), *Measuring Corruption* (Aldershot: Ashgate, 2006), p. 45–56.

Pinheiro, Paulo Sérgio, 'Musings of a UN Special Rapporteur on Human Rights', *Global Governance,* 9 (2003), p. 7–13.

Pinheiro, Paulo Sérgio, 'Being a Special Rapporteur: A Delicate Balancing Act', *The International Journal of Human Rights,* 15/2 (2011), p. 162–711.

Picarta, <www.picarta.nl>.

Pickholz, Marvin G., 'The United States Foreign Corrupt Practices Act as a Civil Remedy', in Barry Rider (ed.), *Corruption: The Enemy Within* (The Hague/London/Boston: Kluwer Law International 1997), p. 231–252.

Pieth, Mark, 'Taking Stock: Making the OECD Initiative against Corruption Work', <www.oas.org/juridico/english/pieth2000.htm>, accessed 6 March 2008.

Pieth, Mark, 'Introduction', in Mark Pieth, Lucinda A. Low, and Peter J. Cullen (eds.), *The OECD Convention on Bribery. A Commentary* (Cambridge: Cambridge University Press 2007), p. 3–41.

Pieth, Mark, 'Article 2. The Responsibility of Legal Persons', in Mark Pieth, Lucinda A. Low, and Peter J. Cullen (eds.), *The OECD Convention on Bribery: A Commentary* (Cambridge: Cambridge University Press, 2007), p. 173–206.

Pieth, Mark, 'Article 7. Money Laundering', in Mark Pieth, Lucinda A. Low, and Peter J. Cullen (eds.), *The OECD Convention on Bribery: A Commentary* (Cambridge: Cambridge University Press, 2007), p. 355–376.

Piragoff, Donald K. and Robinson, Darryl, 'Article 30: Mental Element', in Otto Triffterer (ed.), *Commentary on the Rome Statute of the International Criminal Court. Observers' Notes, Article by Article* (2nd edn.; München: C.H. Beck, 2008), p. 849–961.

Politi, Mauro, 'Elements of Crimes', in Antonio Cassese, Paola Gaeta, and John R.W.D. Jones (eds.), *The Rome Statute of the International Criminal Court: A Commentary* (1; Oxford: Oxford University Press, 2002), p. 443–473.

Pope, Jeremy, *TI Source Book 2000. Confronting Corruption: The Elements of a National Integrity System* (Berlin: Transparency International, 2000).

Posadas, Alejandro, 'Combating Corruption under International Law', *Duke Journal of Comparative & International Law,* 10 (2000), p. 345–414.

Pritchard, R. John, 'The International Military Tribunal for the Far East and the Allied National War Crimes Trials in Asia', in M. Cherif Bassiouni (ed.), *International criminal law: enforcement* (2nd edn., III; Ardsley, New York: Transnational Publishers, 1999), p. 109–146.

Raj Kumar, C, 'Corruption as a Human Rights Issue in South Asia: Law, Development and Governance', *Human Rights 2006: the Year in Review* (Castan Centre for Human Rights Law, Monash University, Melbourne, 1 December 2006).

Raj Kumar, C, 'Corruption and Human Rights – I', *Frontline*, 19/19 (14–27 September 2002).

Raj Kumar, C, 'Corruption and Human Rights – II', *Frontline*, 19/20 (12–25 October 2002).

Raj Kumar, C, 'Corruption and Human Rights: Promoting Transparency in Governance and the Fundamental Right to Corruption – Free Service in India', *Columbia Journal of Asian Law,* 17 (2003), p. 31–72.

Rajesh Babu, R, 'The United Nations Convention against Corruption: A Critical Overview', *Social Science Research Network,* (1 March 2006).

Ramcharan, Bert G., 'Follow-up of the Treaty Body Conclusions by the Treaty Mechanisms and the UN Mechanisms Beyond', in Anne F. Bayefsky (ed.), *The UN Human Rights Treaty System in the 21st Century* (The Hague: Kluwer Law International, 2000), p. 277–283.

Rayar, Louise and Wadsworth, Stafford, *The Dutch Penal Code* (The American Series of Foreign Penal Codes, 30; Littleton, Colorado: Rothman & Co, 1997).

Reuters Africa, 'Tunisian Court Sentences Ben Ali for Corruption', <http://af.reuters.com/article/topNews/idAFJOE76S02V20110729>, accessed 29 July 2011.

Roach, Steven R., *Politicizing the International Criminal Court: The Convergence of Politics, Ethics, and Law* (Lanham: Rowman & Littlefield Publishers, 2006).

Robinson, Darryl, 'The Elements of Crimes against Humanity – III. Elements of the Specific Forms of Crime against Humanity: Article 7(1)(a)-Article 7(G)', in Roy S. Lee (ed.), *The International Criminal Court: Elements of Crimes and Rules of Procedure and Evidence* (Ardsley: Transnational Publishers, 2001), p. 80–93.

Robinson, Mary, 'Foreword', in Transparency International (ed.), *Global Corruption Report 2006: Corruption and Health* (London – Ann Arbor, Michigan: Pluto Press, 2006).

Rodley, Nigel and Pollard, Matt *The Treatment of Prisoners under International Law* (Oxford: Oxford University Press, 2009).

Roos, de Th. A., *Strafbaarstelling van Economische Delicten: een Crimineel-Politieke Studie* (Arnhem: Gouda Quint, 1987).

Rose-Ackerman, Susan, 'The Political Economy of Corruption', in Kimberley Ann Elliott (ed.), *Corruption and the Global Economy* (Washington, D.C.: Institute for International Economics, 1997), p. 31–60.

Rose-Ackerman, Susan, *Corruption and Government: Causes, Consequences and Reform* (Cambridge: Cambridge University Press, 1999).

Rossbacher, Henry H. and Young, Tracy W., 'The Foreign Corrupt Practices Act: An American Response to Corruption', in Barry Rider (ed.), *Corruption: The Enemy Within* (The Hague/London/Boston: Kluwer Law International, 1997), p. 209–230.

Ruzindana, Augustine, 'The Importance of Leadership in Fighting Corruption in Uganda', in Kimberley Ann Elliott (ed.), *Corruption and the Global Economy* (Washington, D.C.: Institute for International Economics, 1997), p. 133–145.

Safaralieva, Rena, 'Azerbaijan's Yawning Gap between Reforms on Paper and in Practice', in Transparency International (ed.), *Global Corruption Report 2007: Corruption in Judicial Systems* (Cambridge: Cambridge University Press, 2007), p. 175–178.

Salbu, Steven R., 'Bribery in the Global Market: A Critical Analysis of the Foreign Corrupt Practices Act', *Washington and Lee Law Review,* 54 (1997), p. 229–287.

Salbu, Steven R., 'Extraterritorial Restriction of Bribery: A Premature Evocation of the Normative Global Village', *Yale Journal of International Law,* 24 (1999), p. 223–255.

Salbu, Steven R., 'The Foreign Corrupt Practices Act as a Threat to Global Harmony', *Michigan Journal of International Law,* 20 (1999), p. 419–449.

Samuel, Linda M., 'Repatriation Obligations under the United Nations Convention against Corruption', *Resource Material Series,* 65 (2005), p. 58–64.

Sandoz, Yves, 'The history of the grave breaches regime', *Journal of International Criminal Justice,* 7 (2009), p. 657–682.

Savedoff, William D., 'Pay for Honesty? Lessons on Wages and Corruption from Public Hospitals', in Taryn Vian, William D. Savedoff, and Harald Mathisen (eds.), *Anticorruption in the Health Sector: Strategies for Transparency and Accountability* (Sterling, VA: Kumarian Press, 2010), p. 69–76.

Savedoff, William D. and Joselow, Ethan, 'Budget Transparency, Civil Society and Public Expenditure Tracking Surveys', in Taryn Vian, William D. Savedoff, and Harald Mathisen (eds.), *Anticorruption in the Health Sector: Strategies for Transparency and Accountability* (Sterling, VA: Kumarian Press, 2010), p. 123–136.

Scarpa, Silvia, *Trafficking in Human Beings: Modern Slavery* (Oxford: Oxford University Press, 2008).

SCHABAS, WILLIAM A., 'War Economies, Economic Actors, and International Criminal Law', in Karen Ballentine and Heiko Nitzschke (eds.), *Profiting from Peace: Managing the Resource Dimension of Civil War* (Boulder: Lynne Rienner Publishers 2005), p. 425–443.

SCHABAS, WILLIAM A., 'Travaux Préparatoires of the Rome Statute' (9 April 2008), <http://humanrightsdoctorate.blogspot.com/2008/04/travaux-prparatoires-of-rome-statute.html>, accessed 11 January 2010.

SCHARF, MICHAEL P., 'The Draft Statute for an International Criminal Court', in M. Cherif Bassiouni (ed.), *International criminal law: enforcement* (2nd edn., III; Ardsley, New York: Transnational Publishers, 1999), p. 637–653.

SERAP NIGERIA, <www.serap-nigeria.org/cases-in-court>.

SHAW, MALCOLM N., *International Law* (6th edn.; Cambridge: Cambridge University Press, 2008).

SCHEININ, MARTIN, 'Impact on the Law of Treaties', in Menno T. Kamminga and Martin Scheinin (eds.), *The Impact of Human Rights Law on General International Law* (Oxford: Oxford University Press, 2009), p. 23–36.

SCHMIDT, MARKUS G., 'Follow-up Mechanisms before UN Human Rights Treaty Bodies and the UN Mechanisms Beyond', in Anne F. Bayefsky (ed.), *The UN Human Rights Treaty System in the 21st Century* (The Hague: Kluwer Law International, 2000), p. 233–249.

SCHROTH, PETER W., 'The African Union Convention on Preventing and Combating Corruption', *Journal of African Law,* 49 (2005), p. 24–38.

SECURITIES AND EXHANGE COMMISSION WEBSITE, <www.sec.gov>, accessed 7 October 2008.

SEGAL, PHILIP, 'Coming Clean on Dirty Dealing: Time for a Fact-Based Evaluation of the Foreign Corrupt Practices Act', *Florida Journal of International Law,* 18 (2006), p. 169–210.

SENTURIA, J.J, 'Corruption, Political', in E.R.A. Seligman (ed.), *Encyclopaedia of the Social Sciences* (New York: Macmillan, 1931), p. 448–452.

SEPPÄNEN, MAARIA and VIRTANEN, PEKKA, *Corruption, Poverty and Gender. With Case Studies of Nicaragua and Tanzania* (Finland Ministry for Foreign Affairs, 2008).

SEPÚLVEDA, MAGDALENA, *The Nature of the Obligations under the International Covenant on Economic, Social and Cultural Rights* (School of Human Rights Research, 18; Antwerpen: Intersentia, 2003).

SEPÚLVEDA CARMONA, MAGDALENA and BACIO TERRACINO, JULIO, 'Corruption and Human Rights: Making the Connection', in Martine Boersma and Hans Nelen (eds.), *Corruption & Human Rights: Interdisciplinary Perspectives* (Antwerp: Intersentia, 2010), p. 25–49.

SHALEV, CARMEL, 'State Reporting and the Convention on the Elimination of All Forms of Discrimination against Women', in Anne F. Bayefsky (ed.), *The UN Human Rights Treaty System in the 21st Century* (The Hague: Kluwer Law International, 2000), p. 23–34.

SHEPHERD, CHRIS R and NIJMAN, VINCENT, 'Elephant and Ivory Trade in Myanmar', (Petaling Jaya, Selangor, Malaysia: TRAFFIC Southeast Asia, 2008).

SHORE, CRIS and HALLER, DIETER, 'Introduction – Sharp Practice: Anthropology and the Study of Corruption', in Dieter Haller and Cris Shore (eds.), *Corruption: Anthropological Perspectives* (London: Pluto Press, 2005), p. 1–26.

SIERRA LEONE TRUTH & RECONCILIATION COMMISSION, 'Witness to Truth: Volume 2', (2004).

SIKKEMA, E., 'De Strafrechtelijke Corruptiewetgeving; Opmerkingen naar Aanleiding van Wetsvoorstel 31 391', *Strafblad,* 7/1 (20 February 2009), p. 5–13.

SINGER, PETER, *Animal Liberation* (New York: Harper Collins, 1975).

SISSENER, TONE KRISTIN, 'Anthropological Perspectives on Corruption', *Working Paper, 2001:5* (Bergen: Chr. Michelsen Institute, 2001).

SKOGLY, S, 'Crimes against humanity – revisited: is there a role for economic, social and cultural rights?' *The International Journal of Human Rights,* 5 (2001), p. 58–80.

SLIEDREGT, E. VAN, *The Criminal Responsibility of Individuals for Violations of International Humanitarian Law* (The Hague: TMC Asser Press, 2003).

SLIEDREGT, E. VAN, 'Criminal Responsibility in International Law: Liability Shaped by Policy Goals and Moral Outrage', *European Journal of Crime, Criminal Law and Criminal Justice,* 14 (2006), p. 81–114.

SLOANE, ROBERT D., 'The Expressive Capacity of International Punishment: The Limits of the National Law Analogy and the Potential of International Criminal Law', *Stanford Journal of International Law,* 43 (2007), p. 39–94.

SLYE, RONALD C. and SCHAACK, BETH VAN, *International Criminal Law: The Essentials* (New York: Aspen Publishers, 2009).

SMITH, JACK, PIETH, MARK, and JORGE, GUILLERMO, 'The Recovery of Stolen Assets: A Fundamental Principle of the UN Convention Against Corruption', *U4 Brief* (Bergen, Norway: Chr. Michelsen Institute, February 2007).

SNIDER, THOMAS R. and KIDANE, WON 'Combating Corruption through International Law in Africa: A Comparative Analysis', *Cornell International Law Journal,* 40 (2007), p. 691–748.

SOUTHERN AFRICAN DEVELOPMENT COMMUNITY WEBSITE, accessed 7 October 2008

SPORKIN, STANLEY, 'The Worldwide Banning of Schmiergeld: A Look at the Foreign Corrupt Practices Act on Its Twentieth Birthday', *Northwestern Journal of International Law & Business,* 18 (1998), p. 269–281.

SUBEDI, SURYA P., 'The UN Human Rights Mandate in Cambodia: the Challenge of a Country in Transition and the Experience of the Special Rapporteur for the Country', *The International Journal of Human Rights,* 15/2 (2011), p. 249–264.

SUBEDI, SURYA P., *et al.*, 'The Role of the Special Rapporteurs of the United Nations Human Rights Council in the Development and Promotion of International Human Rights Norms', *The International Journal of Human Rights,* 15/2 (2011), p. 155–161.

SUNGA, LYAL S., 'The Special Procedures of the UN Commission on Human Rights: Should They Be Scrapped?' in Gudmundur Alfredsson, *et al.* (eds.), *International Human Rights Monitoring Mechanisms. Essays in Honour of Jakob Th. Möller* (The Raoul Wallenberg Institute Human Rights Library, 7; The Hague: Kluwer Law International 2001), p. 233–277.

SURJADINATA, KENNETH U., 'Revisiting Corrupt Practices from a Market Perspective', *Emory International Law Review,* 12 (1998), p. 1021–1090.

SMITH, DANIEL JORDAN, *A Culture of Corruption. Everyday Deception and Popular Discontent in Nigeria* (Princeton: Princeton University Press, 2007).

SMITH, JOYOTEE, *et al.*, 'Illegal Logging, Collusive Corruption and Fragmented Governments in Kalimantan, Indonesia', in Luca Tacconi (ed.), *Illegal Logging: Law Enforcement, Livelihoods and the Timber Trade* (London: Earthscan, 2007), p. 91–109.

SMITH, R.J., *et al.*, 'Governance and the Loss of Biodiversity', *Nature,* 426 (6 November 2003), p. 67–70.

SMITH, R.J. and WALPOLE, M.J., 'Should Conservationists Pay More Attention to Corruption?' *Oryx,* 39 (2005), p. 251–256.

SOKWANELE, 'Corruption in the Passport Office', <www.sokwanele.com/thisiszimbabwe/archives/591>, accessed 6 July 2011.

SOUTH AFRICAN HUMAN RIGHTS COMMISSION, 'The Right of Access to Adequate Housing', *5th Economic and Social Rights Report Series, 2002/2003 Financial Year* (21 June 2004).

SØREIDE, TINA, 'Corruption in Public Procurement. Causes, Consequences and Cures', *CMI Report, R 2002:1* (Bergen,: Chr. Michelsen Institute, 2002).

STARR, SONJA, 'Extraordinary Crimes at Ordinary Times: International Justice Beyond Crisis Situations', *Northwestern University Law Review,* 101 (2007), p. 1257–1314.

STEINER, HENRY J., 'Individual Claims in a World of Massive Violations: What Role for the Human Rights Committee?' in Philip Alston and James Crawford (eds.), *The Future of UN Human Rights Treaty Monitoring* (Cambridge: Cambridge University Press, 2000), p. 15–53.

STOITCHKOVA, DESISLAVA, *Towards Corporate Liability in International Criminal Law* (School of Human Rights Research Series, 38; Antwerp: Intersentia, 2010).

SUKSI, MARKKU, 'Good Governance in the Electoral Process', in Hans-Otto Sano and Gudmundur Alfredsson (eds.), *Human Rights and Good Governance. Building Bridges* (The Raoul Wallenberg Institute Human Rights Library, 9; The Hague: Kluwer Law International, 2002), p. 203–227.

SUNGA, LYAL S. and BOTTIGLIERO, ILARIA, 'In-Depth Study on the Linkages between Anti-Corruption and Human Rights for the United Nations Development Program'(Raoul Wallenberg Institute, 15 January 2007).

TALLGREN, IMMI, 'The Sensibility and Sense of International Criminal Law', *European Journal of International Law,* 13 (2002), p. 561–595.

TARULLO, DANIEL K., 'The Limits of Institutional Design: Implementing the OECD Anti-Bribery Convention', *Virginia Journal of International Law,* 44 (2004), p. 665–710.

THE NEW ZIMBABWEAN, 11 December 2009, 'Spend it like Grace', <www.newzimbabwe.com/pages/shopper6.11592.html>, accessed 7 January 2012.

THEYTAZ-BERGMAN, LAURA, 'State Reporting and the Role of Non-Governmental Organizations', in: Anne F. Bayefsky (ed.), *The UN Human Rights Treaty System in the 21st Century* (The Hague: Kluwer Law International, 2000), p. 45–56.

THOMSON, MARK, 'Defining the Role of Non-Governmental Organizations: Splendid Isolation or Better Use of NGO Expertise?' in Anne F. Bayefsky (ed.), *The UN Human Rights Treaty System in the 21st Century* (The Hague: Kluwer Law International, 2000), p. 219–226.

TIJSSEN, HERVÉ, *De Juridische Dissertatie Onder de Loep. De Verantwoording Van Methodologische Keuzes in Juridische Dissertaties* (Den Haag: Boom Juridische Uitgevers, 2009).

TOEBES, BRIGIT, 'The Impact of Acts of Corruption on the Enjoyment of the Right to Health', *Working Paper* (Geneva: International Council on Human Rights Policy, 2007).

TOEBES, BRIGIT, *The Right to Health as a Human Right in International Law* (School of Human Rights Research Series, 1; Antwerp: Intersentia, 1999).

TOEBES, BRIGIT, 'Health Sector Corruption and Human Rights: A Case Study', in Martine Boersma and Hans Nelen (eds.), *Corruption and Human Rights: Interdisciplinary Perspectives* (Maastricht Series in Human Rights; Antwerp: Intersentia, 2010), p. 91–123.

TOEBES, BRIGIT, 'Human Rights, Health Sector Abuse and Corruption', *Human Rights & Human Welfare working papers, no. 64* (1 April 2011).

TOMASEVSKI, KATARINA, *Human Rights Obligations in Education: The 4-a Scheme* (Nijmegen: Wolf Legal Publishers, 2006).

TOMBS, STEVE and WHYTE, DAVE, 'White Collar Crime', in Eugene McLaughlin and John Muncie (eds.), *The Sage Dictionary of Criminology* (2nd edn.; London: SAGE Publications, 2005), p. 462–464.

TOMUSCHAT, CHRISTIAN, *Human Rights: Between Idealism and Realism* (2nd edn., The Collected Courses of the Academy of European Law, XIII/1; Oxford: Oxford University Press, 2008).

TRANSPARENCY INTERNATIONAL, *Global Corruption Report 2006: Corruption and Health* (London – Ann Arbor, Michigan: Pluto Press, 2006).

TRANSPARENCY INTERNATIONAL, *Global Corruption Report 2007: Corruption in Judicial Systems* (Cambridge: Cambridge University Press, 2007).

TRANSPARENCY INTERNATIONAL, 'Executive Summary: Key Judicial Corruption Problems', in Transparency International (ed.), *Global Corruption Report 2007: Corruption in Judicial Systems* (Cambridge: Cambridge University Press, 2007), p. xxi-xxviii.

TRANSPARENCY INTERNATIONAL, 'Human Rights and Corruption', *Working Paper* (2008).

TRANSPARENCY INTERNATIONAL, 'Frequently Asked Questions on Corruption and Africa', <www.transparency.org/news_room/in_focus/2005/g8_summit/faq>23 May 2011.

TRANSPARENCY INTERNATIONAL, 'Frequently Asked Questions About Corruption', <www.transparency.org/news_room/faq/corruption_faq>, accessed 20 May 2011.

TRANSPARENCY INTERNATIONAL, 'Poverty and Corruption', *Working Paper 02/2008* (2008).

TRANSPARENCY INTERNATIONAL, 'UN Corruption Conference: Failure to Act on Critical Issue a 'Major Setback' for the Fight against Corruption', *Press Release* (1 February 2008).

TRANSPARENCY INTERNATIONAL, 'Effectively Monitoring the United Nations Convention against Corruption', *Policy Position Paper 1* (2008).

TRANSPARENCY INTERNATIONAL, 'Inter-American Anti-Corruption Convention Strengthened by Member States', <www.transparency.org/news_room/latest_news/press_releases/2010/2010_12_15_cosp_third_meeting_en>, accessed 25 May 2011.

TRANSPARENCY INTERNATIONAL, ECOWAS Protocol, <www.transparency.org/global_priorities/international_conventions/conventions_instruments/ecowas_protocol>, accessed 24 May 2011.

Transparency International Croatia, 'Croatia: Still in Transition', in Transparency International (ed.), *Global Corruption Report 2007: Corruption in Judicial Systems* (Cambridge: Cambridge University Press, 2007), p. 194–197.

Transparency International Paraguay, 'Politics and Nepotism Plague Paraguay's Courts', in Transparency International (ed.), *Global Corruption Report 2007: Corruption in Judicial Systems* (Cambridge: Cambridge University Press, 2007), p. 255–258.

Travaux Préparatoires <http://untreaty.un.org/cod/icc/rome/proceedings/contents.htm>.

Trochim, William M.K. (Cornell University), 'Research Methods Knowledge Base', <www.socialresearchmethods.net/kb/dedind.php>, accessed 26 May 2009

Tyagi, Yogesh, *The UN Human Rights Committee: Practice and Procedure* (Cambridge: Cambridge University Press, 2011).

Udombana, Nsongurua J., 'Fighting Corruption Seriously? Africa's Anti-Corruption Convention', *Singapore Journal of International and Comparative Law,* 7 (2003), p. 447–488.

United Nations Office on Drugs and Crime, 'Signatories to the United Nations Convention against Corruption', <www.unodc.org/unodc/en/treaties/CAC/signatories.html>, accessed 26 May 2011.

United Nations Office on Drugs and Crime ---, 'Signatories to the United Nations Convention against Transnational Organized Crime', <www.unodc.org/unodc/en/treaties/CTOC/countrylist.html>, accessed 26 May 2011.

United Nations Office on Drugs and Crime (Regional Office for Southern Africa). Edited by Ugljesa Zvekic, 'Corruption & Anti-Corruption in Southern Africa. Analysis Based on the Results of the Regional Seminar on Anti-Corruption Investigating Strategies with Particular Regard to Drug Control for the SADC Member States.' <www.unodc.org/pdf/southafrica/southafrica_corruption.pdf>, accessed 21 October 2008.

United Nations Treaty Collection, <http://treaties.un.org>.

United Nations, Universal Human Rights Index, <www.universalhumanrightsindex.org>.

UN.GIFT, <www.ungift.org>.

United Nations Global Initiative to Fight Human Trafficking, 'Corruption and Human Trafficking: The Grease That Facilitates the Crime', *The Vienna Forum to fight Human Trafficking* (Austria Center Vienna, 13–15 February 2008).

United States Department of Justice, 'Lay-Person's Guide to FCPA', (Washington United States Department of Justice).

University of Minnesota Human Rights Library, <www1.umn.edu/humanrts/google/localsearch.html>. and <www1.umn.edu/humanrts/cases/commissn.htm>.

UPR Info, 'Analytical Assessment of the Universal Periodic Review', (Geneva, 2010). <www.upr-info.org/database/> accessed 21 June 2011.

U4 Anti-Corruption Resource Centre, 'Corruption in the Education Sector', *U4 Issue* (Bergen: Chr. Michelsen Institute, 2006).

U4 Anti-Corruption Resource Centre, 'Corruption in the Health Sector', *U4 Brief* (Bergen: Chr. Michelsen Institute, 2008).

U4 Anti-Corruption Resource Centre, 'Corruption Glossary', <www.u4.no/document/glossary.cfm>, accessed 18 May 2011.

U4 Anti-Corruption Resource Centre, 'FAQs: Causes and Consequences of Corruption', <www.u4.no/helpdesk/faq/faqs1.cfm>20 May 2011.

U4 Anti-Corruption Resource Centre, 'Special Courts for Corruption Cases', *U4 Helpdesk Query* <www.u4.no/helpdesk/helpdesk/query.cfm?id=19>, accessed 10 June 2011.

Vallini, Antonio, 'Mens Rea', in Antonio Cassese (ed.), *The Oxford Companion to International Criminal Justice* (Oxford: Oxford University Press, 2009), p. 412–415.

Vel, Guy de and Csonka, Peter, 'The Council of Europe Activities against Corruption', in Cyrille Fijnaut and Leo Huberts (eds.), *Corruption, Integrity and Law Enforcement* (The Hague: Kluwer Law International, 2002), p. 361–380.

Vian, Taryn, Savedoff, William D., and Mathisen, Harald (eds.), *Anticorruption in the Health Sector: Strategies for Transparency and Accountability* (Sterling, VA: Kumarian Press, 2010).

Vian, Taryn, Savedoff, William D., and Mathisen, Harald, 'Introduction: Closing Opportunities for Corruption in the Health Sector', in Taryn Vian, William D. Savedoff, and Harald Mathisen (eds.), *Anticorruption in the Health Sector: Strategies for Transparency and Accountability* (Sterling, VA: Kumarian Press, 2010), p. 3–15.

Vian, Taryn, Savedoff, William D., and Mathisen, Harald, 'Preventing Drug Diversion through Supply Chain Management', in Taryn Vian, William D. Savedoff, and Harald Mathisen (eds.), *Anticorruption in the Health Sector: Strategies for Transparency and Accountability* (Sterling, VA: Kumarian Press, 2010), p. 77–84.

Viljoen, Frans, *International Human Rights Law in Africa* (Oxford: Oxford University Press, 2007).

Wachira, George Mukundi, 'African Court on Human and Peoples' Rights: Ten Years on and Still No Justice', (Minority Rights Group International 2008).

Way, Sally-Anne, 'The Role of the UN Human Rights Bodies in Promoting and Protecting the Right to Food', in Wende Barth Eide and Uwe Kracht (eds.), *Food and Human Rights in Development, Volume I* (Antwerp: Intersentia, 2005), p. 205–228.

Webb, Philippa, 'The United Nations Convention against Corruption: Global Achievement or Missed Opportunity?' *Journal of International Economic Law,* 8 (2005), p. 191–229.

Wei, Shang-Jin, 'How Taxing Is Corruption on International Investors?' *NBER Working Papers, number 6030* (Cambridge, Massachusetts: National Bureau of Economic Research, February 1997).

Weissbrodt, David, *The Right to a Fair Trial under the Universal Declaration of Human Rights and the International Covenant on Civil and Political Rights*, ed. Hurst Hannum (The Universal Declaration of Human Rights, 1; The Hague: Martinus Nijhoff Publishers, 2001).

Werle, Gerhard, *Principles of International Criminal Law* (The Hague: TMC Asser Press, 2009).

Werle, Gerhard and Jessberger, Florian, '"Unless Otherwise Provided": Article 30 of the ICC Statute and the Mental Element of Crimes under International Criminal Law', *Journal of International Criminal Justice,* 3 (2005), p. 35–55.

Westendorp, Ingrid, *Women and Housing: Gender Makes a Difference* (School of Human Rights Research Series, 23; Antwerp: Intersentia, 2007).

Westlaw, <www.westlaw.com>

WIERDA, MARIEKE, 'Special Tribunal for Lebanon', in Antonio Cassese (ed.), *The Oxford Companion to International Criminal Justice* (Oxford: Oxford University Press, 2009), p. 519–520.

WILSON, RICHARD J., 'Researching the Jurisprudence of the Inter-American Commission on Human Rights: A Litigator's Perspective'; <www1.umn.edu/humanrts/iachr/first.html>.

WINDSOR, DUANE and GETZ, KATHLEEN A., 'Multilateral Cooperation to Combat Corruption: Normative Regimes Despite Mixed Motives and Diverse Values', *Cornell International Law Journal,* 33 (2000), p. 731–772.

WORLD BANK, *World Development Report 1997: The State in a Changing World* (New York: Oxford University Press, 1997).

WORLD BANK (ed.), *Voice for the World's Poor: Selected Speeches and Writings of World Bank President James D. Wolfensohn, 1995–2005* (Washington, DC, 2005).

WORLD BANK, 'Helping Countries Combat Corruption. The Role of the World Bank', <www1.worldbank.org/publicsector/anticorrupt/corruptn/corrptn.pdf>, accessed 12 April 2010.

YARNOLD, BARBARA M., 'The Doctrinal Basis for the International Criminalisation Process', in M. Cherif Bassiouni (ed.), *International criminal law: crimes* (2nd edn., I; Ardsley, New York: Transnational Publishers, 1999), p. 127–152.

ZERVOS, ALEXANDROS, 'Amending the Foreign Corrupt Practices Act: Repealing the Exemption For "Routine Government Action" Payments', *Penn State International Law Review,* 25 (2006–2007), p. 251–294.

ZHANG, SHELDON X. and PINEDA, SAMUEL L., 'Corruption as a Causal Factor in Human Trafficking', in Dina Siegel and Hans Nelen (eds.), *Organized Crime: Culture, Markets and Policies* (Studies of Organized Crime: Springer, 2008), p. 41–55.

United Nations Documents

UN Human Rights Treaty Bodies

Human Rights Committee (HRC)

General Comments

General Comment No. 18 on non-discrimination, Thirty-seventh session (1989).

General Comment No. 25 on the right to participate in public affairs, voting rights and the right of equal access to public service (Article 25), Fifty-seventh session (12 July 1996), UN Doc. CCPR/C/21/Rev.1/Add.7.

General Comment No. 27 on freedom of movement (Article 12), Sixty-seventh session (18 October 1999), UN Doc. CCPR/C/21/Rev.1/Add.9.

General Comment No. 28, Sixty-eighth session, Article 3: equality of rights between men and women, (2000) UN Doc. A/55/40, §12.

General Comment No. 32 on the right to equality before courts and tribunals and to a fair trial (Article 14), Ninetieth session (23 August 2007), UN Doc. CCPR/C/GC/32.

Concluding Observations

Italy 3 August 1994, UN Doc. CCPR/C/79/Add.37

Georgia 5 May 1997, UN Doc. CCPR/C/79/Add.75

Portugal (Macau) 5 May 1997, UN Doc. CCPR/C/79/Add.77

Algeria 18 August 1998, UN Doc. CCPR/C/79/Add.95

Cambodia 27 July 1999, UN Doc. CCPR/C/79/Add.108

Portugal (Macau) 4 November 1999, UN Doc. CCPR/C/79/Add.115

Kyrgyzstan 24 July 2000, UN Doc. CCPR/CO/69/KGZ

Trinidad and Tobago 10 November 2000, UN Doc. CCPR/CO/70/TTO

Argentina 15 November 2000, UN Doc. CCPR/CO/70/ARG

Georgia 19 April 2002, UN Doc. CCPR/CO/74/GEO

Benin 1 December 2004, UN Doc. CCPR/CO/82/BEN

Albania 2 December 2004, UN Doc. CCPR/CO/82/ALB

Kenya 29 April 2005, UN Doc. CCPR/CO/83/KEN

Brazil 1 December 2005, UN Doc. CCPR/C/BRA/CO/2

Congo 26 April 2006, UN Doc. CCPR/C/COD/CO/3

Central African Republic 27 July 2006, UN Doc. CCPR/C/CAF/CO/2

Kosovo 14 August 2006, UN Doc. CCPR/C/UNK/CO/1

Bosnia and Herzegovina 22 November 2006, UN Doc. CCPR/C/BIH/CO/1

Ukraine 28 November 2006, UN Doc. CCPR/C/UKR/CO/6

Georgia 15 November 2007, UN Doc. CCPR/C/GEO/CO/3

Macedonia 17 April 2008, UN Doc. CCPR/C/MKD/CO/2

Rwanda 31 March 2009, UN Doc. CCPR/C/RWA/CO/3

Chad 11 August 2009, UN Doc. CCPR/C/TCD/CO/1

Azerbaijan 13 August 2009, UN Doc. CCPR/C/AZE/CO/3
Moldova 4 November 2009, UN Doc. CCPR/C/MDA/CO/2
Russia 24 November 2009, UN Doc. CCPR/C/RUS/CO/6
Uzbekistan 7 April 2010, CCPR/C/UZB/CO/3
Mongolia 2 May 2011, UN Doc. CCPR/C/MNG/CO/5

Views on Individual Complaints
Communication no. 526/1993, *Michael and Brian Hill v. Spain*, views of 22 June 1997, UN Doc. CCPR/C/59/D/526/1993.
Communication no. 933/2000, *Mundyo Busyo et al. v. Democratic Republic of Congo*, views of 31 July 2003, U.N. Doc. CCPR/C/78/D/933/2000.
Communication no. 1128/2002, *Rafael Marques de Morais v. Angola*, views of 29 March 2005, UN Doc. CCPR/C/83/D/1128/2002.
Communication no. 1037/2001, *Zdzislaw Bator v. Poland*, inadmissibility decision of 22 July 2005, UN Doc. CCPR/C/84/D/1037/2001.
Communication no. 1353/2005, *Philip Afuson Njaru v. Cameroon*, views of 19 March 2007, UN Doc. CCPR/C/89/D/1353/2005.
Communication no. 1520/2006, *Munguwambuto Kabwe Peter Mwamba v. Zambia*, views of 10 March 2010, UN Doc. CCPR/C/98/D/1520/2006.

Committee on Economic, Social and Cultural Rights (CESCR)

General Comments
General Comment No. 3 on the nature of States Parties' obligations (Art. 2, par. 1 of the Covenant), Fifth session (1990).
General Comment No. 4 on the right to housing (Art. 11(1)), Sixth session, 1991.
General Comment No. 7 on the right to adequate housing (Article 11(1)): forced evictions, Sixteenth session, 1997.
General Comment No. 11 on plans of action for primary education (Art. 14), Twentieth session (1999) UN
Doc. E/C.12/1999/4.
General Comment No. 12 on the right to adequate food (Article 11), Twentieth session (1999), UN Doc. E/C.12/1999/5.
General Comment No. 13 on the right to education (Art. 13), Twenty-first session (1999), UN Doc. E/C.12/1999/10.
General Comment No. 14 on the right to the highest attainable standard of health (Art. 12), Twenty-second session (2000), UN Doc. E/C.12/2000/4.

Concluding Observations
Dominican Republic 3 December 1996, UN Doc. E/C.12/1/Add.6
Russia 20 May 1997, UN Doc. E/C.12/1/Add.13
Dominican Republic 12 December 1997, UN Doc. E/C.12/1/Add.16
Azerbaijan 22 December 1997, UN Doc. E/C.12/1/Add.20
Nigeria 13 May 1998, UN Doc. E/C.12/1/Add.23
Mexico 8 December 1999, UN Doc. E/C.12/1/Add.41

Bolivia 21 May 2001, UN Doc. E/C.12/1/Add.60
Georgia 19 December 2002, UN Doc. E/C.12/1/Add.83
Guatemala 12 December 2003, UN Doc. E/C.12/1/Add.93
Moldova 12 December 2003, UN Doc. E/C.12/1/Add.91
Azerbaijan 14 December 2004, UN Doc. E/C.12/1/Add.104
Serbia and Montenegro 23 June 2005, UN Doc. E/C.12/1/Add.108
Albania 21 November 2006, UN Doc. E/C.12/ALB/CO/1
Tajikistan 24 November 2006, UN Doc. E/C.12/TJK/CO/1
Latvia 7 January 2008, UN Doc. E/C.12/LVA/CO/1
India May 2008, UN Doc. E/C.12/IND/CO/5
Kenya 1 December 2008, UN Doc. E/C.12/KEN/CO/1
Angola 1 December 2008, UN Doc. E/C.12/AGO/CO/3
Philippines 1 December 2008, UN Doc. E/C.12/PHL/CO/4
Cambodia 22 May 2009, UN Doc. E/C.12/KHM/CO/1
Congo 20 November 2009, UN Doc. E/C.12/COD/CO/4
Madagascar 16 December 2009, UN Doc. E/C.12/MDG/CO/2
Chad 16 December 2009, UN Doc. E/C.12/TCD/CO/3
Colombia 21 May 2010, UN Doc. E/C.12/COL/CO/5
Algeria 7 June 2010, UN Doc. E/C.12/DZA/CO/4
Afghanistan 7 June 2010, UN Doc. E/C.12/AFG/CO/2–4
Kazakhstan 7 June 2010, UN Doc. E/C.12/KAZ/CO/1
Mauritius 8 June 2010, UN Doc. E/C.12/MUS/CO/4
Sri Lanka 9 December 2010, UN Doc. E/C.12/LKA/CO/2–4
Russia 1 June 2011, UN Doc. E/C.12/RUS/CO/5
Yemen 1 June 2011, UN Doc. E/C.12/YEM/CO/2

Miscellaneous

Compilation of guidelines on the form and content of reports to be submitted by State Parties to the international human rights treaties, 3 June 2009, UN Doc. HRI/GEN/2/Rev.6.

Committee on the Rights of the Child (CRC)

Concluding Observations
Thailand 26 October 1998, UN Doc. CRC/C/15/Add.97
Georgia 28 June 2000, UN Doc. CRC/C/15/Add.124
Cambodia 28 June 2000, UN Doc. CRC/C/15/Add.128
Tajikistan 23 October 2000, UN Doc. CRC/C/15/Add.136
Cameroon 6 November 2001, UN Doc. CRC/C/15/Add.164
Kenya 7 November 2001, UN Doc. CRC/C/15/Add.160
Malawi 2 April 2002, UN Doc. CRC/C/15/Add.174
Gabon 3 April 2002, UN Doc. CRC/C/15/Add.171
Mozambique 3 April 2002, UN Doc. CRC/C/15/Add.172
Zambia 2 July 2003, UN Doc. CRC/C/15/Add.206
Georgia 27 October 2003, UN Doc. CRC/C/15/Add.222

Pakistan 27 October 2003, UN Doc. CRC/C/15/Add.217
Liberia 4 June 2004, UN Doc. CRC/C/15/Add.236
Sao Tome and Principe 1 July 2004, UN Doc. CRC/C/15/Add.235
Kyrgyzstan 3 November 2004, UN Doc. CRC/C/15/Add.244
Angola 3 November 2004, UN Doc. CRC/C/15/Add.246
Albania 31 March 2005, UN Doc. CRC/C/15/Add.249
Togo 31 March 2005, UN Doc. CRC/C/15/Add.255
Nigeria 13 April 2005, UN Doc. CRC/C/15/Add.257,
Mongolia 21 September 2005, UN Doc. CRC/C/15/Add.264
Russia 23 November 2005, UN Doc. CRC/C/RUS/CO/3
Kazakhstan 17 March 2006, UN Doc. CRC/C/OPSC/KAZ/CO/1,
Uzbekistan 2 June 2006, UN Doc. CRC/C/UZB/CO/2
Benin 20 October 2006, UN Doc. CRC/C/BEN/CO/2
Congo 20 October 2006, UN Doc. CRC/C/COG/CO/1
Kyrgyzstan 4 May 2007, UN Doc. CRC/C/OPSC/KGZ/CO/1
Kenya 19 June 2007, UN Doc. CRC/C/KEN/CO/2
Ukraine 28 June 2007, UN Doc. CRC/C/OPSC/UKR/CO/1
Sierra Leone 20 June 2008, UN Doc. CRC/C/SLE/CO/2,
Bulgaria 21 January 2008, UN Doc. CRC/C/OPSC/BGR/CO/1
Bulgaria 23 June 2008, UN Doc. CRC/C/BGR/CO/2
Moldova 30 January 2009, UN Doc. CRC/C/MDA/CO/3
Bangladesh 12 June 2009, UN Doc. CRC/C/BGD/CO/4
Niger 12 June 2009, UN Doc. CRC/C/NER/CO/2
Romania 12 June 2009, UN Doc. CRC/C/ROM/CO/4
Philippines 22 October 2009, UN Doc. CRC/C/PHL/CO/3–4
Mozambique 4 November 2009, UN Doc. CRC/C/MOZ/CO/2
Mongolia 29 January 2010, UN Doc. CRC/C/MNG/CO/3–4
Tajikistan 5 February 2010, UN Doc. CRC/C/TJK/CO/2
Burkina Faso 9 February 2010, UN Doc. CRC/C/BFA/CO/3–4
El Salvador 17 February 2010, UN Doc. CRC/C/SLV/CO/3–4
Cameroon 18 February 2010, UN Doc. CRC/C/CMR/CO/2
Nigeria 11 June 2010, UN Doc. CRC/C/NGA/CO3–4
Burundi 1 October 2010, UN Doc. CRC/C/BDI/CO/2
Guatemala 1 October 2010, UN Doc. CRC/C/GTM/CO/3–4
Sierra Leone, 14 October 2010, UN Doc. CRC/C/OPSC/SLE/CO/1
Sri Lanka 19 October 2010, UN Doc. CRC/C/LKA/CO/3–4
Mexico 7 April 2011, UN Doc. CRC/C/OPSC/MEX/CO/1
Afghanistan 8 April 2011, UN Doc. CRC/C/AFG/CO/1
Ukraine 21 April 2011, UN Doc. CRC/C/UKR/CO/3–4

Committee on the Elimination of All Forms of Discrimination Against Women (CEDAW)

Concluding Observations
China 5 February 1999, UN Doc. CEDAW/C/1999/I/L.1/Add.7

Thailand 3 February 2006, UN Doc. CEDAW/C/THA/CO/5
Uganda 5 November 2010, UN Doc. CEDAW/C/UGA/CO/7

Committee on the Elimination of Racial Discrimination (CERD)

Concluding Observations

Albania 10 December 2003, UN Doc. CERD/C/63/CO/1
Madagascar 10 December 2004, UN Doc. CERD/C/65/CO/4
Uzbekistan 4 April 2006, UN Doc. CERD/C/UZB/CO/5
Bulgaria 23 March 2009, UN Doc. CERD/C/BGR/CO/19
Azerbaijan 26 August 2009, UN Doc. CERD/C/AZE/CO/6
Chad 21 September 2009, UN Doc. CERD/C/TCD/15
Cambodia 16 March 2010, UN Doc. CERD/C/KHM/CO/8–13.

Committee Against Torture (CAT)

Concluding Observations

Italy 26 July 1995, UN Doc. A/50/44
Cambodia 5 February 2004, UN Doc. CAT/C/CR/31/7
Ecuador 8 February 2006, UN Doc. CAT/C/ECU/CO/3
Tajikistan 7 December 2006, UN Doc. CAT/C/TJK/CO/1
Nepal 13 April 2007, UN Doc. CAT/C/NPL/CO/2
Benin 19 February 2008, UN Doc. CAT/C/BEN/CO/2
Indonesia 2 July 2008, UN Doc. CAT/C/IDN/CO/2
Kenya 19 January 2009, UN Doc. CAT/C/KEN/CO/1
Chad 19 May 2009, UN Doc. CAT/C/TCD/CO/1
Austria 20 May 2010, UN Doc. CAT/C/AUT/CO/2–5
Cameroon 19 May 2010, UN Doc. CAT/C/CMR/CO/4,
Cambodia 20 January 2011, UN Doc. CAT/C/KHM/CO/2

Views on Individual Complaints

Communication no. 221/2002, *M.M.K. v. Sweden*, decision of 15 May 2005, UN Doc. CAT/C/34/D/221/2002.

General Assembly

General Assembly Resolution 52/135, 27 February 1998, UN Doc. A/RES/52/135.
General Assembly Resolution 55/116, 12 March 2001, UN Doc. A/RES/55/116.
General Assembly Resolution 56/169, 28 February 2002, 56th session, UN Doc. A/RES/56/169.
General Assembly Resolution 56/175, 28 February 2002, UN Doc. A/RES/56/175.
General Assembly Res. 60/251, UN Doc. A/RES/60/251 (Establishment of the UN Human Rights Council)

Commission on Human Rights
Resolution 1999/15, 23 April 1999, UN Doc. E/CN.4/RES/1999/15.
Resolution 2000/27, 18 April 2000, UN Doc. E/CN.4/RES/2000/27.
Resolution 2001/18, 20 April 2001, UN Doc. E/CN.4/RES/2001/18.
Resolution 2001/82, 25 April 2001, UN Doc. E/CN.4/RES/2001/82.
Resolution 2002/16, 19 April 2002, UN Doc. E/CN.4/RES/2002/16.
Resolution 2003/79, 25 April 2003, UN Doc. E/CN.4/RES/2003/79.

Sub-Commission on the Promotion and Protection of Human Rights
Sub-Commission on the Promotion and Protection of Human Rights, Resolution 2003/2, UN Doc. E/CN.4/Sub.2/RES/2003/2
Sub-Commission on Human Rights Resolution, 5 August 2005, UN Doc. E/CN.4/Sub.2/2005/L.24/Rev.1.

UN Human Rights Council
Human Rights Council document 8/PRST/1, titled Modalities and practices for the universal periodic review process.
Human Rights Council Resolution 15/20, 8 October 2010, UN Doc. A/HRC/RES/15/20.

Universal Periodic Review
UPR Working Group outcome report Brazil, 1st session (2008), UN Doc. A/HRC/8/27
UPR Working Group outcome report Czech Republic, 1st session (2008), UN Doc. A/HRC/8/33
UPR Working Group outcome report Ghana, 1st session (2008), UN Doc. A/HRC/8/36,
UPR Working Group outcome report Poland, 1st session (2008), UN Doc. A/HRC/8/30
UPR Working Group outcome report Benin, 2nd session (2008), UN Doc. A/HRC/8/39
UPR Working Group outcome report Korea, 2nd session (2008), UN Doc. A/HRC/8/40
UPR Working Group outcome report Mali, 2nd session (2008), UN Doc. A/HRC/8/50
UPR Working Group outcome report Guatemala, 2nd session (2008), UN Doc. A/HRC/8/38
UPR Working Group outcome report Peru, 2nd session (2008), UN Doc A/HRC/8/37
UPR Working Group outcome report Romania, 2nd session (2008), UN Doc. A/HRC/8/49
UPR Working Group outcome report Tonga, 2nd session (2008), UN Doc. A/HRC/8/48
UPR Working Group outcome report Zambia, 2nd session (2008), UN Doc. A/HRC/8/43
UPR Working Group outcome report Burundi, 3rd session (2008), UN Doc. A/HRC/10/71
UPR Working Group outcome report Serbia, 3rd session (2008), UN Doc. A/HRC/10/78
UPR Working Group outcome report Montenegro, 3rd session (2008), UN Doc. A/HRC/10/74
UPR Working Group outcome report Germany, 4th session (2009). UN Doc. A/HRC/11/15
UPR Working Group outcome report Malaysia, 4th session (2009), UN Doc. A/HRC/11/30
UPR Working Group outcome report Mexico, 4th session (2009), UN Doc. A/HRC/11/27
UPR Working Group outcome report Afghanistan, 5th session (2009), UN Doc. A/HRC/12/9
UPR Working Group outcome report Belize, 5th session (2009), UN Doc. A/HRC/12/4
UPR Working Group outcome report Chad, 5th session (2009), UN Doc. A/HRC/12/5
UPR Working Group outcome report Macedonia, 5th session (2009), UN Doc. A/HRC/12/15
UPR Working Group outcome report Uruguay, 5th session (2009), UN Doc. A/HRC/12/12

UPR Working Group outcome report Vanuatu, 5th session (2009), UN Doc. A/HRC/12/14
UPR Working Group outcome report Vietnam, 5th session (2009), UN Doc. A/HRC/12/11
UPR Working Group outcome report Yemen, 5th session (2009), UN Doc. A/HRC/12/13
UPR Working Group outcome report Albania, 6th session (2009), UN Doc. A/HRC/13/6
UPR Working Group outcome report Cambodia, 6th session (2009), UN Doc. A/HRC/13/4
UPR Working Group outcome report Dominican Republic, 6th session (2010), UN Doc. A/HRC/13/3
UPR Working Group outcome report Equatorial Guinea, 6th session (2010), UN Doc. A/HRC/13/16
UPR Working Group outcome report Norway, 6th session (2009), UN Doc. A/HRC/13/5
UPR Working Group outcome report Angola, 7th session (2010), UN Doc. A/HRC/14/11
UPR Working Group outcome report El Salvador, 7th session (2010), UN Doc. A/HRC/14/5
UPR Working Group outcome report Bosnia and Herzegovina, 7th session (2010), UN Doc. A/HRC/14/16
UPR Working Group outcome report Madagascar, 7th session (2010), UN Doc. A/HRC/14/13
UPR Working Group outcome report Nicaragua, 7th session (2010), UN Doc. A/HRC/14/3
UPR Working Group outcome report Grenada, 8th session (2010), UN Doc. A/HRC/15/12
UPR Working Group outcome report Guinea-Bissau, 8th session (2010), UN Doc. A/HRC/15/10
UPR Working Group outcome report Kenya, 8th session (2010), UN Doc. A/HRC/15/8
UPR Working Group outcome report Kyrgyzstan, 8th session (2010), UN Doc. A/HRC/15/2
UPR Working Group outcome report Turkey, 8th session (2010), UN Doc. A/HRC/15/13

National Report submitted by Albania, UN Doc. A/HRC/WG.6/6/ALB/1

SPECIAL PROCEDURES

Special Rapporteur on Corruption and Its Impact on Human Rights

Working paper submitted by Ms. Christy Mbonu in accordance with Sub-Commission decision 2002/106, 14 May 2003, UN Doc. E/CN.4/Sub.2/2003/18.
Preliminary report of the Special Rapporteur on corruption and its impact on the full enjoyment of human rights, in particular economic, social and cultural rights, Sub-Cion 56th session, 7 July 2004, UN Doc. E/CN.4/Sub.2/2004/23.
Progress report submitted by the Special Rapporteur on corruption and its impact on the full enjoyment of human rights, in particular economic, social and cultural rights, Sub-Cion 57th session, 22 June 2005, UN Doc. E/CN.4/Sub.2/2005/18.
Final report of the Special Rapporteur on corruption and its impact on the full enjoyment of human rights, in particular economic, social and cultural rights, Sub-Cion 58th session, 8 August 2006, UN Doc. A/HRC/Sub.1/58/CRP.10.

Special Rapporteur on the Independence of Judges and Lawyers

Report CHR 54th session, 12 February 1998, UN Doc. E/CN.4/1998/39.
Report CHR 56th session, 21 February 2000, UN Doc. E/CN.4/2000/61.
Report CHR 57th session, 1 February 2001, UN Doc. E/CN.4/2001/65.

Report CHR 58th session, 11 February 2002, UN Doc. E/CN.4/2002/72.
Report CHR 59th session, 25 February 2003, UN Doc. E/CN.4/2003/65/Add.1.
Report CHR 60th session, 31 December 2003, UN Doc. E/CN.4/2004/60.
Report HRC 4th session, 18 January 2007, UN Doc. A/HRC/4/25.
Report GA 63rd session, 12 August 2008, UN Doc. A/63/271.
Report HRC 11th session, 24 March 2009, UN Doc. A/HRC/11/41.
Report HRC 14th session, 25 March 2010, UN Doc. A/HRC/14/26.
Report, Addendum: Communications to and from governments, HRC 14th session, 18 June 2010, UN Doc. A/HRC/14/26/Add.1.
Report GA 65th session, 10 August 2010, UN Doc. A/65/274

Special Rapporteur on Trafficking in Persons, Especially Women and Children
Report HRC 10th session, 20 February 2009, UN Doc. A/HRC/10/16.
Report, Mission to Bosnia and Herzegovina, CHR 62nd session, 30 November 2005, UN Doc. E/CN.4/2006/62/Add.2.
Report, Summary of cases transmitted to Governments and replies received, CHR 62nd session, 27 March 2006, UN Doc. E/CN.4/2006/62/Add.1.
Report, Summary of cases transmitted to Governments and replies received, HRC 4th session, 30 May 2007, UN Doc. A/HRC/4/23/Add.1.
Report, Mission to Japan, HRC 14th session, 12 May 2010, UN Doc. A/HRC/14/32/Add.4.

Special Rapporteur on the Sale of Children, Child Prostitution and Child Pornography
Report, Mission to Nepal, CHR 50th session, 20 January 1994, UN Doc. E/CN.4/1994/84/Add.1.
Report, Mission to Kenya, 28 January 1998, UN Doc. E/CN.4/1998/101/Add.1.
Report, Mission to Mexico, CHR 54th session, 23 February 1998, UN Doc. E/CN.4/1998/101/Add.2.
Report, Mission to Belgium, CHR 56th session, 22 December 1999, UN Doc. E/CN.4/2000/73/Add.1.
Report, Mission to Guatemala, CHR 56th session, 27 January 2000, UN Doc. E/CN.4/2000/73/Add.2.
Report, Mission to Morocco, CHR 57th session, 7 November 2000, UN Doc. E/CN.4/2001/78/Add.1
Report, Mission to Russia, CHR 57th session, 6 February 2001, UN Doc. E/CN.4/2001/78/Add.2.
Report, Mission to South Africa, CHR 59th session, 9 January 2003, UN Doc. E/CN.4/2003/79/Add.1.
Report, Mission to Brazil, CHR 60th session, 3 February 2004, UN Doc. E/CN.4/2004/9/Add.2.
Report, Mission to Paraguay, CHR 61st session, 9 December 2004, UN Doc. E/CN.4/2005/78/Add.1.
Report, Mission to Romania, CHR 61st session, 26 January 2005, UN Doc. E/CN.4/2005/78/Add.2.
Report, CHR 62nd session, 27 March 2006, UN Doc. E/CN.4/2006/67/Add.1.

Report, Mission to Albania, CHR 62nd session, 27 March 2006, UN Doc. E/CN.4/2006/67/Add.2.
Report, Mission to Ukraine, HRC 4th session, 27 January 2007, UN Doc. A/HRC/4/Add.2.
Report, on the mission to Mexico, HRC 7th session, 28 January 2008, UN Doc. A/HRC/7/8/Add.2.

Special Rapporteur on the Right to Adequate Housing
Report CHR 58th Session, 1 March 2002, UN Doc. E/CN.4/2002/59.
Report CHR 62nd Session, 14 March 2006, UN Doc. E/CN.4/2006/41.
Report HRC 7th Session, 13 February 2008, UN Doc. A/HRC/7/16.
Report GA 63rd Session, 13 August 2008, UN Doc. A/63/275
Report, Mission to Afghanistan, CHR 60th session, 4 March 2004, UN Doc. E/CN.4/2004/48/Add.2
Report, Mission to Spain, HRC 7th session, 7 February 2008, UN Doc. A/HRC/7/16/Add.2

Special Rapporteur on the Right to Education
Report, Mission to Uganda, CHR 56th session, 9 August 1999, UN Doc. E/CN.4/2000/6/Add.1.
Report, Mission to Turkey, CHR 58th session, 27 March 2002, UN Doc. E/CN.4/2002/60/Add.2.
Report, Mission to Indonesia, CHR 59th session, 4 November 2002, UN Doc. E/CN.4/2003/9/Add.1.
Report, Mission to China, CHR 60th session, 21 November 2003, UN Doc. E/CN.4/2004/45/Add.1.
Report CHR 60th Session, 15 January 2004, UN Doc. E/CN.4/2004/45.

Special Rapporteur on the Right to Food
Report CHR 57th session, 7 February 2001, UN Doc. E/CN.4/2001/53.
Report CHR 59th session, 10 January 2003, UN Doc. E/CN.4/2003/54.
Report, Mission to Niger, CHR 58th session, 23 January 2002, UN Doc. E/CN.4/2002/58/Add.1.
Report, Mission to Bangladesh, CHR 60th session, 29 October 2003, UN Doc. E/CN.4/2004/10/Add.1
Report, Mission to India, CHR 62nd session, 20 March 2006, UN Doc. E/CN.4/2006/44/Add.2.
Report HRC 7th session, 29 February 2008, UN Doc. A/HRC/7/5/Add.1.

Special Rapporteur on the Right to Health
Report CHR 59th session, 13 February 2003, UN Doc. E/CN.4/2003/58.
Report GA 59th session, 8 October 2004, UN Doc. A/59/422.
Report, Mission to Mozambique, CHR 61st session, 4 January 2005, UN Doc. E/CN.4/2005/51/Add.2.
Report, Mission to Peru, CHR 61st session, 4 February 2005, UN Doc. E/CN.4/2005/51/Add.3.

Report, Mission to Romania, CHR 61st session, 21 February 2005, UN Doc. E/CN.4/2005/51/Add.4.
Report, Mission to Uganda, CHR 62nd session, 19 January 2006, UN Doc. E/CN.4/2006/48/Add.2.
Report CHR 62nd Session, 3 March 2006, UN Doc. E/CN.4/2006/48.
Report GA 61st session, 13 September 2006, UN Doc. A/61/338.
Report HRC 7th session, 31 January 2008, UN Doc. A/HRC/7/11.
Report GA 63rd session, 11 August 2008, UN Doc. A/63/263.
Report, Mission to India, HRC 14th session, 15 April 2010, UN Doc. A/HRC/14/20/Add.2.

Independent Expert on the Question of Human Rights and Extreme Poverty
Report CHR 55th session, 29 January 1999, UN Doc. E/CN.4/1999/48.
Report CHR 56th session, 25 February 2000, UN Doc. E/CN.4/2000/52.
Report GA 63rd session, 13 August 2008, UN Doc. A/63/274.
Report HRC 14th session, 11 May 2010, UN Doc. A/HRC/14/31/Add.1.

Special Representative of the S-G on the Issue of Human Rights and Transnational Corporations and Other Business Enterprises
Report HRC 4th session, 8 February 2007, UN Doc. A/HRC/4/35/Add.4.
Interim report CHR 62nd session, 22 February 2006, UN Doc. E/CN.4/2006/97.
Report HRC 8th session, 23 May 2008, UN Doc. A/HRC/8/5/Add.2.

Special Rapporteur on the Situation of Human Rights in Burundi
Interim report GA 55th session, 7 September 2000, UN Doc. A/55/358.
Report CHR 57th session, 19 March 2001, UN Doc. E/CN.4/2001/44
Interim report GA 56th session, 17 October 2001, UN Doc. A/56/479.

Independent Expert on the Situation of Human Rights in Burundi
Interim report GA 61st session, 19 September 2006, UN Doc. A/61/360.
Interim report HRC 4th session, 26 February 2007, UN Doc. A/HRC/4/5.
Report GA 8 August 2007, 62nd session, UN Doc. A/62/213.
Report HRC 9th session, 15 August 2008.

Independent Expert on the Situation of Human Rights in Haiti
Report GA 50th session, 1 November 1995, UN Doc. A/50/714.
Report CHR 52nd session, 24 January 1996, UN Doc. E/CN.4/1996/94.
Report CHR 53rd session, 7 February 1997, UN Doc. E/CN.4/1997/89.
Report HRC 11th session, 26 March 2009, UN Doc. A/HRC/11/5
Report HRC 14th session, 3 May 2010, UN Doc. A/HRC/14/44.

Special Representative of the Secretary-General on Cambodia
Report CHR 50th session, 21 February 1994, UN Doc. E/CN.4/1994/73/Add.1
Report GA 49th session, 3 November 1994, UN Doc. A/49/635.
Report CHR 52nd session, 26 February 1996, UN Doc. E/CN.4/1996/93.
Report GA 53rd session, 17 October 1997, UN Doc. A/52/489.
Report CHR 54th session, 20 February 1998, UN Doc. E/CN.4/1998/95.

Report CHR 55th session, 26 February 1999, UN Doc. E/CN.4/1999/101.
Report CHR 57th session, 24 January 2001, UN Doc. E/CN.4/2001/103.
Report GA 56th session 26 July 2001, UN Doc. A/56/209.
Report CHR 59th session, 18 December 2002, UN Doc. E/CN.4/2003/114.
Report CHR 60th session, 19 December 2003, UN Doc. E/CN.4/105.
Report CHR 61st session 20 December 2004, UN Doc. E/CN.4/2005/116.
Report HRC 4th session, 30 January 2007, UN Doc. A/HRC/4/36.
Report of the Secretary-General, CHR 23 December 2004, UN Doc. E/CN.4/2005/111.

Independent Expert on the Situation of Human Rights in Somalia
Report CHR 54th session, 16 January 1998, UN Doc. E/CN.4/1998/96.
Report CHR 55th session, 18 February 1999, UN Doc. E/CN.4/1999/103.
Report CHR, 55th session, 17 May 1999, UN Doc. E/CN.4/1999/38/Add.1.
Report CHR 56th session, 26 January 2000, UN Doc. E/CN.4/2000/110.
Report CHR 58th session, 14 January 2002, UN Doc. E/CN.4/2002/119.
Report CHR 59th session, 31 December 2003, UN Doc. E/CN.4/2003/115.
Report HRC 12th session, 17 September 2009, UN Doc. A/HRC/12/49.
Report HRC 13th session, 22 March 2010, UN Doc. A/HRC/13/65.

Special Rapporteur on the Situation of Human Rights in the Sudan
Report GA 54th session, 14 October 1999, UN Doc. A/54/467.
Report CHR 56th session, 19 April 2000, UN Doc. E/CN.4/2000/36.
Report GA 62nd session, 24 September 2007, UN Doc. A/62/354.
Final report on the situation of human rights in Darfur prepared by the group of experts mandated by the HRC in its resolution 4/8, HRC 62nd session, 24 September 2007, UN Doc. A/HRC/6/19.

Special Rapporteur on the Situation of Human Rights in the DPR of Korea
Report HRC 10th session, 24 February 2009, UN Doc. A/HRC/10/18.
Report HRC 13th session, 17 February 2010, UN Doc. A/HRC/13/47.

Special Rapporteur on the Situation of Human Rights in Myanmar
Report CHR 52nd session, 2 May 1996, UN Doc. E/CN.4/1996/95.
Report CHR 53rd session, 6 February 1997, UN Doc. E/CN.4/1997/64.
Report CHR 55th session, 22 January 1999, UN Doc. E/CN.4/1999/35.
Interim report GA 55th session, 22 August 2000, UN Doc. A/HRC/55/359.
Report CHR 58th session, 10 January 2002, UN Doc. E/CN.4/2002/45.
Report CHR 60th session, 5 January 2004, UN Doc. E/CN.4/2004/33.
Report CHR 61st session, 2 December 2004, UN Doc. E/CN.4/2005/36.
Report GA 60th session, 29 August 2005, UN Doc. A/60/306.
Report GA 61st session, 21 September 2006, UN Doc. A/61/369.
Report HRC 4th session, 12 February 2007, UN Doc. A/HRC/4/14.
Report GA 62nd session, 13 August 2007, UN Doc. A/62/223.
Report HRC 6th session, 7 December 2007, UN Doc. A/HRC/6/14.
President's Statement, HRC 6th session, 28 September 2007, UN Doc. A/HRC/PRST/6/1.

Table of Cases

European Court of Human Rights

Lietzow v. Germany, 13 February 2001, Application no. 24479/94.
Thoma v. Luxembourg, 29 June 2001, Application no. 38432/97.
Craxi v. Italy (No. 2), 17 July 2003, Application no. 25337/94.
Sabou and Pîrcaleb v. Romania, 28 September 2004, Application no. 46572/99.
Cumpana and Mazare v. Romania, Grand Chamber 17 December 2004, Application no. 33348/96.
Stângu and Scutelnicu v. Romania, 31 January 2006, Application no. 53899/00.
Gorelishvili v. Georgia, 5 June 2007, Application no. 12979/04.
Diena and Ozolins v. Latvia, 12 July 2007, Application no. 16657/03.
Dyuldin and Kislov v. Russia, 31 July 2007, Application no. 25968/02.
Timpul Info-Magazin and Anghel v. Moldova, 27 November 2007, Application no. 42864/05.
Ramanauskas v. Lithuania, 5 February 2008, Application no. 74420/01.
Guja v. Moldova, Grand Chamber 12 February 2008, Application no. 14277/04.
Ünel v. Turkey, 27 May 2008, Application no. 35686/02.
Milinienè v. Lithuania, 24 June 2008, Application no. 74335/01.
Barb v. Romania, 7 October 2008, Application no. 5945/03.
Alithia Publishing Company Ltd & Constantinides v. Cyprus, 22 May 2008, Application no. 17550/03.
Kudeshkina v. Russia, 26 February 2009, Application no. 29492/05.
Fedchenko v. Russia (no. 2), 11 February 2010, Application no. 48195/06.
Mahmudov and Agazade v. Azerbaijan, 18 December 2008, Application no. 35877/04.

Inter-American Commission on Human Rights

Cases

Santiago Marzioni v. Argentina, case 11.673, report no. 39/96.
Juan Milla Bermúdez v. Honduras, case 11.206, report no. 46/96.
Oscar Vila-Masot v. Venezuela, case 11.216, report no. 87/98.
Gustavo Gomez Lopez v. Venezuela, case 11.703, report no. 82/98.
Victor Manuel Oropeza v. Mexico, case 11.740, report no. 130/99.
Horacio Verbitsky et al. v. Argentia, case 12.128, report no. 3/04.

Other Documents

Report on the situation of human rights in Mexico, 24 September 1998, OEA/Ser.L/V/II.100, Doc. 7 rev. 1, chapter V.
Second report on the situation of human rights in Peru, 2 June 2000, OEA/Ser.L/V/II.106, Doc. 59.
Third report on the situation of human rights in Paraguay, 9 March 2001, OEA/Ser.L/V/II.110.

Fifth report on the situation of human rights in Guatemala, 6 April 2001, OEA/Ser.L/V/II.111, Doc. 21 rev., chapter VIII.
Democracy and Human Rights in Venezuela, 30 December 2009, OEA/Ser.L/V/II. Doc 54.
Guidelines for Preparation of Progress Indicators in the Area of Economic, Social and Cultural Rights, 19 July 2008, OEA/Ser.L/V/II.132, Doc. 14.
Haïti: Failed Justice or the Rule of Law? Challenges Ahead for Haïti and the International Community, 26 October 2005, OEA/Ser/L/V/II.123, Doc. 6 rev 1.
Report on Citizen Security and Human Rights, 31 December 2009, OEA/Ser.L/V/II, Doc. 57.
Resolution 1/08, Principles and Best Practices on the Protection of Persons Deprived of Liberty in the Americas.
Resolution 1/03 on trial for international crimes, mentioning the Inter-American Convention Against Corruption.

INTER-AMERICAN COURT OF HUMAN RIGHTS
Ivcher Bronstein v. Peru, Judgment of 6 February 2001.
Ricardo Canese v. Paraguay, Judgment of 31 August 2004.
Acevedo-Jaramillo et al. v. Peru, Judgment of 7 February 2006.
Apitz Barbera et al. v. Venezuela, Judgment of 5 August 2008.

AFRICAN COMMISSION ON HUMAN AND PEOPLES' RIGHTS
Ilesanmi v. Nigeria, Communication 268/2003.

INTERNATIONAL CRIMINAL COURT
ICC *Prosecutor v. Lubanga Dyilo*, Decision Pre-Trial Chamber I, 29 January 2007, ICC–01/04–01/06–803.
Prosecutor v. Katanga and Ngudjolo Chui, Pre-Trial Chamber Decision of 30 September 2008, ICC–01/04–01/07.
ICC *Prosecutor v. Jean-Pierre Bemba Gombo*, Decision Pre-Trial Chamber II, 15 June 2009, ICC–01/05–01/08.
ICC *Prosecutor v. Thomas Lubanga Dyilo*, Judgment Pursuant to Article 74 of the Statute, Trial Chamber 14 March 2012, ICC–01/04–01/06.

INTERNATIONAL CRIMINAL TRIBUNAL FOR RWANDA
ICTR *Prosecutor v. Akayesu,* ICTR–96–4-T, Trial Chamber Judgment 2 September 1998.

INTERNATIONAL CRIMINAL TRIBUNAL FOR THE FORMER YUGOSLAVIA
ICTY *Prosecutor v. Tadić,* IT–94–1-AR72, Appeals Chamber Judgment 2 October 1995.
ICTY *Prosecutor v. Delalic* (aka *Celebici* Trial Chamber Judgment), IT–96–21-T, Trial Chamber Judgment 16 November 1998.

SPECIAL COURT FOR SIERRA LEONE
Prosecutor v. Brima et al., SCSL (Appeals Chamber), Judgment of 22 February 2008.

PERMANENT COURT OF INTERNATIONAL JUSTICE
Lotus Case (1927), PCIJ Ser. A No. 10. See *Ibid.* at p. 31–32.

INTERNATIONAL COURT OF JUSTICE
Anglo-Norwegian Fisheries Case (1951), ICJ Rep 116.

ECOWAS COMMUNITY COURT OF JUSTICE
Judgment *The Registered Trustees of the Socio-Economic Rights and Accountability Project (SERAP) v. The Federal Republic of Nigeria and Universal Basic Education Commission (UBEC)*, 30 November 2010, ECW/CCJ/APP/12/07; ECW/CCJ/JUD/07/10.

Index

A

Abuse of functions 36, 316, 370
African Union Convention on Preventing and Combating Corruption 33, 35, 36, 38, 88-92
Armed conflict, Role of corruption in 41 *et seq.*

B

Bribe Payers Index (BPI) 39, 51, 61, 354, 384
Bribery 33-36, 51, 65-67 *et seq.*
Burundi, Special Rapporteur on the Situation of Human Rights in 166-167

C

Cambodia, Special Representative of the S-G on the Situation of Human Right in 168-170
Children's rights 122, 123, 244
Collusion 30, 31, 51, 184, 354
Committee Against Torture (CAT) 13, 14, 107-109, 128-130, 132, 133, 222, 269, 357, 359
Committee on the Elimination of all Forms of Racial Discrimination (CERD) 14, 103, 107-109, 126, 127, 131, 132, 134, 269, 357, 359
Committee on the Rights of the Child (CRC) 13, 14, 103, 108, 120-125, 132, 216, 221, 228, 244, 252, 357, 358
Consequences 26, 40-51, 96, 148, 157, 282, 336, 354, 355
Economic 42, 45, 48
  Environmental 49, 50
  Political 41, 42, 148
  Social 48, 157
Consequentialism 309-311
Corruption Perceptions Index (CPI) 38, 39
Council of Europe Criminal Law Convention on Corruption 81
Council of Europe Civil Law Convention on Corruption 82
Cultural aspects of corruption 32

D

Democratic People's Republic of Korea, Special Rapporteur on the Situation of Human Rights in 171
Detainees, Rights of 128, 132, 222, 224, 358, 366
Deterrence 280, 309-311, 313, 318
Dolus eventualis 323-325, 332, 337, 338, 343, 344, 371, 373
Domestic human rights litigation 271, 272, 367

E

ECOWAS Protocol on the Fight Against Corruption 88
Education, Right to 15, 123, 151, 157, 172, 244-248, 250, 251, 267, 270, 272, 361, 366, 376
Embezzlement 31, 33, 35, 36, 41, 51, 67, 68, 83, 90, 95, 99, 167, 206, 224, 230, 232, 233, 238, 241, 244, 247, 255, 264, 270, 272, 316-319, 333, 336, 340, 344, 349, 354, 355, 361, 367, 370, 373, 374, 376
Equal access to public service, Right to 216
Equality before courts and tribunals, Right to 109, 110, 132, 148, 149, 202-205, 207-209, 267, 357, 360, 366
European Court of Human Rights 16, 177, 178, 193, 197, 270, 363, 367, 379
Expressivism 11, 311, 313, 318
Extermination 8, 11, 320, 329-333, 336, 338, 371-373

F

Fair trial, Right to a 110, 133, 149, 182, 186, 191, 193, 196, 198, 205, 207, 209, 210, 212, 271, 358, 360, 364, 365, 375, 376
Feasibility and motivation of harm 295, 296, 299, 301, 306, 308, 369
Food, Right to 15, 132, 151, 157, 158, 164, 234-239, 267, 294, 358, 361, 366
Foreign Corrupt Practices Act (FCPA) 53-55, 57-63, 75, 77, 87, 347
Fraud 30, 31, 39, 40, 51, 71-73, 354
Freedom of movement, Right to 112, 113, 127, 132, 224, 225, 267, 358, 366

G

Global Corruption Barometer (GCB) 40, 51, 354
Grand corruption 29, 30
GRECO 74, 85, 86, 138, 356

H

Health, Right to 15, 151, 159-162, 164, 175, 196, 242, 252-264, 267, 361, 362, 366, 367, 376
Housing, Right to 105, 165, 239-244, 267, 294, 361, 366
Human Rights Committee (HRC) 12-14, 18, 103, 107-114, 116, 118, 132, 133, 204, 205, 207, 213, 216, 219, 220, 222, 224, 225, 227, 249, 269, 357, 358, 377
Human trafficking 112, 118, 132, 141, 153, 154, 169, 216-221, 267, 358, 359, 361, 366, 369

I

Illicit enrichment 33, 38, 51, 66, 68, 90, 95, 198, 316, 317, 354, 370
Incapacitation 309, 311
Indigenous spoliation 29
Inter-American Convention Against Corruption 33, 35, 38, 65, 139, 140, 189, 355
Inter-American Court of Human Rights 190-192

K

Kleptocracy 29, 30, 336, 339

L
Legality 11, 295, 305, 306, 308, 316, 341, 349, 369

M
Maximum available resources 122, 123, 132, 150, 229, 231, 237, 255, 358
MESICIC 68, 70, 356
Myanmar, Special Rapporteur on the Situation of Human Rights in 171

N
National Human Rights Institutions 272
Natural resources 3, 41-44, 49, 52, 236, 238, 266, 304, 355

O
Objectives of punishment 11, 277, 282, 308, 309, 313, 317, 318, 368, 370
OECD Convention on the Combating of Bribery in International Business Transactions 73-80
Other inhumane act 8, 333, 334, 336-338, 372, 373

P
Patrimonicide 29
Patronage 36, 37, 48, 189, 354
Petty Corruption 29, 30, 33, 40, 51, 65, 89, 100, 199, 272, 300, 311, 314, 315, 340, 354, 357, 367
PFI Convention 71-73
Political participation, Rights of 148, 149, 212-216
Practical Applicability and Effectivity 295, 306-308, 369
Presumption of innocence 38, 198, 199, 211
Proportionality 11, 226, 227, 295, 304-306, 308, 369
Public interest litigation 269, 271, 367

R
Rehabilitation 129, 223, 309, 311
Remedy, Right to a 212
Retributivism 11, 309

S
SADC Protocol Against Corruption 86, 355
Somalia, Independent Expert on the Situation of Human Rights in 170
Special Procedures of the Human Rights Council 356, 360, 367, 378
  Independent Expert on the question of Human Rights and Extreme Poverty 15, 151, 162, 362
  Special Rapporteur on Corruption 15, 147, 151, 174, 228, 360, 378
  Special Rapporteur on the Independence of Judges and Lawyers 15, 16, 151, 164, 361
  Special Rapporteur on the Right to Adequate Housing 15, 151, 156, 239, 243, 361
  Special Rapporteur on the Right to Food 15, 151, 157, 234, 361
  Special Rapporteur on the Right to Health 15, 151, 162, 252, 261, 361, 362

Special Rapporteur on the Sale of Children, Child Prostitution and Child Pornography 15, 151, 153, 154, 164, 165, 216, 361
Special Rapporteur on Trafficking in Persons, especially in Women and Children 15, 151, 153, 361
State capture 29, 30
Subsidiarity 11, 295, 302, 306, 308, 369
Sudan, Independent Expert on the Situation of Human Rights in 170

T
Tolerance 4, 11, 113, 141, 295, 301, 302, 306, 308, 369
Trading in influence 33, 35, 36, 51, 82, 83, 87, 90, 95, 316, 354, 370

U
United Nations Convention Against Corruption (UNCAC) 11, 26, 32-36, 38, 51, 94-99, 128, 138, 139, 141-143, 160, 169, 171, 179, 198, 230, 268, 279, 281, 295, 302, 303, 314, 316, 318, 341, 344, 348-350, 354, 356, 359, 373, 374, 380
United Nations Convention Against Transnational Organised Crime (UNCTOC) 93, 94, 218
Universal Periodic Review 10, 15, 135, 356, 359, 378

V
Vote, Right to 214, 215

W
White-collar crime 51

Curriculum Vitae

Martine Elisabeth Victor Boersma (Maastricht, 1984) studied law at Maastricht University. In 2005, she obtained a Bachelor in Dutch Law (*cum laude*). The following year, she finished a Master in Dutch Law, with a specialisation in company and commercial law (*cum laude*), and in 2007 she finished the Master Law, Labour & Health (*cum laude*). During her studies, Martine worked as a volunteer for the Stichting Vrouwenrechtswinkel Maastricht, and did an internship at the company law department of a major law firm.

Martine started working at the Faculty of Law of Maastricht University as a Ph.D. researcher with the Maastricht Centre for Human Rights in September 2007. During her appointment, she taught various courses at the Faculty of Law and the University College, mainly in the field of international and European law. Next to her research and teaching, she was active in the Board and the Graduate Programme Committee of the Netherlands School of Human Rights Research, and in the Board of the Maastricht Centre for Human Rights. In 2008, Martine attended the Public International Law Summer Course at the Hague Academy of International Law.

In September 2011, Martine began working at a law firm as a practising lawyer, dealing with cases in various fields of law. She continues to follow developments in the area of human rights with great interest.

School of Human Rights Research Series

The School of Human Rights Research is a joint effort by human rights researchers in the Netherlands. Its central research theme is the nature and meaning of international standards in the field of human rights, their application and promotion in the national legal order, their interplay with national standards, and the international supervision of such application. The School of Human Rights Research Series only includes English titles that contribute to a better understanding of the different aspects of human rights.

For previous volumes in the series, please visit http://shr.intersentia.com.

Published titles within the Series:

47. Otto Spijkers, *The United Nations, the Evolution of Global Values and International Law*
    ISBN 978-1-78068-036-1
48. Karin Veegens, *A Disrupted Balance? Prevention of terrorism and compliance with fundamental legal rights and principles of law – the Dutch antiterrorism legislation*
    ISBN 978-1-78068-042-2
49. Antenor Hallo de Wolf, *Reconciling Privatization with Human Rights*
    ISBN 978-1-78068-049-1
50. Marie-José van der Heijden, *Transnational Corporations and Human Rights Liabilities*
    ISBN 978-9-40000-195-4
51. Marthe Lot Vermeulen, *Enforced Disappearance*
    ISBN 978-1-78068-065-1
52. Vera Vriezen, *Amnesty Justified?*
    ISBN 978-1-78068-075-1
53 Maite San Giorgi, *The Human Right to Equal Access to Heath Care*
    ISBN 978-1-78068-081-1
54. Jeroen Blomsma, *Mens rea and defences in European Criminal Law*
    ISBN 978-1-78068-104-7
55. Masha Fedorova, *The Principle of Equality of Arms in International Criminal Proceedings*
    ISBN 978-1-78068-111-5
56. Martine Boersma, *Corruption: A Violation of Human Rights and a Crime Under International Law?*
    ISBN 978-1-78068-105-4

www.ingramcontent.com/pod-product-compliance
Ingram Content Group UK Ltd.
Pitfield, Milton Keynes, MK11 3LW, UK
UKHW051918100926
8556IPUK00021B/1245

9 781780 681054

Corruption: A Violation of Human Rights and a Crime Under International Law?

School of Human Rights Research Series, Volume 56

The titles published in this series are listed at the end of this volume.